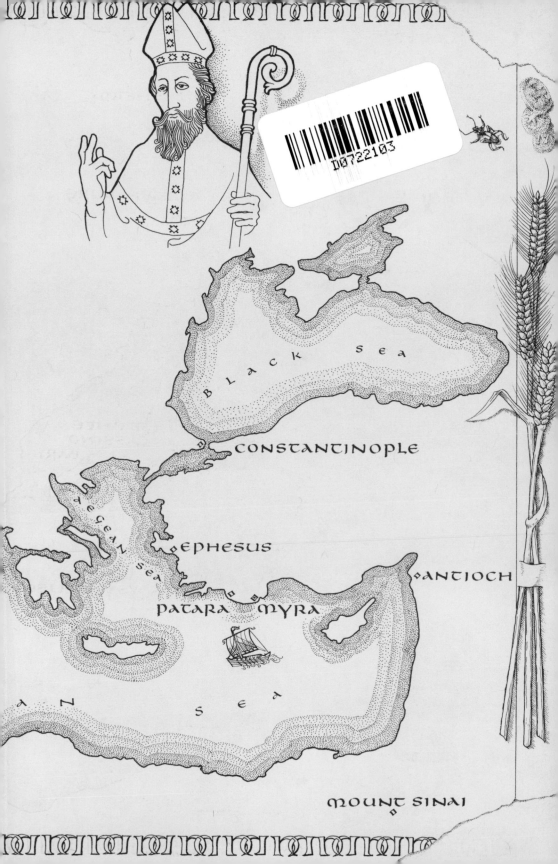

BLACK SEA

CONSTANTINOPLE

Aegean sea

EPHESUS

ANTIOCH

PATARA   MYRA

N   SEA

MOUNT SINAI

SAINT NICHOLAS

OF MYRA, BARI, AND

MANHATTAN

SAINT NICHOLAS

OF MYRA, BARI, AND MANHATTAN

*Biography of
a Legend*

CHARLES W. JONES

THE UNIVERSITY OF CHICAGO PRESS
Chicago & London

THE UNIVERSITY OF CHICAGO PRESS, CHICAGO 60637
THE UNIVERSITY OF CHICAGO PRESS, LTD., LONDON

Printed in the United States of America
82 81 80 79 78 5 4 3 2 1

CHARLES W. JONES is Professor Emeritus at the
University of California, Berkeley. Among his previous books are
*Saints' Lives and Chronicles of Early England; Medieval Literature
in Translation; The St. Nicholas Liturgy; Bedae Opera de
Temporibus; Bedae Opera Exegetica: In Genesim;* and
Opera Didascalica.

Library of Congress Cataloging in Publication Data

Jones, Charles Williams, 1905 -
  Saint Nicholas of Myra, Bari, and Manhattan.

  Bibliography: p.
  Includes indexes.
    1. Nicholas, Saint, Bp. of Myra.   2. Christian saints
—Turkey—Lysia—Biography.   3. Lysia—Biography.   I. Title.
BX4700.N55J63   282'.092'4   [B]   77 - 51487
ISBN 0-226-40699-7

To

SARAH

beloved companion for seven squared years plus one

CONTENTS

ACKNOWLEDGMENTS

This book has been produced only with the cooperation of staffs of libraries, institutions, and shrines too numerous to mention; but I especially thank the New-York Historical Society and its late director Robert Vail, the Byzantine Institute at Dumbarton Oaks, Biblioteca Vaticana, Bibliothèque Royale de Belgique, British Museum, Princeton Index of Christian Art, Cornell University Library—particularly Felix Reichmann—and the Libraries of the University of California and the Graduate Theological Union.

I acknowledge the generous interest and help of many colleagues and other friends, but especially the dearest of all, George R. Stewart, who read the whole text, as did also Frederick Amory, David J. A. Ross, and Frederick E. Prinz. Those who read generous portions are Paul Alexander, Charles Muscatine, my inspiring coworker in many ventures Walter Horn and his artistic alter ego Ernest Born. For other favors I thank Ruth Iodice, Robert Cathcart, Bryce Boyer, Jan de Vries, and most especially Reuben Frodin, Elizabeth Dow Pritchett, and Jane Eshleman Conant. My assistant Pat Clark with patience and humor modified (she could scarce expunge) my veniality. Excepting the lady of the dedication, my encouragement from the first has been my children and then grandchildren, who have grown along with N.

C.W.J.

PROLOGUE

One man in his time plays many parts,
His acts being seven ages.
As You Like It, II, vii

The world's a stage, and the stage is a world. Shadow and substance, macrocosm and microcosm—which is the image or visible representation and which the reality? We shrug and answer both are both. But an answer does not end the mystery. As humans have their seven ages, do not their images, icons, similacra, figures, fables, fictions, types, myths and legends, which are their imaginative selves, have their seven ages too? We like to think that for a cosmic moment a human being leaves a vacuum when he crumbles into dust, perhaps a footprint on the sand. Is a legend less material a part of things?

A biographer traces the vestiges of his human subject with such senses as he has and creates a legend. In what follows I propose to reverse the process—not to find the human at the end of the legend, but somehow to apprehend the force which makes a fiction bestride this earth as if it were a man.

My organic analogy is intended, in the words of Henry Adams, to serve as a fatal weapon if it succeeds, and as an innocent toy if it fails. It is traditional to discuss society as if it were an organism. Why not also the image which society creates? Croce said no: "All doctrines that represent the history of nations as proceeding according to the stages of development of the individual, of his psychological development, of the categories of the spirit, or of anything else, are due to the same error, which is that of rendering periodization external or natural. All are mythological." But there is room for doubt. Mendeleev's and Seaborg's Periodic Tables seem to us as natural as the men who invented them. Those who believe that myths are vacuous will not read this book anyway; but I hope that readers will find that the framework of biography at least permits fewer words at many points than if I presented a history of *Nikolausbrauch* without it.

To fulfill my purpose, which is to appreciate the macrocosmic imagination through observation of a microcosmic image, the legend of Nicholas has, in Milton's phrase, pleased me long choosing. It has

1

the proper attributes. It has been robust, long-lived, important. It seems to have been self-made, growing by nature more than art (though I write to test that inference). It has depended less than rival legends on any party or sect. To be sure, the Church was often the mode of transmission, but normally to its embarrassment. Even the catholicity of the Church was stretched to contain this *nihil alienum*. Nicholas was never canonized. This volume ends with the year when the Papal Court, attendant on Rome II's militant effort to be ecumenical, removed Saint Nicholas from its calendar of saints.

With the Nicholas legend we run the least chance of confusing imagination with fact. A legend of a man in the White House may have its image tarnished by some brush with actuality. With Nicholas we need not worry: he is essential poetry with no beclouding historicity. We are dealing with an image on the scale of Lady Luck. However, to help the reader keep this truth in mind, throughout the book I call the legend, with all its attributes, N,* thereby distinguishing it from any historic, i.e., organic, Nicholas. If the reader is sometimes led to disagree with my decisions, N or Nicholas, a purpose will be served.

N is a legend rather than a myth or image or symbol according to both technical and general definition. "*Legenda* applies essentially to lessons of the second nocturn of matins in the breviary," wrote Professor Aigrain. "Thus understood in the liturgical sense, which is its proper and technical sense, the word *legend* implies no judgment of value regarding the historic or fictive character of the statement." "Legends, in contradistinction to myths or tales," wrote Père Delehaye, "presuppose an historical fact as basis or pretext: such is the first essential of the species. This historical fact may either be developed or disfigured by popular imagination: and here we have the second element. According as the preponderance is to be found on the side of fact or on that of fiction, the narrative may be classed as history or as legend." These quasi-official definitions neglect one essential of this biography: that a legend in its technical or liturgical sense may be static, perhaps dead, whereas a legend outside the liturgy is a living thing. Students of Man often use the formula *creator,*

*N [omen] has only in recent centuries been displaced in writing by X as symbol for a hypothetical agent.

creatus, creandus—the creator, the created, but what for *creandus?* "To be created"? *Creandus* has in fact defied easy interpretation. Hence *N creandus* is the subject of this book, and the book is intended to be a definition of the word *creandus*.

N artifacts are vestiges of *N creandus*. Their infinite variety has led some historians to remark that N has been the most popular nonbiblical saint in Christendom, though Saint Martin might challenge the claim. Some years ago Professor Meisen of Bonn mapped the public monuments dedicated to N erected before the year 1500 only in France, Germany, and the Low Countries. He tabulated 2,137 monuments. Yet his list was notably incomplete. Professor Börsting immediately named fifty in the single diocese of Münster, where Meisen listed but nine.

These monuments were usually religious; for religion and poetry are inseparable, especially before the year 1500. Faith and myth are of imagination all compact. Of the fifty-odd windows in Chartres Cathedral, four are devoted exclusively to N: the separate medallions in them depict some twenty-five different N-tales—only a few of the many which people loved to tell. The windows were donated by nonclerical artisans, merchants, and nobles. That the monuments were churches or in churches is an accident of a time when churches were intended to express all culture, equivalent with yesterday's Tuileries or today's Lincoln Center. When bishops accepted N-monuments, they were not accepting creed or dogma.

The oldest *Western* artifact of N to survive is one frescoed figure among many in the basilica of ninth-century Santa Maria Antiqua in Rome. Like Dante in the Bargello fresco, that N has barely made his mark. But he is among those judged by the composer as most likely to succeed. We like best to see and remember him as painted by the artists of his prime, when he was the cynosure of artists' eyes. Fra Angelico caught N in a studious moment (as always, in his iconographic bishop's robes)—the humane master, the patron of all scholars, whose ghost today gives out diplomas at Cologne and Aberdeen. Veronese saw him as spokesman for the most powerful party of his day: he ranged N as front man before the Carmelite Madonna in her glory. Ghirlandaio caught him as a pillar of the state, the way Borglum caught Washington, Jefferson, Lincoln, and Roosevelt the First. Along with Peter, John the Baptist, and Martin, he is Power. Titian followed

N with his brush as Stuart followed Washington, producing a variety of results. In one, N dominates his committee, made up of Catherine of Alexandria, as well as Peter, Anthony of Padua, Francis, and Sebastian. But in a lovely drawing he catches N alone and solitary, as the wisdom of the ages. Bellini sees N as overshadowing Augustine—the kind of invidious comparison that news photographers nowadays are trained to snap.

Above all is Rafael's Ansidei Madonna, with N and John the Baptist. Here is a Christian trinity just short of godhead—the Virgin as apex of a triangle which lowly Man can comprehend, supported and supporting in a mysterious triangulation the dichotomized states of being that western culture loved above all others: John and N, ascetic and secular, contemplative and active, claustral and worldly, individual and collective, monastic and episcopal, soul and body. Rafael brings out many traits of N: worldliness without pomposity, judiciousness softened by charity. Like a true head of the establishment, this N carries a book but never reads. Note how lightly the book is held, as he listens for the phone to ring.

Is it a tragedy of man and legend that life prolongs itself into senility and then oblivion? Biography but turns from Rafael's so-lovely portrait to images of Santa Claus. Men and legends strut and fret their poor hour upon the stage, but then no more.

Unfortunately, as in any serious biography, the flow of the story often has to be broken to "establish credibility" in the face of misinformation or distortion or scholarly neglect. I have tried to err on the side of under- rather than overdemonstration and have excised from the script masses of supporting data. Like any serious biographer I pray that I remove more misconception than I create. May the reader find on this world's stage a humane personality who became such, according to Riezler's formula, in intercourse with men, things, and gods, in the passion of life, in fighting and conquering, in acting and resisting, and never without suffering. That personality could not help creating an atmosphere around himself whose impact others found difficult to resist, in the end full of scars. Such a personality has exercised a force that no mere man, however charismatic or obstinate, can match.

"When shall we have a full comparative treatment of individual saints who, like Saint Brendan, Saint Mary the Egyptian, Saint Nicholas, and Saint Margaret, figure not only in Latin versions but also in numerous versions in the different vernaculars?" asked President Aston of the Modern Humanities Research Association.[1] To take "full" literally, the answer is never. To exhaust the literature of Saint Nicholas—that is, N, the legend of Nicholas—would be foolhardy, if possible. But to treat the legend without the life—the artifacts, the arts, and the sciences, the whole operation of man's imagination on a single image—would be unbalanced. I have tried to suggest the life without ever attempting to treat it, or any phase of it, fully.

Imagination is both ontogenetic and multifarious. If "inspired by" and "indebted to" are common phrases for criticizing creative art, how much more derivative is popular art, which breeds upon as it feeds upon! A legend gives rise to a legend about a legend about a legend, like nested chinese boxes—a process as inevitable as folk etymology. Though historians have written books and monographs about N, they are either so slight as to be simply memorials (like that of Ancelet-Hustache) or so rare as to be unobtainable (like that of Meisen). Though not my primary purpose, I want this book to supply reasonably accurate historical information about a congeries of our images of the Advent Season, to satisfy the curiosity of those many who now perforce must consult one or a dozen potboilers composed by hacks as little interested in evidence as was a Metaphrast or a Deacon John. Meisen's monumental study, which was pulped and the plates destroyed during a Nazi shortage before it achieved its deserved circulation, is not the only work not readily available. For example, there are not a dozen copies of Anrich's edition of the Greek sources in all of North America. And some sources exist only in manuscript. Hence I have perhaps too generously verbally translated rather than summarized documents, and have retained stilted hagiographic style that does not make pleasant reading. But *vera lex historiae* has determined me to retain such literality.

Finally, though I have tried to interpret the evidence without bias, as Meisen admirably tried to do, I find my story different from his. I have not selected evidence to demonstrate the principle, but this biography may well suggest to readers that in the wake of the Grimms we have attributed too much creative power to the "folk," to the denigration of art. Since imagination is not sense, and its operation cannot be weighed, no conclusion can be reached whether folk or poets created the images which I call N, but I have from this study come to thank the poets, both the known and the unidentified.

ınfancy

*At first the infant
Mewling and puking in the nurse's arms.*

I WAS THERE A HISTORIC NICHOLAS?

By derivation *infant* means "not speaking." *Fant* is from the same root as *fate* and *fable* and *fame*. What does one know about the infancy of a great man, a Christ or Socrates? Even the emperors of almighty Rome are without childhood in history unless they were prophyrogenites, palace-born, and such were the exceptions. When the infant acquires the Word, the unique dignity of man, he is no longer infant. Then we take the half-recalled insights and imaginations of his infancy, however fanciful, and say that's what his infancy was.

A legend is "what should be read." It is a document and not a speaker. To find the infancy of legend N we take later documents and work back. At best they suggest what might have been.

The common belief is that Saint Nicholas lived at Myra in the first half of the fourth century, but there is no evidence or document before the reign of the emperor Justinian in the mid-sixth century. The Church's authorities, the Bollandists, conclude that they know nothing of that man named Nicholas: "In fact we know nothing about the actions of that renowned miracle-worker."[1] Fourth- and fifth-century documents tell us some slight thing about shadowy characters like saints George, Symeon Stylites, the Seven Sleepers of Ephesus, and such acts as Thomas's mission to India; but nothing about a Nicholas of Myra. Nevertheless a most scholarly N student, Gustav Anrich, concluded: "To dispute the historicity of a bishop of Myra named Nicholas would be a methodological error. We can grant a bishop of that name who had a great impact on his homeland. We can also accept December 6 as the day of his death and burial. These are all the facts we can hold to. Further we cannot go."[2]

In this chapter I will clear the way for the maturing N by looking at the data that Anrich accepted for the infant N. But first, a look at "Nicholas," "Myra," "bishop," and "December 6."

"Nicholas" may be an abstract, the Greek word for "people's

victor."[3] The name could have attracted N, or N the name. St. Sophia (Wisdom, 18 Sept.), was an abstract before a legend; St. Veronica was first a name and then an abstract (*Vera icon*) and a legend (4 Feb.).[4] Cults of nonexistent saints like Saint Pistis (Faith), Saint Agape (Love), Saint Renatus (Reborn), etc., are very old; such cults precede Christianity.[5] Saints have originated not only from abstracts but from misinterpreted Roman milestones (e.g., Saint [Praefectus] Viar[um]),[6] from half-heard prayers, typographical errors, and of course from folklore.

To us the name "People's Victor" seems quite appropriate for a hero saint. But ancient Greeks did not like people's victors. They coined pejorative words like "demagogue" for them. In tragedies such nicholases were apt to come to bad ends. Hence there are very few pagan Nicholases of record.[7] Nicholas of Damascus (philosopher and historian at the court of Herod I, friend and biographer of the emperor Augustus) is rather an exception.[8] But he came from the appropriate region: all pagan Nicholases except for a Syracusan who slipped into Diodorus' history, were natives of the Antiochene shore, where Myra was.[9]

The Christian tradition started well. A Nicholas, native of Antioch, was among the first seven deacons appointed by the Apostles.[10] But then John of Patmos damned a sect of Nicolaites, whoever they were.[11] Irenaeus, one of the earliest of the Fathers (2d cent.), said these Nicolaites were heretical followers of that first deacon Nicholas, and many Christians thereafter believed him. That opprobrious association, which later became a tag for clerical sexual laxity, has remained an active tradition in the Church. *The Acts of Andrew* (ca. 260) name two Nicholases, one a too-rich burgher, the other a libertine.[12] Saint Jerome at the beginning of the fifth century wrote to a friend: "Not all bishops are true bishops. You notice Peter; but mark Judas well. You look up to Stephen; but consider also Nicholas, whom the Lord in His Apocalypse abominates."[13]

A slight suggestion that the good Nicholas of Myra never lived in the flesh is that Jerome, who had lived near Damascus and later in Bethlehem and who, as John Milton once remarked, seems to have known more than anyone about anything, knew nothing of our N.

More obscure than these connections with N is the presumed link with a troll, demon, or what you will, rather commonly called Nix,

Nikke, Nikker in early Teutonic dialects. Philologists and folklorists have not successfully sorted out the interrelations between Old Nick and old N, both very active around water. But when the froth is cleared away, nothing remains to show that N could have come from the troll image. Our particular term "Old Nick" is inspired by N, as we shall see.[14]

N's town of Myra, more recently Dembre and now Kale, was a secondary seaport in the mountain massif on the south coast of Asia Minor between Rhodes and Cyprus. Andriake, two miles away, was Myra's Ostia, now silted up. Saint Paul passed or stopped there on his Second Journey and certainly transshipped there on his Third, from Alexandria to Rome.[15] There the saintly romance of Paul and Thecla began.[16] Myra comes at the end of the Greek isles. Mountains rise to six thousand feet within ten miles behind it. The surviving church, with a pavement well below the present level of the town that in part goes back to the fifth century, was partially restored by Russians in the nineteenth century, and some work progresses now.[17]

In the eastern Mediterranean, always subject—sometimes desperately—to piracy and violent storms as well as imperial skirmishing for naval hegemony, such havens have their special veneration. Roman ships might make their dash from Alexandria or Antioch to the lee of the protective isles at Myra, or vice versa. If preparing to dash south across the open sea, sailors could burn a candle at the local shrine while praying for safety. On safe return, the sailors would devote their thanksgiving for safe passage to the local spirit, demigod, or saint. Poseidon, Artemis, Thetis, and other pagan patrons fared well in those ports.

Hence in Christian times Myra was strategically situated for developing a cult.[18] Normally a cult developed for the missionary founder(s) of a diocese. It seems likely enough that there was a local Saint Nicholas, founder of the Christian cult in the period immediately following the Emperor Constantine's edict of toleration (A.D. 311).[19] Anrich believed that an N *martyrion,* or tomb which was an object of cult, existed there well before the reign of Justinian.[20] At about the moment that Christianity emerged from persecution, the Byzantine emperors began to consolidate and foster Lycia, making Myra a capital. Eventually Byzantium created a theme that included Attalia, Myra, lesser Antioch, and Rhodes into Cibyrraeot.[21] As some kind of provincial capital, Myra lasted until Haroun-al-Raschid, hero of the *Arabian Nights,* took it from the Romans in the year 808. Then the port silted up and the populace languished. Doubtless the omnipresent earthquakes of the region assisted.

Nicholas Day is December 6 in the Roman calendar. Few matters are so perdurable as the saints' days in a solar calendar. Before Christian saints, pagan heroes and demigods were honored on equally unalterable anniversaries. The earth may shake, but seasons endure. What is tied to a Julian date lasts though the Colossus crumble and leave no trace. Hagiologists may disbelieve a name, an act, a virtue, but not a solar date. Something happened on some December 6 in some year to make it Nicholas Day.

Normally, a saint's day marks the date of his death on earth and rebirth in heaven. But there are times when the festival existed long before the saint whose day is honored. Often so meaningful is the seasonal point as compared with the virtue of the saint that the day determines what the saint's virtues may be. Christ, who was born in a dark world to bring light, had His Mass determined by the winter solstice; His Resurrection by that annual day of perfect light when the equinoctial sun and full moon conjoin. But conversely, Saint Martin is the Thanksgiving saint and Martinmas the day of geese and pies because he happened to die on November 11, the end of the harvest season. February 2 has been sulfur-and-molasses day through history: a Feast of Purification for the pagans, Candlemas for Christians, Groundhog Day for Americans. Such solar incidences are more eternal than any manmade laws.

In Christian primitivism before the Nicene Council (A.D. 325), the Fathers kept pagan cults of heroes severely at bay. They condemned anything more than *honor* accorded to venerated mortals. But Delehaye remarks that "the years 325 to 400 bring all the basic forms of hagiolatry."[22] Saints began to become godlike.

Whether Christian saints are in fact successors of the pagan gods was a white-hot debate a century ago.[23] It was quite as hot in A.D. 404 when the great Jerome tried to slay an old acquaintance, Vigilantius of Aquitaine, with his pen. Vigilantius had issued a pamphlet protesting that "under the cloak of religion we see really a heathen ceremony introduced into the churches: while the sun is shining, heaps of tapers are lighted and, everywhere, I know not what paltry bit of powder, wrapped in a costly cloth, is kissed and worshiped. Great honor do men of this sort pay to the blessed martyrs, who, as they think, are to be glorified by trumpery tapers."[24] Jerome defended the cultists; he based his doctrine on what was to become the orthodox distinction—between *latria* (worship paid to God alone) and *dulia* (veneration paid to saints). But even the most orthodox defenders of the saints' uniqueness—of the irrelevance of comparison with pagan acts—did not hesitate to list innumerable "coincidences" between adoration of gods and demigods and veneration of saints. Some of these practices were fundamental to Christian cult. For example, the practice of "incubation," of nights passed beside the altar awaiting a healing vision.[25] We are familiar enough in the world of art with Sebastian, successor of Apollo, or with George, successor of Apollo the Python slayer or Perseus.

The solar calendar is a record of many such coincidences. Christians, like pagans, kept their festal calendars, their immutable records of anniversaries. In the middle of the third century Cyprian required his clergy in Carthage to preserve and protect the calendar: "Mark the days on which the martyrs depart, that we may celebrate their memories . . . the days on which our blessed brethren in prison pass by way of a glorious death to immortality. And oblations and sacrifices in commemoration of them are here celebrated by us, which, the Lord protecting, we shall soon celebrate with you."[26] Cyprian's own name was to be added to that "martyrology," which often combined the names of pagan gods and Christian saints on the same Julian dates. A most famous edict is that of the Third Council of Carthage (A.D. 397): "Let the Passions of the Martyrs be read at their anniversary celebrations" (*Liceat etiam legi passiones martyrum, cum anniversarii dies eorum celebrantur*).[27]

Around December 6 the seasonal winter storms began, and the maritime folk of the Hellenic shores propitiated their meaningful sea gods.[28] Feasts for Poseidon were most common.

The Julian calendar was solar, but the Hellenic and Semitic calendars were lunar. Consequently they wavered in their relation to the sun. Nevertheless, Greek proverbs survive that indicate that people regarded just about December 6 as the symbolic start of winter. It was a traditional date for close of navigation or special invocation to some deity for protection on wintry seas. It is not amiss to compare the date of close of navigation on the Great Lakes: to sail beyond it a shipper must invoke the special action of the insurance carriers, in ancient times the appropriate gods. Along the islands and coast, the Poseidonia (feasts honoring Poseidon) were held then.[29]

If there was a founder-bishop of an important port city whose name was People's Victor, and God took the bishop's spirit on December 6, his name would inevitably be linked with Poseidon's and he would be a peculiarly suitable candidate for a maritime cult once accorded to the pagan god. The Emperor Theodosius II (A.D. 401 - 450) ordered a great church built at Myra, dedication unknown, which in much later times was known as the Nicholas Church. He probably would not have done so had not he and the citizens of Myra had a common interest in maritime success.

December 6, what year? According to *The Golden Legend* (13th cent.), Nicholas died A.D. 343. At the time of the Translation, A.D. 1087 (see below, chap. 4, iv), a historian said that his holy body had been entombed at Myra for 746 years; that would make his death A.D. 341. Another (Nicephorus) said 775 years, or A.D. 312; another (Harley 3091) 800 years, or A.D. 287; the *Vendôme Annals* say Anno Passionis 317 (= A.D. 345).[30] There are other documents that point to A.D. 345 and 351. Réau's *Iconographie* (1958) unhesitatingly says 342, but papal commissions of modern times have stated that no date is certain.

To determine the spread of the Roland legend historians have traced in records the rise in number of twins christened Roland and Oliver. I believe that the appearance of the name Nicholas outside the Antiochene coast is a clue to the spread of N, either directly or through chains of Nicholases. Often the intermediate namesakes are saints in their own right. Whatever the opprobrium attached to the Nicolaitans of the Apocalypse, we note that the name Nicholas begins to appear in pious circles after the year 450. The Pauly-Wissowa encyclopedia records a growing number of deacons, priests, bishops, and archimandrites from that time, centering in Lycia—indeed, in Myra, but spreading to Tarsus, Thessalonica, and Constantinople, no further.[31] Among seculars was a comic poet and sophist at Constantinople.

Yet the first "fact" regarding N is a statement of the historian Procopius (ca. A.D. 555) that the emperor Justinian (A.D. 527 - 565) codifier of Roman law and builder of Hagia Sophia, in order to restore a Church of Saints Priskos and Nikolaos had to erect a platform out over the sea.[32] These saints had two days, one possibly the Day of Dedication of the Church, September 22, the other December 7. Procopius remarks that the citizens crowded the church, for they quite adopted these foreign saints. The church was outside the walls beyond the palace of the Blachernes. The double dedication and confusion in feast days obscure the testimony. This Nicholas could have been another, unknown, Nicholas. However, current archaeologists usually accept the statement as earliest evidence of a church later positively identified as Saint Nicholas Blachernes (Ἅγιος Νικολαος των Βλαχερνων) burned by the Slavs and Avars in 626 but restored and still standing in 1350. Its position over the Golden Horn next to what grew to be the primary imperial palace suited N, patron of sea trade and politics.

There are a few other artifacts of N that have without certainty been assigned to this same period, the reign of Justinian. For example, an invocation in a church on Crete[33] and N's effigy on a glyph now in the British Museum.[34]

II LEGENDS

Some anonymous writings about N survive that just possibly may have been penned before the ninth century. But the eastern tradition of texts of Christian cult in the century and a half following Justinian is complex and obscure, irrevocably disturbed by the iconoclastic disorders of the eighth century. We can best simply accept Gustav Anrich's conclusions. It took him one large volume to print all the texts about N extant in Greek, but a larger volume to clarify their meanings and values. Throughout this book I will refer to the texts as they are catalogued in the Bollandists' *Bibliotheca Hagiographica Graeca,*[1] based upon Anrich's results. In nearly all instances the statements of this chapter express likelihood, not certainty.

Père Delehaye, a most accomplished hagiologist, stated as a principle that legends arise from cult, not cult from legends: It is the love of a hero that inspires loving tales about him, a love not primarily generated by actions narrated in those tales. True, we have all in our own communities observed individuals who are "born saints," to whom are attributed exemplary actions, fables, and moral dicta, not theirs by right and perhaps quite contrary to their actual dispositions.

13

But I doubt that many would accept "Delehaye's Principle" as universally applicable. We cannot confirm nor refute that principle in the instance of Saint Nicholas. What seems to be the action earliest attributed to that saint, *Stratilates 3,** to be discussed later in this chapter, is so attractive an action that it might justly be regarded as the seed of a cult. Yet not all can believe that any man performed it—Nicholas or another. It is the kind of tale that might equally well float about looking for a hero to attach itself to.

No matter how legends originated, in antiquity they were classed as eloquence, and as such were subject to the principles of rhetoric. Of the three Aristotelian classes of rhetoric—forensic, deliberative, and epideictic—those designed to *edify*[2] were monumental. By exalting a *homo* to a *vir* and demigod, the pagans by persuasive example "built up" (*aedificere*) the feeling of confidence in a common cause or community, which might be called patriotism, sociability, or cult. The product of cult would be culture, the purpose of epideictic rhetoric. An instance is Thucydides' *Funeral Oration of Pericles,* which has become part of our culture.[3] Christianity inherited from the pagans a comparatively trite and formulated tradition of epideictic art. The rhetorical rules of Aristotle had become the rigidities of an elder Seneca and the fables and fictions of early hagiographers of diverse sects. Only a most exceptional *Life of Saint Anthony* could rise above the simple vulgarity of later epideictic composition. From such, the saintly legend easily evolved.

The conscious purpose of early legendaries was to inflame through the medium of words, to edify with no more substantiation than an underlying ethical verity. In them sanctity was measured by moral, not historical, standards. Legend found itself cast into colorful biography suggesting human sensibilities, but unbound by mundane limitations. Symeon's Preamble to his *Life of Nicholas* expresses this purpose:

The Father Be Praised 1
It is a skilled and wise thing, the hand of a painter. It knows

Throughout the volume, I refer to the separate anecdotes, as narrated in a specific text, by catchphrase and Verbal Relic number. At the end of the volume, p. ooo, these 85 Verbal Relics or anecdotes are listed in numerical order—e.g., *Stratilates* is no. 3 in the list. Primary discussions of each Verbal Relic are indexed in the General Index according to catch phrase.

so beautifully how to reflect the truth and to externalize the significance of things. But a more skilled thing is the faculty of speech, by far a more effective instrument than painting for expressing that which man desires and making it clear. For it is better able to induce and motivate the minds of men to imitation, and to stir them to proper ends. Indeed, the life of one of those men who have lived according to God's will, expressed in speech, draws and summons many men to virtue and will completely inflame them to similar zeal. An example of this, to be sure, is the life of our father Nicholas. His life more than another's both delights our ears and causes our souls to be happy, and stirs us to the performance of good deeds. Therefore the story of his life should be related and recounted in speech for reconsideration of the merits. Even if they have been known to many before and on that count need no telling (if not for recalling and refreshing your memories), then to gladden your souls, which love virtue.[4]

Here is the cultist's interest in the relation of shadow and substance, known to us from antiquity through exegesis of the Second Commandment, Plato's debates about poets in politics, the Second Book of Aristotle's *Rhetoric,* the tracts of the Gnostics and Neoplatonists, and Christian allegory. This interest often stirred men to action, as in the bloody christological and iconoclastic controversies. Christian piety developed in lands traditionally committed to religious *mysteria.* When we look for the forms and purposes of Christian hagiography, we have to ask many of the same questions about the relation of faith and fiction, figure and fact, that the Apostolic Fathers asked of the Eleusinian or Orphic *drama mysticon.*

The Hellenistic world cultivated epideictic art, that is, the exemplary reflection of the Idea. Although the graven image and the verbal image alike incite belief, the Second Commandment forbids the graven image, though the very Commandment is itself verbal imagery. Moslem and Iconoclast, both following Mosaic law, forbade visual images but not spoken ones. A saint's Life is *legenda,* "what ought to be read," because it is truer than depiction.

In "the life of those who draw that life from God," art hangs on a point of grammar: "the life" or "lives"? A legend is a life of saints, for all things are common in the communion of saints, and what is essentially true of one is true of all. The figuration extends far beyond the scriptural types and antitypes. The common spiritual goodness forms a common material appearance which to a theologian may be only symbolic but to many worshipers is reality itself. If Peter walks upon water, every saint walks or may walk upon water. Every true Christian is a saint. His life, stamped or typed by God, has in some way been prefigured by N, as N is prefigured by the Gospel. The Gospel is prefigured by the Prophets, as Prophecy by Law, in one everlasting Life in which all postapostolic saints likewise commune. Hence Père Delehaye called legends "un genre où le plagiat est la règle."[5] Epideictic art is legendary, that is, what ought to be read as multiple and diverse reflections of unity.

A Life of a saint, an *encomium,* was normally built to rhetorical formula, graduated in a series of steps from birth to death. Aristotle had treated the characteristics of three *loci* or ages of man: youth, prime, and eld.[6] Early Christianity added more ages, sometimes totaling six or seven. The Lifes* of saints were normally constructed on a chronologically arranged sequence of such ages. The seven ages which form this volume are such steps. Each was illustrated by actions, incidents, tales, examples, usually circulating in an oral tradition—the kind of homely illustration that suits the ethics of the home. It may be fathered on one member of the family or another without losing its essential truth; for human memory is carefree about the who's and when's but is apt to retain settings and features that "fit the picture."

The first such Life of N was not composed until an incompletely identified Michael the Archimandrite wrote shortly before the year 842.[7] His was followed by a spate of Lifes to be discussed below in chapter 2, ii. The Iconoclastic upheaval of the eighth century, which destroyed the bulk of evidence of the Christian cult of saints existing in the Hellenic world before that time, seems an obvious reason for N's prolonged *infantia*. That period of inexpressiveness concurrent with Iconoclasm began to disappear about the time of the Second Council of Nicea, A.D. 787, an event which her-

---

*The spelling, which I shall continue throughout, may seem an affectation. But it emphasizes that the many authors conceived of their act of composition as retelling the same life without change of fact or emphasis. And not only the Life of N but the Life of a Saint, since all saints' lifes should essentially be one.

alded the demise of the icon breakers and the rebirth of hagiography.

However, these boyhood Lifes do incorporate a few tales and incidents for which there is evidence of earlier existence, sometimes inferential rather than documentary. They so conform with N's emerging personality that a biographer sees in them an infancy that fathers the man. They deal with pagan gods that N displaced in men's affections—Poseidon and the Ephesian Artemis—and with the relation of Church and State which the prelatical N exemplified.

III N AND THE PAGAN GODS

An early tale is *Diana* or *Artemis 4.* Its spiritual message is extirpation of paganism. There is a kind of dramatic propriety in the conflict between N, to become the most popular Christian saint along the Ionian shore, and Artemis, the most renowned of pagan gods along that shore: "Great is Diana of the Ephesians, whom all the world worshippeth," says Acts xix, in recording Saint Paul's founding of the Church of the Ephesians. When N drew devotion away from the pagan cult, battle lines were drawn on which he and Artemis fought.

The Ephesian Artemis, possibly Phoenician, was not the chaste Artemis of Athens; but both together were associated with the moon, and therefore sailed the stellar sea, as does the moonship in its quarter phases.[1] Though an early epithet for the Ephesian goddess was Potamia, and the Ephesian temple was more than a mile from the sea, up the fertile marshy valley of the Maeander, Lactantius records[2] that she was the seamen's patron, and Strabo writes that on sea trade her city grew richer every day. Pliny made a revealing error in stating that the Artemesion was washed by the sea;[3] to a Pliny she and the sea were one. As archeologists have recently discovered, five Artemesia were built in succession on the same spot, the last and greatest one of the Seven Wonders. "Kings, states, and individuals with treasury or money to deposit banked it here, happy in the security provided by her sanctity."[4] The Goths destroyed the temple in A.D. 262, but the cult persistently lingered on. *Firebomb 5* suggests that N usurped her patronage.

Christian doctrine normally encouraged the faithful to observe and collect in "one body" the attributes of good in human beings as a reflection of God the Creator: "He gave some apostles; and some, prophets; and some, evangelists; and some, pastors and teachers; for the perfecting of the saints, for the work of the ministry, for the edifying of the body of Christ" (Rom. iv, 11 - 12). It was a Christian duty to visualize, impersonate, divine attributes in flesh wherever found. So the Christian Fathers seldom discouraged the assignment to saints of traits of thought and deed which had been deified by pagans before them. Nevertheless, they abhorred the customs of pagan cult whenever the act might suggest a literal belief in a pagan mythology, or result in the adoration in their own right of natural forces created by God, or induce moral disorder. In the early, or pre-imperial, Church it was common to proscribe an action or belief on any of those three counts.[5] But by the fourth century, Christian tradition was becoming a part of imperial culture. The Edict of Toleration (A.D. 311) opened the door to acceptance among Christians as well as pagans of a mythology which might well have scandalized many Apostolic Fathers. But its growth was gargantuan.

We possess a monumental folklore of godly battles over shrines and temples, when Christians tore apart the temples stone by stone to destroy the lurking evils, conceived as devils. Pagan emperor Hadrian failed in his effort to maintain effigies of Jupiter at Christ's tomb, and of Venus at Calvary; the Christian emperor Constantine wholly eradicated a temple of Venus before building Holy Sepulcher on the site.[6]

As might be expected, on the Lycian and Pamphylian shore, which depended on commerce between Ephesus and Antioch, Artemis was the center of battle.[7] According to his legend, Saint Daniel the Stylite (5th cent.) defeated her minions, who used a Syrian church as a staging place for sinking ships and injuring the passers-by. Daniel lived in the church and wrestled with the demons, who resented dispossession. The Devil even enlisted the help of neighboring priests; but the archbishop supported Daniel, who stayed there nine years, healing those who were haunted by the demons.[8] Artemis' sway extended far beyond that coast. Saint Theodore drove her and her demons from her temple near Corinth by reciting psalms at terce through two summer months.[9] Such instances of root-and-branch extirpation especially characterize legends of fourth-century saints, though the actual destruction culminated in the fifth.[10]

We may set the change of spirit among Christians at about the year 400. Up to that time, they speak of temples and statues with a kind of fear because they think of them as the haunts of demons who lustfully breathe the smoke of sacrifices and the scent of incense. But then a "rationalist" point of view supplants those feelings of terror. The temples are viewed as storehouses of duperies and fakes. According to the contemporary historian Rufinus, in the Serapeum at Alexandria (which was destroyed A.D. 390), the statue of Serapis was placed in the west, and an aperture of the east wall let in a ray of sun which at an announced moment played on the lips of the idol, to the marvel of the people.[11] Such acts led polemicists to depict temples as palaces of illusion, caverns of debauchery and ritual sin.

This phase preceded one of tolerance marked by methods of conversion of pagan haunts to Christian uses. Best known in this connection is the letter of Gregory the Great (A.D. 598 - 604), who in the year 601 recommended to Augustine of Canterbury that with holy water he rededicate pagan temples to Christian uses: "Some solemnity must be exchanged for the pagan rites, so that on the day of rededication or the nativities of the holy martyrs whose relics are there deposited . . ., whilst some gratifications are outwardly permitted the people, they may the more easily consent to the universal consolations of the grace of God."[12] The Parthenon had just been rededicated to Hagia Sophia, and in 609 the Pantheon would become Santa Maria. We still tour to Syracuse to see how the columns of the temple of Minerva became the supports of the bishop's Duomo.

The infant N seems to have undergone both sorts of action. The early tales suggest that N is not only the eradicator of Artemis but Poseidon's converted self.

Here is *Artemis 4,* according to Symeon:

> When every land subject to his rule had received Constantine's decrees of toleration, all Christians and confessors returned to their own states. Thus the citizens of Myra received back their pontiff Nicholas, an unbloodied Victor though by nature and will a martyr. Strengthened by the gifts which God had granted him, he cured all the infirm from everywhere.
>
> So famous and renowned did he quickly become not only among the faithful but among many of the infidels as well that in all minds he was admired beyond the power of words.
>
> Now when he discovered that many of the shrines of the

N✝

idols still existed, and that great broods of demons dwelt
therein and were disturbing some of the citizens of Myra,
incensed in mind he set out with force and holy zeal to
range through the whole infested region. Wherever he
found such a shrine, he tore it down, reducing it to dust. In
this way he drove the mass of demons away and brought
about tranquillity for the folk to enjoy.[13] Understand, when
the saint as adversary of the Evil Spirit thus waged war, it
was the inspiration of the Supreme Being and a more divine
Intelligence that effected these results for him. Eventually he
did not even abstain from the temple of Artemis, but attacked it also, doing with it as he had done with the others.

That temple was outstanding—remarkably beautiful and
unsurpassed in magnitude. It had been a most felicitous resort for demons. But when Nicholas launched his attack
against the temple, an attack both vigorous and devastating,
he not only destroyed everything that towered aloft, and
hurled that to earth, but he uprooted the whole from its
very foundations. Indeed, what was highest, at the very pin-
nacle of the temple, was embedded in earth, and what was
in the earth was impelled into the air.

The evil demons, who had no way of withstanding the
attacking saint, fled shrieking aloud. And they protested that
they had suffered great agony at his hands and were driven
mercilessly from their possessions. Clearly, the saint's force
in effecting this campaign, and the attack which he
launched against the demons, brought about a good result.[14]

These sentences are so typical as to seem merely hagiographic formula, remote in time and place from actuality, as indeed they are. Yet
they fit the character of infant N in time, place, and circumstance—
like the Cid born in a good hour (en buen ora naçido).

"Martyr" is the Greek word, "confessor" the Latin word, for
"witness." In the days of persecution, from Nero to Diocletian, the
faithful Christian who was tried in the Roman court and executed was
the witness, the public example of the viability of Christianity. Hence
"martyr" came to assume that special meaning of one who physically
died for the faith. All ardent Christians wanted to be martyrs (Origen

is a dramatic instance), but would not anticipate the Providence of God by seeking martyrdom.

When toleration came, there were presumably no more martyrs. But piety still needed witnesses, the fleshly exemplars of the good of Christian living. For these new witnesses, who died in bed rather than in the arena, a convention arose of using the Latin synonym, "confessor." On hearing the news that Martin of Tours was dead (A.D. 397), Sulpicius wrote:

> Cleansed from every stain, he walks in the throng whose leader is the Lamb. For although the character of our times has been such as not to afford him the opportunity of martyrdom, he nonetheless will share the martyr's glory. If it had been given to him to have a part in those struggles which were waged in the days of Nero and Decius, then (I call the God of heaven and earth to witness) he would have mounted of his own free will upon the rack or he would have flung himself spontaneously into the fire . . . . Though he was assailed by every kind of trial, his will to conquer, his patience in waiting, his serenity in enduring, always gave him the victory.[15]

The unmartyred Christian shepherds who had been harried from their sees during persecution now returned, confessors. The common word for martyrs and confessors became "saints," a word originally used for any true Christian, that is, all baptized or elect.

The frenzied destruction which *Artemis 4* describes is also general truth. Demons, which are latent power, inhabit the very temple stones, which are relics, encasing the same kind of vigor to be found in N's bones, locks of Byron's hair, or shreds of Valentino's clothes. Though early Christians shunned pagan relic hunting, they did so because the relics were potent, not impotent. No material vestige may remain, to be preserved by infidels as haven for demonic power. N's aerating of the temple's foundation stones represents dramatic truth, as does a depiction of the shrines as rural, away from the metropolis, for, etymologically speaking, a pagan is a peasant, and dark superstition lurks in sylvan glades of the *pagus* or "backwoods."

A second tale of Artemis, *Firebomb 5*, depicts a culture later than the stage of extirpation. The Christian N, now People's Victor, has settled into his Miltonic battle with the powers of Pandemonium. In *Artemis 4* Nicholas acted when alive; in *Firebomb 5* his spirit acted after death:

N̈

Pilgrims flocked to Myra from all parts of the earth as numerous partakers of his grace. It happened that some lived in the remote regions of Lycia and therefore had to travel for many days; nonetheless undeterred, they resolved to visit the tomb of the saint and partake of sanctification.

So they raised their sails and set out on the sea for the metropolis.

A malignant demon that once dwelt in the temple of Artemis but had been expelled with many another when glorious Nicholas had toppled the shrine to earth became aware of their sea journey. Partly in hatred for the saint, because Nicholas had destroyed his temple and thereby made him homeless, by his powers trying to exterminate him, but partly also in wanting to keep the pilgrims from the exercise of sanctification, with a wish to undo their plans he disguised himself as a woman, carrying a jar apparently full of oil.

The "woman" said to the pilgrims that she would very much like to carry the jar to the saint's tomb, but that she feared the thought of making so long a voyage. For, she said, it is not possible that any woman alive would be so brave as to undertake the difficult sea voyage. "Therefore I ask you to take this jar and present it at the tomb of the saint. There you can fill his lamps with the oil."

The horrible demon made this request in words, handing over the jar to the pilgrims. However, as I shall shortly relate, this was the first step in an evil action and one truly worthy of the demon who made it.

Then they received it, and the first day of their voyage passed. O faithful servant of God and egregious defender of those in jeopardy, Nicholas! This too was thy task, which was performed miraculously and beyond the power of imagination! For in the night Nicholas appeared to one of them and ordered the jar to be thrown into the deep.

When they arose at first light, they did as he said and cast it into the sea. At once the sky lit up in flame, and the most terrific stench followed. Then the waters began to split apart, booming like hell broken loose, with a tremor like an earthquake, emitting a rumbling; and drops of water glistened in the morning light. Then the ship, buffeted by the huge waves, began to sink.

The men, stunned by such an unbelievable prodigy, lamenting as one, and clearly hopeless, looked at each other but found no way out of their plight.

Yet he who from afar had taken account of their safety and had ordered that the jar be cast into the sea now appeared before them. He freed them from that evil instance and from the peril at sea; for at once the ship, without further interruption, moved from that spot, and the men had their fears assuaged.

A gentle and fragrant breeze wafted them, and they delighted in the balm. Their hearts were filled with the greatest joy.[16]

Was this story in circulation before the Byzantine employment of "Greek fire," which *Firebomb 5* vividly describes? "Life follows art," and many an invention has been preceded by its fable. According to one prevalent belief, Greek fire was invented by the engineer Kallinikos in the year 678. It revolutionized warfare scarcely less than did gunpowder 650 years later.[17] At first it was packed in clay jars and hurled, to break on enemy decks and explode. (In 941 the Russian attackers of Constantinople jumped into the sea in full armor to drown rather than to face it.) Applications of the substance spread, and it was used on land in the Crusades, often with the image of N in men's minds, as a chronicle records. At all events, Greek fire saved the Roman Empire from the Moslem navy, or so it is generally understood.[18] Throughout the Middle Ages the meteorological phenomena now more commonly called Saint Elmo's (or Helme's or Telme's) Fire were named for N.[19] When the devil took a devilish form for pageants and other drama, N, the protector against explosives, often controlled his fire. Exorcism, too, attached itself to N's personality, as to that of many another saint in imitation of Christ. But N's exorcisms were

generally of a violent and explosive type, as we shall see. The Collect
for Nicholas Day in the Roman liturgy says: "We beg that we may be
freed through his merits and prayers from the fires of hell."[20]

IV N AS PATRON OF MARINERS

N was sometimes conceived not as Artemis' enemy and destroyer but
as her reincarnation, a saint successor to a goddess. This human trait
of converting images reminds us of Saint Ciappelletto in the first story
of the Decameron and many another.[1] In Aitolia, on the Gulf of
Patras, a ruined chapel of Saint Nicholas stands on the site of a temple
of Artemis; near Chalcis at what was Aulis, a little Byzantine church of
Saint Nicholas has replaced the Artemisium.[2]

The temple of Poseidon on the island of Eleusa, now Saint
Nicholas Church, might seem a similar instance, but inversion is not
involved. N is the Christian Poseidon, a white-horsed rider of the
waves. A cluster of N tales of rescue at sea are mostly trite—a last
stage of degraded Homeric myth. What is probably the earliest of
these, *Mariners 6,* tells how the living bishop N, invoked by foundering
sailors, appeared to calm the waves. The rescued sailors then voyaged
on to Myra, where they found the saint performing his normal diocesan
duties. They threw themselves at his feet in thanksgiving, but he
said, "What happened is the mercy of God alone. Because of the
strength of your faith, in His clemency He deigned to save you." After
further instruction from the good shepherd, "they went on their way,
marveling at his humility of spirit, niggardly garb, adeptness of speech,
and overpowering virtue."[3] There is no evidence that the tale circulated
before the eighth century, but it was ubiquitous thereafter.
Except in the one remarkable respect, that the miracle took place
while N was still alive, it seems an unimaginative coinage designed to
deify by upbuilding N as a kindly patron of the sea—a Poseidon-
Neptune—rather than the destroyer of Artemis and her dark, ugly
powers. The remarkable appearance of the living N is doubtless a
borrowing from *Stratilates 3* to be discussed shortly.

Orderic, the Norman chronicler, adapted *Mariners 6* so as to have N
rescue William the Conqueror on the English Channel.[4] Trite though
the tale might be, it kept its popularity until Columbus's time and was
used by the best of verbal and graphic artists, as we shall see. Columbus's
contemporary, the Italian poet Mantuan, verbalized it:

> *Cum turbine nautae*
> When some Cilician sailors,
> *Deprensi Cilices magno clamore vocarent*
> Swamped in a hurricane, invoked the aid
> *Nicolai viventis opem, descendere quidam*
> Of living Nicholas, one thought he saw
> *Coelituum visus sancti sub imagine patris:*
> The father-saint descend from upper air
> *Qui freta depulso fecit pacidissima vento.*
> To drive away the wind and calm the waves.[5]

Mantuan only updated his patron Virgil, who described the venerable wild olive on the Laurentine shore on which rescued sailors hung their votive offerings to Neptune.[6] Such ex votos were standard paganism, as lines of Horace show:

> *Me tabula sacer*
> Me in my vowed
> *Votiva paries indicat uvida*
> Picture the sacred wall declares to have hung
> *Suspendisse potenti*
> My dark and dripping weeds
> *Vestimenta maris deo.*[7]
> To the stern God of sea.

Consistently among Christians the thanks are turned to N. "All ships and boats carry his icon with an ever-burning lamp, and in his chapels models of boats, coils of cables, anchors, and such things are given as votive offerings."[8] Regularly in Greek ports (e.g., Piraeus, Mykonos) the church on the quay is dedicated to him. The newly discovered American shores were dotted with Saint Nicholas Ports, Saint Nicholas Ferries, and the like. Among the maritime protectors, only Sancta Maria Stella Maris has been more generally invoked. (As we shall see, N and Saint Mary often travel hand-in-hand.) The Greek Isles are filled with ports and promontories bearing one name, or the other, or both as at, e.g., Saint Euboca, island of Kea, West Pylos. At La Pointe Saint-Nicolas, on the approach to the port of Moribhan in Brittany, sailors alternated the chant *Ave Maris Stella* with prayers to N.

Andrew of Crete (d. 740?) in his Encomium to N thought that Noah was N's prototype: "Noah was just and beloved of God for his sacrifices. In his wooden Ark he saved all species of the irrational animals. But you, Nicholas, offer to God spiritual sacrifices, your mystic adorations; and you display to the human race, in the flux of Arian heresy, the Church of Christ, the new Ark of Salvation, saving it by your true and earnest doctrine."[9] Noah and Nicholas appear together in medieval painting and sculpture.[10] Though the pagan Noah was commonly Deucalion, in this range of images Poseidon was the pagan Noah. Among the Christian Fathers, Poseidon was, like Noah, believed to be a figure from history, for euhemerism was orthodox.[11] Enveloping the community of saints, in which all things are common, is the community of man: "Above all nations is humanity." What Noah and Poseidon could do, N does. We shall come to see N ride a white horse (the spume of the cresting wave) as did Poseidon. He rides as easily as he controlled Greek fire.[12]

N the Seaman seems a natural product of the Byzantine sixth and seventh centuries.[13] Roman emperors had given no serious thought to an imperial navy. Hannibal's travel by elephant did not strike the ancients as absurd. Julius Caesar's getting to Britain betrays an active mind at work but a mediocre naval tradition.

Naval historians tend to think that the fleet of the Vandals of North Africa, which controlled much of the Mediterranean in the fifth century, awakened the Roman emperors. Anastasius (A.D. 491 - 518) was the first to show even a tepid interest in a navy. Some historians like Lewis maintain what other historians like A. H. M. Jones deny, that when in 536 Justinian reorganized the Asiatic shores he did so for naval reasons; at all events, even he suffered from the Vandals' sea strength in the west. After the Vandals' hegemony, the Persians, Avars, and others from the east began to threaten on the sea. In 626 the Slavs were defeated on water after they had destroyed the "Church of Saint Nicholas" at Myra, already mentioned.

Then came the Arab inundation: In 634 - 636 Syria fell; 640 - 642, Egypt; 643 - 708, Africa; and in 711, Spain. Indeed, the wave washed all the way to Poitiers, France, in 732. In 649 Cyprus fell to the Arabs, and in 652 the Greek fleet was defeated off Alexandria. In 655 the Emperor Constans II personally led his navy to a disaster off the Lycian coast in which he lost five hundred ships.

Despite the invention of Greek fire, the Byzantine fleets habitually lost engagements and needed all the divine aid they could muster. In 698 the navy deposed the emperor Leontius and placed an admiral on the throne; in 711 they did the same thing, deposing Justinian II. In the year 718, which Bury called "an oecumenical date," the Moslem fleet and army besieged Constantinople itself for a full year before being driven off by the new emperor, Leo III the Isaurian. Thereafter western and eastern forces, the sons of Sarah and Hagar, battled rather equally for sea control, but battled nonetheless.

During those years from Justinian I to Leo III, Constantinople assumed the patronage of N. Every text of the infant legend in whatever form bears that city's stamp, as do the proper liturgies. One reason surely must have been his control of the sea lanes. According to Janin, before Constantinople fell in 1453 there were in the city twenty-five Nicholas churches of record; their dates of construction are not clearly known.[14]

In circulation in the sixth century, possibly older than *Mariners 6,* was *Grainships 7,* which was recorded by Symeon; it made of N a modern Joseph:[15]

> Once when famine spread over the whole of Lycia, the city
> of Myra exhausted its food supply and struggled against
> those same evils. Then to a certain seaman who had dealt in
> grain, the great Nicholas appeared in the night. After giving
> him three measures of gold in pledge, Nicholas ordered him
> to approach the city of Myra and sell the grain to the citi-
> zens there. The merchant, astonished at finding the gold in
> his hand, pondered the vision, marveling at what had hap-
> pened. Nevertheless he went to Myra, where he sold his
> grain in the city. Those who live in the city ascribe the relief
> of famine in that instance to God and the great Nicholas (as
> they do much else).[16]

The theme of *three* may be inspired by the earlier *Stratilates 3,* which we will consider next. Three, especially in three measures of gold, is an identifiable part of N's developing personality, as is his night visit. Here, N may be a disembodied spirit, or he could be a living bishop; but he is a ubiquitous rectifier of economic distribution.

Another version of *Grainships 7* has three imperial galleys putting in at Andriake, the port of Myra. N hastens from Myra and begs the captain for some of his cargo, but is refused because the emperor's agents have already weighed the grain. N promises the captain immunity from punishment. The grain which N acquired miraculously lasts for two years, with seed corn for a third. Yet more miraculously, the ships deliver the full weight of grain when they arrive at Byzantium.[17] *Stratilates 3* even more obviously casts its shadow on this version.

To indicate in what way simple images in infant legend may grow in size and complexity, if not in import, I paraphrase a much later version:

> Five years after the death of N, a great famine struck. N then appeared to a relative, Theodulos, and bade him establish a public prayer service in the N sanctuary. Around midnight at the service there is a notable earthquake. The coffin of the saint opens; from the outstreaming perfume of the myrrh, the pangs of hunger are assuaged. The blind and lame are healed. The next day N appears, in the guise of a patriarch with keenly flashing eyes, a staff with flames of fire in his hand, walking on the sea to five grainships going from Cyprus to Constantinople. N buys the grain, pays the price, and bids the sailors sail to Myra. At the instigation of the Devil, they all deceitfully pocket the money and change from the prescribed course. When they are hit by a terrific storm, they repent and promise to fulfill their contracts. They land at Myra, calm the fears of the Myrians, tell them what happened, and sell them the grain. At the tomb of N they recognize him when he appears to them. They lay the money at his tomb, with which to institute a great feast for the saint.[18]

It is by *Grainships 7* that the first iconographic symbol of N is inspired: three loaves of bread. "Saint Nicholas loaves" becomes a standard phrase and commodity. A report of the seventeenth century confirms that Mediterranean sailors would not embark without a supply of such loaves, which they threw into the sea at first sign of tempest.[19]

V *STRATILATES* AND THE THEME OF CHURCH AND STATE

Undoubtedly the most distinguished incident in the whole life of N appears in infancy and may well have been his earliest. It was the only one specified in the official Roman Martyrology, which reads as follows:

> *VIII id. Dec.,* the birthday of Nicholas, bishop and confessor, at Myra, which is a chief city of Lycia. Among the many egregious miracles related of him, that one is especially memorable which reports that, though stationed far away, by appearance in vision through warnings and threats he deflected the emperor Constantine from destruction to compassion for certain men who had invoked him.[1]

Following some predecessors, I choose the Greek word for "military line officers," *Stratilates 3,* as catch-title. This narrative circulated separately in the seventh century, before any of the Lifes, not only in Greek but in Latin and Syriac as well.[2] By the tenth century at least five Greek versions were known. As Byzantium, New Rome, symbolized stable government throughout the known world, so did *Stratilates 3* come to symbolize a perilously maintained balance between the powers of State and the Church within it. Since from Constantine to Pope Urban II this balance was the predominant concern of western civilization, we will find it dominating N's personality in his first three ages, and setting his habits of choice and action for life; almost solely to it we may attribute N's exceptional growth in popularity and power.

Stratilates seems to have been the first action of N to receive liturgical notice. Even in the Latin west it found its place in a passional of the seventh century, which eventually penetrated to the transalpine north. I translate the complete narrative from that Latin version. For reasons that will become evident in the reading, I divide the story, calling the first half *Citizens of Myra 2* and the whole story *Stratilates 3.*

> In the days of the great emperor Constantine there was unrest and dissension in Frigia Adaifalorum,[3] and it was suggested to the most benign emperor that the evils be ex-   N⧾

terminated. At once he sent an army with the officers in command who were called Nepotianus, Ursus, and Eupoleonis. Crossing the strait from their station in Constantinople, they eventually sailed into the Lycian prefecture.

They came to a place called Andriake, which constituted the port for the metropolis of Myra lying three miles, more or less, from it. There they took shore leave from their anchored ship because there was no wind for sailing. Some of the soldiers separated from the main group, to find food and recreation—ostensibly to buy food for the whole party. Shortly some looters, impersonating those soldiers, were arrested for looting and pilfering. As a result a great crowd started to riot in a plaza called Placomatus. Even the Myrians at the metropolis heard the crowd, who were mobbing the soldiers as if they were the lawbreakers.

The tumult and noise were great indeed. Hearing it, the servant of God Nicholas, who administered the Holy Church of God there as bishop, walked down to quiet the disturbance, asking whether anything wrong or illegal had been done. As he arrived at Andriake, the officers of the army saw him and hailed him, drawing him into conference. The soldiers who knew him and the others who met him for the first time greeted him and embraced him with great affection. He asked them: "Where do you come from, and on whose business do you come, and for what reason do you come?"

They told him: "We are peaceful. Our most benign emperor sent us to engage in battle with some lawbreakers, and we are on our way. Pray for us, most holy father, that we may prosper on our journey."

Then the holy bishop invited them to go back to Myra with him, there to receive his blessing and to partake of food. The soldiers, admiring both the most holy bishop himself and his softspokenness, commanded everybody to quiet the tumult and thereby avoid arrest. Then Nicholas urged the soldiers to climb with him to the bishop's palace.

Just then some people came from the city to that most

holy man, saying: "Lord, if you had been in the city, three innocents would not have been handed over to death as they were, because Judge Datianus, taking those three men into custody, has ordered them beheaded. The whole city is in a turmoil because Your Sanctity was not to be found there."

On hearing this, the most holy bishop became downcast. After speaking with the soldiers, he took their leaders and crossed the city.

Coming to a plaza named Leonti, he asked those who were coming away from those who had received sentence whether they were still alive. They told him that the men still lived and were directly ahead at a place known as Dioscorus, which they would find at the martyrium of the brother confessors Crescentius and Dioscorus. As they were talking, Nicholas said that the victims ought by now to be coming out. When they got to the gate, some told him that they were in a place called Byrra: that was to be place of the beheading.

Saint Nicholas, now running, found a great crowd of people before the executioner, who was holding his sword up, anticipating the coming of the holy man. When Nicholas came up to the place of the confessors of Christ, he found the three men with their faces covered with linen cloths. They had been placed in position, with their hands tied behind them. They were bending their knees and bowing their heads, expecting death.

At that moment Saint Nicholas, according as it is written, "The righteous are bold as a lion" (Proverbs xxviii, 1), fearlessly grabbed the sword from the executioner and cast it to the ground. Loosening the men from their chains, he took them with him to the city.

Walking down to the Pretorium, he thrust open the door and entered the presence of Eustathius the Praeses. The Praeses, hearing from a guard what had been done, now walked up to honor the holy man. But the servant of God, Nicholas, turned away from him saying: "Sacrilegious blood shedder! How dare you confront me, apprehended in so many and such evil acts! I will not spare or forgive you, but will let the mighty emperor Constantine know about you—how many and how serious are the sins which you have been discovered in, and in what fashion you administer your princely prefecture."

Then Eustathius the Praeses fell to his knees and begged him: "Be not wrathful with thy servant, lord, but speak the truth, that I am not the guilty one, but the heads of state, Eudoxius and Simonides."

Nonetheless the holy man answered: "It is not Eudoxius and Simonides who did this, but silver and gold." For the holy man had learned that the Praeses was to receive more than two hundred pounds of silver to execute the citizens for crime. Yet the most holy man, after the officers of the army had earnestly spoken in behalf of the Praeses, granted him pardon, once the charges which the Praeses had leveled against the three men were cleared.

Then the army chiefs, during their refection with the very holy man, asked him to pray for them, and received from him his benediction. After prayers, they bade good-bye and sailed away. Finally coming to Frigia and pacifying the tumultous populace, they returned to their quarters at Constantinople. A great reception was prepared by those who were in the city. As if taking the triumphs away from the master of the forces, and the emperor and his whole court, they came to be lionized in the palace.

N But the Devil instilled immoderate envy of them in the heart of the man who was master of forces. He rendered a writ to the prefect, Ablabius, who on hearsay evidence could betray them to their death, promising him one thousand, seven hundred pounds of gold. The prefect Ablabius, agreeing to the proposal, entered the presence of the emperor Constantine and said to him:

"Most pious lord, a great sedition and conspiracy has been formed against Your Potency by the officers of the army who were sent to Frigia. For I learn as a fact that they have engaged themselves to rise up against Your Clemency.

They make pretence that they are acting in your behalf while they work for money and bribes and create high honors for themselves. When I learned of this, I could not keep silent; for such iniquity is contrary to my principles. Now, immediately, if it please Your Clemency, act!"

The emperor was consumed with wrath. He immediately ordered the officers to be placed in custody without inquiry.

After a short time, those who were plotting against the officers put great pressure upon the prefect Ablabius, saying, "Why do you remand them to prison but leave them alive? As long as they stay in prison they can help their own cause."

So the prefect, after listening to them, announced himself to the emperor and said: "Most pious lord, behold how those men whom you ordered to be incarcerated, Nepotianus, Ursus, and Eupoleonis, live on in prison, developing their intrigues throughout the imperial rule of Your Amplitude and Potency!"

When the emperor heard these assertions, he ordered the officers to be beheaded by the sword during the night.

The prefect, on obtaining this order, immediately left the palace and instructed the warden of the prison, saying: "These three men, whom you have safe in prison, should be prepared for the decree of death this night."

The warden went at once to the officers on hearing this, and with bitter tears cried out to the three men: "Men and my lords, sorrow grips me, and fear and trembling. Ay me, would that I had never seen or heard of you! But now I do speak, and do you listen! Tomorrow we shall be separated one from another, for you are ordered to die. Whatever you possess, silver or gold or anything else that you can give away, send off. For this night you have been ordered to die!"

The men, hearing these words from him, tore their clothes and hair from their heads, and threw themselves in the dust, crying aloud, "What evil did we do, that we should perish so miserably?"

One of them, Nepotianus, remembering what the holy

man of God Nicholas did in the case of the three men, crying out with tears said, "Lord God of Saint Nicholas, have mercy upon us; and just as Thou didst with the three men who were iniquitously and unjustly adjudged to death in Lycia, when Thou didst save them, now in like fashion save us. Saint Nicholas, servant of Christ, though you be far from us, bring your intercession the nearer to us, and your behest to Thy Lord God and Our Lord Savior Jesus Christ. Intercede for us that we be rescued from iniquity and the deathbearing tempest, that we may be deemed worthy to come and adore the most holy tokens of thy paternity."

When Nepotianus had uttered this and more in the same vein, then all three as if with one voice prayed to the same effect.

Then Saint Nicholas himself appeared on that very night to the emperor. He said to him:

"Constantine, emperor, rise and free those three men whom you have remanded to prison, Nepotianus and Ursus and Eupoleonis, officers of the army, who have been condemned on hearsay. If you do not obey me, I will stir up an uncontrollable revolt against you, and hand over your carcass and your entrails to the wild beasts for food, bearing witness against you before the celestial King Christ."

Then said the emperor, "Who are you, and how did you get into my palace?"

Said the holy man, "I am Bishop Nicholas, a sinner, who lives in the metropolis of Lycia."

With these words he disappeared. Nevertheless, the same night he made his way to confront Ablabius the prefect, saying to him: "Ablabius, stricken in neither conscience nor mind, rise and free those three men, officers of the army, whom you hold in custody, though innocent. But if you do not wish to listen to me and to resolve to free them, I shall bear witness against you before the immortal King Christ. You will fall ill and end as food for worms, and your whole family will perish evilly."

Ablabius said to him, "But who are you and where do you come from, to speak so?"

Then Saint Nicholas said, "I am Nicholas, a sinner, servant of God. I am the Metropolitan in Myra." Having said this, he disappeared in the same fashion as before.

When the emperor awoke, he sent for Ablabius, saying, "Go, call the prefect Ablabius, and tell him what I saw and heard." As soon as he had told the messenger all that had happened, he sent him away.

Similarly the prefect sent the same nuncio back to the emperor, telling the same story. And immediately the emperor ordered the three officers of the army to be presented to him in the presence of his court and commoners as well as the prefect.

When they had all assembled, he said to the officers: "Tell me, what kind of magic do you do, that you can so affect us in our sleep?"

But they stood silent, staring at the ground. Then he asked them the same thing again.

One of them, Nepotianus, said: "Most pious lord, your servants know nothing of magic. But if we had thought of any such thing, or if we have done any evil against the majesty of Your Pious Emperorship, may Your Benign Potency order us to undergo the most horrible torments and punishment of torture."

The emperor said to him, "Tell me, do you know anyone by the name of Nicholas?"

Hearing that name Nicholas, the officers were inspired and uplifted in heart. As if with one voice they said: "Lord God of Saint Nicholas, hear us. And as Thou didst save those three men who unjustly faced death in Myra, the metropolis of Lycia, so do Thou now save us who unjustly and unfairly face death."

But the emperor said to them, "Tell me, who is this Nicholas?" Then Nepotianus told him what Saint Nicholas had done.

And the emperor said to them: "Now understand this, it is not I who have granted to you your life, but he whom you did invoke, Saint Nicholas, to whom you are devoted. Cut the hair of your head, and don your proper uniforms.

35

Then render thanks to him. And be charitable toward me."

The emperor ordained that they should take several holy vessels and a Gospel all of gold, and two golden candelabra and a gold patina studded with precious stones. Then he sent them away.

They made their way to Myra, the metropolis of Lycia, where they venerated Saint Nicholas. They cut the hairs of their heads and changed their vestments. Amid tears they distributed largesse to the poor from among their own goods, even gold and silver and raiment. And they continued such acts through many years, glorifying and praising Father, Son, and Holy Ghost, now and for ever, world without end. Amen.[4]

The two halves of this story are marked by differences: *Citizens of Myra 2* is laid in Myra, is remarkably circumstantial about names and places, and tells a story which is credible despite idealization. The second half is laid in Constantinople, has all the marks of composition of a fable, with abstract names and unvisualized locales, and tells an incredible story. The names of Constantine and his prefect Ablabius were linked in tradition, the latter executed by Constantine's successor in A.D. 337.[5] If we discount those, the only particulars are the names of the stratilates, carried over from the first part. In the absence of all external evidence, we easily surmise that *Citizens of Myra 2* was composed first and that the second tale, a sequel, was added by a different author, or at least for so different a purpose as to change the form and quality of the writing. In the existing world of pious fiction to which the early Acts and Passions of the martyrs or saints belong, such sequential additions were common.

If there is any truth in that surmise, then we can easily imagine *Citizens of Myra 2* as a legend based on a document (possibly an epistle) reporting a historical incident at Myra centering in a reigning bishop. This bishop called Nicholas was almost certainly not the missionary founder of the diocese. The name may have been his own or an epithet arising from the incident described. A sense of historical action permeates the narrative. We can imagine ourselves in the presence of a real and saintly bishop at the moment of his greatest triumph. Using such a document as basis and suggestion for a fable, a second author then invented a miraculous tale, an epiphany, using in his narration the traditional epic machinery.

Stratilates 3 incorporates traits that we have already observed. They are becoming the unalterable personality of N. Foremost is his unusual ability to be invoked from far places while still performing his mundane duties in the flesh at Myra.[6] In early versions of *Stratilates 3* he is described as "angel-like" (ἰσάγγελος), a "heavenly man" (αἰθέριος),[7] like Habacuc of "Bel and the Dragon"[8] and Philip.[9] Early commentators refer to Habacuc as clearly the prototype for this aspect; yet Habacuc was carried from place to place by an angel, not self-propelled.[10] There are no certain precedents in the Christian tradition for N's miraculous power. Hence the epithet of "thaumaturge."

Second, in conformity with his name, N is the people's champion and victor against an overweening establishment. More by his evident virtue than by prelacy, he renders malleable the imperial bureaucracy. His justice is rough and ready, as it is in *Grainships 7* when he provides food.

Third, he is the exemplary secular bishop, or shepherd of his flock. Among saints, bishops are usually of low esteem: "A Saint in Crape is twice a Saint in Lawn."[11] Most saintly confessors were either pure monk or priest with ascetic attributes. Not N. No recluse, no scholar, not even overtly a man of prayer, he is instantly alert to the safety and well-being of his innocent lambs. A not wholly convincing saint perhaps, but hero yes.

In this instance, the threat against the spirit is government and its officials. Before *Stratilates 3* can be seen in true perspective, we need to review what is to westerners a difficult tradition to understand: that centering of powers and responsibilities in the person of the emperor—a tradition now generally known as *caesaropapism.* [12]

Separation of Church and State is not an ancient idea. Melchizedech was both king of Salem and priest of the Most High God.[13] The Old Testament Judges might concurrently be priests; Saul as king dominated the priests; David was king and priest—a theocrat. Christ, teaching "my kingdom is not of this world," was untraditional. In Graeco-Roman culture the head of state, in addition to other duties, performed sometimes as earthly god, sometimes as high priest; but in any case his will was the ultimate expression of religion. The emperor was *divus* and *invictus*.[14] When Constantine decided to patronize the Christian Church, he acted as president, sitting in the chair at the First Oecumenical Council at Nicea, recognizing from the chair those he allowed to have an opinion. Bréhier remarks, "That extreme adulation astonishes and shocks us, but it was in accord with an official doctrine confirmed by very specific testimony."

There were few precedents for the theme of *Citizens of Myra 2,* let alone *Stratilates 3* as a whole, but historians have cited the instance of the monk Eutychius (or Eutychianus), a contemporary of Constantine. In the early fifth century, the Church historians Socrates[15] and Sozomen[16] tell the same tale of Eutychius, who lived on Olympus in Bithynia. According to Sozomen,

> he healed diseases and wrought miracles, and the fame of
> his virtuous life induced Constantine to seek his intimacy
> and friendship. It so happened that, about this period, a
> certain person who was suspected of plotting against the
> Emperor was apprehended near Olympus and imprisoned.
> Eutychius was besought to intercede in his behalf with the
> emperor, and, in the meantime, to direct that the prisoner's
> chains might be loosened, lest he should perish beneath
> their weight. It is related that Eutychius accordingly sent to
> the officers who held the man in custody, desiring them to
> loosen the chains; and that, on their refusal, he went himself
> to the prison, where the doors, though fastened, opened of
> their own accord, and the bonds of the prisoner fell off.
> Eutychius afterward repaired to the emperor, who was then
> residing in Byzantium, and easily obtained a pardon; for
> Constantine esteemed him too highly to refuse his requests.

Eutychius was Novatian rather than Orthodox, so that with the triumph of Orthodoxy he could not remain an ideal for later emulation. We should not be surprised to have this part of his legend, entertaining as it is, adapted to another protagonist.

Caesaropapism was not without mitigations.[17] Athanasius, constantly in and out of the patriarchate of Alexandria, had resisted the spiritual rule of a series of emperors.[18] To be sure, in his day Christianity was as yet but insecurely knit to the imperial throne; yet the image of his struggle with Constantine and all his sons was transmitted by all Christian historians as antidote for the overweening power of emperors. John Chrysostom as patriarch of Constantinople was powerful enough to inform the emperor's conscience.[19] Emperor Justin I on his coronation promised the clergy to govern them justly and mildly. But Justinian, who followed him on the throne, was unrestrained; he "was one of the most characteristic representatives of the caesaropapist tendency," according to Vasiliev and many others.[20] Though many of the emperors flattered themselves as theologians, Justinian published long tracts on theological questions. He chose the prelates of the Church. For patriarch of Constantinople he would receive a list of three nominations, but he could and did go beyond it. And he could depose his creature for either religious or civil reasons.[21]

His empress Theodora, whom he married out of "a life of the lowest degradation," with the help of Belesarius banished Pope Silverius to N's native city of Patara, in favor of Vigilius. The bishop of Patara journeyed from Lycia to Constantinople to protest against their intrigue to Justinian himself, who ordered an investigation. This historical instance may well have inspired N's legendary action. Some interested contemporary could have composed the second half of *Stratilates* 3 at that time.

But caesar continued pope: Silverius was temporarily restored to the papal chair, but was shortly exiled again, by Justinian himself. Justinian eventually banished Vigilius, who succeeded Silverius. Justinian's patriarch of Constantinople, Menas, opined that "Nothing can be done in Holy Church against the opinion and orders of the emperor."[22]

The Justinian Code of Roman Law comprises what we now call canon as well as civil law. However, Justinian would not have been able to understand such a distinction. As Diehl points out,[23] where modern legislators set a statement of principles at the head of a legal code, in his Code Justinian placed the rubric: "On the very Holy Trinity and the Catholic Faith." It was the rubric for the text of the Nicene Creed. "Be of my opinion," he said to Pope Agapitus, "or I will exile you." In return for obedience, he unreservedly put to the bishops' use public goods and authority for both propagation of faith and repression of heresy. He munificently endowed the Church Temporal, building throughout the land edifices such as Santa Sophia, and the Church of Saint Nicholas which I have mentioned.[24] No legal subterfuges such as characterized the later Inquisition beclouded his acts as protector of the faith. His written assertions on this topic have come down to us: *as the pious and orthodox emperors have always had in their hearts the extirpation of heresies and maintenance of peace in the Holy Church of God, so the first duty of a sovereign is to conserve intact the pure Christian Faith.*[25] Wrote Leontius of Byzantium in the sixth century: "The emperor is predestined in the designs of God to govern the world, as the eye is set in the body to direct it. The emperor has need of God alone, with no intermediary whatsoever between God and him."[26]

Absolutism may have preserved the Roman Empire for fifteen hundred years, but at a high price in rulers. Perhaps the populace accepted the principle, but they did not need to like it. In the four centuries from Julius Caesar to Valentinian II (44 B.C. - A.D. 392), thirty-nine emperors were assassinated or dethroned; five were killed in battle; only nineteen died in their beds. According to Bréhier, almost the same proportions held for the next 1,058 years to the Fall of New Rome in 1453.[27]

But in the imagination of the people, God always governs through intermediaries—angels and His more mundane saints. If the eye sleeps, whence cometh vigilance? *Stratilates 3* is a beautifully framed vehicle for consolidating the hopes of a populace under the species of tyranny described. An effective myth has often checked despotic powers. Small wonder that *Stratilates 3* spread wherever the Roman emperor held sway. It was an imaginative surrogate for violent rule, personifying the Christian shepherd of sailors and merchants as moderator of imperial will. N like Christ scourged the moneychangers but rendered Caesar his due. Hence he ameliorated absolutism without disturbing its foundations, and imperial benignity became a virtue in the seventh century.

Whatever may have been the nonspeaking experiences of N's infancy, *Praxis de Stratelatis* is the first literary text, the first rational or composed words of the growing N. By the best authority the composition is assigned to Justinian's reign.[28]

When Islam exploded and threatened to engulf the West, the patriarch of Constantinople became even more the single voice of religious conscience beneath the emperor; for the Apostolic Sees of Alexandria, Jerusalem, and Antioch fell into Arab hands. Shortly before Alexandria fell, its patriarch Eulogius (A.D. 579 - 607) had been called "vice emperor." But now the patriarch of Constantinople was the only representative, except the pope in Rome, of the apostolic tradition, though his claim to that apostolate was never clear. He was in the secular world a deterrent to imperial absolutism, in the religious world to the growing pretensions of the pope, who after A.D. 476 began to assume secular responsibilities.[29] The patriarch was acknowledged head of fifty-seven metropolitanates, forty-nine archbishoprics, and 514 bishoprics—a formidable hegemony. *Stratilates 3,* the image of the perfectly just and therefore potent shepherd, expressed a proper relationship. The emperors came to use the patriarch of Constantinople as adviser in matters of welfare *and* justice. In the next chapter we shall see in an important instance how the patriarch acted according to the example of N.

The unknown author or arranger of *Stratilates 3* excites our admiration. To N's traits of personality already observed we may add:

N is orthodox. The emphasis of the story is upon *three,* which since Nicea was becoming the orthodox number: three *stratilates,* three citizens of Myra. We have met three ships in one version of *Grainships 7,* almost certainly composed after *Stratilates 3.* From now on, three is N's symbolic number.

N is the protector of *innocentes.* The word *innocentes* is used for both the condemned citizens of Myra and the stratilates in all versions. In the Christian tradition the word is ambiguous—imaging misjudged men and children at the same time. Sidrach, Misach, and Abednego, who are *innocentes* in Daniel iii, are there called men (*viri*) in one verse and boys (*pueri*) in another. Not only because they are a trio, but because they are the prototypes of innocents, they haunt N through his life. The Church's traditional prayer for the protection of the innocents (*Innocentium protectio*) runs:

> God, Who didst grace the blessed Nicholas as protector of
> imperiled innocence whilst he lived, and after his death by
> countless miracles, grant that by his merits we may be freed
> from perversion of justice while alive and from the fires of
> hell (*a gehennae incendiis*) after death.

Obviously this prayer depends upon *Stratilates 3,* but *a gehennae incendiis* refers to *Firebomb 5.*

As protector of *innocentes,* N becomes patron of prisoners.[30] The earliest known dedication to him in Rome was the church beside the civil prison.[31] The Byzantine princess-historian Anna Comnena (A.D. 1083 - ca. 1148) writes of the Nicholas *temenos* called "The Sanctuary," "founded long ago as a refuge for the protection of those being taken for crimes."[32] As champion of *innocentes,* N also becomes patron of lawyers and judges, as we shall see. But as a judge he is the most charitable of Christians, merciful at the expense of the Letter of the Law, as in the instance of the Praeses.[33]

The personality apparent in *Stratilates 3* inspired an early tale, effective in the East but not the West, *The Charter (Praxis de Tributo 8),*[34] which I mention only to confirm the evidence of N's character as he emerges from the Age of Infancy. In this tale N goes to Constantinople to ask for a charter of liberties for the citizens of Myra. When he receives it, he throws it into the sea. Later, when the emperor challenges him, N states that the charter was delivered. Constantine, unbelieving, sends legates to Myra to determine the truth. They find that the charter had been washed up on the shore at Myra, where it was found and delivered by fishermen the very day it had been signed at the capital.

What was not in the early versions of *Stratilates 3*, but soon became attached to the tale as a stage property, is N's whip, switch, or scourge, with which he threatens, indeed chastises, Ablabius and Eustathius the Praeses. There is a promising leaven of low comedy in the potential terror of the villain prefect and his surprise and dismay at the unprecedented apparition. In early retellings, N becomes fierce. In an N hymn of the eighth century, Theodore Studites, the hymnographer, has N rip (*eripuisti*) the innocents from the chains of the "terrible" emperor, certainly the prefect.[35] We shall watch the theme of the switch mature.

An infant at birth, we are told, possesses about twelve million nerve cells, all that he will ever have. They have been fixed in their pattern by perhaps a million years of repetitive organic growth. The infant is not yet himself but a formulated structure of the most essential achievements of life. He is at once nothing but an entity and the inheritor of all that has been. Yet by the time he emerges from infancy, by the time he can speak for himself, he has a personality—not predictable, for Fortune has not yet turned her wheel—but unique. The infant N might live briefly, obscurely, or long and magnificently. He is a bundle of all the legends that ever were born, lived, and died. Yet he now has a way of his own. As behaviorists are apt to say, environmental factors support, inflect, and modify the personality, but they do not generate the progressions of development, which come from within the organism:

> quamvis doctrina politos
> constituat pariter quosdam, tamen illa relinquit
> naturae cuiusque animi vestigia prima.

> Though training may a certain polish bring
> Yet everyone's innately churl or king.[36]

Some traits are identifiable: his thaumaturgic power—especially his power to be present at more than one place at one instant in time; his ingenuous material solutions of complex human relations, with a touch of the macabre; his love of the sea and especially of its commerce, with the sunshine and storms that make life and property the ultimate speculation; his disruption of darkness and its powers through sheer energy; his determinative position between the establishments of Church and State. Once he becomes a man, the universe may well be his.[37]

Boyhood

And then the whining school-boy, with his satchel,
And shining morning face, creeping like a snail
Unwillingly to school.

I BOYHOOD

The traditional date of beginning of boyhood among ancients was seven years.[1] Having learned to speak at home, the little Greek boy was put in charge of a pedagogue, who took him to a master for "discipline." Some Greek authors suggest that while the boy was protected from worldliness during his hours in school, he was apt to be introduced to a very earthy world by the pedagogue on their walks back and forth. There was both action and lore on the byways to entice a pedagogue as well as a boy. "Littered under Mercury," schoolboys like Autolycus and his father before him were curious snapper-ups of unconsidered trifles.[2] Once Autolycus was deposited in school, the master would whip some of these trifles away by forming or conforming the boy to an academic and traditional pattern. Yet he would be a fanatic master indeed who could or would clean away all the dust of the byways that the boy acquired.

Christianity did not alter the traditional age of initiation into boyhood. That was the "age of oblation" for boys dedicated to the religious life, when they were taken inside the cloister (lit. "the barrier") to stay, away from the corrupting world. But few Christian boys were oblates; they remained in "the world." N is the legend of a secular bishop, a man of the world, never cloistered. Although his biographers constantly repeat that he was born of pious parents, no instance of parental piety appears in the legend. They did leave their only child rich in the goods of the world (*Parentage 10*). N was ambient and ambitious, literally "one who got around," as curious as Autolycus. He attached to himself more adventurous tales than did other legendary figures, especially ascetic saints.

The infant of the preceding chapter stayed in the congenial Byzantine world, with a geographical axis no longer than from Myra to Constantinople; and his infancy extended to the time of the Hegira (A.D. 622) and the Iconoclastic Controversy. In this chapter the boy will move on an axis stretching from the Black to the Tyrrhenian Sea from the eighth to the tenth century. I shall treat first the formal training or shaping that N underwent at the hands of his masters, the authors of the Lifes; then describe some of N's extracurricular acquirements; and finally present the young graduate as he stepped into the world.

II The Lifes

Throughout the eighth century, the Iconoclasts held all cult of saints in abeyance, but the reins began to slacken in the ninth, even before the restoration of the icons under Theodora in 843.[1] The masters who disciplined N were those authors already mentioned who wrote Lifes of N, imposing literary form on the matter available to them. Michael the Archimandrite, otherwise unknown, wrote the first Life between the years 814 and 842. The work[2] exists today in a number of MSS, and was the primary source for all subsequent Greek Lifes. Directly or indirectly through later borrowers, Michael's Life became second in importance only to *Stratilates 3*.

Another Life, written very shortly thereafter, professedly by Methodios to Theodoros,[3] was the source for the influential Latin Life written by John the Deacon of Naples about the year 880.[4] Methodios to Theodoros exists in a single MS,[5] probably from southern Italy. It remained unused in the Greek world. There is good reason to believe that this Methodios was the icon-restoring patriarch of Constantinople (843 - 847), known as a panegyrist and hymnographer. His origin in Syracuse may explain why the Neapolitan John used this otherwise neglected work.

To an author of the same name was attributed the *Encomium Methodii,* composed after 860, twice as long as the work to Theodore, and very popular. It exists as a whole or in part in many MSS and was early translated into Armenian and Old Slavic. But there can be no direct connection between the two works of "Methodios."[6] As the title suggests, the second is highly panegyric. It retells Michael's story and adds other incidents. Many other N encomia followed, including one composed by the emperor Leo the Wise (886 - 911).

One more of the many Greek Lifes directly affects our narrative, composed by Symeon Logotheta in the later tenth century.[7] He is known as the Metaphrast, from his habit of altering or paraphrasing the pieces which he assembled in a comprehensive legendary. He had slight concern with authenticity, preoccupied as he was with assembling a library of pious reading of immense scope. It has been his work which most influenced the Renaissance West through the early printed legendaries of Leonard Justinian,[8] Aloysius Lipoman,[9] and Lawrence Surius.[10]

The Lifes were designed for pious meditation. Another genre was what the Byzantine world called synaxaries and the Latin world legendaries. These were Lifes arranged according to the ecclesiastical calendar for congregational or liturgical lections. The "Greater Synaxarion,"[11] shaped about the year 900, digests the earlier Lifes, to be sure, but adds incidents, including one we shall discuss, *Nicea 15*.

Another liturgical genre was hymns. The first identifiable hymnographer to mention N was Theodore the Studite (A.D. 759 - 826). His hymn contains no narrative beyond a reference to *Stratilates 3*.[12] A remarkable hymn *Apud Myros, O sancte 9*, falsely attributed to the famous hymnographer Romanos, was composed in the ninth century, probably in the first half.[13] The hymnographer Joseph, who died at Constantinople A.D. 883, was exceptionally devoted to N.[14]

An unconsidered trifle of the byway which proved infectious is the legend of Nicholas of Sion, which became incorporated in tenth-century Lifes of N, for example, Metaphrastes and the *Vita Compilata*.[15] This kind of confusion of persons haunts every legend of stature, whenever there are heroes of the same name to be commemorated. How many Johns, Jameses, and Peters! Cyprian of Antioch takes on the acts of Cyprian of Carthage. And at a later date Felixes, Benedicts, and Louises. Calabrians trace the journey of Saint Louis, on his return from the Sixth Crusade, through the several towns in which he slept, like Washington. But in fact he did not set foot in Italy, sailing directly from Sidon to Provence.[16] It was Louis VII who returned through Italy, but through Campania, not Calabria. Alexander the Great and Charlemagne absorbed the achievement of all their namesakes.[17] Many of N's traits have become attached to the legends of Saint Nicholas of Trani, of Tolentino—even of Cusa.

Nothing is known of Saint Nicholas of Sion except his legend,[18] but from internal evidence Anrich deduced that he was a holy monk who built and was archimandrite of a cloister of Sion (likewise a common and confusing name) set in the hills behind Myra. He died bishop of

Pinara, December 10, 564. The extensive but naive Life must have been composed at that Sion shortly after the saint died. It seemed to Anrich that one purpose of the Life was the common one of exalting, and attracting pilgrims to, the local relics. The author of this Life of Saint Nicholas of Sion tended to uncultured folkspeech, employing only the more trite rhetorical patterns. Nicholas of Sion was nephew and ward of a Nicholas who was archimandrite of Akalissos, about twenty-five air miles northeast of Myra. The legend is peopled with still more Nicholases, a name undoubtedly popularized by the local cult of N.

N needed his Life to be written in the language of the West, for after the sixth century Greek was seldom understood there. This need was supplied by John, a deacon of the Church of Saint Januarius at Naples, who as a young man of twenty-five about the year 880 loosely translated *Methodios ad Theodorum,* adding rhetorical flourish, and especially a new rendering of *Stratilates 3.*[19] The many Lifes of N of the Latin and Teutonic worlds all owe their basis to this Life by John.[20] Naples was managing somehow to exist precariously in a kind of independence among Romans, Saracens, Lombards, the remnants of Ostrogoths, and occasional intrusions of Carolingians. Its dukes, especially John III, encouraged letters and the collection of Greek MSS. Naples was the primary portal through which a little Greek knowledge sifted into the West.[21]

As I have said, in forming or disciplining N these authors followed the generic patterns of epideictic biography. "The epideictic form," wrote Delehaye, "as it was conceived by the sophists, tended to erase personal and concrete traits and to replace them by abstract qualities. The method of development by the *common places* and the substitution of the universal for the particular create the same difference between the hero of the panegyric and the hero of the historical work as between an authentic portrait from life and the hieratic image where all details are idealized."[22] The biographical common places (*loci communes*) were apt to be six or seven Ages, terminating in a climactic birth-death, to which were appended postmortem evidences of a continuing spiritual guidance and mediation, usually stories of miraculous manifestations.

Since no Lifes of N were composed until five centuries after his presumptive *floruit,* any biographer lacked precise sensible data for his need. But since his biography was an idealization, and in the communion of saints proper biographical details were available in legends of other good and holy men, N was disciplined to conform to them by making him act in well-known saintly ways. Authors seldom explained their epideictic methods, which were traditional, as it were axiomatic. However, Agnellus of Ravenna (b. ca. 805) was an exception and I quote him. He was ordered to write the Lifes of all the bishops of Ravenna for eight hundred years! At one point in his long narration, as a kind of interlude, he stepped aside to explain to his readers:

> If by any chance you readers should find the treatment in this part of the book vague and should be moved to ask, "Why didn't he depict the deeds of this pontiff as he did his predecessors?" listen to my reasons: I, Agnellus, likewise called Andrew, lowly priest of my holy Church of Ravenna, have put together this book which covers nearly eight hundred years or more from the time of the death of the blessed Apollinaris, by inquiry and research among the brothers of the see. Wherever I found material that they were sure about, I have presented it to you; and anything that I have heard from the elderly gray-beards I have not withheld from you. Where I could not uncover a story or determine what kind of a life they led, either from the most aged or from inscriptions or from any other source, to avoid a blank place in my list of holy pontiffs in their due order according to their ordination to the see one after the other, I have with the assistance of God through your prayers invented a Life for them. And I believe that no deception is involved; for they were chaste and almsgiving preachers and procurers of men's souls for God. If any among you should wonder how I was able to create what I have written down, you should know that a picture taught me. Images were always made in their likeness in their lifetime. To anyone who may raise a question about whether a picture is sufficient warrant for a description, St. Ambrose, bishop of Milan, in his *Passion of the Blessed Martyrs Gervase and Protasius,* says of the description he drew of blessed Paul the Apostle, "A picture taught me his features."[23]

Byzantium, New Rome, to which Ravenna was closely attached, held a confirmed principle that under the guidance of the Holy Spirit artisans so precisely copied icons that the very features of early saints (Luke, for example) were precisely delineated. The number of stories—about N as much as others—of visionaries who could immediately identify their spiritual visitors by their resemblance to icons is countless. Luckily Agnellus had all those mosaic figures to inspire him that still inspire us in the churches of Ravenna. Though none of the bishop figures were older than the fifth century and they were few, it sufficed that they were effigies of angels and saintly men. Doubtless the eighth-century Iconoclasts, who had destroyed many of the effigies of angels and saintly men, had destroyed many of the effigies of N, but not all; and effigies of other saints, especially those in scriptures, were recognized inspiration. Moreover, the everlasting tales which N picked up in the world on his way to school could be preserved in his Lifes. When their provenience escapes us, we call them folklore, but the ancients called them poetry.[24]

III THEIR CONTENT

Parentage 10

According to Symeon the Metaphrast:

The home of his admirable father was Patara, the foremost famous city of Lycia. His parents were of substantial lineage, holding property enough without superfluity. To be sure they had had more than a taste of worldly pomp and circumstance. But they nobly exemplified for their son how he should own nothing for his own selfish purposes by devoting themselves wholly to that which is good and following it in all ways. When they "had planted near the running waters and brought forth fruit in due season,"[1] the divine Nicholas, the mother ceased to bear—sterile from that day, producing no more children, as if Nature, having lavished such bounty, could give no more. When the mother brought him into the light as at once the first and the last noble offspring, a fruit of true spiritual union, the parents endowed the world with the acme of the virtues, that truly beautiful and bounteous issue—Nicholas (I repeat), the admirable! Although their son typified with his conception

N⳨

49

that of the Baptist, whose mother, though sterile, brought him forth,[2] yet John, when he was brought into the world, unlocked his mother's womb, but Nicholas, conversely, closed his.[3]

Legendary secular saints are apt to be born to successful burghers although there are many exceptions (for example, Saint Theodore the Studite was son of a courtesan and a hippodrome performer). In contrast the ascetic saints, even in birth, are often born in unworldly environments. Their types, Elijah and John the Baptist, one from the wilds, the other from the priests, counterbalance N in medieval art and thought. N is of the type of Jacob. But whether secular or ascetic, all were plainly predestined. Neckham (d. 1217) wrote:

Ornat Remensem sanctus Remigius urbem,
   He glorifies the town of Reims, does Saint Remi,
Qui nondum natus sanctificatus erat.
   Who yet unborn was marked for sanctity.
Conformatus in hoc, Baptistae cum Ieremiae.
   Thus he conformed with John and Jeremy,
Luctantique Iacob, et, Nicolai, tibi.[4]
   The wrestling Jacob and, Nicholas, with thee.

Some of the Lifes depict the predestination of N by suggesting the type of Isaac, son of the barren Sarah who bore him at the age of one hundred.[5]

Lactation 11

To fill out the common places of Infancy and Boyhood, some biographer attached to N incidents unknown before. The first such incident, *Lactation 11,* thereafter appeared in many other legends (e.g., Saint Roch, d. 1327),[6] but nevertheless was peculiarly N's. According to Symeon:

N When it came time to nurse the infant and he was placed at the maternal breast, God signified to all what kind of man Nicholas was to be when he should come to the age of discretion. For it is a fact that though throughout the rest of the week he would nurse at the breast like any infant, when Wednesday and Friday came he would take milk but once on each of them. Thus from the earliest moment, self-disciplined by rigid rule even before boyhood and from the very beginning, Nicholas showed how abstinence was a familiar token. And so he grew, the model of good behavior—in part reflecting the habits of his parents, but also in part developing a goodness from within.[7]

Lactation 11 was rather steadily employed as an example of restraint in sermons against gluttony. Here is a bit from the pen of twelfth-century Peter, a bishop of Chartres and abbot of Celle:

By Grace preoperating, he reined in the vice of gluttony, and before he was old enough to sin venially, he had throttled guilt. How weak, Nicholas lying at the teat! How strong, abstaining from the teat! If the boy is known by his studies, what of the infant and his milk! What can you do through your power—you who can do so magnificently, though as yet you can do nothing? How desirous, how greedy as an adult you will become over heavenly affairs, who as yet scarcely born raise a hand against the first serpentine enticements which deceived our parents in paradise![8]

And so on, to full sermon length. At the moment of that sermon, the trouvère Wace, the first vernacular poet of the King Arthur stories, was devoting no fewer than thirty-five lines to Lactation 11 in his verse Life of N.[9] Senator Thomas Reed set a quite different tone in 1901 at the annual banquet of the Saint Nicholas Society in New York City:

The child in its earliest infancy refused every Friday to absorb the sustenance suitable to that period of life; and as I looked over the tables this Friday evening and saw the abstention from all food and drink by this company, I marveled at the influence of pious example. Here was a man dead 1,559 years ago, and yet across the centuries, and across three thousand miles of distance, his example as a child makes go to bed hungry a whole nation distinguished in poetry and song for breadth of beam and for the generous portion of the earth's surface they cover when they sit down.[10]

It is often asserted that *Lactation 11* inspired N's patronage of children. So slight an invention would not enlarge the personality of N from its typical form of worldly shepherd, champion of the people, commercial agent, chastizer of emperors, to lover of infants. *Lactation* became popular in the later Middle Age, not as the cause but as the result of a patronage of children which N acquired for other reasons, reasons that exist in embryo not here but in the ambiguity of *innocentes* in *Stratilates 3*.

Yet inherent in *Lactation 11,* though certainly not yet realized in Symeon's version, is what Peter of Celle made clear, that by fasting the child N overcame the Devil, and by overcoming the Devil N added to a power already manifested in *Firebomb 5*. Even in the ninth century the hymn *Apud Myros, O Sancte, 9* shows that some predecessor of *Lombard Son, 64* was in circulation: "Fashioning a cross, Moses repelled the Amalikites; but thou hast cut to pieces the Devil with the Cross. That boy whom he had already done to death, thou didst restore to life by thy prayers, O Nicholas, and didst restore to his own land." These are tales true to the personality which N now but adumbrates—suggesting the tension, later to be examined, between childhood with guiltlessness and the macabre of unnatural life and death. The Encomium of pseudo-Andrew, composed not long after the first of our Lifes, exclaims: "Happy the city of Myra, to receive such a shepherd as you, full of love for the children, such a protector."[11] These words seem almost certainly to have been inspired by the ambiguity of *innocentes* in *Stratilates 3* rather than by *Lactation 11*.

Education 12

According to Symeon:

N Then, like some good and fertile soil, when he reached the proper age he was sent to the grammaticus for schooling. Under him and from his keen and subtle genius, in a short time Nicholas mastered the many disciplines, although all those of political and mercantile nature he rejected. He avoided immoderate companions and consorting and conversing with women. Refusing even so much as to turn his eyes in their direction, he bade them goodbye. Taking leave of worldly ways, he spent all his time in holy churches, according to the saying of the divine David preferring to be abject in them (Ps. lxxxiii [lxxxiv], 11).[12]

Emphasis on training under a *grammaticus* is proper in the Life of an exemplary secular bishop. The young Nicholas unimaginatively received the best conventional training of the day suitable for the son of a burgher of the Roman Empire. His shunning of practical studies of politics and business is also conventional. From this class of Roman gentlemen were drawn the fourth-century bishops whom the ascetic desert fathers most despised. N was disciplined in the ἐγκύκλιος παιδεία or *artes liberales*, whereas Anthony and Benedict in their legends revolted against such irrelevance. And his shunning women was also in character; the ascetics were apt to seek out women, that they might preserve their chastity under most trying conditions.

At this point the Lifes of N frequently treat a related topic, discussion of youthful virtue, but so unimaginatively—that is, so in conformity with scholastic formulas, and so slightly contributing to his personality—as to warrant our neglect.

Three Daughters 13

Even if Delehaye's principle were valid, that a legend arises from a persistent cult, not a cult from a legend,[13] nevertheless an appealing fable or image may change the personality or the object of a cult. *Three Daughters 13* is one of the best-known actions of N, determining to no slight extent his eventual effectiveness. Like *Parentage 10, Lactation 11,* and *Education 12,* there seems no reason for its incorporation in the Life of N beyond the need to represent the *common place,* this one of adolescence. It has no clear antecedents in pagan or Christian lore; it belongs to N alone. We know it first in Michael's Life. The infant or boyhood character of N would not attract it. Rather, it seems a vacation from discipline, a kind of truancy, an episode of adolescent and romantic affection quite outside the norm of discipline. N encounters a new experience that broadens and modifies his personality. Let us believe that here we find a key to N's unique vigor. *Stratilates 3* gave N the muscle for affairs; now *Three Daughters 13* modifies his legend, opening the door to sentiment. A great hero, as the romantic formula has it, must be both valiant and courteous.

According to Symeon:

N There was a man, once famous, who had fallen into obscurity and from riches to poverty. He had been reduced to extreme want in all material ways. When the day came that he lacked the very essentials of life (ah, shame! to what extreme does poverty progress!), he determined to sell into prostitution at a price his three beautiful daughters to whoever were willing to buy, with the profit from each to sustain himself and them. It was impossible for him to marry them off; for because of their excessive poverty, all beaux disdained them.

Now once having convinced himself, he pondered the disreputable plan, and was already making the first move toward that shameless act. But Thou, Lord, Who art by nature both good and the source of every good, and dost benignly hearken to our needs, didst convey news of this plight to the ears of Nicholas. And Thou didst send him like a good angel and ready helper to that poor man, who had already reached the point of decision, that Nicholas might at one and the same time relieve his poverty and free him from that which was more oppressive than poverty.

Let us scrutinize together the compassion mingled with good sense of this saint. For Nicholas could not bear either to approach him to discuss the matter (however briefly), or show him the hand that would rescue him, as those are wont to do who bare that hand for philanthropy but with a mean and earthbound heart. For he sensed what arrogance it would be to approach one who had fallen from riches and glory into want—how it would cover one with shame and too vividly recall his one-time felicity. Rather, just as Nicholas was striving to live up to the evangelic precept that a good deèd must not be identified as the act of a Christian lest the Christian use his beneficence for his own gain, so he should divorce himself from this deed and not seek glory from men.[14] Indeed, whenever he did anything good, he tried harder to hide his actions than do those who do evil.

So, after he had bagged a sum of gold, in the dead of night he went to that man's home. The minute he had thrown the bag through the window, he hastily returned to his home, disquieted at the thought of being seen. When the poor man arose later in the morning, he found the gold. Loosing the string with difficulty, he was dumfounded, thinking himself deluded and fearing that what he saw before him was fool's gold. For in such circumstances how could he imagine that a benefactor would be willing for him to benefit without knowing the source of the benefaction? Then assaying the gold with the sensitive tips of his fingers and scrupulously testing it, he concluded that it was in fact gold. He was elated, he marveled, he was transported. In the realization of such joy he shed warm tears. Mentally checking down the roll of all his many acquaintances, he could find none to whom he could ascribe what had been done. He attributed this gift to God, incessantly and tearfully rendering thanks to Him.

Then with overflowing heart he strove before all else to erase the mischief of his sin against God. He married off one of his daughters, the eldest of course, providing as dowry for her the mysterious gold which had so abundantly been supplied.

Yet at a later time it came to the attention of the remarkable Nicholas, and he verified the fact, that the man was preparing to carry through a resolve to sell the second of his daughters, despite his vain hope that through marriage he might avert a second such evil occasion. Thereupon, unperceived by anyone, during the night Nicholas threw an equally valuable bag of gold through the same window. And so again, when the man arose in the morning and found the gold as before, he was once more dumfounded. Prostrate on the ground he wet the earth with his hot tears, saying: "God, Who dost gladden the wretched and art the font of our wellbeing, Who even once didst become man for my disobedience, and now hast freed me and my daughters from the snare of the Enemy, show Thou me the one who obeyest Thy will, who is angel among men and reflector of Thy goodness. Who is this man who has snatched us from the poverty which overwhelms us, and freed us from our loathsome intentions? For lo, out of Thy mercy I now give a daughter to wed, conjoined in lawful matrimony. Till now she has escaped becoming the prey of the Devil and a source of profit for me. What a sorrow, that—more overwhelming than any other catastrophe to me!" He uttered this prayer, and forthwith arranged for the marriage of his second daughter.

He was now consumed by a firm belief and high hope that the same evil occasion would not arise with respect to the third daughter. Surely a bridegroom could not be lacking! Because of the previous happenings he confidently imagined that in the instance of this daughter he would have her dowry ready at hand. As a peer of her sisters she should receive equal generosity. This time he waited, watchfully, night after night on guard, to anticipate that singular disburser of money when he came again unannounced. If and when he should come again, he would learn from that person who he was and why he was distributing gold in this way.

The father watched very carefully, awaiting the unknown's appearance. Then at the third hour in the dead of night, the servant of God Nicholas came to the now-customary spot with silent tread, and now again threw a tied bag of gold through the same window, swiftly retreating toward home.

The girls' father, when he heard the sound of gold as it struck and realized that it was the anticipated gift of wealth, as fast as he could ran after the man. When he caught up with him and recognized who it was (for because of his family's position and celebrity Nicholas could not hide his identity) he dropped to Nicholas's feet, calling him redeemer, reviver, savior of souls who were foundering in dire peril. "For had not," he said, "the good Lord in His compassion awakened thy pity, then long ere this, alas unhappy me!, I would have perished with my three daughters. But now through you God has granted salvation to us and freed us from the mischievous mischance of sin. He has lifted the indigent from the mire and caused the poor to rise from the earth."[15]

These words he uttered with tears of joy and in the
warm glow of faith. Then Nicholas, as soon as he realized
that he had failed to keep his identity hidden from the man,
made him arise. He bound the man by an oath never in the
whole course of his life to relate to others what had occurred, or to make known the benevolent act. Now of all
the actions of the marvelous Nicholas, this one is the most
charitable and the best known.[16]

The number *three* is beginning to characterize tales of N, though it
is not essential in this instance: in the Ethiopic version there are four
daughters, and in a version from Wallonia seven.[17] Nor is the *persona*
of all-knowing, all-protecting bishop present; for the narrators always
set the dramatic time in N's youth, when as a rich orphan he had not
yet taken ecclesiastical orders. Indeed, a purpose of the story is to
depict a class of innately good and charitable youths from among
whom the order of priests needs to be drawn. There are evidences of
homiletic style in all the retellings, as in this version of Symeon.

May we presume that a devotee of N, most probably a preacher,
knew a fine story and believed that to add it to N's Life would honor
both story and hero, as Washington was wedded to the equally
inexplicable cherry tree? It is a premonitory sign that just as the first
evidence of N in the Latin West is circulation of the text of *Stratilates
3*, the most effective of the tales, so the second evidence should be of
the almost equally effective *Three Daughters 13*. In the Church of Santa
Maria Antiqua in Rome, to which we shall return, is a fresco of three
women, usually but not certainly identified as a rendering of *Three
Daughters*, painted in the eighth or ninth century.[18] In the tenth
century there were two important convents dedicated to N in Rome.
One, on via Lata, founded ca. 940, was among the wealthiest and most
influential in the city;[19] the other, before 992, was at the foot of the
Aventine.[20] We may be reasonably certain that their cult was inspired
by *Three Daughters*.

Simplicity and dramatic cogency made *Three Daughters 13* a feature
of every Life of N, East and West. It was the first episode to be
dramatized—indeed, the very first medieval nonritual drama. It has
been a staple of Sunday-school and Yuletide pageants, including radio
and television. The three bags of gold for a time ran even with three

loaves of bread (*Grainships 7*) as an iconographic symbol for N, but then outdistanced them. The symbol for pawnbrokers is normally declared to come from this story of N; at all events, in London the Church of Saint Nicholas was on Lombard Street, and had three golden balls on its spire. In the late Middle Age the Lombards had replaced the Jews as English moneylenders, and Lombard Street fore-ran the financial City.[21]

A folk trait arising from this ubiquitous tale affects N from his boyhood to old age: his patronage of maidens. Indeed N comes in time to control fertility and marriage rites in a wide variety of customs scattered throughout both East and West.[22] It helped to involve N in psychoanalysis. The association is paradoxical because all complete Lifes, even as late as the *Golden Legend* (13th cent.), make N virginal: "He avoided association with women."[23] Nevertheless the imperial superman became the hope of quaking women in many a province in the West. He provided marriage, conception, parturition, and milk. His patronage of conception—perhaps the most famous instance is that of the birth of Saint Nicholas of Tolentino (d. 1305)—may derive from *Parentage 10* or *Son of Getron 46,* but at all events it rapidly became one of N's important powers. In the most popular of Western tales, *Three Clerks 44,* N promises the innkeeper's wife that God will send her a son. The cult of N as marriage broker and baby bringer, though spread throughout Europe, centers in France.[24]

Bishop 14

According to Symeon:

N⳩ After the incumbent bishop of Myra had in a single instant yielded up both his see and his life and had set out on the path to God, a holy desire suffused all the bishops and the most eminent of the clergy subject to him to discover the one man most worthy to be appointed to that charge. When all of them had assembled in the church, one urged that the matter be entrusted in prayer to the will and wisdom of God. All concurred as warmly as if each had presented the idea himself. Then God, Who fulfills the desire of those fearing Him and hears their prayers, revealed to one of them who would lead the church in the future;

for in due course He appeared to him in a holy vision
enjoining him to go stand at the entrance of the temple,
there to greet the first man to enter. That man would be
the one who was inspired to his action by His own Divine
Spirit. Then the clergy should receive him (his name would
be Nicholas) and ordain him bishop, as the one predestined
for the post. When the holy man had experienced the mysterious vision, he communicated it to the clergy and synod.

While all the rest devoutly prayed, he to whom this great
revelation had been vouchsafed went to the stipulated place.
At about the hour of Matins our estimable Nicholas, impelled by the Holy Spirit, came to the church. In its ves-
tibule the man deemed worthy of the vision received him.
"What do people call you, my son?" he earnestly inquired.
"Nicholas the sinner," he simply and unaffectedly answered,
"and I am the servant of Your Sanctity."

At these humble and courteous words of our exemplary
man, to be sure partly because of the name of Nicholas
which his vision had foretold when it appeared, but partly
also because of the extraordinary, unmistakable modesty (for
the holy man knew the saying, "Whom does God look to
here below, except the meek and the peaceable?"), he knew
that this was the man whom God was signifying.

At that, joy suffused him, just as if he had stumbled on
some precious treasure. He thought of this disclosure as
pure wealth. "Follow me, son," he directed. Taking him by
the hand, he led him to the bishops, who recognized at once
what had already been foretold to them by their colleague.
They, too, filled with holy joy, recognized that the virtue of
the man was in accord with the will of God.

Then they immediately conducted the saint to the
sanctuary of the temple. When news of this affair had
spread about (for it is natural for news to circulate in such
important matters and to employ swift wings), uncounted
masses poured into the church. In a loud voice the bishops
proclaimed: "Accept, our sons, this man as your shepherd,
whom the Holy Spirit has anointed for you and to whom

He has submitted your souls for guidance and instruction.
He has been made our leader not by human but by divine
determination. He whom we have been longing for we have;
whom we were seeking now we receive. As long as we may
truly be shepherded and protected by him, we need not lack
hope that in the day of the Coming and the Revelation we
may stand firm as a people beloved of God."

To these words the people added their own expression of
gratitude, and addressed to God those jubilees which cannot
be expressed in words. Then the holy synod of bishops,
together with the clergy, at once invested him with what
belonged to the office by law and what by custom. They
appointed him Pontiff, though he was very slow and hesi-
tant to accept that pontifical honor. Because of a truly
praiseworthy sense of constraint, he could hardly ascend the
bishop's throne and assume the prefecture and presidency of
Myra, the proper dissemination of the Word of Truth and
Piety, adherence to orthodoxy, and the right teaching of
it.[25]

It seems that in its earliest and simplest form, the choosing of N as
Bishop 14 was a simple tale. He was chosen because his appearance at
the earliest morning service vouched for his piety just as his social
grace vouched for eligibility to rule. But by the time of Symeon the
tale had become elaborated into a miraculous intervention of a par-
ticipating God. What had started, perhaps, as merely an invention to
complete a common place became a powerful image.

The hymn *Apud Myros, O sancte 9* places N in the tradition of Moses,
Aaron, Levi, and Samuel, all God-chosen.[26] The Lifes idealize N the
bishop: devout, self-effacing, dutiful, predestined, but also wealthy,
physically attractive, and energetic.

This hagiological theme of reluctance and chance reflects a historical social situation in the Church of the Fathers. The Christian congregation (often the total citizenry of a city) normally chose its
shepherds by acclamation. Lotteries, whose results were the manifest
Will of God, were common: three different children drew the name
of John of Alexandria from the hat on three successive occasions to
determine his appointment.[27] Did not God Himself say: "I will give

you pastors according to my own heart; and they shall feed you with knowledge and doctrine"?[28] And the appointment of Matthias to replace Judas was also a model.[29]

Many a wealthy man was forcibly frocked in order that his property might be confiscated for the benefit of the poor: the poet Paulinus of Nola is an instance. Sometimes a political magnate of senatorial distinction was impressed into episcopal service: Ambrose, the preeminent Roman civil official, was forced into the archepiscopacy (relates his legend)[30] by the cry of a child in the forum at Milan, "Let Ambrose be bishop!" Gregory the Great, a reluctant monk, according to legend fled from Rome to the forest to avoid the mob that would make him pope; but a pillar of fire directed the mob to him.[31] Such supernatural choice is a topos in the legends of all saints who were, according to historical record, outstanding administrators of their charge. In patristic times the populace was apt to force leadership on the conspicuously innocent, if not ignorant, in revolt against the manifest corruption of those trained and established. The depiction of N as a rich lay orphan of Patara, wandering into Myra at the divine moment through no will of his own, conforms with the manners of the times.

As has been mentioned,[32] in *Stratilates 3* N began to assume the traits which made him the exemplary shepherd-bishop of all Christianity, manifested especially in the polarities of benevolence and willingness to resort to violent corporal discipline. This duality will in his old age evolve into a folklore trait, with N carrying gifts in one hand and switches in the other. Pope Gregory the Great (d. 604), whose legendary traits seem often to have been inspired by events in his young manhood at Constantinople at a moment when in fact N of *Stratilates 3* was attracting attention, became a western counterpart of N as exemplary secular bishop, despite Gregory's historical addiction to claustral life. His legend (G) was written by a famous historian-poet, Paul the Deacon of Monte Cassino,[33] but then again by John the Deacon of Rome, known as Hymnonides.[34] Since John of Rome (G) and John of Naples (N) were contemporaries, neighbors, deacons, and Greek students together, the two Johns and the two subjects of their separate legends were easily confused and their exploits intermingled. N's polarity is also a trait in the legend of G,[35] who appeared like N at night before his corrupt successor as pope. In exasperation at his successor's malevolence, G lethally kicked him in the head.[36] From some such evolution of an imaginative communion of saints, James of Voragine in his thirteenth-century *Golden Legend* drew the following tale:

N John the Deacon, who compiled the Life of Blessed Gregory, tells how, while he was polishing up his draft of the
Life, a man appeared to him in priestly dress. The outer
cope of white was so thin that he could see the black tunic
underneath. The stranger came up to the deacon and started
to laugh. When John asked him why a man of so serious a
calling should burst into laughter that way, the man replied:
"At the sight of you writing the history of men now dead
that you didn't even know when they were alive." And John
answered: "True, I did not know Saint Gregory personally,
but what I am writing has been transmitted in writing."
Then he added: "Never mind, it doesn't matter much to me
what you do, for it's my business to do what I am capable
of doing." At that he snatched up the lamp that the deacon
was writing by, and struck him so hard that the poor deacon thought himself killed. At that, Saint Gregory appeared
before him with blessed Nicholas on his right and deacon
Peter[37] on his left. Gregory said to him, "Man of little faith,
why have you doubted?" Since the stranger had hid himself
under the bed, Gregory took the huge torch from the hands
of Peter and thrust it into the unknown's face until he had
burned the face as black as an Ethiopian's. A spark lighted
on the white mantle and burned it up. There stood the
stranger, who was none other than the Devil, as black as
soot. Deacon Peter exclaimed to blessed Gregory, "We have
blackened him for sure!" And Gregory: "No, we haven't
blackened him; we've simply made him appear as he is." At
that they departed, leaving a great light behind them.[38]

Nicea 15

Although *Parentage 10, Lactation 11, Education 12,* and *Bishop 14* contribute to the emergent personality of N, they seem modest hagiological inventions for making the puerile N conform with legendary

discipline. On the other hand, *Three Daughters 13* is something picked up out of school which the masters let N keep. It has no more than the justification of all poetry: instruction and delight.

Another kind of accretion, not part of the scholastic hagiographical pattern, is the episode of *Nicea 15*. According to Symeon:

> At the time when Constantine the First, who chose the true
> religion, was administering the Roman Empire, and the
> great pontiff Nicholas was training his people to accept
> righteous dogma and, if anything alien or weakening were to
> be found in it, to root it out and destroy it, at that time all
> the Orthodox were gathered at Nicea to establish a true
> Constitution of the Faith and to drive away the blasphe-
> mous doctrine of Arius, with a view to peaceful conciliation
> of the whole Church. It was effected by the determination
> that the Son was equal in honor with the Father and that
> both Persons were conjoint. The admirable Nicholas helped
> to bring this about as a member of the sacred synod, and he
> strenuously resisted the casuistry of Arius, reducing to
> naught his every tenet. Then when the correct rule of Faith
> had been transmitted to all, he left Nicea and returned to
> his own flock. There, by precept and example he acutely
> and fervently set forth the doctrine of Faith, leading all
> toward virtue.[39]

The First Oecumenical Council, Nicea A.D. 325, is possibly the most famous event in postapostolic Christian history. Pope Urban II, for example, spoke of "the authority of the Nicene Synod, which we should venerate as equal to Holy Gospel."[40] It determined, among other decisions, that thereafter for ever the Christian belief should be the orthodox Trinitarianism then defined and championed by Athanasius against the pretentions of the followers of Arius. Granted that threes and triplets are central to all narrative and especially to hagiography, the appearance of three in tales of N is so especially prevalent that most commentators have regarded N as the exemplary exponent of the Trinitarian orthodoxy established by the Council.[41]

It seems clear that since N's presumed *floruit* was the time when the Council was held, so exemplary a Christian must have been present, active, and influential during those discussions.[42] This form of historical association, so common in legends, is the bane of factual historians, equivalent with the "folk etymologies" that trouble lexicographers. Because Milton, who in his writings showed interest in Galileo, visited Florence when Galileo was alive, Miltonic legend reports that the two met and exchanged views. In folkloristic circles the attraction to invention of this sort is naturally greater.

The lists of bishops who did attend (according to the strongest tradition, 318 of them) are fragmentary and unreliable; but N appears on no such list except as a name inserted after the thirteenth century, under the influence of the legend itself.[43] Nor is there any allusion to his presence in contemporary documents or for the next four centuries.[44] The early hymn *Apud Myros O sancte 9* says that like David he slew the Goliaths of Sabellian, Nestorian, and Arian heresies;[45] had the hymnographer known about *Nicea 15* he would have been more specific at that point. Only with Symeon and the synaxaries around the year 900 does the incident appear.

Even after the connection between N and the Council was established, there was seldom agreement among the Lifes about the actions at the Council. A myth found in the fourteenth century is that with that characteristic love of direct action, N struck a certain Arian in the jaw, and for that reason the Council deprived him of mitre and pallium.[46] There are Western effigies which depict him without them. By the sixteenth century, hagiographers like Petrus Equilinus report that the Blessed Virgin, to whom N was especially devoted, had two angels restore them.[47] This late invention, as we might expect, was immediately popular among Renaissance painters, for whom the mitre and pallium supplied texture, the persons of Mary and N dramatic contrast, and the tale a doctrinal orthodoxy in the age of the Carmelites. Père de Bralion in 1646 renders him full justice: Christ and Mother Mary appear to the disgraced bishop in prison, as in *Stratilates 3*.[48] In a still later embellishment, N had his beard forcibly shorn in prison, but as he said Mass it was instantaneously restored.[49] *Nicea 15* is the subject of a series of seventeenth-century frescoes on the ceiling of N Basilica at Bari, together with an additional scene of N's going to Rome to meet *Pope Sylvester 16*.[50]

Death 17

The sanctuary at Myra in the sixth century was called a "martyrion," and later writers speak of the bones of N in a "martyrion," "ecclesia," "naos," "temenos," and "sakos." Although these terms might, but seldom did, refer to the same kind of building, any one of them might without solecism refer to the church at Myra that Emperor Theodosius II (A.D. 408—450) erected. Even the earliest of the ninth-century masters agree that N was entombed therein, and it is hard for us to disbelieve that the corpse of a Bishop Nicholas, translated from that church to Bari in the year 1087, was not entombed there when the church was built.

The climax in the Life of a saint is his death or rebirth, parallel with the Crucifixion and Resurrection. Authors of Lifes fall roughly into two groups, understaters and overstaters. At no point in a Life is the difference of taste more marked than at the common place of Death. Though eloquent descriptions of death served religious exercise, they also stimulated relic hunters. Probably for this reason Athanasius, in his model *Life of Saint Anthony,* completely underplayed Anthony's death—even refusing to specify the time and place of burial. N, who in the Lifes was becoming the most potent of thaumaturges, the most effective of rulers, the most respected of God's agents, still felt no celestial premonitions of death, no agonies of the flesh; his angelic ascent and vision of glory is remarkably restrained. He is depicted less as a phenomenon and more as a comparatively imperceptible, irresistible force. According to Symeon:

> Now after he had long lived in this manner, renowned for his virtuous conduct, he asperged the metropolis of Myra with sweet and lovely unction distilled from the blossoms of divine Grace. When he came to the very advanced age, full of days both heavenly and earthly, he needs must comply with the common law of nature, as is man's lot. He was ill but a short time. In the grip of that illness, while rendering those lauds and thanksgivings to God which are said in death, he happily yielded up his spirit (for while he desired to remain in the flesh, Nicholas equally desired to be un-yoked from it). He left this brief and transitory life to cross over to that blessed everlasting life where he rejoices with the angels while more clearly and openly contemplating the light of Truth. But his previous body, borne by the holy

hands of bishops and all the clergy with torches and with lights, was rested in the *temenos* which is at Myra.[51]

Myrrh 18

This underplaying of the earthly demise was compensated; for N became a myroblyte ($\mu\nu\rho\alpha\beta\lambda\acute{\nu}\tau\sigma\varsigma$) a saint whose relic exudes a myrrh, oil, balm, or liquid.[52] Symeon continues: "There to this very day the unguent flows which beneficially is used for the uplifting of spirits and the healing of bodies." Symeon's literary figure, in the passage above, of "sweet and lovely unction distilled from the blossoms of divine Grace" was traditional. The "odor of sanctity"[53] clung to demigods and heroes, in life and death, from earliest times. But both Michael and Theodore the Studite (d. 826) recorded, and Symeon repeated, an unusual attribute of the relics of N: that they incessantly generated a transportable, healing potion.

This theme quickly became embroidered. According to an anonymous addition to the Life by John the Deacon:

N Then after most blessed Nicholas had departed from this world to the Lord, the tomb in which his venerable corpse was enclosed never ceased to distill an oleaginous liquid, even to this day. To the spot come multitudes of weak, lame, blind, withered, deaf and dumb, and ones who are vexed by unclean spirits. When they are anointed with that holy liquor, they are restored to their original state of health.

To this addendum a second witness appended:

I stand witness that once, and then a second time, when I was in pain, I took a potion of that humor. While beside the tomb itself, I would invoke Nicholas to propitiate the Lord in my behalf. The temple of holy Sion where that confessor is at rest is about three miles distant from the walls of the city of Myra, along the road to the seaport which is called Andriake.[54]

To such notices was often added a tale that the myrrh miraculously ceased to flow when a later bishop of Myra was unjustly deposed. When he was restored to his see, the myrrh flowed again.[55]

Even as N emerged from boyhood he became the best-known myroblyte, though the number of his lesser peers multiplied. For example, Abbot Theofrid of Epternach (1078 - 1106) composed for his religious encyclopedia a chapter (III, v) entitled "The Fluids Water, Wine, and Oil, and the Tomb of Nicholas," neglecting all other myroblytes.[56] According to *Apud Myros O sancte 9*:

> Surely thou wert made the repository of the unguents of
> Christ, bathing all men who hasted to thee with the sweet
> savor of Grace of the most Holy Spirit, O venerable one.
> Thou art the mystic balm which brings light to those who
> are anointed in the faith, who have received the divine unc-
> tion of the true Christ. Here stand forth as patron of the
> men of Myra, O high pontiff.[57]

The liquid was variously termed liquor, oil, balm, balsam, unguent, manna, and so forth; but the most popular term in N is myrrh ($\mu\acute{\upsilon}\rho\rho\alpha$). Hence a common explanation is that the miracle results from a word play—myrrh and Myra ($M\acute{\upsilon}\rho\alpha$).[58]

Epideictic writing stresses such formal parallelism as the healing unction of the true shepherd in life and in death. But this effluence from the corpse was not merely a literary figure. So far as our evidence goes, pilgrims went to Myra to be awestruck by a physical manifestation and to carry away a droplet or a phial to their faraway home. Such visits were not made for health alone. Pilgrims are insatiable collectors of souvenirs, talismans, and artifacts in every age. An everflowing distillate might be collected or bought by those of meager purse, whereas only the rich could gather relics professedly unique, which required expensive authentication. Yet wherever a droplet went it became an object of some cult.[59]

Applied ritually in all religions and among all races, savage and civilized, oil (*oleum*) and ointment (*unguen*) were always meliorative— feeding, purging, exorcising, cleansing, healing, comforting, enriching, enlightening. Though the olive tree and its oil was Athena's gift to mankind and her triumph was over Poseidon, Aphrodite claimed and sometimes received a similar credit. Unguents, balm, and myrrh were cosmetic and luxurious; oils, humors, and solvents were therapeutic and restorative. The holy chrism of Catholic Christianity combines oil and balm and is called *myron* (μύρον) in the Eastern Church.[60] According to the oldest surviving Roman missal (the Gelasian Sacramentary, 6th cent.), the bishop with solemn ceremony consecrates the mixture with the following formula:

> Send forth, O Lord, we beseech Thee, Thy Holy Spirit the Paraclete from Heaven into this fatness of oil, which Thou hast deigned to bring forth out of the green wood for the refreshing of mind and body, of soul and spirit, for the expulsion of all pains, of every infirmity, of every sickness of mind and body. For with the same Thou hast anointed priests, kings, and prophets and martyrs with this Thy chrism, perfected by Thee, O Lord, blessed, abiding within our bowels in the name of our Lord Jesus Christ.

The formula calls up ancient, indeed, prechristian sensibilities. But the image of a corpse rather than a font, a cloud, or a herb, distilling healing liquor is not so ancient. It seems to have entered Christian cult well after the time of Constantine, and all early myroblytes were levantine.[61] Modern rationalists, who explain the odor of sanctity as the smell of embalming fluid, account for liquifying relics by the porous rock formation of levantine shores, which allows free and often untraceable passage of feldspar and limewater. There have been many less rational explanations as well.

Evidence unearthed in this century suggests another possibility—that a boyhood companion, Saint Menas, taught N (and other eastern myroblytes, like Saints Matthew and Andrew) how to exude liquor, somewhat as Huck Finn taught Tom how to smoke—by the sheer accident of association.

Saint Menas is purely legendary and may here be called M. M is indeed a vagabond to both archeologists and historians, who continue to dispute almost his every move. This is no place to chart his peregrinations and adventures, but only to relate such relevant details as knowledgeable students seem to agree about.[62] I choose only what relates to M's association with N, which in fact continued into their middle age.

Menas (or Mina), an Egyptian soldier, according to the *Hieronymian*

Martyrology, was executed after torture in the arena at Alexandria 11 November.[63] He became object of a cult at an oasis and crossroad (Mareotis Libya = Karm Abu Mina), some thirty miles from Alexandria, where he lay entombed. So intense was the cult, we know not why, that the emperor Arcadius (A.D. 383 - 408) built a sumptuous basilica there, which was subsequently embellished and enlarged, especially with hospitals and guesthouses for pilgrims. A working community of great size centered in a pottery works which produced ampules, cruets, lamps, and figurines estimated to have numbered in the millions.[64]

This extraordinary city fell into ruins after the Arabs under Omar overran it in 641. The Bedouins looked upon the ruins as haunted by evil spirits, and no one dared approach the place after sunset.[65]

All knowledge of M eventually disappeared from Egypt, only to be partially recovered after 1905 when C.-M. Kaufmann began excavations at the site. The extent and complexity of that community and cult were then revealed.[66] In addition to water courses and sacred fonts, Kaufmann uncovered a vast crypt housing a cistern with a Castalian inscription: "Take the water of Saint Menas if you wish to end your illness."[67] Clearly, pilgrims took away the healing water in ceramic containers of local manufacture.

The ampules, cruets, and lamps, often bearing the effigy of the saint and an inscription, "Glory to Saint Menas," discovered in modern times as far away as the Balkans, Morocco, and France, indicate that the healing water was at least sometimes oleaginous.[68] Such a change is characteristic in popular forms of reverence. The flow from many a sacred font insensibly becomes enriched. Healing oil customarily is drawn from the lamps lit before the altar of a therapeutic saint, to which a peculiar virtue is attributed. Such oil was part of M's tradition. In the sixth and twelfth miracles of his legend, invalids were healed through M's intercession by means of oil.[69] The social pressure to add greater dignity to the healing liquid could well have been intense in a cult of such dimension. Oil carried in the ampules to far countries, described as "from the tomb of Saint Menas," can well account for the quick spread of the cult. But there is no evidence that M became a myroblyte; no literary Act or Passion endows him with the attribute.

In the fifth to seventh centuries M traveled the Mediterranean.

Several cities contended that they possessed his corpse, for example Jerusalem and Rome.[70] Early in the seventh century a Passion was composed at Cotyaeum in Phrygia, midway by land between Myra and Constantinople.[71] Constantinople had a great church dedicated to him, by common belief erected by the emperor Constantine himself.[72] The Cotyaean legend added confusion to obscurity by reporting that he was executed there. Could this be the Menas entombed in Egypt? Was he miraculously transported? The author of the Passion had an answer: after the execution of Menas at Cotyaeum his body was carried "to the desert"—a report sufficiently vague to satisfy the Egyptian constituency. Since they had no written authority of their own and were just collapsing into Islam, they accepted the Cotyaean Passion as their authority.[73] Indeed, the fall of Egypt and the ubiquity of the ampules made M's vagabondage credible. In disordered times legends, like men, "hit the road." Constantinople's M church was a martyrion containing relics, reputedly M's corpse. Perhaps they originated as an ampule, but one of several explanations for their presence, which appeared first in the ninth century, was that M was translated from Egypt in a floating iron coffin which an angry emperor had thrown into the sea.[74] How many of the devout accepted such words as conventional literary imagination and how many as historical fact is no longer capable of authentication. Legends like humans travel without passports in anarchic times.

If evidence of M's oil is strictly archeological, and if, despite the ampules, he was in fact no myroblyte, why associate his cult with that of N? M's Acts and Miracles as they survive accent holy oil, but do not name his relics as the source. Conversely, N was known as a myroblyte at the beginning of the ninth century only by grace of hagiographers; there are no shards of ampules from Myra. But there are overlapping areas of cult. For example, though Menas was a soldier and in legend a cameleer, his martyrion in Constantinople supplanted a temple of Poseidon;[75] thereby his cult was rather nautical. Second, though not the theme of myrrh, several other N themes were borrowed, even verbatim, from M, most especially *Broken Staff 61, Substituted Cup 62,* and *Murdered Merchant 65,*[76] to be discussed below. Third, M and the adolescent N traveled much the same paths from Asia Minor and Constantinople to the west; in transalpine Europe the manuscripts of M appear in codexes which contain N as well. Finally, the two legends in their unembroidered forms are contemporaneous. One of the two is the earliest instance of a myroblyte. The *genius* of the theme fits M especially; he was from the first the object of a pilgrimage cult which surely preceded the invention of the theme.[77]

'M and N met during the period of Roman contraction and Islamic expansion, primarily during the century between the Justinianean and Isaurian dynasties. In the milieu of that period myrrh would especially attract the devout. For centuries pagan and Christian traffic in relics had been impeded by Roman laws against violation of interred remains. These stringent laws were repeated and reinterpreted in Christian context in the Constitution of A.D. 386 and its repetition in the Theodosian Code (A.D. 438). They were, for example, cited as late as A.D. 594 by Gregory the Great when he refused to send relics to the wife of the emperor Maurice.[78]

Yet from the time of the establishment of Constantinople the emperors had been above their own laws. Constantine was only the first of the Byzantine rulers who filled New Rome with relics. Clearly the laws were breaking down as Old Rome collapsed. Then the Islamic explosion following the Hegira blew open the burial grounds of apostolic saints, scattering the remains and shattering all legal barriers to traffic in relics.[79]

Already the doctrine had spread that churches should not be consecrated without relics.[80] Any locally venerated remains would serve, but the pretentious would look toward holier lands and holier relics. Even in the seventh and eighth centuries many devout Christians retained their ancestors' compunction against disturbing bodies of interred saints despite their rulers' model. Yet they could satisfy their longing for physical contact with sanctity by means of representative relics.[81] Not the least attractive of these was N's myrrh—a freely-flowing gift to ardent man from his mediating saint.

Though in the high Middle Ages the number of Western myroblytes was legion, all evidence suggests that they acquired their power by direct or secondary association with N. In the Byzantine world of the ninth and tenth centuries that power came from either N or M. At the end of chapter 3 we shall discuss the myrrh again as we watch the interaction of N and the legend of Saint Catherine. In that instance the data will be less obscure, but the conclusions much the same.

This long treatment of M and N illustrates a trait of popular imagination: a legend, however auspiciously launched, will not sustain its popularity indefinitely unless it is adaptable to change of taste or manners. There are styles in hagiography as there are styles in heroism. How many promising youths, heroic players on the stage of life, lose their public for no more reason than a change in taste? The myroblytic power of M could attract favor in the fifth and sixth centuries; there are, for example, allusions to it in such faraway western authors as Sulpicius Severus, Paulinus of Perigieux, Fortunatus, Gregory of Tours, and Gregory the Great.[82] Yet M was soon forgotten: "The instance of the cult of Saint Menas, of his immense popularity, and of his total neglect may be counted among the most curious and instructive," wrote Père Leclercq. N acquired the power, but only as one in several. During the centuries when M's popularity declined, N rode the crest by help of *Grainships 7* and *Firebomb 5*. M, a soldier and desert saint, lost his deserts to Islam as his army lost its preeminence to a navy equipped with Greek Fire. M was a martyr, N a confessor; M a recluse, N active in the forum. Political dissenters, which martyrs were, lost their charisma in the centuries of migration and iconoclasm, when political order was prized for its rarity. Deserts lost their romantic attraction during centuries of infertility and famine. Popularity went to saints who controlled the grainships, sailing now from Scythia. Egypt lost its attraction when the southern Mediterranean was held by Islam. Unlike the saintly M, the boyish and adolescent N had the political acuity of *Stratilates 3,* combined with the Cinderella fascination of *Three Daughters 13*. Later, when an age of pilgrimage reappeared, especially in the century preceding the First Crusade, and tourists once more demanded souvenirs from pilgrim shrines, N's myrrh was at the ready. Indeed, so great was the demand that other legendary saints then learned the art from N, and even M recovered some of his forgotten strength.

Whatever the origin, N's remains continued to exude after their Translation to Bari in 1087. Myrrh flowed for Emperor Frederick I Barbarossa and his Empress Beatrix in 1163. A finger or finger bone, also myroblyte, initiated the cult of Saint-Nicolas-de-Port, to be discussed in chapter 5. Pilgrims obtained phials at Bari as late as 1940, though even in the seventeenth century Tillemont denied that myrrh flowed there; yet Tillemont agreed that it occasionally flowed from the finger at Worms.[83] In the first half of the last century a spate of chemists analyzed the myrrh without reaching any memorable conclusions.[84] In addition to the phials, pilgrims carried away bone chips and fingers, vended by attendants at the tomb. At Worms, Bishop Arnold dedicated an N chapel 30 September 1058, with a finger of the saint: *digitus salutare oleum distillans.* That finger must have come, or have been believed to have come, from Myra; for the relics had not yet been translated to Bari. At the abbey of Bec, where Lanfranc and Anselm taught, a chapel was built to house a phial.[85] A phial worth mentioning was deposited in the N altar in Saint Peter's, 6 October 1672. The altar was designed by Bernini and executed by the famous mosaicist Fabio Christopheri.[86]

From *Myrrh 18* N became patron of perfumers (the scriptural type is Judges xv, 19). An eleventh-century hymn for Vespers has the stanza:

> *Cuius tumba fert oleum*
> *Matris olivae nescium;*
> *Quod natura non protulit,*
> *Marmor sudando parturit.* [87]

His tomb yields an oil which is wholly different from that of olive oil. Nature does not produce it, but the very marble sweats it out.

IV THE BYZANTINE-ARABIC BORDER

Greek Cult

The disciplined, scholastic ensemble of Lifes, Synaxaries, hymns, and other liturgical and paraliturgical texts imposed order on the floating and flowing imagination. By the ninth century N was a recognizable personality, a schoolboy most likely to succeed, and his features were recorded in many a book.[1] The *Encomium Methodii*[2] repeats a hymn attributed to John of Damascus (d. 750)[3] that "it is easier to count the waves of the sea, the drops of rain, the stars, and with a glance see all the Atlantic than to recount in detail God's marvels accomplished through Saint Nicholas." Yet the boy led an increasingly active extracurricular life. The Roman Empire, Constantinople at its head, had contracted in size. Even during the lifespan of Michael and Methodios it lost Sicily and beyond,[4] Crete and beyond, the Black Sea and beyond, the Danube and beyond. Everywhere the interior land masses were yielded to other peoples, while the City maintained a precarious trade; but with the help of N and the mariners, it held the Aegean, the Peloponnesus, and the Adriatic, though a novel disruptive force was appearing in Venice. It disputed the Black Sea only with the Russes, or Rhós. The image of N more than any other saint is found on Byzantine seals.[5]

If one looks at a historical map of the Mediterranean at this period, he sees that the coast was divided between two naval powers, Byzantium and the Arabs. They were rival sea merchants. By their location they commanded the oriental land routes as well. The mercantile N was bound to thrive, and thrive he did, within the full limits of remaining Byzantine naval hegemony, primarily the Greek Aegean ports.

I have mentioned that a twentieth-century census of 4,637 Greek churches finds 752 dedications to the Virgin, 359 to N, 291 to George, 196 to Athanasius, and 189 to John the Baptist.[6] There were six dedications to N on Mount Athos, about thirty in Constantinople.[7] The Chrysostom Liturgy (one of three Orthodox liturgies used throughout the world), after memorials to Theotokos (Our Lady) and the taxiarchs Michael and Gabriel, has a third to "our Fathers among the Saints, great Hierarchs and Oecumenical Doctors, Basil the Great, Gregory the Theologian, and Chrysostom, Athanasius and Cyril, Nicholas of Myra, and all holy Hierarchs."[8] This number is often reduced to four—Basil, Chrysostom, Gregory Nazienzen, and N—as at the Monastery of Saint Luke in Phokis.[9] For one who never wrote a word, N is in very distinguished company. In the Parakletike, the daily Office, Sunday is given to the Resurrection, Monday to the Angels, Tuesday to John the Baptist, Wednesday to the Cross and Theotokos, Thursday to the Apostles and Saint Nicholas, Friday to the Cross and Theotokos, and Saturday to All Saints and the Dead. In Greek Orthodox formulations John the Baptist is the type of all prophets, while Nicholas is the type of all bishops, confessors, and fathers of the Church.

This Greek cult of N was produced by strife. About 824, the strategic island of Crete was lost from the empire; for one hundred and thirty years it·was the base for Arabic piracy. Each spring Crete vomited out like a monstrous war machine fleets of armored ships with black sails of marvelous speed. Cruising their *mare nostrum,* the freebooters burned cities and decimated towns before imperial forces could arrive. "Only hours sufficed for these remarkable corsairs, of agilit〉, audacity, incomparable precision, to transform a flourishing Byzantine city into a smoking ruin." The goods and slaves were marketed in the bazaars of the Asian and African coasts. In the single year 825, five Byzantine expeditions were vainly launched against the island.[10]

This frontier condition extended over the entire north shore of the Mediterranean, but especially to the boot of Italy and to Sicily, which the Arabs largely held. On 4 July 836 Naples and the emirs of Sicily signed an alliance which kept open to the Arabs the ports of Amalfi, Naples, and Gaeta for the next half-century. The native Latins and Greeks of all southern Italy were helpless before the constant Arab raids, and only in the tenth century did concerted efforts against them assume "the aspect of a veritable crusade."[11] The Byzantine commander who mounted that crusade was named Nicholas.[12] The anarchy of littoral and sea forced merchants to seek insurance where they could, for assuredly the civil authorities were powerless. Supply and demand determined that commerce must exist, but only the marvels of N, the Christian replacement for the Goddess Fortuna, could survive the uncontrolled greed and rapine.

The following tales of N, existing in Greek texts, appear to have been put into circulation no later than this period of Byzantine-Arabic rivalry of the ninth and tenth century:

I. PETER THE SCHOLAR 19. A Roman soldier, captured by the Caliph, thinks that his capture is God's punishment for his breaking a vow to become a monk. N intercedes with Symeon the Righteous, John the Baptist, and the Mother of God to bring it about that Pope Nicholas I consecrates Peter as monk.[13]

II. THE CAPPADOCIAN CAPTAIN 20. Rather like *19.* A Cappadocian leader's son is freed from the Manichaeism which he learned at the emperor's court.[14]

III. THE PRIEST OF MITYLENE 21. Christopher, a priest of Lesbos, on his way to Myra to venerate N and acquire myrrh,

75

is captured by Saracen Cretans and condemned to death. N seizes the sword from the executioner's hand and returns the priest to his home. Related to *Stratilates 3* and *Peter the Scholar 19*. [15]

N✝ IV. BASILEOS 22. A peasant's son from country near Myra is abducted by Cretan Arabs on N Eve, and is made cupbearer for the emir of Crete. A year later the brokenhearted parents go to the N church, to find Basileos standing before the facade, beaker in hand. He had been snatched away by N and restored.[16] This tale, a most popular Byzantine marvel, survives not only in many N versions but also in legends of Saint George, the Saints of Edessa, etc. In the West it appears as *Son of Getron 46*[17] and *Adeodatus 75*, to mention only the most important instances. Its relation to *Demetrios 29* is close. These are variants:

iv[a]. *The Euboean Laborer 23.*[18] Employs Cretan Arabs.
iv[b]. *The Sicilian Priest 24.*[19]   Employs African Arabs.
iv[c]. *The Catanian Image 25.*[20]   Also Sicily, with African Arabs.

N✝ V. JOSEPH THE HYMNOGRAPHER 26. This historical saint (d. 883) flees from Arabs in Sicily. On an embassy from Constantinople to Rome during the affair of Leo the Armenian, Joseph is captured by Cretan pirates. On Christmas Eve, after a night of hymns and offices, he is visited by N, who announces the death of Leo and transports Joseph back to Constantinople.[21]

N✝ VI. FATHER JOHN 27. The author of *Encomium Methodii*[22] wrote that his rich patrician father, drowning in a shipwreck, went under with an invocation to N on his lips. N spread his bishop's mantle on the sea as a float, which buoyed up the drowning man.[23]

N✝ VII. MONK JOHN 28. During a tempest John invokes N in unison with the sailors. He speaks to a figure on the water, who disappears; but the storm is quelled.[24]

N✝ VIII. DEMETRIOS 29. Embarked for Athyr, Demetrios sinks with a call for N on his lips. N restores him to his house, and then again to a street, where the neighbors witness his dripping clothes.[25]

IX. THE LONE SAILOR 30. An Egyptian Arab fisherman invokes N during a storm, promising to turn Christian if
rescued. N carries him to Attalia, where the fisherman recognizes his rescuer in an icon of N.[26]

X. THE CRETAN BOYS 31. N rescues three boys playing in a
skiff on Good Friday, and returns them on Easter.[27] The
weeping mothers are foreshadowed or typed not only by the
Three Marys, but also by Niobe, Procne, and Philomela. The
time interval is, of course, typed by Jonah and Christ's
entombment. Such overt instances of scriptural analogies are
apt to originate in homilies.

XI. THE SARACEN TRADER 32. A Saracen trader returning
from the Orient loses his caravan over an abyss during a
storm. Invoking N, he finds his caravan unharmed twelve
miles away. He gives a golden icon of N to Seleucia.[28]

XII. THE GOLDPIECE 33. A pauper grieves that he has nothing
to offer on N Day. In his sleep he sees a venerable old man
draw out a goldpiece, which he finds on waking. The emperor, when he hears, takes the gold piece and gives the
pauper twenty-four others to take its place.[29] This is only one
of the many variants of a story which is itself a variant of *Three
Daughters 13.*

I have listed these episodes as evidence of the deepening and
solidifying personality of N. He has lent himself to narrative imagination in the following range of topics:

Christian secular piety, i, iii, iv, ix, xi
sailors, iii, v, vi, vii, viii
merchants, x
gold and coinage, banking, xi
innocentes (children, or falsely accused adults), ii, iv, v, ix
Saracens, Hagarenes, Paynims, Barbarians, i, iii, iv, viii, x
physical action and chastisement, iii
patron of poor, iv, viii, xi
patron of military, i, ii
trinity, ix, x

Though monks are twice involved (i, vii), there is no representation of asceticism in the tales; the religious vocation is accidental. Nor is there any fierce ostracism of the Hagarenes such as is found in comparable legends, chansons, or romance. The authors may regard the Saracens as pirates, conquerors, enemies, but not devils. In several instances N is voluntarily invoked by professed Moslems.

In addition to these twelve, the oft-mentioned hymn *Apud Myros, O sancte 9* contains evidence of a lost episode in which N revived a dead boy through prayer, an episode that will recur in *Lombard Son 64.*[30] *Basileos 22* and the *Cretan Boys 31* are not apparent versions of that lost work. Though they show that N at this age did not neglect youngsters, since they are only two among many similar tales we do not yet find any special emphasis on youth.

The *Encomium Methodii* asserted:

> Let anyone approach his image, invoke him in prayer, only call upon him by name; he comes, performs marvelous works, shows his power in all things and all places in all times; he cures the sick, succors the needy, consoles the afflicted; he makes himself available to all, to the end that all may be saved and that no one shall languish from sorrow after having besought his aid.

The center of this boyhood personality of N was *Stratilates 3.* May God ameliorate the yoke of society and its rulers on each of us! A fantasy, a surrogate, a mediator is in the making, being schooled for his wide reign over the imagination. Like the Moses to whom N was so often compared, by miraculous resolution of material obstacles he will lead God's children from abject want to promised plenty. His range of action both compares and contrasts with that of Theotokos, Stella Maris, who affords God's children an imaginative escape from theological quicksands. Both easily attract an abnormal number of marine images, for the sea is one of the most readily available comparisons with human life.

Iconia 34[31]

The icons of the Eastern Church continue the tradition of Egyptian funerary portraits which replaced the death masks of the Hellenistic age. The oldest, according to Bréhier, reproduced first the effigies of the martyrs, then the saints, then apostles, then the Virgin, and finally

Christ. From the fourth century the celestial character of the individual was indicated by the nimbus.[32] From Syria a rich apochryphal literature developed in which certain figures of Christ and the Virgin were considered as authentic portraits, such as the icon brought from Palestine by the empress Pulcheria, reportedly painted by Saint Luke, or the *acheiropoietes* (not made by hand of man) of Christ, a portrait presumed to have resulted from contact of a cloth with the Savior's face (later called *veronica*).[33] Such excesses led to Iconoclasm, a reaction from cult of saints. Under Emperor Leo III (717 - 740) the smashing of images reached epic proportions, though from 781 (Empress Irene) strictures were relaxed in part. Icons were only fully restored under Empress Theodora and Patriarch Methodios, who instituted Orthodoxy Day, 11 March 843. On that day thereafter annually was read the *Synodicon* to celebrate the full restoration of images. Even before this event Theodore the Studite (d. 826) composed a hymn, "If anyone place himself before thy painted image, Nicholas, he will have what he wants."[34]

In the Greek region of southern Italy, on the border between iconoclastic Islam and iconodulic Byzantium, where Methodios grew up, arose one of the most popular and influential tales of N, *Iconia 34,* in its Greek form, which is probably the earliest, known as *Thauma de imagine.*[35] Anrich would not date its appearance more precisely than A.D. 871 - 1077,[36] but almost certainly it appeared right around the year 900,[37] for the following version circulated widely in Latin as an almost immediate appendix to the Life by John the Deacon:

> When the Vandal army invaded Calabria from Africa and set fire to the whole countryside, one of the barbarians found in a Christian home an image of Saint Nicholas, carefully painted on a plaque. Concealing it in his garment, he hurriedly ran off, without knowing what he had. When he had rejoined those who were guarding the bound Christian captives, he said to one of the captives, "I would like to have you tell me whose face is so beautifully painted on this plaque." As he spoke he uncovered the icon. As the Christians looked at it, they said with weeping and tears, "That image before us is said to be that of Saint Nicholas. His many famous miracles and deeds with God and man clearly

manifest that he lives on, even after death." When the barbarian grasped what was being said, he straightway hid the image from his own company, telling them nothing about it.

After the Vandal army had returned to Africa with their many captives and extensive booty, the barbarian kept the plaque of Saint Nicholas in his own home. He was also the collector of customs. One day he brought out the icon and put it in front of his depository, containing all that he had—gold, silver, vestments. Then he spoke to the icon as follows: "Nicholas, supervise the protection of this treasure, for I have to go away." With these words to the image, he left. Though the depository was entirely unlocked, he went his way without a care, just as if he had set many guards over it.

Unfortunately some thieves passed by and saw the depository wide open, unguarded. They promised each other that they would come back at night and steal everything that was in it. And so they did. Coming in the night, they took everything—gold, silver, vestments, and all—and made off. The icon remained hanging in front of the depository as the only witness. Now these happenings occurred through the dispensation of God, that He might by a misfortune of this kind clearly manifest throughout all regions of Africa what the merit of Nicholas was.

When the barbarian who owned the treasure returned and found the treasury empty, with nothing at all left except the icon of Saint Nicholas, he raged and shook, letting out fearful cries. With distorted features he turned on the imaged likeness of Saint Nicholas as if he were addressing a live and rational man, saying: "O Nicholas, I left you as a trusted guardian of my treasure. What have you done? Return my goods to me. Otherwise I will scourge you thoroughly." Saying that, he took up a whip and beat the image of Saint Nicholas. Then when he was exhausted from beating, he said to the icon, "Rest assured, I will throw you into the fire if you do not return my property."

That most religious and blessed confessor Nicholas, spurred on by the treatment of the icon as if he himself had been whipped, went speedily to a place nearby where the thieves were dividing all the loot which they had stolen from the Saracen's depository. He said to them: "What are you doing, you miserable wretches? Did you not know that I myself was there when you perpetrated this evil? For my eyes were watching when you stole these things, and those."

Enumerating to them even the amount and worth of every last item which they had taken from the depository, he went on to say: "But remember that if you do not make satisfaction to me for the robbery which you committed, so that everything which you stole is replaced, I will make it my business to declare the theft publicly. That whole lot has been placed under my care. On that account I, though perfectly guiltless, have been scourged more than a little for your crime. Take my word for it, I will not spare you if you do not follow my directions. Otherwise tomorrow I'll see that you are sentenced to death."

The thieves, when they found themselves apprehended, thinking that he was one of the citizens who had spied upon them, were thrown into panic—more terrified than can easily be believed. Spurred on by fear of death, they carried back everything in the long hours of the silent night, replacing it in the depository.

When morning came, the barbarian appeared and saw all the property which he had lost. He began to weep for joy that he should have been involved in so great a miracle through Saint Nicholas. Grasping the icon, he began to kiss it, saying: "O Saint Nicholas, faithful and just, most pious and compassionate servant of the High God, how exalted, how sublime, how great, how powerful you have been made, as close attendant on the immortal God the King. When alive you never ceased to fight for Him from Whom you have deservedly received your power to effect such actions—acts which you deigned to accomplish out of thin air for me, an infidel. From this day I believe in Christ. And in you."

He believed in Christ the Lord and was baptized, he and

his whole household. And he built a church in honor of
Saint Nicholas in which he worshiped together with his wife
and sons, glorifying the Lord and Saint Nicholas. This was
the first occasion through which blessed Nicholas became
known in African lands.[38]

The Temple of Diana of the Ephesians was the public treasury of
the city, and was used by private individuals as the safest bank; from
such business the temple drew its income.[39] Christ only temporarily
drove the moneychangers out in Palestine. Religion and moneylending were more than tangential in antiquity. The reader may be reminded of the *Aulularia* of Plautus, in which the miser hides his gold in
the shrine of his domestic Lar, from which it is stolen. A Latin script
Querolus, composed in Gaul about the time the Vandals were passing
through, is another version of the same theme. Nevertheless, the
imaginative difference in effect between such pagan comic inventions
and this product of iconolatry is marked.

Pope Adrian wrote to the Seventh Oecumenical Council (Nicea II,
A.D. 787) that the emperor Constantine had seen two men in a dream.
When Pope Silvester showed him the icon of the apostles Peter and
Paul, Constantine cried out in amazement that they were his dream
visitors. At the council the patriarch of Constantinople asserted that
images exercised miraculous powers.[40] Bishop Theodore of Myra, a
delegate to that council, testified on the floor that his archdeacon had
seen in a dream a man whom he took to be the patriarch; but
afterward he saw the icon of N and knew that it was N whom he had
seen.[41] According to Ostrogorsky, the canons of the Byzantine and
Russian communions required such evidence of the piety of painters
of icons that the Church might be assured that the image was,
through the inspiration of the Holy Spirit, a real depiction of the
saint.[42] Our narrative seems an iconodulic reinforcement of the spirit
of Nicea II.

Iconia 34 did not stay in the Mediterranean world but became
exceptionally important in the transalpine West. Why? It is a better-
than-average tale, with such dramatic possibilities as to make it the
font or basis of Romance drama (Jean Bodel's *Jeu de Saint-Nicolas*). And
it characterizes N in his sudden miraculous appearances, his righteous
anger, his rough justice, his scourge, his due respect for the material

things of life. *Stratilates 3* might prove in the long run to be slightly exotic to Westerners, but *Iconia 34* did not. It seems to have been the primary source for N's emergence as the hero of the Western tales of thieves and judges. In the Mediterranean, the association of banking and sanctuaries was ancient indeed.

V VENICE

While N was adventuring on the Byzantine-Arabic border, Venice too was undergoing schooling, being shaped as a legend as well as a fact. When, in the year 1087, N's relics were translated to the rival port of Bari in Apulia, two legends as well as two maritime polities met in conflict. To be sure, this conflict really flared only after the Norman conquest of southern Italy and therefore belongs in a later age of N, but he had been schooled for it as a boy.

The Roman Venetians who had fled their mainland homes to escape the barbarians in the sixth and seventh centuries, settling on the sandbars of the Adriatic, had in A.D. 814 achieved a special political status, when Byzantium and the Franks agreed to their virtual freedom under a nominal Byzantine jurisdiction.[1] Venice was already a protégé of Saint Mark, evangelist and founder of the see of Alexandria. As early as A.D. 629, before the Arabs arrived in Alexandria, Emperor Heraclius had acknowledged Mark's patronage of Venetia by sending the patriarchal chair from Alexandria to Grado. Though some of the evidence adduced is dubious, there was and is a general belief that in A.D. 828 the relics of Saint Mark were rescued from Islamic Alexandria and translated to Venice.[2] In the ninth century Venice monopolized the traffic between Constantinople and France, Bavaria, and Lombardy. Under Doge Peter Tribuno (888 - 920), the *civitas Venetiarum* was established—an independent trading state of wholly bourgeois-mercantile dedication. With Saint Mark, missionary and seaman, as their patron, the Venetians had only a secondary interest in N.

But merchantmen can never have too much insurance. The developing ostentation and arrogance of the Venice which housed the body of Saint Mark, untimely ripp'd, were making their impact on the world. There were countless precedents, pagan and Christian, for their act. Constantine and succeeding emperors had enriched Constantinople by translation of relics from the Holy Land. Timothy was translated in A.D. 356, and Andrew and Luke the next year. In the West the great Fathers Ambrose and Augustine and their contemporaries in one way or another had blessed such translations. When the Moslems came to occupy half or more of what had been the christendom of the saints, some further traffic in relics began. In the chaotic days we have been examining in this chapter, it would hardly escape attention that the Constantinople of the True Cross and the Venice of Saint Mark were enjoying more than average commercial success. Every Mediterranean port began to search for saintly patrons.

Evidence of a marine cult of N as well as Saint Mark at Venice is substantial. In 1044 the doge Domenico Contarini erected San Niccolò del Lido, "when the Republic of Saint Mark was at the apogee of its civil and military glory."[3]

VI THE SLAVIC WORLD

The missionaries to the Slavs began their first mission, to Moravia, in 864—opening up a new Christian world to the north and east of Byzantium at a moment when the Byzantine cult of N reached its height.[1] N became patron saint of virtually all Slavic peoples and those allied with them. It does not serve my purpose to treat the Slavic cult, other than to indicate at this point how some split in N's personality occurred as the Eastern and Western traditions parted company.[2]

It was in the year 860 that Byzantium, the "God-guarded city," was saved by an eyelash from capture by an immense fleet of Russians. The "Russians" were an aggregate of tribes under the leadership of Scandinavian migrants.[3] Photios, patriarch of Constantinople, seems to have sensed that Christianization of these enemies of Byzantium would in the long run be New Rome's salvation. His was the first effective support of the missionaries Constantine (Cyril) and his brother Methodius, who in Moravia translated the Gospels into Slavic, inventing for the purpose the present Russian Cyrillic alphabet. They prepared a Slavic liturgy, preached in Slavic, and ordained a Slavic clergy.[4] The independent language separated to no inconsiderable extent the Slavic from both the Greek and Latin communions. Yet since the mission took place at the moment of reaction from Iconoclasm, the separate communion embodies that trait of the older churches: for example, the doctrine of the undeviating likeness of icon and subject. Not only decreed, but implemented, was the demand that any artist of icons must be spiritually inspired to record the unchanged and unchanging tradition. This juncture explains, at least to many students, why the N of Eastern countries is at once more rigid inside the church precincts and more unrestrained in field and forum than he is in the West.[5]

Pope Nicholas I, contesting with the patriarch Photius for hegemony, sponsored a mission of Latin priests under Formosus in Bulgaria (866 - 867). He began to woo Cyril and Methodius for support. In 867 the brothers spent several months in Venice on their way to visit the papal court. Pope Nicholas died before they arrived in Rome, but his successor Adrian II immediately formally approved the missionaries' actions.[6]

The Nestorchronicle reports the building of a Church of Saint Nicholas in Kiev in 882, which the Russian count said "shall be the mother of the Russian state."[7] The patriarch at the moment was named Nicholas (Chrysobergios).[8] There is still an N church on the spot. Christianity became the Russian religion of state A.D. 988, but the grandduchess Olga (d. 969) had already been Christian. An N mosaic of 1046 survives in the Kiev cathedral, and a calendar of 1056/7 marks December 6 a festival.[9]

Eastern records for several centuries are so incomplete that we cannot measure the extent of the Slavic cult. All we know is that after these first manifestations it was proportionately intense centuries later. Masaryk said that "Russia has preserved the infancy of Europe. She presents the Christian Middle Age, and more particularly the Byzantine Christian Middle Age."[10] And Dvornik added: "But that Middle Age is more particularly that of the first half of the ninth century."[11]

The Russians—at least their leaders, who have the name—were Scandinavian freebooters (Vikings) who had settled, primarily near Kiev, for piracy, conquest, and commerce;[12] but the tribes amalgamated under them were pastoral or peasant. All took on the patron of sailors, "An icon of N on every Russian merchantman."[13] Anichkof reports a piquant Serbian story, sung as a carol: Once all the saints were enjoying wine together. When the circulating cup reached N, he was too sleepy to hold it and let it drop. Saint Elias shook him by the arm to arouse him. "O, I beg the company's pardon," said N, "but I have been very busy and was absent from your festival. The sea was rough, and I had to give my help to three hundred ships that were in danger. That is the reason for my being tired, and letting the cup fall out of my hands."[14]

But toward the interior, away from the sea, N guarded the fields. The northerners simply liked "the Helper" (*Nikolai ugondniker*) not for his law and order, his bags of gold, his shoring up of mercantilism, but for attributes that they invented: his shepherd's friendliness, his companionship in loneliness. He became protector against wolves and wild beasts; indeed, 'during the twenty-four hours of N Day, the wolves will not snatch even a chicken.[15] In the empire, N was ameliorator of the tyranny of the czars, according to the image of *Stratilates 3*.

The folklorist Louis Katona says that as Russian missionaries spread Christianity eastward they would capture the interest of the nomads of Central Asia by showing the serene and amiable effigy of N.[16] Frazer reported: "Near Kursk a patch of rye is usually left in honour of the Prophet Elijah, and in another district one of oats is consecrated to St. Nicholas. It is well known that both the Saint and the Prophet have succeeded to the place once held in the estimation of the Russian people by Perun [the Slavonic thundergod]."[17]

Graven images are not allowed in the Russian churches, being held to be in violation of the Second Commandment.[18] But there is one exception, that of N. It is reported that when the patriarch Philaret removed the holy statues from the churches, all went well until hands were laid upon a representation of N. When the statue was broken from its pedestal, the image of the saint reappeared. N is the only figure seen in high relief in the Church, and is usually made with the model of a church in his hand.[19]

VII POPE NICHOLAS I AND THE PATRIARCH NICHOLAS MYSTICUS

The boyhood of N draws to a close in a time period of two dominant prelates, Pope Nicholas (A.D. 858 - 867)[1] and Patriarch Nicholas (901 - 925).

It is likely that all occurrences of the name Nicholas from the time of Justinian find an inspiration, direct or indirect, in N.[2] The appearance of Nicholas as the name of the Gothic father of Bishop Eugenius II of Toledo (A.D. 646 - 657) is quite exceptional in its time and place.[3]

To be sure, the Goths had lived in the shadow of Byzantium only two centuries before, but as explanation that fact is unconvincing. Between him and Pope Nicholas I, I have not met with the name Nicholas in the Latin world. Nevertheless, there was an immature cult in the city of Rome, especially in the Greek quarter. Rome was Grecized in the seventh century as emigrants swarmed in from the East, where Arabs had overrun their homes after the Hegira.[4] It was Grecized again in the eighth century by migrants forced west by Iconoclasm.[5]

We have noted[6] that *Stratilates 3* existed from the seventh century in Latin form. The Roman church of S. Nicolai in Carcere, next to the prison, may have been built in the seventh century, and almost certainly before Pope Nicholas's birth.[7] It served the Greek quarter. On N Day each year its clergy had the privilege of pardoning one prisoner sentenced to death, on the model of the Crucifixion story.[8] There probably is some connection with N's later cult of prisoners, but I have no direct evidence. There was an oratory dedicated to N built about the year 795.[9] The frescoes in Santa Maria Antiqua[10] which certainly depict N and perhaps depict *Three Daughters 13* may have preceded the pope,[11] though the Life of Pope Nicholas unambiguously states that he had them painted.[12] Nevertheless, it was not until about 880 that John the Deacon published the first Latin Life. The only documentary Latin source was the version of *Stratilates 3*. It circulated not only in Rome but beyond the Alps, at least before the year 842,[13] so presumably *Stratilates 3* was the unique source of N's cult in the West during the first half of the ninth century.

Where did Pope Nicholas get his name? We know nothing of him before he entered papal service as a subdeacon in 844 - 847 except that his father Theodore, a *regionarius,* is presumed to have been a member of the Conti family.[14] Whether he was christened Nicholas or acquired the name in religion, we do not know. Popes did not, on assuming the Chair, change their names at that time;[15] but rededication or change of lifestyle was often accompanied by change of name, as with the Slavic missionary Constantine, who became Cyril. At all events, Pope Nicholas was under the patronage of N.[16] As pope, he built an oratory to N in Santa Maria in Cosmedin and "lavishly endowed it."[17] It was called Saint Nicolai in Schola Graeca.[18] There are a number of less certain evidences of the Pope's devotion.[19]

The decisions of Pope Benedict III (855 - 858) were largely made by his lieutenant Nicholas. Nevertheless, Nicholas needed the powerful presence of Emperor Louis II (in Rome at the time) to assure his succession to office. Like Becket, Nicholas immediately threw off the yoke of his sponsor.[20] He fostered the career of Anastasius, once antipope (855) and his own rival, making him an abbot, papal secretary, and librarian. Anastasius's friends thought him the best Greek scholar in the West, though friends of John Scotus thought otherwise; certainly Pope Nicholas valued him for his knowledge of Greek. As early as the year 905 Regino of Prüm wrote[21] that Nicholas was unquestionably the most important pope after Gregory the Great (d. 604). No successor equaled him in assuring the primacy of his office until the eleventh-century Hildebrand (Gregory VII), who constantly appealed to Nicholas's precedents.

By virtue of the withdrawal or expulsion of imperial Byzantine troops from the Latin West beginning in the fifth century, Caesaropapism did not exist in Rome. In most provinces the migrant barbarians who took over military government left ecclesiastical government to the Old Roman families. To their ecclesiastical governments, headed by the bishops, fell nearly all public social responsibilities. By circumstance the bishops were forced to rescue, reorganize, staff, and administer the agencies that dealt with health, poverty, food supply, curial decisions eventuating in canon law, education, art, and letters. By the great power and personal dynamism of the early Carolingians, such then-traditional episcopal powers were being assimilated to the political state, rather on the model of Davidic theocracy; for a strong emperor like Charlemagne, the episcopacy was his right arm in his body politic. But when he died (A.D. 814), the prelates began to eat away at this theocracy, unsystematically and quarrelsomely assuming prerogatives where they could. The Papal Curia, slow to realize that under Louis I and his sons the theocratic grip was weakening, was laggard in controlling this dispersal of power.[22]

It was Pope Nicholas who, virtually single-handed, curbed the anarchical tendencies. His model was not Byzantine Caesaropapism, though he borrowed aspects of it that suited him. He expressed in forthright fashion the existence of balanced powers, each in its own domain. Here was born the Gregorian doctrine of two ruling powers—the light-bringing sun of the Church and the light-receiving moon of the Empire.[23] But, like Gregory in his turn, he was essentially not satisfied with balance, for he demanded civil support for clerical decisions without an equalizing clerical support for civil decisions. Wrote the malcontent Gunther of Cologne, whom he deposed: "Nicholas, who is called pope and who counts himself an apostle among apostles, has made himself emperor of the whole world."[24]

Stratilates 3 became a model for modifying the theocracy of the West. Writes Amann:

> That benevolent neutrality did not sufficiently satisfy Nicholas I. He wanted a positive intervention of the secular powers in favor of the Church. Without yet having arrived clearly at that conception that the civil power is an executive instrument in the hands of the Church, he was on the road that led to it . . . . A text which recurs frequently is Psalm xliv, 17: "Thou shalt make them princes over all the earth." He emphatically affirms the primacy of the spiritual on the temporal. The idea is not new. Many popes of the fifth and sixth centuries had advanced it. What is novel is the application. If the sovereigns failed in their duties, it was the Church that reprimanded them and kept them in line by excommunication. The emperor Michael on one side and Lothaire II on the other were threatened by that punishment. We would therefore not be much amiss in making Nicholas one of the partisans (if not one of the theoreticians) of the law which the Church exercised in temporal matters: *ratione peccati.* He was a very great pope who appears on the eve of the *siècle de fer,* a very forceful and very noble incarnation of the ecclesiastical ideal.[25]

Pope Nicholas was the first to use the spurious Donation of Constantine and the pseudo-Isidoran Decretals as a code of papal rights.[26] Gregorovius calls him "the founder of the papal monarchy." He was inaccessible to fear. To temporal arms he opposed spiritual arms, especially prayer. One day the partisans of Louis II overran a great procession moving toward Saint Peter's; they beat the pilgrims and trampled down the sacred banners. In the dead of night, the pope left the Lateran, avoiding the guard, and spent two days in prayer, prostrate at Saint Peter's tomb, without food. God heard him. One of the soldiers who had thrown the processional cross in the mud was suddenly struck dead. The emperor ran a fever. The pope, still at prayer, was visited by the empress Ingelberge, who took him to the emperor's bedside. Louis II renounced his partisans and yielded to Nicholas full liberty in ecclesiastical law. Behold the art of *Stratilates 3!*

The pope's relations with all rulers exemplified the vigor of his patron saint. His chastisement of Lothaire II in divorce proceedings is a crux in history; in the course of it he degraded the archbishops of Cologne and Treves. He snatched Bulgaria from Byzantine hegemony (it reverted immediately after his death).[27] He forced the great patriarch Photios from his see under excommunication, with resulting estrangement of the Eastern and Western Communions.[28] He disciplined the Byzantine emperor Michael III, showing himself an extreme iconodule. His words to Michael affected the cult of saints for centuries: "You ought with utter concentration of mind and exertion of utmost desire to venerate and adore the venerable images, not only of Our Lord Jesus Christ but also the Most Holy Mother and the blessed Apostles and all Saints . . . . We ought to do outstanding honor not only to the bodies but also to their clothes or even the painted images of their features, wherever found."[29]

Pope Nicholas I was to the papacy what N was to the populace, the model of pastoral care.[30] *Grainships 7* typifies his feeding of the populace of the City, his issuing food tickets to the indigent. His letter replying to the Bulgarian king Boris's hundred and six questions and petitions in converting a pagan citizenry to Christianity is a practical casebook to accompany Gregory the Great's *Pastoral Care* and his letters to Augustine of Canterbury.[31]

According to the contemporary Life of Pope Nicholas in the *Pontifical Book,* "He was loved by the clergy, praised by the nobility, and magnified by the people."[32] And Anastasius the Librarian wrote to the archbishop of Vienne at the pope's death, "Alas, how late the Church acquired so great a man, how quickly it lost him."[33]

Patriarch Photios, in his fury, held a council at Constantinople to pronounce the deposition of Pope Nicholas.[34] To gain support he tried diligently to enlist the help of the Western emperor, Louis II, and the empress Ingelberge. Indeed, that council voted them the titles

Augustus and *Augusta,* thereby legitimizing the Western Empire, so illegally established Christmas Day, A.D. 800.[35] But as the Byzantine legation went to Aachen late in 867, Nicholas died and the Byzantine revolution overthrew Photios. Almost at once the revolt collapsed.

The pope was not the only Nicholas to tangle with Photios. He exiled the Archimandrite of the Studium, also a Nicholas. The Studium was the most important and troublesome convent in Constantinople. Photios harried Nicholas from place to place. When Photios fell from power, Nicholas the Studite was returned from exile to take his place, but shortly died.[36]

However, our chapter on N's boyhood should end, not with Nicholas the Studite, a professed recluse, but with Nicholas Mysticus, who was Photios's most important disciple, possibly a nephew.[37] "Mysticus" ($\mu\nu\sigma\tau\iota\kappa\grave{o}\varsigma$) does not in this instance refer to things metaphysical, quite the contrary; it was a Greek term for secretary and intimate. When Emperor Leo VI, "the Wise" (886 - 912), came to the throne, he called his old schoolmate to the palace, and subsequently appointed him patriarch (1 March 901). Here was another of the many anticipations of the Becket story, or perhaps in this instance more appropriately Saint Thomas More; for Nicholas, like the pope before him, ruled against the emperor in his marriage.[38]

Leo found Nicholas a doughty foe. In changing from layman to pastor, Nicholas assumed the personality of his namesake and patron saint in all the visible ways. In his pastoral and missionary duties he demonstrated an intense charity that historians tend to overlook in their attention to his political interventions. Like N, he proselytized even in Islam, corresponding with the Emir of Crete and Byzantium's enemy Andronicus Doucas.[39]

But it was as typed by *Stratilates 3* that Patriarch Nicholas too became a legend. In 906 he refused communion and entry to the emperor, writing: "If the Emperor, under inspiration of the Devil, orders something contrary to the Law of God, we do not have to obey him at all; we must hold as naught an impious order from an impious man." On the following 1 February 907, he was seized and incarcerated in a convent near Chalcedon. His successor Euthymius, by bowing to the will of the emperor, divided the Eastern clergy into two parties, Nicolaïtes and Euthymians.[40]

In the course of these quarrels, Nicholas became estranged from

Rome.[41] When, after Emperor Leo's death, he was restored to power, he began to demand justification from the papal court.[42] The already dangerous rift between the Eastern and Western communions again widened. But the benevolence and charity of Nicholas's patron N manifested itself, doubtless under some civil pressure. The patriarch evolved an accommodation: "To underestimate the autonomy of the pope," he wrote, "is to do injury to the Prince of the Apostles." Nevertheless, he did not take the position of a loser, and confirmed the right of the Apostolic Patriarchate of Constantinople to autocephalous government.

Nicholas *papa* and Nicholas *mysticus,* like N, exist in history as saintly exemplars of business, of the forum, the world of action, not contemplation. Endowed with Christian charity and sympathy, *ambitious* in its original sense of "getting around," circulating, they are never at a loss for an answer, easily dividing experience into good and evil, sweets and switches, east and west, making sensible by their acts what less practical men might leave in the realm of the spirit. They typify in history an awakening consciousness of power, an unconventional irascibility and assertiveness, a chafing against civil authority, and a desire to sample the greater world. This is the dawn of adolescence.

N's school days are over, the discipline past. As an adolescent he chafes at the rod, eager to roam, choosing even inconsistently to deny his own innate characteristics. Before the middle of the ninth century, N's master Methodios wrote of the boy: "If in the Indies some man is afflicted, or if there be in the British Isles some victim of calumny, if he but invoke the name of Nicholas, then Nicholas will arrive to succor him." This is a very fine letter of recommendation to be gained by a boy on graduation from school. Like all such recommendations the boy's abilities are yet to be substantiated. Though N was being called to adventure at further and further points of the compass, he was in fact still unnoticed in Britain and India.

THREE
aòolescence

And then the lover
Sighing like a furnace, with a woeful ballad
Made to his mistress' eyebrow.

I ADOLESCENCE

The Old Testament type of adolescent is the David who slew Goliath, "for he was a youth, pink-cheeked and fair."[1] And the New Testament type is the unnamed *adolescens* who had done what he was told since he was a boy: What more did men want? Jesus told him. "But he went away sorrowful, for he had great possessions."[2] The adolescent, which means "in the process of growing up," leaves home to see the world, without moving to a new home of his own. On the whole, the ancients extended the age of adolescence beyond our formulas—normally to the age of thirty, in Christianity the canonical age of priesthood. But Brutus and Cassius were called *adulescens* at age forty, and Cicero called himself adolescent at age forty-four. The typical medieval adolescent was the subdeacon, canonically of age eighteen or twenty to age twenty-five.[3]

Adolescence is a time for wandering without great purpose, for searching for friends of any kind—social, intellectual, sexual—for probing and experimenting without assurance of success. N's age of adolescence extends from Pope Nicholas I to Pope Nicholas II or, better, to the Translation to Bari in the year 1087. According to some facile historical analogies, the tenth and eleventh centuries are also the adolescence of the West—the barbarous age, the age of iron, or anarchy, of the man on horseback—too late for "Roman," too early for "Romanesque." Decadent Italy has then disappeared into a shadowy "empire," dominated by those barbarian tribes, races, clans, nations, peoples—themselves in the adolescence of thoughtless pushing, searching for a place in the sun. These are primarily the transalpine Franks, the Saxons, and the Normans. At that time our Western tradition belonged to young Davids, quite fresh on the northern pastures. Their stories are told in chansons de geste. It was the adolescence of two other images, "Europe" and "Christendom," which were only conceived as effective entities in a *Lebenszeit* parallel with that of N.

The adolescent finds friends without conscious discrimination, hence easily. So this chapter will be dominated by personages—friends of N, unpredictably joined together in a kind of patchwork that suggests connection without design.

Encyclopedists (the authors of *The Oxford Dictionary of the Christian Church,* for instance) are apt to suggest that N's cult "became popular in the West after the inhabitants of Bari claimed to have got possession of his remains on 9 May 1087." But that Translation was more the result than the cause. Divinity had pretty well shaped his ends before he emerged from adolescence. By the time of his Translation, the lineaments of N's puissant personality were set.

The formative documents started with the Latin version of *Stratilates 3,* which circulated in the seventh century.[4] It is more than an accident that the Western version comes to us in two German MSS; Germany was the first transalpine state to receive N. He was officially recognized by the foremost Church official of the ninth century, Hraban Maur, abbot of Fulda, archbishop of Mainz, teacher, author, adviser and at times commander of princes. In the year 818 Hraban wrote a set of verses about relics of seventeen saints as well as of a fragment of the True Cross, Sponge, and so forth, that had been assembled at the tomb of Boniface, the missionary founder of the German Church. Among the relics was something of N; we may guess a phial of *Myrrh 18.*[5] There follow N entries in the martyrologies of the next half-century: those of Florus of Lyons, Hraban (after 840), Wandalbert of Prüm, Ado of Vienne, and Usuard of St.-Germain-des-Prés.[6]

Usuard's entry, composed A.D. 859 - 875, contained: "The Nativity of blessed Nicholas, shepherd of the Myrans of Lycia. Among the many miraculous signs reported of him is that memorable instance whereby, though living far away, yet by warnings and threats through an apparition he dissuaded the emperor Constantine from the destruction of certain men. (*Natalis beati Nicolai episcopi Mirorum Liciae, de quo inter plura miraculorum insignia illud memorabile fertur, quod imperatorem Constantinum ab interitu quorundam, longe constitutus, ad misericordiam et monitis per visum deflexit et minis.*)"[7] This statement grew into pages of lauds and litanies as N's popularity developed in subsequent centuries.

But it was these words of Usuard only that the papal commission returned to in the Roman Martyrology issued by Pope Gregory XIII in 1584. It continued until 1969, N's death knell.

Usuard's notice, like all the notices preceding his, including a more extensive account written by Hraban, referred to no adventure of N except *Stratilates* 3. The Papal Curia has never endorsed N beyond that limit, though it sometimes conferred upon him unspecified thaumaturgic and miraculous power, as in the passage above.

So in the ninth century N earned votive rights in the West. There is a question whether the N Church at Metz was dedicated to him in the ninth century or later.[8] But we may measure how feeble was his standing by a litany of saints composed at Lorsch under Louis the German and Queen Emma, about the time of Pope Nicholas I, in which the misspelled *Nicolus* is merely one of 534 invoked saints.[9] Two calendars written at Mainz in the early tenth century do not even include the name, though a liturgy for reconciliation of penitents does.[10] Nevertheless, that he appeared at all is remarkable. Few of the oriental saints of intense cult in the later Middle Age find mention at all in Carolingian times; we shall treat a typical instance, of Saint Catherine, at the end of this chapter. However, the true martyrs of the Moslem frontier in Spain, where Carolingian armies fought, also received scant attention. Eulogius, archbishop of Toledo in the ninth century, has left us a vivid account of the Saracen persecutions and of those Christians who earned martyrs' crowns.[11] Indeed, Eulogius himself was eventually martyred. Yet none he eulogized found place in the catholic martyrologies.

Wanderlust is the first of adolescent traits. *Peregrinatio,* "pilgrimage," and "tour" are synonymous. The biography of sailors, merchants, and travelers fittingly treats peregrination, from pilgrimages to the temple of Diana to weekends at Santa Claus Village. A French count, Black Fulk of Anjou, "The Jerusalem Traveler," will symbolize for us the tourism that expanded medieval roads, hostelries, shops, and banditry. Europe was emerging from the economic collapse of Rome, and the merchant seaman N emerged with it.

The steady increase of pilgrims on the roads to Palestine, Rome, Compostella, and Tours from the eighth to the eleventh century is a fact often given as a primary explanation for the Crusades (themselves a form of pilgrimage).

Pilgrimage to Jerusalem had peaked about A.D. 400, in the era of Gregory of Nyssa, Basil, and Jerome, who lamented the touristic waifs and strays: "Stay home! The Holy City has become worse than Sodom. Do people still believe that the Holy Spirit dwells in Jerusalem and cannot come to us?"[12] They cried out to no avail. "Sorrow, modesty, and virtue," wrote Gregorovius, "were too often condemned to make the journey in company with shameless vice and cunning fraud and, while on the very way to salvation, through contact with evil, to become themselves corrupt."[13] What exhortation could not stifle, poverty did. The economic collapse of the Western empire slowed travel to a trickle in the sixth and seventh centuries, though it never stopped.

But already at the beginning of the ninth century Charlemagne found it necessary to enter into a rather ineffectual treaty with the Moslem Haroun-al-Raschid to govern access to the Holy Sepulcher. The Roman Emperor at Constantinople was more effective. His staff dealt with Islam in a diplomacy based on acute experience. Despite constant sporadic border warfare, Holy Sepulcher was kept open, though under the best of conditions access was problematic. For instance, in 870 the French monk Bernard penetrated Bari (then in the hands of Saracens), where he bought passports to Alexandria and Cairo. Afterward he paid six gold pieces for passage to Alexandria; then another thirty deniers for new passports. Nevertheless he spent six days in prison at Cairo, being released on payment of thirty more deniers for another set of passports. The same levy was thereafter exacted at every major city he passed through.[14]

The dangers were such that men began to regard pilgrimage as the Justice of God. Courts sentenced their peers to it. The Council of Tours, A.D. 813, decreed that a pilgrimage could cancel guilt.[15] Judges sentenced culprits to leave home with chains forged around their necks, belt, and arms. In the unlikely event that the criminal survived, he seldom had stomach for further evil. In the mid-ninth century a parricide, Frotmond, returned after seven years of such sentence, to end his broken life in a cloister near Rennes. God had determined the weight of punishment.[16]

From the year 1000, when Saint Stephen became first king of Hungary, the Danube land route, which inevitably led through Constantinople, was opened up.[17] The West from that moment moved closer to Byzantium.[18] The isolation of the West was breaking down in a variety of ways. A protection for the Roman emperor at Constantinople was his Varangian Guard of Scandinavians; many of them gladly accepted his palace training and then returned to indoctrinate their native lands with tag ends of eastern culture. The N church at Wisby, on the Baltic island of Gothland, has been said to have roots in this period. It was the earliest of the many Hanseatic cities with a pronounced cult of N. The Normans of France regularly welcomed Eastern legates to their courts; I will soon treat their early cult of N. Bishop Gerard of Toul before 994 set up Greek communities in his diocese, where the Greek rite was maintained.[19]

But for a time conditions in Palestine dampened pious desires. The years 1009 to 1020 marked Hakem's organized pogrom against Christians and Jews in Palestine, Syria, and Egypt. What had formerly been mere levies and accidental hazards now were legalized attacks on pilgrims.[20] Then at the termination of that persecution, gold was sent from the West, Normandy especially, for rebuilding the Holy Places. Duke Richard II sent one hundred *livres d'or*.[21] In the peculiar internationalism of the times, the Roman emperor assumed the responsibility for rebuilding Jerusalem. Runciman thinks that he was allowed to keep his own officials at the door of the Holy Sepulcher to extract tolls from pilgrims to pay for the work.

Pilgrimage became *tout à fait à la mode*.[22] In place of pilgrimage groups comprising three or four, there were tours of hundreds. In 1027 abbot Richard of Vannes shepherded seven hundred; in 1032 bishop Avesgand of Le Mans set out with more. In 1064 there was a pilgrimage organized by German bishops numbering seven thousand, of whom four thousand returned.[23]

Most pilgrims were poorly schooled against the rigors of the journey. The number of unprotected women ran high. Like Fulk, Robert of Normandy was surrounded by hundreds of pilgrims at the gates of Jerusalem, weeping and crying out because they had no money to enter. According to accounts, only one in a thousand who arrived had enough for his needs, for most of them had lost their provisions en route and had saved only their bodies from the countless perils. Lietbert, bishop of Cambrai, crossed Hungary and the Hellespont without great misfortune. But at Laodicea (Latakia, Syria) he had to wait three months because the roads were blocked. He decided to sail, but a tempest cast him on Cyprus. The Catapan retained him some weeks on the excuse that he feared for his safety. Lietbert returned to Laodicea, where he was persuaded by returning pilgrims to give up the attempt and return home.[24] Bréhier says that those who could not complete the long voyage consoled themselves by swallowing the oriental tales which circulated throughout Europe, by venerating relics allegedly from Jerusalem, and by praying in churches now being built all over Europe on the model of the rotunda of Holy Sepulcher.[25]

So Pope Urban II, in preaching the First Crusade at the Council of Clermont, is reported to have said:

> What can I say for those who, having lost everything and trusting in their poverty, undertake the voyage because they seem to have nothing to lose but their bodies. The infidels submit them to horrible torments in trying to steal the money they don't have. They tear off their nails to search under the skin for some hidden piece of gold. They force them to drink scammony to induce vomiting to make them cough up any gold or silver they might have been able to swallow. With instruments they open the stomach to examine the most secret recesses of the body. Can you tell how many millions have died in such frightful fashion?[26]

Such conditions made a harvest for guardian saints, whose patronage was about the only form of insurance at that time. N was but one who was invoked; others were George and Christopher.

The climactic period of pilgrimage before the Crusades coincided with the peak of admiration for N the Thaumaturge throughout the Byzantine world, and it was that world that western pilgrims had to cross in dangerous times. Invocation on land as well as sea assured N's fame. For example, it was then, apparently, that "Saint Nicholas water" came into being. As late as 1533 Griffin Affagart, a pilgrim, was recommending that all travelers should carry a "jar of the sweet water of Saint Nicholas, which keeps sweet longer at sea."[27] In the central decades of the eleventh century, pilgrims vowed many shrines to N; and some of them returned to their homes in the West to fulfill their vows.

II THE ANGEVIN COUNTS

Typical of the Age of Iron are two counts of Anjou, Fulk Nerra and his son Geoffrey Martel, "the Hammer." They were early founders of that House of Anjou which filled many thrones of Europe and Jerusalem. Today's château country is filled with their names and their works. As I report the relevant portion of their story I am aware that it sounds fabulous. Nevertheless I draw it from documents regarded as standard for their age: the letters and pronouncements,[1] monastic and county annals,[2] contemporary historians,[3] the half-century-later history of William of Malmesbury,[4] and a century-later history composed by a later Angevin count.[5] To be sure, it was not an age that valued sheer information. No statement here is in itself quite reliable as political or social history, but I deem each to be essential in a biography of a legend. Each appears elsewhere in modern histories.[6] For example, I speak of Fulk Nerra as if the words meant, as they do now, "Black Falcon," though the epithet *Nerra* appeared first only a century after his death, and there is no etymological justification for *Nerra* or *Noera* as identical with *Niger*.[7] Yet if those who learned of N learned from the Angevin shrine of the Black Falcon, what matters etymology?

The Carolingian Empire had been hastily put together by three strong Frankish magnates in the eighth century from a loose aggregation of aborigines, Celts, decadent Romans, commerical and migrant Greeks and Syrians, with Teutonic overlords not very remote from barbarity. Like other such forced growth, the first change of weather withered it. The change was a northern blast of Scandinavians, Normans, Vikings, with cross winds of eastern Magyars and southern Moslems, to whom the rest of this age primarily belongs. The Northmen settled Greenland and prowled about Newfoundland and perhaps America, flowed over Ireland, Scotland, and England, settled in Spain, conquered Sicily and southern Italy, marched into the heart of Greece, threatening Byzantium from the west as a century before they had threatened it from the east.

The Norman wave rushed up two main valleys of France, the Seine toward Paris (leaving as tidal deposit the Duchy of Normandy), and the Loire. In this second wave the Angevin line sprouted, the *homines novi*.[8] A desperate king, far inland at Laon, helped an effective guerilla leader, a forester named Ingelger, to gain power by arranging noble marriages and lending political support. The inherited title changed from viscount to count in 919 with Fulk the Red.[9] In 987, exactly a century before N's Translation, the year that Hugh Capet, Duke of the Franks, went to Paris to be King of France, Fulk Nerra succeeded to the countship, which he held for fifty-three years. "A strange and complex figure," wrote LeMoy, "indefatigable, athirst for vengeance, brutal in moments of reprisal, quick to remorse, hurrying to Palestine, making his own servants beat him, and despite those penances always the bandit, builder of castles and churches, including some marvels, feared and adored by all, uniting in his person all contrasts."[10]

Centering in "black Angers," from Roman days the home of slate processing, young Fulk started with a country roughly fifty miles square. He was pinched by rapacious Normandy and Maine to the north, Chartres and Blois to the east, Poitou to the south, and the kingdom of Britanny to the west. But in fifty-three years of rule he taught them all to tremble and by the time his son Geoffrey died Anjou held the balance of power in France. A case can be made that their work forced William the Conqueror to turn north to England, since the south was closed. It mattered little, because in the long run Henry II of Anjou took all—and then some.

This age of anarchy was also an age of castle building, and Fulk was preeminent in this activity. Today we may stand and marvel at his towering keeps of Loches and Montrichard.[11] His grandson listed fourteen such, and more ambitious historians have pushed the number above twenty.[12] At Langeais, where Rabelais and Ronsard lived, beside the château of Louis, built in 1460, is Fulk's square donjon.[13]

Lacking the finesse of later civilization, Fulk seems both choleric and barbaric to us. I need mention only a few instances to set the stage. Hè won outer Maine by an ambuscade that caught his brother-in-law, the Duke of Rennes, under a tower that ever since has been called the Tower of the Squashed Bretons.[14] In the melee, Fulk killed two of his nephews and captured the other two. He joined with the outlaw Duke of Perigord in sacking Tours.[15] In sudden choler at a canon who got in his way at the cathedral, he rode his horse in pursuit through the sanctuary of Saint Martin.[16] Four hundred years earlier a royal legate had done the same, and Saint Martin had palsied him so severely that he abandoned church and city.[17] In dealing with Fulk, the clergy played on that traditional image. They sealed the tomb of Saint Martin, closed the doors of the basilica to all pilgrims, and stopped the flow of gold to the richest shrine in France. Fulk had to crawl barefoot with many knights, pledging respect. But the evil remained. The chroniclers are strangely silent about how Fulk lost Tours, but in less than a year he had withdrawn, never to enter the city as its lord again.[18] Yet within four years of his death his son held Tours and all Touraine.[19]

According to local annals Fulk put to death his first wife, Elizabeth of Vendôme, who had failed to bear him a son. A few days later the whole city of Angers burned to the ground.[20] Angers had been leveled by the Normans more than a century before, and the new city, evidently having been jerry-built, burned freely. Very shortly the two events were linked, with Fulk as the evil agent.[21]

Finally there is the instance of Fulk's treatment of Hugh of Beauvais. Fulk's niece Constance married King Robert Capet, who had Hugh as a favorite. In her hatred of Hugh she called on her uncle for help. Without hesitation he arrived at the royal court with a dozen picked Angevin knights. One day when the king and his favorite were hunting in the forest and had paused to rest, Fulk's knights surrounded them, and even as they did obeisance to the king they cut off Hugh's head. Robert, evidently more in piety than in sorrow, complained to the bishops, who sat on the case at Chelles.[22]

There is another, and more charitable, picture of Fulk which might well be made up from a different set of selections from chroniclers. But such acts as we have mentioned were the cause of Fulk's sobriquet, "Jerusalem traveler."[23] He made at least three pilgrimages to the Holy Land in penance and expiation.[24] Ever since Charlemagne had negotiated with Haroun-al-Raschid, the Holy Land had been open to western pilgrims, and the trip was a favorite form of imposed penance.

The documents seem to agree that Fulk was seized with a dreadful fear of hell (*metu gehennae territus*) after his mistreatment of his wife Elizabeth and the burning of Angers. With contrite heart he set out on his first trip. Glaber says that Fulk returned mellowed. At all events he immediately began to build his magnificent abbey at Beaulieu, near Loches, which was to house his Palestinian souvenirs and, eventually, his corpse.[25] Who would dedicate the abbey? The Archbishop of Tours, still smarting from Fulk's desecration, refused.[26] His refusal, and that of the strongest prelates of France, eventually drove Fulk into the hands of the Romanizing party. Naturally enough, the history of the involvement of the Curia comes to us from the pens of Fulk's near-contemporaries only as a legend replete with miracles and fictional devices. The papal legate dedicated Beaulieu, but consecration proved insufficient:

> Even as the ninth hour of the day neared, the sky was everywhere clear and only a gentle breeze was blowing. But suddenly a violent cyclone came up out of the south and struck the church. Filled with the wind, it shook violently again and again. Then as the cyclone loosened the ceilings and timbers of the complete structure, the entire roof of the western gable was overturned and went hurtling to the ground.[27]

The pope sent the bishop of Viterbo to reconsecrate it, but the foundation continued to be plagued. That it housed the bones of Fulk Nerra did nothing to stabilize it. Later on, Pope Urban II, while traveling through France preaching the First Crusade, again reconsecrated it—an act of beneficence that calmed its spirit.[28]

Fulk's killing of Hugh of Beauvais occasioned his second journey. The jury at Chelles, headed by the renowned and venerable Fulbert of Chartres (*mirabilis modernorum temporum doctor*) required him to name the authors of the crime and to disavow them or else to go to the Holy Sepulcher. According to Fulbert's letter, "You will go purge yourself and give humble satisfaction."[29] Evidently Fulk named no accessories, because he set out alone in penance in the same year 1008.[30] This second journey, probably because of the great publicity of the trial, turned into an epic under the pens of near-contemporaries.[31]

First, Fulk went to Rome, then Constantinople. Later chroniclers wrongly report that it was this trip, not Fulk's third (or fourth) on which he traveled in Palestine with the ill-fated Duke Robert (*le Diable*) of Normandy, father of William the Conqueror, who died and was buried at Nicea.[32] In fact, Fulk arrived alone at Jerusalem during the pogrom of the Fatimate Caliph Hakim, whom Bréhier describes as a crowned madman.[33] It was in 1010, after Fulk's visit, that the caliph's governor reduced the superstructure of the Holy Sepulcher to rubble and destroyed the adjacent monastery, the Church of Saint Mary, and Golgotha. But the flow of Christian pilgrims had already been stemmed by excessive persecution. When we consider that Fulk survived this chaos to return to Angers, we must forgive our chroniclers for stretching credibility. A sample retelling bears repeating to indicate the aura surrounding Saint-Nicolas d'Angers:[34]

> Outside the city gates were Christian pilgrims of every class from all Europe, who had survived the perils of ship and land travel, the storms, the robbery and piracy, the imprisonments, the wars and rapine, the zealots, and, most of all, the grafting officials who made pilgrimage so speculative a venture. Here at the very door of their destination, they were barred. But Fulk, with personal magnetism and full purse, bought their way into the city. He found the Holy Sepulcher covered with a heap of stones, but there were ways of descending to the vault. The Arabs would consent to his making his way through the rubble to the tomb on one condition only—that he would desecrate the tomb by letting water upon it. Fulk went to his lodgings to scheme. He filled a small phial with rosewater [another chronicler says white wine], which he attached to his garter. The next day he went through an apparent act of desecration, to the glee of the assembled Arabs. Then as he stooped to kiss the tomb, God, in reward for his abject repentance, wrought a miracle in his behalf. Fulk's tears softened the stone of the tomb. Feeling the yielding substance he covertly took a bite, bringing away in his teeth a precious fragment of the sepulcher.[35]

Fulk's encounter with N on the Antiochene coast is attested by early, quite reliable, authorities.[36] Leaving Jerusalem, he made his way to Antioch and then set sail for the west by the common route along the Lycian coast. The ship was struck by a violent tempest. Each man aboard, as he awaited his approaching death, invoked the saints of his special affection. In the babble, the name of Saint Nicholas stood out. Though strange to Fulk, he was not one to neglect a favorite. He fell on his knees to implore the aid of the blessed confessor, promising him that if it pleased him in that necessity to deliver him from death, he, Fulk, on his return to Angers would build a church to him. N then saw him safely home.[37]

According to the early fabulists, the pope received him on his return through Rome before all bishops and cardinals assembled. Fulk was assured of a seat in heaven beside the archangel Michael himself. The pope loaded Fulk with relics, including the corpses of Saints Chrysanthus and Daria.[38] One destined for the angelic hierarchy by the successor of Saint Peter could afford to be Olympian about his contracts with lesser saints, and after his return to Angers Fulk rather neglected his vow to N. But one day as he stood staring at the rugged countryside across the River Maine from a window in his castle at Angers, he saw a dove carrying rubble in its beak to fill up a hole in a rock. That edifying bird recalled to Fulk his duties as a builder.[39] He mounted his horse to survey the site which the nesting bird had providentially marked. But his horse started in sudden fright and threw his rider. The count saw in this accident demonic power at work, and cried out: "Satan, I had intended only a chapel to Saint Nicholas, but now I will build a monastery."[40] This foundation, dedicated 1 December 1020, so far as I can tell, was the beginning in western France of the cult of N.[41] Almost at once King Robert, the indirect cause of Fulk's journey and dedication, built a chapel to N in his palace at Paris.[42]

According to Fulk's own testimony: "I, Fulk, Count of Anjou, albeit one of the lowliest and most sinful of men, in the name of God and the heavenly hierarchy decreed that a church should be built within view of the city of Angers, and in the year 1020 I had it consecrated by the Lord President Herbert of that city. Not long after its consecration, I installed as abbot one of the monks of the great Monastery of Saint Martin at Tours, Baldric by name, and I took pains to endow it from my own goods for the support of the brothers and of the poor." Fulk listed the endowments, of which he was rightfully proud: vineyards and plantations on the banks of the Brianneau, twelve arpents near Alloyau, the land of Adesière, a clearing at Villenière, a vineyard between the Maine and the Brianneau and other vineyards near the Maine; the exemption from restrictions of wine sale on this side of the Barre; the right to administer justice for the tenants of the monastery; exemption from military service except in war; and exemption from requisition of carts, oxen, and asses.[43]

But Satan was not idle. Abbot Baldric almost immediately found administration not to his liking. (Many a college president has discovered the inconvenience of having his millionaire donor living in the same town.) So Baldric retired to a spiritual life—furtively, wrote Fulk in his account. Then Fulk consulted the abbot of Marmoutier, who nominated his rising young monk Renaud. But before Renaud could even be consecrated, Fulk's son Geoffrey Martel dazzled the new appointee with promise of the abbacy of Holy Trinity at Vendôme, which Geoffrey had begun to build at a spot where he had seen a meteorite fall. Renaud was evidently especially desirable because he was an architect. Without ever attending his consecration at Saint-Nicolas and without asking authorization from his abbot Albert, Renaud went to Vendôme to be with Geoffrey, now Count of Vendôme.[44] Fulk flew into a black rage (*valde iratus,* he says himself). He canceled all contracts and sent the monks of Saint-Nicolas back to Marmoutier, in violation of rules of tenure. He demanded an abbot and monks from Gautier, abbot of Saint-Aubin. Since Saint-Aubin was within the city walls of Angers, Gautier was constrained to comply. With that settlement, Satan left the monastery in comparative tranquillity.

This contention with Geoffrey the Hammer brings us to the lasting quarrel between Fulk and his son.[45] The Vendôme annalist calls it a *bellum plus quam civile,*[46] and it stayed in the Angevin memory for centuries. One hundred and forty years later, when the sons of King Henry II broke out in civil war against their father, Henry's son Geoffrey exclaimed: "It is the destiny of our family that we do not love one another. That is our heritage, and not one of us has ever renounced it." And Richard the Lion-hearted, a second rebellious son, said: "Is this strife astonishing in what comes from such stock, we who live badly, one with another? What comes from the Devil must return to the Devil."[47] They were conforming with the epic pattern of Fulk and his son Geoffrey; and Queen Eleanor, in urging them on, aped Fulk's niece, Queen Constance, who raised a war between sons and husband.

Fulk had killed one wife to get a son. His second wife Adela obliged by bearing Geoffrey, but had the good sense not to repeat the mistake.[48] I quote the brief account of Geoffrey as given by his nephew and successor, Count Fulk Rechin:

> My uncle Geoffrey became a knight in his father's lifetime, and began his knighthood by wars against his neighbors, one against the Poitevins, whose count he captured, and another against the people of Maine, whose count he also took. He also carried on war against his own father, in the course of which he committed many evil deeds of which he afterward bitterly repented. After his father died on his return from Jerusalem, Geoffrey possessed his lands and the city of Angers, and fought Count Thibaut of Blois, son of Count Odo. By gift of King Henry he received the city of Tours, which led to another war with Count Thibaut, in the course of which, at a battle between Tours and Amboise, Thibaud was captured with a thousand of his knights. And so besides the part of Touraine inherited from his father, he acquired Tours and the castles round about—Chinon, l'Ile Bouchard, Chateaurenault, and Saint-Aignan. After this he had a war with William of Normandy, who later conquered England and was a magnificent king, and with the people of France and Bourges. And he warred with William Count of Angoulême, and Aimeri Viscount of Thouars, and Hoel Count of Nantes, and the Breton counts of Rennes, and with Hugh Count of Maine, who had thrown off his fealty . . . . In the year that King Henry died, my uncle Geoffrey on the third day after Martinmas came to a good end. For on the night which preceded his death, laying aside all care for knighthood and secular things, he became a monk in the monastery of Saint Nicholas, which his father and he had built with much devotion and endowed with their goods.[49]

Let William of Malmesbury tell the story now of the "war more than civil":

> In his latter days, Fulk ceded his principality to Geoffrey his son. Geoffrey conducted himself with excessive barbarity to the inhabitants, and with equal haughtiness even to the per-

son who had conferred this honor upon him. On being ordered by his father to lay down the government and insignia of authority, he was arrogant enough to take up arms against him. The blood of the old man, though grown cold and languid, yet boiled with indignation. In the course of a few days, by canny planning, he so brought down the spirit of his son that, after carrying his saddle on his back for some days, he cast himself with his burden at his father's feet.[50] [This incident of saddling his son is an epic convention in the twelfth century, contained in *Garin of Lorraine, Girard of Vienne,* and elsewhere.] Fulk, fired once more with his ancient irascibility, rising up and kicking the prostrate youth with his foot, exclaimed, *Victus es tandem, victus*! [you're still beaten! Beaten!], repeating the word *victus* three or four times. Yet the applicant had enough spark to make this admirable reply: "I am vanquished by you alone, because you are my father; by others I am utterly invincible." With this reply, Fulk's rage was quenched, and having assuaged the mortification of his son by show of paternal affection, he restored him to his principality, with admonitions to conduct himself more wisely—telling him that the prosperity and tranquillity of the people were creditable to him abroad as well as advantageous at home. In the same year the old man made provisions for his soul by proceeding to Jerusalem. There, compelling two servants by an oath to do whatever he commanded, he was by them publicly dragged naked, in the sight of the Turks, to the Holy Sepulcher. One of them had twisted a withe about his neck, the other with a rod scourged his bare back, while he cried out, "Lord, receive the wretched Fulk, Thy perfidious scoundrel; look to my repentant soul, O Lord Jesus Christ."[51]

These are the words of William of Malmesbury, the most reliable historian of his day. He wrote about ninety years after Fulk's death. Fulk died on a fourth (or fifth) journey back from Jerusalem, at Metz, 21 June 1040.[52] The archbishop of Metz buried his entrails there in all honor, then shipped his bones to his beloved Beaulieu.[53] Fulk has been equated with Thierry d'Angers of the *Song of Roland,* but seems to be more the historical counterpart of Raoul of Cambrai, in whose chanson Geoffrey and Herbert are designated actors.[54]

Geoffrey's death and burial in sanctity, A.D. 1060, was followed by his son's, who died only three years after him from battle wounds.[55] Their noble relics,[56] together with an endowment, made N abbey a cultural force for the next several centuries. Abbot Johel of Le Mans, when he was a monk there before 1080, composed an N Life containing accounts of local miracles.[57] One of the most important surviving MSS for both provincial and general N cult in the west is Angers MD. 121 (anc. 113).[58] Under the Normans the abbey acquired property in England, such as a church at Newhold, a manor at Crowston, a farm in Bedfordshire. Its most important holding was Monks Keiby in Warwickshire, founded A.D. 1077 by Geoffrey de la Guerchi; it was built under the personal supervision of the Abbot of Saint Nicholas of Angers.[59] Pope Urban II visited Saint Nicholas and confirmed its possessions, *Letter of Privilege* 56 below. The grounds at Angers, still quite traceable, now house the *Maison de retrait de Saint-Nicolas.* However, I found on a visit there several years ago that the authorities, in anticipation of N's recent demise, were unostentatiously substituting *du Bon Pasteur* (of the Good Shepherd) for *de Saint-Nicolas* in the title.

III EMPRESS THEOPHANO

Two events in tenth-century Germany determined that the N cult would be intensified there. The first was the marriage of the Byzantine princess Theophano in 972 to the future Western emperor Otto II;[1] the second was the composition of the N liturgy. Theophano's origins are obscure, though she is now generally regarded as a niece of the Byzantine emperor.[2] Coming to the West with a considerable entourage, she toured widely and effectively. After the year 983 she became a strong force in politics as regent, indeed de facto imperatrix, for her son Otto III.[3] Her circle, including the duchess Hadwig of Bavaria, the abbess Gerberge of Gandersheim, and Burchard the future abbot of Saint Gall, revived the use of Greek.[4] Today there are Greek books in the library of Bamberg given to the young Otto by John Philajathor of Calabria, who later (997) became Gregory V's antipope.[5] Her most powerful courtiers were devotees of N: Bishop Hildward of Halberstadt, who erected an N altar in the crypt of his cathedral and an N church;[6] Archbishop Willigis of Mainz, who dedicated an N church at

Weende bei Göttingen;[7] Bishop Bernward, who was Godehard's predecessor at Hildesheim; and Bishop Notger of Liège, to be treated later. Meisen lists thirteen German churches dedicated to N after the arrival of Theophano.[8]

Let the *Burtscheid Icon 37* symbolize these effects.[9] Before the year 1000 Emperor Otto III built a monastery at *Burtscheid 36* then a suburb but now incorporated in Aachen. He appointed as abbot a monk Gregory, whose home monastery in Byzantine Italy had been destroyed, possibly by Otto's armies. Gregory built two new chapels. One was dedicated to Saint Apollinaris, doubtless the saint of that name who was first bishop of Ravenna, for whom two remarkable sixth-century Ravennese basilicas are named. The other chapel was dedicated to N.[10] At that time it acquired an N icon, unquestionably painted in Constantinople or in a wholly similar atelier. In the autumn of 1971 I examined the icon, still possessed by the church at Aachen-Burtscheid.

Here is a story about the *Burtscheid Icon 37* from the Dialogue on Miracles of Caesarius of Heisterbach, who was born ca. 1180:

> NOVICE.——Because Saint Nicholas is represented in churches both in sculpture and in pictures more frequently than any other pontiff, I should be glad to know if it is possible to see any real likeness of his face, so that his memory may be more lastingly impressed upon my mind.
>
> MONK.——I will show you a certain image of wonderful workmanship which is said to have been wrought by one who saw Saint Nicholas in the flesh, and sculptured it according to his likeness.
>
> In the monastery of Burtscheid, which is near Aachen, is a picture about a foot and a half long, representing the likeness of the blessed pontiff Nicholas from the waist upward, which the blessed Gregory, the son of the king of Greece and the founder and first abbot of that monastery, brought thither. It is said to be the same picture which a barbarian, as we read in the Miracles of Saint Nicholas, carried off and set up to guard his tolls and was by its means converted to the faith, after he had lost his goods and recovered them on beating the image [*Iconia 34*]. Many won-

ders were wrought through it, especially in the case of women who were with child. On one occasion it was carried to the house of a certain noble matron who was in childbed, and was hung up opposite her on the wall. And at the season when she was delivered, in the sight of all who were present, the picture turned its face to the wall, as though to avoid seeing the woman in her labor. Now the face of the picture is long and emaciated, very earnest and venerable. The brow is bold, the hair of the head and beard quite white. Lately when the monks retired, nuns of our Order came into possession both of the shrine and of the picture.[11]

Here is the earliest datable evidence of N's connection with childbirth, which will form a topic of chapters 6 and 7 below. Otto III also founded a collegiate convent in the center of Aachen, the capital, with an N chapel.

In recording the founding of *Burtscheid 36,* the Acts of the Founding of the Abbey of Brauweiler[12] tells that Matilda, daughter of Emperor Otto II and close adviser of Theophano, and her husband Palatine Count Ezo dedicated their new monastic foundation at Brauweiler, just outside Cologne, to N and Saint Medard (Medard soon lost his influence). The party of Theophano had by then dispersed, since she was long dead, but,

> nonetheless the venerable hero Ezo pressed on with the project he had so zealously begun, and in the fifth year thereafter the monastery was entirely completed. The bishop Pilgrim of Cologne performed its dedication, and as was customary confirmed its possessions on 8 November [A.D. 1028]. With the permission of his children, the pious founder and originator of the shrine himself devoted it to the preeminent confessors of Christ, that is, Saint Nicholas and Saint Medard, and by his ban confirmed as an endowment in perpetuity the estates which he had previously willed to his heirs.[13]

A daughter of Ezo, who had been a handmaiden of Theophano and afterward became Queen of Poland, was a most generous supporter of

Brauweiler. When she died in the odor of sanctity, the then archbishop of Cologne, Anno, exercising his hegemony, entombed her
corpse in the Church of Saint Mary in Cologne. The monks of
Brauweiler, deprived of precious relics which they had been led to
believe would be theirs, joined with their abbot in composing, in the
name and person of their patron N, an open letter of castigation of
Anno (*N's Letter 38*). This letter is remarkably characteristic of the N
of *Iconia 34*, patron of bankers:

> As you fear the judgments of God, which are most pro-
> found, do not irritate Him by diverting His goods from His
> saints, lest it turn out that the Advocate for *all* men, aroused
> by our laments, should take *you* from among us and hand
> you over to everlasting torment. For much is asked of us:
> we are terribly pushed around and chivied on every side,
> and constantly cursed because the Lord has prolonged *your*
> life. Indeed, the longer you retain your high position among
> men, the more your image suffers among all.[14]

The verbal scourging is inventive and unrestrained. Nine centuries
later we flinch at so physical an image. But more importantly, it is an
early instance in Northern literature of deliberate *impersonation,* the
soul of drama. As we shall see below (3, v), N was the first subject of
Western scholastic and secular drama; he was, as it were, drama's
patron saint. The Hildesheim plays of N were already in existence
when this letter was composed.

Subsequently the archbishop patched up some sort of truce, but a
chaplain Otto, who for money had been helpful in the machinations,
was struck by lightning and disintegrated.

A description of the pre-Translation miracles wrought at
Brauweiler through the ministrations of N has survived.[15] Most of the
miracles are common physical cures, but one, where N rescues a
homicide from hanging, develops the personality of N. It employs the
innocentes motif of *Stratilates 3,* including the word itself; and N is the
rescuer of those unjustly accused. But now N no longer works
through an official or, as in *Iconia 34,* persuades; he is beginning to be
judge and executioner both. This story became popular, and in embroidered form was thereafter attached to the legends of many saints,
especially to the Miracles of the Virgin.[16]

IV REGINOLD AND THE N LITURGY[1]

What very probably contributed most to swelling the cult of N in western Europe was the composition of his proper liturgy shortly before the arrival of the empress Theophano. Its background, its composer and composition, its melodiousness, and its dissemination are as stagy, in the way Shakespeare's Jacques meant, as the N legend itself.

"Historia" was a new term[2] in the tenth century,[3] denoting any entire liturgy of proper anthems and responses, sometimes together with lections and prayers, for a particular saint's day. These parts were interrelated, usually in a loose representation of the saint's life. Despite quite intensive study during the past century by historians, liturgists, and musicologists, the origins and evolution of such liturgies, often composed in rhyme or rhythm, are rather obscure.[4] The N Office, or historia, came very early in the evolution of this very popular form of liturgy. Probably, but not certainly, some historiae were in use before that of N. One for Saint Stephen has more convincing claim to priority.[5] However, it had no such popular acceptance. The N historia not only spread the cult of the saint, but the popularity of the liturgical form as well.

In any religious tradition, the form of worship is subject to waves and troughs of conservatism and innovation. In liturgy as in politics, military men are usually conservative: their central aim is deployment, maneuverability, and dependability of human masses. That aim is most easily achieved by adhering to what has been. The military Charlemagne, while trying to govern all Latin Europe as a theocracy, did all in his power to arrive at uniformity in social forms: in homiletics, scriptural texts, monastic rules, letter writing, court manners. So he insisted on a single conservative liturgy, undeviating from parish to parish and diocese to diocese. It was to be the "Roman Rite," insofar as his lieutenants could determine what that rite might be. His agents pressed for a *usus pristinus:* "They must sing the Roman chant end-to-end and perform the nocturnal and sacramental office without deviation from the text as defined by our father King Pippin of blessed memory."[6] Or, as the bishop of Basle interpreted the order: "Nothing is to be read or chanted in church except what has divine authority (i.e., Holy Scripture) and what has been sanctioned by the authority of the orthodox Fathers."[7] But after Charlemagne's death, choirmasters developed as artists, and congregations became audiences; innovation increased. The Compiègne MS, Paris, B.N. lat. 17436, the earliest to contain the seeds of historiae, was written for Emperor Charles II (d. 877),[8] and Stephen of Liège (d. 920) is presumed to have composed a complete historia for Saint Stephen and for Saint Lambert.[9]

According to the so-called *Anonymus Haserensis 39*,[10] a literary history of the diocese of Eichstätt, composed about 1075, the N liturgy was composed by Reginold of Eichstätt,[11] "of noble blood, but even nobler in learning—not alone in Latin and Greek literature but even somewhat trained in Hebrew; and, what was unique and exceptional indeed, he was the first musician of his day. His first act was to make a historia of Saint Nicholas, and for this he earned appointment as bishop."[12] As bishop (A.D. 966 - 991), he composed songs for Saint Willibald, founder of the see, and a historia for Willibald's brother Saint Wunebald, and thereafter one for Saint Blase.[13]

Anonymous Haserensis 39 proves out to be accurate in details. The text of the Willibald songs, which he describes in their technical details, exists still and checks with his description.[14] In the records of the see of Eichstätt Reginold appears as an active and successful bishop.[15] *Anonymous Haserensis 39* ends with a statement that I quote in full, for it is the bud from which a full romance will blossom later:

> Moreover that same bishop loved (*diligebat*) a very important lady named Pia, who is reputed to have incomparably surpassed all women of her day by the distinction of her handicraft. She adorned our church with many a marvelous ornament, not only by working and setting a model for herself, but also by teaching many others many varieties of artistry. At last, giving herself over wholly to the Lord, she built nearby a convent for nuns, called Bergen, which she enriched with an endowment befitting royalty (for she was extremely rich) and adorned with every kind of art object before she turned it over to the special protection of the Church of Rome. John, the Apostolic Vicar, confirmed this deed with his privilege, which is in our possession today; and proclaimed a most terrible anathema against everyone doing any injustice to that convent.

Eichstätt, halfway between Augsburg and Nuremberg, in a romantic valley of the Altmühl, was a foundation of the English missionary Saint Boniface. Its first bishop, the English Willibald, had left Britain about the year 720 to travel with his brother Wunebald and a father (in later legend to become Saint "King Richard of England"), who died at Lucca.[16] Wunebald dropped out of the party at Rome, but Willibald pushed on to the holy places of the East. On the way his ship ran ashore in Lycia, where he passed the winter.[17] On his way back he again sailed past Myra. Such facts suggest that he may have become a devotee of N. After ten years of such travel he spent ten years more as a monk at Monte Cassino. Then Pope Gregory III sent him to help Boniface. He was bishop of Eichstätt ca. 741 - 786. His sister Saint Walburga, made famous by the Walpurgis Night of *Faust,* became abbess of Heidenheim, and her legend incorporates symbols and cult of the pagan Walburg, the Earth Mother. This whole family of saints became myroblyte in later cult.[18]

As *Anonymous Haserensis 39* says, Reginold composed the extant chants of Willibald partly in Latin, partly in Greek, and partly in Hebrew.[19] That fact lends credence to the assertion that Reginold was acquainted with both foreign languages, though we may question how well acquainted he was. Haserensis also states that he had traveled extensively in Greece and was *chrisostomus noster.*[20] In Upper Germany at the time, Reginold "of noble blood, but even nobler in learning" would normally have received his education in an external monastic school, but such education could not have included training in Greek or Hebrew. He would have had to travel at least to Lombardy to learn Greek. Chances are great that he learned Greek and any smattering of Hebrew in the polyglot regions of Apulia, Calabria, and Sicily, home of "Methodios" and John the Deacon. There he could well have been a civil representative of the Ottonian court, though possibly he could have been a pilgrim to the Holy Land who, like so many others, tarried long in southern Italy.

The remarkable statement that "his first act was to make a historia of Saint Nicholas, and for this he earned appointment as bishop" can be explained only on grounds that the historia was artistically exceptional.[21] Like a catchy new tune, it seems to have swept the world.[22] Historia denotes both words and music, but since the words (which have come down to us) do not seem distinguished, indeed are largely copied from John the Deacon, the distinction seems to have lain in the melodies.[23] Unfortunately neumes, the only form of musical notation at the time, are a very loose and ambiguous record, and musicologists have not yet successfully transposed the N liturgy into modern notation. We must accept the inference from other evidence that there was something new, exciting, and disturbing to traditionalists about Reginold's composition. It suggests youth or adolescence, the "rock liturgy" of his age. We possess it in a large number of MSS; several of these also record the melodic lines in neumes. Reginold could possibly have composed "new music" for his new historia.[24]

Not only were all the lections in N Liturgy 40 drawn verbatim from Deacon John's Life of N, but some content of the anthems and responses were also.[25] Reginold copied words, phrases, and a few whole sentences from John. The following episodes are mentioned: Stratilates 3, Artemis 4, Firebomb 5, Mariner 6, Grainships 7, Parentage 10, Lactation 11, Three Daughters 13, Bishop 14, Myrrh 18. Reginold flavored his Western music with melodies and musical devices acquired from the Greek communion, but too little evidence survives to allow us to judge how much this exotic strain had to do with its popularity. The Eastern Church had long cultivated proper services for the saints, and their popularity in the East is well authenticated. The very novelty of such a service in the West would add to popularity. For whatever reason, Reginold was unrivaled in the tenth century as a popular composer of music. The office of Saint Nicholas has served as the model for many another. As one instance, Saint Thomas Aquinas, in composing the Office for Corpus Christi, borrowed at second hand (through Gaude felix parens of Saint Dominic) Reginold's melody of the anthem O Christi pietas 45.[26]

To repeat, his plainchant melodies were so novel and attractive that they earnèd him a bishopric. To a lesser extent his melodies spread the cults of all the other saints that he honored, first in Germany and then in Britain. Blase (3 Feb.) became a folklore figure in both lands, especially in Scotland: "Patron of woolweavers and carvers, builders and stonecutters, also invoked against wild beasts, coughs, whooping cough, goiter, and throat diseases in general." The heath fires burned on Saint Blase Day make it "little Candlemas." A Cappadocian martyr, presumably A.D. 316, he was patron of Ragusa,

Sicily, but wholly neglected in the Latin world until Reginold composed his historia.[27]

This popularity of the N liturgy is substantiated by two legendary texts which have survived: *The Cross Legend 41* and *The Bari Widow 73*. [28] In their different ways both accent the worldliness of the composer, the catchy melodies, and their appeal to the young if not to the profane. The eleventh century was a period of youthful ebullience which witnessed the rise of the troubadours and trouvères in France and of the "Cambridge Songs" in Germany. Fulk's niece Constance, when she became queen of France, was a center of contention in the staid royal palace because she imported "jongleurs" from her native southland. The cloisters had to guard against such infection. *The Cross Legend 41* is appended to a MS of John the Deacon's Life of N:

N   Among the countless indications of those powers by which the blessed Nicholas shines among the spiritual fathers with the unique radiance of the morning star, as if in the stellar reaches, it seems proper to include evidence from our own day as well. It will show how he favors his devout servants while being displeased with the detractors from his service. How this actuality came about, I will carefully but briefly describe.

Although, to be sure, the new historia of Saint Nicholas's life and miracles was composed by a man, he was a man who was divinely inspired. Yet even when, because of its overwhelming sweetness, it was being devoutly chanted far and wide among the churches of Christ throughout the whole of the Latin world, it had never been instituted in a cell named Cross, subject of Saint Mary of Charity,[29] because of the acedia of the inmates. There came a day when the elders of the establishment appeared in a body before Dom Ytherius, that is, their prior, and humbly requested that he permit them to psalm the responses of the blessed Nicholas. Far from acquiescing to their petitions, he replied that it would be totally out of order in this way to change the ancient custom by any such innovations.[30]

While pondering this harsh decision of their father, they began to argue the matter with words of this sort: "Why, father, do you disdain to listen to your sons? Why, when the historia of Saint Nicholas, full of sweet spiritual honey, is already honored through nearly the whole globe, cannot we chant it? Why cannot we, like others, be refreshed at such a feast? Do you suffer us to fast in the presence of such a spiritually reviving refection? Why, with all the churches committed to jubilation through this new leaven, must this cell alone now remain in mute silence?"

When these and other like queries had sufficiently annoyed the prior, he burst out with blasphemies in this vein: "Leave, brothers. For I certainly will never give you the right to abandon the ancient rite and to admit new songs of worldly clerks, indeed of a kind of jonglerie, into a church in which I serve at the command of God."

When they heard his words of rejection, they were quite overwhelmed with blushes. Not being able to protest further, the disciples kept their peace, and at the subsequent feast they carried through the evening and morning office according to custom, though not without some sorrow. Then when the vigils were over, they went to their own beds to sleep.

But when the prior lay down on his cot as did the others, lo, the blessed Nicholas appeared visibly before him with a fearful demeanor and upbraided him in the bitterest terms for his obstinacy and pride. Dragging him from bed by the hair, he shoved him to the floor of the dormitory. Beginning the anthem *O pastor aeterne,* and with each modulation inflicting most severe blows on the back of the sufferer with the switches which he held in his hand, he taught the wayward prior to sing the whole from beginning to end.

Hysterical from such blows and from the strange vision, the prior began to cry out unintelligibly, and at the cries the brothers quickly ran together before him. Seeing him alone but prostrate, they solicitously tried to find out what he had seen or suffered. But he, as if he were beside himself, was not able to give any answer to their inquiries.

Lifted up by the hands of the brothers, he was carried to the infirmary and for some days was in the grip of a profound lethargy. At last, restored by divine compassion and the intervention of the blessed Nicholas, he addressed the brothers in congregation: "Observe, my dearest sons, that after I refused to obey you I underwent severe punishment ·for my hardness of heart. Now do I not only freely accord with your request, but as long as I live I will be the first and most accomplished chanter of the historia of that great father."[31]

The Cross Legend 41 appears to have been coined and disseminated in order to justify the inclusion of a dubious but desirable rite in the services of somewhat puritanical Cluniac houses. The Cluniac monastic reforms were the most exciting innovations in Western religion and art of the time. They especially centered in development and artistic exaltation of the liturgy. Acceptance in Cluniac houses assured the popularity of Reginold's N liturgy.[32]

In the rather deft phrasing of this legend we recognize the personality of N in action. There is, of course, considerable humor in the image of a saint armed with a cat-o'-nine-tails, leading a recalcitrant prior through the very long liturgy (per ordinem morose canendo ad finem usque perduxit). The anthem O pastor aeterne identifies Reginold's First Anthem [ad Vesperas]: "O Eternal Shepherd, O Kindly and Good Guardian, who dost attend the prayers of the devoted flock, with a word released from Heaven Thou hast shown Thy servant Nicholas worthy of the most holy position." Such humorous conjunction of the "kindly and good guardian" with a whip wielder ushers in the period of parody and satire of the twelfth and thirteenth centuries. It is in accord with the image of Stratilates 3 and Iconia 34 and directly refers to Bishop 14.

The prior specified that the composer was a worldly clerk, not then a bishop or even priest, and he condemned the liturgy as a kind of jonglerie—a confirmation that conservatives thought the melodies irreligious. In a second recension of this legend the prior says, "In your church the service will be chanted like a chant, and no more." Very plainsong, as it were. Just before the year 1000, the Cluniac reform tended, as in this legend, to polarize the religious orders. "New songs of worldly clerks" (nova saecularium cantica clericorum) expresses the voice of reaction. But the young radicals soon prevailed, as the provenience of MSS of the N liturgy shows; a number copied in Cluniac scriptoria survive today.

I repeat that N conforms with *Stratilates 3,* but the rod is wielded with the force of *Iconia 34.* Another recension[33] of this episode is even more flagellant. In it N "began to thrash the prior soundly, in the way masters customarily drill letters into an unwilling boy." Meisen thought this sentence to be the earliest known suggestion of N's patronage of scholars—a topic to be treated shortly.[34] Even Methodios and Deacon John had N threaten to call upon God to administer dire punishment in their versions of *Stratilates.* But that was N in his puerile years; the adolescent becomes more fractious. As early as Symeon's Life of N, N threatened in very physical terms to administer punishment in person. Now N's scourge has become formalized. This addition to N's personality may have been abetted by the painters of scenes in which N tore the executioner's sword from his hand and hurled it to the ground. Switches and whips, often associated in the imagination with schoolboys and classrooms, are especially common in German storytelling. N is fully equipped with whips in Otloh's Lives of N, shortly to be mentioned.[35]

Even in adolescence we note this weakness in N: a tendency to play God—not unexpected in a thaumaturge, to be sure, but hardly pious. The legend shows him "businesslike," as befits a patron of commerce; but faith, hope, and charity are not stressed in his legends. Orthodoxy maintains that all action is of God, with the invoked saint an intercessor only. But N is becoming a law unto himself. Thus early in his youth we may anticipate the tragic fall.

N Liturgy 40 brings out an important element of N's success, his tunefulness. As in the Greek world, the eleventh-century Latin world whistled his name. The most popular of all N songs, the sequence (or prose) *Congaudentes 47* is of uncertain date and provenience:

> *Congaudentes exultemus*
>> Let us lift our joyful voices
> *vocali concordia*
>> in vocalic harmony
> *Ad beati Nicolai*
>> On the day of blessed Nich'las,
> *festive sollemnia*
>> marked with due festivity.

N⳨

Qui in cunis adhuc iacens
    He, still clinging to his cradle,
servando ieiunia
    practiced abstinence by fast,
Ad papillas coepit summa
    At his mother's breast beginning
promereri gaudia.
    to gain merits that would last.

Adulescens amplexatur
    As a youth he concentrated
literarum studia,
    on close study of the Word,
Alienus et immunis
    Shunning like the plague those bordels
ab omni lascivia.
    where gross acts of sin occurred.

Felix confessor,
    Exemplar benign,
cuius fuit dignitatis
    whose worth was of such verity
vox de caelo nuntia,
    'twas manifestly God's decree,
Per quam provectus
    By which straightway
praesulatus sublimitur
    in bishop's robes by merit he
ad summa fastigia.
    exalted was to high degree.

Erat in eius animo
    Character in him was marked
pietas eximia,
    by notable benevolence.
Et oppressis impendebat
    He relieved oppression's victims
multa beneficia.
    with a true munificence.

Auro per eum virginum
    With the gold which he expended
tollitur infamia,
    he removed the maidens' shame;
Atque patris earundem
    indigence alleviated
levatur inopia.
    of the father with the same.

Quidam nautae navigantes
    Certain sailors navigating
et contra fluctuum
    against a hostile tide,
saevitiam luctantes
    battling savage counterwinds,
navi paene dissoluta,
    with their vessel might have died,
Iam de vita desperantes
    Losing hope of this existence,
in tanto positi
    in jeopardy constrained,
periculo clamantes
    crying out in chorus
voce dicunt omnes una:
    praying with a fear unfeigned:

"O beate Nicolae
    "O most blessed Nicholáos,
nos ad portum maris trahe
    draw us toward a peaceful haven
de mortis angustia;
    from this ghastly threat of hell.
Trahe nos ad portum maris,
    Draw us toward a peaceful haven
tu qui tot auxiliaris
    by thy marv'lous mediation,
pietatis gratia."
    call on God, Who know'st thee well."

Dum clamarent nec incassum,
 While they clamored, not unheeded,
ecce, quidam dicens: "Assum .
 someone said, "Lo, here I speeded
ad vestra praesidia."
 to your rescue from the deep."
Statim aura datur grata
 Then the force of wind was lightened,
et tempestas fit sedata,
 tempest calmed and heavens brightened,
quieverunt maria.
 and the waves reclined in sleep.

Et ipsius tumba manat
 From his tomb there flows an unction
unctionis copia,
 rich in healing cordial
Quae infirmos omnes sanat
 Which cures ev'ry ill on contact
per eius suffragia.
 through his graciousness to all.

Nos, qui sumus in hoc mundo
 We who suffer in this world,
vitiorum in profundo
 in this sin-full vortex whirled
iam passi naufragia,
 e'en to foundering in the deep,
Gloriose Nicolae,
 Pray to heav'nly Nicholáos
ad salutis portum trahe,
 to a port of safety draw us,
ubi pax et gloria;
 glorious hav'n of peaceful sleep.

Illam nobis unctionem
 Yield to us that healing unction,
impetres ad Dominum
 granted through the Lord's injunction,

prece pia,
    His loving boon—
Qui sanavit laesionem
    He Who healed the lacerations
multorum peccaminum
    of our many divagations
in Maria.
    through Mary's womb.

Huius festum celebrantes
    Celebrants, this Feast of Nich'las,
gaudeant per saecula
    may they all rejoice this day,
Et coronet eos Christus
    And may Christ grant halos to them
post vitae curricula.
    when from life they pass away.[36]

The earliest extant MS of *Congaudentes* was copied at least as early as the eleventh century.[37] It is not impossible that its composer was the man who became Pope Leo IX, who will appear in the next chapter.[38] The development of "sequences," a unique form of musical and verbal composition, in the ninth and tenth centuries, is one of the lively topics of musicology. *Congaudentes* 47 was a product of this new art and helped to perpetuate it. An only slightly less popular N sequence was *Perpes laus et honor tibi,* which seems to have been composed at Saint Gall in Godehard's youth; it echoes the N *liturgy 40.*[39] A successor of Reginold, Bishop Heribert of Eichstätt (1021 - 1042), composed a well-known N hymn, *Plaudat laetitia lux hodierna,* borrowing freely from the N liturgy.[40] Perhaps N's good fortune in musician friends resulted from his uncomplicated worldliness, which attracted adventurous youth. The eleventh century is filled with new music of an awakening world, and N was singing and sung about.

V GODEHARD AND *THE THREE CLERKS*

Reginold and Theophano characterize the "Ottonian Renaissance" of the tenth century. While France was lapsing into the anarchy of the last Carolingians, the Saxon emperors reached an accommodation with clergy and barons at home and with papal Italy across the Alps. What had been the culture of the Rhine provinces extended itself to Franconia and Bavaria as far as Salzburg. The once-impoverished abbeys prospered as centers of feudal power. Fulda, Saint Gall, and Reichenau were not solitudes, but arms of governmental and agricultural administration—great landlords, purveyors of professional knowledge and leaders in palatine, if not military, service. By their internal order they were models for a disordered citizenry. From the middle of the ninth century to the beginning of the eleventh, the abbeys and regularized sees grew in dependability.

Charlemagne, in his campaign for literacy, had rather forced upon the cloisters a responsibility for public education which they were often most reluctant to assume (adolescents *are* noisy and not instinctively reverent). But the foundations were well repaid in gifts and lands. The provinces where the Church and the hierarchy were newest, east of the Rhine and far from the old Gallican tradition, most easily evolved a pedagogy to meet the times. With education came the arts of culture, and European artistic innovations most often spread out from German centers: in music the sequence, in architecture the bay system, in literature vernacular verse and prose. In earlier centuries the outstanding pedagogues came from the West (Isidore, Bede, Alcuin), but now from the East (Hraban, Notker, Gerbert). Our eyes need to center on Godehard.

Emperor Otto III, son of Theophano, died in A.D. 1002. He was succeeded by Henry, Duke of Bavaria, who in a fait accompli was crowned king of the Germans by Archbishop Willigis of Mainz, whose cult of N we have noted.[1] Henry, who eventually became emperor, was educated in the Bavarian schools. Contemporaries lauded him above all others for his science and discipline in the different arts. His sponsorship of pious letters, in which his empress Cunegund and his abbess niece Uta shared, quickly earned him the informal title "Saint," which was formalized by canonization in 1146. Saint Stephen, king of Hungary, was a brother-in-law.

The Bavarian schools thrived under his ducal patronage, especially Saint Emmeram at Ratisbon and the diocesan school at Bamberg, Henry's foundation. Liturgical calendars such as CLM 21557, fo. 22$^{\text{r}2}$, show that by the year 1000 N Day was red-letter throughout Bavaria, doubtless primarily because of Reginold's historia. Henry's chief of ecclesiastical and scholastic reform was his old master Godehard, a Bavarian born about 960, who was later canonized. As prior he reformed Altaich, then Hersfeld, Tegernsee, and other claustral schools.[3] In the year 1022, Henry appointed him bishop of Hildesheim. Under Godehard's predecessor, Bernward, Hildesheim had become the artistic center of northern Germany, the center of devotion and education for the Saxon royal house. Emperor Otto III had been educated there.

Two of Godehard's students wrote about him, Otloh of Ratisbon and Wolfery, who composed Godehard's Life.

Otloh (ca. 1010 - 1070) became *le premier polygraphe d'Allemagne*.[4] After schooling at Tegernsee and Hersfeld and time spent at Fulda, he settled at Saint Emmeram in Regensburg.[5] He composed two different Lives of N, one for his brothers at Saint Emmeram,[6] the other at the request of Wicrad, abbot of Fulda.[7] For both he used Reginold's historia and John the Deacon's Life, to which had been appended *Son of Getron 46* and *Iconia 34*, which he retold. But for both he also used a Life transmitted by some unknown, who said "he had acquired it far away on the Greek borders."[8] Otloh abridged both his Eastern and Western sources, "editing out rusticity and prolixity," begging his readers to forgive the scholastic flourish, poetic license, and verbosity of *tirunculus* John the Deacon, and the incredible, indeed mendacious, tales of the unknown Eastern author. Then he added to both his Lives a local miracle, *The Thief 42*, a tale of stolen property which N returned to the brothers of Saint Emmeram after they devoted three days to continuous masses in prayer for his assistance.[9] Under the inspiration of *Iconia 34* N is fast becoming a banker who protects property from theft. In addition, Otloh composed a narrative hymn to N in unrhymed trochaic septenarii.[10]

In his *Book of Visions* Otloh related an experience told him at Hersfeld by Wolfery, who would become the biographer of Godehard. In it an angel of the Lord more than superficially resembles the switch-bearing N in his nightly visitations. He told how at Hildesheim before Godehard's arrival it was customary for the clergy ostentatiously to display their personal wealth in vestments, jewelry, choirstalls, and even hangings:

125

An angel appeared to a clerk in a vision, saying, "Go tell the
bishop of this city that he should check his own and his
clerks' immoderate and irregular ostentation, or else divine
vengeance will be visited upon them." The clerk disregarded
the mandates as delusions of sleep. But the angel appeared
again and said, "I tell you for certain that if you do not
reform, you will not go unpunished." Though shaken, the
clerk did nothing. On the third visit the angel brutally
shook him, "How dare you disregard my admonition so
consistently? Did I not tell you that if you disregarded me
further you would suffer?" The clerk replied: "I did not act,
my lord, in contempt, but because I knew how mad the
bishop, my superior, would be unless I gave him some convincing proof." "If you need proof, take this," replied the
angel, grasping a whip and striking the clerk long and hard.
"Mark you the proof you asked for. If this isn't enough,
we'll give you a sign that anybody will understand." The
clerk hurried to the bishop and told the story.

The bishop and his clergy, failing to comply, were severely punished,
as it were with the whip of N.[11]

This legend embodies some history. Godehard, when placed at
Hersfeld, not Hildesheim, by the zealously reforming Henry, ordered
the monks either to strip down their finery or get out. Unable to
contend against an official with most powerful regal backing, all but
two or three of the monks left. Henry then shifted the corporate lands
N of Hersfeld from the jurisdiction of the monks to that of the abbot.

In composing his *Life of Godehard 43,*[12] Wolfery, like Otloh when he
composed his Lifes of N, copied passages from N *Liturgy 40.* When he
commented upon Godehard's induction into his see of Hildesheim, at
N vigil 5 December, Wolfery underlined the significance by quoting
Reginold's anthem, *Beatus Nicolaus pontificatus.* He described how
Godehard assembled a library at Altaich, of wondrous size and beauty,
but especially useful for singing and reciting the liturgy throughout
the year, an exaltation of the cult of saints. And he wrote:

It was wonderful how patient and kind he could be to de-
linquents and troublemakers—so much so that whenever
any of that sort ran to him for confession and penance, he

immediately extended clemency to those wrongdoers and watched over them to see that they were freed from temptations of that sort thereafter. He foresaw every future contingency, in the pattern and model of the holy bishop Nicholas, his patron, who with his almsgold removed the maidens' incest, the poverty of their father, and the foul reputation of the whole household; and with his pious clemency he relieved the sufferings of whatever poor might come in contact with him for whatever reason. In that model, I say, our prelate labored to console the needy ever and everywhere.[13]

Wolfery's *auro virginum incestus et patris earum inopiam et totius familiae detestabilem ademit infamiam* is a direct quotation from Anthem 7 of Reginold's historia. But the word *incestus* was not an invention of Reginold; it was taken by him from the Life by John the Deacon.[14]

Wolfery specified N as the patron of the best-known educational reformer and teacher of the German Empire. From the time of Godehard and his famous students, the tales of N and schoolboys multiply. In the year 1061, N relics were imported for the occasion of reconstruction and reconsecration of Hildesheim's main church.[15]

It is a fact that before Godehard there was no observable scholastic cult of N, and that from Godehard the cult quickly spread in all directions. Nor is that fact surprising. In Bavaria tales of youthful scholars had become firmly appended to Deacon John's legend: *Basileos 22* = *Adeodatus 75* and *Son of Getron 46*.[16] The German schools which Godehard, the outstanding master of the most powerful polity of the time, dominated were exporting masters and their learning to the rest of Europe. Only after a full generation, at the moment when Abelard went up to Paris, did the center of scholarship shift to the Ile de France; even then, it carried with it, through the swinging door of Lotharingia, the cult of N.

Coincidentally, the adolescent N made a special appeal to adolescent scholars. "Boyhood" was as yet unrecognized: "Medieval art until about the twelfth century did not know childhood or did not attempt to portray it . . . . In a French miniature of the late eleventh century the three children brought to life by Saint Nicholas are also reduced to a smaller scale than the adults, without any other difference in expression or features . . . . In medieval society the idea of childhood did not exist; this is not to suggest that children were neglected, forsaken or despised."[17] At first, therefore, "the schoolboy cult of N" was imagined as a cult of adolescents, the twenty-year-old subdeacons. Of importance in the artistic life of Europe is the birth, or first appearance at Hildesheim, of its incorporation in a new legend destined to become the most popular of all, and its expression in a new art form, scholastic drama.[18]

A MS of the eleventh or twelfth century now in London[19] bears the inscription "Lib. sci. Godehardi in Hild."[20] Internal evidence indicates that it is a copy, not an autograph of the composer. It contains scripts of two plays, which are the earliest existing drama of the kind which medieval and modern writers call "miracle plays." The inscription may indicate ownership by the Abbey of Saint Godehard (founded 1146), not by the bishop.

The first play tells the story of *Three Daughters* 13 in seventeen strophes, each with four end-rhymed decasyllabics and one unrhymed tetrasyllabic coda.[21] Speeches ranging from one to three strophes in length are assigned to each of the speakers: the father, each of three daughters, and N. The second drama tells a story new to the N legend, the *Three Clerks* 44:[22]

N✝

PRIMUS CLERICUS: FIRST CLERK:

Hospes care, tres sumus socii
    Gentle innkeeper, three scholars are we,
litterarum quos causa studii
    En route to learn God's Word and liturgy.
cogit ferre penas exilii
    To bear the pains of imposed vagrancy
nos sub tui tectis hospitii
    We're forced to ask your hospitality.
    hospitare.
      Be host to us.

SECUNDUS CLERICUS: SECOND CLERK:

Fessi sumus longo itinere
    Worn out and tired are we from travel long,
tempus esset iam nos quiescere
    'Tis past the hour for sounding vesper gong.

nobis velis amoris federe
>   To grant us charity could not be wrong.

hospitium noctu concedere
>   Allow us place to sleep till morning song,

>   *quo egimus.*
>   As is our need.

TERTIUS CLERICUS: THIRD CLERK:

>   *Summo mane cras hospes ibimus*
>   We'll leave tomorrow, host, at break of day.

non de tuo vivere querimus
>   Nor will we strain your larder by our stay,

quia victum nobiscum gerimus
>   For we have food sufficient for the way;

hospitium tantum deposcimus
>   And beg from you but shelter, if we may.

>   *causa Dei.*
>   For love of God.

RESPONDEAT HOSPES: LET THE HOST REPLY:

>   *Cum vos ita fessos conspiciam*
>   Since I can plainly see that you're worn out,

propter summam Dei clementiam
>   By grace of the high God without a doubt

vos hic intus noctu suscipiam
>   I'll save you further wandering about,

vobis ignem cum lecto faciam
>   Fixing a bed and fire as shelter from without.

>   *ite sessum.*
>   Now rest yourselves.

HOSPES AD UXOREM: THE HOST TO HIS WIFE:

>   *Uxor audi meum consilium*
>   Woman, please listen to the plan I've laid.

isti censum gerunt eximium
>   These have more money than I've ever made.

inpendamus eis exitium
>   We'll plot their death—see that you're not afraid

ut eorum tesauri pretium
>To have their treasure in our coffers paid.

habeamus.
>>Let's get it!

UXOR: WIFE:

Tantum nefas coniunx si fieret
>A crime so bold, my man, if carried through

creator nimis offenderet
>Will bring immeasurable wrath of God on you;

et si quisquam forte perciperet
>And if perchance someone should glimpse us two

nos per orbis spatium gereret
>He'll tell the world the act he saw us do

infamia.
>>In infamy.

RESPONDEAT HOSPES: LET THE HOST REPLY:

Frustra times bene celabitur
>Your useless fears will change to joy, indeed.

nemo sciet si pertractabitur
>No one shall know just how our crimes proceed.

horum nobis morte parabitur
>Gold from their deaths will purchase every need.

in manticis qui clauditur
>Their mantles hide the reason for our deed—

opum census.
>>A spate of wealth.

UXOR RESPONDEAT: LET THE WIFE REPLY:

Fiat quod vis ego consentiam
>Do what you will, I follow in your wake.

que pro posse tibi subveniam
>I'll help in any plan you undertake.

tam infeste cladis nequitiam
>However loathsome be the scheme you make,

caute tecum coniunx incipiam
>Your trembling mate is with you for your sake,

uxor tua.
>>Ever thy wife.

VERBA SANCTI NICOLAI: WORDS OF SAINT NICHOLAS:

Ad te gradu nocturno venio
    To you I come along the path at night
tuo pauper admotus hostio
    Disguised as beggar, guided by the light.
hic exoro frui hospitio
    I pray mine host here, Furnish me a bite:
fave mihi pro Dei Filio.
    In God's Son's name, may your care set me right.

HOSPES: HOST:

Precor hospes intra hospitium
    Enter, my guest, within the tavern's wall,
ut per noctis istium spatium
    Resting the night until the cock's first call.
meum tibi prosit auxilium
    You'll profit from my charity withal,
quod exigis habe remedium
    And satisfy your wants within this hall.
    vade sessum.
        Go rest yourself.

NICOLAUS: NICHOLAS:

Nove carnis si quidquam habeas
    If you by chance have some fresh meat out back,
inde mihi parumper tribuas
    You might grant me a morsel from the rack.
quam si mihi prebere valeas
    If you could graciously supply my lack,
adiuro te per Deum nequeas.
    I ask you in God's name, do not hold back.

RESPONSIO: REPLY:

Que tu poscis, hospes, non habeo
    That which you ask for, guest, I don't possess;
nec hanc tibi prebere valeo
    I cannot serve you so. I must confess
non sum dives, sed pauper maneo
    The larder's empty, and there's no redress.

multis enim semper indigeo
> At inns like mine you'll meet with no success.
diutius.
> > Ever in need.

SANCTUS NICOLAUS: SAINT NICHOLAS:
Falsum refers atque mendacium
> You're speaking falsehood, fakery, and lies.
nuper enim per infortunium
> But recently, by deed that God defies
peregisti opus nefarium
> (Such as we pray may never more arise),
clericorum fundens exitium
> You sent three clerks, amid their tears and sighs,
> *per corpora.*
> > To corp'ral death.
Ergo prece mentis sollicite
> Solicitously now with prayerful mind
nostro simul pectora tundite
> And contrite hearts, fast intertwined
et Dominum mecum deposcite
> With mine, ask from the Savior of mankind
indulgere vobis illicite
> Indulgence for yourselves from laws that bind
> *crimen mortis.*
> > All homicides.

ORATIO SANCTI NICOLAI: PRAYER OF SAINT NICHOLAS:
Miserere nostri, Rex Glorie;
> Have mercy on us, Righteous King of Glory;
Nobis locum concede venie
> Grant us forgiv'ness, we do implore Thee.
et clericis peremptis impie
> By Thy power free the clerks from purgatory,
per virtutem tue potentie
> Thus bringing joyful ending to this story.
> *redde vitam.*
> > Grant them their life.

CHORUS: ANTHEM: N✝

O Christi pietas [omni pro-
    O lovingkindness of Christ [adorned by all
sequenda laude, qui sui famuli
    hymns of praise, Thou dost make manifest
Nicolai merita longe lateque
    far and wide the merits of Thy servant
declarat, nam ex tumba eius
    Nicholas, for from his tomb the oil trickles
oleum manat, cunctosque languidos sanat]
    and heals all invalids.][23]

ANGELUS: ANGEL:

Nicolae vita fidelibus
    Nicholas, through you True God will tender
reddita esta a Deo precibus.
    Eternal life to all who prayers will render.

The word "Clerk" in the title of this drama is from κλῦρος, clerus, clericus, denoting the Christian clergy or ministry.[24] Because of the scriptural context from which it was drawn, it commonly specified the younger orders, *adolescentes*, especially those still being educated: subdeacon or reader. In the early Middle Age the specific business of schools was to train boys in Scriptures and Liturgy (*literarum studium*); consequently the connection between school and choir was very close. All major schools and their curricula were extensions of clerical training for choir. The decasyllabics with coda, which is the verse form of these plays, comes from a tradition of writing proper hymns for saints in a modified form of Horatian sapphics.[25]

This drama represents three scholars on their cross-country way to a religious school, who stop for lodgings at a desolate inn. The host, with connivance of his wife, kills them for their money. But N, appearing in disguise, invokes God's help to resurrect them.

These new dramas seem to have developed in the classroom as grammatical exercises. For many centuries Terence's plays had been used as models of style. But in the tenth century the poetess Hrotsvita composed a number of imitations of Terence for the convent school of Gandersheim, dramatizing as her subjects the early monks and nuns of the desert.[26] A good example is that of the reformed courtesan Thais, in a drama entitled *Paphnutius.* In her work Hrotsvita hoped to create a Terentian grammatical model while eliminating his impious fables. The convent at Gandersheim was a retreat for princesses of the Saxon house of the Ottos and Henry II; it was near Godehard's Hildesheim, which served the Saxon princes.

The two Hildesheim plays, *Three Daughters 13* and *Three Clerks 44,* appear to be masculine substitutes for the rather feminine approach of Hrotsvita's scripts. The low quality of verse and diction makes Karl Young's remark convincing: "A schoolboy might have been assigned this or that prose legend for versifying."[27] Neither the verse nor the diction is, in itself, anything to praise, but both are important in the history of Western literature. The verse form is prototype of the dramatic decasyllabic verse that became traditional, and the diction is the religious tongue of scripture and the hymns of the choir school that perpetuated itself in French and English drama of the sixteenth century and lent it distinction. These two dramas are the earliest extant texts of miracle plays, from which modern drama took some of its rise.

Although in the text above I have filled in some missing rubrics, enough rubrics survive in the Hildesheim MS to show that the parts were spoken, in other words "acted." Evidence of two MSS from the eleventh and twelfth centuries, one from Freising and one from Saint Martial, Limoges, shows that dramatic texts of the Slaughter of the Innocents, with Rachel's Lament, were being developed concurrently with these N plays, apparently also of German inspiration. They, too, are December and childrens' plays, doubtless prepared for the Nativity Season of the schools. And two others, *Lazarus* and *Conversio S. Pauli,* use the neo-sapphic verse form.[28]

In other writing which survives from the eleventh century there are remarks about strolling players and minstrels in Germany.[29] Dramatic action and acting of a variety of kinds were therefore not unknown, although we are ignorant of the forms of presentation. However, Godehard's group could hardly have intended their scripts for public edification and enjoyment. Rather, we see here the embryo of collegiate dramatic associations (obvious in France as confreries) and of university revels, which come to play a vital part in N's existence.[30] A traditional role of scholars is to present pageantry on charter days, legends of appropriately scholastic heroes, and edifying manners and morals, usually in the artificial language of inept translators and adapters. Nonetheless, scholastic drama, though played before captive audiences, does have an audience, in all ages since Godehard. It quickly became popular, and N (who seems always to ride the wave of the future) was the first to become known through this art. Out of the choir which chanted the historiae and the classes of the choir school where the clerks were trained arose the nonliturgical, or secular, or miracle, plays; and out of the miracle plays arose romantic comedy. Already in the twelfth century, Thibaut of Clairvaux could remark in passing, "This we see on Nicholas Day when people (aliqui) represent his person as performing the miracles of the clerks or maidens, which the Lord performed through him."[31] This was N's first overtly dramatic role. His histrionic powers and repertoire will develop in maturity.

Of even greater importance in N's life is the legend, fable, or story line dramatized. From the time of the Hildesheim play, N becomes the symbol of scholasticism, then of youth and childhood, and *Three Clerks 44* is its most popular expression.[32]

Where and how did *Three Clerks 44* become a part of N's biography? No one knows, and none of the innumerable guesses is wholly satisfactory.[33] Most historians surmise that the tale was coined as a result of misinterpreted iconography; for example, that a picture of a bishop raising three children from baptismal waters suggested raising the three clerks from the dead.[34] There is, however, no evidence of such a picture or a corresponding N tale. An alternative is that three men in the crow's nest of a ship[35] suggest three boys rising from a pickling tub. True, late versions of the legend include the host's cutting up the bodies and salting them down in a tub, from which they are raised by N. But the variant does not appear before the thirteenth century. Slightly more convincing is the statement that depictions of the three *Citizens of Myra 2* in stocks suggested dismembered limbs, as they do in paintings which survive, but again only from later centuries.[36] Some critics believe that the story of the boys dismembered and placed in a pickle barrel was inspired by the famines of the early eleventh century, when cannibalism was an attested fact.[37] But again, the pickle barrel is a much later addition to the legend of the *Three Clerks 44*, though it had long existed in the tradition of storytelling.[38] Eleventh-century lawlessness and famine may have revived the popularity of murdering innkeepers and their vats, but why N?

A more convincing theory about the origin of *Three Clerks 44* may be drawn from hymnology, not painting. The first Western composers of hymns, Saints Hilary and Ambrose, employed verse patterns which became rigid frameworks for a kind of substantive phrasing as a substitute for classical predicative syntax; that is, short linear statements with terminal rhyme forced composers away from developing rational statements of thought hung upon finite verbs of action into sequences of labels (nouns, verbals, vocatives) which *named* without activating. An analogy is the cinema, consisting of exposed stills rather than live representation. In cinema the optical afterglow convinces the observer that he is seeing live action, not shadows. In medieval hymnography lists of substantives of discrete action are crowded together to suggest, but not to express, activity. Between each substantive lies a blank filled by an afterglow, which is only a meaning supplied by the mind of the reader. Between one such still photograph and the next lies ambiguity. Medieval hymns suggest life by naming its parts; they do not narrate life.[39] Lines which must be phrasably complete in eight or even six syllables turn into billboard slogans, tolerating almost certain ambiguity. This ambiguity was in fact the artistic aim of medieval christendom—a part of the cultural pattern of polysemous typology. Hymnologists strove to find phrases which would suggest in any one locution a large number of disparate incidents or myths. It is not surprising that more recent hymnologists are guilty of fastening on only one or two meanings in a medieval hymn where several were intended.

Hence it is not surprising that critics have often misinterpreted medieval hymns as referring to *Three Clerks 44* when originally *Stratilates 3* was intended, e.g.:

Ave que de funere
trium puerorum
venditam pro munere
vitam non reorum
liberasti prospere.

or

Homicidam visitat
tres occisos suscitat
tres ereptos vinculis
fert ad domum consulis.

The number of such hymns is very great.

What recent critics do, medieval congregations could do as well. They could imagine a legend other than the one the composer had in mind. Verses written to index *Stratilates 3* called up a more contemporary floating myth of murder and resurrection; for by the eleventh century caesaropapism was moribund (we shall consider its revival below) but resurrection tales, especially in scholastic circles, were lively indeed.

The legend or fable of *Three Clerks 44* had long been known in hagiography. We have noted, for example, how the legend of Saint Menas yields a parallel for *Myrrh 18;* it has many other affiliations with N. It contains the tale of a traveler on pilgrimage to a martyrium, who was dismembered by an innkeeper for his money. Menas, accompanied by many saints, entered the inn, pieced the man together, breathed life into him, and chided the innkeeper.[40] There are similar tales of Saint George and other saints of the Eastern communion. At Einsiedeln, Switzerland, a MS only slightly younger than that of Hildesheim contains a narrative dialogue in trochaic septenarii.[41] Modern editors have assumed, without evidence, that it is a fragment of N's *Three Clerks* drama. It tells of an unidentified *sanctus pater* entering a house (perhaps an inn, but that is not specified) of a man and wife. He asks for fresh meat. The *pater* restores *tres iuvenes* to life and sends them away. However, there is no indication that the *tres iuvenes* of that incident were scholars or clerks, or that any theft was involved. Indeed, *iuvenes,* the age of young manhood, normally refers (as in this book) to those who have outlived adolescence, young priests for example, not to *clerici.* That the verse form is septenarius suggests that the composition was a classroom literary exercise, but not scholastic drama which, as we have seen, was normally composed in decasyllabic sapphics.[42]

The tale of a homicidal host and resurrection of his victims was common enough; at least it had no particularized relation to N. Also the number three, as in a narrative trilogy of threefold repetition of an action, was common in legends. Nevertheless, the incidence of threes is higher in the legend of the Nicean N, rescuer of the three maidens, than in other legends. But what is strikingly relevant to N is the ambiguity of three *innocentes,* the *Three Clerks* who are also three *Citizens of Myra 2* and three *Stratilates 3.* All such *innocentes* may be *viri* or *pueri;* indeed, Otloh, in his Life of N, changes the *cives* and *innocentes Myrae* into *pueri,* seemingly unconsciously, in the very course of writing, though clearly under the influence of Reginold's N liturgy. It is a word that spread through the West in N contexts, from the very early Latin translation of *Stratilates 3.* We have seen and will see it caught up in new N legends as they are coined.

The three *innocentes* of most common parlance are those of the *Benedicite* or *Song of the Three Boys:* Shadrach, Meshach, and Abednego, who "walked in the midst of the flame."[43] Their song became a part of the Christian rite, central to the rite "from earliest times," said the church historian Rufinus. The Fourth Council of Toledo (A.D. 633) required it to be sung at every Mass, directly after the Epistle. Except for *Te Deum* it was probably the best known canticle in a choirboy's repertoire. These "three boys," together with "the form of the fourth who is like the Son of God," became in religious allegory the type and prefiguration of the Trinity,[44] together with the "three men in one" of Abraham.[45] To this Trinitarian tradition had now been intermingled the N image.[46] The typological traditions of Abraham and the angels, Daniel's three boys, and Bishop N's trios were fast becoming the homiletic exposition of trinitarian orthodoxy. That N came out of the East at the time of the Nicene Council additionally lent conviction.[47]

Daniel's story of the calculated puericide of three divine protégés became a staple of the Nativity season, normally a season of intensely religious pathos. It extended from harvest thanksgiving and the beginning of Advent (Saint Andrew's Day) to Purification or Candlemas. In this dead season of the year, people huddled around the fire and filled their minds with Persephone images like Daniel's three boys in the furnace. Such evocation recurred especially in the days just before Innocents' Day (28 Dec.), when all minds, particularly scholars' minds, were on Herod's puericide.

N, whose day fell at the center of this season, was now being especially associated with this Resurrection-Restoration complex because of the fast-spreading popularity of the N tale of *Basileos 22,* which in its Latin version as *Son of Getron 46* had become appended to Deacon John's Life of N. *Basileos 22* is a legend from the Byzantine-Moslem border.[48] It is a kind of Proserpine myth. Depictions of N's flight through the air and across the sea, with cope spread like wings, are reminiscent of the depictions of *Mariners 6,* especially a fresco among the disputed works of Giotto at Assisi[49] which seems to have acted as model for the Superman cartoons of the 1930s. The anonymous author of the Johannine *Son of Getron 46* used the simile, "Just as N freed those three innocents [the Citizens of Myra} from the snare of death, so will he summon our son back to life."[50] Since the *innocentes* of Daniel, of the Gospels, and of N were all central to the liturgy of the Nativity Season, they now echoed each other. To anticipate, this story of *Son of Getron 46* appealed to dramatists (undoubtedly because the miracle dramas were scholastic products and the hero was a model schoolboy) and is one of the four N plays surviving in the "Fleury Playbook" of early drama.[51] The other three are *Three Daughters 13, Three Clerks 44,* and *Iconia 34.* Drama and the schoolboy cult of N were thus inextricably interlinked.

As we have seen, Wolfery asserted that N, as Godehard's patron, was particularly imagined with *Three Daughters 13.* In making this statement Wolfery quoted Reginold's fourth anthem, *Auro virginum.* Godehard's disciple Otloh also quoted from most of Reginold's songs. Now in one of the anthems (*Muneribus datis*) Reginold referred to the *Citizens of Myra 2* as *iuvenes innocentes.* Then in unusual fashion he departed from the diction of his source, John the Deacon, and composed what became his most popular Respond, the Verse of which is: *Qui tres pueros morti deditos illesos abire fecisti* ("Thou who hast made three boys committed to death to go out unharmed"). This is not only a move from *innocentes* to *pueros,* but a direct allusion to the Book of Wisdom xix, 6, recounting the rising to life of the Children of Israel out of the grave of the Red Sea. The *Three Clerks 44* conforms to the scriptural type.

Of like bits of colored stones are the majestic mosaics of Hagia Sophia formed. The tale of *Three Clerks 44* depends not on one source but on a fusion of images under appropriate social conditions. In Godehard's lifetime the tradition of education was being passed from abbot to bishop, from monastic to episcopal schools. It may be doubted that a secular bishop like N would or could have become the scholars' ideal in previous centuries. And he would not have been so readily available before Reginold composed his liturgy. During the twelfth century the many newly-composed hymns begin to refer to the *Three Clerks 44;* praises of N, the rescuer of slaughtered scholars, are chanted wherever a boys' choir sings from an angel gallery. The incident was carved on all the "Tournai fonts," which were marketed throughout England, Belgium, and northern France as part of the growing wool trade.[52] The first known illustration in glass is a window at Civray of about the year 1175.[53] Wace's treatment in Romance octosyllabics about the year 1150 is the first of what will become a spate of literary renderings.[54] And the iconographic symbol for N, that is, three boys in a tub, begins to replace the symbol of three bags of gold or three loaves of bread.

VI Lotharingia and Early England

Shortly after the year 1000 western Europe began to stabilize itself. The Northmen had accommodated themselves to the British Isles and the shores of the English Channel in the Netherlands and Normandy. The anarchic barons of France had moved into stone castles. Islam had been pushed back enough to open up some Mediterranean trade. The Poles, Bohemians, Magyars, Avars, and other nomad and rustic peoples that had separated East and West were converted. Schools and the scholastic arts began to flourish. The sea lanes surrounding the lowlands were becoming the preserve of merchantmen more than pirates and marauders, and their ships went up the estuaries to freshwater ports. Each of them welcomed the wandering adolescent, who had some reputation as the sailors' friend.

For reasons that we had best leave to the economic and political historians, Lower Lotharingia, centering in the three great episcopal sees of Cologne, Reims, and Liège, momentarily emerged as the cynosure of the literate.[1] There were over six hundred priests in Liège alone, not to mention disciples whose numbers cannot be estimated, divided among one cathedral and six collegial schools.[2] The Lotharingian abbey schools were dominated by the bishops, and their epis-

copal school was attracting laity whose aims were secular.[3] Saint
Dunstan, the great restorer of the English Church, studied under
Bishop Eracle (959 - 991), who began Liège's leap forward in numbers, quality, and fame, to become peer of Cologne and Reims.[4] Of
the tenth-century graduates of Reims I mention only two: Fulbert,
who became the venerated master and archbishop of Chartres, and
Gerbert, who became Pope Sylvester II, "the wizard."[5]

Hildesheim and Low Lotharingia were artistically very close at this
time.[6] We have seen how the Greek empress Theophano spread the N
cult through the low countries.[7] The population of Lotharingia was
divided in its speech into romance and teutonic dialects, about an
equal number speaking each.[8] But it was at the moment a most active
part of the German Empire, and fully participated in Germany's
political, religious, and aesthetic life. "It is therefore necessary to look
to Germany for the types of Liègeois art," wrote Kurth.[9]

Modern Lorraine still claims N as its tutelary saint. Its cult was well
established in the early eleventh century. Meisen lists many Lotharingian dedications before the Translation, scattered from Altdorf to
Arras.[10] The groundwork for that claim was laid in the late tenth
century, when Theophano was regent for Otto III. We remember the
Burtscheid icon at Aachen. Archbishop Willigis of Mainz, the N
devotee, extended his hegemony from Cambrai to Salzburg.[11] His
companion Notger, bishop of Liège 982 - 1008, came from High Germany (Saint Gall).[12] With the liturgist Heriger, he accompanied
Theophano to Italy,[13] and thereafter was Italian ambassador for the
emperor several times. A chapel of N *ante scholas* is attributed to him.[14]
A Liège calendar of the early eleventh century marks N Day as a
red-letter feast,[15] as does a slightly later calendar of Cambrai, now at
Cologne.[16]

At a later date, when Lorraine became renowned for its N patronage, the Liègeois boasted[17] that Liège was the first town in Lotharingia
to have an N church. This was Saint-Nicolas-aux-Mouches, built A.D.
1030 under the episcopacy of Reginold because an epidemic of flies in
the city was stopped by N's intervention. Indeed, Iohannes Ultramosanus says quite mistakenly that it was the first N church in all
Germany.[18] There were two other churches built later, Saint-
Nicolas-Outremeuse (Ultramosanus) and Saint-Nicolas-au-Trait.
There were altars, oratories, and relics in nearby abbeys before the

Translation. The important abbey of Stavelot had separate N dedications in 1030 and 1037;[19] Saint-Vannes in Verdun, in 1045.[20] Later we shall speak of a cult at Toul.[21] N is a familiar image in the chanson *Raoul of Cambrai*.[22] Burtscheid, and especially Brauweiler, combined to spread their cults through the region; the Brauweiler Acts specify a number of N dedications along the Rhine.[23] At the abbey of Gorze, most active in monastic reform, an N relic arrived in 1065. The reforming, ascetic movement did not dampen the N cult there, which prepared the ground for a great event after the Translation, when Saint-Nicolas-de-Port, the patron church of all Lorraine, was built.[24]

Godehard, *Three Clerks 44,* and the bishops of Liège may have kept N ashore, away from the swashbuckling life of sailors, merchants, and thieves, in the quiet world of education. But it will be yet awhile before adolescent N becomes a confirmed pedant. He was by nature drawn toward the water. An N cult originated in England before the Norman Conquest. It led to eventual dedication of 385 English churches to N, even before the time of discovery of America.[25] To put this number in due perspective, I note that there were only 202 dedicated to England's patron, Saint George, 69 to the "holy blisful martir" of Chaucer's pilgrims, and a mere 28 to England's missionary saint, Gregory the Great. N as sailor was responsible for about two-thirds of these dedications, which are located along the seaboard; yet it was the schoolmasters who began the fad.

I have mentioned that tenth-century Bishop Dunstan was educated at Liège. In the eleventh century Bishop Leofric of Exeter (1046 - 1072), who is renowned among students of English literature for the library he established,[26] reformed his see by rules he learned abroad. But he was only one of many Englishmen educated in Lotharingia before the Conquest. We are apt to think that England was tied to Normandy because our images of the period are dominated by the Northman Canute, the romantic Edward the Confessor, and William the Conqueror. However, closer examination of works of art shows that at least until the arrival of the Conqueror the stream of culture flowed into England most richly from Low Countries, in part because of the wool trade.

Wulfstan of Worcester, "the last of the Anglo-Saxon bishops," after being master and prior, became bishop in 1062 and died in 1092.[27] Although he retained his see after the Conquest while some of his compatriots were losing theirs, he was not especially in favor with King William. He received his bishop's pallium from Pope Nicholas II, who will appear as an actor below. Wulfstan was one of the few prelates in southwest England who was not educated in Lotharingia. Gisa, bishop of Wells (1061-1088),[28] Walter of Hereford (1061-1070),[29] the Lotharingian-born Walcer, bishop of Durham,[30] and Herbert de Losinga, first bishop of Norwich, whose father Robert became abbot of Winchester, were all educated there.[31] Others (e.g., Ealdred, 1054) traveled there.[32]

Wulfstan's devotion to N manifests itself in many ways. In his *Portiforium* he introduces only three foreign saints (Jerome, Martin, Nicholas) into his list of English subjects for proper prayer.[33] The earliest surviving MS of Reginold's *N Liturgy* 40[34] was written under his direction, doubtless before he was ordained bishop and possibly when he was still master of the Cathedral School. He had a hand in the creation of other MSS closely related in content.[35] Dewick was only the first of the scholars to find in these MSS "a most remarkable agreement with Liège use . . . . The influence of lower Lorraine is very strongly marked in *Harl. 2961*. There is no trace of the influence of Normandy."[36] From these service books the N liturgy spread.[37] By the same route, naturally, we trace the appearance of N in liturgical calendars.[38] Deacon John's Life was rendered into Old English.[39] A Durham MS, ca. 1100, contains an initial miniature of N rescuing sailors.

Wulfstan had a favorite disciple whose name was probably originally Aethelred, but was changed to Nicholas.[40] According to the historian William of Malmesbury, who wrote Wulfstan's Life: "In speaking of the master, our pages should mention his worthy disciple Nicholas, coming from one of the best English families. His parents venerated the holy Wulfstan profoundly. They had proof of his friendship in many ways. He baptized their boy; constantly he taught the boy his letters as he grew up, and always had him at his side."[41] Nicholas was William of Malmesbury's primary informant for the Life of Wulfstan, in which Wulfstan appears constantly to have the traits of N:[42] "In the seas between Bristol and Ireland, Wulfstan rivaled even Saint Nicholas as a protector of sailors during his lifetime."[43] Indeed, William baldly transferred *Mariners* 6 from N to Wulfstan, without any change except the name.[44] His statements also confirm what we know from the Nero MS, that Wulfstan introduced historiae into the Winchester liturgy. In short, the cult of N was well planted in England out of Lotharingia before the Norman Conquest. When William marched in, a band of English nobles, probably led by Siward, fled to Constantinople to enter the emperor's service. Beside the imperial palace they built a basilican church dedicated jointly to N and Saint Augustine of Canterbury. The adolescent had wandered to the farthest reaches of christendom and returned.[45]

VII The Norman Cults of N and Saint Catherine[1]

Any account of an adolescent hero would be incomplete without a heroine. It was at Norman Rouen that N acquired a helpmeet in Saint Catherine of Alexandria, whose companionship he never wholly lost.

The two images, of Catherine and of Nicholas, are very different—one a martyr, learned philosopher, and type of conventual chastity; the other a confessor, bourgeois poseidon, and type of secular episcopacy. Though N appeared in universal Latin calendars in the ninth century, Catherine's feast was entered in the calendar by Pope John XXII about the year 1335. Nevertheless they have notable similarities. They are among those exotic saints of Hellenic origin and Latin veneration who were deleted from the Calendar in the wake of Rome II. Though reputed to have lived in the early fourth century, no extant document earlier than the fall of the Iconoclasts supports their historicity. They are not named in ancient calendars and legendaries. They are saints of the Advent Season (25 Nov., 6 Dec.), together with Andrew (30 Nov.). Catherine and Nicholas together are the leading tutelary saints of scholars and schools, so officially denominated by the University of Paris and others.[2] They are patrons, too, of children and (in lands once Neustrian and Lotharingian) of lovers—cults preserved in folk custom by Catherine wheels and Sinterklaeses (see chap. 6, vi). They are of such common tradition that, I believe, Catherine and Nicholas has been the most popular combination in names of twins; so named are the Siberian tigers in my local (San Francisco) zoo. In the century of the Reformation, their only rivals among nonbiblical saints were Lawrence, George, and Martin.[3] They are the original subjects of scholastic drama, called miracle plays. Each is an outstanding thaumaturge and *Haushüter*. They are often depicted together by renaissance painters. But above all Catherine is, like N, μυρόβλυτα, or myroblyte.

The reader will have already encountered numerous instances of intersanctoral loan of stories, motifs, and images among legends, "un genre où le plagiat est la règle." Such borrowing is properly basic to hagiographic art, for its essential purpose is to accent that Christian life is imitation of Christ and His saints and that all is common in the communion of saints.

But I choose this instance for a more intensely documentary and circumstantial demonstration of the principle as especially appropriate to the theme of this book.[4] Biographers, though unpoetical, needs must attempt to give to airy nothings a local habitation and a name.

The received legend of Saint Catherine (hereafter called C) can most briefly be stated in the words of *The Oxford Dictionary of the Christian Church*:

> Acc. to tradition, she was a virgin martyred at Alexandria in the early 4th century; but though she is among the most widely venerated of women saints, she is not mentioned before the 10th cent. Legend represents her as of a noble family and of exceptional learning, who, as a result of her protest against the persecution of Christians by Maxentius, was tied to a wheel, tortured, and finally beheaded. Her body was said to have been discovered *c.* 800 on Mount Sinai, whither, acc. to her acts, it was transported by angels after her death. The monastery on the site, however, goes back to 527, and the earlier pilgrims knew nothing of its connexion with St. Catherine. There was great devotion to her in the Middle Ages, notably in France during the Crusades.[5]

The action I describe is the duplication at Rouen in the eleventh century, well before the First Crusade and N's Translation from Myra to Bari, of N's myroblytic power in C. From Rouen it was conveyed to Sinai by crusaders and pilgrims. It effectively spread the cult of C, with the N traits of scholastic patronage, dramatic subject, and thaumaturgic healing, through transalpine Europe.

C's *name* was known in the West (but only as Ekatarina) by the year 840,[6] and Latin versions of a Greek *Passio* came into circulation at some time thereafter.[7] That *Passio* recounts the martyrdom at Alexandria but not the legend that C's corpse was conveyed by angels to Mount Sinai and entombed in a sepulcher of their making. A part of the later legend is that the sepulcher remained unknown for centuries until a shepherd, on heavenly inspiration, discovered it. As we shall see, the whole story of translation to Sinai almost certainly was coined after the year 1030. There is no substantial evidence of a cult of C at Sinai before the Third Crusade.[8]

Beyond the *Passio,* which was paraphrased in Greek by Metaphrast, the first indication of cult is the foundation outside Rouen, A.D. 1024 - 1030, of the cloister of Sainte-Trinité-du-Mont, which after two generations acquired the popular, even quasi-legal, name of Saint Catherine's.[9] That event is described by a brother of the convent who wrote between 1054 and 1090.[10]

Briefly, that anonymous author says that Symeon, a monk at Mount Sinai, during his turn to collect the oil emanating from Catherine's tomb, was graced by having three bone particles flow into his phial. These he secreted. Later, when he was commissioned with a party of four monks and several servants to journey to Rouen to collect the alms which Duke Richard II owed the convent,[11] he took the precious relics along.[12] At Rouen the reigning Duke Robert[13] housed him with his magnate Goscelin and wife Emaline, pious philanthropists who were contemplating the establishment of a monastery. As encouragement, Symeon gave them the relics, which continued to exude oil. After the embassy had received its payment, it returned to Sinai, but without Symeon, who after two years moved on to stay at Verdun with Abbot Richard of Saint-Vannes, whom Symeon had met in Antioch.[14] Thereafter he went to Trier, to live under Archbishop Poppo as a recluse in the Porta Nigra. He became object of a local cult (evident to all who visit Trier today), and on his death[15] Poppo erected beside the gate a cloister dedicated to him, and secured his canonization by Pope Benedict IX.

The principals in this story were outstanding figures of the time, and their activities were well documented; few events of that century were more amply attested: deeds and charters, saints' lives and chronicles, sermons and letters, hymns and liturgy. The witnesses do not agree. What I report here is what the evidence seems to say: that the oldest center of C cult in the West was Sainte-Trinité, Rouen, A.D. 1030, and that it became renowned through the instrumentality of Saint Symeon.[16]

Symeon's biographer, Abbot Eberwin of Saint Martin's, Trier, wrote at the request of Archbishop Poppo to substantiate the papal canonization. He was factually reliable and a good friend of his subject, whom he knew in the Holy Land as well as in Trier.[17] Indeed, Symeon died in his arms. According to Eberwin, Symeon was born in Syracuse, learned his letters in Constantinople, and was for seven years a pilgrim guide before entering a cloister on Mount Sinai. He was sent with a delegation of brothers and servants "for money which was owed to the monastery from the territory of Richard, Count of Normandy."[18] Eberwin never mentions C or C relics, at Sinai or anywhere.[19] Symeon arrived at Rouen late in 1027: "Lacking all human companionship, he went alone to Rouen, which is the most noble Norman city, widely renowned by the body and merits of Saint Ouen Confessor. There he found Count Richard already dead, and no one would be responsible to him for the money and kind which the prince owed the monastery in alms."[20] Very shortly after his visit Sainte-Trinité was opened (1030), and in due season C relics began to display their miracle-working power. In fact, the first abbot of Sainte-Trinité, the German Isambert (d. 1054), was healed through mediatory C relics.[21]

The basic statement of the Anonymous that Symeon brought the relics to Rouen cannot easily be disputed. But if so, then the contradictions among contemporary authorities, as Weigand says, "can only be explained in a manner as little favorable for Symeon as for the relics."[22] It seems most probable that, broke and with his patron Duke Richard dead, Symeon at Rouen trafficked in relics of an undocumented and obscure saint who was just then coming to slight attention in the East and could have been known in the West only through the mouths of Palestine pilgrims and through an anonymous translation of a *Passio* of unidentified origin.[23]

According to the charter of foundation, A.D. 1030, confirmed by Duke Robert, the cloister was dedicated to Holy Trinity.[24] It still bore that name in an abbatial document of 1196, but already around 1120 to 1140 it was popularly called "Sainte-Catherine à la Trinité au Mont," and definitely in 1233 *Sanctae Trinitatis sanctaeque Catherine de monte Rothomagi.*[25]

But N had reached transalpine Europe and Rouen well before C. As we have seen, the Norman dukes were avid Jerusalem travelers, with and without Black Fulk. According to Meisen,[26] the first bearer of the name Nicholas north of the Alps was the son of Duke Richard II. He was born in 1026 and became abbot of Saint Ouen.[27] By 1040 a large number of Norman Nicholases are on record.

The first abbot of Sainte-Trinité was choirmaster of Saint Ouen before the abbot Nicholas was born. He was Isambert, to whom Dom Pothier mistakenly attributed Reginold's Office.[28] What Isambert almost certainly composed was the N Prose *Sospitati dedit aegros olei perfusio*[29] attached to Reginold's Response (No. 31) *Ex eius tumba marmorea sacrum resudat oleum.*[30] At all events, Isambert was and is intensely associated with the spread of the N liturgy and cult.

We have already charted the course of the theme of myroblytes as attached to the boyish N.[31] How did C become a myroblyte?

Those who attributed the N Office to Isambert did so because he was one of the really effective and known scholar-composers of his generation, and such evidence as was available pointed to a Norman birthplace for that Office. The scholars and musicians whom Isambert trained also added their names to history.[32] Of them, only Ainard, who became first abbot of Saint Peter's at Dives, is important here. Both he and Isambert bore the epithet *Teutonicus.* According to Orderic Vitalis, the best of Norman historians, Ainard composed the Offices for Saint Kilian and C.[33] The reference to Saint Kilian strongly suggests that both scholars originated in Franconia, home of the N liturgy.[34] When Isambert migrated at the beginning of the century, he probably brought along the N Office. Ainard migrated in the 1030s, to submit to Isambert's discipline at the new Holy Trinity. Doubtless Ainard composed the C Office there, taught the skill by his master, before he became abbot of the new foundation which Countess Lescelina established at Dives.

As there were several common words for the fluid—*myrrha, balsamum, manna, humor, unguen, liquor*—but in the C cult and liturgy only *oleum* is common,[35] so for other parts of the action the diction of

Response 31, drawn from the N lections,[36] is the diction of the C cult:[37] *tumba* or *sarcofagus* (rather than *sepulchrum, tumulus, monumentum, sepulta, humatum, funus,* etc.); *manare* (rather than *fluere, diffundere, liquere,* etc.); *distillatio* (rather than *fluidus, fluxus,* etc., *sudor, gutta, aestus, stillicidium,* etc.); *sospitas* (rather than *salus,* etc., *sanitas,* etc., *valetudo, medicamen*). Isambert's only line about the N myrrh in the Prose which he presumably composed is *Sospitati dedit aegros olei perfusio,* which follows the diction of Response 31.

C was the most hymned of all nonbiblical saints,[38] even more so than N. Convincing evidence of the descent of the healing oil from N to C lies in her hymns. I cite a very few of many representative examples. The most popular N sequence, *Congaudentes 47,*[39] directly derived from Reginold's Office, has:

> *Ex ipsius tumba manat unctionis copia*
> *Quae infirmos omnes sanat per eius suffragia . . . .*
> *Illam nobis unctionem impetres ad dominum prece pia*
> *Quia sanavit laesionem multorum peccaminum in Maria.*[40]
>> From his tomb flowed ointment in abundance, which through his intercessions cleanses all invalids . . . . May you by pious solicitation of our Lord Who in Mary cleansed the pollution wrought by manifold sins procure that ointment for us.

A C sequence of the eleventh century with similar transalpine range, which borrowed its musical form directly from *Congaudentes 47,* reads:

> *Stillis oleum, oleum laetitiae, medicina gratiae.*[41]
>> Oil in droplets, oil of happiness, gracious means of healing.

The hymn which Chevalier erroneously dated s.x is similarly phrased:[42]

Sepulchrum marmoreum	*Sacrum stillat oleum*
Inde salus languidis	*Venit multis multimodis.*
Caecis lumen redditur	*Claudus inde graditur*
Illuc 'perge debilis	*Et sospes inde resilis.*

> The marble tomb exudes the holy oil. So the
> restoration of the feeble comes in many
> forms.
>
> Sight is restored to the blind and the lame
> are made to walk again. Carry on there,
> weak one; and through it add still more
> strength, fortunate one.

In other hymns of the eleventh and twelfth centuries the line *Oleum ex ipsa manat* often occurs verbatim.

Only from the thirteenth century does the oil work back to a specifically Sinaitic locale:

Salve decubans in Sina salutaris medicina prece te quaerentium;
Salve cuius tumba manat oleum, quod morbos sanat cunctorum languentium.[43]

> Hail, healing restorative, inhumed for postu-
> lants seeking you in prayer! Hail, you from
> whose tomb flows the oil which cures the
> maladies of all enfeebled!

Perhaps Ainard's C historia contained only the themes of the *Passio,* with no mention of the oil.[44] But far more probably, in the presence of the Symeon relics,[45] Ainard copied Reginold's theme and wording precisely, thus generating a new legend for a yet unestablished saint.[46]

In the 1030s the demand for new offices exceeded supply. Accumulating wealth was stimulating pilgrimage, voyages, tours, as never before; the form and subjects of this new genre were exotic. A wave of new romanesque cloisters and oratories was rolling over the West. Released manpower allowed, or would come to allow, for expanding public schools, Norman conquests at three points of the compass, and crusades both south and east. As monks deserted labor in the fields for labor in choir, they expanded the liturgy. *Laus perennis* became an even more popular ideal than before. As does the N Office, Ainard's C Office may well account for the phenomenal popularity of a previously uncultivated foreign saint and patron of scholarship.

The one version of the *Passio* which circulated in the West before Isambert,[47] attributed to "Athanasius," said nothing of the oil; but that fact has long been obscured because to several MSS of it[48] an

addition was appended: "Siquidem de sepulchro eius fons olei indeficienter manare videtur, quo peruncta debilium corpora optate
sospitatis gaudia reportant prestante domino nostro Ihesu
Christo . . ." (Since indeed from her sepulcher a font of oil appears to
flow incessantly, by which through the operation of our Lord Jesus
Christ the anointed bodies of the ailing are restored to longed for joys
of health . . .). The sentence appears in no MSS earlier than the
twelfth century.[49] An additional confusion occurs because one single
MS has a still further addition: "This Passion, first composed in the
Greek tongue by the aforesaid Athanasius, existed thereafter in a form
so corrupted by its various translators that it could scarcely be read
among the ranks of believers. *Ego arechis,* impelled by the devotion of
religious brothers and by the love of that most holy martyr herself,
rescuing it from its inept phrasing, following the meaning more
strictly than the words, deleting the superfluous and adding what was
needed, have taken pains to transmit it fully to Latinate ears to the
praise and glory of Our Lord Jesus Christ."

How old is that passage? Readers have interpreted *arechis* as a
proper name, and none has challenged Varnhagen's identification[50] of
Arechis as the brother of Paul the Deacon, who died A.D. 799.[51]
Varnhagen offered no support whatever for that identification. It
seems probable that he fixed on it as the only name, so spelled, in his
onomasticon. Since Paul's brother was not a monk, or in orders of any
kind, such an identification is incredible. Inevitably subject to wide
variations in spelling, the name represents the north Teutonic names
Eric and Heiric, amongst others. But chances are that it is not a
baptismal name, but a place name for *Arcus* = Arques (Normandy).
Indeed, Goscelin, founder of the Abbey of Holy Trinity, was *vicecomes
archacensis* or *de Archis.*[52]

In short, the evidence is that C's oil, and consequently her cult,
first appeared at Rouen after the visit of Saint Symeon, and probably
after Ainard's composition of the *historia S. Catherine* in the 1030s.

The kind of contagion that made C a myroblyte by contact with
the N legend and Office, emanating from its home at Eichstätt,
created a track of myroblytes along the way. The dripping fluid
appears in the legends of no fewer than four saints of Eichstätt
veneration: Willibald (7 Jul.), founder of the see; Abbess Walburga his
sister (25 Feb.); and Abbot Wunebald (18 Dec.) his brother. They

acquired the trait long after Reginold's time. Indeed, hagiographers invented a father for them, King Richard, also a myroblyte.[53] Strangely enough, the grace passed over Bishop Reginold, composer of the Office, and Pope Victor II, his successor in the see of Eichstätt, but attached itself to Bishop Gundechar (1057 - 1075).

The most famous Western myroblyte after N and C was Saint Elizabeth of Hungary (19 Nov.):

> *Ob pietatis opera tu oleo manasti*
> *Post mortem et innumera miracula patrasti.* [54]
> Because of your works of piety, you flow
> with oil, and thereby accomplish countless
> miracles after death.

Her activity before her move to Marburg centered in Würzburg, home of the musician-bishop Heribert and presumptively of Isambert and Ainard. She made a special pilgrimage to N's tomb at Bari,[55] doubtless bringing back a phial of myrrh. Indeed, the *Golden Legend* points out the debt: "Then keep Saint Nicholas in mind, because he is paired with her as companion and partner in her miracles."[56]

It was the crusaders who created a demand for oil at Sinai, which then began to flow.[57] The first of these to record his experience, Thietmar, A.D. 1217, would not have taken "No" for an answer: "Desiderio autem desiderans desiderantissime corpus beate Katerine, sacro sudans oleo, visitare, eoque ardentius, quo id in animo meo proposueram diuturnius, totum me, corpus beate Katerine submisi auxilio, quelibet pericula et casuales eventus no abhorrens."[58] (But desiring with a most desirous desire to visit the body of blessed Catherine, dripping with holy oil—the more ardently because I had for an excessively long time debated the question in my own mind,—not shrinking from any perils or mishaps, I submitted the whole of me to the ministration of the body of blessed Catherine). He could then testify that the C relics "swam (*membra et ossa natant*) in oil." The *tumba marmorea* that he and subsequent crusaders found there derives from Reginold's N liturgy, Responses 31 and 46, in turn drawn verbatim from Deacon John's Life.

From eleventh-century Rouen the cults of C and N, though sometimes traveling together and interchanging images, pursued their individual paths, deepening their inherently disparate personalities but never wholly losing the traits acquired in adolescence.[59] The first record of a "miracle play" in the British Isles is a Play of Saint Catherine.[60] The script is lost, but clearly it was in the form of the N plays, now gathering momentum. It was produced at Dunstable by a Norman émigré named Geoffrey of Le Mans, "a Norman of distinguished family." He borrowed costumes from the nearby abbey of Saint Albans, but they were lost in a fire. For repayment Geoffrey offered himself as a suitable holocaust, and eventually (A.D. 1119) became the abbot of that richest of all English monasteries.

In 1325, when miracle plays were already degenerating into farces, the statutes of the College of Navarre in the University of Paris decreed that "on the feasts of Saint Nicholas and of Blessed Catherine no unseemly play may be produced."

The invocation of N in marital and sexual relations, arising from *Three Daughters 13,* was shared with C from the eleventh century. The Anonymous, in his *Miraculum X,* makes her a patron of fecundity in men as N had become in women. Three men whom she relieved of sterility are specifically identified. The folklorist Van Gennep has noted that Saint Andrew (whose name means "man") shared this power with N and C. On that basis he elaborated a theory of a prewinter love cycle.[61] Saint Andrew's Day, 30 November, begins the Advent Season. In schools the winter vacation from formal instruction, relieving the choirs so that they might have time for the heavy Nativity duties, began at some point in the double-octave of these three saints. It lasted through Innocents' Day. We shall look at that season more carefully subsequently.

The cults of all three saints exchange their seasonal traits. It is of special interest that in some Western churches the Translation of Saint Andrew, which 30 November is supposed to mark, is observed on 9 May in places where 30 November is regarded as the day of his death. May 9, as we shall see in the next chapter, is in fact both the historical and festal Day of Translation of N. As I have remarked, Days as such virtually never change in the Julian calendar; but festal customs easily slip from one day to another by proximity. For example, by virtue of the Gunpowder Plot in England, the use of the "Catherine wheel" shifted from 25 November to 5 November, Guy Fawkes Day.

Now that N had acquired a scholastic personality through Godehard, the *Three Clerks 44,* and the schools of Liège, he was the more appealing in a Rouen which at the moment was the most lively scholastic center in Normandy, thanks in large part to the migration of such German scholars as we have identified. As both Henry Adams and Charles Homer Haskins have stated, "The Normans of the eleventh century stood more fully in the center of the world's history than their English descendents ever did."[62] The Bretons are wont to say that there has never been a Norman saint; but they made up for that lack by cultivating C and N from Greenland to the steppes.

So N's period of adolescence was coming to an end. He had wandered far from home, and had experimented with a variety of stances and endeavors, and had made new and important friends. Not many of those friends were preeminent for religious fervor or moral responsibility; but all of them were energetic and, like N, getting along in the world. Songs to and about him were in every throat, it would seem. Invocations for his influence with Higher Power were taking shape. He had become central not only to the old arts but to the new art of drama. To his political and prelatical following and his ancient nautical and commercial friends, he now had added school-mates who were to spread his name through the bulging cathedral schools and embryonic universities. He was ready to leave his birth-place for good, to find his fortune in a world of affairs.

knighthood

Then a soldier
Full of strange oaths, and bearded like the pard,
Jealous in honour, sudden and quick in quarrel,
Seeking the bubble reputation
Even in the cannon's mouth.

I KNIGHTHOOD

Man's fourth, or middle, age is knighthood, the halfway point in the book of life. In ancient descriptions of the ages, it was sometimes called *iuvenilitas* and the individual was called *iuvenis,* cognate with *cnicht* or *Knecht* in northern vernaculars and its state of being, *cnihthád.* The primary meaning, youth, was quite consistently maintained through Indo-European early tongues,[1] as was a secondary meaning of service and attendancy. *Iuvenis* and *miles* were as regularly interchangable as were *cnicht* and *thegn.* The ideal warrior was virile, admirable, companionable, servicable; hence he was, though perhaps not noble, of noble quality. Isidore of Seville, who composed the *Britanica Junior* of the Middle Age, wrote that a knight is called *iuvenis* because he is acquiring the power of helping (*iuvare posse incipit*); as one who has reached the very apex of life, he is equipped to support, for it is the business of a vassal (*homo conferens*) to assist.[2] The knight has reached the apex of his physical strength, but not of judgment. This is the connotation of German *Junker*: wisdom and judiciousness are not in his armory. "Young men are fitter to invent than to judge; fitter for execution than for counsel; and fitter for new projects than for settled business," wrote Bacon.[3] Ferocity and impetuosity stamped the knight.[4] He was a *iunior* as distinguished from the *senior* that he would become should he survive.

Our term "middle age" is now a patronizing euphemism, but not in the days of knighthood, when virility was recognized as juvenile. Though a knight might vary in age, abstract treatments usually mentioned the years twenty or twenty-five to forty, "draft age." Even the *seniores* who were still active in the field and therefore retained the primary quality of knighthood did not much exceed forty. Of the six or seven primary *duces* or *principes* of the First Crusade the oldest,

Raymond of Saint Gilles, may have approached fifty-five, while the youngest, Baldwin, was but thirty-three. Their companion knights, *gesiths,* were regularly but not invariably younger. The title "knight" would cling on after one had ceased campaigning, as had Chaucer's perfect, gentle knight's, or gentle man's.

In the Romance vernaculars the equivalent of *cnicht* was *chevalier, caballaro, cavaliere,* which has its Teutonic equivalent in *Ritter* or *rider.* Horsemanship was the primary quality of Frankish knights and the foremost discipline of the "palace schools," whose masters were *equites.* It is a paradox, perhaps, that ideal seamen like Poseidon and N were horsemen, riding spume as if it were a white horse, as they appeared in their terrestrial effigies. The *caballarius* was essential to a barter economy, in which service was demanded in kind. His practical use of the horse, as in warfare and hunting, determined his efficiency; but he had also to be marksman, engineer, architect, veterinarian, and physician or nurse as well.[5]

In the eleventh century, which begins N's middle age, and possibly the Middle Age of all christendom as well, appeared several conditions which produced a new, or very much expanded, class of knights that give us the terms freelance, knight errant, landless knight, or mercenary. Some of these conditions were acceptance of primogeniture, a population explosion, increased use of money, the Crusades and other trade and communication with Byzantium and Islam, and a spread of the kind of freebooting and brigandage exemplified and perhaps popularized by the Normans. Younger sons, no longer sharing in the familiar holdings, hired out to neighboring or foreign warlords or carved out holdings for themselves by piracy. Increasingly their eldest brothers, who owed military service to their princes, bought out (*scutage*), and their princes paid for their replacements. Knighthood could no longer be taken for granted as wedded to the soil, as N left his soil at Myra for Bari; it became a profession with identifiable credentials: ribbons, medals, and flags; shield, horse, and retinue; demonstrations of power in tournaments; recommendations and passports of palatine masters, and the like. The Eastern emperor, always short on manpower and long on gold, was a notable employer who welcomed trainees (i.e., *scutifers,* squires) and paid an elite corps of *varangians* (βαραγγοι), primarily Scandinavians but intermingled with knights from all western Europe, especially displaced Anglo-Saxons.

In any age unemployed rovers of whatever profession are a threat to the establishment. The Church, as primary preserver of social order, found it necessary to attempt to control knights and knighthood. Hence arose the paradoxical union of church and knighthood—one devoted to preservation of God's creatures and the other to their destruction. Accreditation for knighthood became religious as well as martial. Crusading orders like the Templars and Hospitalers are only one of infinite manifestations of the linkage. Nobility took second place in this new kind of knighthood. It should therefore not surprise us that an N—seaman, merchant, banker, and pedagogue—should be thought of as a knight. He had been an arbiter between Church and State (*Stratilates 3*) and a mediator between God and men (*Artemis 4, Bishop 14*), and, as a saint of the Antiochene shore, a conciliator between East and West, Byzantium and Islam, and both with Rome. In an age of crusading he was a predestined bourgeois knight, as Saint George was the aristocratic dragon slayer.[6]

Indeed, prelates were often in all essentials knights. Prelates were usually drawn from the noble class, and nearly all the nobles, like Pope Leo IX, had knightly training. Archbishop Turpin of the chansons is our most familiar instance of the prelatical horseman, and he exhorts: "Christendom is in peril, lend it your aid. You will now have battle, for you see the Saracens before you. Confess your sins and ask God for pardon. *I* will absolve you and save your souls; if you die, you will be holy martyrs and will win a place in Paradise the Great."[7] As the Church was catholic, so was knighthood; it recognized no boundaries.[8]

To compare the middle age of an incorporeal image with a knight will seem a tour de force only to such readers as are not at home with the polysemous view of creation that medieval man evolved and immersed himself in. For him, God created at every level of being at once. Essence and substance have their *integritas,* true as both abstract and concrete, as macrocosm and microcosm, as spirit and body, however viewed. The human and humanity are created one, as is the knight and knighthood. If a man has an ideal, he is to that extent the ideal; if he possesses an image or a legend, he is the legend, and the legend is the man. Nominalist readers perforce must think that the theme of this book is sophistical. But the topic of this chapter is that the image N happened to be a knight at just that chronological point when knighthood was in flower, and that in his knightly age he happened to become the image of Pope and Norman, who above all impersonate the world of knighthood.

Knights were never Nominalists but, by profession, Realists, and Roscellinus had few followers when knighthood was in flower.[9] Rather, God is Truth no matter how He may be viewed, and His creations are always His creatures, whether flesh or spirit or fleeting thought, for all ideas, ideals, images, legends are God's creatures. "If there was an element of collective hysteria behind the phenomenon of the Crusade," wrote Zoé Oldenbourg,[10] "it was provoked by an involuntary confusion between the elements of time and eternity, between the earthly and the heavenly Jerusalem."

So N is not alone in being both timed and timeless. That his knighthood, which lies at the center of his biography, should coincide with the age of knighthood would surprise no medieval writer, for instance, Dante, however surprising to some readers now. Any victory of Nominalism over Realism marked the defeat of Knighthood.

The landless knight, the political arbiter of the age, as exemplified by the Angevins and Normans we have treated, was only socially as responsible as his own *parole*.[11] Beyond that he was responsible to the higher law of God or his own imagination. The word "parole," curiously, is somewhat akin in derivation to the word parable, and the tales of N were Christian parables. They caught the imagination of the knights because in the crusading age not only political but natural law was practically suspended. Some have called it an age of superstition, but it is perhaps better to speak of anarchy in its widest sense.

Who could be more representative, indeed ideal, for such an age than N? He, too, became landless with his Translation; he, too, became a Norman, or Viking, or Varangian, as you please. From earliest infancy he was the image of that fulcrum on which balanced the counterweights of politics and religion. His means of resolving that ambivalence was thaumaturgic power, not as a disembodied spirit but as a superman. And his acceptance in the seats of power slowly changed his humility toward hypocrisy and a casual acceptance that the means justify the ends. Like the Cid, N was born in a good hour.

It was a time for fighters: in the struggle between Pope and Emperor, Bari and Venice, Cross and Crescent. When N stepped into the world as a knight in shining armor, eyes were dazzled. A homily from which I quote only the introductory words is attributed to Saint Peter Damian (d. 1072), Cardinal Bishop of Ostia, the most articulate preacher of his day. The attribution may be false, but not false in time or spirit; for we know on other counts how zealous Damian was for N.

That Nicholas of mine, and indeed of yours, elect from the uterus, saint from boyhood, glory of youth, reverence of age, honor of the clergy, splendor of the pontiffs, fills us all with joy on this his Feast. Here is Nicholas, whose miracles spread throughout the world, whom the whole earth and those who live on it praise. So many and so astonishing are the known miracles that all the cunning of poets does not suffice to describe them or for us to read them. And even if a team of scholars should forge the tale in Quintilianic rhetoric, or with Ciceronian hammer beat it out into the most subtle laminations, the glory of the Confessor would belie the words, the meaning, the tongue, and the art. For the marvels daily grow brighter; and the Spirit of God never rests from multiplying His miracles as a memorial for His champion. He is glorified on the sea, praised on earth, invoked in every danger. "They that go down to the sea in ships, that do business in great waters; these see the works of the Lord, and His wonders in the deep."[12] They see the works of the Lord, and the miracles of Nicholas through God's power in the deep.

Is it not true that, except in consideration of the Virgin, such sweet piety or pious sweetness fills the hearts of believers, that in the day of trial the name of Nicholas rests on the tongue and lingers in the heart? If lightning flares and thundrous hurricanes rage from the skies, Nicholas steps in as patron and Nicholas quiets the storm. If savage tempest and cruel seas threaten death for the seamen, their tearful cries turn to Nicholas, who hears; at their supplications he comes; in compassion he rescues them as they cry out his name. If we are stricken by troubles or blocked by obstacles, the holy name at once springs to our lips, "Nicholas." Again and again we beseech Nicholas's patronage.

Don't think me oratorical, or loading my words with gilded commonplaces; for the whole world feels the bene-factions of that confessor. Pilgrims to his holy corpse from the ends of the known world testify to the miracles they have seen wrought through him. Not only among Christians but even among pagans such authority speeds to the invocation of his holy name that they eagerly become one in praise and glorification of his holiness. And especially is there such a host of priests and clergy devotedly attached to his cult that throughout the whole wide world everyone everywhere gives himself over to the observance of this great holiday. Boys are happy, knights give thanks, maids bedeck themselves, old men quicken their step, and every age makes carnival. But each has reason to celebrate: the boys laud the fasting boy (*Lactation 11*), the knights the free-ing of the knights (*Stratilates 3*), the maids the release of the maids from shame (*Three Daughters 13*), the old men the compassion for the old man's poverty (*Iconia 34*). "Both young men and maidens, old men and children: Let them praise the name of the Lord."[13]

To call the roll of the social and vocational classes that had come to invoke him, at first sight seems exhaustive: preachers, courtiers, lawyers (and thieves), prisoners, merchants, transporters on sea and land, maids, swains, wives, and now scholars, clerks, schoolboys, and infants. He was the companion for iconodules (and hence the plastic artists), musicians, and mimes. From the days of Fulk of Anjou and his traveling companion Robert of Normandy he appealed to those war-riors whose heavenly protector was Saint Michael and battlefield companion was Saint George. Cynics might find his thaumaturgy no defensible resolution of troubles of this world; but shrewd men found it useful, and their vassals and assistants found it credible. N con-trolled the powers of darkness by using their own mechanistic methods. He owed fealty only to the source of his prowess.[14] The roll of professions does not include physicians, who despite some strange empiricism, had slight use for miracles. N's close connection with the great seats of power—the Eastern emperor and his patriarchs, the Western popes and their guelphic lieges—made courtiers and provincial bishops suspect him; they depended upon the powers of local saints who remained loyal to the land. As the most vital exemplar of secular prelacy, benign toward wealth and creature comforts, N was shunned by cloistered ascetics.[15]

We who have the benefit of hindsight can see even in his first three ages the tragic weaknesses, in the Age of Knighthood first manifest, that would eventually bring about his decline and death: his secularity and materialism, his willingness to sponsor men of overtly corrupt desires, his growing reliance upon ostentatious miracles and cheap metamorphoses, his delight in Power and its Possessors.

II THE NORMANS IN SOUTHERN ITALY

The cult of N in Italy, especially southern Italy and Sicily, was omitted from its natural place in chapter 3 because it forms a necessary introduction here to the great changes that occurred in the South in the eleventh and twelfth centuries. Note, however, that the virile Norman invaders, the singers of Reginold's, Isambert's, and Ainard's songs, stepped into an already flourishing cult of N there.[1] The land had produced our authorities, the Greek Methodios and the Latin John the Deacon. It was the meeting place of all the cultures of the Mediterranean, Christian and Moslem, Teutonic, Italic, Hellenic, Coptic, Arabic, African. The catalytic Normans set this mixture seething and consumed the brew.

Neapolitan John the Deacon had been followed by John of Amalfi, a monk who translated and paraphrased N narratives in his Book of Miracles, a rich source of oriental tales transmitted to the West.[2] When John found himself in Constantinople, he translated into Latin a sermon for N Day. Already N's fame was inspiring scholars to search the archives for fresh or neglected material, as he said: "Spurred on by love, I sought and found, and not in rough notes of any kind but in archives and closely edited codexes."[3] John tells a story, *Magnentius 49*, in which the flow of N's myrrh at the now-popular pilgrimage resort of Myra ceased because an enemy had expelled one of the archbishops from his see; the flow resumed when the archbishop was restored.[4] John terminated his sermon with twelve epanaleptic distichs, one of the many intensely artificial verse forms with which ascetics relieved monotony, e.g.:

Ordine quoque potes, Nikolae, tuere rogantes,
    Laity in a line   seek you, Nicholas divine;
Nos superis socies, ordine quoque potes.
    To the heavenly angels you join   laity in a line.

An Amalfitan like John would find himself on both Byzantine and Arabic seas. Citizens of the port cities of Sicily and the Italian peninsula were intermediaries among three worlds.[5] South of Rome the merchant and ruling classes quite zealously traced back their bloodlines not only to preclassical Greek and Levantine trading colonies but to later waves of invaders including Goths, Lombards, and Vandals, as well as Moslems and Byzantine Greeks and Asians, and even Slavs. Assimilation among these "races" was not great, but their accommodation to each other was. Roughly speaking, at the time when the Normans first appeared, Sicily was dominated by the Saracens, Apulia and Calabria by the Byzantines. Benevento, Capua, and Salerno were Lombard principalities, while Gaeta, Naples, and Amalfi claimed a tenuous independence.[6] Taxes were paid to whatever horseman could batter down the gate to collect them.

If one thinks of Italy only as Latin in language and imagination, let him look at a very lovely hymn in modified iambic trimeter composed by Bartholomew IV, abbot of Grottaferrata, a dozen miles from Rome.[7] This Canon, composed according to Orthodox form, evidently for his own monks and other Greek monks of northern Italy, consists of nine odes, each of four strophes followed by single strophes in praise of the Trinity and the Mother of God. For example:

ODE VI

The whole world, luminous in the light of
thy wondrous deeds, is a brilliant opposite
from the blindness of passions and darkness
of evil spirits; and with glad spirit, Oh Father
Nicholas, it solemnizes thy memory, glorifying the God Who glorifies thee.

Holy is thy temple, Oh Father, and admirable for justice while it possesses thy most

holy image. Pray! with thy prayers sanctify, Oh leader, all those who with faith there avow thee blessed.

Enlighten with thy light, Oh Father, those who celebrate thy splendid feast, and for thy suppliants pray, Oh Wise One, that having become splendid in the whiteness of purity and innocence they succeed in celebrating with joy and without reproach the marvelous feasts of the Lord's apparition.

Thou art, Oh Leader Nicholas, like the mystic dawn, as thou dispelest the darkness of the evil spirits and the night of passions; therefore, Oh Father, give light with thy intercession to those who celebrate with affection thy luminous image.

To the Trinity
Devoutly I worship Thee, Who art Father without beginning and inborn, and I recognize Thy Son eternal and born, and confessed I adore and glorify also the eternal almighty Divine Spirit Which proceedeth from the Father.

To the Mother of God
To Him Who is like His eternal Father and has the same nature and eternity, He, the Lord God, having taken flesh from thee, Oh Virgin, who appeareth like unto mortals in order to sanctify those who piously pay homage to thy sanctity.[8]

But N was praised in Latin hymns as well outside the Norman fiefs. The best known hymnographer, Alphanus of Salerno, abbot and archbishop who died in 1085, composed several N hymns.[9] Salerno was a Lombard state, but a Greek church dedicated to N had existed there from the tenth century.[10]

The Northmen had settled in many lands, taking over some. They were typically ferocious and rapacious. "From the fury of the North-men preserve us, O God," was a standard invocation. Those who carved out the Duchy of Normandy soon found it too restricted for their generative proclivities, and so they spread to Italy and to England. They were rather given to ostentatious piety and, as we have seen, were singing N tunes and invoking his aid along the English Channel. Most of the Normans first learned as Jeruselem travelers that southern Italy was comparatively defenseless against their kind of brigandage. They hired out to princes as mercenaries, only to end as princes themselves. By 1017 they were in battle; in 1030 Sergius, Prince of Naples, granted the Norman Rainulf the territory of Aversa as his fief.[11]

As camels edging into the tent, they were ruthless. Leo Ostiensis of Monte Cassino, chronicling events before 1039, tells how one Nor-man, "swollen in mind and inflated with pride," accosted the abbey's fishermen. "Inasmuch as Normans are greedy of rapine and insatiably anxious to invade other people's possessions," the Norman seized one man's coat, entered a skiff, and ordered the boatman to draw up his net so that he might steal the fish. When the boatman refused, the Norman threw him into the sea; but the greedy Norman, in pulling at the net, fell overboard and drowned, to Leo's normanophobic joy.[12] The historian Maitland called attention that *Monasteries Burned, Sacked, and Destroyed by the Normans* is the longest item of its kind in the Index to Mabillon's Annals. The Normans maintained their racial unity North and South: the N of Rouen but strengthened the cult of the Byzantine N in Apulia.[13]

At Rainulf's Aversa, just above Naples, eight sons of Tancred de Hauteville equipped themselves for their careers. Tancred, a minor noble near Coutances in the duchy of Normandy, had a dozen sons, five by one wife, seven by another. Of the first family William of the Iron Arm, Drogo, and Humphrey distinguished themselves in Italy. Then came the second wave, led by Robert, called Guiscard ("the Wily"),[14] and his younger brother Roger. Before their deaths, all Sicily and Italy south of the papal state was in their realm.[15] We must neglect Sicily, where Roger won the last great city only the year Guiscard died (1085), despite the statement of the *Catholic Encyclopaedia* that "Sicily honors him as a patron." The esteem was moderate at best.[16] However, it is relevant that the Palatine Chapel of

Roger II at Palermo has N depicted together with the four warrior saints.[17] But N did not sacrifice all to knighthood, for on the outer wall of that same chapel his mosaic image rests between those of the scholar Saint Jerome and the archbishop Maximus of Naples.[18]

Rather, we turn from Roger to the older Robert, who took Apulia and Calabria especially as his own. On 5 August 1068 he laid siege to Bari, center of Byzantine rule through its catapan. He was not able to take it, despite Roger's help, until 16 April 1071, a date that marks the last rule of New Rome in Italy.[19] It marks also the birth of a Norman fleet in the Mediterranean. It is remarkable what landlubbers the Vikings had become during their little more than a century's residence in Normandy. The invaders of southern Italy regularly arrived there by the land route. But Guiscard learned in the siege of Bari that he could not gain it by land force alone. His brother Roger sailed into the Adriatic with Sicilian ships and defeated the Byzantine fleet.[20] It had been Saint George who opened Sicily to Roger at the battle of Cerami, A.D. 1063; but N unlocked Bari.

Bari was the prize of the lower Adriatic. Since Justinian it had been Byzantine except for a period in the ninth century. At that time the Arabs took it in 841 while moving toward Rome. In 871 the western emperor, Louis II, with the fleets of the Venetians and Byzantines recovered it. Louis was too weak to hold it against Emperor Basil's seizure in 876.[21]

Bari was again relieved by the Venetians when the Saracens, who seldom yielded gracefully, launched a great siege by land and sea in A.D. 1003. By early May, the citizens were ready to surrender. Had the assault succeeded, Bari would have been set afire by the Africans and "the whole immense population, rich, elegant, refined, transported captive to Sicily and Africa, devoted to the most infamous slavery."[22] But the white rescue sails of the Venetians appeared. An indecisive battle continued until September, when Doge Peter Orseolo took personal command and employed Greek Fire. For his victory Bari accorded him greatest honor and respect, according to the local historian. But the Venetians were nonetheless excluded from the city as having exceeded the authority granted them in the Byzantine Chrysobulle of 992; as a major port in direct service to Constantinople, Bari was not to be handed over to the growing Venetian power.[23] A company of Russian varangians arrived in 1066 to enforce the claim. Documents of 1086 indicate that Barian ships were plying a steady trade in fruits and other goods to Moslem Antioch as well as to Constantinople. Peter the Hermit, on his early trip to Jerusalem, took a Barian ship back from the Levant.

N's icon of about the year 1000 at Bari is Eastern.[24] Nevertheless, by the peculiar accommodations of the age, from around the year 950 the archdiocese was Latin, with a Latin rite. The archbishop exercised hegemony over most of lower Italy: the saffragens of Canosa, Bitonto, Giovenazzo, Molfetta, Trani, Canne, Aquatetta, Lavello, Rapolla, Melfi, Vitalba, Conversano, Polignano. Between 1035 and 1062 the archbishop's name was Nicholas, of ancient Greek family, who built near Bari two N churches, both, it seems, because of specific acts of N's benevolence.[25] In 1075 the records of Archbishop Peter mention still another N church—dei Monte. The emperor at Constantinople, Constantine IX Monomachos (1042 - 1054), who built a church to N inside the Barian walls, served by Basilian monks, had officially placed the city under N's patronage. We note Nicholases as archbishop of Canosa and bishop of Temoli; and the patriarch of Alexandria when Guiscard's daughter went into the convent was named Nicholas. Slight wonder that Guiscard in the year of his death should contribute an icon of N as "protective patron of the state of Bari."[26]

With Bari in 1071 came most of southern Italy, though Salerno, home of Bishop Alphanus II, who composed the impressive hymn to N, *Rex regum, Deus omnium,* did not fall until 1076. So convincing was this Norman ascendancy that the Byzantine emperor, Michael VII, betrothed his son Constantine to one of Guiscard's daughters, possibly thinking that he could recover by marriage what he had lost by arms. But before the actual ceremony, Nicephoros had seized the imperial throne (1078), sending Michael to a monastery and Guiscard's daughter to a convent.[27] This act was an open excuse for Guiscard to invade the Greek peninsula, with a view to seizing Constantinople (no less!). The expedition failed, partly because his son Bohemond, whom he left in command, was not yet experienced enough, and partly because Greece was defended by skillful Venetians.[28]

Anna Comnena, the historian daughter of Emperor Alexius, reported the Greek campaign. When Robert took Dyrrachium, Alexius "moved on to the chapel dedicated to the memory of Nicholas, greatest of all bishops,"[29] which he made his headquarters. Robert took it, including the imperial tent and all the army equipment. "He sent off all the strongest men he had to pursue the emperor, while he stayed where he was, picturing to himself the capture of the emperor—for such ideas inflamed his overweening pride."[30] We can see him speaking to N, as Brutus spoke to the spirit at Abydos: "Thou shalt see me at Philippi." But Guiscard did not get so far.

Some modern historians think that Alexius never called for the West to crusade, and that that universal belief arose from his asking the Count of Flanders for five hundred knights to withstand Guiscard. At the very moment that the Normans took Bari from it, Byzantium suffered its worst defeat, at the hands of the Seljuk Turks at Mantzikert.[31] New Rome was toppling. According to the Anglo-Norman chronicler Orderic, Alexius depended in the war on the Greek peninsula not only on Slavs and Turks but on the Scandinavian varangians, a corps which now included many Englishmen who came as mercenaries driven from Britain by William the Conqueror's usurpations. Such was knighthood that Norman fought against Norman in these campaigns.[32]

However unsuccessful in Greece, the campaign focused the eyes of Guiscard and Bohemond on the east. Theirs form a goodly part of the energies and ambitions poured into the First Crusade. They would have more land, whether from Greeks, Arabs, or Turks. Guiscard finally in October 1084 returned to Greece to try to salvage the expedition, but contracted the plague and died. At his death his militia "burst into a wild stampede for the shore"[33] and Italy.

The Venetians had already received from New Rome the inflated trade preferences of the chrysobulle, which, as Vasiliev remarks, "ought for a long time to render impossible the appearance of any rivals." But now they raised their ante, and Alexius conceded. To be sure, Guiscard had defeated them one last time before his death; but even so, Bari needed some miracle to even up its competition with Venice. When the Barians set out for Antioch in the year 1087, the civic honor of Bari was at low ebb.

III THE PAPACY IN THE GENERATION OF NICHOLAS II

N had guarded Pope Nicholas I and his court, but he was not a force in papal politics after that pope's death. The court became a tool of whatever lay power was dominant. It is often remarked that no pope between Nicholas I and Leo IX had any claim to saintliness. N's cult continued to be religiously and socially acceptable in Rome. Huelson records nearly a dozen church dedications before the Translation, and I have already mentioned two influential convents that were operating early in the eleventh century. Rome was sometimes a refuge for oriental Christians, and communities of Basilian monks and their *familiae,* scattered through the Italian peninsula, maintained the cult.

Pope Leo IX[1] was devoted to many saints, N foremost among them. Born (21 June 1002) Bruno, of a family of counts of Upper Alsace, and a second cousin of the German emperor,[2] he was an oblate at Toul. He acted like a Lotharingian all his life. Though an oblate he evidently obtained knightly training. In time he became bishop of Toul, already mentioned as a center of N cult. He was a most able musician, composing at least five *historiae,* including one for Gregory the Great, and lauds for N.[3] I have hazarded that he might have composed the N sequence *Congaudentes 47.* Musicologists attribute to him the *Gloria* which is No. 1 *ad libitum* in the Vatican edition of the Roman Gradual. As Bishop of Toul he was a militant reformer.[4]

In 1048, Emperor Henry III named him pope. Bruno, now forty-six years old, immediately showed his reforming zeal. He would accept the position only at the hands of the Roman citizens, not the emperor. He stated an unprecedented principle: "If he should hear that all the clergy and the Roman people were in agreement, then he would not draw back."[5] So he went to Rome to await the City's acclamation as pilgrim Bruno, Bishop of Toul, and not as Pope Leo IX.[6]

He took with him a whole company of Lotharingians, including Frederick of Lorraine, archdeacon of Liège, who was later Pope Stephen IX. Having received Roman election, he declared war against simony and clerical incontinence (which in a later day would be called *nicolaitism,* nòt for N but for the deacon in the Apocalypse).[7] As chevalier of God, Leo was constantly on the road. He held reforming councils in France and Swabia, and also in southern Italy, where he met the Norman brigands head on. In 1049 he dedicated N relics at the monasteries of Altdorf in Alsace and Saint Emmeram at Regensburg.[8] In 1052 he dedicated an N chapel on the Nagold bridge in Calw (Württemberg).

There is, says Donnet,[9] a relation between the consecration of the hospice to N on the Great Saint Bernard Pass and the frequent trips[10] of Pope Leo IX in the years 1049 - 1050. He suggests that Leo's cult of N inspired Saint Bernard of Menthon. Others have said that N's patronage of commerce was responsible. The well-known hospice cared for the main commercial route, heavily fortified, across the Alps.

As early as Charlemagne a monastery at the foot of the Pass furnished guides to travelers,[11] but the Saracens who operated from a base on the Mediterranean held the pass from 940 on for a generation. After 988 the bishop of Geneva rebuilt Saint Peter, the monastery, and in 1020 the Normans emigrating to southern Italy forced passage against those exacting tribute.[12] Bernard (d. 1081) founded the hospice at the summit of Mont Joux (Jupiter), dedicating it to N.[13] Already by the year 1139 a pilgrim guidebook for Saint James of Compostella named it one of the three greatest hospices.[14] In the Life of Bernard by Richard, archdeacon of Aosta,[15] he is depicted as being counseled by N at every step. This Life was dramatized in French vernacular—one of the many N mystery plays.[16] In both, emphasis is placed on Bernard as scholar, inspired by the patron of scholars.[17] A Sequence tells the story, beginning:

> Nicholas appeared then standing
> In a pilgrim's guise, demanding
>   Of the saint in much this mode:
> "Come, we'll scale Mont Joux together
> And on topmost rock or near there
>   Build a hospice by the road . . ."[18]

Amann calls Leo a very pious pontiff, very religious, very *bon,* full of mercy toward the weak and poor; but especially a *grand* pope, having a very elevated conception of his role. Too elevated: he became the Pope on Horseback. Scandalized by the Normans, lay contemners of moral law, he appealed to Henry III and Byzantium for aid to quell them. Henry's hands were bound by Hungary at the moment, but he allowed Leo to levy troops in Alsace and Swabia, which Leo *personally* led into battle, together with a scattering of Romans. He was supposed to be joined by the Venetians and Byzantines, but they never arrived. He met the Normans in the valley of Fortore 16 June 1053, and was captured. Held prisoner in Benevento until he signed what the Normans wanted, legitimizing their rapine, he did not return to Rome until 12 March 1054, and died 19 April. The Christians of the West were humiliated. Preachers, Peter Damian in the lead, condemned a fighting pope.[19]

At this moment a delegation which Leo had dispatched to Constantinople to deal with the differences between the churches appeared in Hagia Sophia 15 July 1054. They placed on the high altar a bull excommunicating the patriarch. The pope's legates were two Lotharingians, Humbert and Frederick,[20] along with the archbishop of Amalfi. The emperor Michael five days later laid the legates under anathema. The Schism was on.[21] N's allegiance was divided.

It took a year to get a new pope. Victor II's place in our theme is as Bishop Gebhard of Eichstätt, home of the N liturgy. As pope he was little more than a house chaplain for the Western emperor. Frederick of Lorrain, perhaps shaken by his Byzantine mission, retired as a monk in Monte Cassino. In 1057 he was made abbot, but just then Victor II died and Frederick succeeded, though he shared his family's opposition to the German emperor.[22] As Pope Stephen IX he enlivened the papal opposition to the emperor on the north but also to the Normans on the south. However, he died within eight months, having effected little more than declarations of intent.[23] Like all of Leo's Lotharingian entourage, he was a devotee of N.

A cardinal-bishop was elected Pope Benedict X, but the Northerners in the court, especially Hildebrand, who was now leader in the curia, would not have him. Meeting in Siena, they chose a Burgundian, Gerard, bishop of Florence, in his place.[24] With the aid of Empress Agnes, regent for the infant emperor Henry IV, the Duke of Lorrain and Tuscany marched the new pope into Rome as Benedict fled.

It is commonly explained that Gerard chose the name Nicholas (II) because he was elected on N Day; but in fact the day, even the month, of his election is not certain. What *is* obvious is that the Lotharingian reformers looked back on two interlocked images, N and Pope Nicholas I, as their model. In choosing the name, Gerard set high standards in relations of prelacy to royalty, though his premature death prevents our measuring him by them. Despite its brevity, his pontificate was of capital importance. We have already noted the relation to the N cultist, Wulfstan of Worcester. His acts in 1061, when he joined hands with the southern Normans, were a mighty step in bringing on the Norman Conquest, and his ex post facto dispensation for the marriage of William the Conqueror and Matilda had as its price the erection of those mighty abbeys at Caen, the fancied scenes of the mythical Arthur's marriage to Guenivere.[25] His Lateran Council of 1059, in trying and condemning Berenger,[26] set the direction of Eucharistic theology. Under the lashing tongue of Peter Damian, rebellious Milan fell into line with him. At the stroke of two synodal letters, he regulated clerical and lay marital and extramarital morality.[27]

But still, his most important reform, which controls all present legislation governing the election of the pope, was the decree centering all power of election in the college of cardinals, thereafter at the very heart of the warfare between pope and emperor.[28] It immediately dashed all hope of accommodation with the German emperor. To maintain his power, Pope Nicholas had to woo France and the dastardly Normans. He met with Richard of Aversa and Robert Guiscard at Melfi and received their allegiance in return for his legitimizing their rule—Richard as Prince of Capua and Robert as Duke of Apulia, Calabria, and Sicily.[29] Thus N, through his namesake, became a patron of opportunists. As *Stratilates 3* had for so many centuries promised, he typified secular priest, bishop, prelate, pontiff, pope par excellence, as would be memorialized at a later date by Calixtus II in building the N Chapel in the Lateran Palace.

Pope Nicholas II died at Florence 27 July 1061. In the development of our special theme, we may skip over papal history for the next quarter-century—a grave omission on any other count, for Alexander II (d. 1073) and Gregory VII (d. 1085) are deeply graven in the history of mankind.[30] Perhaps that deep incising that made common the phrase "the Age of Hildebrand" left no energy for extending the legendary imagination. Note, however, that after his days barefoot at Canossa the emperor Henry IV retired with the papal representatives to "the Chapel of Saint Nicholas."[31] All energy in this period was devoted to very material matters: popes and antipopes, emperors and treasonous barons, rabblerousers and charlatans, torchbearers and slashers. The short occupation of Rome by Robert Guiscard and his Normans in May 1084, ostensibly on the pope's behalf, was most destructive of all. "The monuments of ancient Rome suffered more from the Normans than from the Vandals."[32] Not N alone, but every patron saint, seems to have turned his eyes away. It was not a time for sanctity.

The only profit went to the freebooters whom Nicholas II had legitimized. At odds with Eastern and Western emperors alike, and finally deserted even by the baronry of France, the pope must compromise with those who kidnaped him, imprisoned him, made a pawn of him, whom he despised as Saracenic despoilers of God and moral law, and had excommunicated and anathematized. Popes and Normans, nonetheless, had in common the image of N, who controlled emperors, as both parties desired to do. The Normans represented Necessary Force, which more than once in this world's history has been called upon to back up spiritual reform. Alexander II and Gregory VII did not deviate from the path of Leo IX, Stephen IX, and Nicholas II. Pope Calixtus II (1119 - 1124) embodied the aspirations of these popes in stone when he began the Chapel of Saint Nicholas in the Lateran Palace, completed under Anacletus II (1130 - 1138).[33]

IV THE TRANSLATION

Myra

It is pointless to discuss the knightly fever for holy relics, which reached its climax with the Sack of Constantinople in the year 1204. There have been unsuccessful efforts to inventory the caravan loads of relics ripped from the walls of Constantinople to titillate Western society. Relics were the Old Masters of the age, with a comparable latent power to stir the best and worst instincts in the beholders.[1]

Saint Augustine had testified to the extrasensory energy of tombs and relics: "I myself know how, at Milan, at the tombs of the saints, where demons are brought in a most marvelous and awful manner to confess their deeds, a thief who had come with the intention to deceive by perjury was compelled to own his theft and what he had taken away."[2] Gregory the Great's letter to Empress Constantina[3] might well be read in its entirety in this connection. Contrary to the scriptural words of Saint Peter,[4] from the fifth to the fifteenth centuries God was a confirmed respecter of persons, or at least of His Saints. Yet as Augustine said, "Even the gift of healing and the gift of discerning of spirits are not given to all saints, as the Apostle declares;[5] so it is not to all the tombs of the saints that it has pleased Him who divideth to each severally as He will to cause such miracles to be wrought."[6]

It pleased Him especially to distinguish N's tomb. The miracles performed in the presence of the relics more than befitted a great thaumaturge. Before the Turks arrived, the tomb was one of the popular pilgrim shrines of the Antiochene coast.[7] Not only myrrh but other N relics penetrated the west and all other regions of christendom.[8] Myra's shrine had supernatural protection. The chronicler Theophanes recorded that in the year 808 the Caliph Haroun-al-Raschid dispatched a fleet to ravage Rhodes. His admiral Koumeid ordered the fleet to put in at Myra to violate the tomb, but he lost his fleet in the consequent storm. Koumeid's life was saved that he might testify to the puissance of N.[9] According to Landulf Sagax, in 801 the Arab leader Aaron (Haroun-al-Raschid), in trying to destroy N's sepulcher, destroyed another by mistake—manifestly an act of divine protection.[10] It is possible that Landulf, whose reliability may be questioned, was only repeating a mutilated version of the Koumeid story, but no matter. *Fama* was N's ally.[11]

For several centuries the Byzantines and Saracens had alternated as nominal masters of Myra; their accommodation left the tomb comparatively unscathed.[12] The Myrans profited from the pilgrims. But after the battle of Mantzikert in 1071 and the fall of Nicea in 1080, the Seljuks swept across Lycia.[13] In 1084 Antioch fell. Thereafter the Turks rolled back and forth in waves. Though they maintained a rule over Myra itself, they left the shrine, beside the sea and outside the walls, unravaged. The leading citizens of Myra fled to the citadel up the mountainside.

Pagans though they were, the Turks had no desire to destroy N's relics. Sanctity in relics knows no sects: a good corpse is efficacious, whatever his communion. For example, when Simeon Stylites died in the fifth century, the desert nomads, Hagarenes not yet Mohammedans, rushed up to seize his body by force of arms; open war with Roman imperial troops followed.[14] The desire for contact with the evidences of heroism transcends sects and faiths; when religion fails, economics may preserve a shrine. In 1087 the Turks were taking the cash and letting the credit go—N was cash, and would go unscathed as long as he filled the alms box. He still lived in Myra, but precariously, for the Turks but loosely policed the land while the Arab navy had collapsed and the Byzantine forces were overextended.

Hence outsiders needed no exceptional incentive to plan the "translation," that is, the stealing of N's bones.[15] *Translatio,* as first used by Ambrose in the fourth century, had a faintly pleasant connotation; it suggested the experience of the patriarch Enoch, who had walked with God and was translated.[16] The word's subsequent use in cult and liturgy suggested that the established practice was blessed by prelates and presumably approved by Divine Providence. Among famous "translations" were Saint Benedict from Monte Cassino (A.D. 672 or 703) to Fleury in France,[17] Saint Mark from Alexandria to Venice, Saint Matthew from Paestum to Salerno (A.D. 954).[18] In 1076 Salerno fell to Guiscard, and in 1080 Matthew's relics were "rediscovered."[19] Pope Gregory VII wrote in congratulation to Archbishop Alphanus, and Guiscard built a new cathedral to house his bones, consecrated by Gregory VII during his famous exile from Rome.[20]

As the experience of the Arab Aaron, just mentioned, suggests, the "translators" were very apt to abscond with the wrong bones—or at least so their rivals might (and always did) maintain. Bodies of saints multiplied like loaves and fishes, for the saint's relics professedly stolen lived on to be stolen again and again.[21] After the Bari translation of N, Venetian merchants also professed to translate his bones; and much later they were again taken from Myra for deposit in Moscow. Saewulf, who described his pilgrimage to Palestine in 1102, wrote of stopping to venerate N's corpse at Myra, fifteen years after the translation to Bari.[22] The shrine at Myra, though in ruins much of the time, never entirely ceased to be a goal of pilgrimage until an earthquake devastated the city. The church was buried in the silt which the waters carried down from above. Only the tops of the vaults could be seen, which, in the course of time, cracked open.[23]

A chamberlain of the Russian emperor, Andrew Mourawiew, on his return from Jerusalem in the nineteenth century, visited the site of Myra and uncovered the wall of the basilica. Home in Russia he made a collection to cover the cost of the venture, and he carried on excavations for five years until he died in 1858, having spent a hundred thousand francs. Today some restoration proceeds under Turkish direction. At a museum in nearby Antalya a few small bones and an icon allegedly left behind by the Barian sailors are displayed. There are excellent photographs of them in the French weekly *Match* for 25 December 1965, which reported that there had been about one thousand visitors during that year. That same year the Associated Press reported:

> No Christmas services in downtown Demre (ancient Myra) are held in the Church of St. Nicholas because there are no priests or other Christians here now. The church, with a gendarme station and trees blocking its view from the street, has now been completely restored by the Moslem Turks. The interior is lighted through glass-covered arched windows behind the altar. Mosaics on the floor of the 48 by 24-foot nave and frescoes of saints on the walls inside the church and the courtyard are still visible. In one of the two side aisles of the church is the sarcophagus of Santa Claus [sic] with a marble cover on which two reclining figures have been carved—that of an adult, perhaps St. Nicholas, and a child—but both have been decapitated by vandals. There is a big hole in the side of the marble tomb, probably made by those who stole the remains.

A magnificent Roman amphitheater built into the mountain has survived.

The Documents

Translations of relics elicit documents to authenticate the event and to be read at public commemorations. Such a well-known document is the versified report of the historian Einhard of the translation of the relics of Saints Marcellinus and Petrus from Rome to Seligenstadt in the year 827. But no saint's translation has been graced with such international documentation as N's.

Practically every Western chronicler of the generation reported this event of 1087. The eminent historians Orderic[24] and William of Malmesbury gave it thorough attention; other Anglo-Norman historians like Matthew Paris[25] noted it. The Cotton MS Tiberius B V contains the story in twenty-seven tetrameter couplets.[26] The continental historians were only slightly less appreciative.[27] In after years there were elaborate accounts by popular authors like Vincent of Beauvais and James of Voragine.[28]

But four documents have claim as independent evidence—two in Latin, one Greek, and one Russian. All but the Greek versions were written shortly after the event. Just as N was exceptionally graced by the providential composition of his liturgy by the young musician Reginold, so was he now equally graced by having as first narrator the young *Nicephorus 50,* "Lowliest of the clerks of Bari." In recent centuries his artistry has been too much neglected. He is a good reporter—honest, graphic, inquisitive, and sensitive. The other three authors, whatever their independent contributions, largely depend on him.

Here is his complete statement:[29]

From Vatican MS. lat. 5074, fos. 5^v - 10^v

N

Here begins the Prologue which Nicephorus, the least of all clerks, composed for

THE TRANSLATION OF SAINT NICHOLAS, CONFESSOR

Just as the hand of the sculptor is dextrous in giving shape to a bust of his subject, so is it adept in objectifying the inherent worth of his creation. Just as it is hard to endow a conception with life, however comparable it is with the life of the true object, and to unify all that is apprehended by the artist's several discrete senses, so perhaps may it be realized how hard it is to treat particularities meaningfully with the worthless tools of physics, ethics, and logic. To such demanding representation only those should devote themselves who, according to the accepted categories of active and contemplative life, can sing out with the sweet voice of the muse and make it their care step-by-step to match feeling with feeling, word with word, according to the sophistic principles of the Peripatetics. In this instance I, Nicephorus, the lowliest of all clerks in Bari, am unskilled in art and untrained in the lucid style required to express the inexpressible virtues as well as the leonine actions of this confessor of God. Yet however unworthy, steadied by his support I shall begin to condense into brief form a written report of his Translation.

Lord Curcorius, the perspicacious judge, together with other Barian magnates, and even officials of the holy churches, exercised the greatest pressure to get me to compose this work. Yielding to their requests because of my love for this saint, supported by the faith they had in me even though I felt that I was too unskilled for a task of such finesse, I agreed to put my hand to the plow. Under these conditions, I beg the learned readers and masters trained in the liberal arts that they bear only the slightest animosity against this extenuated verbal exercise.

END OF PROLOGUE

When Almighty God, in His indulgent but secret Providence, once determined that the city of Bari and the whole province of Apulia was to be visited and ennobled by a most propitious and lasting splendor, His Divine Providence was the very act itself: It was His Providence that determined that some wise and illustrious men of Bari should make their way to Antioch with their ships laden with grain and other merchandise. With the favor of God, they discussed together how they might take away from the city of Myra, either going or coming, the body of the most blessed confessor of Christ, Nicholas. Devoting themselves and their possessions to this consuming desire, they conspired together. While all of them, with the help of God, eagerly began to lay the groundwork and to shape their plans, it came about that they learned that the Venetians wanted to carry out the very same project that they were meditating. At that moment the Venetians, too, were headed for Antioch for similar commercial reasons. When the Barians had verified that fact, in checking on the Venetians' actions they found out that the Venetians had equipped themselves with iron instruments with which they might, if they could get there first, enter the Myran shrine of blessed Nicholas the confessor. If the Lord should favor them, they could break open the floor of the church and carry away the holy corpse.

After the plans of the Venetians had been bared, the Barians pledged each other to work so energetically that they would outdo not only the Venetians but all those stationed in Myra. So they quickly put up their merchandise for sale and bought whatever was most available to them at the moment. Quickly finishing up both the buying and the selling, they hurried on their way to the city of Myra. Gaining port, they made fast their ships in the normal manner.

Then they sent out two Jerusalem pilgrims whom they had picked up at Antioch. One of them was Greek, but the other was of French birth. These two could more intelligently explore the surroundings, being wary of the Turks, who had villainously ravaged the district. After they had made their way to the holy body and discovered that the Turks were not there, they swiftly returned to announce that their company could carry out their plan very safely. Immediately on receiving this welcome advice, forty-seven of them, well armed, devoutly hurried to the holy corpse. However, others not dissimilarly clad in arms stayed behind to guard the ships for fear of the Turks, who had invaded that region and cruelly depopulated it. Having wisely divided in two companies in this way, they set about gaining their desire.

Now the forty-seven, on coming to the holy see of the pious confessor, when they discovered as many as four custodians around the place, politely entered the reverend shrine and worshiped at the holy altar. Then in an excess of holy, burning desire, they said to the custodians, "Brothers, show us where lies the physical body of the holy confessor." Thinking because of an inadequate mastery of languages that they were asking for the place of oblation, the guardians first showed them the place from which with a sponge they extracted the holy liquor. Then they showed how the holy body was hidden away at that place.

Yet because the holy basilica was set apart from the habitations of men, the guardians began to fear that the holy body might be taken from them. They anxiously queried the Barians, "Why do you ask these questions? Can it be that you want to take the body? Don't you know that we cannot possibly assent to such a thing—indeed, we would rather die than permit him to be taken?"

To these queries the Barians replied, "Know for a fact that we have come to your shores for that very purpose; and therefore we ask you to show us the true location, so that our efforts will not be wasted."

Then the custodians, seeing that the Barians were doubtful about the place they had been shown, reaffirmed what had been said, adding, "We are sorry that we told you the truth about the holy liquor and the corpse. But whether it be the place or not, the holy confessor of God will never let you touch him. So leave before these actions come to the ears of the citizens."

The Barians now realized that their courteous requests would not soften the guards. They changed to hot arguments. But yet, they chose their words with saintly ingenuity—words which seemed as blameless as possible—according to the saying of scripture, "Good is the deceit which harms no one."[30] So they said, "You should know that when the pope of the city of Rome came to our city of Bari, accompanied by many archbishops and a retinue of clergy and laity, he himself sent us to these parts to transfer this sacred body there. He did all this because that confessor of God appeared to him in his sleep and requested to be transported to our land. However, even though ships cannot sail on good will alone, we are prepared to pay you any price you name for this great treasure, in order that we may receive your benediction and leave here peacefully."

When the custodians saw them prepared to smash the pavement of the church and carry away the body, they were very nearly struck dumb.

The color left their faces, and blood drained
    from their veins.
They wailed and rent their priestly garments
    from their breasts.
In sorrow they tried to pull hair from their heads
    and beards,
And desired more to depart from this life on earth
Than to give over the saint they had for so many ages
    cherished.

What more can I say? The offering of gold is tossed aside like dung, the blandishing words shunned like adders' venom. The custodians tried every means of escape, to let the townsfolk know the whole course of events. When the Barians realized what they were trying to do, they cannily ordered some of their number to bind the custodians and others to guard the gates of the basilica, as well as the plazas and roads, so that none of the inhabitants of the district could learn of their acts. The custodians were to be held until everything they planned had been done.

After this, one of the two priests who were taking part, holding in his hands a glass phial full of the holy liquid, wanted to join his companions' parley, to help the process along. He placed the phial on top of a not-very-high column which rested on the altar stead. As he mingled with them while they wasted time in various discussions about what they should do, a very startling thing happened: the phial fell from its place on top of the column and with a loud clang struck the marble pavement under which the saint exuded the liquid. At this accident, all of them crowded around. When they found the phial whole and unbroken, full of wonder the Barians broke into praises to the high lord. At that point they knew for a fact that the confessor of God himself had gotten their attention by that sound, and was saying, "Why are you so slothful in performing your duty? It is my will that I leave here with you. This is the spot in which I have rested through many cycles of years. Regard that as a miracle; but now leave, taking my body with you. For under my protection all Barians will prosper. You will lead happy lives under my rule."

Thereupon a very daring young man broke out of the group, anxious to perform the duty. He threateningly clutched one of the custodians, with drawn sword, and swore that he would run him through if he did not indicate the sepulcher containing the holy body. When another of the custodians, more prudent and saintly than the rest, saw how the sailor raged, he approached the threatener and implored him to moderate his remarks: "Why," he said, "do you manhandle a servant of God in this way? Look there at the place where the holy liquid comes out. Obviously the body of the saint must lie in that same place. But we know this for a fact from the tales of men of old and also from our own experience: that many emperors and other potentates have done their best to carry out what you now plan; but they had no luck because the saint of God was unwilling. [Cf. *Magnentius 48*]. Yet perhaps it may happen through you, because the confessor of God himself last year warned us in a vision that his abode would be moved elsewhere."

When the Barians heard that, they plied the custodian with questions about the meaning of the vision. He replied to them, "Already a year has passed since Nicholas, the servant of God, made himself known to three residents. He admonished them through a vision to inform the inhabitants of the city of Myra, who had fled in fear of the Turks to a mountain twelve stades away, that they should return to live and guard the city. Otherwise they should know that he would migrate elsewhere. How true that prediction was we now see. So put up the sword, soften your threats, once for all rid yourself of those belligerent looks. If it is granted to you that the confessor of God cooperate in your actions, then depart in peace without anger or hurt on our part. But though by his holy admonitions he holds us blameworthy, we believe that by the will of God he will not thus easily desert his own humble servants."

Thereupon the young man we have told about, whose

name was Matthew, agreed to what had been said, together with his company. He put away the sword and took up the iron mallet. Manfully striking the marble slab of the pavement which stretched out above the holy body, he broke it away bit by bit. He had not dug a very deep hole before his companions insisted on working with him. They found a very white marble tomb which covered an interior coffin. They were exceedingly fearful of striking it, dreading the something terrible that might happen to them. But Matthew, who was more audacious than the others, could not longer restrain his hot intent; he scoffed at the notion that any evil would come to him.

Bravely taking the hammer from his fellows, he struck savagely. When the tomb was open, he found the whole coffin full of holy liquid up to the umbilicus of the saintly body. Both of the priests, who had ordered the smashing, and some of the sailors and others of the company who had taken part in the action, were standing there. Immediately such a wave of delightful perfume arose that everyone thought himself to be standing in God's paradise. This scent not only permeated the sanctuary where they were, but it was borne on the breezes that played round about the way to the sea, nearly three miles away, to the other company. As they breathed it in, each was at once overwhelmed with joy, knowing that the holy confessor of Christ had consented to join their company.

After this, Matthew conducted himself even more rashly. In the whole episode he had daringly stopped at nothing, so to speak. Now, still clad in shoes, he impetuously lowered himself into the sacred sarcophagus. Once down, he bathed both hands in the liquid. He found the holy relics swimming in an envelopment of all perfumes, which licked at the venerable priests as if in insatiable embrace. This envelopment made it perfectly clear that the authentic confessor of Christ was freely granting himself to the Barians. As they watched, the local guardians most reverently began to weep, saying, "The saint is yours, for he has never accorded such treatment to others. Alas for sorrow, how great an evil has happened to our fatherland."

And they chokingly addressed the saint: "Our lord, dearest father, why dost thou desert us when we are afflicted by so many miseries? Here thou art, pious to strangers, impious to thy children. Lo, as we see, thou deemest as nothing all the tokens of our service, which our fathers and we have meted out to thy glory. Dost thou thus repay thy subjects for such benefits? Alas, now thou wilt cast a dark curtain over the whole province of Lycia. Lord, why didst thou not before this adjudge thy servants to death rather than accept thy separation from us? From kind father thou showest thyself unkind stepfather, and dost cast off thy beloved sons as if the worst of stepsons. Alas, how lamentably will we lead all the days of our lives while we view ourselves and our sons together with all our goods evilly effaced! How can we escape?"

Meanwhile Matthew, who was carefully examining the relics of the most holy body, found them all intact. Another, the priest whose name was Grimoald, very carefully arranged them in a new silk covering for the body. Some others in the company wanted to take away an ancient wonder-working icon painted in the likeness of Saint Nicholas. But they were definitely forbidden to do so. With respect to the icon, it was promptly made plain that the confessor of Christ never wished to have the parties there at Myra completely bereft.

Then the Barians, filled with joy, quickly took up their arms and, while the first priest led the chant, they lifted the holy body onto their shoulders and walked back to the ships, singing praises to God. Their fellows, hearing the sounds of the processional hymns, which were being rendered to God for the gift of a shepherd, advanced to meet them. Gaily congratulating each other, they praised Almighty God in unison for the great gift with which he had crowned the Barians. Certainly they shed many tears that day, knowing themselves to be unworthy of such goodness.

183

Meanwhile, all these events had been broadcast by those custodians who had been held prisoners, but who were freed as the Barians left. Why should I prolong the story? Almost at once a countless crowd of men and women of all ages gathered at the seashore, all in the grip of heavy sorrow. Weepingly they bemoaned their evil loss of so much good. And they cried out to our Barians in these words: "Who are you, and from where do you come here, daring to commit such ravage on our possessions? What is the source of such savagery stirring within you, that you should dare to touch our possession, hallowed from antiquity, deposited in this sacred spot? Look you, according to our Aeolic chronograph, 775 years have passed in which no one has committed such an act, be he representative of emperors or of whatever human quality. The high-thundering Lord has clearly approved this unprecedented act for you; and His most blessed confessor Nicholas, who has left us orphaned, has completely reestablished his fatherhood among you unknowns."

Not being able to contain themselves, clad and shod they waded into the sea, and as they wailed they grabbed the rails of the ships, crying out to the rowers, "Give back our father and our lord, our master and nourisher, who in every way has by his protection kept us safe from visible foes. If you would give all or even a part of his body to us, we would not be so completely divorced from our great patron."

At these dirges the Barians who were close enough to hear sympathized with the tender words. They said in reply, "You should know that we have come out of the territories of Apulia and have made our way here from the city of Bari because of a revelation that we should take the holy body to that place. Why do you so irrationally flay yourselves for these calamitous happenings? Just as you have said, since the time that the holy confessor of God died, 775 years have passed. It is enough that you have had his benefits, not you alone but your progenitors. Now it is his desire to leave here and to shed his light on other parts of the world.

Surely you can be abundantly comforted by the fact that you have a sepulcher full of the holy liquid, which is left for you. Moreover, you have the icon, from which you have derived many benefits.[31] It is only right that so important and illustrious a state as Bari should enjoy this great patronage."

While this parley was going on, the bereaved, catching sight of one of the almsmen of that orphaned and desolated church, seized him. While they pounded him, blow after blow, they accused him of trading the holy body for money, in league with his associates. But then the most blessed confessor of Christ freed him from their pounding, and they stood dumbfounded, acknowledging that he was blameless.

Then the holy body was honorifically settled in a very small alcove of the ship. As the sun set upon the waves, with favorable wind the Barians began quietly to sail into deep water. At that point the natives, seeing that they were separated from their great patron by distance and that the Barians had left port to return to us with God and the saint . . . they were overwhelmed with chagrin. They filled both shore and air with their sorrowful dirges, which on the testimony of the Barians they could hear echoing nearly two miles away. Indeed there were very few among them who could even with great effort keep themselves from tears, as they sympathized with such wretchedness.

Holding their course for a long distance, they rested that night at a place called Caccavus. Then after crossing a craggy stretch, they came to the deep sea. They began to be very much impeded by tides and by the north wind which is called Aquilo, which blew against them all the way to the state of Patara, where the confessor of God was born. Since they were being driven from their course with great danger to themselves, they began to think that the saint of God had never wished to go with them, and would keep them from going further unless they returned him.

After expending every bit of energy they had, yet not being able to proceed beyond, possibly, twenty-four miles, they unwillingly altered their course to a place called Perdikca, with all their strength gone. When they disembarked, they saw that the sea was as peaceful as they could have wanted. Not having the strength to start out, they began to accuse each other that some one among them had pilfered something from the relics of the saint. At once the sailors decided that they should bring out the Gospels and that every sailor should swear in turn that no one of them had stolen anything from them. Because, if any had dared to do so, they would have to consider what could be done with whatever came from the holy body so that they could return it to its proper place. Then five of the sailors made known that they had something from the holy relics. When they had returned it and put it down with the lot, both these five and all the rest of the company swore that no one of them had any more of the holy relics. By this incident, no one was left in doubt that it was in accordance with the will of God. It was God's will that they should be delayed until the relics of the holy body were rendered intact. They were thereby given to understand that the confessor of God himself willed that his relics should never in any way be divided.

O wondrous God, how ineffable is Thy power, since not through the voice of any angel nor through the revelation of any saint whatsoever, nor through the most saintly Nicholas himself (who in this affair rises in esteem), indeed not even through dreams of Thy seamen, didst Thou impart understanding, but through the inanimate elements. Up to the moment when they returned to the saint his own, Thou didst hide the answer from them.

Then, after celebrating mass, with quieted winds and becalmed seaswell, they left the shore under swollen sails. With joy among them all, they came to a place which is called Markiano.

At length, after they had passed Culfus Trachiae, it happened that one of the sailors named Disigius sank into a deep sleep in which Saint Nicholas appeared to him and said, "Don't fear, for I am with you. At the end of twenty days we will all arrive together at the city of Bari." When he had awakened and told his associates what he had seen, they were all joyful and greatly delighted.

They came to Ceresanus and there, after they had eaten, they took to the water. After they had sailed a fast course for two days and one night, covering fifty miles, they came to the island of Milos, where they rested for the night. Leaving at dawn, they pursued their course.

I cannot pass over a marvelous thing that happened to them, telling it just as those who saw it narrated it to me. While they were holding to the open sea, a single little bird rather like a lark settled on the starboard of the ship, where the holy body was being carried, and hopped over the casket as if it were looking for food from the men. He calmly landed on the hand of one of the sailors, the one who was then officer of that deck. From there he turned and made his way to where the holy body lay at rest. Softly singing, he gently touched the carrier in which the holy relics lay. Now, my good brethren, how much is to be praised Almighty God, who shows not only men but even dumb animals how to praise and venerate His saintly confessor. For the song of the bird was laudation, and the kiss of the beak is to be taken as the touch which he extended in faith to the holy body. Then he circled the whole ship and its crew as he sang. He seemed to be extending to them all his praise and blessing for what they had done to the magnificent, miracle-working shepherd. Then, having rendered his compliant oblation, he flew away and they saw him no more.

Not long thereafter they came to an island which in Aeolic is called Staphnu, in Latin Bonapolla. Then they came to the primary port called Geraca, from which they quite lightheartedly entered the city of Monobasia. Leaving there, they went a short distance to Methon, where they bought wine and some necessities. Thereafter they came to Sukea, where they rested for a short while. They did not deviate from their course at any point, for the holy confessor of Christ was their cheer. When they arrived at the port of

Saint George, the martyr of Christ, which is four miles away from the city of Bari, they built a casket in which they arranged the holy body, removing it from its carrier.

How many glories are associated with that city of Bari! That it should transcend others as does the Samaritan, I will try to set forth in fewest words: O Bari with all thy residents, at one with the angelic Jerusalem, exultingly rejoice in thy infinite favors! Rejoice Bari without restraint, full of delight! Rejoice Bari, overwhelmed with so many eulogies! Rejoice Bari, drawing to thyself this new legacy of salvation! Rejoice that thou shouldst prove more worthy of praise than all the strong points of Apulia! Rejoice that thou art crowned in triumphant victory! For "Nicholas" in Greek means "Victory of the People" in Latin. He truly was Victor when he acquired the Barians and Apulians as protector, freeing them from the grip of infirmities. Rejoice that through most blessed Nicholas thou mayest come to learn of thy leaders enrolled among the choirs of angels! Rejoice that thou wilt be known through all zones of the world through news of thy celebrity! O with what reverence the Omnipotent looks upon thee! O with what sweet savor He subjects thee to his lovingkindness! O with what clear light of His aspect He illumines thee, as He commends thee to the care of the holy angels! O with what watchful guard day and night, hours and moments, He most carefully hovers over thee—but assuredly not through thee, who art weighed down with mighty mountains of sin, but through His most blessed confessor Nicholas, with whom the legions of the angels attend!

Most beloved brothers, let us all take stock, and with every fiber let us turn together to the loving Lord, who has with true love made us shine white with the beauty of this ethereal pearl. For if with whole heart we shall have been converted to the Lord Himself, not only will we rejoice in this egregious gift but we will be rewarded with the ultimate gift of heavenly good to come. Our witnesses may be the Lycian land—his states of Myra and Patara. If the ancient precepts and present powers of this confessor of God follow their true course, that cynosure will not diminish one jot in his power. And therefore we must liberate ourselves from every form of adultery, perjury, homicide, thievery, animosity, falsity, malignity, false accusation, detraction, pride, and whatsoever beclouds our faith. Interposing against these evils the lovable virtues, strengthening our faithfulness, but always in behalf of God and with love of His confessor, coming together here from every direction to make our oblations and offer our sacred prayers, no one of us should be guilty of any malice or evil, or commit any underhand act; for if that saint of God should observe in us, his own humble servants, scorn of evil and striving for good, not only will he manifest his traditional powers in our behalf, but through his own intervention he will effect our possession of the heavenly kingdom.

Now after these Barians had set their course for the port of their city, their relatives came to meet them in little boats. They were told how the mariners had brought with them the body of the most blessed confessor. When some of the greeters came to understand that fact, they quickly returned to shore, shouting it at the top of their voices to all those standing around. As the news spread everywhere through the city, everyone ran together in a crowd to witness the marvelous and heartwarming spectacle. The Barian clergy, dressed in their sacred vestments, extending the blessings of heaven, walked down with hurried steps to the port, looking to receive the holy body.

Meanwhile, the naval officers and men, through an appointed representative, made an announcement to the citizens, saying, "In the course of conveying the holy body, we pledged ourselves that, together with you, we would erect a church worthy of him in the domanial court which is called the Court of the Catapan. We ask your approval of our pledge."

At this announcement, a violent dissent sprang up among the listeners. Some (who seemed to be a plurality) praised the proposals; others said nay, hoping that the holy confessor of God would be borne to the episcopal see. While the

two parties were quarreling, Dom Elias, the venerable abbot
of the monastery of Saint Benedict in this city, boarded the
ships. After bestowing holy kisses, he addressed the leaders:

You intelligent men here at hand, may He stir your hearts
To grant to me the cherished saint—
He to whom we most truly must strive to render thanks
Until that populace joins with you
In what you have pledged to the saint and seek
　　for the people,
The domanial court, which should form a home for dear
　　Nicholas.

Everyone in conscience agreed with his thoughtful
request. They took up the holy body. Then it was ordered
that all the church bells should ring in honor of the saint.
Gently lowering the holy relic, with vigilant care they
placed it on the altar of Saint Benedict. In order to manifest
that no force was being exercised by any party in the city,
all of the sailors had disposed of their arms ahead of time.

Then word was hastily sent to Lord Urso, archbishop of
Bari, that he should hurry back as fast as possible to this
marvellous and most exalted event. At the moment he was
away at Canusia [Canosa], carrying out holy obligations. At
once he retraced his steps to the city of Bari. His horse did
not gallop as fast as his ardent desire made him pant to get
back. When he entered the city he went at once to the holy
body. Upon rendering due devotion to it, he moved on to
his own see, rejoicing in such a prize. He directed that it
should reverently be conveyed to his episcopal palace.

The minute that the sailors and their associates heard
about his directive, they and the people who had agreed to
their proposal all ran together to oppose the change. When
the prelate learned of their antagonism, he drew back from
immediate action. Then the most noble and sagacious leaders of Bari were sent to him as legates, with the request that
he accede to their desire.

But when the legates returned to their clients without a
favorable response, they began to be seriously aroused by

the thought that the prelate was himself plotting to carry away the body by force or guile. So when both parties quickly had armed themselves, they set to fighting. As the struggle went on, it came about that two adolescents, one from each camp, were killed. We truly believe and affirm that by the high favor of the Lord their souls will be placed in eternal blessedness because both died in their very commendable quest for the holy corpse. The antagonists carried them with highest honor to the monastery, with the armed men and other people chanting *Kyrie eleison* and singing other hymns.

With bared heads they took the body of the saint through the back gate of the monastery, on the seaward side, and bore it to the designated domanial court, into the Church of Saint Eustratius the Martyr of Christ. (That church,* together with churches of other saints, was leveled to the ground some days later. On their sites and on some other space from the same court, the Barians erected the most glorious and magnificent church in honor of most blessed Nicholas and of those saints. This project was managed from the beginning by Dom Abbot Elias together with some nobles of Bari. It was at the request of the archbishop himself and of all the citizens that he had charge of the holy body. In order that it should not be disturbed by anyone wanting to take it by force, it was guarded day and night by different detachments of armed men as long as it was honorifically resting in that church.)

The most sacred body of Saint Nicholas, confessor of Jesus Christ, who was inclined to leave the city of Myra, was borne away on the eleventh day of April, and on the ninth day of May he now had a fresh start, one thousand and eighty-seven years having passed from the Incarnation of the Lord, Indiction X.

And now, if God will allow it, I will record how the Translation first affected the people.

Invalids possessed of all kinds of illnesses, who had

---

*This parenthetical statement may well have been added later.

191

flocked from all parts of the city, were restored to health when in deep devotion they rested beside the body in the monastery. Among them that night and on Monday, forty-seven people of both sexes and differing ages: among these a very noble Barian and an *armenius* [pauper?] with his whole left side withered, three lunatics and a deaf and dumb man, two cripples, two humpbacked children, three blind, a man of Pisan blood with withered arm and hand and clubbed feet. There were others, too numerous to list here.

Then on Tuesday nine infirm were cured at the monastery, out of the great multitude of people flowing in from the villages and towns and cities round about. Up to the fourth hour of that day, through the saint a very small infant with arm and hand withered and with a spotted eye, and a deaf beggarwoman lame in both feet, and another small infant infested with a demon, and an infant girl who was a demoniac *armenia,* a woman *invenaciensis* [?] wholly withered, and another woman possessed of a grave disease, and a lunatic woman also bedridden with a very bad infirmity; a paralytic lunatic and a pilgrim with a withered left hand and blind eyes. Later that day we had taken the holy body to the court. Fourteen infirm, too many to describe here, were cured.

On Wednesday, twenty-nine were cured: first, a woman from the village called Tellizzus [Terlizzi] who was totally withered, and a girl from the city of Betuntus [Bitonto], and a demoniac from the city of Ascalon [Ascoli Satriano], and a woman from the state of Taranto; three lunatics; two blind men; and another woman bent over double; and a woman from the town of Saint Vitus, which is under the castle of Mount Scagiosus, who, gravely troubled, many times had been given up for dead. I earnestly queried her when she was healed concerning what she had seen. She said that a great hawk had flown over her, and had landed on her breast and spread his wings to cover her. As he left, suddenly an odor followed, so sweet that she thought she was in the garden of paradise. Some others who were cured said the same thing. In this regard, undoubtedly it is to be believed that it was the angel of that holy confessor, who guards over the holy body day after day. A Barian girl, suffering very much from pains in the knees. And others whom we haven't time to tell about.

On Thursday the confessor of God revealed himself through a vision to a venerable monk, directing him to speak to everyone who might despair of healing, because by the wish of the Omnipotent Lord he had to go away to parts of Greece; yet before he went, they would see a great miracle performed. And so it happened, for on that very day a young man was made whole who had been possessed by a demon for five years and was deaf, dumb, and blind.

On Friday Ernulphus, bishop of Betuntus, came to the holy body with a great procession, in prayer to the Lord and to the holy confessor Nicholas. Now on that day the bishop of Bari, with bishop Guidonius Oritanus and Leo, bishop of Cupersanus, and with three other bishops and all their clergy and countless people, peacefully came in all humility to adore the holy corpse. Likewise at the ninth hour of the Sabbath eleven infirm persons, on approaching Saint Nicholas, recovered their lost health.

Dearest brethren, we ought reverently and piously to love God and the Lord profoundly and earnestly, and to follow His precepts, Who, after a brief sojourn in this life, made His saints possessors of the heavenly reaches, while lighting up their relics with great and renowned gifts of miracles.

Jesus Christ, God and our Lord, Who with God the Father and the Holy Ghost, lives and reigns for ever, world without end. AMEN. Here ends the tract on the Translation of Saint Nicholas, confessor and bishop.

The rhetorical proem, filled with wholly irrelevant scholastic commonplaces of the type "unexpressibility topos," specifies the commemorative purpose. Evidently two political parties had been battling over the relics. Nicephorus wrote at the request of Lord Curcorius and magnates of Bari, that is, the still essentially Byzantine burghers. Nicephorus is a Greek name; we may assume that he was of the Byzantine party. Probably Nicephorus completed his account in little more than a week after 9 May 1087. The party that at that moment possessed the relics, that is, the Byzantine burghers, the crews that performed the feat, and the Greek aristocracy, were rushing a document into circulation which would confirm their claim and their plans.

The opposite party was headed by Archbishop Ursus, who was Guiscard's man and rode by his side. He had been bishop of Rapolla, but Gregory VII promoted him to Bari on Guiscard's demand. Ursus seems to have been a political busybody, seldom in his see; he was occupied with such matters as conducting to Spain the espoused of the Count of Barcelona. At Bari he completed the cathedral begun by Archbishop Nicholas, and he continued to load the diocese with new churches, a sign of growth, rising prosperity, and ambition. The antagonistic merchants and sailors also wanted church building, but not to the enrichment of the archbishop. It is one of the piquancies of true history, unmatched in legend, that the ambitious Ursus was caught absent from his post of duty at the most important moment of his life.

N A rival account was composed very shortly thereafter by *John the Archdeacon* 51 at the request of his archbishop.[32] John's sympathies are clear. He emphasized the rivalry with the Venetians, who were Norman foes. Nicephorus had piously depicted Ursus as bustling around among his suffragans at Canosa, vaguely "carrying out pious obligations," a damnation with faint praise. John showed him at Trani, already embarked on a pious pilgrimage to the Holy Land, carefully described as for the purpose of prayer (*causa orationis*). Certainly the Translation caught Ursus napping. He hurried home to bolster his party.

As befits the voice of organized religion, John is a peacemaker. He easily slides over the partisan disputes which led to the deaths of two youths. His archbishop is a benevolent and pacific shepherd (who, by a sardonic fate, was christened Ursus, the Bear). John is a more accomplished rhetorician and versifier than Nicephorus, but a less graphic reporter. Though he borrowed from Nicephorus, the two accounts do not always agree. John asserts that there were three guards at the church, not four. The pilfered fragments are specified as two teeth and some bone splinters. The emperor who wanted to translate N to Constantinople is identified as Basil, though whether Basil I or II is not known. John tells us that the ships were three in number, and that they actually stopped at Myra on their way to Antioch, but that the sailors withdrew when they found Turks in town. The money offered to the guards was three hundred gold bars, one hundred from each ship.[33]

A few concluding sentences sufficiently indicate how he differs from Nicephorus:

> When the ships arrived at port, the sailors who had brought the corpse did not know to what reliable churchman they should take the great treasure for committal; for Ursus, the archbishop of the Barians, a righteous man worthy of God, widely known and a close friend of the Italian rulers, was just then at Trani. We ourselves were with him on that day. There the ship stood ready to sail which he had boarded on the previous day for the purpose of going to Jerusalem for prayer. However, at the last moment a legate with letters from the citizens of Bari caught him there. The letters told that Omnipotent God had in His own time granted a miraculous gift to His church. Canceling the passage which he had contracted, Ursus arranged to hurry to Bari by direct route.
>
> However, the sailors had commended the coffin containing the holy relics to Abbot Elias of the Convent of Saint Benedict. This deposition occurred on the ninth day of the month of May, the day which was set as a solemn feast. For three days and nights he responsibly and vigilantly guarded the corpse with his brethren. Thereafter it was taken away and carried to the court which is called the Catapan's. This change resulted from the civil strife and discord which arose among the citizens of Bari, dividing them into two factions. Some wanted the saint to be placed in one part of the city and some in another. We are unwilling to sadden the generations to come by telling what happened between these factions. We prefer to maintain everlasting silence and let amnesty breed ignorance. When the archbishop finally arrived, the sailors and townsfolk asked him whether the coffer

should, by his favor, be left inside the court, a place which was suitable and capacious, and have its own church built there. He finally decided the issue.

Going together barefoot with the bishops and clergy and the whole populace of the city, he took the coffer from the midst of the court and deposed it in the Church of the Blessed Martyr Stephen, which had been erected in only a few months three years before. Then the cortege began to consider which suitable, worthy, and faithful man should be entrusted with the custody of this marvelous treasure. That man would receive the offerings of the faithful* and take full responsibility for the necessary services of the basilica. As diligent steward, he would be in charge of all income. At this time they could find no one more worthy of this great honor than Abbot Elias. And so with the consent and approbation of everyone, the archbishop committed the location and the listed duties to him and directed that he be in charge of everything done there.

Up to this point we have put down in words, however uncouth our style and insufficient our powers of mind, virtually everything which Omnipotent Majesty deigned to perform through mortal acts. All else that followed was His works—countless and wondrous signs, that is, of His powers. For it was pleasing to Divine Omnipotence to confirm by His own miraculous works what had seemed to be done by rash act. Many Christians were dubious, not firmly convinced that such grace and glory and sublimity had come to Bari by divine dispensation, to the illumination of all Italy. As we said, many a prince had tried in vain to effect such a project. So if anyone should question, or even silently wonder to himself, why God conceded to our men what He had so long denied to others, he can be answered, "We don't know why. Who knows the mind of God? Who can be His confidant? We know only this, that He did not formerly

---

*We can judge the income for a saint of pilgrim veneration by comparing a record from Canterbury: In one year not a penny was left at the altar of God, £4. 1. 8. was left at the altar of the Virgin, and £950. 6. 3. at the altar of Saint Thomas.[34]

wish to concede to others what He has now conceded to us, as has been evident. So we need to take this concession for granted, without questioning, because the Provider of All Things clearly ordained that this gracious bequest be translated from Asia to Europe for the salvation of Italy—indeed, for all Europe. For only in this one part of the world—Europe, that is—is catholic piety so fully and so perfectly observed."

Nicephorus wrote as agent of the old bourgeoisie, those who still regarded Apulia as theirs despite a current setback at the hands of upstart and (be it hoped!) short-lived Normans. He wrote for the sponsors of the new basilica which was soon to rise and house N's relics within the old Greek palace. His account was designed not only to protect the relics from all possible duplication and rivalry, but to attract pilgrims to Apulia and the palace as a thaumaturgic shrine. In contrast, John may have written to defend his archbishop's good name; certainly he meant his work to serve as lections in the liturgy for Translation Day (9 May), which immediately became a major feast of the Basilica and promptly spread throughout Latin Europe. John's text was composed before Ursus died 14 February 1089.

A third version, *Greek Account 52*,[35] is anonymous. It is based on Nicephorus and John and is shorter than either. Its point of view is not immediately intelligible. Byzantium should have been greatly shamed by the Translation. As father-protector of the Greek communion and the Aegean isles, as author of the cult of N, as profound enemy of the Normans, as leader of the recent schism with the Roman Church, Byzantium should have expressed rancor and protested the Latin seizure of its favorite child. But the politics of the 1080s were not simple. Even the emperors and patriarchs rejoiced that N had found safe haven outside the now-Turkish world. The accommodation of Mediterranean Islam and Christendom that had endured for four centuries was just now being replaced by the polarity expressed in the Chanson de Roland. The Seljuk Turks were demons, children of Satan, as the Arabs had not been. The Greek account ends in a glorification of the Translation. To be sure, it does not hide the Greek hatred of the Romans, but that hatred does not spread to other Occidentals. John, in the last sentences quoted above,

might undermine the Eastern communion; the Greeks did not recip-
rocate. Nor did the author suggest any commercial motives. His pious
Barians, filled with the Holy Spirit, planned the rescue before sailing
from Bari.

N   The fourth version is *Russian Account 53*. The Feast of Translation
was introduced into Russia from Constantinople as early as the year
1091.[36] According to this Russian account and also the Byzantine
Synaxarion: "This Translation took place in the year 1087 from the
Incarnation of the Son of God, under Alexis, emperor of the Greeks,
and the patriarch Nicholas, with our beloved Princes of Christ, Husvold of Kiev and Bladimir of Tchernigov his son, reigning in Russia."[37]
The Russian account is one of the oldest monuments of Russian
literature.[38] Its point of view is that the Translation was a victory of
the West over the oriental infidels and Turks. The Russians, who
evidently still communicated with their relatives who as varangians
had settled at Bari, felt that they shared in this direct manifestation of
God's interest. Their participation continued.[39] Until the twentieth-
century Revolution, the Russian government supported a church,
hospital, and hospice in Bari. Indeed, in 1896, the czar chose the
Basilica for the czarina's profession of Roman faith, followed by the
wedding. The czar donated the new pavement of variegated marble in
the crypt.[40]

The Russian author, whose name may have been Ephrem, relied
upon Archdeacon John:

> The Turks had destroyed the whole country from Antioch
> to Jerusalem, the towns and the villages; everywhere slaugh-
> ter and slavery reigned, pillage and arson; everywhere
> churches and monasteries were devastated. Lycia and the
> town of Myra, where the relics of Saint Nicholas reposed,
> had not been spared. At that moment the great thaumaturge
> appeared to an "orthodox" priest, who lived across the sea
> on the coast of Apulia at Bari, a Norman city, and ordered
> him to translate his body to that city . . . . That was a day of
> triumph. The city of Bari is in joy, and with her the whole
> world breathes forth its joy in hymns and holy song, for
> they observe the holy solemnity of the Translation of the

precious and miracle-working remains of Saint Nicholas the
Thaumaturge—that sun which radiates its refulgent beams
and hides them not, who from afar dissipates the shadows
of temptation and of misery from those who invoke him
with faith . . . . Like a star thy relics have crossed the sea
from East to West, the waves have been hallowed by their
passage, and the city of Bari is crowned with favors from
thy grace; for, through love for us, thou hast appeared to us
as a puissant and merciful thaumaturge . . . . Already his
miracles illuminate all countries; clearly it is not from Bari
that it is necessary to attain all favors, but from the heavenly
Jerusalem, where he shares the felicity of the angels, the
prophets, and the saints . . . . If now the land of Myra is
silent, the whole world, enlightened by the holy thaumaturge, invokes him with tuneful praise.

According to the author, the reliquary of the saint was discovered
and transported from East to West with the aid of the monks who
guarded the tomb and who, after having indicated the spot, followed
the relics to their destination:

Sanctified by thy perfect life, thou hast shown thyself high
among the saints of God, strengthened by Him; thou hast
silenced the heretics, thy Translation is a splendid feast
which glorifies the Christ of God . . . . O father, pastor of
the flock of Christ, thou hast been sent amongst the foreign
ewes in a land of Latin tongue; make thou all to marvel by
thy miracles and lead them happily to Christ. Beseech Him
incessantly in our name . . . . Saint Nicholas heals everyone,
as much in Lycia as in the Latin land, and he extends his
benevolence to the confines of Russia . . . . He has allowed
his body to depart for Bari that he may heap his favors upon
us.

The account ends with the dedication of the Basilica in 1089 by
Urban II, whom the author calls "Germain." Since Prince Husvold
died in 1093, the author must have written within the four years,
1089 - 1093.

Comments on the Documents

Remarkably, the names of all participants in the adventure have come down to us in a list brilliantly reconstructed by Monsignor Nitti.[41] Archbishop Elias had rewarded them all with perquisites for self and heirs, such as burial place next to the wall of the Basilica, pew for man and wife, clerical appointment in the college without fee if desired at regular stipend, full support as pensioner on quitting secular habit.[42] In the year 1105, Leo Pilillus sold his rights for fifty *solidi michalati,* claiming pressure of extreme poverty. With this document as a basis, Monsignor Nitti was able from all surviving evidence to authenticate sixty-two names of holders of these veterans' preferences, extant in a census copied in the second half of the twelfth century. (There are other extant twelfth-century lists, more or less in agreement.) About half of the rights issued eventually reverted or were bought in by the college.

I have mentioned Gregory the Great's letter to the Roman empress Constantia, which fully describes how a saint cooperates or negates men's actions in translation. The examples of both are innumerable.[43] In this instance, though we may grant that tombs lose their identity as soon as man's memory fails or inscriptions dim, and more than one saint has thereby taken on another's body, N's tomb in the popular pilgrimage shrine at Myra could hardly have been unidentifiable. But life follows art, and if the sailors were not actually puzzled, in conformity with legend, then even so honest a reporter as Nicephorus must make them so. How else than by such complexity can ancient bones be authenticated for the future? According to Gregory of Tours (6th cent.), to tell which tomb was Saint Valerius's, the inquirers placed a flagon of wine on the two possible tombs; the next day one flagon was nearly dry, the other overflowing. The inquirers felt that God through His saint had answered their question, though Gregory did not bother to tell us whether empty or full was the answer. For saints who refused cooperation a hagiological formula developed: *feretrum fit immobile* (he makes his bier immovable).[44]

The incident in *Nicephorus* 50 of the sailors' pilfering the relics is one of the most frequently employed common places, according to Delehaye, *un lieu commun légendaire des plus usités,*[45] doubtless developed to discourage multiplication of relics; if a saint allows no pilfering, then all duplicates are fake. A monk of N Angers, according to Orderic, stole the arm of N at Bari.[46] It had been encased in a silver reliquary which, when carried in procession, served to bless the people. But N exposed his theft and he had to return it. Such stories are countless. Nevertheless we shall encounter innumerable efficacious relics of N spread through western Europe after the Translation (not counting the phials of myrrh); they were subject to challenge and defense.

When a legend emphasizes a part of the body, the emphasis inevitably stimulates multiplication of that part. A nineteenth-century census of relics revealed the existence of more than thirty heads of John the Baptist. The large number of N's teeth scattered about doubtless goes back to John's report: "All the crew held out the particles they had taken from the body. A man called Romoaldus held out two teeth and a number of small particles of the body." But even earlier in his account, *John the Archdeacon 51* related a traditional tale. When the emperor's man, dispatched to Myra to take away the body, found that he could not do so, he entreated N for some small token:

> When the deacon of the church extracted the sacred liquor from the urn, as he was accustomed to do, one tooth came out too. The emissary snatched the tooth, gave thanks to God and to His servant Nicholas, and began to plant numerous kisses upon the relic. Then he enclosed it in a small gold box and placed the box upon the church altar. After he had gazed upon it for a while, he noticed that a large quantity of oil was trickling out of the box, so he wrapped the box in his cloak, thinking by that means to prevent more oil from dripping out. But in vain. The more tightly he bound it up, the more oil dripped out from the drenched cloak. He was in despair since he was not able to hide the box as he had hoped. Consequently he recognized God's presence in the act. The blessed Nicholas himself is said to have appeared to him in a dream and, holding the tooth before him in his hands, to have said, "Behold, I granted your wish. But you cannot take the tooth away with you as you wanted, because I do not permit even the smallest portion of my body to be

N⸸

separated from the rest." When the emissary awakened and grasped the fact that he had been dreaming,
he could not find the tooth. We have found this noted in
Greek volumes and prefixed it to our account to show that
through all these centuries the Omnipotent Lord never
allowed the body of His servant to be moved.[47]

The twelfth-century trouvère Wace set this incident to Romance
octosyllabics (lines 1377 - 1484).[48] The Norman historian Orderic concluded his account with additional tales, one about William of Pantoul's securing a tooth for the monastic cell at Noyon.[49] Caesarius of
Heisterbach tells of some covetous priests who obtained N's tooth
from the monks of Brauweiler; they carried it around the land,
milking the populace, until the indignant N broke the crystal of the
reliquary.[50] The Brauweiler monks resolved never to let the tooth
wander again. Despite these precautionary tales there were plenty of
N's teeth in circulation: my informal count totals seventeen teeth
separated from bodies. Some of these were sent from Constantinople
in the Sack of the Fourth Crusade, one to Corbie and one to Mont
Saint-Quentin.[51] Fingers were nearly as common because of
Nicephorus's remarks: one taken from Santa Sophia and sent to
Halberstadt, one to Toulouse, one to Soissons, one to Saint-Vincent-
au-Bois.

V THE BASILICA AND CULT AT BARI

The N cult burgeoned inside and outside Bari.[1] Nicholas had been a
common name in southern Italy since the ninth century,[2] but after the
Translation the number of citizens named Nicholas rose sharply—
more numerous than Peters, Pauls, or Benedicts.[3] In a deed of 1096 of
Duke Roger I, over 115 peasants (*villani*) recorded were named
Nicholas.[4] Meisen says that there were more than 200 N churches,
chapels, and convents in Norman Italy built before 1500.[5] After 1130
N's effigy graced the coins of Roger II.[6]

Elias emerges from the Translation as the strong character. Once a
monk of La Cava, he had been imported to Bari as the abbot of Saint
Benedict's. He seems to have enlisted the confidence of all parties,
especially that of Bohemond. Elias, *Account 54*, wrote in 1089: "I
agreed to supervise the construction of a church dedicated to the

honor of blessed Nicholas in the court which once was that of the civil governor. This church by the will of God I began . . . . Not long thereafter Boamund, Lord of Bari, and all the inhabitants of Bari, sent legates to the Apostolic Urban of the City of Rome, asking him to come to Bari and transfer and entomb the body of the most holy Nicholas, which had not been suitably deposed, within the martyrium in which he is now seen to rest. Consequently that venerable pope came and honorably and reverently interred the holy relics."[7] Elias's own tomb, with epitaph, can now be seen in that basilica, and his abbatial baton is in the treasury.[8] A letter of Pope Urban reports and authenticates the whole procedure, which included consecration of Elias as archbishop. The letter stipulates the feasts at which Elias is to wear the papal pallium; 6 December (N Day) and 9 May (Translation Day) are both included.

Elias's epitaph testifies that in designing and building the basilica he was the driving force. In 1087 Bari was under the rule of Bohemond's younger half-brother, Roger Prince of Apulia, whom Guiscard had put over Bohemond.[9] In June Roger gave Archbishop Ursus the catapan's court with entitlements to build N's church, but under terms suitable to the sailors, free from all episcopal jurisdiction and under direct protection of the prince.[10] Roger gave personal gifts to the basilica thereafter. Elias held two offices—archbishop, and abbot of the basilica—but the offices were never regarded as one. At his death in 1105, Abbot Eustachius of Saint Benedict's succeeded to both, but separately. On 18 November 1105, Pope Paschalis II confirmed all the independent liberties of the basilica.[11] After Eustachius's abbacy ended, a regular college of canons responsible only to Rome and headed by a rector was formed to assume full responsibility for N's shrine.[12]

Archbishop Ursus was not the only magnate who was caught off balance by the Translation. So was the pope. At that moment the papacy was in ebb. Before Gregory VII died (25 May 1085) he named three possible successors, but the southern Italians would have none of them. Nearly two years later the pressured cardinals, surrounded by Cencius the Roman consul, Prince Jordan of Capua, and Duke Roger, designated Abbot Desiderius of Monte Cassino as Pope Victor III. It took that reluctant and ineffective pope forty days to reach Rome. There he was consecrated on 9 May 1087 by Odo, cardinal-bishop of Ostia, one of the three named by Gregory VII. As the primary historian, Peter of Monte Cassino took the pains to note that was the day that N's relics arrived in Bari.[13] Odo was shortly to become Pope Urban II.

Hád a strong pope like Nicholas II or Urban II been in office in 1087 and had Archbishop Ursus been in Bari when the ship arrived from Myra, the cult might have been somewhat different. The relics of the chastener of emperors, the representative of papacy and of secular episcopacy, would have been housed in the cathedral—a pillar of the Visible Church and Petrine episcopacy. Instead, N's basilican monument and tomb, erected but a short distance away from the cathedral as a separated convent, expressed the caprice and disorder of the Norman horsemen and maritime traders rather than the stability of the establishment.

Gifts and grants flowed in immediately, of course.[14] Three small churches included in the catapan's curia were among the buildings razed to make room for the new basilica, which is unchanged in basic structure today, though inside it has undergone renovations and restorations.[15] Pope Urban II consecrated it on 9 May 1089, Translation Day. Urban consecrated a complete crypt. The basilica was roofed before Elias died.[16] One reason for the later renovations is the pilfering of souvenirs.[17] N himself is said to have changed one pillar from wood to iron because relic hunters had fragmented it, as the True Cross was fragmented.[18]

The emphasis of Greek authors of Lives upon N as light spreader to the world is carried out by sculpture on the facade. A human figure mounted on a chariot with four horses holds in one hand a sun and moon. The other hand holds a torch. At Saint Mark's, Venice, the figure of Perseverance holds the sun and moon in one hand.[19] Just at this moment the papal partisans were promulgating their exceptionally effective image of the Church as sun and the Empire as moon.[20] According to common belief, it was an image coined by Pope Gregory VII (Hildebrand). At all events, the N who holds in one hand both sun and moon is the N of *Stratilates 3*, who holds together both Church and State.

As at Angers, the powers at Bari seem to have had doubts about the efficacy of the papal consecration. Is it a sign of waywardness that N's shrines were apt to be reconsecrated with change of power? On 22

June 1197, Bishop Conrad of Hildesheim reconsecrated the basilica in the presence of numerous troops of German Crusaders. He was the chancellor and right hand of Emperor Henry VI. At the moment all the ports of Apulia and Sicily were crowded with transports for the Fourth Crusade. On the previous 20 March Conrad had signed at Barletta a charter of exemptions for the church. The consecration is commemorated by an inscribed plaque, still to the right of the main door, which states that "many prelates of Apulia and Germany, five archbishops, twenty-eight bishops, seven abbots, a host of clergy, and a countless multitude of Germans and diverse races" were present.[21] Neither party, emperors or popes, diminished their cult of N. Frederick II called the basilica *nostra specialis capella;* in 1228 he had led forty galleys of Crusaders along the Lycian coast, stopping the night at Patara "in which was born the Confessor of the Lord," and Myra. The year before his great defection, Manfred ordered that sixty pounds of wax for candles for Translation Day be paid out of customs income of the port.[22] On 15 April 1296 King Charles II of Anjou made noteworthy gifts "for adding to and enlarging the church."[23]

The altar of the crypt, once covered in silver by King Urosius of Serbia, is now protected by an impermeable wall and metal grill. Pope Nicholas IV was instrumental in drawing King Urosius from schism into the Roman orbit, though the formal change of faith took place under a later pope. In 1318, while battling against King Charles of Hungary, he had invoked and received N's aid. In consequence, in 1319 he contracted with two Byzantine artists then working in Bari to cover the whole altar of the crypt and the vault above it with silver. The vault thus formed a baldachin. The whole was meant to rival the famous *pala d'oro* of Saint Mark's at Venice. The silver icon which was part of the contract is now preserved in the treasury. In 1346 Urosius's nephew confirmed a perpetual gift of wax for that altar.[24]

The flow of *Myrrh 18* continued without diminution at Bari. Of course it was a vital element in increasing N's popularity. Already early in the twelfth century Honorius of Autun was retelling *Magnentius 49,* but with Bari rather than Myra as the mise en scène.[25] Pope Clement V issued a bull (26 July 1306) encouraging "those who desire to go to the Church of Blessed Nicholas of Bari, Confessor, in which the body of the blessed Nicholas, Confessor, venerably rests, and to which because of the distillation of liquor which unceasingly emanates, as is piously believed, from the bones of that most glorious confessor, there should be a great concourse of people from different parts of the world, to attend with due honors, . . . etc."[26] Indeed, the flow at times reached staggering amounts. In the sixteenth century a rich Flemish pilgrim, Georges Languerant, reported that he had returned from Bari with three phials—but his companion received twelve from the archbishop.[27]

Nicolas de Bralion (1646) was the first who, under the impact of the Counterreformation and the new science, issued a "controlled" report of the flow.[28] Thereafter no half-century and usually no decade passed without a "scientific" inquiry regarding its authenticity, chemistry, and remedial power. Monsignor Barbier de Montault (*Myrrh at Bari* 55) described the nineteenth-century procedures for extracting it:

N⚔ Four canons appointed as *custodes* appear each morning to collect the manna. They chant a Collect, then *De profundis*. Prayer for the sailors of the Translation. One canon opens the silver shutters of the altar. He reclines on the front step of the altar and lowers into the sarcophagus a silver chain with a sponge and candle attached. When the sponge has absorbed the liquor, the canon draws it up and squeezes its content into a silver bowl. The operation is continued from 7 to 9 A.M., the moment when the worshipers are allowed to enter the crypt, which closes at noon. When the bowl is full, the canons empty it into a square strainer in white marble. The strainer is needed to catch pieces of bone which sometimes appear. Several ounces of the filtered myrrh, kept in large white glass jars, are given to each pilgrim, who comes with a flat phial with effigy of N in Eastern garb, sold by the merchants of Bari. The church has a collection of phials going back three centuries; in them the myrrh varies in color and sometimes has a deposit or vegetation that might be algae.[29]

The pilgrimage route to Bari rivaled the equally recent route to Compostella.[30] In competition is born prosperity, and the new rage for pilgrimage coincided with the dramatic rise in Western prosperity. Cluniac monks were the primary agents for Compostella; the

Norman network so acted for Bari. It is unnecessary to document the notoriety from the host of surviving notices. At Cambrai in the year 1090, when a priory and oratory were dedicated to Holy Trinity and N, it was written that "the incredible tales attendant on his recent Translation have by now been popularized throughout the globe." On Pentecost 1137, Pope Innocent II celebrated Mass there with Emperor Lothair III and Bernard of Clairvaux.

In recent times the number of spirituals active under the prior is fixed at one hundred: forty-two canons, twenty-eight of the middle, and thirty of the lower orders.[31] The canons of the basilica operated a "German House" (domus teutonicorum) outside Barletta. The shrine of Saint Michael on Monte Gargano was a favored station on the route.[32] The Life of Saint Stephen of Thiers tells how his father, the Viscount of Thiers, took him as a boy of twelve on pilgrimage to Bari.[33] The story is unhistorical, but does indicate that a hundred years after the Translation the route to Bari was regarded as appropriate, physically and spiritually, for such a father and son. Famous pilgrims to Apulia who died and were buried in a shrine of their devotion intensified the veneration for that pilgrimage resort.[34]

Internal as well as external rivalry was constant. Trani, a suffragan diocese, in 1094 acquired its own Saint Nicholas, protégé of N, called also Saint Peregrinus.[35] According to his legend, he was a poor illiterate shepherd boy of Achaia who formed a special veneration for the Kyrie eleison. He was forever persecuted for his stupidity. At thirteen he entered the abbey of Styros, which he left on the inspiration of the Lord at the age of seventeen, to make his way to southern Italy. According to one version, he crossed the Adriatic on the back of a dolphin; hence he became a patron of sailors. In Italy his cultivated witlessness and humility and his gift for miracles stimulated excesses of adoration and persecution. On the Saturday after Ascension Day, 20 May 1094, he entered Trani bearing the cross. As usual the children, whom he treated to fruit bought with alms, gathered around him, and he exhorted them to chant the Kyrie in Greek after him. Bishop Bisanius, who arrived to question him, promised him haven for a time but, after striking up a cult especially virulent among the children, he died from the results of flagellation of the scorners and his own excessive asceticism.[36]

Almost at once the fervor he had generated was diverted to political use. In 1099, Pope Urban II held a last council in his lifelong effort to end the Great Schism. One hundred and fifty bishops assembled at Rome in the basilica of Saint Peter. According to Ruinart,[37] the business of greatest moment was canonization of Nicolaus Peregrinus, a dolphin-borne saint who might manifest the one Holy Spirit Who spoke in tongues to Greeks and Latins across the Adriatic Sea.[38] Bishop Bisanius was advocate, reciting an extensive list of miracles.[39] The pope was easily convinced, for the Greek Pilgrim had stirred the imaginations of the Greek colonists in Italy and might well stir the Greeks at home. Then he granted canonization.[40] The relics of Nicholas Pilgrim lie in the crypt at Trani, and the legend is represented on the bronze doors of that superb cathedral by the sea.[41] Indeed, the renowned Byzantine-Romanesque cathedrals of these Apulian towns (Bitonto, Molfetta, Barletta, Altamura), which resulted from the affluence of this Norman period, are all in some way monuments to the cult of N.[42]

A more overt rivalry was Benevento's, where an N church had existed long before the Translation. Before the year 1096, someone composed there *The Advent of Saint Nicholas to Benevento*,[43] with the purpose of showing that though Bari possessed the body, N worked his miracles primarily in Benevento. Moreover, "Bari is an unmerciful place, without water, lacking wine, and short of bread," whereas Benevento has an abundance of bread, all the wine one can drink, plenty of meat, a proper scorn of fish, the juiciest fruit, and an unfailing abundance of water.[44]

The rivalry involved many saints of other names, but I will cite only one, Saint Mennas of Samnium, not the one whose legend so often crosses N's.[45] In 1094, Count Robert of Caiazzo, near Capua, discovered Mennas's body on Mount Taburnus and translated it to Caiazzo. Leo Marsicanus of Monte Cassino was commissioned to write the account, to which the historian Peter later appended miracle tales. One of these tales tells of a Lombard woman with a demented son whom she took to N at Bari. As she slept, prostrated by prayer and tears, before the altar, a man in white appeared to her, chiding her for wasting her time when her son could be cured by Saint Mennas. She went up Mount Taburnus, to Sant' Agata di' Goti, only to find the relics translated. Despite their fatigue, they hurried on to Caiazzo where, even before reaching the shrine, as they came within the gates, her son was restored to sound mind.[46]

And of course the great rival, Venice, failed in 1087. It found by the end of the century that even Saint Mark was not alone sufficient, that Bari had indeed stolen a march on it. As I have noted, the Lido had long been Nicholas's Isle because of the N abbey existing there, at least before 1053. A monk of that abbey shortly after 1116 composed a *History of the Translation of Great Nicholas, Glorious for His Miracles on Land and Sea, and of His Uncle, Another Nicholas, and of the Precious Martyr Theodore,* from the city of Myra to the monastery of Saint Nicholas on the Lido of Venice.[47] On the tomb of "Great Nicholas" is inscribed: *Hic requiescat magnus episcopus Nicolaus, terra marique miraculis gloriosus.* The *History,* a patent steal from Nicephorus and John, recounts the finding of the relics at Myra in the year 1100 by Venetians returning from the Crusade. *The Brief Annals of Venice* records the event for the year A.D. 1096. Stealing relics had become a Venetian habit which some French writers have called *une dévotion des corsaires.*

The Fourth Crusaders stood in the presence of N at Bari while Bishop Conrad reconsecrated the basilica, but those who went from Venice had even closer contact. Since they had paid in advance only a small fraction of the 85,000 silver marks owed for passage, the doge Henri Dandolo interned them on the island of Saint-Nicolas-du-Lido. To work off their debt they first crusaded against a Christian people—the town of Zara in Dalmatia, which the doge coveted.[48]

The Venetians have sporadically tried to make the *History* stick, publishing "true accounts" in 1698, 1709, etc.[49] But a modern critic remarks, "Pious Venetians who have made a vow sometimes give the saint of Bari the benefit of the doubt by repeating at his tomb the devotions they have already paid at the church on the Lido. I have never heard of a man of Bari returning the compliment." At all events, all occasions do inform in favor of N; for Meisen lists some sixty sanctuaries in northern Italy which partake of this particular light from Venice.[50]

VI POPE URBAN II

In time, Odo became Pope Urban II. He was a Cluniac monk of noble blood. The worldly N is not likely to have been in his devotions at

Cluny, which had reluctantly accepted the N liturgy, but not more. Late in life when Urban issued a privilege for Cluny,[1] he listed more than fifty Cluniac churches and priories, not one of them dedicated to N. But when he reached Rome, as a member of Hildebrand's party, N began to become a force in his life.

He was elected pope in March 1088 but could not enter Rome for more than a year.[2] The city and the Lateran were held by the emperor and his antipope, Clement III, who was archbishop of Ravenna. Clement precariously held onto his spurious title until he died—a year after Urban. Because Urban was seldom safe in his own see, he traveled more often and more extensively than even Leo IX; and N, patron of travelers, was ever at his side. In a temperate way he carried through what Gregory VII's abrasiveness could never effect. Nevertheless, he was not soft. At one same moment he held the three most powerful secular rulers of the West outside the communion: Emperor Henry IV, King Philip of France, and King William II of England.

Urban first entered Rome 3 July 1089, taking the city and his opponents rather by surprise, and thereafter holding enough of the city to be regarded as its head. Yet within a month he found it safer to live at Capua, while he knitted together his secular support, consisting in the South of the Normans, especially Roger I of Sicily, and in the North of Countess Matilda of Tuscany—she who married Welf V of Bavaria in August of that year, thereby inaugurating the parties of Guelfs and Ghibellines. At Capua he received an invitation of Roger of Apulia, pressured by Bohemond, to come to Bari to consecrate N in his new tomb.[3] At a council at Melfi 10 - 15 September, he tied together political loose ends. After the pattern of Nicholas II, he exchanged with the Norman leaders homage for legitimacy, endowing Guiscard's son Roger with the title of Duke in the presence of the excluded older son Bohemond, who bided his time as Lord of Taranto. Then they all moved on to Bari. That city saw Urban near the beginning and again near the end of his papal career.

We can imagine that the journey to Bari suited Urban's already established aims. If one can find consistency in the life of any ruler, we find it in Urban's desire, with which he died, to heal the schism of Eastern and Western churches.[4] Many attempts had vainly been made since that day in 1054 when the legates of an already deceased Leo IX excommunicated the patriarch and the emperor anathematized the pope. In 1073 the emperor had promised Pope Gregory VII a reunion of churches in exchange for help against his enemies (including the Normans). Gregory wanted to lead an army of fifty thousand personally to Michael's rescue; but the existing papal federation with the Normans killed that initiative. Apulia, the last Italian stronghold of Byzantium to fall, still cultivated its Greek aristocracy. Now it was the new home for that saint of universal and especially oriental veneration, N. Who better to invoke for healing the wounds of a dissevered Church?

On 30 September Urban ordained Abbot Elias as archbishop of Bari in the cathedral, explaining in his Letter of Privilege[5] that he had violated all tradition in the Church by consecrating an archbishop in his own see, "in reverence for blessed Nicholas, against the custom of the Roman and Apostolic Church." He wrote of his "excessive love for the blessed confessor Nicholas." The next day he moved over to N's independent new basilica, for which the crypt was complete, and blessed the new resting place, again consecrating Elias, this time as abbot of the basilica. He decreed that 9 May should be a major feast for Bari and approved it as a feast for all christendom.[6] Elias proved a faithful servant; he was, for example, among the prelates present at Clermont.[7]

Urban was back in Rome for Christmas. However, Clement's troops still held Angel Castle, and in 1092 he was strong enough to convene a council in the city. Urban gained the Lateran, but during most of the five years he operated from safe havens outside Rome. In the main, like other reforming popes, he drew his support from feudal barons and abbots, against kings and prelates. In his extant writings[8] he quoted Pope Nicholas I more than he quoted Gregory the Great or Gregory VII or any other prelate.

With Rome nominally secure, Urban started north, and on 1 March 1095 held council at Piacenza.[9] According to reliable estimate, more than four thousand clergy and three thousand laity were in attendance from Italy, Burgundy, France, and Germany.[10] Here probably the floating ideas congealed which patterned the Crusade, though doubtless that council's primary purpose was the reordering of the German imperial church. For years Urban had been in the presence of the Translation doctrine of Nicephorus, that "God wills it." God had rescued the Byzantine N from the Turks through the agency of the

Latins. For God such things were possible. The hearts of Byzantium and even far Russia had beat in concord with the Italian adventurers. Could not a similar venture be launched for the sake of unity in the Church?

At Piacenza he received ambassadors from Emperor Alexius, asking for troops to recover that part of christendom lost to the Turks. He listened to harrowing tales of Christian hardship. The news of the campaign against the infidels in Spain, to which Cluny had dedicated its special talents and activity, was promise of glory to come. Toledo had fallen in 1085, Valencia 1092, Lisbon 1093. Neither Alexius nor Urban as yet thought in an image of Crusade, but rather of rescue of faithful sufferers. Writes Augustin Fliche: "It was much less a question of holy war than of bringing aid to Eastern brethren. The thought of succor for Christian communities certainly seems to have dominated Urban II—the concept of holy war, in our opinion, being born of the Crusade rather than engendering it."[11] Urban felt the pathos of deserted Hagar and Ishmael; the Turks were benighted, but they were creatures of God and not actively satanic. At the moment N's rescue of *Basileos 22* and the *Son of Getron 46* from the Hagarenes is a most prominent theme among N stories.

It was a full six months from Piacenza to Clermont:[12] Cremona, Milan (6 - 26 May), Asti (27 June), Saint Nicholas Pass, Valence (5 August), LePuy, the see of bishop Adhémar (15 August), Tarascon (where he blessed the excavations for a new N convent 11 September),[13] Saint-Gilles, base for Duke Raymond IV (18 August - 1 September),[14] Avignon, Lyons, Macon, and home to Cluny on 25 October to relax in the congeniality of brotherhood before the great French Council opened at Clermont 18 November.[15] At every station he spread the doctrine of reunion of East and West, and we must believe that the translated N was a living image. To this day in Arles, the urchins who cadge pennies in the street sing:

> *Caritate, Senyora, caritate si os plau!*
>> Alms, Signora, alms please!
> *Que venim de Roma,*
>> For us who come from Rome,
> *I portem Corona*
>> Bringing the *Corona*

De Sant Nicolau!
Of Saint Nicholas![16]

Because of the three-way meaning of *Corona* (glory, coin, clerical tonsure) the word does not yield to translation. Doubtless all three were meant if that chant was a product of Urban's day. *Corona* expresses Crusade. These six months were a gestation period before the God who willed N's Translation west should will the flower of Europe east.

The most conservative historians guess that Urban faced at least twelve archbishops, eighty bishops, ninety or more abbots, and un-counted priests and laymen at Clermont; but Bréhier says forty arch-bishops, two hundred and fifty bishops, and four hundred abbots, almost entirely French, and Spanish from the recovered lands.[17] The only English representative was Anselm's legate Boso. A first order of business was a decision about the marital affairs of King Philip I. Bishop Ivo of Chartres had brought suit on behalf of Fulk Rechin, Count of Anjou, nephew of Geoffrey Martel and like him to be buried in Saint-Nicolas d'Angers. He was the aggrieved husband because Philip had bigamously married his wife Bertrada and had been ex-communicated in 1094. That sentence was now renewed, as it was again in 1097 and 1101.[18]

Urban's speech of the last day, preaching the Crusade, is variously reported, and the reports do not agree. If we can believe Robert the Monk, who claimed to have been present at the speech,[19] Urban talked like a knight-errant: "Enter upon the road to the Holy Sepulcher; wrest that land from the wicked race, and subject it to yourselves. That land which Scripture says 'floweth with milk and honey' was given by God into the possession of the children of Israel . . . . From you especially she asks succor, because, as we have already said, God has conferred upon you above all nations great glory in arms . . . . When an armed attack is made upon the enemy, let this one cry be raised by all the soldiers of God: 'It is the will of God! It is the will of God!' " About this time Urban wrote to Godefrid, bishop of Lucania:[20] "We do not regard men as homicides when, in their zealous fervor for the Catholic Mother against the excommunicate, they may happen to butcher some of them." Intolerance was growing with empurpled speech.

N Urban made his way to Angers in February,[21] ostensibly to preach the Crusade.[22] On the 10th he rededicated the sanctuary in Black Fulk's N abbey. He decreed, as confirmed in his *Letter of Privilege 56,*[23] issued 14 February, that a fair should be held every year at that season at Saint-Nicolas; we may imagine that it was meant to be a Mardi Gras. One-seventh of their penance was to be commuted for all who attended. He decreed perpetual possession of its holdings, which were now remarkable.[24] For example, Matilda, daughter of King Henry I of England, who had married Geoffrey Plantagenet, thereby initiating the Angevin line of English kings, endowed N d'Angers with very substantial English holdings, scattered through the countryside.[25] They intensified the cult of N in midland England. Urban's Privilege can be compared with a Bull of Pope Eugenius III (A.D. 1145 - 1153) which, in specifying many continental holdings placed under papal protection, shows how fast the abbey was becoming wealthy.

With Urban at the dedication were the most influential of the prelates who opposed King Philip: Hugh of Lyons, Amatus of Bordeaux, Ivo of Chartres, Hoel of Le Mans, Walter of Albi, Geoffrey of Angers, Bruno of Segni, as well as three cardinals, Teuthio, Albertus, and Rangerius, and *magna senatus Romani pars.*[26] They were spellbound by a sermon of Robert d'Arbrissel, a local zealot who held offices at Rennes and Angers and who had founded the abbey of La Roë.[27] On the spot Urban gave him the unique title of "Apostolic Preacher," or wandering preacher—a precedent for the Dominican Order.[28] This act set Robert on the path to fame, and like Damian he became a notorious pied piper. Rich and poor, repentent and sinners, noble dames, mothers with children in arms followed him from place to place while he made the word *pitié* the keystone of the French language. The wayfaring of these long-haired children of God was marked by some violence, and Robert settled them in a wilderness commune beside the spring of Evraldus (Fontevrault), which became famous for many reasons, perhaps foremost as tomb for Henry II and Eleanor of Aquitaine.[29] Within a generation Hildebert, preeminent poet and bishop of Le Mans, spoke from the pulpit of N d'Angers:

> Every Christian should venerate this church, the possessor
> of memorials of that most precious confessor, blessed and
> venerable Saint Nicholas. He began to serve God from

babyhood when against the very law of nature he fasted at the breast [*Lactation 11*]. Furthermore this church has a special prerogative for your due reverence and honor. You should especially serve it because Blessed Peter through his vicar, the pope of the Roman Church, visited it, sanctified it, dedicated it, and granted everlasting forgiveness to those who each year attend the anniversary of its dedication. Consider, dearest brothers; consider, believers, the having of saints of God as intercessors! And especially the precious confessor Nicholas, that by his merits you may merit the everlasting home, by the assent of Our Lord Jesus Christ.[30]

Not Urban's piety for N, intense though it might be, but pure politics was responsible for this rededication of Saint-Nicolas d'Angers. His own secretary Milo, who had once been a monk at Saint-Aubin d'Angers, had persuaded him to consecrate that latter abbey. But the brothers of that abbey did not share Milo's enthusiasm for the pope and would have none of it.[31] There were vicious politics involved: the pope was not universally respected, especially among French royalists. The chronicler of Saint-Serge, another local abbey, took occasion to remark how famine seemed to follow in Urban's wake, and the Chronicle of Angers noted "a fearful eclipse" on 11 February, when he was still in town.[32] Rejected by Saint-Aubin, the Pope (or Milo) turned to Saint-Nicolas. The current Count Fulk, whose case had been favorably acted on at Clermont, then gave a large gift to Saint-Nicolas. Yet the fraternity at Saint-Aubin contended for a portion of that gift, *Forestae Catiae,* as belonging to them.[33] The dispute resulted in litigation.

Saint-Nicolas d'Angers continued to spread the cult of N. A Life of N, written by Joel of Le Mans, consists largely of accounts of local miracles. It inspired a steady but not dramatic flow of pilgrims from central France. And some familial ties with cultists elsewhere were maintained. When, on 13 July 1875, Barbier de Montault, prélat de la Maison de Sa Sainteté, together with the Chapter of the N basilica at Bari, opened the casket of cedar planks which the sailors of the translation had made, he sent fragments of the planks (together with four ampules of myrrh) to Pope Pius IX for transmittal to Saint-Nicolas d'Angers.[34]

On 11 March, the chronicler of Tours states, "The pope himself sprinkled holy water on the Cemetery of Saint Nicholas, and at his command Archbishop Hugh of Lyons and Lord Cardinal Rangerius consecrated the cemetery, sprinkling holy water everywhere along the banks of the Loire up to the wooden cross which is above our mill," etc.[35] Then he made his way back to Rome, to direct what was now turning into the First Crusade. Though the documents of the French trip show him involved in the affairs of about twenty other N establishments,[36] N nevertheless ran a rather poor second to Saint Martin in France.[37]

On 3 October 1098, Urban convoked a council at Bari of 183 Latin and Greek bishops, still trying to bring schism to an end.[38] Now finally powerful enough to be able to choose where he would go, he chose the corpse of N as the point of union: *apud Barum ante corpus beati Nicolai.* Urban was making N an ecumenical symbol, invoking his miraculous powers to reunite East and West. As the sailors of the Translation auspiciously had found, N had himself chosen to move his visible members from East to West.[39]

Elias was still alive. Present at the council was Anselm, archbishop of Canterbury, who had come to seek the pope's aid against his king, William Rufus.[40] On the way to Bari, Anselm finished his epochal *Cur Deus Homo?*[41] At Urban's request he composed *De Processione Spiritus Sancti,*[42] with which he vainly hoped to convince the Byzantine theologians that the *Filioque* clause was not an intrusion in the Creed (a bone of contention between communions since Carolingian days).[43] According to Anselm's biographer, Eadmer, who was with him, Pope Urban said in the course of the council, "You have been sent here by God to rescue us with the truth."[44] Anselm was new to Bari, but not to N. There had been an active N cult at the abbey of Bec, where Anselm was abbot before an anonymous Life of N was composed there. When Anselm transferred to England in 1092, he found the English cult and liturgy as I have already described them. Anselm, before he left Bec, put together a long and extremely effusive prayer to N (*Anselm* 57).[45] He thought enough of it to send back from England for a copy,[46] of which this is a fragment:

N   So gross, so illimitable, are my derelictions that nothing can avail nor can my prayer be received without an intercessor.

I will implore one of the great servants of God, if God
might heed him in my behalf. I will call upon Nicholas, that
great confessor, whose name is glorified throughout the
globe. Nicholas! O if he would but hear me! You, that great
Nicholas! If God turns away from me, who will turn toward
me? If God hides His countenance from me, who unmasks
His to me? . . . Saint Nicholas, I pray Thee through him
who makes the whole world venerate Thy name: Do not
deny Thy help to the needy and suppliant. Why wouldst
thou, my lord, be invoked by everyone throughout the
world unless thou art advocate for every postulant? Why do
we hear on every lip, "My lord Saint Nicholas, my lord
Saint Nicholas, my mediator Saint Nicholas"? How could
thy name spread everywhere unless through that name some
mighty good might spread through the world? Thy renown
calls me to thee, thy works draw me to thy side.[47]

Herein he depicted N as a spiritual guide through Hell and Purgatory.
This may well be the seed of a later image of N as guide through
nether regions, an image that evolved into the *Vision of the Monk of
Eynsham 72,* to be treated below.[48]

The Bari chronicle reports that Archbishop Elias built for Pope
Urban II a marvelous golden throne in N basilica for the occasion of
this council.[49] The council, with its 183 bishops seated directly in
front of the tomb with its effusion of myrrh, lasted for eight days. The
English historian William of Malmesbury wrote of "the body of Saint
Nicholas thatched with stolls and pallia. The Apostolic Vicar mounted
a tribunal built upon the sepulcher."[50] On 30 May (Pentecost) 1137,
Pope Innocent II celebrated Mass there in the presence of the emperor, Lothair III.

Pope Urban II died 29 July 1099 "while staying at the home of
Peter Leo, next door to the Church of Saint Nicholas *in carcere
tulliano,*" the ancient church of N next door to the city prison mentioned above in chapter 2.[51]

VII BOHEMOND AND THE FIRST CRUSADE

Guiscard passed over his first wife's only son Marc (b. 1050 - 1058),
nicknamed Bohemond—leaving the duchy to the eldest son of his

217

Lombard second wife Sigelgaita, who is sometimes figured by historians as a valkyrie.[1] From Guiscard's Greek campaign Bohemond had acquired an Eastern inclination, and he was land-hungry. If he were blocked by his relatives in Italy, he could emulate the Turks and steal land from infidels. Meanwhile as Lord of Taranto he attended conclaves at his half-brother's side. Undoubtedly he lusted for Bari, the central port on the east, and in 1089 he effected an exchange of Cosenza for Bari with Roger.[2]

From the start, Bohemond had generously endowed N Basilica.[3] Elias could not have been so prosperous without him. Until 1089 most of the Norman rulers' grants to the basilica were co-signed by Sigelgaita and Roger, but there are reasons for believing that Bohemond drove many of them through. Though Roger officially asked Urban II to consecrate the basilica that year, the chroniclers tend to credit Bohemond, as we may too. After Bari became his, Bohemond appears in the charters as the great benevolent.[4] Throughout western Europe, the name Portus S. Nicolai often supplanted that of Bari, as in the Angevin Chronicle.[5]

There is an early hymn:

O beate Nicolae
Oh, our blessed Nicolaus,
Nos ad portum coeli trahe,
To the heavenly haven draw us
De maris angustiis . . . .
From the perils of the sea . . . .

which with a slight shift of words became a Crusaders' song:

O beate Nicolae,
Nos ad maris portum trahe
De mortis angustiis . . . .[6]

Despite the French dislike, if not fear, of the southern Normans, Apulia became the route of many of the French contingents of the First Crusade who were not logistically attached to the Danube route.[7] Consequently, all towns on the pilgrimage road to Bari were enriched by passing Crusaders. Indeed, chronicles of the Crusade (both Fulcher of Chartres and the Monk of Bec) record that the Portus S. Nicolai was regarded as a sufficiently pious end in itself—

sufficient for penance if the pilgrim could not or did not go to the Holy Land.[8]

There are historians both early (e.g., William of Malmesbury)[9] and late (e.g., Sir Francis Palgrave) who credit Bohemond with single-handedly plotting the whole Crusade. Certainly the Portus S. Nicolai had been thoroughly advertised to the pope and all his court as the proper staging place, and N as an insurance underwriter second only to Lloyds of London.[10] As Bohemond's modern biographer Yewdale says, the preaching of the Crusade disclosed new prospects to the ambitious and dissatisfied Bohemond. The chronicler Lupus says that a shower of meteors in April 1095, six months before Clermont, was seen throughout Apulia: "From that time on, the people of Gaul and indeed of all Italy too, began to proceed with their arms to the Sepulcher of the Lord, bearing on their right shoulders the sign of the Cross." This looks to be a direct outcome of the Council of Piacenza in March 1095.

Bohemond, occupied with consolidating his Italian gains and protecting his rear, waited until August 1096 at the siege of Amalfi to announce his taking the Cross. He followed his announcement by abandoning his part in the siege of Amalfi, leaving it to the two Rogers, but not until he had lured some notable portions of the ducal armies to take the Cross with him. Though an advance corps appeared on the Greek coast at once, Bohemond himself did not land with his main force until late in the year.[11] According to Urban's Letter 212, which may well be spurious, Bohemond led seven thousand "of the choicest knights of Italy." (Fulk of Anjou wrote in his chronicle that Bohemond's army was 30,000.) A fire which he set to a city gate in Constantinople threatened, wrote Anna Comnena, "the church built long ago by one of the emperors to the memory of Nicholas, the greatest saint in the hierarchy."[12] Almost certainly this was Saint Nicholas Blachernes, treated in chapter 1.

Pope Urban II must at all cost preserve his alliance with the Normans in the South. But the old Cluniac monk saw his salvation in a united France that as yet was not really aware that it existed as an entity. Urban's Council of Piacenza may have been primarily Germanic, but was international at all events. On the other hand, the Council of Clermont was remarkably French. The national feeling expressed later in the *Song of Roland*—"douce, belle France"—is anticipated in Urban's treatment there of the French as a nation. Nationalism, on the contrary, was never a part of N's personality; perhaps that is one reason why his cult was more intense among Normans, who were wandering knights, than anywhere else. There is much of Bohemond in his image. In France N is constantly seen in the mind's eye as a patron of merchants and scholars, children and lovers, jurists and fées—never as a saint of national aspiration. The same is true of other emergent nations of the west. Among territories, only Lorrain and Sicily invoked a patriotic N, and both failed in all national aspirations.

The French leaders of the Crusade, after Raymond of Saint-Gilles, Count of Toulouse, and Bishop Adhémar of Le Puy, were variously listed, but included Hugh the Great,[13] brother of King Philip, Duke Robert of Normandy, Count Robert of Flanders, Count Stephen of Blois, Godfrey of Bouillon Duke of Lorrain, and his brother Count Eustache of Bologne. According to Fulk's chronicle, "Many took the shorter route through Pannonia, but more still through the Portum Sancti Nicolai"; that is, they went from Apulia to Constantinople.[14] We know that Robert of Normandy and Stephen of Blois, after staging at Bari, sailed from Brindisi. Hugh went from Bari to Durazzo.[15] If on this chaotic movement of men, women, and children, camp followers and horses, supply trains and beggars, visionaries and fortune hunters, imperial troops and brigands, we can impose an unrealistic concept of four armies on the march (Provençaux under Raymond, Lotharingians under Godfrey, Flemish and Normans under Robert, Apulians under Bohemond), only the first came from a land where the cult of N was not the vogue.

They were all anticipated by Peter the Hermit, whose even more chaotic motley following arrived by the Danube many months before.[16] He had been a pilgrim to Jerusalem. The comparatively reliable historian William of Tyre states[17] that the patriarch of Jerusalem commissioned him to return by way of Rome to stir Pope Urban to action. At all events he appears to have landed at Bari and stayed at the N hospice erected by Elias and Bohemond, placing his crusading enterprise under N's protection. According to unreliable historians writing after the event,[18] he stimulated Bohemond to act as a rescuer of the Holy Land before he moved on to Berry,[19] where his presence is first reliably documented.[20]

Bohemond's seizure of Antioch as his own is a key point in the

Crusade, and fits his character.[21] At Antioch the True Lance was uncovered.[22] One Peter Bartholomew, under the inspiration of Saint Andrew, miraculously discovered it in the church of Saint Peter. Believers asserted that it brought a mighty victory over the Saracen Kerbogha; Raymond and his Provençaux, confident in its strength, pushed on toward Jerusalem. The other armies straggled after them in time. All but Bohemond and his Apulians, who remained in Syria to carve out a feudality.

Bohemond was the most adaptable of Normans. In seizing the territory he persuaded the leaders to adopt a bitter policy of terrorization of inhabitants, including threats of cannibalism.[23] Yet he established a most tolerant, though almost certainly most tax-ridden, new Latin state, adopting a policy of retaining the existing civil service of whatever race or creed.[24] Eventually the Greek patriarch of Antioch found it expedient to desert his see,[25] but otherwise the Greek, Latin, and Syriac clergy mingled freely in ritual and politics under the complacent patronage of N and his vicar Bohemond.[26] But Latin Jerusalem, where the French held sway, had a different history. Though Bohemond was for three years captive of the Turks, he never lost the loyalty of his subjects, doubtless because of his relaxed attitude toward inherited customs and beliefs.

He returned to Italy in 1105,[27] bringing the Turkish emir Kerbogha's tent as a gift to N Basilica. This does not show exclusive veneration, for he also brought two thorns from the crown of Christ, still bearing traces of Christ's blood, to the church at Canosa where later he was buried. Making his way to Rome, he elicited a new privilege for the N Basilica from Pope Paschal II, who declared its independence of every prelate except the pope himself.[28] Ostensibly to visit Saint Leonard's tomb at Limoges, but in fact to marry the daughter of King Philip, he moved on to France. After the marriage he went to Angers, where he visited the abbey of Saint Nicholas.[29] In September 1107 Bohemond, back home, heard Mass in the N Basilica and then mustered an army that the local chronicler called thirty-four thousand men to sail ostensibly for Antioch but really to attack Byzantium through Albania. The failure of that enterprise brought about the loss of all his power.[30] In 1108 he confirmed the possessions of N. In 1111 he died.[31]

Two of Bohemond's auxiliary ports were Brindisi and Otranto, both graced by N sanctuaries. I want to glance at the story of Otranto (San Nicolo di Casole), as told by Charles Diehl.[32] On a cliff that dominates the sea there is now only a little chapel with Greek inscriptions to N and to Saints Cosmas and Damian. Ravaged by the Turks in 1483, the peasants in Diehl's time (1886) used the chapel for a granary. The Basilean monastery of N was founded by a Greek monk Joseph in 1099 under, and doubtless with the help of, Bohemond. It quickly became "the foyer for classical studies" for the West. The monks operated a boarding school, rich library, active scriptorium, and scholarly institute. A century later they were still praying for the souls of Bohemond I, his wife, and son Bohemond II. A Nicholas was abbot 1153 - 1190: "Philosopher and diplomat, bibliophile and scholar, polemicist and statesman, he took an active part in the dissensions between Latins and Greeks. At the same time he worked to increase the splendor of his monastery. He collected previous MSS . . . like the *Typicon* and *Hypotyposis* preserved at Turin. Other libraries still possess testimony of his activity." The monks at Otranto kept close relations with the land of Basil. One monk, Luke, became the patriarch of Antioch. At least seven cells or priories of San Nicolo di Casole in Italy are known by name. Cardinal Bessarion (d. 1472), protector of Italian Greek convents, had the richest treasures of the abbey transported to Rome and later to Venice.

N had reached manhood—young manhood—seeking the bubble reputation. His active participation in the First Crusade and those to follow was in one sense but a continuation and fulfillment of his boyhood on the Christian-Moslem border. He emerged from the crusading era as the most successful of legends, despite the competition of such doughty legendaires, real or imaginary, as George, Louis, and Francis.

His image is anchored in the soil of the Levant in unpredictable ways. For example, though since the time of Peter the Hermit there had been several children's crusades, the model of young Stephen of Vendôme, who led a thousand children away to die in June 1212, inspired a rascal father and a ten-year-old child who called himself Nicholas to lead twenty thousand from the region of Cologne over the Alps toward Apulia and Bari. They starved and died throughout Italy, and "Nicholas" disappeared; but on the coast of the island of San Pietro, Pope Gregory IX erected a "Church of the New Innocents" to preserve young Nicholas's tale.[33] The Villehardouins built three N chapels in connection with their crusade.[34] Among N tales of shipwreck and rescue there is none so eloquent, so unforgettable, as that told of the party of Saint Louis˜by Joinville.[35] And in the Latin Kingdom of˙Jerusalem outside the walls of Acre, the Church of N was a favorite burial ground, where the bones of Count Philip of Flanders were venerated.[36] After Jerusalem fell, the King of Jerusalem was traditionally crowned in the "Church of N of the Latins" at Famagusta, on Cyprus (founded 1308).[37] So, for example, was King Peter de Lusignan, Count of Tripoli (A.D. 1372). The Chronicle of Makhairas records that the King of Cyprus in 1362 sent a fleet of fourteen ships to sack Myra "where Saint Nicholas was, and they besieged the Turks and by the help of God took the castle and ravaged and slaughtered as much as they could; and they took away also the picture of the great Nicholas and brought it to Famagusta and put it in the Church of Saint Nicholas of the Latins."[38]

But N suffered from his own success. The Crusades were the phenomenal product of anarchic feudalism. The followers of Bohemond, that Apulian ethnic conglomerate, carried in their minds images and legends not congruant with those of the new nationalists. N's companionship with the Bohemonds made him unacceptable to some other social circles.[39] And as the Western people in revulsion from crusading and the Turks turned their eyes away from the East, so did they start to shun an N with exotic Eastern habits. Nevertheless an anthology of vernacular songs which celebrate N's patronage of mariners gathered by Babudri from Balkan and Adriatic provinces suggests how deeply and widely N's crusading presence affected later centuries.[40]

To achieve dramatic impact, the Elizabethans shortened man's seven ages to five for their two hours' traffic of the stage. But the peak between rise and fall was still achieved at the midway point, as we have reached it now.

FIVE
ΩATURITY

And then the justice,
In fair round belly with good capon lined,
With eyes serene and beard of formal cut,
Full of wise saws and modern instances;
And so he plays his part.

Life, viewed as a tragedy, is an action serious, complete in itself, and of adequate magnitude. Tragedy has an apex—a point, no more—of no magnitude, movement, or interest, except that on it heroism turns from ascent to descent. He who has acquired a fair round belly has gained his figure, but lost his sense of direction.

Created half to rise, and half to fall;
Great lord of all things, yet a prey to all.[1]

Maturity is *ens,* not *esse*; it is a Dantesque heaven where a saint can merely glow. Hence this chapter is not a tale of action and consequently has little biography. It reduces itself to a listing under several headings of the substance that makes the sedentary, bellied justice. Later chapters will again narrate action, but decrescendo. "Let us," wrote Robert Ulich in an analogous work,[2] "acknowledge the artificiality of this procedure. If anything is a *Gestalt,* or a configuration, man is. Yet the discursive character of language does not allow us to represent in one comprehensive symbol the simultaneity of various factors, their oneness in variety, their independence and interdependence. We have to describe one quality after the other, though in reality there is no strict chronological sequence." At some point in every biography the organic subject is violently anatomized into topics, as if life were a card file.

The thirteenth to the sixteenth centuries marked N's maturity:

When a man's age and spirit have matured
He trades his lusts for high society,
Shining up honor's boots, fearing assent
To anything he soon might have to change.[3]

It seemed probable at that time that N had made no mistakes, though mistakes we see on looking backward. Those centuries were centuries of growth of towns, banking and commerce, exploitation and orientalizing, scholasticism and universities, Gothic art and theology, vernacular literature and song. Those were the centuries of taking stock, when newer, more worldly saints usurped the cults of the old: Becket at the expense of Benedict, Francis at the expense of Anthony.[4] But N had a universality that allowed him to survive both worlds. As an instance, in the year 1290, King Edward I ordered all Jews from England, and the Lombards moved in to take over the Jews' moneylending functions. They brought with them as a sign of their trade N's three golden moneybags (*Three Daughters 13*). In the past N had led the saints of Britain as a mariner and Crusader, but he was now equally capable as a banker.

I THE LITERARY LIFES

The important Lifes of N assembled or composed in the West before the thirteenth century were the standard Life by John the Deacon of Naples, two Lifes by Otloh of Saint Emmeram (Regensburg), an anonymous Life largely corrupted by adventures of Nicholas of Sion surviving in a Paris MS, and two Lifes that were really gatherings of local miracles, one by Joel of Le Mans, written for Angers,[5] and the other by a monk of Brauweiler.[6]

These Lifes established N's personality, but they needed reinterpretation for each new generation, for each generation rewrites history in its own image. The passing from feudal to bourgeois age, from abbeys to cathedrals, from schools to universities, from castles to cities, from the simplicity of barbarism to the complexity of humanism, allowed the adaptable N to reach his height; for he was the patron of rich men, poor men, vagrants, and thieves. The evidence is too abundant to be listed here: artifacts, reports, and Lifes. To cope with such overabundance, let us narrow our range. Already we have virtually deserted the Asian, Hellenic, and Slavic worlds. Now let us center in those provinces most obviously affected by returning Crusaders: Italy, the Rhineland and Low Countries, northern France, and Britain.

Nearly every diocese now had a thriving school and every diocesan library a copy of the Latin Life by John the Deacon, with Mediterra-

nean additions like *Iconia 34* and *Son of Getron 46.* Their calendars
marked N Day in red to indicate a major feast, quite usually an
Octave, when the Life of N would be read publicly. The need arose to
extend John's Life in order to supply lections for a full week. That
action alone would explain the rapid increase in the number of stories
we find appended to MSS.[7] Most of them make dull reading for us;
they are records of miraculous cures effected through the N relics in
the local shrine. They have no necessary place in this biography.

The mature, established N was no longer to be edified, that is,
built up as a model of Christian culture; he had acquired a full
momentum to which the force of artistic creation could add little if
anything. He was in fact the established culture, or that part of it
wherein he moved. He was now to be used, not developed. His name
had become a recommendation for almost any course of action that
ambitious authors might invoke him for. Among the more elaborate
of the new Lives was one composed by a monk of the abbey of Bec in
the year 1103.[8] Bec was a Norman center of learning where two
famous archbishops of Canterbury, Lanfranc and Anselm (who venerated N at Bari), studied and taught. Like Godehard, this Anglo-
Norman author at Bec emphasized N's patronage of scholars. Two
episodes show that the cult now embraced both scholars and infants.
The Thunderstorm 59 tells how the youngest of the scholars in the
dormitory quelled his fellows' panic by invoking N during a fearsome
storm—an extension of *Mariners 6.*[9] *The Infant Touch 60* tells how N
himself, at the age of *Lactation 11,* was momentarily set on the lap of a
halt and blind man and how his touch effected a cure.[10]

One aim of the anonymous Bec author was to control abuses in the
relic market. He tells of a man who took a wax impression of the Bari
key while the guard slept and stole *N's Arm 58,* enclosing it in a
jewel-encrusted gold capsule.[11] But as the thief fled he was paralyzed
until pursuers arrived to recover the arm. As is common with red-
letter bishop saints, N grew arms like hydra heads. The arm expresses
benediction. Another Bec story of the same arm has the thief, a monk,
immobilized and blinded as he flees along the Apulian shore. The
blinding power becalmed seven passing ships as well. The pursuing
duke of Bari and the bishop recovered the arm, and the monk spent
his life in penance.[12] The author writes:

No one could possibly doubt that what we say is true, for
the Lord can do whatever He wishes and however He
wishes to succor men. And the miracles of blessed Nicholas,
the glorious confessor of Christ, are always more marvelous
and exotic than the miracles of other saints . . . . Indeed, it
would be sheer stupidity and madness for anyone to commit
to writing anything regarding so glorious a confessor which
might not be true, since there would be still more important and remarkable truths about him left unsaid. Anyone
who might wish to tell them fully would scarcely be able to
find in common parlance enough, I do not say letters, but
words for the purpose.[13]

This was an open invitation to compose the grossest fables with N as
the protagonist. And so it came to be.

The earliest and most important of all the Lifes written in Britain is
anonymous.[14] The single surviving MS, now in London,[15] was once at
that Battle Abbey which William the Conqueror vowed to build if
victorious at Hastings. In 1067 he drew monks from Marmoutier-
les-Tours, on the Loire, to start it. The enigma of this MS has not yet
been solved. Within the single binding is a variety of material in
various hands and ages. One gathering, copied in one scribal hand,
seems to have originally comprised a single book of geography. But on
the flyleaves the same or a contemporary scribe copied a unique Latin
Life of N in 8 + 8 rhymed couplets. Some paleographers maintain that
this part of the codex was written before the Conquest, that is, before
Battle Abbey existed.[16] As already noted, the Conqueror owed his life
and therefore special fealty to N; perhaps this text was connected
with his personal cult. Twenty years after the formation of Battle
Abbey, its brotherhood established a priory at Exeter, dedicated to
N.[17] There is a tradition that the Conqueror was instrumental in its
establishment. At all events, the MS is known to have been at that
priory for at least a time shortly after its foundation.

In this Life is evidence again of N's unusual power of catching the
popular rhythm. Just as the N Liturgy 40 was full of tuneful melodies
and his legend fitted the crusading humor, so this Life was composed
in popular new verse forms.[18] Most of its episodes were traditional

because the author versified the content of John the Deacon's Life, specifically *Lactation 11, Three Daughters 13, Bishop 14, Mariners 6, Grainships 7, Artemis 4, Stratilates 3,* and the appended *Iconia 34.* But two episodes are novel: *Broken Staff 61* and *Substituted Cup 62.*[34]

N *Broken Staff 61*[19] resembles *Iconia 34.* A Christian borrower swears on an N icon to repay on N Day money lent by a Jew, but he does not pay. When hailed to court, he conceals the borrowed gold in a hollow cane. When he is asked to testify, he hands the cane to the Jew while taking the oath that he gave the Jew his money. As he leaves the court, he is run down by a wagon and dies, but the cane is broken by the wheel and the gold spills into the street. Thus the trick is exposed. The Jew, with faith in N confirmed, turns Christian and prays through N for God to restore the life of the cheating Christian.

There may be many reasons for one story to inspire another. One such reason is to be found in hymnology. As shown above, stories are usually so briefly sketched in hymns as to suggest a variety of plots. For example, in a sequence probably composed in the eleventh century, *Iconia 34* is ambiguously mentioned: *Auro dato stuprum dessuasit* (By the very act of handing over the gold, he exposed the dishonorable act). That line is derived from a hymn of a century earlier regarding *Three Daughters 13: Auro patris infamiam / Stuprum redemit virginum* (By the gold he averted the disgrace of the father, the dishonor of the maidens).[20] Such ambiguity might help to authenticate any number of floating anecdotes. The broken staff is an ancient folklore motif, but its application to N increased its popularity.[21] An altered version appears in a Namur MS of the twelfth century:[22]

> *Ligno fracto fraus probatur*
>> With the breaking of the stick, the deceit is exposed.
> *Aurum cernens baptizatur*
>> The Jew, on sighting the gold,
> *Judaeus, cum suscitatur*
>> Is baptized. And the dead man
> *Defunctus in bivio.*[23]
>> Is revived, there at the crossroads.

The first vernacular Lives in English and French, the twelfth-century sermons, and the earliest stained-glass storied windows all contain *Broken Staff 61.*[24] In the same period it was carved on a capital in the cloister at Tarragona in Spain. Readers of Cervantes[25] will remember a thinly disguised paraphrase in which Sancho, acting as a judge, plays N's part.[26] *Broken Staff 61* had the inherent power to make N patron of judges, law courts, and lawyers.[27] By a delightful caprice of late medieval imagination, the thieves whom they judged also invoked him.

Already the monk of Bec recorded variations of *Iconia 34,* particularly a story of gold deposited in an N church in Picardy, stolen by some "youths of ready wit."[28] A London MS [29] tells how a rich man, mounted on a gelding, found himself pursued by enemies (*Horse Value 63*). He vowed to donate his mount to N should he escape. After escape he tried equivocation: he left the horse at the church door, entered, and deposited twelve marks on the N altar as a redemption fee. But the horse could not be moved until the rider had deposited four marks more. The rich man acquired fresh admiration for N, as bargainer as well as rescuer. The story appeared at just the time when bankers and lawyers were beginning to control the society and art of the cities.

In somewhat later versions of *Broken Staff 61,* the N icon is made surety for the loan, another borrowing from *Iconia 34.* N thus became patron of pawnbrokers, and his symbol, the three golden balls derived from *Three Daughters 13,*[30] became theirs. As mentioned, a century after the verses were written in the Battle Abbey MS, the Lombards supplanted the Jews as moneylenders in the west. Simultaneously the mise-en-scène of *Broken Staff 61* changed to Lombardy,[31] as did the other new Battle Abbey story, *Substituted Cup 62.* Later stories (*Lombard Son 64* and *Murdered Merchant 65*) were also laid in Lombardy, which was becoming the center of goldsmithing as well as moneylending. So we begin to have stories of N and Lombard goldsmiths.

I mention one further effect of *Broken Staff 61:* the oath taken in the name of N. Within a century, oaths by N became common.[32] Says Franke, "*Foy que je doy a Dieu et a saint Nicollay* appears to be as stereotyped an expression as on my word of honor."[33] Joinville, on crusade with Saint Louis, swears by Saint Nicholas.

The second new tale in the Battle Abbey Life is *Substituted Cup 62.*[34] A devotee of N promised his altar a chalice of marvelous workmanship, but when the goldsmith delivered it the buyer was so enchanted with its beauty that he kept it for himself and ordered a second for N.

On the ship to Myra to deliver it, his young son, beautiful chalice in hand, fell overboard and was drowned. The man and wife proceeded to Myra, where they placed the substitute cup on the altar, only to have it crash to the pavement. Contrite, they confessed their acts. N restored the boy and the original chalice.

Now we can see the mature personality of N fulfilling the promise of his youth.[35] N had become restorer of lost boys in *Demetrios 29* in the East and *Son of Getron 46* in the West. Such episodes came into the west from the Greek-speaking world at least as early as Gregory of Tours in the sixth century, though not then applied to N. The Blessed Virgin, sharing many an action with N, was a constant rescuer of children from the sins of their fathers. The lost boy of Chaucer's *Prioress's Tale* goes back to that same Greek world in which N was active.

Substituted Cup 62 parallels an episode in the legend of Saint Menas,[36] which has already supplied us with parallels for *Myrrh 18* and *Three Clerks 44*. A citizen of Alexandria, Eutrope, bade a goldsmith make two silver plates, one to be offered at the altar of Saint Menas. On the ship to Alexandria, he ate from the plate to be offered. The slave boy who washed it let it slip into the sea and in fear and despair threw himself after the plate. Eutrope invoked Saint Menas. When he arrived at the basilica, the slave appeared, carrying the plate, which was given to the altar.[37]

Though doubtless helping to intensify N's patronage of children, *Substituted Cup 62* does not appear in children's exercises—drama or song, for instance. Rather, deceit and fraud apparently were regarded as the point of the story, and it traveled together with *Broken Staff 61* throughout the West and even to parts of the East where Crusaders penetrated.[38]

The first artistic Life written in a modern vernacular was composed in French. It exists in a Paris MS written before A.D. 1100. Then John of Saint Ouen in Rouen wrote a metrical Life in Norman French before the year 1119.[39] There was a Life written in English in the twelfth century,[40] and thirteenth-century Lifes in German and Norse (Nik[1] and Nik[2]).[41] But best known[42] is the Anglo-Norman verse Life composed by Master Wace. He is especially remembered for his Romance of Rollo (*Roman de Rou*), a chronicle of the deeds of the first dukes of Normandy, and his Romance of Brut (*Roman de Brut*), the first vernacular rendering of the matter of Arthur and the British kings. By publishing about A.D. 1150 three "romances," that is, narratives written in French end-rhymed octosyllabics, about Saint Nicholas,[43] Saint Margaret, and the Conception of Our Lady, Wace attracted as patrons the English king Henry of Anjou and Queen Eleanor of Aquitaine.

Wace professed to have merely versified and romanticized an existing Latin Life for those who did not understand Latin.[44] In the French recension Wace ended with mention of "Robert son of Tiout," in the English with "Osbert son of Thiout." Since the romance survives in two French and three English MSS, we may judge that it was equally popular on both sides of the Channel and that its audience was essentially noble and courtly.[45] Seven of the twenty-three episodes[46] appear in Wace for the first time, three of them negligible. Of three others (*Boiled Infant 66, Murdered Merchant 65,* and *Lombard Son 64*) there exist Latin versions only slightly later than Wace.

Boiled Infant 66[47] tells how a mother left her infant in a tub of hot water placed over a fire while she attended the installation of N as the new bishop of Myra. When she returned she found her child playing in the boiling water, miraculously preserved from death. It resembles in some details *Lactation 11,* which tells how N stood upright in his bathwater the first day. It falls into a group with other N stories of restored children, like *Son of Getron 46. Boiled Infant 66* is akin to an episode in the sixth-century Life of Saint Theodore of Sykeon.[48] Do such Byzantine parallels reveal some continuous N tradition now lost to our understanding, or a new tradition that originated with the Crusaders? Or do they merely illustrate that man's storytelling mind reinvents actions consonant with the personality of a legendary hero? A variant of *Boiled Infant 66,* drawing also from *Artemis 4,* tells that the child fell accidentally into a tub of boiling water and was dead when the mother returned from pontifical Mass. N brought him back to life. This version illustrates N's power over flames, a source of his patronage of Parisian *pompiers.* [49]

Evidences of these later fictions, which we might well call the N Apocrypha, survive more by chance than do the earlier stories. In 1930 André Royer, working at the church of Saint-Nicholas in Mesuil-sur-Oger (Marne), found under an eighteenth-century wainscoting an early fourteenth-century polychrome altar frontal

with N centered as bishop, flanked by depictions of *Three Clerks 44,*
Three Daughters 13, Substituted Cup 62, and *Boiled Infant 66.*[50] This is a
more popular, less orthodox, selection than windows in the great
Notre Dames. In 1932 Professor Douillet published, with musical
notation by M. Dahler, a folksong he had recovered from oral tradition near Epinal in the Vosges.[51] The scene is laid at Orleans, where a
nurse leaves an infant in the heating tub while she washes clothes in
the river. N accosts her and sends her home, where she finds the
infant safe. A refrain for the eight epanaleptic stanzas is:

> *Jésus, aidez-moi*
> *Douce Vierge Marie*
> *Saint Nicolas!*

Murdered Merchant 65[52] is like *Three Clerks 44,* which Wace also tells.
An innkeeper murders a traveling salesman for his money and pickles
the body, which N then restores. The innkeeper repents. A variation
of this variation, as in a Ghent MS of ca. 1200, has one business
associate murdering his partner (*Murdered Partner 68*).[53]

In *Lombard Son 64,* a man attends church on N Day with his wife,
who has been troubled by an evil dream. Their boy, left at home, is
killed by the Devil, who comes to the house disguised as a pilgrim.
The mother sees the murder as fulfillment of her dream. Nevertheless
the father and mother join with clergy and laity to celebrate N's feast,
while the corpse lies unguarded in the next room. N appears as a
pilgrim, who desires to eat in the room where the dead child lies. He
revivifies the child and vanishes. In this version *Lombard Son 64* is a
work of art by a highly competent rhetorician, who creates a brief
epic of the Fall of Angels and Salvation of Man. But that version is
quickly corrupted into a vulgate version which is no more than a
repulsive amalgam of *Three Clerks 44* and *Son of Getron 46,* with overtones of *Artemis 4,* as in Bohnstedt's French Life, strophes 43 - 62.[54]

N's personality fitted or was adapted to a number of consummate
fads of the day: a new sentimentality about youngsters, a cult among a
fast-growing vocational class of clerks, a new interest in witchcraft
and demonology, a neobarbarism in narrative. Back of these lay the
new wealth and leisure which allowed for the copying and circulation
of trifling literature. "Courtiers' Trifles (*Nugae Curialium*)" was becoming a popular form of literature.[55]

There is also a universal reason for images of murder to coagulate around N Day. The scholar Bede tells us that the pagan English called November (which overlapped December in their reckoning) "Blood-month."[56] After the grain harvest came the slaughter of animals, depicted in the conventional medieval miniatures in books of the month. A psalter at Cividale copied about 1200 has on its calendar page for December pictures of (1) a man raising an ax above a hog, (2) the Zodiac sign of the Goat, (3) N with three figures that may be *Three Daughters 13* or *Stratilates 3,* and (4) a Nativity scene. These are four primary images of the winter season. Rather-frequently-identical murder stories appear in legendaries of N and of the Virgin containing analogues of these four.

Perhaps John the Deacon was partially responsible for this burgeoning of N murder stories. In his youthful anxiety to attract attention to his rhetoric, he composed the following outburst regarding the City of Patara, which he likened to Sodom and Gomorrah:

> God dragged Lot from the midst; the others he condemned
> to trial by sulphur. And rightly, that they might spread the
> stink of their actions far and wide, destroyed with a fetor as
> repugnant as the actions themselves. Lo, now likewise the
> unhappy inhabitants of Patara, because they indulge in every
> debauchery and abuse themselves with every lust, wretch-
> edly undergo for their correction this foretaste of the im-
> pending Last Judgment. We are given to understand that if
> they had not proved themselves deserving of punishment,
> they would never have undergone that horrible extermina-
> tion. Alas, alas, evil pestilence, such are your retributions,
> such are your rewards—that as you have evilly enticed
> others, so do you evilly create your own extinction. It will
> come, it will come, believe me—that day when both you
> and your author the Devil will be damned in eternal fire.
> The fire of that aforesaid city has his image, and impeni-
> tent he will burn.[57]

These and similar lines were read every year on N Day in the major churches of the West.

Of several other Lifes in French vernacular, one composed in 169 octosyllabic rhymed quatrains was published by Bohnstedt.[58] Among

233

the tales it adds to the tradition is one[59] laid in Myra when N was alive, in which one confidence man feigns death on the highway while a second collects alms to bury him. After N passes by, the second man finds the first truly dead. N later restores him to life.

Trouvères and troubadours, often on crusade, united vernacular song and chivalry; minnesingers found welcome livings in German courts. The nobles spread such poetry and courtliness among the rising bourgeoisie, while the religious taught the lower classes how to sing at fairs and festivals and crowded street corners. Mendicant friars, with Saint Francis as model, sang vernacular songs while they preached. In all these circumstances the lurid tales of N could catch, if not hold, attention.

The earliest extant English lyrics of any kind after the Norman Conquest are those of Saint Godric (d. 1170), a Saxon who at age forty became a hermit in a cave in the wilds of Finchale in County Durham.[60] Among his few surviving compositions is a prayer to N:

> Sainte Nicholaes, Godas druth,
> Tymbre us faire scone hous.
> At thi burth, at thi bare,
> Saint Nicholaes, bring us wel thare.[61]

Godric had been a merchant-peddler, a pirate, and a pilgrim; he had captained a North Sea craft and had transported Baldwin I, king of Jerusalem, to Jaffa in 1102; he had prayed for his sins at Raymond's Saint Gilles, at Rome, and at Compostella. His biographer Reginald recorded[62] that N once visited Godric in a dream: N and an angelic chorus urged Godric to sing with them, a reminiscence of *The Cross Legend 41.*[63] The earliest extant beast-debate, *The Owl and the Nightingale,* is attributed to a Nicholas (of Guildford, ca. 1250), who is also the leading human actor in it.

The *South English Legendary*[64] is an accumulation of the products of many authors of the twelfth and thirteenth centuries. The earliest surviving MS (at Oxford) was copied about 1300.[65] Of its sixty-seven legends, all are of biblical saints, martyrs (Catherine among them), and Insular confessors, except those of N, Martin, Scholastica, Sylvester, Francis, and Dominic.[66] All of the stories in the N legend are found also in Wace, though five of Wace's[67] are omitted. Apparently the South English adapter(s) used a common source.[68] An account of N's demise with the Thirtieth Psalm on his lips first appears in Wace[69] and this legendary:[70]

I ween there never was a saint who was St. Nicholas' peer,
That so many fair miracles in his life did here,
For to penetrate so strong a palace and go upon the sea also
Great wonder that anybody such miracles might do!
Many of the Host of Heaven our Lord here them send
Since it is our Lord's will that they hence should wend.
When he saw the angels to him come, he thanked our Lord fast.
The Thirtieth Psalm of the Psalter he began thus at last:
"In Thee, Lord, I have hoped, that I not confounded be,
Thine holy ear bend down to me. Hie and deliver me."
He died at the sixth verse that in English words would go,
"My soul, Lord, I betake to Thee; Thou redeemed it, I know."
The soul outwent upon that word, and the angels forth him bear;
The fellowship of heaven all right glad to have him there.
He died in the three hundredth year, with three and forty more,
After that God was y-born, as the Book records the lore.

This account was derived from a passage in the *Golden Legend*[71] which may have inspired a very effective passage in the *Commedia*.[72] The following couplet from the *South English Legendary* adequately sums up the whole:

Fairore miracle on earthe, no mighte we nevere i-wite
Than we of Saint Nicholas findeth ofte i-write.[73]

The influence on Western imagination of Bishop James of Voragine's *Legenda Sanctorum,* later called *Legenda Aurea,* the *Golden Legend,* has been incalculable and cannot be discussed here beyond brief notice; the facts about the whole, in which the Life of N is but a day in the cycle of the year, appear in common reference books. Its popularity may be gauged by the number of MSS surviving, more than seven times as many as those of Dante's *Commedia* or Chaucer's *Canterbury Tales,* and by the more than 150 editions and translations that appeared during the first century of printing.[74] The *Golden Legend* had already been translated into English, as into all the main European languages, before Caxton retranslated it for the first English press.[75] James, a Dominican, had his verbal images preached to the populace by the Blackfriars. In the fifteenth and sixteenth centuries, Renaissance painters then translated James's verbal images into visualizations.[76]

James's selection of stories was almost exactly that of the *South English Legendary*. However, local librarians who possessed a copy of the *Golden Legend* were apt to add to it, thereby creating a local legendary. Of these countless additions, I mention only one, *Dazed Thieves 69,*[77] to illustrate N's waxing patronage of both lawbreakers and their victims.[78] The narrative, quite dramatically composed, tells

N how, during a local war, the prefect's wife hid his two sacks of property in the balcony of the N church. Youths hunting birds' nests sighted the sacks and returned in the night to steal them. But time after time in their attempt to escape they lost their way in the woods and circled back to the church. At dawn, having circled once too often, in fear of apprehension they buried the goods, dropping the sacks in the churchyard as they retreated to their homes. A neighbor discovered one of them washing away the night's ravages and made him confess. Prefect and wife recovered their property and rendered thanks to N.

Until printing, such N Lifes reached the public, who could not or would not afford books, only as retellings by the preachers and street singers. There was but slight distinction between them, for they cultivated each others' arts. This form of popular delivery stifled originality, required broad chromatic effects, and easily assimilated commonplaces and thoughtless sequences of unimaginative action. The more the populace heard hagiography, the more its relation to reality, whether human or divine, was distilled away. The old tales of N and their reshapings equally lost all hold on men's credulity and became irresponsible lore without the saving grace of novelty. Occasionally a poet endowed some fragment with a plastic beauty or an elegant period and in this way exalted the subject. And sometimes some entertaining and even instructive anecdotes were caught up by the serious historians of the time. Such an episode is an account of *The*

N *Pigeon Drop 70,* incorporated in the Annals of Winton for A.D. 1201, which is the earliest description of this ruse, still used by confidence men. In it the confidence men impersonate N and Saint Andrew; N eventually appears to administer justice.[79]

II AMONG THE POETS

N's chromatic quality made him congenial to songwriters, who must in a phrase or a line suggest but not narrate experience, and to itinerant preachers, who must by means of the fantastic catch and hold the fancy of passers-by. Such a quality would not attract humane poets. Dante's disinclination has been mentioned. Nevertheless, as poets held up their mirror to nature, N's presence was caught in the image. Such ubiquity could not be blotted out. Two dissimilar instances will suffice to demonstrate what happened.

The Vision of Eynsham

Visions are a literary genre older than Enoch and Plato. Texts like Macrobius' *Commentary on the Dream of Scipio* and Boethius' *Consolation of Philosophy* perpetuated them in medieval schools. The Christian hagiographical tradition blossomed with visions in the tradition of the Apochryphal New Testament, most especially the *Apocalypse of Saint Peter* and the *Vision of Saint Paul*. The exegetes treated two main classes of religious vision, the mystic and the prophetic, and the rhetoricians treated two others, the amorous and the utopian. Less aesthetic and philosophical than these were the fabulous visions of popular morality and entertainment, usually eschatological.

N appears massively in the visionary literature.[1] Possibly the juncture made by Revelation ii, 14 - 15, caused his sporadic connection with the early visionary Balaam.[2] At all events medieval *Palmesels*—the carved wooden asses on which an impersonator of Christ rode on Palm Sunday—were ridden by Balaams in Processions of Prophets and by Nicholas Bishops on Innocents' Days.

I will not catalogue N's connections with visions. Suffice it to mention *Peter Bartholomew 71,*[3] who in the First Crusade (A.D. 1099) was the instrument for finding the Blessed Lance of Christ, without which—so the camp tales ran—the Crusaders could not have gained Antioch. Later Peter, lying in the chapel of his overlord, Raymond of Saint Gilles, had a vision of Christ's being lowered from the Cross by Peter on the right, Andrew on the left, and a third figure at His back who eventually proved to be N. Peter narrated the vision and the extensive admonitions of the Lord spoken from the Cross. According to the Chronicle of Raymond:

N̄

But when we reported these things to the brothers, some
began to say that they would never believe that God had
spoken in this fashion, bypassing the prince-bishops, showing Himself to a rude man. For the same reason they also
disbelieved the spear of the Lord. Hence we called together
those brothers to whom the matter of the spear had previously been revealed. Shortly Arnulf, the chaplain of the
Norman count, emerged as the apparent leader of all those
who disbelieved.[4]

This Norman count was Bohemond, N's protégé of chapter 4 above,
rival and overt enemy of Raymond. We may infer that this bitter
rivalry between two leaders of the First Crusade in some minor way
involved N.

And because Arnulf was a lettered man, some believed him.
And we inquired of him why he doubted. When he said
that the bishop of LePuy had questioned the fact, a priest
named Peter Desiderius replied, "I myself saw the bishop of
LePuy after his death, and blessed Nicholas was with him.
After quite a long discussion that bishop said this to me, 'I
am in the same choir with blessed Nicholas, but because I
was dubious regarding the spear of the Lord, which I certainly ought to have accepted, I was led off to Hell, where
the hair on the right side of my head and half of my beard
were burned off. And though I am not now in punishment,
yet I cannot see God clearly until my hair and beard have
grown out to their former length.'" This and much else
regarding God's afterworld that priest preached to us, as it
had happened before but could not be revealed until now.

N   One of the most famous medieval eschatological visions is an
account written by Adam, *Monk of Eynsham 72,*[5] chaplain and biographer of Saint Hugh, bishop of Lincoln, at Hugh's instigation.[6] Eynsham in Oxfordshire was, at the time, in Hugh's jurisdiction.[7] Just
before this vision and composition, another Nicholas (de Romanis),
bishop of Frascati and cardinal legate in England, had deposed a hated
abbot of Eynsham. The original Latin text survives in many MSS,
British and Continental. The doctor Ecstaticus, Dionysius the Carthu-

sian, used it.[8] The first printer in the City of London, William de Machlinia, translated it into English and published it in A.D. 1482.[9]

The subject of the vision was Eadmund, a monk of the abbey of Eynsham, who was entranced for forty hours, from Good Friday Vespers to Easter Lauds in the year 1196. The modern editor of the Latin text, Father Thurston, very credibly surmised that the visionary was Edmund Rich, who became archbishop of Canterbury in the year 1233.[10] Contemporary historians like Matthew Paris[11] and Roger of Wendover[12] reported the vision in full. From the beginning of the thirteenth century, especially from the fall of Constantinople in 1204, Greek migration to England can be noted. Indeed, a Greek named Nicholas assisted Robert Grossteste in his Greek studies.[13] Robert, who later became bishop of Lincoln, was then prebendary there.

Many have believed that *Monk of Eynsham 72* was a model for Dante. Like Dante's, Edmund's vision took place at Eastertide. It involves a contest for souls[14] and like *The Comedy* it embodies the theme of *one little tear*. The ethical standards are high. Though pilgrim and guide first travel through a schematized Hell, the center of interest is Purgatory, a hill as in Dante. In the journey through it the redeemed have their burdens lightened. The therapy is homeopathic. Specific clerics and even a pope are punished. The transition from misery to health is gradual, and during it the greatest suffering results from uncertainty of salvation. Periods of purgation are fixed periods of time, though the periods are shorter than are Dante's. There are the same nightly rests.

The guide, equivalent with Virgil, is N, who leads Edmund not only through Hell and Purgatory but Paradise as well.[15] There is no evident reason for his appearance as philosophical guide; he is not visualized as patron of clerks. It is possible that Edmund was inspired by the *senex venerabilis* of Reginold's N *Liturgy 40*. According to Matthew Paris,[16] ten years after the Eynsham vision, Thurcill of Essex had a vision in which Saint Julian was guide; in that instance N was overseer of Purgatory, not wholly unlike the Cato figure of Dante.[17]

The Bari Widow 73 and Chaucer

Important poets, East or West, ancient, medieval, or modern, have not found N as suitable a subject as Saint Anthony, Saint Thomas à Becket, or even Saint George. The *bürgerlich,* however redolent of the marvelous, hardly inspires burghers, let alone poets. At the height of his fame N attracted few serious poets,[18] though many a painter and musician. Satirists and comic poets depicted him: Nicolaus de Bibera,[19] Walter of Chatillon, Jean de Meung, Rabelais. At Bonn a vagrant clerk named Nicholas was called the Archpoet.[20] When he was at death's door he "assumed the cowl with great contrition; yet no sooner was the danger past than he quickly put it off, with a mocking jest."[21] A round belly with good capon lined, no matter how just the justice who bears it, is not a proper image for serious poetry even though, as mentioned, Justice Nicholas of Guildford sits on the bench in *The Owl and the Nightingale*. Chaucer's thin wall between jest and earnest was sometimes breached: "Nicholas" is his typical clerk in the *Miller's Tale*,[22] and the *Prioress's Tale* is as much an N as a Virgin legend.

Chaucer's kindly idiom of excess in *Troilus and Criseyde* is fashionably called "the language of courtly love." That language had a rich tradition from Asian fiction, transmitted to the West by hagiographers. In the twelfth century clerks who had learned this idiom in diocesan classrooms parodied and satirized it for their worldly masters. N, who lent himself so easily to every new popular movement, was himself an Asian and fitted naturally into the idiom of Romance. He was a useful tool for spreading it, through popular songs out of hymnology, anecdotes out of homiletics, and fiction out of hagiography. I will center on what is perhaps the most piquant example.[23]

The composition of the N *Liturgy 40* by Reginold of Eichstätt inspired *The Cross Legend 41,* a legend about a legend.[24] It also N inspired a subsequent legend, adapted to courtly idiom and the emergent secular taste. That legend, *The Bari Widow 73,* survives in only one MS (13th cent.), but that copy appears to be several times removed from the archetype.[25] Though in this narrative the mise-en-scène is Bari, doubtless the author was a transalpine clerk. The other contemporary N material in the same codex comes from the Low Countries. The Latin style is the scholastic jargon that flourished from Cologne to Angers in the time of Abelard and subsequently. The work could have been composed at any time between 1087 and 1225, but probably not later than 1150.

The *Bari Widow 73* begins:

There was a man of noble birth and handsome features who breathed forth the sum of Helicon in both rhyme and meter. In the city of Bari, to which the blessed Nicholas had been translated, this man ran a school in those first years after the Translation, when laments for the loss of Nicholas had as yet scarcely dwindled in Myra and the signs of dolor were dissipating in thin air, like wisps of smoke after a funeral pyre.

In that same city lived a widow preeminently endowed in mind, though even richer in wealth and loveliness. In either grace she was so surpassing that by a look she could have enticed a stony Demosthenes to the nuptial bed or have aroused passion in the most chaste Lucrece. But since she was both honest and true, she feared God and venerated all the saints with profound piety. Yet principally did she turn all her love to blessed Nicholas; and that she might preserve that treasure of holy love from rust and moth and flames, she frequently held precious vigils before the tomb of the beloved corpse.

Reginold, the rich young man-about-town of Eichstätt, yet to become bishop, can faintly be recognized in the "noble birth and handsome features " of the clerk. Says the authoritative chronicle of Reginold: "He loved a very important lady named Pia who . . . adorned our church, extremely rich"—who eventually evolved into the Bari widow. The clerk "saw her and was stricken to the marrow":

As is the curse of that disease, he would at one moment in self-accusation execrate his imperiled soul for its tempestuous waywardness, and the next moment recall it from self-banishment to the cauldron of an anguished heart, with tears and punctuating sighs. Woe enveloped him, and tumult of mind: it urged him to confession of his tide of love; then decency and despair recalled him to concealing his desires. Yet the more he smothered it, the more the fire exploded. Back and forth he warred with himself, but remained enmeshed in his sinfulness. Here is that *amor*, famed in every page of the poets, worthy of scorn, to be sure, lawless and merciless. It scorches its victim, yet presents a glozing front. Thus the wind sinks the bark by gusts which a steady force would have brought to port. Indeed, the vicious mind transforms the countenance, and as the face loses its refinement, the latent corruption is expressed. It is chained to its error, and itself betrays what it lusts for.

Pale and wan, he eventually confesses his love and is unequivocally rejected. Only by exercise of will does he survive, but barely. At a dinner party which the widow held annually on N Day to honor her patron, she chides the clerks present because they have never composed "a single responsory or prose suitable for praise of that good friend of God, or even a canticle to joyfully honor his festive holy day."

Her languishing clerk, who had not been invited, heard of her remarks. He took on new life. In a short time, with accompanying fellows, he called upon her and played and sang some compositions honoring N. The lady promised any gift to the clerk who would complete the liturgy thus begun.

With that pledge before witnesses, the clerk composed the whole *historia*. The author specifies particularly the prose *Congaudentes 47,* which Reginold did not compose, and the response *Confessor Dei Nicolaus,* which he did. The Bari clerk showed his work to many, who judged it "pure gold," and then to the delighted widow, who asked him to name his reward. When he demanded her love she "deplored the price of her delusory promise with tears such as they say Phoebus shed at his hasty judgment in the vengeful and total cremation of Phaëton."

No offer of money or power could divert him. Conferences, letters, pleas and pledges were of no avail. She was granted a truce of one day.

> Having thereby obtained that little respite, she sat all the day in hairshirt and ashes; then she turned her whole concentration on him who was created refuge for her grace and for us: on the subsequent night she prostrated herself before the tomb of her hope, that is to say, of the blessed Nicholas. By the benign mercy of God, even before she prayed she was heard, for, herself righteous, she but besought righteousness. Yet not knowing that she would have been saved, she dissolved her anguish in words broken with sobs, and seasoned her piteous petitions with the sweet savor acceptable to God. Indeed, she forgot that she should pray

to God, Who had already heard and to that fountain of
mercy, His mother. Instead, he whom They held within
their enveloping essence was wholly and completely on her
lips—Nicholas: that name is sweet to her above all others;
that name which she had repeated a thousand times over
she now repeats beseechingly; that name is the beginning
and end of each sob; that name before all others is drawn
from her fevered brain by her sighs.

And so swiftly the good Nicholas, ever indefatigable in
response to good vows and the suffrages of his devotees,
stood at the bed of the clerk in his episcopal garb. He found
the clerk awake and cursing the night's delay with many a
sigh; for a night is long to those to whom a mistress has
promised the following night. She was wakeful in the hope
of avoiding shame, he that he might create it; she wept for
fear that she commit weepful acts, he sighed that he might
give himself up to sighs.

But in the end iniquity was vanquished by justice, as is
ever the result of such warfare—wisdom wins out over
folly. Not tolerating so unfair a conflict either to hang long
in the balance or to become an unkind victory, blessed
Nicholas seized the youth by the hair and held him aloft,
then dropped him with a thud. Harshly he chastized the
man's sinfulness with the whip which he carried—yet not
mercilessly, for he kept himself within bounds of the fright
of his victim. Now chastened and wretched, the youth could
scarce raise his tearful eyes and blood-drained visage; with
frightened and whispering voice he begged forgiveness, asking how he had transgressed and who his visitor was. (For
the saint of the Lord and his majestic appearance struck
terror; and though his whole countenance glowed with
compassion, yet he said nothing kindly or affectionate, so
that his silence added the more to the other's stupefaction,
while he had vengeance written in his eyes and whole face.)
That wretch, but blessed in his very wretchedness, rolled
back his eyes as if sunstruck, and prone on the floor tearfully exclaimed with the publican: "Lord, have mercy on
me, a sinner." At this the glorious man of the Lord: "I am

he, Nicholas, whom you honor with your lips, though your
heart beat against me, since you have subverted your words
to concupiscence. But daughter Jude has sustained not your
iniquity. Your evil intents have ensnared her; to her great
sorrow mingled with tears your deceit granted nothing.
Now come to your senses and correct every act, that these
floggings may cease; and by my intercession you may have
that reward for your masterpiece from Him from Whom
you have received the gift of composition, Who alone grants
and repays such, gifts." At these words Nicholas disappeared.

Quickly the chastened youth arose, and hastened to the
tomb of his castigator. There at vigils he found her whom
for his own pleasure he had rashly lusted after. Casting himself at her feet, he told her what had transpired, and begged
her forgiveness and intercession with the blessed saint.

Awestruck, they separated prayerfully and lived out their separate
lives in devotion to N. The early chronicler recorded that the lady Pia
"at last giving herself over wholly to the Lord, built a convent for
nuns which she enriched with an endowment befitting royalty (for she
was extremely wealthy)."[26]

Why was *The Bari Widow 73* composed? Not for a noble or
bourgeois audience, who were no longer interested in Latin and could
not read it. Nor would it have been composed, as was *The Cross Legend
41,* for influencing action; the N liturgy was now everywhere accepted. Nor was it a classroom exercise like the early N dramas,
though scholastic rhetoric ("draw Venus from the breast of Pallas") is
apparent enough. Doubtless it was extracurricular.

About the year 1100 the popularity of cathedral schools quite
suddenly rose. In Paris the Latin Quarter took shape. Goliardic songs
of wine and women flowed through Europe. Abelard's students, like
Hilarius, who dramatized *Iconia 34,* wrote pretentious compositions to
display their wit to possible employers.[27] Those who had not yet sold
their wits carried them in their scrips for instant display. The patrons
of the Left Bank, N and Catherine, were subjects ready at hand,
lending themselves to parody of themes that pious ecclesiastical masters had taught their impious scholars. The author of *The Bari Widow
73* was practicing the craft of a Benoit de Saint-Maure or a Walter de

Chatillon; for in the twelfth century the clerks practiced in Latin what they would later preach in Romance.

This was the language which the tradition-loving Chaucer practiced two centuries later, dated though it was.[28] His *Troilus and Criseyde* is, through Benoit, a kind of *Bari Widow*. Chaucer, like other studious humanists, practiced and perpetuated archaism: his Troilus is delightfully out of date, *remisse et humiliter* to use Dante's phrase—the Bari clerk tossing on his lovesick bed two centuries too late.

Chaucer's Prioress is equally conventional—she and her nun both speaking in rime royal, an overly emphatic conventionality suggesting the remoteness of time and place of the conventuals. N is her patron and stands at her elbow as she composes:

> But ay, when I remember on this mateere,
> Saint Nicholas stant evere in my presence,
> For he so yong to Crist did reverence.[29]

Her schoolmarm pedantry suggests the classroom dominated by N; her unnatural precision in the Prologue matches the discordant irrelevance of the Tale. She narrates among the spring blossoms of the pilgrimage a frigid "calendar legend," tied to the folklore of the winter season, which is far older than Christianity and as worldwide as frost and barren fields.

From Hallowe'en to Marymas the Days of All Souls, Leonard, Martin, Clement, Catherine, Andrew, Barbara, Nicholas, Nativity, Stephen, John, Innocents, Genevieve, and Hilary are associated with supernatural, pathetic, and all violent forms of birth and death. Sir James Frazer's twelve volumes of *The Golden Bough* are keyed to the traditional associations of this sort and explain the seasonal temperaments to be treated in the next chapter. For example, it is a Northern folk custom to hang a "grainchild" in the barn over the threshed corn, to be taken down (revived) on Marymas (= *Purificatio* = Candlemas = Groundhog Day).[30] This was a folk custom to preserve the dead spirit through the frozen stillness, and the token might be the effigy of a child. It seems possible that the grain on the tongue of the Prioress's little *clergeon* reflects this custom.[31] By the time of Chaucer "good Bishop Nicholas" was acquiring these folkish traits. The Innocents, like little Hugh, were grainchildren resurrected through the merits of the Virgin Mother or good Bishop N or both. The accident of the ecclesiastical calendar is one reason why N, of 6 December, should have attracted stories of violence and death as did all the saints of the season. But N, already a patron of infants and scholars, was more appropriate than the others. Was it part of Chaucer's mild humor that his pedantic Prioress should tell a tale somewhat improper to the April Pilgrimage when Innocents were no longer under threat of death? The *clergeon* did not have a Paschal resurrection but "yaf up the goost." The irrelevance of the Tale is quite as discordant as the precision of the Prioress's table manners. Though similar stories, we know, occasionally started to be attached to the legends of April saints like George and Mary of Egypt, they never really caught on; for the Christian West, unlike the Semitic East, did not make a spring cult of the Paschal slaying of firstborn. Winter was a time for Balders and Herods and ritual sacrifices of litel clergeons.

III WORDS AND MUSIC

The close relationship of music and religion, of poetry and ritual, of drama and the liturgy, has been written about at least since the time of Aristotle. It is perhaps too much a commonplace that modern drama originated in the medieval sanctuary, evolving from Christian ritual—too much, for as we have observed the "miracles" came from the classroom, not the church.[1]

Whatever period of history, even the ages of Menander and Seneca, few dramatic scripts survive their time. Two Hildesheim plays composed about 1100, *Three Daughters 13* and *Three Clerks 44*, might be accidental survivors of a rich dramatic period, but their naive form suggests rather that they are the very seed of drama, at least of the kind of dramatized legends called "miracles." In his play, yet to be mentioned, Bodel links these two N subjects together as if they were classed by themselves, to the exclusion of other tales. And in a sermon, Thibaut of Clairvaux says "We see on the Feast of Saint Nicholas how some represent his person, as in the miracles of the clerks or the maidens, which the Lord effected through him."[2] The context suggests that Thibaut was choosing almost the only common dramatic miracles of his day. The two stories, so contrasting in time, place, and manner of invention, now are linked in popular imagination. Three golden balls of the daughters and three murdered clerks become the almost-exclusive iconographic symbols for N. The two tales are among the first to be represented in church windows and such mass-produced wares as the Tournai Fonts.[3]

The Hildesheim MS allows us one insight into N's connection with drama, the "Fleury Playbook" another.[4] Orleans MS 201, which once belonged to Fleury (abbey of Saint-Benoit-sur-Loire), was copied roughly about the year 1200, doubtless somewhere in northern France if not in Fleury itself.[5] There is no reason to believe that all or even any of the ten plays which the MS contains were composed there.[6] All speeches in this codex are neumed, that is, accompanied with the primitive musical notation that had neither staff nor measure. The stage directions indicate that they are truly play scripts, not grammatical exercises, though written in Latin. The Fleury MS is the earliest known script for only two of them (*Conversion of Paul, Getron*).

The Fleury *Three Daughters* repeats its Hildesheim predecessor, nearly completely word for word but with addition of both persons and speeches, some of the additions in a different verse form. Contrariwise, the Fleury *Three Clerks* is a wholly new and more sophisticated composition. Though its verse form resembles the Hildesheim sapphic, the stanzas lack codas. Here dramatic verse took a big step toward the Shakespearean accentual decasyllabic.

Three Daughters 13 belonged to N's infancy.[7] It illustrated the gift-giving side of N's personality and was consonant with the gift-giving habits of man in the winter season.[8] Now very quickly the new tale, *Three Clerks 44,* becomes equally popular. *Three Daughters* was linked with maiden rites; *Three Clerks* was indissolubly linked with youths and scholars. Both accent youth. The cult of N as patron of scholars, beginning with Godehard in the third decade of the eleventh century, spread rapidly. The Guild of Saint Nicholas of Parish Clerks, founded in London in 1233, is merely typical.[9]

A Limoges MS (Paris, B.N. Lat. 1139) copied no later than the year 1100 contains a hymn with this refrain:

> *Festum ergo pontificis*
>> The feast day of the bishop good
> *iam sociati caelicis*
>> Now in celestial brotherhood—
> *cum cantibus mirificis*
>> When chants in every tonic mode

atque modis organicis
    Tales of his wondrous works include—
festinanter a clericis
    Is by the clerks and scholars viewed
et maxime scholasticis.
    As time when homage is renewed.[10]

In all twelfth-century hymns which include reference to *Three Clerks,* the number three is as unalterable as in *Three Daughters.* It identifies the boys not only with *Stratilates 3* but with the *Canticle of the Three Boys* (Daniel v, 35 - 66),[11] which became the *Benedicite* of the Western Church. Later, when *Three Clerks* had grown strong in its own right, trinity became less important; late medieval and renaissance artists altered the number to fit, for example, spatial requirements, or for other equally valid reasons. A sermon once attributed to Bonaventure, and contemporary with him, has two noble and rich Athenian students of philosophy as actors; it is the earliest known document employing the pickling tub.[12] An altar frontal ca. 1300, now in Barcelona, contains all particulars of that sermon version.

Three Clerks 44 spread wherever Westerners went.[13] It was as popular in the inexpensive pious effigies before the Age of Enlightenment as Christopher medals have been since. Nevertheless the clergy seems not to have received *Three Clerks* happily. It is not mentioned in the *Golden Legend,* a compilation seldom censorious. Though many hymns include it, at least as many pass it by. Considering its documented ubiquity, such omissions must have been purposeful.

The popular cult led to its becoming the subject of a number of timeless ballads. Professor Sadoul gathered a ballad of ten strophes, of which the first and last are:

> *Saint Nicolas a trois clériaux*
> Saint Nicholas has three clerks;
> *Sont tous les trois du même arreau.*
> All three are in the same class at school.
> *Un jour ont demandé congé*
> One day they asked permission
> *Pour aller sur la mer jouer,*
> To go for a vacation cruise.

Saint Nicolas leur y a donné.
    Saint Nicholas granted their request.

C'est la chanson d'saint Nicolas
    This is the ballad of Saint Nicholas.
Ce ou cell' qui la chantera
    He or she who will chant it
Quinze pardons il gagnera
    Will receive fifteen credits;
Ceux ou cell' qui l'écouteront
    Hes or shes who hear it
Tout autant ils en gagneront. [14]
    Will receive just as many.

Another from Artois begins:

Saint Nicolas, patron des enfants sages,
    Saint Nicholas, patron of good children,
Pour te prier je me mets à genoux;
    I kneel for you to intercede.
Entends ma voix à travers les nuages,
    Hear my voice through the clouds
Et cette nuit donne-moi des joujoux.
    And this night give me some toys.
Je voudrais bien une ménagerie
    I want most of all a playhouse
Avec des fleurs et des petits oiseaux,
    With some flowers and little birds,
Une montagne, une verte prairie,
    A mountain, a green meadow,
Et des moutons buvant dans les ruisseaux. [15]
    And some sheep drinking in the brooks.

But most popular by far is one that Gérard de Nerval caught up from folk balladry in his masterpiece *Sylvie*. [16] To this day it is sung throughout France, normally in seven couplets (*Trois enfants 74*) beginning:

Il etait trois petits enfants
Qui s'en allaient glaner aux champs. [17]

249

It has not become popular in the English-speaking world, though often translated. Here is a Victorian version of James Henry Dixon:

Three little children sought the plain
Gleaners of the golden grain.

They lingered past the angel-song,
And dewy shadows swept along.

'Mid the silence of the wood
The butcher's lonely cottage stood,

"Butcher! lodge us for the night,
Lodge us till the morning light."

"Enter in, ye children small,
I can find a place for all."

The butcher seized a knife straightway,
And did the little creatures slay.

He put them in his tub of brine,
In pieces small as they were swine.

St. Nicholas, at seven years end,
His way did to the forest wend.

He sought the butcher's cottage drear:
"Butcher! I would rest me here!"

"Enter! enter St. Nicholas!
You are welcome, St. Nicholas!

Enter! enter St. Nicholas!
There's place for you the night to pass."

Scarce had the Saint his entrance made,
He would the supper board was laid.

"Will you have of ham a slice?"
"I will not, for it is not nice!"

"Of this veal you'll take a bit?"
"No! I do not relish it.

"Give me of the little swine,
For seven long years have laid in brine!"

The butcher caught the words he said,
And forthwith from the portal fled.

"Butcher! butcher! do not flee,
Repent and God will pardon thee!"

St. Nicholas the tub drew near,
And lo! he placed three fingers there.

The first one said, "I sweetly rest!"
The second said, "I too am blest!"

The third replied, "'Tis well with me,
In Paradise I seem to be!"

It was this ballad, no doubt, that inspired Anatole France's *Le Miracle du Grand Saint Nicolas.*[18] With true Anatolian irony he tells how N adopted the three clerks he had revived. They grew up to be inconceivable scoundrels, violating his niece, inducing a war which devastated the land, and inspiring a papal bull of excommunication, *Maleficus pastor,* against N himself. Broken in health and spirit, N wandered into the forest, where he found the once-homicidal inn-keeper, now reformed by N's Christian act and thoroughly sanctified. N exclaims more than once, "Seigneur, votre sagesse est adorable; mais vos voies sont obscures et vos desseins mystérieux."

We have strayed from the Fleury Playbook, but now return. *Adeodatus 75*[19] is a dramatic version of *Son of Getron 46,*[20] derived from *Basileos 22.*[21] All versions are basically the tale of Christian parents, devoted to N, whose son is captured by infidels on one N Day and miraculously returned the next. The boy spent the year as cupbearer to the foreign leader or king. In both East and West the tale evolved in the retelling. Another Eastern version, *The Youngest Son 76,* tells of a widow, Constantia, whose youngest of three sons is rescued.[22]

Adeodatus 75 consists of 171 lines of chanted dialogue and chorus.[23] The characters are pure types: Eufrosina (= Grace), Marmorinus (= Stony), Adeodatus (= God-given). A chorus of *Consolatrices* is more platitudinous than the Trojan Women:

Thy sorrow, misery, and desperation
Harm you and give your son no consolation.
Instead, for him pour out your affluence
On needy clerks and other indigents.

251

> Pray for compassion from that excellent
> Saint Nicholas, that he may represent
> Your loneliness before the seat of God
> And your request receive a favoring nod.

We cannot know whether the self-seeking reference to clerks was a joke or not.

Of special interest are the more than fifty lines of stage directions, which indicate a self-conscious and expansive setting in three *loci:* Getron's home, the N church, and the infidel king's banquet hall. N is himself a silent but effective agent: "Let someone in the likeness of Nicholas pick up the boy, who is still holding the goblet with cooled wine, and carry him in his arms to the doors of the church and then disappear as if unobserved." The aerial N of *Stratilates 3* is now assuming a definite shape (*in similitudine*) or iconography.

The banquet scene with the Saracen leader, Marmorinus, pulling his beard in rage and throwing dishes, is the dramatic origin of many a popular staging to come: Herod ("out-Herod Herod"), Antichrist, and Nebuchadnezzar (in which the king rails at the three *innocentes*). The dramatic lament of Eufrosina, Getron's wife, with her chorus of consolatrices, is like the lament of Rachel in another play in the Fleury Playbook.[24]

The narrow range of themes and images, repeated in the several plays under various guises, the elaborate staging, and the broad humor suggest that many of the Fleury plays, however scholastic, were intended for outdoor presentation to very large groups. N is the only nonscriptural subject among the ten plays, and his Day, which symbolically and actually stood for inclement weather, does not make him a suitable subject. His presence can only be accounted for because he was patron of clerks. From other sources we know that Catherine plays ranked second to N plays in popularity. A text from the fifteenth century changes the type of presentation from a miracle to a morality, though the story line is essentially the same. In it Getron is called Simon de Borgoys, "the burgess's boy."

Most effective of the four Fleury scripts was *Iconia 34.*[25] The story was discussed in chapter 2. The wholly Latin script, in 157 lines of a great variety of measures, like *Adeodatus* has quite extensive stage directions, with speaking parts for three thieves as well as for the Jew and N.

A second, contemporary dramatic version of *Iconia* was composed by the Anglo-French poet Hilary, who had been a student of Abelard, contemporary with Wace.[26] His play has only two speaking parts but a number of silent persons and two locales. The protagonist is Barbarus rather than Judaeus of the Fleury play and Wace. Vernacular refrains vary the Latin speeches.[27] As in Hilary's other surviving verse,[28] his secular wit marks the departure of literature from shrine and cloister for castle and marketplace.[29] There is some slight evidence that Hilary composed *Iconia* at and for Angers, a town often visited in this biography of N.

The trouvère Jean Bodel of Arras wrote the first truly vernacular drama, and a very successful one, *Li Jeu de Saint Nicolas,* about the year 1200.[30] We are lucky to have it, for a copy of any script for public and popular entertainment would survive by merest chance.[31] Sometimes called the first medieval work of dramatic originality, its more than 1,400 lines in a variety of measures are only suggested by the earlier versions. The dramatic impact is unique. Lost is all the old sense of a fluid Byzantine-Arabian front, where the tales discussed in chapter 2 first appeared. In its place is the white-black, Christian-Saracen oppugnancy of the chansons.

Into an oriental court of a king, a seneschal, and four extravagant emirs, Bodel injects a lone surviving Crusader, *li preudons*, whose faith rests on two rocks, God and Saint Nicholas. The action is rather like horse opera: the lone ranger ("the good man") ropes in the whole court of potentates, and icon N outgallops idol Tervagan. Bodel cast the tavern scenes[32] with drunks, gamblers, and robbers, a host with a heart of iron, a dromio, and a posse of criers—each anticipating cowboy types. He enlivened the plot by constant local personal and geographical allusion, current patois (food for many a philological dissertation), and slapstick humor (the messenger travels from Africa to Artois "swifter than a camel").[33] Here begins in drama the overt interpretation of scriptural and legendary lore in contemporary terms, familiar to English audiences of somewhat later date in the *Second Shepherd's Play*. Small wonder that *Iconia* 34 was the most popular theme of later dramatists. Picaresque adventure has been a staple of dramatic entertainment ever since. Another rendering exists in a fifteenth-century MS now at Florence;[34] a surviving document shows that still another was played by schoolboys in a cemetery near Blois.[35]

The productions of the *basoche* and advocates, to be mentioned later, regularly included it.

There are a large number of surviving records of sixteenth-century productions of N miracles. All of the four Fleury subjects except *Adeodatus 75* have a continuing dramatic history.[36]

The drama, though both audible and visual, happened only occasionally; liturgy and hymn singing were constant. People may have heard the tuneful N liturgy but once a year, yet it was whistled frequently.[37] As we shall see, N was the cynosure of guilds and confraternities. A measure of N's stature is the surviving hymns. A rough, possibly misleading, statistic is the number of inches which each major saint takes in the Index of Chevalier's *Repertorium Hymnologicum*:[38]

Agnes	5.25	Denis	2.00	Sebastian	2.50
Ambrose	1.75	Francis	4.00	Thomas	
Anthony	2.75	George	2.75	(Aquinas)	1.60
Augustine	5.75	Jerome	3.00	Thomas	
Barbara	6.00	Lawrence	4.00	(Becket)	3.00
Benedict	5.75	Margaret		Ursula	5.75
Bernard	2.50	(Antioch)	4.50	Vincent	3.75
Catherine	8.00	Martin	5.75		
Christopher	1.35	Nicholas	5.75*	*284 separate entries.	

Though Chevalier was an indefatigible compiler, the list is incomplete and somewhat provincial. The female saints (Agnes, Barbara, Catherine, Margaret, Ursula) are hymned rather out of proportion to their fame as measured by other standards; I do not find that liturgists have told us why. The monastic saints (Anthony, Benedict, Bernard, Jerome) bulk larger than life because the monasteries were the special homes of hymnography.[39]

The earliest N hymns were composed in the ninth century,[40] hardly later than the *Apud Myros, O sancte 9*, one of the earliest hymns in Greek. As might be expected, the period of most intense composition was shortly before, during, and immediately after the Reformation. The Catholics sang in Latin, the Protestants in vernacular. Their hymns are not represented in the list above, but inclusion would not alter the figures much, for nearly all Protestants were violently hagiophobic, and I know of no hymns to N or to any other of the nonbiblical saints listed above. Of N music, the sequence *Congaudentes* 47 seems to have been most popular, though *Laude Christo debita / Celebremus inclita / Nicolaus merita* outshone it in parts of Germany.

In the twelfth century, French writers discovered the pleasure of writing *macaronic* verse, that is, in two or more languages. We have already noticed that Hilary so composed the drama *Iconia*. A hymn in Picard dialect, about 1300, has six stanzas in end-rhymed 7's (*aaa/ ababa*), the first three lines Latin, the rest in Romance:

> *Nicolaus hodie*
> *Fit causa leticie:*
> *Filii ecclesie,*
> > *Loés le roi de glorie.*
> *Del Signor qui feste est hui*
> > *Joiose est la memorie:*
> *Grans vertus fist Deus por lui,*
> > *Si com nos dit l'estorie.*[41]

We have had occasion enough to note N's attraction for medieval musicians. Among the moderns I mention only Haydn's *Mass in Honor of Saint Nicholas* and Benjamin Britten's *Cantata for Saint Nicholas*.[42]

IV VISUAL ARTS

Within the compass of this book, visual arts, like music, can be treated only somewhat statistically. The *Index of Christian Art,* established at Princeton University by Charles Rufus Morey,[1] has indexed and photographically reproduced under *Nicholas* the artifacts surviving from the period before the Reformation. It forms a kind of descant for this biography.

Medieval painters and sculptors, despite the variety of their individual styles, did not really affect the personality of N. In the main their patrons allowed only what was traditional, for no one is so conservative as a pious patron. The Eastern tradition of unchangeability in the iconic image reenforced this natural trait. By the time painting had left this purely iconographic stage, N had matured and his habits had been formalized by the legend makers in pulpit or forum. "Saints and saints and saints again!" despaired Browning's Fra Lippo Lippi. When he began to depict personalities rather than symbols the Prior protested: "Make them forget there's such a thing as flesh. Paint the soul!" But the saints of legends had lost their souls. During the fourteenth and fifteenth centuries in the main, like fashionable painters of almost any historical period, the artists depicted ethical types. Saints could be differentiated one from another, not by physical traits or an evanescent individualization or even by narrative subject, but only by an inscribed name (as in Byzantine mosaics) or by iconographic symbol.

Indeed, the iconographic symbol appeared only contemporaneously with emblems and heraldry in the centuries between Romanesque realism and Humanistic nominalism. In the earlier Middle Age sanctity had been ineffable and indivisible; therefore identification of a saint was nugatory. In fact, I believe that N was among the very earliest to attract a humanizing symbol. An exemplary secular bishop, he had from the time of Santa Maria Antiqua been depicted with crozier and mitre. When narrative symbols came in, N was differentiated from other symbolic bishops by three golden balls (occasionally three bread loaves) or by three boys in a tub, as already stated. He is credited with eight different arrangements of three or six gold balls, loaves, or apples; two of anchor or ship; two of tubbed boys; two of purses; one of a church.[2]

A prehumanistic saint's personality had been determined by where his portrait hung on the wall, his *degree* or position in the celestial hierarchy. Only position distinguishes saints like Beatrice in Dante's Great Rose. A story line would not help in that era, for a narrative scene was only a depiction of God's work being done, as the phrase goes "through the merits of N." The merits were not his but belonged to the communion of saints, to any member of the interchangeable soldiery. Saints sparkled in unison, and their light was common to the full communion. To repeat, medieval artists of the Carolingian and Romanesque eras cared little about differentiating one saint from another. So depictions of N's "character" such as those mentioned in the Prologue were products of Renaissance and Reformation, when men came to believe that artistic genius could make a dead past look like a living present. Moral doctrine could be related to character, if one were interested, through such devices as Bishop Joseph Hall's revival of Theophrastus' "Characters"; otherwise individuality was the vogue.

N was a constant subject for painters in the days of his maturity. Caesarius of Heisterbach (d. 1240) wrote that N "is represented in churches both in sculpture and in pictures more frequently than any other pontiff."[3] More recently Mrs. Jameson found N's ubiquity beyond her descriptive powers: "So widely diffused and of such long standing is his fame, that a collection of his effigies and the subjects from his legend would comprise a history of art, of manners, of costume, for the last thousand years." A history of all those, but not of him. Medieval painters expunged his personality; Renaissance painters, on the contrary, strove to make each of their depictions a unique conception without regard for the personality of the legend, which is our theme.

Nevertheless, in most Renaissance representations N takes on the attributes of maturity, a round-bellied justice in mitre and crozier. Though the Gothic Notre Dames expressed the infinite power of the Virgin, or tried to, the only somewhat fewer N shrines expressed his ultimate lack of power. As in the verbal documents, the depictions suggest a tool of God's creatures, not their servant. He might have been the saintly counterpart of any pope, archbishop, or bishop in christendom; but he is instead a cipher. The Crusading popes may have tried to persuade others that he was a vital force, but only as they could use him for their purposes. One of the most remarkable facts of this biography is that there are very few (Fribourg, Soest) cathedrals in the Roman communion dedicated to him, in sharp contrast with the overwhelming number of other western church dedications to him (parishes, shrines, chapels, hospitals), and dedications of cathedrals in the Orthodox East.[4]

The monumental parish churches dedicated to N are concentrated in the centers where commerce expanded in the fourteenth to the sixteenth centuries—in the port cities of the Hanseatic League and the Channel and Rhine ports of the Low Countries: Wisby, Lund, Wissant, Bergen, Lübeck, Hamburg, Aberdeen, Newcastle, Yarmouth (dedicated 1119; present building from 1190), Hull, Ipswich, Brighton, Amsterdam, Bruges, Antwerp,[5] Ghent, Brussels, Barfleur— extravagant Late Gothic creations set at crossroads between shipping and banking.[6] Each was a mighty story now more or less in dust. Wisby, on the west coast of the island of Gotland (Sweden), was the capital, as it were, of the Hanseatic League, which was formed in

1241. In the tenth and eleventh centuries it was a proud seaport. Its N church (which was at that time a cathedral) was built in 1097 in Norman Romanesque style. When King Waldemar III of Denmark sacked the city in 1361, killing 1,800 of its citizens, he loaded two ships with booty, no small part the property of N. But N saw that one of the ships was wrecked on its route home.[7] Wisby never recovered from that sack.[8]

Elsewhere N was paid for favors with parish churches, chapels, and altars.[9] Unlike cathedrals, they could be and were disregarded when tastes changed.[10] The most impressive N churches, in the Low Countries, are Gothic of the fifteenth century, built more for love of material than for love of spirit. Many of them have been notably refurbished only in the touristic affluence of the twentieth century.

A word about miniatures, the hand-drawn or painted illustrations in codices. The earliest surviving examples are probably those of the ninth-to-tenth-century Bible of Leo and the tenth-century Menaloge of Basil II, both in the Vatican. The Latin Slavic world almost exclusively adhered to the Eastern iconic form of representation; for example, a thirteenth-century miniature in the Belgrade library shows N flanked by Christ extending the Gospel and the Virgin extending a bishop's vestment (cf. *Nicea 15*), all statuesque. The early narrative miniatures in Germany largely represent *Stratilates 3* in some pose, as in a Stuttgart MS in which Constantine's young officers appear in stocks. Outside Germany *Three Daughters 13* is the most popular subject, as in the "Psalter of Isabelle," now in the Fitzwilliam Museum at Cambridge. We remember that the first N story illustration may be the *Three Daughters* of Santa Maria Antiqua in Rome. Miniatures of *Three Daughters* multiplied in psalters from the late thirteenth century on as an illustration of Psalm lxxx, 8: "Thou calledst upon me in affliction, and I delivered thee: I heard thee in the secret place of tempest; I proved thee at the waters of contradiction." Although *Three Clerks 44* appears in a thirteenth-century Fitzwilliam MS, the tale seldom appealed to miniaturists. Early Western miniatures do not reveal the kind of doctrinal commitments found further East. Probably the miniatures most widely reproduced in modern copies, and imaginatively most effective, are those of "Queen Mary's Psalter,"[11] drawn early in the fourteenth century. Few of the famous Books of Hours (e.g., Anne de Bretagne) neglect N.

Enamel panels survive from the ninth century; ivories are nearly all of the tenth and eleventh. Ecclesiastical textiles are apt to illustrate narratives.[12] I have mentioned baptismal fonts, especially those mass-produced at Tournai. In the east a fashion for *mosaïques portatives* extended through the tenth to the fourteenth century; one such, depicting N, has found its way into the museum at Vich (Spain).

Emile Mâle specified N's ubiquity among French stained-glass windows. Imposing storied windows survive in cathedrals at Bourges, Le Mans, Tours, Auxerre, and Rouen. The thirteenth-century window in the choir clerestory of Tours Cathedral has twenty-five scenes.[13] But the most extensive survival is the glass at Chartres Cathedral.[14] In addition to the windows, the south portal is devoted to sculpture of Saint Martin and N, with the tympanum depicting N's *Myrrh 18,* the lintel *Three Daughters 13,* and the embrasure on the left an unidentifiable incident. Fulbert's crypt contains a frescoed figure that some have identified as N.

Why is N so disproportionately represented in glass? Probably because there was usually less theological (i.e., clerical) control over its designs. Whereas the clergy exercised judgment within the ambulatory of the choir and apse and the carving and glass of the western front, it seldom restrained choice of subjects elsewhere, especially in the naves. It could be firm about subjects of art intimately associated with the sacraments and liturgy. But windows cast only a dim religious light, seldom channeling doctrine. The medallions in clerestories of Gothic cathedrals tell their stories now only through binoculars. Of 171 windows of all kinds in Chartres, the donors of 116 have been roughly identified: 44 were donated by crown and nobility, 42 by guilds, 16 by ecclesiastics, and 14 by portrayed but not identified individuals. Of the five N windows, three were donated by guilds and a fourth by a burger. The Diana window was donated by Étienne Chardonel, member of a local family but canon of Notre-Dame de Paris.

Simply because in port towns the N cult expressed itself in overpowering stone we need not infer that it was not very intense elsewhere. Meisen lists fourteen N sanctuaries or other dedications in the inland diocese of Chartres. N's protégés outside port cities were not so rich: the scholars and clerks created intangible verses and songs; lawyers composed mimicry and drama; the artisans made N boats, domestic shrines, and cakes and cookies. As the Middle Age waned, Giotto, Fra Angelico, Cranach the Elder painted their tributes to N. But we may presume that as the disenchantment of Humanism and Reformation spread, the great Renaissance artists mentioned in the Prologue were confined by patrons' conservative tastes regarding subject while imposing their own interest in personality.

N had lived long and acquired his status, which no single artist could alter. N the subject was a miracle-working mercantile prince, no matter what the artist tried to imagine. The fallen angel whom Milton made to say, "In my choice to reign is worth ambition, though in Hell," advised

> If at great things thou wouldst arrive,
> Get riches first, get wealth, and treasure heap,
> Not difficult, if thou hearken to me;
> Riches are mine, fortune is in my hand,
> They whom I favor thrive in wealth amain
> While virtue, valor, wisdom, sit in want.[15]

V ECCLESIASTICAL LIFE

We are apt to think that the Church was N's path to success.[1] At crucial moments it may well have led him to wealth and honor. But if so, it was as some inchoate, unidentifiable body of faithful, not as diffident clergy, that it opened a path to his door. We cannot imagine the caesaropapist Justinian, except under duress, building a shrine to an N who tongue-lashed his model Constantine. Nor can we imagine a Cluniac prior accepting the novel rhythms of N liturgy except as prodded from below. Archbishop Ursus of Bari surely did not advocate the stealing of N's relics; he simply tried to use the event to inflate his position. The papacy was not diffident, but N was thrust upon it by the world, as the Angevin and Norman counts thrust him on Urban II.

N symbolically "arrived" when his namesake Pope Nicholas III (John Cajetan Orsini, d. 1280) at long last introduced Reginold's liturgy into the papal chapel, more than three centuries after its composition. But he also built a new chapel into the Vatican palace which would eventuate in the Sistine,[2] to cast into inferior place the N chapel in the Lateran.

Of five popes named Nicholas, he is the type of greed and venality. Dante placed him in the Malebolge among the Simoniacs.[3] The pope took his papal name, it is believed, because he had been cardinal-deacon of the church of Saint Nicholas in Carcere Tulliano. His bull *Exiit qui seminat* (14 August 1279), prepared with the help of the future Nicholas IV, was drawn in favor of the Franciscans, who, as we shall see, were becoming N's friends.[4] Like his patron, Pope Nicholas IV added to his wealth and political power in office.

We may take the churches of Rome as an indication of N's overwhelming position in western Christianity. In a listing made at the time of Leo III (A.D. 806), not one was dedicated to N; but a census of A.D. 1192 lists twenty.[5] A record compiled about 1230 has the following numbers of dedications: Saint Mary 73, Savior 34, N 22, Lawrence 20, Andrew 18, Stephen 15, John (not distinguished) 13, Blase 11, Martin 6 or 7, George 2, and one apiece for Gregory, Cecilia, Anastasius, Benedict, Sylvester, and Lucia. Huelsen identifies twenty-five Roman N churches in that period,[6] Armellini thirty-one.[7]

Following the papal victory embodied in the Concordat of Worms, Calixtus II convened the First Lateran Council on 18 March 1122 to confirm the pact. Immediately thereafter he began the erection of a new chapel to N.[8] In its tribune were painted the portraits of all his predecessors from Alexander II. And in the arch at the feet of the Savior, Calixtus added Leo "first of the popes," Gregory the Great, and himself. "The chapel might serve as a monument of all the popes who had waged the battle with the empire."[9] These popes had prospered only as they walked hand-in-hand with N the whip wielder (*Stratilates* 3) and the Normans. They were predominately Cluniac and Gallophile. They set the pace of the Church Militant.

Yet such glory as the N chapel symbolized could not last. In the eighteenth century the whole oratory with all it contained of ancient art was demolished, to the lasting regret of archaeologists and historians, if not of artists.[10] The new world of the Jesuits replaced neoroman with rococo. Like N himself, the Lateran Palace was old and ready for the discard in the eighteenth century; yet it was in fact Pope Nicholas III in the thirteenth who prepared for that eventual shift by advocating a Vatican Palace which would eclipse the Lateran. According to an inscription of A.D. 1278 an act of his first year was to order an *aulam maiorem et capellam* to be built at Saint Peter's. The papal expansion in the first half of the thirteenth century brought on the pressure for new quarters for the enlarged bureaucracy in the second half—a common form of middle-aged spread. The Two Laws, Canon and Civil, occupied its attention as it professed to render justice to the world: "Supreme in Europe, the papacy gathered into a body of doctrine the decisions given in virtue of its enormous de facto power, and promulgated its collected decrees and *oracula* to form the immutable law of the Christian world."[11] A more apposite ideal than N, the patron of Parisian doctors of law, would be hard for the popes of that period to find.

The abbeys, being seats of wealth and power, often accepted N's patronage despite their traditional dislike of prelacy and its saints. There were more than six hundred N cloisters in the Latin world.[12] Saint Stephen of Muret (d. 1124), founder of the Order of Grandmont, was under N's tutelage, as his burial panel shows.[13] Even Bernard of Clairvaux advocated turning to N in time of danger.[14] Canon John Myre's Curse (ca. 1420) fairly represents N's ecclesiastical status among the localized clergy: "By the authority of the Father and of the Son and of the Holy Ghost and of our Lady Saint Mary God's Mother of Heaven, and all other Virgins, and Saint Michael and all other Angels, and Saint Peter and all other Apostles, and Saint Stephen and all other Martyrs, and Saint Nicholas and all other Confessors and of all the Holy Saints of Heaven, we accursin and bannen, etc."[15] Caesarius of Heisterbach tells of a priest at Essen who always had the Nicene Creed said on N Day: " . . . and the Prior: 'You did not do rightly, for he was not an Apostle.' To which the priest replied: 'Assuredly, I hold Saint Nicholas the equal of many of the Apostles.' "[16]

However, after the year 1200 the mendicant orders affected society more than did the cloisters. As urban preachers, direct arms of the papacy, the mendicants were attracted to both the commercial and scholastic personality of N. Dominic received the gift of the church of Saint Nicholas of the Vineyards at Bologna and at his own request was buried under a simple slab behind the altar of Saint Nicholas at the entrance to the cloister.[17]

The extraordinary cult of N among Franciscans is not accountable. Many of the local instances seem at this distance to have been purely accidental. The N chapel in the church of Saint Francis at Assisi was the gift of Gian Gaetano Orsini, of the family of Pope Nicholas III.[18] The frescoes are variously attributed to Maestro Stefano, Giotto, school of Giotto, and Giottino. On the south wall N presents the donor, wearing a monk's habit, kneeling with three bishops, to Christ, Saint Francis, and the celestial hierarchy. On the vaults and walls are narrative panels.[19] Between and below the windows of the north wall are the Virgin, Saint Francis, and N, together with angels, prophets, and saints.

In the year 1224 four clerks and five lay brothers of the Friars Minor landed at Dover.[20] The following year John Iwyn, a wealthy mercer, bought for them a plot of land in Stinking Lane, near Newgate, so called because it was in the parish of Saint Nicholas Shambles (in *Macellis*), or the slaughterhouse district. Their evident humility, as in taking such quarters, is one reason for their attracting a popular following, and their numbers rapidly increased; in less than two decades there were eighty brothers. The affluence which followed resulted in a dwarfing of the humble church of Saint Nicholas by a monumental greyfriars church and cloister. But since little was left in the old parish but the Franciscans, the names became in the public usage quite interchanged. Greyfriars, or Saint Nicholas, grew into a center of scholarship, holding its own with Oxford and Cambridge until the Dissolution, when all religious buildings were leveled and "many faire houses" (Stow) erected. A Franciscan scholar of this house, Nicholas Cusack, according to letters of the year 1280, was in person consecrated Bishop of Kildare by Pope Nicholas III and commended to King Edward I.[21] Another Franciscan scholar, Roger Bacon of Oxford, had his writings condemned in 1278 by Jerome d'Ascoli, General of the Franciscans and future Pope Nicholas IV (1288 - 1292); Bacon was in prison for fourteen years, while N, patron of prisoners, looked the other way.

That new pope is said to have chosen Nicholas as his papal title to honor his mentor, Nicholas III. But d'Ascoli had served as papal minister to Constantinople with an eye to uniting the Churches, and indeed he was instrumental in the temporary union of 1274. His life was dominated by two interests, the East and the Franciscans. He was the first Minorite pope. His crusading disasters especially preserve his memory: though he personally commanded twenty ships in naval action, the Christians had lost all Asia Minor except Cyprus and

Armenia by the time he died.[22] Contemporaries might have reasoned from those events that N's supremacy at sea was no longer what it had been.

One of the major acts of Pope Nicholas IV was to crown Charles of Anjou King of Two Sicilies. The scepter which he received from the pope at that time is in the treasury of N Basilica at Bari. Also in that treasury is one of the thorns from Christ's crown which Charles obtained from his brother, Saint Louis. There were twenty-one such thorns distributed through the west.[23] There is a dubious inscription on an effigy at Bari which reads: "Most Serene Charles II of Anjou, King of the Sicilies, captured in naval battle and condemned to death by Constance, Queen of Sicily, was freed by the miracle-working Lord Nicholas; for which reason he endowed this royal basilica munificently. Having preserved sole and canonical dignity for himself and his successors, he prospered from the year 1284 to the year 1309."[24]

The most beloved of all the Franciscan Nicholases was Saint Colette, whose carpenter father of Corbie in Picardy christened her Nicoletta (A.D. 1380). A reformer and a visionary, walking poor and unprotected through war, pestilence, and misery, she was appointed by Pope Benedict XIII as superior-general of the Poor Clares. A contemporary recorded that by her inspiration and effort 380 churches were erected. On the road to Moulins the two most active women of the fifteenth century met: this carpenter's daughter and the peasant's daughter, Joan of Arc, who in company with Dunois was bound for Charité-sur-Loire.

VI PATRONAGE

Names

Any appearance of the name Nikolaos or its variants in the west doubtless is due directly or through intermediaries to N.[1] One of the least "logical" variants is the spelling I use throughout this book, the English form of N with an *h*. This confusion of *x* with *k* betrays the lack of Greek knowledge in the British Isles during N's growth and maturity. The Cambridge Platonists and others who stimulated the study of Greek were interested in eliminating the cult of saints, not in rectifying it. Among English variants are Collins, Cole, and of course Nixon;[2] French are Colas, Colin, Col, Colette, Colinot, Collinot, Collignon, Colesson, Nicol, Nicolete, Niclausse, Nicollay, Nicolon,

Nicholes;[3] the Italian Niccolò, Cola, and Nicola; Spanish Nicolás; Portuguese Nicalao; Catalonian Nicolau; German Niklas, Nickel, Klaus, Klos, Clewi, Claüsli;[4] Dutch Niklass and Klaas; Danish Niels and Nils; Hungarian Miklos; Russian Nikolaï and Kolia.[5] This list is selective; Meisen lists more than eighty variants in France alone;[6] Müller forty-seven for Luxembourg; Jan de Schuyter lists Cool, Cools, Laefke, Luckele, Lykles, Nole, Nols, Noolke, Serclaes. These do not include the inexhaustible number of compounds like Clasmann, Horn-nickel, Sinterklas, or Kleber. And their patronymics like Nelson, Classen, and Nikolaiev. Tom, Dick, and Harry in the Netherlands is "Jan, Piet, en Klaas."[7] Though each variant doubtless has its story, I mention only the popularity of *Cola* in Italy; it seems to have come from Cola di Rienzi, the parvenu dictator of Italy who became tribune in 1347: *Nicolaus, severus et clemens, libertatis pacis justiciaeque tribunus, et sacre Romanae Reipublice liberator* (Nicholas, austere but generous, administrator of liberty, peace, and justice, and liberator of the holy Roman Republic). Did anyone else rise so high and fall so low in one short life? "Rienzi! last of the Romans! with reign, alas! too brief," exclaimed Byron.[8]

We may believe that the incidence of N names corresponds proportionately to other signs of N cult. For example, lists from southwestern France, and of course Spain, show comparatively few N names. And there are confusions. Some English Nicols come from N, but others by metathesis from Lincoln (from *lindum colonia*).[9] Other relationships may be challenged in this very inexact science. It has been observed and authenticated that in ages before mass communication names spread from upper and clerical classes to middle and then lower. So, a list from Vézelay (Dep. Yonne) toward the end of the twelfth century of 170 - 180 names of serfs does not contain a single Nicholas.[10] But a list of ship masters (mainly Dutch) in the *Albany (N.Y.) Balance* for 1 December 1809 also does not contain a single Nicholas or variant as surname or given, though comparable Dutch lists in the seventeenth century averaged 20 percent.

A Cologne list early in the twelfth century shows N in twelfth place; before the end of that century a Wiesbaden list shows it second only to John; in Breslau in the late fourteenth century it was not only first but comprised 26.4 percent of all personal names (1,321 instances) and in Görlitz 33 percent (1,415 instances).[11] Two centuries later it had dropped behind John, George, Martin, Peter, and Jacob. The fourteenth century was the height of the vogue. Simply as an example, many years ago the Princeton Index listed 35 Nicholases; of these, 7 lived before the twelfth century (N of Myra, Pinara, Sebaste, Pope Nicholas I, Mysticus, the Monk, Trani), 2 in the twelfth century, 8 in the thirteenth, 17 in the fourteenth, one in the fifteenth.[12]

No need to indicate the famous men and women who bore the name beyond those who especially illuminate the theme of interplay between image and action. In one sense this book is a behaviorist biography: presumably a behaviorist can find a relationship between a man's actions and his given name. Shuffling through a census of ship captains named N (including the one Gulliver shipped with) suggests the effectiveness of name giving. Is it chance that the Polos were named for the two tutelary saints of Venice, Niccolò and Marco Polo? One of the two friars whom the pope sent with them was named N.

These are baptismal names, and we cannot easily tell whether parents and godparents were honoring N. There are many Saint Nicholases, some of whom we have already discussed: four of the five popes, Nicholas of Sion, Nicholas the Studite, two patriarchs, etc. Nicholas Breakspear was the only English pope, and Dean Colet founded Paul's School—home of poets. They are all saints, but none was canonized, including N himself. However, the rather ephemeral Nicholas of Trani, who entered Italy from Greece on a dolphin's back, was.[13] In 1446 Pope Eugenius IV canonized Saint Nicholas of Tolentino, an Austin Friar (d. 10 Sept. 1310). His barren mother had invoked N for a child.[14] The intertwining of Tolentino's legend with N's cannot really be unraveled;[15] for example, N's *Myrrh 18* is matched by the blood which T's relics shed, and T is the subject of a drama, *Comedia sancti Nicolai,* published in London about 1510.[16]

Other saintly N's, no less the subject of cult for being uncanonized, are de Rupe (22 Mar. ca. 1420), de Flüe (22 Mar. 1487), both of Switzerland; a hermit of Sicily (17 Aug. 1167); a hermit of Naples (11 May 1310); the Carthusian N. Albergati, bishop of Bologna, not to be confused with Cardinal N. Albergatus (9 May 1443); a bishop of Lincoln (1391); de Farnham of Bologna, bishop of Coventry (1239); a bishop of Durham (1240); the Cardinal Bishop of Ostia to whom Dante wrote his First Epistle (1304).[17] Some Nicholases doubtless were named not for N but for some one of these or other saints.

Strangely, the Nicholases of the Western tradition were impressively scholarly rather than thaumaturgic. True, Metaphrast and John the Deacon endowed N with a genteel knowledge of the liberal arts, but only as a transient gesture. Certainly it would not have been easy at the end of chapter 2 to predict that the exemplar of political, commercial, and nautical success would turn scholar. But in any Christian life lies Christian paradox. From the time of Godehard we have watched N's inclination toward pure scholarship. This incompatible combination of forum and study would not, of course, survive, but it was amazingly effective in the early Renaissance. DuCange lists one hundred and one scholastic authors named N, about one-fortieth of all the names he lists. Nicholas Trivet, fourteenth-century commentator on Seneca, Augustine, and Boethius, enjoyed a special English vogue. Pope John XXII sent Friar Nicholas, lecturer in theology at the University of Paris, to China as the second archbishop of Peking.[18] I did not name among the saints Nicholas de Lyra (d. 1340), *doctor, magister, venerabilis, famosissimus cominus, ordinis Minorum,* born a Jew and converted to Christianity. He is popularly counted as a forerunner of Luther:[19]

> *Si Lyra non lyrasset,*
> Had Lyra not played his lyre
> *Luther non saltasset.*
> Luther could not have danced.

He is one of forty-eight biblical exegetes from the twelfth to the fifteenth century named Nicholas (including Popes Nicholas IV and V).[20] Besides Nicholas Copernicus, I shall mention but three scholar-leaders of the time. All contributed to N's tragic fall.

Nicholas of Cusa or Cues (a town on the Moselle) died Cardinal Bishop of Brixen in 1464. After having long labored in Germany on behalf of Pope Eugenius IV, in the Jubilee Year of 1450 he was brought to Rome to receive the cardinal's hat and new commissions from Pope Nicholas V, "who gave powers of legate in Germany, Bohemia, and neighboring lands to the very knowing man, versed in the languages of those countries, known for his apostolic zeal, his virtue, his tact, his eloquence. . . . He started to destroy superstitious practices, the exaggerations of the cult of saintly images, and the abuses arising from pilgrimages."[21] But in company with Denys van

Leeuwen, the *Doctor Ecstaticus,* he preached crusade against the Turks. In his many works outside theology, sermons, and letters, he stressed physical science and mathematics, proposing calendar reform to the Council of Basle in 1436 and asserting the rotation of the earth.[22] The hospital with library, dedicated to N, which he founded in Cusa, still operates.[23] He collected Greek MSS, read Plato and Aristotle, and labored in Constantinople. Perhaps he intensified rather than dispersed the coming cyclone of reform: Ernest Cassirer points to his doctrine of infinity as leading to the repudiation of hierarchy of personality.[24]

A generation earlier than Cusanus, the double N'd Niccolò d'Niccoli, with the close cooperation of Cosmo de Medici, turned Florence into a humanistic pasture for feeding the coming reborn. Vespasiano's Life of Niccolò and Poggio's funeral oration leave no doubt of his literary dictatorship; more renowned testimony few men have had. When Niccolò died (1437), he left eight hundred MSS, a staggering number for that time, the majority transcribed in his own beautiful hand. He had run into debt for books, valued at six thousand golden florins. When Cosmo settled the estate, half of the books went into the Library of Saint Mark which Niccolò had planned, but the rest went to pay his debts.[25]

I have treated four of the five popes named Nicholas, and now the last, who exemplifies the paradox I mentioned.[26] N, the bookless sailor and superman, ends his papal roles with one known to history first of all as founder of the Vatican Library and then as patron of the new skepticism.[27] When Nicholas V died (1455) the library had acquired 352 Greek codexes, 824 Latin.[28] He had earlier advised Cosmo on the foundation of the Medician Library. Under Nicholas V Rome became an *alvearium* of translation, publication, and erudition. But he was in his own way a miracle worker. He spurred on the restoration of churches and walls; his was the plan (stimulated by the actions of two predecessors named N) to tear down old Saint Peter's and erect a vast basilica.[29]

Nicholas V, "the first, and probably the best, of the Renaissance Popes,"[30] had not the slightest interest in N. He took his name from the patron who helped him up the rungs of the ecclesiastical hierarchy, Niccolò degli Albergati, archbishop of Bologna. Indeed, the Cappella di Niccolò V contains Fra Angelico's frescoed legends of Lawrence and Stephen, and representations of the four Evangelists and of Athanasius, Leo, Ambrose, Augustine, Chrysostom, Gregory, Aquinas, and Bonaventure; but no depiction of N. To Nicholas V was due the flocking to the city of Dutch, French, German, Spanish, and Lombard artists. On his deathbed he spoke of the treasures of art and science which he had amassed for the pontificate, assuring the cardinals that he had acted "not from greed, nor for love of pomp, nor from vainglory, nor from ambition to assume immortality for my name." His one care had been to make Rome the capital of the learned world—an ambition that N, for all his powers, had never cherished. Nicholas V's revival of classical culture contributed greatly to N's fall, for the Humanists especially exercised their scholarship with a view to eliminating veneration for the thaumaturgic saints.

The Corporate Life

At the beginning of the thirteenth century Alexander of Villedieu wrote, "There are holidays that the people observe with special attention. The clerk and the soldier, the tiller of the soil, women, the sailor, the merchant, pay thanks to Nicholas. He struck down the executioner and jailer, multiplied the grain. The triplet maids and the thousand perils give plenty of reason to venerate him."[31] And at the beginning of the twentieth century, Eugène Marsau wrote, "Il est le patron de ceux qui s'exposent pour defendre une idée, une croyance, un honneur" (He is the patron of those who lead the defense of an idea, an opinion, a position).[32]

This quest searches for the operation of the corporate imagination, not the sources of hagiolatry. N is an image that not one but many minds working together made into a reality. The center of N's power lay outside the sanctuary. True, when men's hopes and fears were gathered from field, town, and sea to compose a religion, N was gathered into the Church; and for a few centuries all social action centered in the Church. But when social action returned from the altar to the forum, N traveled out with it. There was a guild of N at Ypres at least as early as the twelfth century.[33]

As feudalism, essentially agrarian, gave way beneath the impact of towns and trade,[34] the feudal Church was adapted to make room for bourgeois ways. Guilds and what the French called confréries and the Flemish meerseniers (meersch = corporation) took over the monastic duties of healing and feeding, entertaining and burying.[35] New corporations, no longer "orders," appeared in Italy, France, and then through Europe.[36] A brotherhood formed at Bologna in 1244 was under the patronage of N, perhaps because the purely secular brothers met in a church dedicated to him.

As the Middle Age waned, nations replaced Christendom, and we can no longer choose examples at random from Islam to Ireland to illuminate one culture. Paris, for example, now differs from Rome, Prague, and London. Some kind of change was in the air everywhere. Around 1520 the Parisian theater was still ecclesiastical, but no longer clerically inspired.[37] The federated entrepreneurs now asked civil authorities to stage a play, though the dramatic form was that of the miracles and the expressed intention was still to edify. Those authorities would appoint an appropriate Feast Day for such secularity. At the end of a catastrophe, war, famine, or pestilence, the burgers gave thanks to God, the Virgin, or a saint (predominantly N) by presenting a mystery or miracle. The clergy cooperated: a priest was often author; the cantors and choirboys were singing actors; chapters often set up stage and properties in cloisters, churchyards, cemeteries, and even naves.[38] But in such actions no more allegiance to the Church was involved than is allegiance to the State now when we borrow books from public libraries. As Reformation vigor spread, laymen relieved clergy of such duties more and more.[39]

Guilds and corporations had within them confréries, fellowships, or lodges for social service, usually obligatory on all members. Sometimes the clergy helped to form them. Purely secular confréries might have colors and arms, a chapel, a priest, and annual feast, and assurance of burial, a mass, and perpetual prayers. Occasionally they provided unemployment insurance, and more often hospitalization. At Fécamp the Confrérie Saint-Nicolas gave to their confrères an indemnity to absolve them, to take them on pilgrimage, to bail them out of prison (N, patron of prisoners), and, in case of fire, to help them rebuild their homes.[40] Meisen[41] and others cogently describe how confréries formulated the imagery latent in N's legend and made it common coin for households.[42]

A very large number of such associations were named for N. A census survives from Savoy, very far from the normal centers of N cult and with only modest urban development, that shows more N and

Catherine confréries than for any other martyrs or confessors. In the diocese of Maurienne alone there were seven N confréries.[43] One reason why N cult was relatively weak in southern France was lack of shipping there. The Garonne was little used and passage on the Saône and Rhône was blocked by rapids as well as by sandbars at the mouth. In the north some twenty-five N confréries have been listed for the city of Paris alone. They centered in lawyers, canal and river workers, merchants, bankers, and schoolmen. The dedication of those organizations to social service brought about a host of dedications of hospitals for nursing and healing.

Again we meet a paradox, another apparent inconsistency in personality; for N, like not a few successful businessmen, by nature avoided dealing with the more repulsive aspects of illness. In the Middle Age, the leprous and the palsied did not go unpatronized, but they had to rely on less venerated and bejeweled saints than N. To be sure, there were innumerable phials of *Myrrh 18,* but despite occasional *ex votos* in his shrines that tell of cures for scurvy, the myrrh seems to have been most effective with arthritis, lumbago, and losses of organs of speech, sight, or hearing. Healing of contaminating diseases found small place within his legend. His healing miracles are often spectacles that do not dwell on repugnant physical deformity or pain. There is a remarkable absence of N invocations in records of the Black Plague.

But though N was not by vocation a healing saint, quite paradoxically he often patronized hospitals. One of the earliest evidences is the Bec Life, which tells of a small N church (*ecclesiolam!*) "which is called the Chapel of the Infirm."[44] What in a superman could be attractive to the helpless? It is more than possible that the cult of youngsters and of myrrh combined with this result. We have evidence as early as the Plan of Saint Gall (A.D. 825) that in abbeys the oblates and the infirm brothers were housed and fed in quarters separated from the brotherhood, outside the cloister. The infirm and youthful had discrete sleeping accommodations, but a common chapel and kitchen. The reason was that both groups required extraordinary care and unusual diets. The saint who offered gifts and attention to children and healing myrrh to the infirm would be doubly attractive.

Though one would think that Saint Roch or Saint Lucy would be more sympathetic, new hospitals, secularly established, often were named for N. A reason could be that guilds and brotherhoods, themselves dedicated to N for commercial reasons, in endowing nursing establishments passed along the invocation. When Reformers closed religious convents and many of them were converted to hospitals, the dedication to N carried over. Brauweiler and Burtscheid, two convents discussed in chapter 3, are both thriving N hospitals today.

Sociability and economic advancement were the driving forces behind confréries, which then developed a sense of social responsibility. As with some clubs today, in the desire to justify before the public a possibly selfish existence, they dedicated themselves to "service." They not only served invalids and paupers but became centers of arts of music, drama, comedy, and the like.[45] These arts, starting as byplay, sometimes became the essential reason for existence.

A great variety of occupations invoked N's patronage.[46] In most instances the patronage arose from the legend, but not always. For example, as Sébillot demonstrated, a byword of Norman Calvados about snowfall, "Le bon Dieu plume ses oies," led, through a series of misquotations, to "Nicolas plumait pour marier ses filles," an adjunct of the N cult of maidens.[47] The artisans of the cloth trade seem to have invoked N simply because the cloth trade centered in Flanders and the Low Countries of Lorrain, where large N churches dominated the culture (Bruges, Brussels, Ghent, Tournai, Lille, Amiens). So N became patron of button makers, lace makers, weavers of cotton and linen, cloth shearmen, drapers, cloth merchants.[48] In Flanders the Feast of Translation, 9 May, was termed *Broquelet,* from the *broches* used in processing; in 1877 this once-customary feast was formally revived at Lille, but the observation (a Mass for N, labeled *du Broquelet*) was shifted to May 14. N's patronage of haberdashers seems simply to have arisen from the word *hapertas* (Fr.), which originally meant "any kind of stuff for sale." Since *hapertas* applied to all merchandise, it was properly N's; then N followed the haberdashers into their specialty as *hapertas* narrowed in meaning.

Among groups who invoked N because of *Stratilates 3,* soldiers and knights (*milites*) were among the earliest, but the allegory of fighting for a cause determined that other kinds of fighters became devotees: the religious were "Christ's knights" (*milites Christi*), the nobility were knights by profession, but the bourgeois politicians then became knights by imitation, and hewers of wood and drawers of water were proclaimed "knights of the soil" whenever their masters wanted their votes or vows. *Stratilates* first drew the interest of those attached to law, but *Iconia 34, The Thief 42, Murdered Partner 68,* and other such tales helped.

The Avocats of the Officialité of Paris, a confrérie originally numbering thirty members, was chartered by King Philip VI in 1341 and dedicated to both N and Catherine; but it met only on the two N Days, 6 December and 9 May.[49] Chances are that the fraternity arose from among the law students at the university; hence the dedication to Catherine as well as N. In processions the group was led by the *bâton de Saint Nicolas.*[50] This society was soon matched by the solicitors (*procureurs*); the "Procureurs de la Chambre des Comptes" also met 6 December.[51] The notaries and their clerks (Confrérie des Notaires du Roy) met both days.[52] N patronized as well the registrars, recorders, and clerks of court (*greffiers*), and, of course, prisoners, captives, and those who suffered false judgments. This cult then extended to confessed, indeed boasted, thieves:[53] "The theafe that commits the robery, and is chief clarke to Saint Nicholas, is called the high lawyer."[54]

By far the greatest number of individuals and of organizations invoked N because of *Mariners 6.*[55] These comprised not only sailors and seamen, fishermen, boatmen, ferrymen, longshoremen, bargemen, plankmen, and dockers, but shipwrights, and gaugers.[56] Then it extended to navigators, to sea voyagers, to pilgrims, to those in shipwreck, and to packers.[57] N guarded many bridges, and often N chapels were built on them.[58] The confrérie of coal carriers met on both N Days at the Hôpital Saint-Gervais.[59] Perhaps *Boiled Infant 66* inspired the watermen, pumpers, and firemen;[60] and perhaps *Artemis 4* inspired those who suffered from fires, floods, and other water disasters. Because merchants were seamen in early times, they (especially the shippers and commission merchants) and the wholesalers looked to N. Window 60 at Chartres was given by the merchants. In seaboard towns and ports the patronage extended to the whole town: the archers and arquebusiers of Abbeville all wore a medallion of N.[61] According to Hubert Silvestre: "We have to remember that commerce was at that time basically peddling, horse-trading—the successful method being to dupe everybody. It is not for nothing that the god of thieves and confidence men was also the titular patron of the corporation of merchants."[62]

Artemis 4 attracted tallow merchants and candle makers, wax chandlers and oil merchants.[63] The latter met in Paris at the chapel of Saint Mathurin on both N Days. Possibly they were equally attracted to *Myrrh 18,* as very obviously were the perfumers, bottlers,[64] florists and embalmers; the pharmacists and apothecaries[65] also contributed to window 60 at Chartres. To their guilds or societies belonged the painters, as did Dante in Florence. They invoked N throughout the West, not alone in Paris.[66] An exception to N's aloofness from physical unpleasantness is that he listened to those afflicted with rheums, perhaps because his own myrrh was essentially a rheum.

Grainships 7 drew into his cult the commission grain dealers and merchants (who met at Saint Eustache in Paris on both days), seed merchants, grain carriers, and weighers, millers, grocers, and brewers[67]—who may, too, have been influenced by *Three Clerks 44.*

Three Daughters 13 was the source of veneration by marriageable maids, giftgivers, those who suffered conjugal sterility, and pawnbrokers. Valentine and N are patrons of eager maids; John the Evangelist and N of youths.[68]

It was *Son of Getron 46* and *Substituted Cup 62* that inspired the devotion of wine porters (feast at the church of Saint-Lenfroi), wine merchants (Saint-Jacques), and wine vendors (Saint-Gervais and Saint-Protais).[69] But note that N governed only transport and sale; there is no record that vineyard workers, vintners, or enologists cared for N. It is not surprising that peasants, agricultural workers, and woodsmen, remote from towns and commerce, had little reverence for N.[70]

He was patron of coopers, and brewers with them,[71] because of *Three Clerks 44;* documents attest the cult throughout the West. From this association came the patronage of the tanners, who gave window 13 at Chartres. And, of course, the butchers. Other recorded patrons of butchers are not only Saints Bartholomew and Hubert, but also Holy Sacrament and Annunciation; these latter came from "The Word is made flesh"! N's governance of cooperage may have been the reason that he was guardian of weights and measures. His effigy (usually with boys in the tub) appeared on seals in the West; hence he is of interest to sphragisticists. But his patronage of sealers—that is, those who imposed seals on merchandise—was older than *Three Clerks 44.* Schlumberger says that "of all the holy figures on Byzantine bulles,

Saint Nicholas is the one whose likeness is most constantly reproduced—half the time at least."[72]

Broken Staff 61 appealed to the carters. In Paris there were two brotherhoods of carters, one meeting at Saint-Nicolas du Louvre,[73] the other at Saint-Nicolas-des-Champs. The wood carters met at the Hôpital-de-Quinze-vingts-Aveugles on both N Days; out of this association may have grown the "Confrérie des Six-vingts-douze Aveugles," which feasted on 6 December.

We have watched the purely Western cult of children, scholars, and the schools grow during N's manhood and maturity, from its !rst appearance at Hildesheim in the early eleventh century.[74] Only that patronage will comfort him in his old age, for all other devotees desert him. Though N is kindly to infants in his legend (*Lactation 11, The Infant Touch 60, Boiled Infant 66*), it is only foundlings that seem really to interest him. There were many foundling hospitals, and a "Foundling Tower" at Metz.[75] He seems never to have been invoked for sick or ailing infants, though more than fifty saints are commonly listed who specialize in every kind of malady from slow walking to stillbirth. N especially aided grammarians and mathematical masters. He sympathized with the *vagantes,* the unemployed, the goliards, and became the saint of ragpickers and junkmen because his clerks were garbed so shabbily.[76]

VII SAINT-NICOLAS-DE-PORT

Rome invoked Romulus and Remus, Juno and Aeneas, Numa and Augustus, as we invoke Washington and Lincoln. A few dozen polities invoked N: countries (Russia, Greece), regions (Sicily, Ponthieu), cities (Paris, Moscow). Some were fickle in their veneration, like Venice, which invoked not only Saint Mark, but Peter, Theodore, George, Lawrence, Justinien, Peter Orseolo, Charitine, Justine, and others beside N. Leipzig invoked not only N but Michael, John the Baptist, and Thomas; Copenhagen Notre Dame and Lucius the Pope. But the tale of Saint-Nicolas-de-Port is one of complete devotion.[1]

The N cult was active in Lorrain before the Translation,[2] but omnipresent thereafter. An identified sixty-six parishes dedicated to N existed at the outbreak of the religious wars. Marot says that there were fifty-eight chapels in the diocese of Toul alone, six within the town. A leading abbey, Gorze, outside Metz, cherished an N relic as early as 1065.[3] From the eighth century the abbey had maintained a priory at Varangeville, at a useful ford on the Meurthe, south of Nancy. Three centuries later Abbot Henry (d. 1093) built a chapel dedicated to N at Port, the other end of the bridge on the left bank. Trade had been expanding, and Varangeville was strategically located where French goods could be loaded on boats to travel down the Moselle to the Rhine. The chapel was consecrated by Phibo, bishop of Toul, an act recorded 12 October 1101; the same bishop also consecrated an N church at Neufchâteau.[4]

According to wholly questionable records,[5] a knight, Aubert of Port, returning from crusade, stopped at Bari, where he encountered a fellow citizen, a clerk in the basilica, who decided to desert Bari and return home with him. At that decision, N appeared to the clerk in a vision advising him to take an N relic with him. Using or misusing the keys of office, he carried off a finger bone. On the route the clerk died, and Aubert, unwilling but under divine surveillance, presented the relic to the abbot of Gorze, who thereupon decided to erect the N chapel at Port. This legend, only one of many similar ones accounting for N's widely disseminated finger bones, may possibly be based on a likely fact that the monks of Gorze, wanting to cater to the affluent trade at Port, transferred their N relic from Gorze to the new shrine.

Be that as it may, the N chapel at Port prospered, at least in part because of its strategic location. By the middle of the twelfth century it had become the goal of an important pilgrimage road.[6] The dukes of Lorrain and the abbots of Gorze, sensing the new prosperity, loaded the growing establishment with the liberties and perquisites, together with licenses for fairs. A historian around 1255 wrote that prisoners, the feverish, and all who suffered from any infirmity flocked there from far places. It was the cult of prisoners that particularized the shrine at Port. Descriptions of mounds of chains shed by prisoners, piled within the church, appear about the middle of the fifteenth century; but only in the next century (A.D. 1537) do we read for the first time the famous legend which gave substance to the cult, and only in a document written at the beginning of the seventeenth century do we read the full tale. Briefly it is this: When in A.D. 1240 the Moslems threatened to take Jerusalem from Frederick II, the feudal nobility of France, Lorrain, and Burgundy went to his defense. A knight of Réchicourt, Cuno, was captured by the infidels and held to the prison walls by seven chains welded to a collar iron more than twenty fingers broad and an inch thick. Since he had commended himself to N as patron of prisoners, on N Eve he prayed especially ardently, promising a pilgrimage to Port if N should rescue him. A renegade Christian, his jailer, mocked him, calling his beloved "Colas de Lorraine" a fraud and a fake. While Cuno slept he was miraculously taken from the prison and set down, still in the ponderous chains, before Saint-Nicolas-de-Port. In gratitude he established what became an annual commemorative processional on N Eve and Day, and gave the priory his land of Réchicourt.

Some sense of the instability of the legend comes from Champier's statement in 1537 that the collar was five fingers broad and three thick. Any chance for antiquarian recovery of evidence to authenticate the early cult was wiped out in the great fire of 1635. There is really no place in the genealogy of the lords of Réchicourt for a Cuno, especially around the year 1240; any slight knowledge we possess of the land grants of the period makes the story seem more than dubious. At any rate, by 1674 it had taken full shape. A pilgrim then described a statue of Cuno that stood in the church. Even before that, in 1628, a "tragicomedy" in five acts told of Cuno's adventure.

We may assume that the legend developed after 1255 but before 1537 and was therefore a factor in the prosperity which led to the building of the great church, the bulk of which dominates the plain of the Meurthe, an eastern Chartres visible all the way from Nancy to Luneville.

Cuno and the crusaders of Frederick II were not the only devout Crusaders. Saint Louis's biographer and chronicler, Joinville, whose demesne was not very far from Port, recounts that during a storm on the Mediterranean he advised the frantic French queen to pledge reward to Saint-Nicolas-de-Port for safe passage: "Madam, affirm your vows to Monseignor Saint-Nicolas of Varangeville, and I pledge you that God will return you to France, and the king and your children." She pledged a silver ship weighing five marks, which she had made (*que Diex absoille!*) when she returned safely to France. It cost a hundred pounds. Joinville himself conducted it to Port.[7]

This *nef* was but the first of several given to the treasury. Today only one remains, if indeed even it is authentic. Though the treasury was dispersed during the religious wars and Revolution, on 10

November 1851 a silver ship with a cardinal seated in the poop was offered for sale in Nancy. The curé of Saint-Nicolas at the time, Lebègue de Girmont, solicited money from tithes and gifts to purchase it for one thousand francs, in the belief that it belonged to the church. It is the work of a goldsmith of Nuremberg, Hans Rappolt, who became master craftsman in 1574.

Duke Nicholas of Lorrain (d. 1473) had been explicitly named for N. When he died his successor René II, already a devotee of N, had to flee from the opposing Burgundians. René underwent a miraculous vision as he prayed at Saint-Nicolas-de-Port. At that moment of need he received great financial assistance from the prior. With such auguries he overcame the Burgundians at Nancy, 5 January 1477. The duke, "not wishing to attach any praise to himself, rendered glory for his victory to God, the Virgin His mother, and equally included honor to Monseignor Saint-Nicolas, naming him Father of the Country, Leader and Defender of Lorrain." This is the official origin of N's patronage of Lorrain. Some months after the battle, Le mystère de Saint-Nicolas, composed by the notary Jacquemin Barthélemy, was performed for the duke's delectation.

Almost immediately afterward, work was begun on the great new late-Gothic basilica. At the instance of René's mother, the duchess Yolande d'Anjou, Pope Sixtus IV ordained a Jubilee (27 April 1480); Pope Alexander VI proclaimed a second in 1502. The profits went to construction. Appropriate for a saintly patron of commerce were shops built into the fabric, under the chapels; they were rented to glassmakers, pewterers, painters, and such artisans. The N fairs boomed. Duke Charles III (24 March 1597) approved two fairs of fifteen days each annually, the first opening 20 June, the second 20 December (called the "Nativity Fair" or "New Year's Gift [estrainnes] Fair"), an indication of the fixed association of N and the festive Twelveday season. Why not fifteen days from 9 May and 6 December? Before the Reformation, feasts did not so easily slip around the calendar, but by the sixteenth century political and commercial exigencies came to determine the fixing of annual cycles and festivals, as they do now.

The number of famous pilgrims to the shrine at Port is beyond count. Saint Joan of Arc prayed there to N for help on her way to her first audience with Duke Charles II at Nancy. Incidentally, the story of Joan is full of N imagery, apropos for a native of Lorrain. Catherine was, of course, one of her celestial visitors, Margaret of Antioch the other. When captured, Joan was imprisoned at Compiègne in the keep (now Tour Jeanne d'Arc) on rue Saint-Nicolas (from the N chapel on it).[8] In chapter 3 above the presence of N at Rouen, where Joan was tried and died, was treated.

Margaret of Anjou, daughter of René II, celebrated at Saint-Nicolas-de-Port her betrothal to King Henry VI of England. She ended her days as prisoner in the Tower of London, where she invoked N, patron of prisoners. Did N come to her rescue, or did he not?

> Was I for this night wrack'd upon the sea,
> And twice by awkward wind from England's bank
> Drove back unto my native clime?

yet

> The pretty vaulting sea refus'd to drown me,
> Knowing that thou wouldst have me drown'd on shore
> With ears as salt as sea through thy unkindness.[9]

Francis Xavier was one of a group who stopped in 1536; they had left Paris on foot to join Ignatius Loyola and go on to Rome. May of Austria, the queen of Hungary, came in 1549. Charles IX and his mother Catherine de Medicis in April 1564; she later brought her son, who would be King Henry III. His wife was daughter of Nicholas of Lorrain, once regent. She made a pilgrimage each week afoot from Nancy to Saint-Nicolas. King Henry IV, with his wife Marie de Medicis, came 5 April 1603.

Marguerite of Gonzaga, traveling from Mantua, on 14 June 1616 stayed at Port the night before she was to enter Nancy as wife of Duke Henry II. She gave a chasuble, two tunics, and a silver cloth for the altar front; her husband gave effigies of N and Saint Catherine, in silver. Their daughter, the duchess Nicole, contributed gifts; Henry's sister Catherine, abbess of nearby Remiremont, was a fervent devotee.

A *Confrérie de S. Nicolas de Varanville en Lorraine,* a pilgrim fraternity, met regularly in Paris on 6 December and 9 May at the Hôpital

Saint-Jacques.[10] It is recorded in a calendar of 1621. In that year Nicolas Dumont composed a very popular guidebook to the shrine; it was most recently republished in 1835.[11]

In 1626, despite the religious wars, Pope Urban VIII granted Duke Charles IV the boon of a Great Jubilee for Saint-Nicolas-de-Port. After that occasion the Jesuit professor Léonard Perin dedicated a Life of N to Prince Nicolas-François de Lorrain, Bishop of Toul, in which he stated that despite the poverty and unrest caused by troops massed in the neighborhood for the religious wars, two hundred pilgrims had come to Port.

Those wars brought an end to greatness. On 30 August 1633 the troops of Louis XIII and his Swedish allies occupied Port. On 10 - 11 November they set fire to town and church and sacked the town. Many lives were lost. The responsibility for that disaster has never been determined: the French blamed the Swedes, the Swedes the French, and both blamed the Germans. But the pilgrimage shrine as such was no more. In 1639 an official report, signed by Nicolas du Grant, clerk of the court, directed to the king, said, "Now there remain only two hundred townsmen, very poor indeed."

To cite further history would be redundant. The shrine was slowly repaired—reroofed, at least, but never restored enough to make it worth serious attention by the Republicans of the Revolution, though they helped themselves to whatever poor remains they could find. The affluence of our century has brought about the basilica's renovation but cannot restore its life—it is a very large and empty religious edifice, a relic without relics. There is "La bonne pierre," a granite stone shaped like a cross, where young couples kneel to assure a year's happy marriage. Over the western portal survives a beautiful Gothic effigy of N, his finger (Aubert's finger?) raised in benediction over anyone who passes on the almost empty street.

In Rome at the beginning of the sixteenth century, if not before, there was a confrérie of Lorrainers, with a chapel dedicated to N in the parish of Saint-Louis-des Français. That chapel lasted until 1798. An anti-French party of Lorrainers formed a new confraternity dedicated to N and Catherine. In 1622 they took over the existing church of Saint-Nicolas de Agone on what is now called Lorrain Street (Via dei Lorenesi), leading from the Piazza Navona. They replaced it with a new church in 1635. That building, designed by Olavo Regig de Campos, still stands; the facade inscription across the lower course reads: *In Honorem S. Nicolai Natio Lotharingorum F.* The mediocre altar painting is by Nicolas de Lorrain.[12]

This chapter has been a catalogue of evidence that N grew to become a justice, popular, prosperous, and possibly pompous. While those are attributes of many another public ideal hero, they are not "great." A generation ago Walter Nigg wrote *Great Saints,* a treatment of Nicholas of Flüe, Francis of Assisi, Joan of Arc, Theresa of Avila, John of the Cross, Francis de Sales, Gerhard Tersteegen, and Theresa of Lisieux. But not of N. It seems to be the pattern of modernity to choose its ideals from history, not mythology, and in N's history there is a Nicholas III for every Louis IX.

SIX
OLD AGE

The sixth age shifts
Into the lean and slipper'd pantaloon,
With spectacles on nose and pouch on side,
His youthful hose well sav'd a world too wide
For his shrunk shank; and his big manly voice,
Turning again toward childish treble, pipes
And whistles in his sound.

I DECLINE

Roland Bainton wrote: "The charming picture of a medieval mason taking leave of his labors in the confidence that his well-carven stones would by the favor of Saint Nicholas weight the scales in his favor at the Day of Judgment affords a certain parallel to any leavetaking from long labors at any time. But . . . he who has drunk from Luther will never suppose that any work of man will tip the scales at Doomsday, nor can he invoke the intercession of Saint Nicholas."[1]

How rapidly the strong grow weak! Suppose we stand, as did the archaeologist Birch, before a window in the Hillesden church in Buckinghamshire. It was being glazed at the very moment that Luther was beginning to doubt. TV audiences take greed and violence with their trays now, but sixteenth-century Christians with their prayers. The window is in four lights, each divided into two subjects.[2] The first two are from *Substituted Cup 62*, with inscribed verses that no one but the priest could read. The first shows a youth drowning as he hangs tight to a golden beaker; the second shows N presiding at the altar while the youth, before his kneeling parents, gives the golden cup as an oblation. The second scene is that kind of inversion of values which the Wycliffites were protesting against; instead of man's receiving the Cup from the Lord, the Lord is receiving gold from man: *Tunc offert cyphum grates pro munere reddens* (Then he offers the chalice, rendering thanks for the favor) reads the caption. The third illustrates N's miraculous multiplication of grain (*Grainships 7*). Four, five, and six illustrate the bankers' tale, *Iconia 34*: the theft, the Jew whipping the icon, N in conversation with two robbers, the robber handing a bag of gold to the Jew. The seventh is a scene of utter violence, *Lombard Son 64;* in Birch's words:

> The arch-fiend, with white beard and hoary hair, in the
> guise of a pilgrim with wallet and staff, but having claw-feet
> and hands, strangles a young man-servant who has carried
> off a dish of dainty food (a duck and cube-shaped trimmings)
> from his master, who is seen on a carved parapet with two
> guests in the background clasping their hands in the agony
> of despair: *Strangulat hic Demon puerum pulmenta ferentem.*
> [Here the Demon strangles the boy as he brings in the
> refreshments.] The final picture makes up for the horrors of
> No. 7. The dead youth lies prostrate on the ground before
> the Bishop, who is sitting in a little church-like house, while
> the young man's friends kneel in supplication to beg for the
> intercession of the Saint, which, according to the legend, is
> not asked in vain: *Mortuus ad vitam rediit precibus Nicholai.* [The
> dead man restored to life renders thanksgiving to Nicholas.]

The saints declined in the Renaissance and Reformation, and N, who represents the quiddity, declined the most; but to make Renaissance and Reformation sufficient reason for decline would be circuitous. N's decline *made* the Reformation, for what is an Age but a totalization of its biographies? We all admire Professor Bainton's clear view of the Reformation. At the moment of my quotation he was following an archenemy of sentimental medievalism, G. G. Coulton;[3] strangely enough, they were both charmed by the N of the Hillesden window that I have cited pejoratively: the summation of the mature N. But as summer comes, it brings the fruits of autumn behind.

What makes decline? What makes a career rich in ethical, political, commercial, judicial experiences eventually rich in falsities, frustrations, and failures? What makes the tragedy of man? Is it mere chaos that the patron of Columbus, who gave his name to Cape and Mole Saint Nicholas in Haiti, should be harboring a Cassius? How could gold of the Indies reduce to a farthing N's three bags of gold? What quirk determined that the thaumaturge of *Stratilates 3* should be reasoned out of existence by both the last pope and the first political scientist (Machiavelli) to bear his name? That the myrrh and relics which had endowed transalpine Europe with more than three thousand shrines should be audited and found deficient?

The descent to Avernus is easy, but not predictable. During all N's rise to fame, the image of the Wheel of Fortune shared men's mind with him: Chaucer, Boccaccio, and Caxton studied falls of princes. Mere age may determine that the old hero must be thrust aside, but from accumulated poison the tragic traits that crown an Oedipus will later blind him.

We have described N's flaws. Three bags of gold when thrown into a maiden's bedroom represent charity in youth but prurience in age. Charming sensibility becomes materialism, which very soon comes to demand its quid pro quo (*Iconia 34, Substituted Cup 62*). The *epiphania* in *Stratilates 3* and *Mariners 6* had once been a miracle unknown to even the greatest saints; they might appear after death, perhaps, but not while still ministering on earth. Such miracles turned out to be mere magic in a time of skepticism. And even in an age of faith, what could one do for an encore? N developed tuneful music, theater and spectacle; but as we know, the livelier the art the sooner it begins to cloy.[4] Then men seek out the bitterness of the Cromwells and Loyolas. The whip which was merely a scourge in *Stratilates 3* might become a heathen golden bough as pristine Christian virtue waned. N's involvement in commerce and the forum, in prelacy and politics, could be considered shrewdness more than charity. In a feudal, essentially uncommercial world N's actions inspired wonder and respect, but they paled before the actions of the Medicis. Finally, his patronage of thieves and homicides brought ostracism: established law and order are inviolable in the minds of burghers.[5]

II THE REFORMATION

The New Hebraism

Demand and invention are seldom far apart, but one historical exception is printing. Why did it arrive two centuries late? When art and science of the West had culminated in Aquinas, Giotto, Dante, "no source of inspiration could spring higher because none so profoundly plumbs the depths of humanity."[1] If printing then could have supplied the necessary criticism by spreading a fund of common sense, the West might have been saved from Huizinga. One Bacon might have stepped on the other Bacon's heels. The Grimm Brothers might have lived two centuries earlier if Dante's *De vulgari eloquentia* had had a means of mass circulation.

But without criticism the miracles of thirteenth-century science looked no different from the alleged miracles of a thousand un-criticized thaumaturges who made a farce of all science and belief, as themes of Faust and Paracelsus indicate. Thaumaturgy gave way to wizardry. Pope Innocent VIII issued his famous bull, *Malleus maleficorum,* in 1484, but Salem witchcraft trials remind us that neither poet nor pope can dam a stream in flux. Indeed, two antagonistic spirits, the New Learning and the New Superstition, joined forces to rid themselves of legends such as N.[2]

From Petrarch on, men of perception, to escape the charlatans, buried their heads in ancient sands. Unable to create for lack of criticism, the Humanists merely imitated what the critic Time told them was Truth. They did not create Beauty but exhumed it, and turned their unearthed taste into an esoteric cult. Hapsburgs and Dutch masters determined the course that the new printing, the new nations, the new world would follow. Burghers ruled armadas on the now compassed seas. Tyrants not far removed from robber barons reduced nobles and clergy to a "commons," where they were outvoted when they were not bought. "Commons" though it was, two-thirds of the populace was not there at all. Life was to be whatever earthly power produced, first from slaves and then machines. As the telescope removed the cosmic order, Harvey and Vesalius removed the heart and brain from the imagination. Order was brought down to earth, a rational piety.[3] Holy wells became mineral baths. Bath, in England, recovered not only a name but all the Roman bourgeois grandeur that had sadly puzzled one of the Anglo-Saxon poets. And the Belgian village of Spa began to lend its name, at the expense of Fonts Saint-Nicolas.[4]

Reason entered church as well.[5] The bifurcation at the Reformation was essentially as old as the Church itself. It might be called Hebraism and Hellenism. The Hebrew Christ Who meditated on the Law and Prophets was also a Hellenistic peripatetic Who laid hands on His Disciples as He reasoned about True Philosophy. The first clergy were in the second tradition: Hellenism provided a sacramental system wherein Divinity acted through material forms: holy places, relics under altars, churchyards, sprinklings, Apostolic successions, and transubstantiation. This was the world of the model bishop N, who meditated little on the Scriptures, though he liked to have his picture taken carrying them. But the early monks were Hebraists who, hand in hand with wandering steps and slow, sought the desert with only the Gospels as their guide.

They attacked no instinct or perception so hardily as that of *mediation:*[6] they asserted that the God-Man alone could mediate, not one of His creatures like the Church, and certainly not the saints. The Augsburg Confession (A.D. 1530): "We may follow their faith and good works according to our calling, as the emperor may follow David's example in making war to drive the Turks from his country; for either of them is a king. But scripture teaches us not to invoke the saints, or ask help of them."[7] Luther was silent about the saints in his Ninety-five Theses, but the Thirty-nine Articles were unambiguous: "The Romish doctrine concerning Purgatory, Pardons, Worshiping and Adoration as well of images as of Reliques, and also Invocation of Saints, is a fond thing, vainly invented."[8] The Council of Trent, desperately attempting to hold a severed world together, mildly recommended the assistance of saints while stating, "No divinity or power is thought to be in them for the sake of which they may be worshiped, or anything asked of them, or any trust be put in images."[9] N, imported from the infernal land of Turks and Slavs, was the primary target. Wrote Georg Turberville (d. 1598) about Russia:

> Their Idoles have their hearts, on God they never call,
> Unless it be Nichole Bough that hangs against the wall.[10]

Aquinas, in justifying the comparatively recent regulations centering *canonization* in the Papal Court, scholastically opined: "In the Church a damnable error cannot exist. But it would be a damnable error if one who was a sinner were venerated as a saint; for those knowing his sins would believe their knowledge false. . . . And if this should happen, they could be thoroughly led astray. The Church cannot err in such matters."[11] But the Church obviously did err in such matters.[12] There were those who believed that the Church would have done well to leave canonization or any other judgment of sanctity to the direct action of the Holy Spirit. Back in the eighth century Charlemagne had lessoned the pope: "A story was cited of a monk who lighted a candle before an image of the Virgin and found it still burning even after six months. A story like this, with no date, time, or place, has no authority. A miracle is not necessarily the work of God; it may be due to demons. Nor is the instrument of a miracle ipso facto an object of veneration."[13] If Charlemagne could say that, what could possessors of the New Learning say? In his very act of purifying and rectifying the calendar of saints, Pope Alexander III (d. 1181) canonized Bernard of Clairvaux, the English King Edward, and Thomas à Becket. The New Learning would not unequivocally support even such proper models.[14] Small wonder that the Mosaic writer had made God condemn the very imagination which He had created,[15] or that Calvin burned the hydra by denying sanctity to all: "God saw that the wickedness of man was great in the earth, and that every imagination of the thoughts of his heart was only evil continually."[16]

The New Learning was too subtle for the new merchant class, but the new printing gave them Scripture to their purpose: "Ye men of Athens," said the apostle Paul, "I perceive that in all things ye are too superstitious." "As many things as we wish, so many gods have we made," echoed Erasmus.[17] The saintly hierarchy became for them the popish peril.

Hagiology and Iconoclasm

It is easier to identify abuse than to find a remedy. How can we control the hagiolatrous imagination of mankind? Already in the twelfth century men complained that at worship they never heard Scripture because of the intrusion of uncertain stories and legends, with a multitude of responds, verses, vain repetitions, commemorations, and synodals. Is it truth or falsehood to move the legend of N onto the shoulders of the Lord? Cotton Mather, D.D. (Glasgow, 1710), Fellow of the Royal Society (1714), who inoculated his son against smallpox in the face of bitter attack,[18] in his *Magnalia Christi Americana* (1702) devoted one of its seven parts to pure hagiography without saints, from which I quote one episode, though many another one would do equally well:

> Over and above the number of sea-deliverances intended for this chapter, we will add one more, which is a late and fresh substance, and attested beyond all contradiction.
> On the 16th of October, in this present year, 1697, there arriv'd at New-Haven a sloop of about 50 tuns, whereof Mr.

William Trowbridge was master: The vessel belong'd unto New-Haven, the persons on board were seven; and seventeen long weeks had they now spent since they came from their port, which was Fayal. By so unusually tedious a passage, a terrible famine unavoidably came upon them; and for the five last weeks of their voyage they were so destitute of all food, that thro' faintness they would have chosen death rather than life. But they were a praying and pious company; and when "these poor men cry'd unto the Lord, he heard and sav'd them." God sent his dolphins to attend 'em; and of these they caught still one every day, which was enough to serve 'em: only on Saturdays they still catch'd a couple; and on the Lord's Days they could catch none at all. With all possible skill and care they could not supply themselves with the fish in any other number or order; and indeed with a holy *blush* at last they left off trying to do anything on the Lord's Days, when they were so well supplied on the *Saturdays*. Thus the Lord kept feeding a company that put their trust in him, as he did his Israel with his manna: and this they continu'd until the dolphins came to that change of water, where they us'd to leave the vessels. Then they so strangely surrendred themselves, that the company took twenty-seven of 'em; which not only suffic'd them until they came ashore, but also some of 'em were brought ashore dry'd, as a monument of the divine benignity.[19]

As Père Delehaye wrote: "It is easy enough to accept a principle of internal reform, especially during the upheaval of the sixteenth century; but it is quite another really to re-form the minds of adherents which the Church had done so much to form in the first instance by complacently blinking the preachment of an ill-educated clergy and a prelatry more concerned with the care of property than the cure of souls."[20]

Various means were used to dethrone the aged monarch N.[21] They may loosely be gathered under two heads: the scholarship of hagiology, and the butchery of image smashers. In the main, the scholars who applied methods of New Learning to purging hagiolatry remained within the Roman Church,[22] whereas the schismatic protestants were normally the iconoclasts.

As Luther threw his inkpot at the Devil, his disciples threw hammers at all artifacts of N. It was Luther's great opponent Clichtove who sounded the principles of criticism of the cult of saints:

> The question of Madeleine pertains to history, not to faith. . . . In all questions that relate to history, it is necessary to adhere to authors who wrote at the time of the event. In the absence of such, to those most competent in the interpretation of Scripture. . . . The works of unidentified authors have no value in opposition to ancient writings. . . . The Church cannot forbid, in doubtful cases, the search for truth through study and application of the rules of criticism.[23]

The invention of printing accounts for this confident new note. At last communities possessed documents which they could study and compare. But an invention does not itself have a moral code or spiritual direction. The very presses that poured out documents for the university scholars also poured out as never before fables of ever more debased sensibility. Two generations had passed since Gutenberg. Legends of saints were the property of every literate home, whence they were disseminated to neighboring illiterates. According to one count, of 349 titles printed in England, A.D. 1468 - 1530, 176 were religious, among them an abundance of tiny lives of saints. The dozen or more rivals of the *Golden Legend,* Mombritius and the *Catalogus Sanctorum* in the lead, were like it in piosity though of far greater bulk.

But scholarship slowly made its way.[24] Bishop Aloysius Lipomanus of Verona applied the new canons of scholarship in his eight-volume legendary (*Sanctorum priscorum patrum vitae,* 1551 - 1560). The rich fruit of such scholarship was the Société des Bollandistes, an affiliation of scholars never exceeding seven in number (not counting a very large corps of assistants), formed at Brussels in 1615 under the patronage of the Jesuits. Now, more than three-and-a-half centuries later, despite every discouragement including banishment, several confiscations of parts and all of their precious libraries, and devastating wars, they continue on their path, which is the critical editing of the lives and legends of the saints (*Acta Sanctorum*). The first two volumes (January) were published in 1643; the last volume of November is not yet published, and the volume to contain N (Dec. 6) is indeterminately in the future. But the scholarship of these Bollandist Fathers, published in their own serials and monographs as well as in the *Acta,* has affected every field of learning. Of course, without their work this volume would have been impossible.

It is the tragedy of old age that it so clings to life. "From the first and to this day, more scholarly energy of the Bollandists," wrote Père Delehaye, "goes to the daily answering of objections of the sensitive than to the discovery of truth." By truth undoubtedly he meant the conclusions reached by applying the principles of Clichtove, Rosweyde, Bolland, and Papenbroeck, the Bollandists' founding fathers. Their struggles with the pretentious Carmelites forms a dramatic section of any history of the age. In 1695 the Spanish Inquisition prohibited reading or sale of the *Acta* for March, April, and May. In 1698 the Papal Court imposed silence on both the Carmelites and Bollandists until it could render a court decision. The decision has never come. Sanctified intellect and sanctified imagination are at a standoff, though the proscription of the Inquisition was lifted 13 January, 1715.[25]

Scholarship, even the Bollandists', cannot eradicate the adulatory propensities of man; but it has helpfully controlled that idolatry of man which is for ever insinuating itself into religious exercise.

The second band of revolutionists was the iconoclasts or puritans, for whom Savonarola and Calvin are models. The abuses of hagiolatry were their excuse for barbarous smashing of paintings, sculpture, gold and ivory carving. Though few burned handwritten or printed Lives of saints, they wrapped fish in them. Throughout ecclesiastical history those who would cleanse the stables[26] have been forced by the logic of their positions to smash the mangers. A Wycliffite document of about 1389 asserted: "These ymages of hemselfe may do nouther gode to mennis soules, but thai myghtten warme a man's body in colde, if thai were set upon a fire." That was the voice of reason that led to the decapitation of half the chiseled heads of Europe. Down went the "Bibles of the illiterate"—the documents of N, who could no longer rescue clerks or maidens in window glass or triptych. For example, the troops of Cromwell wrecked the Galway Collegiate Church of N, "destroying all the old stained glass, defacing many monuments, and stabling horses there." However, some of the wall statues or plaques that were defaced or removed found their way later into what is now Saint Nicholas's Pro-Cathedral, where they serve as an unkind memorial.[27] And like the Mosaic God, who in the Second Commandment forbade all graven images, their rationale for smashing them was preserved in verbal images: by their very words of condemnation, the pamphlets of the seventeenth century helped to preserve N's sadly wasted frame.

Already had begun the sardonic inventories of relics which were to be refined through the next three centuries.[28] In 1599 at Geneva was published an antihagiological compendium, its first tract composed by Calvin:

> *Traitté des Reliques: ou, Advertissement trés-utile du grand profit qui reviendroit à la Chrestienté, s'il se faisoit inventaire de tous les Corps saincts et Reliques, qui sont tant en Italie, qu'en France, Allemagne, Espagne et autres Royaumes et pays. Par. I. Calvin (p. 1 - 74).—Autre Traitté, traduit du Latin de M. Chemnicius (p. 75 - 138).—Inventaire des Reliques de Rome: mis d'Italien en francois (p. 138 - 160).—Response aux allégations de Robert Bellarmin Jésuite pour les Reliques (p. 160 - 208). Geneva: Pierre de la Rouiere, 1599. 12mo.*

> Treatise on Relics, or a very useful indication of the great profit which would accrue to all christendom if it would create an inventory of all the saintly bodies and relics, which are as numerous in Italy as in France, Germany, Spain and other kingdoms and districts. Part I. Calvin (p. 1 - 74). —Another treatise, translated from the Latin by Mr. Chemnicius (p. 75 - 138).—Inventory of the Relics of Rome: turned from Italian into French (p. 138 - 160).—Response to the allegations of Robert Bellarmin, S.J., regarding the relics (p. 160 - 168). Geneva: Pierre de la Rouiere, 1599. 12 mo.

It contained the well-known sentence that there existed so much milk of the Holy Virgin that had she been a cow she would have had to be milked every moment of her life to account for it.[29]

But printing, like fission, does not take sides. Antonio Beatillo's *La storia della vita, miracole, translatione e gloria dell' illustr. confessor di Christo*

San Niccolò il Magno, arcivescovo di Mira, patrono e protetore della città di Bari, published in 1620, was enlarged in 1633 and went through some seven new editions in four cities within a century.[30] A living legend, though emaciated, does not die willingly.

III THE WINTER CALENDAR
Holy Days

Most of the early Christian Fathers had frowned on anniversaries and other festivities except the solemn observance of the Lord's Day, but the imperial Church rolled aside objections to them. Easter, Pentecost, and Ascension were almost immediately followed by Epiphany, Nativity, Rogation Days and others.[1] Then came saints' days—at first those of the New Testament (Peter, Paul, Stephen and the four feasts of Mary), then the angel Michael and the martyrs, with confessors close behind. The Laws of King Ina of Wessex (A.D. 693) required men to rest on Sunday (the Lord's Day), and Charlemagne's Capitulary of A.D. 789 made all feasts of the local bishops' calendars obligatory.[2] However, his Capitularies of 794 and 805 already show his mounting fear of excessive observation and the need for firm regulation.[3]

There was no stemming the mounting tide of holidays. In 1232 Pope Gregory IX specified 95 days of universal observance, free from legal business, all but 10 from servile work as well; but every diocese had additional local holidays.[4] Bishop Gayard of Laon was a great exception; in his diocese of Cambrai he abolished observance of days of all nonscriptural saints but Lawrence and Martin.[5] Workers were actually on a four-day week. In 1166 the Byzantine emperor Manuel I Comnenus cut the number of legal holidays from 156 to 119, though 27 more were half-holidays.[6] As the Reformation neared, both the number of holidays and the outcries against them multiplied: country squires bemoaned the rotted grain and urban artisans the unswept lofts.[7] A son of N, Nicholas de Clamages, composed a tract, *That New Feastdays Should Not Be Instituted.*[8] The Chancellor of Paris, Gerson, protested to the Council of Reims in 1408, and Hugh Latimer to a like council in London as late as 1536.[9] *The Hundred Grievances of the German Nation* represented to the emperor in 1522-1523 that "the common layfolk are no little oppressed by so great an abundance of church feasts and holydays."[10]

William, the mayor of N's town of Angers, lamented (A.D. 1311) that the Devil, not God, was worshiped on holy days, that the churches were empty, crimes of every sort were committed, and all public places resounded with curses, fighting, false-swearing, and blasphemy. Even before him, Bishop Grosseteste of Lincoln spoke of the fatalities when the parishes "each with its own saint's banner paraded to the cathedral, jostling and fighting for precedence." These were occasions not only for gang processions but for the spectacles, pageants, mimicries, tumblings, and sports that the abbots and merchants encouraged at fairs and markets established on the holy days.[11] In 1209 the Council of Avignon decreed that "on vigils of saints there must not be in the churches any of those theatrical dances, indecent games, gatherings of singers and singing of secular songs which, most of the time, not only provoke the souls of listeners to sin but defile the ears and eyes of the spectators." N especially laid himself open to such abuse:[12] the gambling scene in the *Jeu de Saint Nicolas* was "dishonorable." In 1436 the Council of Basle forbade "under grievous punishment" participation in scenic plays, representations, *mascarades,* fictions of bishops, kings, and princes, in churches and cemeteries.

Those who cried abuse did so either on religious, moral, and social or on economic grounds.[13] Luther advocated wiping out all but the Lord's Day, which should be preserved for the rest and worship of the workers: "My reason is this. . . . These saints' days inflict bodily injury on the common man in two ways: he loses a day's work and he spends more than usual, besides weakening his body and making himself unfit for labor, as we see every day."[14] When his desires were carried out in Queen Elizabeth's reign,[15] Holinshed gave the history.

> Whereas not long since we had under the pope foure score
> and fifteene called festivall and thirtie called profesti, beside
> the sundaies, they are all brought unto seven and twentie:
> and with them the superfluous numbers of idle waks, guilds,
> fraternities, church-ales, helpe-ales and soule-ales, called
> also dirge-ales, with the heathenish rioting at bride-ales, are
> well diminished and laid aside. And no great matter were it
> if the feasts of all the apostles, evangelists, and martyrs, with
> that of all saints, were brought to the holie daies that follow
> upon Christmasse, Easter and Whitsuntide; and those of the

virgin Marie with the rest utterlie remooved from the
calendars, as neither necessarie nor commendable in a reformed church.[16]

Against such attacks those officials—also abbots, bishops, and
counts—whose budgets, political power, or authority depended on
the saints had many remedies. In the thirteenth century they issued
letters of indulgence "for all penitents and confessors of Truth" on set
days. But an even more effective method was to shore up legend with
legend. An abbot brought from Mount Golgotha in Jerusalem a celestial mandate to keep the festivals "under penalty of showers of stones
and hot water, ravenous beasts, and extermination by pagan
hordes."[17] Legends were coined to support each several holiday; for
instance, the historian Matthew Paris reported for the year 1200 that a
black suckling pig had attached itself to the left breast of a laundress
who had dared to work on a feast day.[18]

Since all was common in the communion of saints, a legend created
for one saint's day was quickly applied to another's. N's status was
well protected by a stream of reports of condign punishment visited on
those who dared to labor on his Day. Guibert of Nogent tells of a
seamstress who violated the feast of Saint Nicaise at Noyon.[19] The
thread pierced her tongue and hung there to her great pain until
fervent prayers to the Virgin (who had impelled the accident to start
with, as protecting Her Martyr) caused it to drop. The bloodied
thread was thereafter displayed to Guibert, who records the recur-
rence of the same crime and punishment in the same diocese in
protection of another feast, Ascension. I have chanced on the same
legend in three different forms applied to N and N Day (*Holiday
Breaking,* 77).[20]

But Protestantism, led by the new captains of trade, prevailed, not
only in provinces eventually reformed but in the loyal catholic provinces that would compete with them economically.[21] Karl Marx has
written that "Protestantism clearly performed an important role in
the genesis of capital by its commutation of nearly all feasts into
working days."[22] When persuasion failed, the Tudors, who would
usher in a brave world of mercantilism, turned to prohibitory law: the
proclamation of Thomas Cromwell in 1536 states that holidays have
multiplied excessively, the source of superstition prejudicial to the

common weal; that they are the occasion of much sloth and idleness, the nurse of thieves and vagabonds, unthriftiness and confusion; the frequent cause of loss of crops, of food, and pernicious to men's souls; that on holy days there is more sin committed in superstitious observance than on other days. Since even the Sabbath was made for man, let alone the holy days, the king, as Supreme Head on earth of the Church of England, with the consent of the prelates and clergy in convocation assembled, orders that for the future (1) all churches shall keep the special feast of their dedication on the same day, to wit, the first Sunday of October; (2) the feast of the patron saint of the parish is not to be observed as a holy day; (3) no feasts falling in harvest time, i.e., between 1 July and 29 September, or within the law terms, are to be kept as holy days, with certain exceptions.[23]

Epiphanytide

Of all feasts, those of fall and winter were most animated, sometimes frenetic. The autumnal saints of harvest and thanksgiving (Michael, All Saints, All Souls, Guy Fawkes, and Martin) tend to meld with saints of winter (Andrew, Nicholas, and Thomas).[24] The mechanics of cult jump from one group to the other; I mentioned that the "Catherine wheel" of 25 November moved up to Gunpowder (Guy Fawkes) Day, 5 November in England. Pelzmartel[25] and Pelznichol both wander about in animal skins at harvestide. Hence we have difficulty keeping our topic in focus, for legend becomes confused with myth, ritual, folklore, learning (actual and pseudo), and mere politics and commercialism.[26] *Festivity* is as old as witchcraft itself, fostered for the whole sweep of generous and selfish purposes, or for no purpose at all. Benevolent patricians around the globe mold their worship of sticks and stones and their intimations of immortality to "what counts" for them and their society.

But when the corn was in the bin, the carcasses in the smokehouse, the log upon the fire, and the wind whistling in the stubble, the lowered activity of mortals brought a new devotion, compounded of ancestral and ghostly presences, inversions of status, fertility rites and other safety measures designed to preserve the stock, whether vegetable, animal, or human.[27] The winter solstice marked the demise of the sun and the growth of omens, spells, prognostications, especially marked at the Julian New Year. It was then that the Green Knight came to Arthur's court to be beheaded and to live again. Shivering man propitiates good and bad equally, taking no chances. In 1410 Brunswick employed a mime (*Schoduvel*) for the whole winter season. During this dark night of the soul man was sent redeemers; but he also relied on his own powers, often vertiginous: mimicry, processional, song, dance, costume, food, drink, gifts, and storytelling of myth, fable, and legend together with their acting out.[28]

All this is inspiration of the dying god of the winter season. In the mumming processionals men put on animal skins.[29] The hobbyhorse is Wodan's and N's white horse, which anthropologists surmise is the folksy substitute for the animal sacrifice of early man.[30] Early man might be pastoral, as with the bloody sacrifices of the butchering season; or agricultural, as with rites of last sheaves made into yulecakes and cornchildren, compounded with fruits and nuts; or domestic, as with good luck tokens of twigs from sacred groves (*ramusculi,* mistletoe, holly), firelogs, and gifts; or neighborly and clannish, as with visitations and mummery; or ancestral, as with invocations to all saints and souls, earth mothers, wild riders, and cults of dead, near-dead, and never-dead. As with the ancestral old, so with the childish young, who indulge in "quêtes," "strenae," and "barring out" of parents and masters.

The winter season brings a frenzied movement against the inevitable flow of death and birth.[31] The most sophisticated can only sublimate this inheritance, so they say, as with the statutes of King's College, Cambridge: "In honour of God or His Mother or some other saint, the fellows are indulged with a fire in Hall at Wintertide. Then it shall be lawful for scholars and fellows, after dinner or supper, to make a decent tarrying in Hall for recreation's sake, with songs and other honest pastimes, and to treat, in no spirit of levity, of poems, chronicles of realms, and wonders of this world, and other things which are consistent with clerical propriety."[32]

"Heaven help the poor sailor on a night like this," mutters man in his onshore cave; as a charm he coins a Poseidon's and a N's Day. Winter brought with it a host of holy days, all flavored with the bittersweet of fear and hope. Depending on the latitude, but also on man's inheritance of palliatives and preventions, the winter season shortens and lengthens. The croppers possibly have a shorter season than the herders. Transalpine Christendom seemed in the Middle Age to feel the effect from Advent to Candlemas in the milder regions and from Hallowe'en to Easter in the harsher and less inventively advanced. But in stable Christian communions the heart of winter was the Twelve-days between the two Christmases of Nativity and Epiphany (the *Dodecahemeron*), between the joyful birth and the magi's gifts, into which death seems to creep.[33]

It is the time of ghost stories, when the spirits return, and it adds a special anxiety tinged with pathos. It is not paradox or contradiction—this jumble of unlike Days in the winter season. We all know that Christ was born into the greatest darkness, the old winter solstice, to bring light. Bede tells us that his pagan Teutonic ancestors called that winter solstice "Mothers' Night."[34] The subjective loveliness of Saint Bernard's hymn *Jesu dulcis memoria* poured over all worshipers at that time of year:

> *Mane nobiscum Domine,*
>> Stay with us till the day break, Lord,
> *Et nos illustra lumine:*
>> Shed light on us, Eternal Word.
> *Pulsa mentis caligine*
>> Dispel black terror with Thy sword
> *Mundum reple dulcedine.*
>> And cleanséd, kindly world afford.
> *Jesu flos Matris Virginis*
>> O Jesus, Virgin Mother's flower,
> *Amor nostrae dulcedinis,*
>> Sweet lover of the Bridegroom's bower,
> *Tibi laus, honor nominis,*
>> To Thee be glory, honor, power,
> *Regnum beatitudinis.*[35]
>> That us Thy blessedness may shower.

December 25 is a symbolic, not historical date, matching the equally popular *Baptizatio* of the churches of the East, which Christians have learned to call Epiphany. The two, twelve days apart, formed an easy combination, for they bracketed the natural winter holidays when ghosts must be appeased, exorcised, and entertained.[36]

The martyr Stephen's Day comes first after Christmas, equally symbolic. Christ's advent leads to martyrdom. Among clerical chapters of the Middle Age it was naturally the Deacons' Day. The prehistorical winter slaughter continued to haunt it. On Stephen's Day throughout Britain and France "the killing of the wren" was customary. Boys would hunt and kill a wren, hang it from a broomstick amid mistletoe or holly, and sing their way from house to house:

> The wren, the wren, the king of all birds,
> St. Stephen's Day was caught in the furze;
> Although he is little his family's great,
> I pray you, good landlady, give us a treat.[37]

A feather exchanged for food was "an effectual preservative from shipwreck for a year, and a fisherman would have been thought very foolhardy who had not one of them."[38] In the pattern of inversion the boys or men might become officials or magistrates for the day.

On the 27th comes the Priests' Day of Saint John the Evangelist. Was it, too, purely symbolic? Or did John truly die on 27 December, an aged bishop of Ephesus so reverenced as the last of the Apostles that the Muse of History could accurately retain memory of the date of his death? Whatever the answer, John's legend was already full of winter stories, tinged with Twelvetide bittersweet by the time of Constantine. His dying words, wrote Jerome, were "Little children, love one another." Augustine tells that on his burial the earth that covered him moved strangely, and when the sarcophagus was opened it was empty: the Lord had reserved him for personal battle with Antichrist at the Second Advent—which doubtless would occur at the winter season.[39]

The tender, thunderous John made way for Innocents' Day (28 Dec.), another symbolic date.[40] What warrant for Herod's slaughter, nine days before Three Kings' Day? Innocents' was Choirboys' Day, of course, with memories of the *Benedicite* sung by Shadrach, Meshach, and Abednego, those *innocentes* in the fiery furnace (Daniel iii) who inspired *Three Clerks 44.* The choirboys sang it constantly at Lauds.

On the next day (29 Dec.) Thomas à Becket was slain, A.D. 1170, the quintessence of martyrdom for Northern peoples, not only the British Isles and France but (by the peculiarity of politics of the time) of the Low Countries and Germany as well. In our century Eliot's *Murder in the Cathedral* has become a common winter-season theatrical.

On 30 December the Northern choirs relaxed, but the 31st was

Saint Sylvester's Day. The Golden Legend for this day tells how Constantine was smitten with leprosy. The pagan priests counseled him to slay three thousand children and bathe in their warm blood. But as the children were gathered, Constantine saw the mothers in terrified tears. With marvelous rhetoric he countermanded the order, resigning himself to death by leprosy. But Peter and Paul in a vision tell him to summon Sylvester (who is exiled in the mountains) and be baptized. After the ceremony Constantine issues seven edicts in seven days, not the famous Donation, but nevertheless largely devoted to protection of the temporalities of the Church. No historian knows what day Constantine was baptized, but James of Voragine designated the story to be read on 31 December.

The last of the days important to our theme is New Year, the old Roman calends devoted to Janus, the two-faced god.[41] It was central to the winter rites, a time for gifts (strenae), processions, inversions, animal mimicry and the rest.[42] "The Christians were hard put to it to uproot these superstitions," says The Golden Legend, so they supplanted Janus with a symbolic octave of Christ and called it Feast of the Circumcision, a memorial that on that day Christ first shed His blood for man, the winter Dying God in a different guise. But the sub-deacons, who were in reality late adolescents, took the day for their own, and it became the Feast of Fools.[43]

The Church thus incorporated the winter psyche in its doctrines, uneasily. In 1473 the Council of Toledo[44] inveighed against "the gauche custom prevailing on Christmas, Saint Stephen's, Saint John's, Innocents' Day, and others, during solemn Masses to introduce into the church hobgoblins, monsters, everything inappropriate, and to diabolize tumultuously, to shout, to sing songs and carry on derisory tales which degrade the office and distract the people's spirit from pious things."[45] But as Newman said: "Quarry the granite rock with razors or moor the vessel with a thread of silk; then may you hope, with such keen and delicate instruments as human knowledge and human reason, to subdue those giants, the passion and pride of man."[46]

Long before Christ was born, the world had ritualized the haunting emotion caused by the image, feeling, or instinct of inverted status.[47] Perhaps the Dying God drew that feeling from the reversal of the winter solstice. Pastors then became animals by dressing in animal skins, farmers became grain by dressing in straw shocks, nobles became serfs for a day and serfs noblemen. The wheel of Fortune, which is for ever turning, spins violently at the winter holy days. The King of Fools, Abbot of Unreason, Lord of Misrule, manages the season's revels. When the parish church or abbey shrine was the center of all society, the clergy led or were drawn in as directors and actors.

As members of an international order, they acquired and perpetuated Tradition.[48] Both ideas and methods were spread by clerical instruction. Polydore Virgil (d. 1555) notes the inversion at Epiphanytide: "For then servants have authority over their masters, and one of the domestics, being made on that occasion a Lord, all the heads of families and their children willingly yield obedience to him." And he adds ex post facto, "We do this to prove that all should be as free as brothers in Christ."[49]

N and the Dodecahemeron

I have said that saints' days hardly ever slip in the solar calendar; but customs easily do. Catherine (25 Nov.), Andrew (30 Nov.), and N (6 Dec.) acquired customs that are hardly distinguishable. Chambers demonstrated exhaustively how all the customs of Christmas and New Year's Day were interchanged.[50] My topic allows me to treat only one aspect of this formulation: the interchange of N Day customs with the Dodecahemeron.

Some anthropologists say that the gods of the conquerors depress those of the conquered—that the Giants become the Lokis and the Pucks. The god of the slaughtered priests of Baal is the Hebraic Beelzebub. When Christian south moved north with the missionaries, depressed northern gods were equated with depressed southern gods as, e.g., names for the days of the week tell us. Holde, Perchta, Bertha, etc., a kind of earthmother who especially haunted the winter season, entered the home on the smoke of hearthfires. A late medieval scribe in Germany glosses Diana in a Latin sermon, "Vrawholde, das teufilsmutter." As N escapes from public life to the safety of the hearth, he will travel down the smoke in a fashion identical with the Diana whom he once destroyed (*Artemis 4*). When the Reformers conquered the Conformers, the saints approached their Götterdämmerung.[51]

N, as a less substantial saint, less easily retained his place in Church and Heaven than, say Ambrose or Gregory I. From rarified religion he declined into the impenetrable mists of superstition.[52] I share with Meisen a disbelief in the great antiquity of N the elf or sprite. Evidence or the absence of it leads me to believe that Old Nick, Nikke, Nikker, and Nix are but dissanctified N and not Aryan daimons.[53] Old age brings on the capricious antics of incipient senility. In the days when he defended popes and emperors, N was no fit subject for a childish yarn. But later when the New Learning sneered at Old Faith and Morals, pygmy tales were told about an image that had once stood close to God.

Learning and logic cannot explain the degradation of magnates. Once senility makes itself evident, the Establishment turns away in embarrassment. This makes it hard for the biographer: no longer are there documents to prove a case. Rather, there is just evidence enough to let us know that N lived on in obscurity but not enough to make us certain why. Suggestions must suffice.

How N, the preeminent theologian, politician, philanthropist, and merchant became patron of students, children, and even infants has been explained. Old age brings back a second childhood, wherein habits long forgotten (like refusing the pap, *Lactation 11,* and throwing gifts around, *Three Daughters 13*) become again of consequence. Peter Comestor, chancellor of the University of Paris, made N the cynosure of scholars: "Intellectually humble, zealously questioning, unruffled, silently observant, poor and unworldly." It would be hard to derive those qualities from the account of John the Deacon, but the head of the greatest university in the world did: "For our Nicholas was himself a scholar and especial champion of scholastic men."[54] When the scholastic bishop Godehard invoked N and made his *Three Clerks 44* and *Three Daughters 13* the theater of the winter season, we were not surprised at the resultant popularity, for the images of the growing legend fitted in their place. The triune clerks and maidens were rescued from a fate of death or worse, as was Christ Himself, the Scapegoat, and the hunted Wren. N was for the boys and girls their visitation, their ancestral apparition of Epiphanytide, their breath of life. December 6 came closer to Nativity than it had before.[55] No severe strain on the imagination was involved, for N Day was well within the Advent season.[56] The rescued clerks and maidens were Daniel's three boys and Herod's innocents. We can mark in hymns and other documents how the Three Daughters, who started as spinsters, were reduced to adolescence and then to childishness.[57]

Giftgiving probably started with a pedagogue, as reward or punishment: Chiron gave herbs to Asclepius and a bow (which proved his undoing) to Heracles. This kind of magistral giftgiving easily assimilated the N who gave money to the maidens with the Northern custom of winter gifts.[58] No document has survived to assure us, but we can easily imagine that the Hildesheim *Three Daughters 13* and *Three Clerks 44*, composed for presentation 6 December, were part of a Saxon commencement exercise at which a dictionary was given to the best speller and exercise bars to the best athlete. Those first scholastic dramas differed very little formally or didactically from the Herod and Rachel dramas of 28 December, Innocents' Day.[59]

There survives a delightful description of how King Conrad of Franconia at the beginning of the tenth century spent Epiphanytide at the abbey of Saint Gall, where he gave gifts, banqueted the monks, and asked for three days of vacation for the scholar-choirboys.[60] As the reporter writes, Mass was hurried, the refectory crowded at dinner hour for the banquet, and the lector had hardly finished the invocation before the monks had dived into the rich and abundant fare provided by the king. Conrad had sent out for minstrels and strolling players (*satyrici*) to entertain the community. There were such capers as had never been seen in the refectory of Saint Gall, and many an elder brother shook his head in disapproval. Solemn convents (and typical early medieval schools were such) were ever subject to their Maecenas' pressure for ribaldry, especially in the winter season of inertia.[61] I can easily imagine that in a desire to ease the strain at emotional Epiphanytide, scholastic elders found it desirable to move the children's portion of the snowballing winter revels forward to convenient N Day.

We have since evolved an Epiphanytide vacation, but there was none then.[62] Guibert of Nogent's tutor was only excessive, not untraditional: "Even on Sundays and Saints' Days I had to submit to the severity of school exercises; on no day, and hardly at any time, was I allowed to take holiday. With him in this fruitless struggle I passed nearly six years."[63] Coulton writes of the later medieval period: "In the new boarding schools the old monastic tradition was still showing. The boys were not allowed to stray from the precincts, and there were no regular vacations, though, of course, the red-letter days of the Church were holidays in the same sense that Sunday was. Sports were rather discouraged than otherwise. It was only on December 6 (Saint Nicholas Day) that the boys had free—not to say riotous—license."[64]

How did the revels of Epiphanytide become attached to 6 December? As early as 1260 severe legislation was being passed against the excesses of Innocents' Day.[65] The Council of Cognac decreed: "As for the dances which historically take place in certain churches on the Feast of Holy Innocents, they are regularly the occasion of brawling and trouble, even during the Holy Office and at other times. We prohibit these amusements on pain of anathema. There will be no bishops created on that feast of Innocents; for it is only a pretext for laughter in the Church of God and a derision of episcopal dignity."[66]

IV SPECTACLES ON NOSE AND POUCH ON SIDE

The Boy Bishop[1]

"There will be no bishops created on that feast of Innocents." The "Boy Bishop" was well-known throughout Christendom, documented at Rouen as early as the eleventh century.[2] Like the King of Fools, the Abbot of Misrule, and all other inversion figures, he was conceived benevolently.[3] Today our elders create Boy Mayors and Presidents-for-a-Day with the laudable aim of educating and edifying the young. But without stringent control the young habitually learn too quickly and become edified too fast. All over Europe Boy Bishops riotously drank up the alms on Innocents' Day and imperiled the bodies as well as the souls of their parishioners.[4] The scandals of the Winter Season inspired various devices for lessening its impact.[5] In 1245 the papal legate forbade the *fastorum antiqua ludibria,*[6] and the next year the chapter at Nevers prohibited the "Feast of Fools on Innocents' Day and New Year."[7] At Viviers in 1365 an effort was made to disband the "Innocents";[8] but ten days before 28 December a group of "Sclaffards" and lower clergy met to elect a mock Abbot, who presided over revels more extensive than ever.[9] In 1444 the Faculty of Theology at Paris ordered the *ludi* to be wiped out throughout France.[10]

One means of alleviating the clerical revels was to move some part of the customs to N Day, as we have already noted.[11] But of course like many reforms, this action simply substituted two days for one, or indeed all the days between 6 December, when an N Bishop was chosen, and Innocents' Day when he officiated.[12] The Nicholas Bishop (as he was often called) became but one aspect of the harvest and winter masques, mummings, and processionals, which were usually begging quests or levies.[13] Folklorists have pointed to the processionals for bringing in the last sheaves and shoats which mark each major harvest day. Our English dictionaries record these gifts, tolls, or extortions as "souling" (2 Nov.), "guys" (5 Nov.), "clemences" (23 Nov.), "catherings" (25 Nov.), "nixies" (6 Dec.), "thomasings" (21 Dec.), and Calènes (1 Jan.).[14] The Boy Bishop custom, in moving forward to N Day, simply helped to bring two seasons closer together.[15]

An overwhelming number of sees, from Italy to Scandinavia and the Hebrides, from Ireland to Hungary, at some time in their history had Nicholas Bishops; the custom reached its height in the sixteenth century but persisted in places to the nineteenth.[16] Meisen found first evidence of a Nicholas Bishop in France A.D. 1291, England 1299, Germany 1304.[17] In Spain:

> Anciently, in cathedral churches, in memory of the Election
> of St. Nicholas, Bishop of Myra [cf. *Bishop 14*], a chorister
> being placed with solemnity in the midst of the choir upon
> a scaffold, there descended from the vaulting of the ceiling a
> cloud, which, stopping midway, opened. Two angels within
> it carried the mitre, and descended just so low as to place it
> on his head, ascending immediately in the same order in
> which they came down. This came to be an occasion of
> some irregularities; for till the day of the Innocents, he had
> a certain jurisdiction, and his prebendaries took secular
> offices, such as alquazils, catchpoles, dog-whippers, and
> sweepsters.[18]

Complaints about the mounting costs both public and private survive.[19] I cite as representative a single account, of York in the year 1396.[20] The warden received for the purpose from the Chapter, the Town, and the Countryside eight pounds, fifteen shillings, and five pence. These included public oblations from Christmas and Innocents' Day and contributions from the precentor, chancellor, treasurer, archdeacon, and masters; from a local abbot and archdeacon outside the Chapter; from nobility and prelates of Yorkshire, including the countess of Northumberland and the abbot of Rievaulx. The excess of receipts over expenses (£6·14.10) reverted to the bishop's treasury. The N Bishop's banquet (6 Dec.) cost 15 shillings and 6 pence including 21 pence for beer and 2 and 3 for wine at the banquet and 7 pence for bread and beer on visitation. Also charged was dinner on Innocents' Day (6 shillings and 7 pence). Other expenses included subsistence on visitation (to Bridlington, Beverley, Feriby, Allerton, Newburgh, etc.), barbering, alms, expenses for horses and grooms, vestments, contributions, and capital expenditures—rather especially for lights and lanterns. Evidently all visitations occurred after dark, as would indeed be natural in Yorkshire in December.[21]

The natural effect of a formula including both days was to spread abuses over a period of a full month. At Lübeck in 1336 Bishop Heinrich limited the *ludus episcopus* to three full weeks.[22] In 1307 the burghers of Worms caused the schools to limit N Bishop processionals, which were degenerating into vagabondage, to N Day, Lucy Eve (12 - 13 Dec.), Nativity, Stephen's, John's, Innocents' and the Innocents' Octave.[23] At Strassburg between 6 December and 4 January the N Bishop in robes sang the collects and bestowed benefactions, while "a masked crowd troubles all right and justice in the churches."[24] And Luther exploded, "God has nothing to do with masked persons and N Bishops!" Almost certainly this masking and mimicry, with and without procession, consolidated local customs that extended far back into paganism, but the heathens had been supplied with no such convenient staging place as N could offer with his schools and bishop's throne and *loci ludorum.* [25]

A ruler who tried to control the custom was as Hercules with the hydra. In reforming nations, the heat of Reformation burned off the heads of old practices as papistical. Henry VIII legislated against the installation ceremonies of the Boy Bishop.[26] Bloody Mary reacted with an edict issued (13 Nov. 1554) by the Bishop of London to all clergy of his diocese to have a Boy Bishop.[27] According to a later historian, "On the 5th of December, or St. Nicholas' Eve, at even song came a commandment that St. Nicholas should not go abroad or about; but notwithstanding, it seems, so much were the citizens taken with the 'mask' of St. Nicholas (that is Boy Bishop) that there went about these St. Nicholases in divers parishes."[28] Then with the Elizabethan Settlement the custom seems to have disappeared from London for good.[29]

But in lands remaining Catholic no such permanent change was wrought.[30] As earlier at Viviers, would-be reformers simply lopped off the head within the church to have many grow in folk custom.[31] For example, as late as the year 1830 in Champagne poor children prepared "epigrams"—that is, rhymes in splendidly calligraphic manuscript with colored arabesques—to present to the wealthy of the region, who would pay and pay. At Mainz an annual parade of thousands of children accompanies the N bishop still, one of the "most important folk festivals in their calendar."[32]

So the reforming spirit grew concurrently with the natural growth of pageantry, exhibitionism, custom, and abuses; as reformers legislated more rigorously, purifying the churches, they encouraged the folk back into a kind of paganism that a Boniface had once eradicated when he chopped down the oak of Thor.[33] The adults could be held in bond of law, but it was not so easy with the children. The shoemakers' revels on Crispin Day and the blacksmiths' on Clement's might disappear. But in abolishing the rites of N Day and Innocents' in public, they forced them back to the sentimental bosom of the home, and sometimes the school. Once give gifts to children, let them out after dark to wear masks and beg, and a precedent is established more enslaving than any law.

N in the Home

Banned from ritual, N survived in school and home. Catholic counter-reformers pressed for elimination of the N liturgy and any residual miming or representation employed for clarifying the lections. Almost no N homilies or sermons survive from 1550 on, even in the centers of most intensive cult. Normally the Mass and Office became limited to a single proper collect and hymn. Such emasculation inexorably succeeded everywhere as N's health declined, though a very few French convents and chapters retained an extensive proper liturgy as late as the Revolution.

In schools N Day remained a holiday, but no longer a holy day;[34] in the *ludi* N lost his place to less pious heroes. The rising nation-states began to impose civil regulations on the schools which determined the recesses and vacations. We can only guess what the masters may have used N for as a subject of classroom exercise.

But localized customs refuse to die in all localities. Up to the middle of the nineteenth century, the young scholars of Namur gathered on 6 December to draw lots for who should play N and his two escorting deacons. The allotted leader was supplied with some kind of cope, a mitre of colored paper, and a diminutive crozier. Then he and his escorts, decorated with colored streamers, went from house to house receiving gifts (sugar candy, eggs, "meelbloem," meat and milk, and money) while they sang a traditional song. The deacons were needed to carry home the loot in large hampers. N's mother then must cook and serve the food to all the boys who had participated in drawing lots, while those who had failed for office fetched wood for the stove. Not far away the Xanten Council ordained (A.D. 1526) that "the parents of the bishop shall not be obliged to donate apples, gloves, and other small presents or to furnish meals [on 6 Dec.]." Nevertheless on 28 December the scholars had to invite the schoolmaster to breakfast, and the council stipulated gifts of beer, herring, fruits and nuts for all the party.[35]

I am not convinced that such public exercises, evident today in the towns of the Low Countries, uniformly represent an unbroken tradition from the seventeenth century.[36] One reads in current tourist propaganda such a press release as this one from Amsterdam:

> Saint Nicholas, the friend of the Dutch children, visits Holland. According to the story, he arrives by boat from Spain. In Amsterdam, for instance, all schools have a holiday on his arrival, when the children go to the harbor to welcome the good bishop. He then rides on his white horse to the City Hall, accompanied by his faithful Moor servants, known as Black Petes. At the City Hall he is officially received by the Mayor of Amsterdam. In other towns, similar celebrations take place. All stores carry special Saint Nicholas items, and the great moment is Saint Nicholas Eve on December 5.

This is a product of our century.[37] Whatever may have been the latent N cult, Dutch officials discovered during the first World War, the later economic depression, and especially in the restoration after the second World War that news releases based on the source of the Santa Claus cult induced both mercantile and philanthropic interest. I can find no reference to N cult in Dutch press releases or advertising, domestic or foreign, in the decade of the 1890s, but they multiply after 1920, to reach a crescendo in 1943 - 1944. For example, the London *Times* reported (31 Dec. 1945) selection of a Boy Bishop at Addlestone in Surrey, obviously an untraditional act.

N   To return to the later Reformation. The aged N, once demigod now demidemon, found refuge in the home. To be sure, New Learning and Mechanical Arts weakened the impact of seedtime, harvest, and winter on human emotions. The purified clergy, whether in or out of Rome, righteously proscribed magic, myth, and legend—at least if they were traditional, not new. And artisans and burghers frowned on whatever limited the gross national product by encouraging holidays.[38] But the new republicanism and common law determined each home to be a castle, impervious and sacrosanct. No householder could be abashed, irreligious, or unproductive if within those walls his activities were childish or for children. N became the Lar of the hearth.

Sir James Frazer spent his powerful rhetoric on this moment of N's life:

> While the fine flower of the religious consciousness in myth,
> ritual, and art is fleeting and evanescent, its simpler forms
> are comparatively stable and permanent, being rooted deep
> in those principles of the common minds which bid fair to
> outlive all the splendid but transient creations of genius. It
> may be that the elaborate theologies, the solemn rites, the
> stately temples, which now attract the reverences or the
> wonder of mankind, are destined themselves to pass away
> like "all Olympus' faded hierarchy," and that the simple folk
> will still cherish the simple names of their nameless and
> dateless forefathers, will still believe in witches and fairies,
> in ghosts and hobgoblins, will still mumble the old spells
> and make the old magic passes, when the muezzin shall
> have ceased to call the faithful to prayer from the minarets
> of St. Sophia, and when the worshippers shall gather no

more in the long-drawn aisles of Notre Dame and under the
dome of St. Peter's.[39]

This childish N is a quite pure folklore hero, and retains the childhood of mankind evident in the dodecahemera: (1) the bittersweet of
pain and laughter, of black and white, of punishment and reward; (2)
the animal disguise; (3) the visitation; (4) the ubiquity and ghostly
chivalry; (5) the gifts; and (6) the tinsel ornaments and chromatic art.
N stirred himself at the domestic hearth on N Eve in many parts of
Europe until this century (*N-Eves* 78).[40]

V THE SHRUNK SHANK

Bittersweet

From birth, N had makings of a pedant, a disciplinarian. The pedant's
aim is balance, and his favorite phrases are "on the other hand" or
"the other side of the coin." He thinks in dualities: Hebraism and
Hellenism, Culture and Anarchy. Leave Unity and Trinity to the
parson; Duality is mine, saith the pedant. He invents Satan as the Ape
of God (*simia Dei*). His season is Winter, when the black soot of the
fireplace sets off the white of snow, of pain and laughter from
punishment and reward. He calls at night (N Eve) when the outer
darkness is offset by the inner light. From *Stratilates 3* on, N administered his lessons with a whip (*Nicea 15, Iconia 34, Cross Legend 41*),
which closely resembled Loki's Mistletoe,[1] the Fertile Twig, the Golden Bough, the Divining Rod, the Rule of Life. It was called *Klasholz*
in the Netherlands and *Klausenbein* in Switzerland, and eventually it
came to be baked as a sweet called *Speculatius*.[2] N thus returned to
primitive pedagogy.[3] A Monte Cassino hymn as early as A.D. 1000:

Terrificas nece dum meritos,
> You frighten to death all those who deserve it,
A nece retrahis immeritos.
> From death snatching those whose good deeds you observéd.[4]

In 1844 the academic Dr. Heinrich Hoffmann, like Clement Moore just
before him, tried his hand at children's verses for the Dodecahemeron, which to his great amazement swept the world: *Struwwelpeter*.
Unlike Moore's diminutive sprite, Hoffmann's Saint Nicholas was "so

tall he almost touched the sky." He possessed a giant inkstand which he used not only for instruction but for rectification:

Bis übern Kopf ins Tintenfass
    Over his head in the pot of ink
tunkt sie der grosse Nikolas.
    great Nicholas forced each one to sink.
Du siehst sie hier
    Here you can see
wie schwarz sie sind,
    how black they be,
viel schwärzer als des Mohren Kind.
    far blacker than the blackamoor.[5]

But the epithets Saint and Bishop of the legend induced mild images of benevolence. Early corruptions of N's name (Samiklaus, Sinterklaes, Klaus, der Niklas, etc.) betoken friendliness, even familiarity.[6] Hence the corporate mind very quickly came to visualize N the pedant as two persons. This was in accord with the continental folkmotif of the Doppelgänger.[7] Until quite recently N and Satan visited together in parts of Hungary; in Swabia Klos and Teufel; in Low Germany "Quaeclaeys" is coined from "Klaai de duivel" (N the Devil). It may be that "Old Nick" grew up in this way. The second person assumed a personality, usually black to balance N's increasing white. "The little black boy" had long been a type of hagiography, running back through Gregory's Dialogues[8] to Athanasius' symbols of abstract sin in his Life of Anthony. At first in Holland the black boy was called Nicodemus, who rode a monkey as N rode a horse.[9] But then came Black Peter, who traveled from Moorish Spain with the Hapsburg N and would carry bad children back to Spain in a burlap sack—an echo of the Spanish Occupation:[10]

. . .Rijd er mee naar Amsterdam,
    Ride he may to Amsterdam,
Van Amsterdam naar Spanje . . .
    From Amsterdam to Spain . . .
Met uw besten tabbaart aan,
    Put your finest tabard on,

310

Gij rijdt er mee naar Spanje
So may you ride to Spain
Om appelkens van Oranje . . .[11]
With little apples from Orange.

There were many inspirations for the *Schwarzer Mann* (Black Man), so common throughout European customs.[12] Most certainly small children saw him in the chimney sweep,[13] that gave Germans the figure of Hans Crouf ("Black Jack").[14] The Black Man had a mummer's part, as did Melchior of the Three Kings (oddly enough, N's companion was sometimes called Caspar, or Black Caspar, but never Melchior). Whether at N Eve or Epiphanytide, the Second Person of N took on a variety of guises, in part drawn from the black pit of folklore and prechristianity, in part from invention of the mummers.[15] When *Barockshausspiele* replaced *Mysterienspiele* in Germany, N was a personage with scary mask. What may once have been the sacrificial goat of Donar, through mummery emerged as Klapperbock, Schnabbuk, Ziege, Habergeiss, or the like. Saint Martin became a depressed god or demon as Pelzmärtel or Schmutzbartel (Lake Constance) or Märte or Bartel (Styria)[16]—all furry, as in Ruprecht's other self Rüpelz, Butzmann (Swabia), Schmutzli (Switzerland), Biggesel (Alsace), Tomte Gubbe (Sweden), Père Fouettard (France), Hans Trapp, Hans Muff ("muffen" was Middle High German for "twist the mouth"), Krampus (Austria), Rumpanz, Klaubauf (= *Klaub auf!* "pick 'em up," from the order issued when the apples and nuts were finally thrown onto the floor before the children), Aschenklas (N with ashes), Putenmandl, Stämpes (Palatinate), Semper (Bavaria). Women might be Budelfrau, Berchtel, Buzebergt, Frau Holle, Perchte, Pudelmutter; these are derivatives, it appears, of Berchta, the wife of Odin.[17] Sometimes in Switzerland Samichlaus is alone; he is a winter demon who haunts the forests, is armed with switches, and carries a sack in which to put infants.[18] A document from Basel, A.D. 1420, specifically equates the *episcopus puerorum* with the Devil. In some localities they carry on a rite of "expulsion of Saint Nicholas" of the same kind as the expulsions of *Démons de l'Hiver.* [19] N and Knecht Ruprecht often travel together, interchanging good and bad personalities; and N is usually bad when he travels with Kris Kringle (= *Christ Kindl* "Christ Child") or Père Noel.[20]

A dozen years ago Fritz Redl informally recalled his boyhood in Vienna:

> On 5 December St. Nicholas would sometimes also bring you a special present or presents, more like Christmas custom would demand, small in nature but usable and beyond the usual plum or candy treat level. In this way he would certainly assume some of the Christmas function—sort of an advance instalment of what later the "Christ-child" (Christkindl) would bring in more abundance.
>
> The other side of the highly ambivalent coin was equally clear in the Austrian myth, but more directly open: The *Krampus* (or Grampus) was quite clearly the Devil or at least his emissary, while the designation as "Krampus" made him more talkable about and more amiable and less threatening than had he been openly called the devil, his devil nature was undisguised. He would be black, have horns, a mephistophelian countenance, a long tail, preferably hooves or their equivalent.
>
> He would have two major props: (a) a "Putten"—a wooden-type rucksack such as people in the country would wear on their backs to carry vegetables up the mountains, etc.—and (b) iron chains, which would rattle with ample delight.[21]

The mummers would have as many persons as were in the company. I have seen a photograph from Oberammergau of a father and two children standing before a doorway with N, Prince Ruprecht, Pelznichol, and Hans Muff.[22] N will order his company to carry off a delinquent for punishment. "The terror and shrieks thus caused have created vast misery among children, and in Munich and some other places the authorities have very properly made such tragedies illegal."[23] In Walloon Belgium "On lî a dné s'Sin-Nikolèie" means "He got a drubbing."[24] The Reformation was accompanied with a remarkably intensified perception of the Devil and his corps, as in the famous incident of Luther; they were the grist of much continental drama and epic, whence the Elizabethans derived them.

In a German sword dance of the sixteenth century was "Klas Rugebart" (Red-bearded N), which some have pointed to as the

source of the confusion of N and Ruprecht in this December season.[25]
According to his First Dresden Diary, Washington Irving found Ruprecht "dressed up grotesquely, knocking at doors and asking how
the children have behaved."[26] Tille said Ruprecht first appeared (to
his knowledge) in a Nuremberg text of a Christmas procession,
printed 1668;[27] but philologists told Hitler that *Hruodperacht* was related to *Ruhmprangende,* which in very ancient Teutonic might have
meant "Glory-vaunter." So Knecht Ruprecht was admitted to Hitler's
pantheon. He was a *Schimmelreiter,* white horse rider, and as such
related to the Northern gods.[28] The Aryan philologists were not clear
about Thor and Woden but agreed that the horse they rode was
white, as was Poseidon's and then N's horse[29]—a reminder of sea
spume.[30] Folklorists of the nineteenth century used this and a few
more parallels of this kind to assert that N was merely a sanctified
Woden.[31]

Though Luther feted N and bought children's presents for N Eve,
he came to regard his practice as idolatrous and gave the children
such presents on Christmas in the name of Jesus.[32] There followed the
reformed custom of Christmas presents (sometimes set for Three
Kings' Day, Epiphany) and the Christmas figures of Weihnachtsmann,
Père Noel,[33] Father Christmas,[34] and Kris Kringle.[35] But these figures
were "square," mere Protestant artifice, apt to get out of order like all
mechanisms. They lacked the life of a legend.

The Nazis spent great effort and no little precious money prop-
agandizing the Weihnachtsmann, together with Knecht Ruprecht and
Frau Holle, whom Hitler regarded as pure Aryan (*Weihnachtsmann*
79).[36] Kris Kringle, who in mummery underwent a transmutation, to
emerge as a tall slim girl with flaxen hair, and therefore a good fairy,
has enjoyed fair health. But in Alsace she is accompanied by Hans
Trapp.[37] The children sing:

> *Christkindele, Christkindele,*
>> Kris Kringle, Kris Kringle,
> *Komm doch zu uns herein!*
>> Come on in to us for sure!
> *Wir haben ein Heubündele*
>> We have set out a truss of hay
> *Und auch ein Gläsele Wein.*
>> As well as a flask of wine:

Das Bündele fürs Esele,
The truss for the sumpter,
Fürs Kindele das Gläsele,
For Kringle the flask;
Und beten können wir auch. [38]
And we can pray as well.

But French nationalism and the leveling effect of communications have practically eliminated Alsacian German.

Animal Disguise and Symbolic Animalism

The reminiscences of pastoral and rural life in these December personages, N at the fore, have already been very considerably explained.[39] The Old Nick may have some dubious association with a primitive water troll, but otherwise the attributes are very late arrivals. Mainly the persons wear emblematic costumes made of animal skins, straw and seeds, and masks. Klaubauf, to choose but one example, is a monster covered with shaggy hide, with horns and a black face, fiery eyes, and long red tongue. He clanks his chains, as did the N of prisoners.[40] In Baden on N Eve the "Niklaus" was a puppet woven of straw to be burned. The good giftbringer N was undeviatingly mimed in episcopal regalia: in modern versions, which quite possibly are mere archaeological revivals, the vestments are all white.[41] But the degraded N is illustrated in the postreformation centuries in comic or scarifying guise, medusa-haired or with birds nesting in his shaggy beard.[42] Every deviation from bishop's regalia brings with it animal skins, which anthropologists would trace to dim pastoral antiquity, to remain in symbolic costume and name (Pelzenbock, Pelznichol).[43]

Chances are that the ass on which N or his doppelgänger rides results from a mere solution of convenience. The church kept a manufactured ass, used for the Palm Sunday processional; it came to be used also for representations or mysteries of Balaam the prophet, then it was tied to the Feast of the Ass in winter revels.

These tales and mummings preserved some sense of propitiation of animals, a feel for the cult of ancestors and of the dead. Ambrose, the great patristic bishop of Milan, chided Santa Monica, Saint Augustine's mother, for placing cakes and wine beside the tombs of

ancestors, and Saint Boniface had a hard time moderating such heathen habits in Germany. Tille maintained that the customs traveled
with Christianity from Egypt and were known to prechristian He-
brews. Tomte Gubbe, who personifies the Northern Penates, received
his due in milk and gruel, perhaps also new clothes, tobacco, and
aquavit.[44] European children set out crackers or a wisp of hay for N's
white horse or ass—a quid pro quo, like exchange of presents between master and scholar.

One reads in newspaper columns these days that N is but a sanctification of Odin or Wodan, who rode a white horse in the winter
night.[45] This is a legend of a legend, and no older than nineteenth-
century anthropologists, whom Professor Meisen very effectively
brought to task;[46] but as we know, popular lore leads a charmed life
outside the range of scholarship and sometimes within it. Wodan
himself is a pretty misty figure, largely created by those same anthropologists. But whether from gods or myths or folklore or mimes
with hobbyhorses, winter is full of horses to ride and personages to
ride them.

Account books from postreformation centuries very occasionally
mention public payment for the visitors. Mummers moved in procession through the streets and in the front doors as proper bishops with
their retinue should, and in Low Germany and Holland pedantic
Bishop N always appeared in full pontificals to catechize the young.
But the *Schimmelreiters* took more ghostly paths, like ancestral spirits.
The Lares and all Northern equivalents were spirits of the hearth
(indeed, the goddess Heortha was one) and followed the savory path
of smoke down the chimney to the fire.[47] N found that acting like
such spirits was not difficult, for from the days of *Stratilates 3* he had
had the power to be in many places at once at the stroke of midnight
hour, and from the days of *Three Daughters 13* of invisibly propelling
gifts from aloft. The diary of Henry Machyn (A.D. 1550 - 1563), an
English Catholic, records that in many places parents on N Eve
secretly conveyed presents of various kinds to their children, and
taught them to believe that they owed the presents to the grace of N
and his train who, going among the towns and villages, came in at
windows even when the windows were bolted shut.[48] In Sweden and
the Teutonic lands that Sweden once held, a giftgiver aping N throws
a "Julknapp" through a door and escapes without revealing his iden-

tity.[49] In parts of France, with or without his doppelgänger, N came
down the chimney on the smoke, riding a horse or ass, to the tune of
children's songs (*French Children's Songs 80*):

> *Saint Nicolas, mon bon patron,*
> Saint Nicholas, my good patron,
> *Apportez-moi quelque chose de bon!*[50]
> Bring me something good!

Drawings and printed broadsides show him riding the smoke above
the roofs.

VI CHILDISH TREBLE

Gifts

In a few transalpine Latin Catholic provinces, bakers, confectioners,
and parents still observe N Eve from tradition;[1] but it is impossible for
any but zealous local historians to say whether such faint respirations
are true signs of life or artificially induced in the dead.[2] In almost
every instance I have tested they are recent revivals, under the impact
of Santa Claus. The Reformation and Counterreformation, which for
simplicity's sake we may call Lutheranism in this instance, diverted
the *strenae* of 1 January and the N gifts of 6 December to
Epiphanytide—New and Old Christmas, or New Year. In the realm of
folk custom, N became, indeed, the Dying God.[3]

Nilsson maintains that the characteristic gifts, apples and nuts, are
"ancient customs of the bucoliasts, a rustic procession of the familiar
kind. This fruitfulness and charms travel down in ballads; according to
the words, they scatter fruits and grain seeds. They are in some sort a
duplication of the life-rod," assimilated with N's switch.[4] The various
Low Country gift songs all center in fruit, nuts, and cakes, efficiently
perpetuated in the "fruitcake":[5]

> Sinterklaes, good noble man,
> Put something in my shoe,
> An apple or a lemon,
> A nut to crack.[6]

N's *Grainships* 7 easily fitted the grain seed pattern, especially where
his image included a home in Spain. In the upsurge of the House of
Orange, oranges and other citrus fruits joined with or supplanted

apples.[7] The fertile grain seeds became cakes and cookies in the towns; bakers competed by elaborating their cookie molds,[8] which they then preserved from generation to generation.[9] In Dortrecht, 1403, honine (honey), claescoeck (N cakes), and taert (tarts) were specially prepared for N Day. All the traditional tales of N were cast in marchpane—N croziered and mitered and mounted, ships, bags of gold, boys in tubs.[10] Children constructed paper or pastry ships to receive the visitation gifts.[11] A spice cake called "parliament bread" was molded into shapes; de Schuyter quotes[12] the Nieuwe Rotterdamse Courant that bakers of Rotterdam baked 162,000 pounds of parliament bread and 70,000 pounds of vrijers (honey cakes shaped like men) between 15 October and 15 December. A common word in the Netherlands for small pieces is klaasjes.[13] Superstitions attached themselves to these several forms, which protected houses against fire, calmed storms, banished fevers of men and beasts, and combated sorcery. All the excessive flames from baking at this season led to the Walloon saying: S'è sin Nikolè ki ku (N is busy cooking).[14]

Children set their shoes by bed or fireplace, to be filled by the saint with these varieties of fruits, nuts, and cakes.[15] But N, the patron of commerce and saint of getting-on, would not leave well enough alone. Small silver medals were coined, with an image of N on one side and rhyme lines on the other, called Saint Nicholas pennies.[16] The small toys manufactured in the seventeenth and eighteenth centuries, called by N's vernacular names, have become collectors' items. As early as 1487, printed sanctjes were mentioned: Nicholas cards, like Christmas cards, used in social calls. An order for one thousand of them in Deylen in Brabant survives from the year 1593.[17] The custom may be some part of the Knickerbocker sociability to be mentioned in the next chapter.

All these gifts, noted for their miniscule proportions, since originally they were hidden in the toes of shoes, had gay and tinsel wrappings, sometimes even gold leaf, but there are few indications of refined art.[18] Jan Steen's painting of Saint Nicholas Eve hanging in Amsterdam's Rijksmuseum (he treated the subject often) portrays N Eve customs that spread far: The mother in green caraco trimmed with ermine and jupon lilas is seated near a table burdened with cookies and sweets; she holds her arms out to a little girl who is carrying presents that N has brought her.[19] Behind her the family oaf cries at the sight of switches that fill his shoe, which a servant presents him with an air of mockery. Some other children display joy or curiosity. The grandmother, standing backstage, calls to the oaf as the grandfather laughs. The father has a baby in his arms who dangles a doll. In Italy and Spain, Zapata (derived from the word for shoe) filled shoes and slippers in the eighteenth century and later.[20] The first appearance of stockings as receptacles for the gifts was in Italian and French convent schools, where the girls hung them at the abbess's door to be filled in the night.[21]

Pumpernickel, as designating the bread of Westphalia, appeared in 1654; further south *Biernickel* is beer and bread.[22] Both descend from N the baker.[23] From Ireland to Yugoslavia N's name is employed variously in children's games. In Sicily the Catanians call licorice "niculizia." There is a popular French parental chant called *Semaine du Paresseux,* "The Sluggard's Week":

> *Lundi, mardi, fête,*
> *Mercredi, peut-être.*
> *Jeudi, la Saint Nicolas.*
> *Vendredi, on n'travaill' pas.*
> *Samedi, on se repose,*
> *Et l'dimanche, on n'fait rien.*[24]

And "Colas est venue" is said to one with gravy on his vest.[25]

The Mating Game

Three Daughters 13 obviously inspired these customs of surreptitious giftgiving, and to it are also regularly attributed the mating customs, especially in France.[26] Of course, mating and giftgiving often overlap.[27] Dutch *vrijers* and sugar hearts, the grist of N Day gifts, were also construed sometimes as mating calls.[28] *Vrijer,* which also has come to denote a suitor or lover, will make its appearance in New York. In Artois the unmarried adults and adolescents receive flowers on N Eve.[29] De Groot believes that the proper phrase for N, *goed-heilig-man,* has given the Dutch their term for "marriage broker," *huwelijksmakelaar.*[30] I have mentioned that N shares with Valentine the lovelife of the young, and that the *Burtscheid Icon 37* helped pregnant women.[31] *Ex votos* of his help in marriage are scattered through the shrines of Europe. A fifteenth-century Latin hymn reads, *Fecundavit hic steriles.* [32] Here are some other evidences in European folklore: In the Alps Samichlaus delivers babies. [33] *Dem Klose beten* (praying to N) or *der Klos' is ko'* (N has come) means being pregnant; "They have a child coming" is *Der Samichlaus hed'ne geschleikt.* [34] In Holland pranksters once sent spiced nuts, symbols of fertility, to childless couples and, cruelly, to spinsters on N Day. [35] There are many N rocks through Europe on which sterile women sat—the Rocher de Saint-Nicolas in Béarn, for example. [36] Sometimes they rub a statuette of N on their body. [37] A legend of Saint-Nicolas-de-Port is that one stone has the power of marrying whoever stands on it within the year, but no one knows which stone. The Lorrainers at their church in Rome used to marry off a poor maid each N Day. [38] *patron des filles, Saint Nicolas/Mariez-vous, ne tardez pas* or a variant is a standard N invocation. [39] De Groot states that in the tidewaters and marinas of Holland "Girl of Sinterniklass" is a euphemism for promiscuity; similar phrases are "go to Saint Nicholas" and "be with Saint Nicholas." And the sailors of Amsterdam had a chanty:

> We shall steer well our little ship
> All over the wild sea
> In the manner of Sinterniklass.
> Thus with us our sweethearts shall be. [40]

In Denmark girls covered his icon with flowers. Folklorists point to phallic symbolism in various N customs; for example, the maids in the town of Provins (Seine-et-Marne) move the bolt of the door to the N chapel back and forth while chanting *Mariez vos,* etc. [41] In some dialects Nicolai means "uxorious," and sometimes "stupid" (perhaps by affinity with Fr. *niais*); in Germany and Holland *domme Kloskopp* and variants are common pejoratives.

But many of these and similar customs are connected not only with N and Valentine, but especially also with Andrew. In Barnaby Googe's well-known list of patron saints in his *Popish Kingdome,* derived from Naogeorgus (Thomas Kirchmayer), A.D. 1570:

To Andrew all the lovers and the lustie woers come.
Believing, through his ayde, and certain ceremonies done,
(While as to him they presentes bring, and conjure all the night,)
To have good luck, and to obtain their chiefe and sweete delight. [42]

Possibly the patronage results from the psychology of the winter season, not from the personality of the legend.

Demigods who fall into senile old age are capricious, and their habits sometimes betray them into opposite action. The Monk of Bec told of an adolescent boy, commended to N as a baby, who was ensnared by a *muliercula,* which probably means a sylphid. Friends advised him to flee the country, but he prayed all night to N and was relieved, as was *The Bari Widow 73.*[43] Later, the degraded N was charged with every variety (it would seem) of malfunctioning love.

We have had occasion enough to note the partnership of N and Catherine. In northern France, centering in Normandy and Flanders, duplicate rites were performed on 25 November and 6 December: decoration of the appropriate effigies, processions with candles and banners, oblations, distribution of consecrated cake and bread. According to Dergny: "Saint Catherine for the girls and Saint Nicholas for the boys have equality of charge. . . . Around 1850 - 1860 the custom was still nearly general in all the parishes. The eve of the feast (24 Nov.) at Inghem, the boys, with the *roi* [king] of N at their head, went to offer a sprig of rosemary to the *reine* [queen] of Saint Catherine. On N Day the *reine* of C and the girls reciprocated in respect to the *roi* of N. Elsewhere the sprig of rosemary was replaced by a bouquet. . . . The *reine* of C and her company had certain prerogatives: they invited the young men to dance, they paid the fiddlers who, at the request of the *reine*, had to play certain pieces; it was also the queen who opened the dance."[44] Demont has recorded the parallel songs as sung in Artois.

Devotees might in their imaginations marry N to Catherine; but James of Voragine, in *The Golden Legend,* thought him the model celibate, *corpus macerabat, mulierum consortia fugiebat,* "he lacerated the body, he fled the company of women."[45] Salimbene the historian borrowed that phrase as a topos for antifeminist diatribes.[46] Early in the eighteenth century, a homicide named Toffania, at Palermo and then at Naples, distributed small glass phials of poison inscribed "Manna of Saint Nicholas of Bari," by way of charity to such wives as wished to have other husbands. Reputedly six hundred husbands died before Toffania was captured in a convent refuge, racked, and shrived before strangulation. Walter Scott used the phrase "eaten of the manna of St. Nicholas" several times in *Kenilworth*. [47]

As the psychoanalysts have remarked, and we shall see in the next chapter, the collected Saint Nicholas legends read something like a textbook of examples for sexual dream symbolism.

VII THE HYBRID COMPOSITION

The hagiophobic puritans wasted energy in browbeating N's aged frame.[1] In the Netherlands after the Hapsburg expulsion, rigid laws were enacted against not only saints' feasts but the folk customs accrued around them, even in Catholic provinces. The N *meersch* or confraternity in Antwerp had built a chapel, but then abandoned it to meet in homes during the Lutheran onslaught; but on 6 December 1585 the feast was restored and all the major guilds held solemn High Mass. In England the Civil War could not end customs, however stringently legislated against, but they caused such disruption of tradition that palsied legends barely survived the shock. The Roundheads brooked no compromise. For example, they gloried in holding Parliament on Christmas Day. John Evelyn wrote in his Diary: "Christmas Day, no sermon anywhere, no church being permitted to open, so observed it at home."[2] The following remarks were recorded on the floor of Parliament 25 December 1656:

COL. MATTHEWS: The House is thin, much, I believe, occasioned by the observance of this day. I have a short Bill to prevent the superstition for the future. I desire it to be read.
MR. ROBINSON: I could get no rest all night for the preparation of this foolish day's solemnity. This renders us in the eyes of the people to be profane. We are, I doubt, returning to Popery.
MAJOR-GENERAL PACKER WITH OTHERS THOUGHT THE BILL "WELL-TIMED": You see how the people keep up these superstitions to your face, stricter in many places than they do the Lord's Day. One may pass from the Tower to Westminster, and not a shop open nor a creature stirring.[3]

Despite proscription of saints' days, wakes and ales and fairs were still allowed on days of a church's dedication.[4] Since more churches were dedicated to N than to any other confessor, N preserved some strength.[5] The standard index shows that in the year 1500 there were 385 N churches in England, as compared with Catherine 57, Augustine of Canterbury 27, Cuthbert 65, Edmund 55, George 106, Helena 113, Lawrence 220, Margaret of Antioch 230, Martin 151, Swithin 52, Thomas à Becket 69. In the eighteenth century, there were 21 new dedications to George, one to Margaret, and none to the others listed, though 10 to John the Baptist, 18 to John the Evangelist, 15 to Mary (B.V.M.), 16 to Paul, and 9 to Thomas the Apostle.[6] In France, where N chapels far outnumbered churches, old dedications disappeared rapidly after the Revolution, their founding and support having been a noble function.[7]

The Church trimmed away the cult until nothing was left of N but a faint geriatric breath.[8] Cardinal Baronius's *Martyrology* (1588) followed the revised breviary of 1568 by including such questionable episodes as *Nicea 15* and *Lactation 11,* and giving the death date (from *The Golden Legend*) as A.D. 343. To it was joined the cardinal's account from the *Annales ecclesiastici,* which called N "the most brilliant among so many brilliant stars" (copied from the N liturgy).[9] He asserted without qualification that the *Myrrh 18* had flowed continuously "to the present day": *Ungentem iugiter ex ossibus eius scatens quod et hunc usque diem manare non desinit.*[10] He placed N's ordination as bishop A.D. 316.

But Pope Gregory XIV's commission sitting 16 May 1591 trimmed back the lections; nothing remained beyond the tenth-century liturgy of Reginold of Eichstätt; it issued an extensive explanation of deletions containing the statement: *Nam lectiones sanctorum in Breviario non ponuntur ut integra historia actionum alicuius sancti sed sunt veluti encomium quoddam* (For the lections of the saints are not put in the breviary as a complete record of actions of any saint, but they are, as it were, a kind of encomium). A Bull of Urban VIII (22 Dec. 1642) drastically curtailed the feasts of obligation. In 1747 Pope Benedict XIV advised that N Day had only a single proper prayer—all else must be drawn from the Common for any confessor-pontiff, "for the legend published by Mombritius is apocryphal."[11]

To summarize this tragic tale of the old age of N, I quote from a Norman antiquary, M. Mancel, A.D. 1857:

A painter born at Bayeux, named Delaunay, in 1789 exhibited at his salon a picture which attracted attention and showed effective promise as a master. But what an example! All the satirical and skeptical spirit of the eighteenth century was exhibited there: a crowd of maids of all ages on their knees around the statue of the saint, behind them hovering some bantering lovers; some men, doubtless their future husbands, hidden in the clouds above the lovers looking at the group with marked interest. We skip the details of an allegory all too apparent. Delaunay died a short time later, but his picture was engraved. Unfortunately the engraver completed his work only about 1793, at the time when anything that recalled the cult of the saints was proscribed. That prohibition did not help the trade of the publisher, and the greater part of the copies ran the risk of remaining in storage, until he thought of an expedient. He had the statue of the saint scratched off and replaced by a Roman with Phrygian headgear, the right hand resting on a lance and the left hand holding a lictor's ax. Then he boldly inscribed on his hybrid composition: *Pèlerinage au Patron de la Liberté.* With that credential the print, which otherwise was of good workmanship, found a ready sale.[12]

SEVEN
second childhood

Last scene of all
That ends this strange eventful history
Is second childishness and mere oblivion
Sans teeth, sans eyes, sans taste, sans everything.

I INTRODUCTION

According to the Church, which is the authority in the field of sanctity, a saint is immortal. According to psychoanalysts, who are accorded a comparable authority in the field of the imagination, myths and legends are equally immortal. Each authority has recently suggested that N now lacks life, though both avoid the word "death." Because death, eternal death, is an uncongenial word, the authorities avoid so absolute a term.

Their flattering unction has ancient source. The author of Genesis brought to an end every day of the Creation but the Seventh, to which he gave no evening.[1] The act of Creation could not terminate, nor can a saint's life. The Sabbath or Seventh Age is in typology the final age of the creative god, of man, and of history, which is the sum of all biographies.[2] The comic Jacques regarded the last scene of all as but second childishness and mere oblivion. Only a tragic hero, Lear, could greet Death with a cry, "I am a very foolish fond old man."[3]

If we invoked the tragic muse we would have to say that N breathed his last on 14 February 1969, when Pope Paul VI wrote *Nihil obstat* to the latest calendar of saints. N's old companion Catherine was among the saints expunged at that time from the Roman calendar on suspicion of never having endured the flesh. But in the words of the *New York Times* in reporting the event: "The anniversary celebrations of 92 other saints, including St. George of England and St. Nicholas, who has been celebrated as Santa Claus, were made optional."[4] The Papal Court, theologically precise, opined that no saint, expunged or optional, was dead: "Saints who lost their places {e.g. Catherine} or whose feast days were demoted from universal to optional [e.g. Nicholas] in the new edition of the liturgical calendar are still to be venerated as they were before the calendar's updating."[5] Holy Scripture reads, "God blessed the seventh day and hallowed it," but does *not* read, "And there was evening, a seventh day." God and His saints, after their creative period, rest in an eveningless Sabbath.

The figure of Seven Ages, whether of the world or of man or of image, has structured this biography. The earliest known rationalists, Pythagoras and before, regarded six as *completion,* a "perfect" number, containing in itself the sum of its aliquot parts. But in the comedy of perfected temporality six is not a proper end. God must rest on the Sabbath and re-view what He has done. In N's Christendom that Sabbath is "the Lord's Day," the Day of Him who said, "Unless you become as little children" there will be an evening after the Sixth Age, death. The tragic hero, the very foolish fond old man, suffers all indignities of the material world before, all passion spent, he dies to memory; the comic hero ends the eventful history in mere oblivion, sans everything including death.

At all events, even in a saint potentiality departs: *pulvis et umbra sumus.* [6] Psychologists observe that the traditional cult of aged parents is quite neglected in these days. The economics of consumption decrees that the obsolete or dated must be scrapped. N's power began to wane with the invention of the compass, the extermination of piracy on the sea, and then the harnessing of steam. Jet flight has eclipsed N's airspeed in *Stratilates 3, Mariners 6,* or *Son of Getron 46;* it is inconceivable that even the most pious would invoke N against skyjacking. Preschool infants may tolerate an aged giftgiver, but by that very token the veneration of adolescent lovers is lost, for what lover could tolerate a childish patron? Movie stars now supply the thaumaturgy and charisma.

N did survive his fellow saints for a time—adjusting to the industrial revolution while saints like Anthony and Catherine faded.[7] N had long been patron of those merchants who had now to sell the goods that new machines poured out; assisted by Santa Claus they did so. But the key to industrial success now is novelty, and even N is not inexhaustible. For centuries he had been imagined flying over rooftops; so he was equipped to enter highrise apartments. Nevertheless his very expansiveness unfitted him for a crowded world. His carols, firesides, mummings, games, processionals, and sleighs had to yield to Hallmark cards, eggnogs, and praesepes. His invisible ubiquity does not lend itself to TV reporting.

Each age of N in this biography has marked an epoch in Western culture. The infant gurgled in nascent Christian orthodoxy; the boy grew muscular with Greek Fire along the Islamic frontier; the adolescent was schooled with the Northern barbarians; the knight rode out on Crusade. In middle age N counted his money with the buyers in the towns; then with the Reformation his troubled conscience drove him toward black dreams. And now senility.

A psychologist describes the senile man: "He may grow confused about his surroundings, particularly at night and in strange places. He tends to become tearful easily, but he can often be cheered up quickly and even made to laugh through his tears. He is easily annoyed and he may have temper tantrums. Sometimes striking changes in general character develop. Usually these are only exaggerations of previous personality traits, but occasionally they appear as something new."[8]

The senile N took on nicknames, usually "Santa Claus," and a new iconography—fat, bearded, "Ho, ho, ho." But the long story of the previous Six Ages is now retold *in senectute,* and readers of a comparative turn of mind can watch "the exaggerations of previous personality traits." "An old man is twice a child," says the platitudinous Rosencrantz.[9] While, in this Second Childhood, we glimpse shadows of the past, let us keep in mind our original purpose: to ponder the impact of men's activities on their imagery and the imagery on their activities. Previously we have been hampered by the remoteness of time, place, and knowledge; now in our own surroundings, though having the same aims we can be more sure of our facts and more precise.[10]

II THE COLONIAL N

We would expect N to be brought to America, and so he was—before the Reformation. The cathedral of the Vikings in Greenland was dedicated to N;[1] Columbus on his first voyage named Saint Nicholas Harbor and Saint Nicholas Mole in Haiti;[2] the Spaniards called what is now Jacksonville, Florida, Saint Nicholas Ferry. A very few other vestiges survive. But the colonizing of North America and the Reformation concurred in time, and the American colonists were preponderantly reformers. Hence in the seventeenth and eighteenth centuries N did not add to the American land or language.

True, European immigrants have sporadically brought N customs to North America with their families. When they combined in ethnic groups, the customs sometimes survived as long as the group. There are shadows of Kris Kringle and Pelznichol (Belshnickle) among the Pennsylvania Dutch to this day. But in Buffalo, where Germans concentrated around 1840, N would call on N Eve to take orders for presents to be delivered for Christmas; the custom lasted for sixty years or so, but has now, I believe, disappeared. In the Dutch communities of Michigan and Iowa, N occasionally called with oranges and switches on N Eve. In the 1930s I knew three families of anti-Nazi immigrants who preserved Teutonic family customs, including some ancient N customs, on uncongenial American soil. Such importations quickly disappear. Like tuberculosis germs, they invade our social body, but germination does not become virulent except as a unique set of men and conditions change latent infection into plague.

If I may now be as fanciful as the subject I approach, the plague, endemic in New York City shortly after the Revolutionary War, peaked in the decade following the Second World War, while spreading throughout the world. As in plagues, a change in germinal form induced or accompanied the virulence. The senile N like a unicellular germ split off a second self.

At its height Santa Claus's power might well compare with N's at the Third Crusade. Take a representative year, 1954. Some thousand emaciated little men, padded out with pillows and other stuffing, ill-fitting cotton beards (washable fireproof nylon beards and wigs for Santa Clauses cost $24.95 at Gimbels), red cheesecloth, and black oilcloth boots, rang bells at seven thousand corners of these United States. A single, unexceptional store spent about $5,000 converting space to a "Santa's Wonderland," where children lined up to sit on Santa's lap, one to five at a time. Two Santas (one hour on, one hour off), with a retinue of six costumed entertainers and six to eight ushers, greeted a reported fifteen thousand children in seven weeks. In New York City there were in that year three schools solely for the training of Santa Clauses. Macy's parade culminated in a Santa Claus.

It has since fissioned into many parades and Santa Clauses, but an agent tells me that the format is now antiquated and will be changed. That year the post office at Santa Claus, Indiana (established 1852, population still below 100), handled nearly five million pieces of mail and was becoming a midsummer tourist trap. According to the *Herald Tribune,* of sixty books specifically about Christmas published in 1952, six had SC as their theme.[3] The Library of Congress listed, for the single year 1947, twenty-two new songs with SC as the first word in the song (how many other songs with SC as theme?). Such oddments suggest plague.

That SC is a bifurcation of N and that the split occurred in New York City is indisputable. But if we momentarily look at SC as a new organism, with a life and biography of its own, we are faced with a nonspeaking infancy such as that of N in chapter 1. Its origins have seemed obscure, and legends about its origins as incredible as N's. Man's ex post facto explanations of his own imaginings are labyrinthine, but let us try to find some facts to guide us.

It is common to remark that N is patron of New York City, as of New Amsterdam before it. There is Saint Nicholas Cathedral on East Ninety-seventh, a grandchild of N's Russian cult; from 1924 to 1952 it was in litigation before our Supreme Court to determine whether it was purely American or the sect of the archdiocese of North America and the Aleutian Islands under the patriarchate of Moscow. A Saint Nicholas stands above the door of the baptistry at the Cathedral of Saint John the Divine. Until fairly recently a Reformed Church of Saint Nicholas graced central Manhattan. Saint Nicholas Avenue, Saint Nicholas Arena, and a number of beauty shops, drugstores, and the like honor the name. The Saint Nicholas Society (founded 1835) in 1885 took over the weathercock from the Saint Nicholas Hotel, which it had helped to found; it has been said with a smile that only those whose names begin with *Van* can be elected to its Board of Stewards.[4] The Saint Nicholas Club (founded 1875), with colonial descent a requirement of membership, is more definitively social. The Saint Nicholas Society of Nassau (Long Island) in 1915 had about two hundred members who customarily banqueted on N Day. The New-York Historical Society meets on N Day, and the Holland, the Long

Island Historical, and the Knickerbocker societies show their devotion to N in their several ways.

These are signs of cult, not of a Bishop of Myra, but of a legend about a Dutch Saint Nicholas, so potent as to create a mindset in conscientious historians as well as sentimental Gothamites. Only for example, the authoritative Wilson, historian of the City, under the influence of the less reliable Stokes, turned Nicholas Street (which was named for a Whig of the seventeenth century, in parallel with the adjacent Hester, Ann, William, Oliver, and Prince streets) into Saint Nicholas Street without authority. This is not the Saint Nicholas Avenue mentioned above, which was laid out about 1869.

The legend of a Dutch SC, which has been essentially static for more than a century, was most clearly stated by Mary L. Booth in 1859. I quote a portion of her statement:

> The Dutch had five national festivals which were observed throughout the city; namely, Kerstrydt (Christmas); Nieuw jar (New Year); Paas (the Passover); Pinxter (Whitsuntide); and Santa Claus (St. Nicholas or Christkinkle day) . . . but Santa Claus day was the best of all in the estimation of the little folk, who, of all others, enjoy holidays the most intensely. It is notable, too, for having been the day sacred to St. Nicholas, the patron saint of New York, who presided at the figure-head of the first emigrant ship that touched her shores, who gave his name to the first church erected within her walls, and who has ever since been regarded as having especial charge of the destinies of his favorite city. To the children, he was a jolly, rosy-cheeked little old man, with a low-crowned hat, a pair of Flemish trunk-hose, and a pipe of immense length, who drove his reindeer sleigh loaded with gifts from the frozen regions of the North over the roofs of New Amsterdam for the benefit of good children. Models of propriety were they for a week preceding the eventful Christmas eve. When it came, they hung their stockings, carefully labelled, that the saint might make no mistakes, in the chimney corner, and went early to bed, chanting the Santa Claus hymn, in addition to their usual

devotions. [Miss Booth then transcribed Pintard's Historical
Society verses, given below, p. 341] . . . These rhymes, Mr.
Valentine tells us, continued to be sung among the children
of the ancient Dutch families as late as the year 1851. But
the custom is passing away, and the Christmas gifts are now
given prosaically without legend or tradition.[5]

After her, only a very few recent academic historians have expressed
doubts about the New Amsterdam origin of Santa Claus,[6] and today it
is commonly stated as fact, not legend.[7]

When we look at the available documents—that is, the newspa-
pers, magazines, diaries, books, broadsides, music, visual aids, and
merchandise of the past—Miss Booth appears to have been correct in
only one particular, that the cult of "Santa Claus" originated in New
York City, from which it spread. There was no N or Christkinkle Day,
no patron saint of New Amsterdam or New York, no figurehead of N
on an emigrant ship, no dedication of the first church to *any* saint, no
iconography, no pipe, reindeer, or North. It is hard to believe in the
face of all evidence from the time that there was any gifting at
Christmas, any knowledge of a name Santa Claus, any hymns or song.
Nothing. Except possibly a prereformation memory carried in some
individual's head or an Old World tradition connected with 6 December, momentarily transplanted only to die.

In the half-century following the establishment of New Amsterdam, the Dutch at home in the Netherlands were hagiophobic to a
preeminent degree. The new colony was controlled by the Dutch
West India Company. As De Vries wrote, in the year 1642 that
company "was deemed to be a principal means of upholding the
Reformed Religion against the tyranny of Spain." Of the many laws
recorded in Holland against public observance of N customs, I quote
but a part of one ordinance (*Dutch Ordinances 81*) from Amsterdam, to
illustrate what I have already treated amply in chapter 6.

N̄   Since the magistrates [of Amsterdam] have learned that in
previous years, notwithstanding the publishing of the
Bylaws, on Saint Nicholas Eve various persons have been
standing on the Dam and other places in the town with
candy, eatables, and other merchandise, so that a large

> crowd from all over town gathered, . . . the same magis-
> trates, to prevent all such disorders and to take the supersti-
> tion and fables of the papacy out of the youths' heads, have
> ordered, regulated, and opined that on Saint Nicholas Eve
> no persons, whoever they may be, are to be allowed on the
> Dam or any other places and streets within this town with
> any kind of candy, eatables, or other merchandise . . . [under
> penalty of very severe fines].[8]

Of course, the very presence of such laws indicates that abuse existed
in Holland. And, as we have already seen, in the late seventeenth
century many a family like Jan Steen's could revive N customs buried
in old soil after the puritan wave had rolled past.

But traditions rooted in native soil and warmed on the native
hearth do not easily transplant to a new soil. George Stewart has
noted that in London "Nicholas" comprised 1.6% of Christian names
in 1540 - 1549 and about the same percentage in 1640 - 1649; but
though that same percentage is, as would be expected, found
among the Massachusetts immigrants of 1640 - 1649, among the
children born in New England in that decade there were only five
among 1288 in Plymouth, and in Boston (1630 - 1669) only one in 675.
"Non-Biblical saints' names approach the vanishing point," he
writes.[9] To be sure, the instance is drawn from New England, but it
illustrates colonial behavior. Moreover, according to a report in 1643,
New Amsterdam, though a small colony, was a complete ethnic
mixture; there were eighteen languages spoken among fewer than five
hundred inhabitants.[10]

The name Saint Nicholas was first given to a Manhattan church in
1906! That church held its final service 24 July 1949. Indeed, the first
shadow of N in Manhattan was the English colonel, named Nicholls,
who presented Charles II's demand that New Amsterdam be surrendered to Governor Stuyvesant in 1664. About the time that Miss
Booth and others (for she was not alone) were recording their version
of history, a Gotham antiquarian of Dutch infancy, Alofsen, was
writing:

> The emigrant from Holland would never have substituted
> Christmas day for St. Nicholas day, for the Dutch do not

celebrate the birthday of our Saviour with pageants of pagan origin, and boistrous buffoonery and masquerade. This takes place, not on the continent of Europe, but in England alone. It is therefore evident that these changes must have been introduced in later days and clearly point to that period in American history when the Georges ruled this country, and opulent Dutchmen adopted English manners, English habits, English customs, English laws, yes, and English church ceremonies too.[11]

As Gulian Verplanck asserted in 1818 to the New-York Historical Society, "From 1674, when this province was finally ceded by treaty to Great Britain, until 1780, when the United Provinces arrayed themselves in our aid in the War of Independence, New York had little direct communication with Holland."[12]

Once we agree that the Miss Booths had no evidence for their assertions, we see that they also had no logic. The anthropologist Moncure Conway stated the principle that colonies anywhere "conscious of fault and failure in the home system enlist the charm of novelty. Every system imported to a foreign land leaves behind its practical shortcomings, puts its best foot forward—namely, its theoretical foot—and has the advantage of suggesting a way of escape from the existing routine which has become oppressive." An escaping malcontent will not willingly shackle himself with the customs which made him malcontented.

The few Dutch in New Amsterdam would find no encouragement from the "foreign" settlers around them to continue old world customs. To the north, New England scorned all old observances save the Lord's Day. They invented occasional days of Thanksgiving or Fasting, annually appointed *pro causis et temporibus.* After the Restoration the North restored a saintless Christmas season; by 1687 Increase Mather could quote Latimer that "men dishonour Christ more in the 12 days of Christmas than in all the 12 months besides."[13] But they did not yet revoke an ordinance of 1643 that forbade pastry, plum cakes, and "sinful dalliance" at Christmastide. To the south the Pennsylvania Germans, doubtless in part to protect themselves from absorption by the Quakers, built walls of custom around themselves that enclosed Kris Kringle and Pelznichol (Belshnickle); but among the customs associated with those names themselves were none recognizably imported from the Old Country. In the southern colonies the new French skepticism seems to have predominated; the settlers welcomed a winter vacation with feasting, but without overt religious or folklore connections. I have not found a single reference to either N or SC in the twelve other colonies. It is easiest to imagine that none was made.

The first surviving mention of N in America is in the New York *Rivington's Gazetteer* for 23 December 1773: "Last Monday the anniversary of St. Nicholas, otherwise called St. a Claus, was celebrated at Protestant Hall, at Mr. Waldron's, where a great number of Sons of that ancient Saint celebrated the day with great joy and festivity." And on 8 December 1774 in the same journal: "Monday next, being the anniversary of St. Nicholas, will be celebrated by the descendents of the ancient Dutch families." These two are the only survivors until well after the Revolution. These "sons" of Saint Nicholas seem not to have known their father's birthday.[14]

This epiphany, and comparable cases, manifests the rampant anti-British feeling of the time. The American Revolution might be called the War Between the Saints.[15]

The eccentricity of early American literature has been treated enough. Because authors centered in Boston at the moment when the American legend was in infancy, we imagine Boston as the beating heart of Revolution. But already New York was the primary commercial port and financial center. Its equally revolutionary spirit was far more aroused by such regulations as the Stamp Act of 1765. A New York committee of one hundred leading citizens, chaired by Isaac Low, addressed the Mayor and Common Council of London: "Americans will not be deceived by conciliatory measures. The minions of power in New York may inform the administration that New York is as one man in the cause of liberty." Among the one hundred signers were Jay, Alsop, Livingston, Duyckman, Beeckman, Roosevelt, Verplanck, Hallet, Benson, Hoffman, Van Dam, Buchanan, and Lewis Pintard. The names suggest the birth of a nation.

In this rational Georgian world the senile saints were being roused to serve new causes. As early as 1657 the Scots immigrants had formed a "Saint Andrew's Society" in Boston and then in Charleston

(1729), Philadelphia (1749), and Savannah (1750). The purpose of these groups was sociability and benevolence, with an aim to ease the path of fellow emigrants. They first met in New York in 1753, forming a society in 1756.[16] Under the leadership of Philip Livingston, signer of the Declaration of Independence, that society numbered many patriots·in the heat following the Stamp Act; but shortly its center became Tory. For example, in the year 1773 its president was Lord Drummond.[17] The Irish military aristocracy was not to be outdone by the Scots. In 1756 the *Post-Boy* reported: "Saint Patrick's Day is observed by Irishmen in the city" with "a grand entertainment at the Crown and Thistle near Whitehall: at which were present his Excellency our Governor, who wore a Cross in Honour of the Day; sundry members of his Majesty's Council, and others of the General Assembly of this Province."[18] On 17 March 1774 *Rivington's* reported the "very elegant banquet" to have already passed, and the next year the group, now formed into the "Friendly Brothers of Saint Patrick," met before 13 January. The constant shift in feast-day for all these cults indicates that the ecclesiastical tradition was of slight account. Even the Welsh joined the act: This being Saint David's Day (reported the *Mercury*, 7 March 1774), the officers of the Royal Welch Fusileers "in honour of their tutelar saint" give an entertainment to the governor, the general, and "the Gentlemen of the military establishment."[19]

These organizations all took their hue of the Establishment from Saint George, patron of British militia. According to the *Mercury* in 1762: "On this day, the Anniversary of St. George, his Excellency Sir Jeffrey Amherst, gave a ball to the Ladies and Gentlemen of this City, at Crawley's New Assembly Room. The Company consisted of 96 Ladies, and as many Gentlemen, all very richly dressed, and 'tis said the Entertainment was the most elegant ever seen in America." The most elegant up to 1763, that is.[20]

The Custom House Calendar, as published in the first *American Register*, New York 1775, shows the unique position of Saint George; it is worth recording in full as a manifestation of the times:

> By order of the Honourable Commissioners of his Majesty's
> Customs in North America, the following days are to be
> kept and observed as Holydays, viz:

JANUARY 1	New Years day
18	Queen's Birthday
30	King Charles' Martyrdom
	Shrove Tuesday
	Ash Wednesday
MARCH 25	Lady Day
	Good Friday
	Easter Monday and Tuesday
	Ascension Day
APRIL 23	St. George's Day
MAY 29	King Charles' Restoration
JUNE 4	King's Birthday
	Whitsun Monday and Tuesday
AUGUST 12	Prince of Wales' Birthday
SEPTEMBER 18	King George 1st and 2nd landed in Great Britain
22	Coronation
OCTOBER 25	Accession
NOVEMBER 1	All Saints day
5	Powder Plot
DECEMBER 25	Christmas Day
26	
27	Christmas Holydays
28	

To the above may be added the following Provincial days: General Fast, General Thanksgiving, General Election, and Commencement at the College.[21]

Personifying patriotism by patron saints was a peculiarly British trait, an aspect of the "Gothic Revival" which spread to America.[22] The enlightenment following the intensity of religious strife had made the traditional poetic imagery a substance for humorous and sardonic prose and verse. Its subjects were adapted to sophisticated games of intellect.

The personifying had, indeed, started at the end of the Middle Age with "Saint David," who, according to legend, had led the British Welsh in a last victory against the English interlopers, back in the sixth century. Thereafter the English degraded the Celts much as, a millennium later, they degraded the American Indians.[23]

In a like range of imagination Saint Andrew and Saint Patrick came to represent other Celts depressed by the English. When the Hanovers came to the English throne, Saint George, already a byword among English militia, added a new Georgian dimension useful in ballroom humor. Such wit uniquely appealed to the English contemporaries of Goldsmith and Sheridan, but only fueled the tempers of the colonists during Stamp Act days.[24] Ostentatious partyings naturally galled the underprivileged patriots, and they reacted as patriots do. Many of them banded together as the Sons of Liberty. Of the variety of reactions throughout the colonies, I describe only one—the Sons of Saint Tammany.[25] Tammany had been a Delaware Indian chief, now useful as a contemporary parallel for the ancient British David.[26] By 1771 the Sons of Saint Tammany were meeting in Philadelphia and Annapolis. Contemporary accounts state that these meetings were intended to counteract the societies of Saint George and other British saints.[27] Derisively the patriots sanctified a non-British, native American and observed his Day on 1 May each year.[28] Tammany, first a chief, started among the patriots as King Tammany in opposition to King George, but in 1772 he became Saint Tammany in opposition to Saint George.[29]

New York, as a different colony, might borrow an attractive idea from its neighbors, but would give it a local relevance. The sardonic humor that led Philadelphians to Saint Tammany led New Yorkers to Saint Nicholas. Religious reform being dead, political reform exalting Natural Man was the current piety. Rousseau's stirring opening words of his dissertation on the Origin and Foundation of the Inequality of Mankind were leading the popular imagination to discovery of the gods Ur and Proto: Tammany, who greeted and treated with William Penn, and Saint Nicholas, who had become a child among the children of the Low Countries. It became easy to imagine that the Quakers and Dutch, few in number but by virtue of downtown real estate now most influential among the urban anti-British, had in happier, pre-British days communed with such saints of nature, who had poured out their bounty without musket or tax.[30]

Who *was* Saint Nicholas? Doubtless he was an N legend as known to the few recent immigrants from what is now Benelux. They were then increasing in the ethnic ratio with the increase of trade. That ratio was especially affected by the Huguenots, largely from Wallonia (eastern Belgium and Holland), a center of N customs as noted in chapter 6.[31] Antwerp and Amsterdam led the world of the eighteenth century in overseas trade—no matter which of the seven seas. When American merchants sailed from the colonies on business, it was to these cities that they went the most. Of all trade, the most active trade was in mass-produced luxuries, including specialties like candies and cakes.

Throughout the eighteenth century, New Years Day was a peculiarly New York holiday. Giftgiving on that day was a custom of Manhattan merchants: "the baker's dozen" evolved in that ritual. As early as 1680, Charles Wolley wrote that the Manhattan (not New England!) English "observed one custom, and that without superstition, I mean the *strenarum commercium,* as Suetonius calls them, a neighbourly commerce of presents every New-Years day." On New Years Day all old Manhattan families (as opposed to militia and governors sent from abroad) served brandy and cookies imported from the best continental bakers. This was the sophisticated colonists' version of the fertility rite, the harvest fruit and grain as object of midwinter cult, as *in saecula saeculorum.*

The calendar and the habits of time suggest that these were certainly N cookies. As we saw in chapter 6, despite the proscriptions of the early seventeenth century the frugal bakers preserved their N molds and pridefully boasted of their use in the late seventeenth century and beyond. The most common design of such cookies was Saint Nicholas with crozier and mitre. From Vienna to Ghent, N was the most famous name in cookies. Indeed, the American word *cookie* is probably Dutch *koekje,* an N cake, rather than the Scots *cooky.*

We have noted that the colonists only loosely observed either the Julian or the ecclesiastical calendar. This laxity reflects the confusion among ethnic groups over the European calendars of the time. The shift from Old Style to New Style occurred province by province over a long period.[32] Without going into details (involving legends of their own) let us say that cookies baked for N Eve (New Style) in the Netherlands would arrive in New York in time (Old Style) for the New Year receptions. To be sure, Britain finally shifted to New Style in 1752/53, but "the larger portion of this country refused to observe the Christmas and New Year according to the New Style,"[33] as in Britain as well, let it be said. Wrote John Pintard (b. 1759) to his daughter Mary in 1819: "In old times [i.e. prerevolutionary] St. Class used to cross the Atlantic and brought immense supplies of cookies etc from Amsterdam."

We cannot know as fact that these cookies gave patriots their saint. What we do know is that by 1773 New York patriots met under the symbol of N just as Philadelphians met under the symbol of Tammany—all because of dislike for the Georges, saint and king, and their Establishment. N had an ethnic background and a humor proper to the new society. Dutch "tradition" did not demand it: the best estimates indicate that in this period the British numbered 90 percent of the population of New York City (22,000), and the Dutch 2.5 percent, outnumbering French, Flemish, Walloons, and Swedes, but only half as numerous as Germans.[34] To be sure, the whole Hudson River colony was somewhat more heavily of Dutch extraction.

These senile images filled the New World vacuum until indigenous ones could take their places. The legend of Saint John, who became patron of American Masons[35] (including George Washington, who was inaugurated on the New York chapter's Bible) is analogous. Indeed, Americans sanctified pagan Roman heroes, as with the Society of Cincinnati, formed in 1783 by American army officers as a Tammany for the brass.[36] On the Philadelphia stage, 4 July 1788, a Mr. Hallam sang of these neo-European symbols, including Saints James (Spanish), Denis (French), Patrick (Irish), Andrew (Scots):

> The savage tribes their jubilee proclaim
> And crown *Saint Tammany* with lasting fame.
> E'en the poor Negro will awhile resign
> His furrows, to adorn Saint Quaco's[37] shrine;
> But while the dupes of legendary strains
> Amuse their fancy, or forget their pains,
> While mimic Saints a transient joy impart,
> That strikes the sense but reaches not the heart,
> Arise, Columbia!—nobler themes await
> Th' auspicious day, that sealed thy glorious fate. . . .
> Thus when revolving time shall sanctify thy name
> And Washington's, great favorite of fame![38]

N, or Santa Claus, was not yet worth mentioning. Incidentally, the form "Santa Claus" is only a characteristically Teutonic corruption, not especially Dutch.[39] The form actually appeared at that time only in documents from around Lake Constance. Both Nick and Claus, as we have seen, were common phonetic changes. Santa is clearly a phonetic change from *Sanct Herr*. The most common Dutch form then, as now, was the analogous *Sinterklaes*. Until Washington Irving, there was no agreement in Gotham about the proper spelling of N's nickname, and variant spelling continued up to the Civil War.

III KNICKERBOCKER SANTA CLAUS

Then came the Revolution. Saint George took over New York with the Redcoats and N retired to the cookie crock. From Philadelphia, which stayed in patriot hands, Saint Tammany exercised his patronage. When the war ended, the first to mention N was a New York burgher, John Pintard, of Huguenot extraction and nephew of Lewis Pintard, the Stamp Act protestor.[1]

A contemporary spoke of John Pintard as "a singular mixture of heterogeneous particles."[2] In the immediate postwar era he inspired the founding of historical societies in this country (starting with the Massachusetts), the Marine Society, the first New York insurance company, the first savings bank, the American Bible Society, the General Theological Seminary. He was in the New York Common Council and the New York State Assembly, where he was "a popular leader."[3] As a staunch Jeffersonian he was engaged in the Louisiana Purchase[4] and planning the Erie Canal. As editor and publisher of the *Daily Advertiser,* he printed the whole of Thomas Paine's *Rights of Man* and the replies of "Publicola" (young John Quincy Adams), with a preliminary note of approval by Thomas Jefferson, secretary of state. "His great work was as a promoter," says the *Dictionary of American Biography*. His biographer Schoville (1863) wrote: "He could indite a handbill that would enflame the minds of the people for any good work. He would call a meeting with the pen of a poet, and before the people met he would have arranged the doings for a perfect success." I note that though nearly always secretary he was never president of whatever he helped to organize.[5]

Already before the victory (1776) he had graduated from the College of New Jersey (later Princeton University) and founded the New Jersey Society of the Sons of Saint Tammany, No. 1.[6] When the British surrendered New York, he returned to inspire the founding of a chapter there,[7] writing its constitution and becoming its Sagamore.[8] He encouraged Belknap to found the Massachusetts Historical, but when momentarily blocked from organizing its equivalent in New York he "engrafted" it, as he himself wrote, onto the Society of Saint Tammany.[9] Tammany was becoming schizophrenic. William Cobbett, in 1794, noted that "the Tammany Society was, as it still is, composed of about forty poor rogues, and about three rich fools"[10]—Pintard doubtless one of the three. The split came in 1797 when an implied rebuke by Washington led the "rich fools" to forsake it, and Aaron Burr took over.[11] Pintard, who in 1817 could write of "the howlings of the Panther Tribe in Tammany's Den,"[12] turned to agitating for the founding of the New-York Historical Society and transferred his favorite ideas, including collecting American social artifacts and a cult of a patron saint.[13] He was one of eleven Gotham burghers at the founding session in the Picture Room of the City Hall, 20 November 1804. Judge Egbert Benson, the Reverend Samuel Miller, and (of course) John Pintard were appointed to write a constitution.[14]

N was running around in Pintard's mind. The first American appearance of the saint's name after the Revolution was an almanac which he created for himself in 1793;[15] it also marked Independence Day and Washington's Birthday long before there was any agitation for their observance. He is known to have been in part responsible for their eventually becoming national holidays. Presumably he was thinking of N in the same patriotic spirit. His patriot uncle may have been at those prerevolutionary meetings of the Sons of Saint Nicholas. At all events, as Saint Tammany had been his patron saint for the nation, Saint Nicholas now became his patron saint for the city.

Though Walloon Huguenot, at this moment he found no difficulty in linking N with Holland. In 1804 the forgotten Dutch colonizing of New Amsterdam was being recalled, and those with Dutch names were sporting their ancestry. A standard toast of the Society of Saint Tammany, not alone in New York but in Philadelphia since 1790, had been to France, Holland, and the United States, "the three republics where freedom rules."[16] Americans were grateful for the revolutionary support of the two continental nations. In the year 1796, for example, the United States owed only one external debt—twelve million dollars to Holland.[17]

We have no meaningful records of the New-York Historical Society before 1810, though statements immediately thereafter suggest that from the date of founding (1804) N Day was observed. We do know that at the annual banquet 10 January 1809, Dr. Hosack offered this toast: "To the memory of Saint Nicholas. May the virtuous habits and simple manners of our Dutch ancestors not be lost in the luxuries and refinements of the present time." At that dinner, Washington Irving's name was proposed for membership. Later in the same year Hosack repeated the toast on the two hundredth anniversary of Hudson's landing—a gala dinner given by the Historical Society, with Governor Tompkins, Mayor Clinton, and the whole Corporation present.[18]

The next year, 6 December 1810, the society inaugurated an anniversary dinner for N, an observance still maintained by the society, though degraded to afternoon tea and cakes. For the first toast, to *Sancte Claus, goed heylig man!* "amidst hilarity, jocundity, and to crown all, fraternity," Pintard distributed a *Broadside 82,*[19] which he had had Alexander Anderson engrave at his expense, imitating the Low Countries' broadsides called *Bilderbogen.*[20] It was rather ambitiously complicated. In the left panel, N, bearded and bald, in pontificals without mitre, carrying a switch, has two iconographic symbols, a beehive and a dog, which he said denoted Industry and Fidelity. But in traditional iconography the beehive[21] signified eloquence (i.e., pious scholarship); the dog[22] disciplinary power. Again we see how slightly the New Yorkers valued theological meaning. In the right panel on a fireplace mantle is a good little girl with apron full of fruits and nuts beside a bad little boy crying from a switching. Below her hangs a stocking—not a shoe as in the Low Countries—jammed with toys, and below him a stocking filled with switches. Tea, waffles, and sausages rest before the roaring fire. Below these depictions were N verses (Dutch and English in parallel columns):

Sancte Claus goed heylig Man!	Saint Nicholas, good holy man!
Trek uwe beste Tabaert aen,	Put on the Tabard,* best you can,
Reiz daer me'e na Amsterdam,	Go, clad therewith, to Amsterdam,

*Kind of jacket.

341

Van Amsterdam na 'Spanje,	From Amsterdam to Hispanje,
Waer Appelen van Oranje,	Where apples *bright* ** of Oranje,
Waer Appelen van granaten,	And likewise those *granate* † surnam'd,
Wie rollen door de Straaten.	Roll through the streets, all free unclaim'd.
SANCTE CLAUS, myn goede	SAINT NICHOLAS, my dear good
Vriend!	friend!
Ik heb U allen tyd gedient,	To serve you ever was my end,
Wille U my nu wat geven,	If you will, now, me something give,
Ik zal U dienen alle myn Leven.	I'll serve you ever while I live.

**Oranges. †Pomegranates.

Pintard later said that Judge Benson had procured these from an "ancient lady 87 years of age. Several, g^dma Brasher and others, knew some lines, but none except Mrs. H. remembered the whole."²³ Mrs. H. is probably Mrs. John Hardenbrook, who died in 1817, aged 87. These words account for the differences from antecedent Dutch texts and tell us how little true Dutch life existed on Manhattan at the time.

We come now to Washington Irving. He must have attended meetings of the New-York Historical Society before the one in 1809 which opened with Hosack's toast to N and Irving's admission to membership. At the moment in January 1808 when Washington and Peter Irving had the inspiration which became *The Knickerbocker History,* their (and Paulding's) journal *Salmagundi* noticed Santa Claus:

N†   In his days, according to my grand-father, were first invented those notable cakes, hight new-year cookies, which originally were impressed on one side with the honest burly countenance of the illustrious Rip [Van Dam]; and on the other with that of the noted St. Nicholas, vulgarly called Santeclaus:——of all the saints of the calendar the most venerated by true Hollanders, and their unsophisticated descendents. These cakes are to this time given on the first of January to all visitors, together with a glass of cherry-bounce or raspberry brandy.²⁴

342

The *Knickerbocker History 83* was inspired, according to Irving, as a take-off on the learned Samuel Latham Mitchell's guide to the city of New York. To readers it is clearly also a takeoff on Mitchell himself. *Sic transit!* Today Mitchell is almost forgotten, but then he was everywhere. He was with Pintard in Tammany, and in 1795 had presented to it an imaginative *Life, Exploits and Precepts of Tammany, the Famous Indian Chief* ("Avaunt then ye boasters! Cease too your prating about St. Patrick, St. George, and St. Louis; and be silent concerning your St. Andrew and St. David. Tammany, though no Saint, was, you see, as valorous, intrepid and heroic as the best of them . . .").[25] One of Mitchell's later books listed 194 famous events of American history that he had graced by his presence. Professor of chemistry and natural philosophy at Columbia College, in those years 1804 - 1809 he was United States senator, not by election but by appointment of Clinton's party as Clinton's successor. As late as the opening of the Erie Canal in 1825, there he was, wedding the waters with polysyllabic words and baroque images.[26] He ended in a bibulous senility, doubtless acquired on the banquet circuit.

Although the doctor was at the height of adulation in 1808, young Irving could see his frailties as fit subjects for his humorous pen. A kindlier disposition than Irving's would be hard to find; yet the learned Mitchell, who looks exasperatingly pretentious to us of another age, must have many a night been cruelly parodied at Cockloft Hall. Now just at that moment he was making a great play for Historicity. He was public orator for Pintard and DeWitt Clinton, and he was the waddling embodiment of the New-York Historical Society. A decade later Gulian Verplanck would write:

> . . . with what a blithe air
> Great H-s-ck usurps the historical chair!
> While Magnanimous M-tch-ll claims as his own
> To sit sov'reign lord on Philosophy's throne.

And so when the *Knickerbocker History 83,* was published, it was derisively dedicated to The New-York Historical Society. And with a care and thought that in no way marked the frenzied composition of the manuscript, Irving purposely published the *History* on N Day, 6 December 1809. Knickerbocker himself (the name means "child's-marble baker") is in certain flashes Mitchell, and in still other flashes Pintard and Hosack and Clinton.

Irving joined the society while composing the *History,* just to see (we may imagine) what made such mortals tick, for the society's old guard doubtless was quite uncongenial to him. But he who came to scoff remained to pray. As Irving's biographer, Williams, records, the act of writing this lovable satire interested the author in history, so that from his pen eventually flowed his *Columbus, Astoria,* and *Washington.* [27] He learned, too, to take his Saint Nicholas prayerfully, so that he was primarily responsible for the founding, in 1835, of the Saint Nicholas Society of New York City.

He later wrote that, at the time the *History* was published, few of his fellow citizens were aware

> that New York had ever been called New Amsterdam or
> had heard of the names of its early Dutch governors or
> cared a straw about their ancient Dutch progenitors. . . .
> The main object of my work . . . was to embody the
> traditions of our city in an amusing form; to illustrate its
> local humors, customs, and peculiarities; to clothe home
> scenes and places and familiar names with those imaginative
> and whimsical associations so seldom met with in our new
> country, but which live like charms and spells about the
> cities of the Old World, binding the heart of the native
> inhabitant to his home. . . . When I find, after a lapse of
> nearly forty years, this haphazard production of my youth
> still cherished among the descendents of Dutch worthies,
> when I find its very name become a household word and
> used to give the home stamp to everything recommended
> for popular acceptation,—such as Knickerbocker societies,
> Knickerbocker insurance companies, Knickerbocker steam-
> boats, Knickerbocker omnibusses, Knickerbocker bread, and
> Knickerbocker ice,—and when I find New Yorkers of
> Dutch descent priding themselves upon being "genuine
> Knickerbockers," I please myself with the persuasion that I
> have struck the right chord.[28]

Without Irving there would be no Santa Claus. The *History* contains two dozen allusions to him,[29] many of them among the most delightful flights of imagination in the volumes. *Here* is the source of all the legends about N in New Amsterdam—of the emigrant ship *Goede Vrouw,* like a Dutch matron as broad as she was long, with a figurehead of Saint Nicholas at the prow; here are the descriptions of festivities on N Day in the colony, and of the church dedicated to him; here is the description of Santa Claus bringing gifts, parking his horse and wagon on the roof while he slides down the chimney—all sheer fictions produced by Irving's *Salmagundi* crowd.

Santa Claus was a local joke with an anti-British sting until 1809; after 1809 the spritely SC spread like a plague.[30] The *History* was nationally hailed as the first notable work of imagination in the New World. Here at last, in an America grasping for its own poetry, was American Literature. "I can remember," wrote William Cullen Bryant, "learning a passage from it for a declamation and drowning myself in laughter, drawing the rebuke of the tutor."

Only three years after its publication a juvenile, *False Stories Corrected,* published by Samuel Wood, tried to debunk "Old Santaclaw, of whom so often little children hear such foolish stories; and once in the year are encouraged to hang their stockings in the Chimney at night, and when they arise in the morning, they find in them cakes, nuts, money, etc. placed there by some of the family, which they are told Old Santaclaw has come down Chimney in the night and put in. Thus the little innocents are imposed on by those who are older than they, and improper ideas take possession, which are not by any means profitable."[31] Said Chauncey Depew in 1885: "It is often better for fame to have eminent historians than to have enacted history. The judgment of mankind upon nations and peoples of the past is never formed from original sources. . . . The Dutch settlers, by the magic pen of the father of American literature, became the victims of a caricature which captivated the fancy of the world, and made the most potent factors in the founding and development of the freedom and prosperity of our country the accepted subjects of good-natured ridicule and merriment. Two generations have been laughing at a marionette."[32] But Santa Claus is the instance that good-natured ridicule and merriment produced the "freedom and prosperity," though of an uncalculated kind.

So Santa Claus was made by Washington Irving. But as if that were not enough, his partner in *Salmagundi* and brother-in-law, James K.

Paulding, who could not leave a good joke alone, repeated it again and again. If we think of Paulding at all, and we should, we probably think of him as a reputable historian and as secretary of the navy under Van Buren (1837 - 1841).[33] We forget the wide circulation of his fiction, which drew the highest advance royalties of the day.[34] Something of his effectiveness can be recalled in his "Peter Piper picked a peck of pickled peppers." He published a volume entitled *The Book of St. Nicholas, Translated from the Original Dutch of Dominie Nicholaus Aegidius Oudenarde,*[35] full of new-coined Santa Claus straight out of the *Salmagundi* workshop. Santa Claus would regularly appear in other books of his.[36]

The moment was propitious for the nationalization of the legend. New York had won the competition with Boston, Charleston, Philadelphia. When the Erie Canal opened, it was the funnel of immigration to the interior. Immigrants, temporarily settled in the city while awaiting an opportunity to migrate westward, energetically shed the manners of the Old World and donned any obvious manners of the New. During the next decades New York became the hub of all lively arts—publishing, design, and song.

Was there a bit of the adolescent personality of N in the senile Santa Claus? a strain of popular melody he could not lose? The next year after the *Knickerbocker History 83,* and hardly a week after Pintard's broadside, verses appeared in the New York *Spectator* obviously derived from both:

> Oh good holy man! whom we Sancte Claus name,
> The Nursery forever your praise shall proclaim:
> The day of your joyful revisit returns,
> When each little bosom with gratitude burns,
> For the gifts which at night you so kindly impart
> To the girls of your love, and the boys of your heart.
> Oh! come with your panniers and pockets well stow'd,
> Our stockings shall help you to lighten your load,
> As close to the fireside gaily we swing,
> While delighted we dream of the presents you bring.
>
> Oh! bring the bright Orange so juicy and sweet,
> Bring almonds and raisins to heighten the treat;
> Rich waffles and dough-nuts must not be forgot,

Nor Crullers and Oley-Cooks fresh from the pot.
But all these fine presents your Saintship can find,
Oh! leave not the famous big Cookies behind.
Or if in your hurry one thing you mislay,
Let that be the Rod—and oh! keep it away.

Then holy St. Nicholas! all of the year,
Our books we will love and our parents revere,
From naughty behavior we'll always refrain,
In hopes that you'll come and reward us again.[37]

Unlike Pintard and Irving, who set the annual visitation on N Day,[38] Paulding set it on New Years Day. As one of his too-frequently-worked jokes, he rather constantly accounted for the shift by N's confusion over the New Style calendar, possibly suggested to him by Aristophanes' wheeze about the gods' being confused by the shift to the Metonic calendar.[39] As we have said, New Year was the Manhattan visiting day, glorified with N cookies. These anticipatory verses which appeared on 15 December suggest New Year, or possibly Christmas—certainly not 6 December. Actually, all the snowballing commercial ads and notices (N had lost none of his appeal to merchants) were now advertising "gifts for Christmas and New Year," taking no sides. As already stated, the Anglicans eschewed New Year as a pagan orgy, whereas many continentals reserved Christmas for reverence.[40] Eventually Christmas won out (not without a thirty-year struggle) because of the most popular verses of all, composed by a staunch Anglican, Clement Moore.[41]

It is said that Moore's verses, *A Visit from St. Nicholas 84,* have been reprinted more than any other in the world. They were composed for his six (eventually nine) children at Christmas 1822. The following autumn a house guest showed them to someone in Troy who read and copied them, later to send them anonymously to Orville Holley, editor of the *Troy Sentinel,* who printed them 23 December 1823 under this foreword: "We know not to whom we are indebted for the following description of that unwearied patron of Children—that homely but delightful personification of parental kindness—Santa Claus, his costume and his equipage, as he hops about visiting the firesides of this happy land, laden with Christmas bounties; but from whomsoever it may have come, we give thanks for it."

In the first ten years it was republished twelve times, appearing within boards first in two almanacs for the year 1824.[42] The *Sentinel* in a later reprinting showed it knew who the author was, but not until the New-York Book of Poetry (1837) did Moore acknowledge it.[43] The first separate children's edition did not appear until 1848.[44]

Moore clearly depended on Irving: "Laying his finger aside of his nose" is a quotation from the *Knickerbocker History 83,* though by that time Irving's words were in such common circulation that the phrase may not have been directly borrowed.

Moore was the erudite son of the Episcopal bishop of New York and president of Columbia College. His group provided intellectual solidity to a newborn nation, claiming all arts and sciences for their domain. Clement, who was both a violinist and an organist, an architect of sorts, and a self-appointed pamphleteer against Jefferson's skepticism,[45] published (in addition to two volumes of collected verse) such diversities as a translation from French of a tract on sheep raising, a cry for peace in the War of 1812, and a life of George Castriot, king of Albania.

The legends about the composition of *A Visit from St. Nicholas 84* have grown nearly as fast as the legends about Santa Claus himself— even legends that Moore was not the author.[46] Not surprising; for Moore, who fancied his more lofty contributions, for fifteen years left those verses unclaimed—a long time to avoid popular fame for the sake of aesthetic conformity.[47] Moore was an admirable man, benevolent, religious, public-spirited, a loving father.[48] But he was conventional and pedantic. In 1822 he was engrossed in the new General (Anglican) Theological Seminary, for which in 1818 he had donated an entire block bounded by Ninth Avenue, Twentieth and Twenty-first streets, and the Hudson River. In 1821 he became its professor of Oriental and Greek literature.[49] While he and Pintard were working together with Bishop Hobart for its establishment, Pintard wrote in his private notebook: "I told him [Moore] not to speak slightly or disrespectfully of what he was totally ignorant. Is he a sample of the professors of the local school— . . . Eheu! professor."

Moore's imagination was derivative. In his volumes of poetic verse his anapests and iambs never faltered, and his diction was time-tested and secure.[50] Yet his delightful rhymes about Saint Nicholas are quite

in character. There is a mood of irresponsibility that overwhelms even
the most pedantic fathers at the Twelveday Season. They turn to
occasional verse, bashfully conscious of their own ineptitudes. At the
hiemal vacation they especially exorcise the wintry ghosts with formulaic rhythms. The ancient N, patron of *Three Clerks 44* and all
schools, including famous universities, smiled over Moore's shoulder
at their common imagery. Pedants properly anonymify their surreptitious bags of gold. *St. Nicholas 84* is thoroughly Moore's, whatever
legends to the contrary. Even *belly-jelly* was good classical rhyme in
Moore's eighteenth-century models.

But the reindeer seem inspired. In Irving's *History 83,* Paulding's
stories, and the like, Santa Claus drove a horse and wagon. Moore's
early biographers said that he invented the reindeer, but no. Conventional imagination is capable of turning one reindeer into eight;
but the reindeer had appeared, as Carson and Brigham discovered,[51]
in an anonymous juvenile called *The Children's Friend,* published on
Broadway the year before Moore composed.[52] That little book, also
notable as the first book published by lithograph in America, had
illustrations to accompany each of eight quatrains about "Santeclaus."
The first,

> Old Santeclaus with much delight
> His reindeer drives this frosty night
> O'er chimney-tops, and tracks of snow,
> To bring his yearly gifts to you,

is illustrated by a sprightly reindeer and sleigh. Chances are that Santa
Claus's reindeer was already a firm part of the Gotham legend by
Christmas 1822, indeed possibly by 1821.

Late in life (after 1856) Moore was glad enough to acknowledge his
authorship. He wrote out several autograph copies of *A Visit* on
request,[53] and told an interviewer that "a portly, rubicund Dutch-
man" living in the neighborhood of his father's country seat, Chelsea,
suggested to him the idea of making Saint Nicholas the hero of this
"Christmas piece" for his children.[54] This gleaning from an elderly
memory has turned into a legend that Moore was depicting the
gardener.[55] He was not depicting, but assembling, and virtually every
detail can be traced to documents in common circulation in 1822.

IV THE EMIGRANT WORLD OF THOMAS NAST

Christmas mercantile revels were unknown before the Knicker-bockers. The Common Council (John Pintard, clerk) on 21 December 1807, at the request of "a number of clergy" recommended that 25 December that year "be observed and set apart as the day of public and special *Thanksgiving and Prayer* to Almighty God for his benevolent dispensations and mercy to this City, and that we carefully abstain from all recreations and secular employments on that day."[1] A very few advertisements solicited sales for "Christmas and New Year Gifts" impartially together, as also Valentine, Easter, and Whitsuntide gifts. In 1766 a publisher had taken a flyer with *Nurse Trueloves Christmas Box and New Years Gift,*[2] but as late as 1815 the *Daily National Intelligencer* had a single mention of Christmas—a nativity poem by Walter Scott. However, New York as a Cavalier, not Puritan, city had long fostered the tradition of the "Christmas log," which drew Anglican eyes toward N's fireplace resort for sentimental family rites.

New York New Year was a big affair, with much firing of guns as well as visitations, "an ancient but foolish custom of ushering in the New Year with merriment and noise," reported the *Packet* in 1785. "We may with safety say that there were more than a thousand guns and pistols fired on Friday night in this city, attended with excessive vociferation and uproar." It was customary for news carriers to deliver New Year's Addresses to their customers, usually receiving a tip. The Addresses were normally verse, and Moore's poem soon became a favorite, starting " 'Twas the night before New Year."[3] The bakers also produced "New Year's Cakes" as presents, for which as we know N was a tradition.[4] Monroe restored the Presidential Reception on New Year's Day that Madison had dispensed with; we can imagine that in the 1820s a Hamiltonian Federalist might say "The Night Before Christmas" and a Jeffersonian Democrat "The Night Before New Year." In the mid-40s Moore's verses were still being printed in either form.[5] Perhaps that is how the compromise greeting, "Merry Christmas and Happy New Year," gained stature. Up to the Civil War a popular joke was to have SC complain about having to work two nights a year.[6]

The English *Gentleman's Magazine* in 1827, after Irving's but before Moore's vogue, reported:

The old Dutch settlers, and those who have fallen insensibly into their habits, have transferred the observance from the Eve of St. Nicholas, whom you know as the especial patron of little children, to that of New Year. Long before the important night arrives, numerous conjectures and inquiries are made by the young urchins respecting the person and being of Sandy Claus (evidently a corruption of St. Nicholas), who, in the opinion of the majority, is represented by a little old negro, who descends the chimney at night, and distributes a variety of rewards with impartial justice. . . . As soon as the little ones are fast asleep, the parents fill a clean stocking near the chimney with all sorts of bon bons, toys, picture-books, etc., and especially with the much-admired eatable of the season, the New Year cookie . . . , a particular sort of cake made at this season of the year, fancifully stamped and shaped, and distributed along with *liqueurs* to visitors on the first of January.[7]

Paulding toasted Saint Nicholas on his Day (*New Mirror for Travellers*):

To whomever fails in due honour and allegiance, be this his fate: never to sip the dew from the lips of the lass he loveth best on new year's eve, or new year's morn; never to taste of hot spiced Santa Cruz; and never to know the delight of mince pies and sausages, swimming in the sauce of honest mirth, and homefelt jollity. . . . St. Nicholas! thrice jolly St. Nicholas. Bacchus of Christian Dutchmen, king of good fellows, patron of holiday fare, inspirer of simple frolic and unsophisticated happiness, saint of all saints that deck the glorious calendar! thou that first awakened the hopes of the prattling infant; dawnest anticipated happiness on the schoolboy; and brightenest the wintry hours of manhood, if I forget thee whatever betide, or whatever fantastic, heartless follies may usurp the place of thy simple celebration, may I lose with the recollection of past pleasures, the anticipation of pleasures to come, yawn at a tea party, petrify at a soiree, and perish, finally overwhelmed, in a deluge of whip syllabub and floating island! Thrice, and three times thrice, jolly St. Nicholas! On this, the first day of the new year 1826, with an honest reverence and a full bumper of cherry bounce, I salute thee! To St. Nicholas! Esto perpetuo.[8]

At the holidays 1841/42 the newspaper *Brother Jonathan*[9] printed Moore's verses with the caption, "St. Nicholas, on his New-Year's Eve Excursion (as Ingham saw him) in the Act of Descending a Chimney." Ingham, the illustrator, saw sleigh, reindeer, chimney, rooftops, bag and toys, short beard, pipe, shortcoat with narrow fur trimming, and the short breeches now coming to be called *knickerbockers*. This iconography to accompany Moore's verses was developing from the *Troy Sentinel's Carrier's Address* for 1829/30, which showed eight reindeer in spans of two, probably created by the local Myron King.[10] In 1837 Robert Weir covered SC's shortcoat with a cape, emphasizing its scarlet hue and white ermine lining and the high black boots.[11] An illustration in *New Mirror,* 1844, moves Weir's version toward the present iconography, especially in modeling the cap.[12] So SC evolved away from Paulding, who would have "a little rascal with a three-cornered cocked hat, decked with old gold lace, a blue Dutch sort of short pea jacket, red waistcoat, breeks of the same colour, yellow stockings, and honest thick-soled shoes, ornamented with a pair of skates" (1837). In Albany "Sinti Klass" wore tricorn and silver-buckled shoes to mid-century.[13]

As the Knickerbocker SC crossed the Mason-Dixon line, it gathered imagery from Pennsylvania and other middle states. An account from North Carolina, recorded 1917, describes an SC of about 1850:

> I can well remember hearing my grandmother tell of a fear-
> ful fire-breathing monster which came and breathed
> through the key-hole on Christmas Eve. He breathed fire on
> bad children. "Once on Christmas Eve I saw him with his
> big eyes that frightened me almost to death. He came into
> the room where we children slept and put down a pack
> which contained toys and a bundle of switches. He went to
> the most mischievous boy of the family and 'haling' him up,
> gave him an awful beating. He treated the other mischie-

vous boys in the same manner, then divided the toys up among the good children and went away. The same thing happened every Christmas, but this was the only time that I saw the creature."[14]

Perhaps some such lack of uniformity in imagery before the Civil War explains why hardly a Christmas passes without journalistic tributes to Thomas Nast as "the man who made Santa Claus." As Vinson wrote, "Nast's ability to command attention and build up a wide audience rendered an incalculable service in showing Americans that their own people could express themselves in art."[15] An elderly, dejected Nast himself helped to foster the notion of his biographer, Albert Bigelow Paine, that Nast made Santa Claus and Santa Claus made Nast.[16]

Paine, the quite reliable man-of-letters, dramatist, and biographer and editor of Mark Twain, succumbed to the legend-creating urge in his biography of Nast. Probably he chose to open and close the biography with benevolent Santa Claus to provide a contrasting high-light for his theme of Nast as a herculean crusader who cleansed the political stables. The first illustration in Nast's book *Christmas Drawings for the Human Race 85* was his two-page spread in *Harper's Weekly* for 1866, depicting a SC visitation scene and some fifteen surrounding vignettes of the by-then-traditional SC appurtenances. But these were not Nast's inventions; they had evolved over more than thirty years. Most of Nast's predecessors and contemporaries were more "Nast" than Nast, except for one vignette which may well have been an invention—"Santa's Workshop." To be sure, like all the other artists, Nast tended to make the benevolent Santa Claus rather strikingly like his own self-portraits, and who can blame him or them? Just to that extent were his figures individualized.

Nast's last publicly circulated SC drawing (1889/90), with its turned-out fur headgear and buckled shoes, goes back to the *New Mirror*. Indeed, the side vignette of King Cole in that drawing (gold crown aside) is nearer the "Nast" SC than the SC in the picture. Like all nineteenth-century icons, his was drawn smaller than a chimney despite the SC girth, in contrast with the more ballooned Santas that have resulted from department-store impersonations in this century. Nast died of yellow fever in 1902 as American consul in

Ecuador.[17] Creator of the Tammany tiger, the Republican elephant, the Democratic donkey, and other lasting symbols though he was, he had lost his political effectiveness and therewith his public. Venerated but neglected, he found solace and a congenial spirit in the senile N, sketching SC in various guises at the request of friends, including a painting for his admiring sponsor Theodore Roosevelt.[18] Mary Boynton, daughter of the naturalist Louis Agassiz Fuertes, generously gave me a sketch which Nast did for him. His last commission for *Harper's* was his *Christmas Drawings for the Human Race 85,* 1889, reprinted from earlier drawings.[19] We are reminded of Moore's preoccupation with SC in later life. N was not alone in enduring a second childhood.

Harper's Weekly began in 1857, and in 1862 appointed a contributor, twenty-two-year-old Nast, as staff illustrator with freedom for invention. He drew a double-page "Christmas Eve," of two Christmas wreaths encircling, on the left, a fatherless family at home and, on the right, a soldier father staring at their pictures in the campfire light. Christmas had come into its own as sentimental focus for the year primarily because of Dickens's *Christmas Carol* in 1843, but almost equally because of his *Christmas Stories* and Irving's *Christmas Sketches.* [20] In none of these volumes was N or SC mentioned, and at that moment the hinterland, as Detroit records show, had not yet heard of SC.[21] But by 1855 even Massachusetts passed a law that "business is to be suspended" on 25 December. In 1865 Christmas was declared to be "a national holiday." Scrooge and Tiny Tim pulled the strings, but fat SC with toys was a popular puppet.

In that year 1862 the North was a bleak loser in a war that disrupted all familial affections, and Nast's drawing hit just the right soothing note: "Letters from every corner of the Union came to the Harper office with messages of thanks for that inspired picture."[22] From that moment the Christmas double-page was Nast's fixture in *Harper's Weekly.* There was no Santa Claus in that picture, but the same issue had as its forepiece "Christmas in Camp," with a Santa garbed in the stars and stripes distributing presents from his reindeered sleigh to cheering soldiers under a triumphal arch, "Welcome Santa Claus." In 1863 Nast's double-page, "A Christmas Furlough," had a center panel of a soldier returning to bring happiness to wife and family before a laden Christmas tree. It was flanked by two vignettes: "Eve" with Santa Claus, toysack on back, bending over two sleeping infants, and "Morning" with the infants finding filled stockings before the fireplace. That same 1863 Nast drew SC with reindeer and sleigh on the roof as illustration for J. M. Gregory's *Christmas Poems.*

Nast was an immigrant, representative of the time. Before the Civil War, and especially around the Year of Revolt 1848, New York harbor welcomed restless exiles from all Europe into the United States. Most of them made their way west by Erie Canal and Erie Railroad to the great plains, but they used the city as a staging place, learning an American argot, strange even to the British, and the fresh view of life that it expressed.[23] Born in Landau in 1840, Nast sailed with his mother and sister from Le Havre in the autumn of 1846 on stormy seas, to settle on Greenwich Street, probably about the Christmas season. Deserters of the Old World, they were avid for the New. Paine fancifully depicted "the German Santa Claus, Pelze-Nicol, leading a child dressed as the Christkind, and distributing toys and cakes, or switches, according as the parents made report. It was this Pelze-Nicol—a fat, fur-clad, bearded old fellow—that the boy in later years was to present to us as his conception of the True Santa Claus."[24] I can find no evidence of Pelznichol in the Landau Kreis (Palatinate) at the time, and nowhere in all Germany as company for Christkind, and never in that guise; for as a derivative of the devil, Pelznichol was normally horned and tailed. Paine's fancy doubtless was stirred by the Pennsylvania Belshnickle.[25]

Rather, Nast would learn his SC in the New York City school, which he immediately entered. The polyglot immigrants, eager to adjust, were annealed in the crucible of the American grammar school. The fur of SC came, not from Old Germany with its traditional presumptions that fur covered God's outcast crew of fallen angels and the sons of Cain, the raging beasts of the mummers' world, but from new presumptions based on the abundant fur trade of the Astors that those who had "made it" in America wore fur in the cold north winter.

In 1850 Manhattan had more than half a million people, Brooklyn another hundred thousand, and Williamsburg and Jersey together another hundred thousand. "The masses" and "the melting pot" were just beginning to be topics on all lips. In the decade 1820 - 1829 there had been 90,077 migrants to the United States; in the decade 1850 -

1859 Ireland alone sent 1,073,065, and Germany 935,171.[26] Not only to schools but to the migrants very doors came charity in the guise of the Knickerbocker Santa Claus, "men and women who, out of their own pockets, reimburse Santa Claus for his outlay, and count it a joy." The teachers in our crowded migrant schools were Santa's spies. Jacob Riis did not write until 1897, but his autobiography has long been the accepted representation of this earlier era: "Santa Claus is established in that Thompson-street alley, for this generation at least. And Santa Claus, got by book or by crook into an Eighth-Ward alley, is as good as the whole Supreme Court bench, with the Court of Appeals thrown in, for backing the Board of Health against the slums."[27] In a single generation New York could engrain in these hopefuls customs more monolithic than Europe's customs of a thousand years.

The sleigh and reindeer of *The Children's Friend* led to a specification in the 1860s that Santa's home was the North Pole. Unquestionably sleighs were Dutch, not English. Midwinter goodies of milk, butter, and juicy steaks came down the Hudson from as far away as Albany in Dutch sleighs long before New England discovered what two runners could do.[28] The sleigh was the fastest mode in the slowest season, and the imagination needed no artist's stimulation to project Santa's home further and further north. In 1845 Sir John Franklin began to make the North Pole notorious. Then New Yorkers tried to make the North Pole their special preserve. An expedition to search for Franklin left New York in 1850, and another in 1853. The American Geographical Society was founded in direct consequence.[29]

New York was now the publishing capital. Dickens and Irving had made Christmas and Santa Claus artistically respectable. In 1846 "Sanctus Klass" was stated to have "recently become a great harvest for the booksellers." Around 1870 the American Bret Harte, lionized in Britain, told of the wild night ride of Dick Bullen to get some tag ends of toys for the Old Man's sick son Johnny ("How Santa Claus Came to Simpson's Bar").

The first issue of *St. Nicholas Magazine* was November, 1873 (the last in 1939).[30] Its first editor, Mrs. Mary Mapes Dodge, published her best-seller *Hans Brinker* (for which SC's Lowland humor paved the way) in that same year. Almost at once she tied *St. Nicholas* to the new and booming Sunday Schools: e.g., Edward Eggleston's "The House of

Santa Claus, A Christmas Fairy Show for Sunday Schools," 1876, which introduced the assisting dwarfs. Mrs. Dodge enlisted the finest children's writers: Howard Pyle, Joel Chandler Harris, Theodore Roosevelt, Dorothy Canfield, Ellis Parker Butler, Henry W. Longfellow, Rudyard Kipling, James Whitcomb Riley, Ralph Henry Barbour, Joaquin Miller, John Kendrick Bangs, Frank Gelett Burgess, Sidney Lanier, Julian Hawthorne, Ben Ames Williams, Wilfred Grenfell, Richard Harding Davis, Jack London, Frances Hodgson Burnett (*Little Lord Fauntleroy* appeared in the issues of 1886), William Dean Howells, and even Alfred Lord Tennyson (with accompanying music by Lady Tennyson).[31] The St. Nicholas League—the column of contributions from child readers—published the childish compositions of almost every American author widely known in the first half of this century.[32]

The magazine was a Cordelia, faithful to the foolish fond old N and dying in his service. Its first words were: "Hurrah for dear St. Nicholas. He has made friends in a moment. And no wonder. Is he not the boys' and girls' own Saint, the especial friend of young Americans? That he is." Then followed Irving's fairytales about the first ship and the first church: "Dear old St. Nicholas, with his pet names—Santa Claus, Kriss Kringle, St. Nick, and we don't know how many others."

The most effective regular contributor to *St. Nicholas Magazine* was Louisa May Alcott, who joined that illustrious group of Thomas Bailey Aldrich, William Cullen Bryant, Bret Harte, Sarah Orne Jewett, and Frank Stockton as contributors in its first year. She is said to have put her very first tales, written for Emerson's daughter, in her mother's Christmas stocking in 1854. SC had appeared in *Little Women* (1868); now the magazine reintroduced Effie, still aged ten, and not one but four Santa Clauses. "Never give up your faith in the sweet old stories, even after you have come to see that they are only the pleasant shadow of a lovely truth."[33] N's second childhood contributed juvenile morality not limited to *St. Nicholas Magazine* or the marketplace; as late as 1946 E. E. Cummings published his *Santa Claus, A Morality.*[34]

In 1891 J. P. McCaskey published *Christmas in Song, Sketch, and Story: Nearly Three Hundred Christmas Songs, Hymns, and Carols;* of these twenty-one were exclusively about Santa Claus. I have mentioned the song production in the 1950s. To his dying day N would sing. But in the twentieth century creators generally turned away from song and print to the mechanisms of cinema, radio, and television. The aged N has not been adjustable, and only the filmed *Miracle of Thirty-fourth Street* has prolonged his life.

V THE NEW BYZANTIUM

Constantinople, which nursed the infant N, was New Rome, oriented to the routes of trade. New York became the capital of world trade by adapting the industrial revolution to the production line. The gold bezant has been found buried in Scotland and Indonesia; the gold dollar traveled even further. The first production line was the baker's cookie tray, the first stamping machine the cookie mold or cutter. N's cheap hideaways fitted naturally into the new tinsel world. Though Uncle Sam supplanted Tammany as a symbol of our nation, at Christmas he gave way to Santa Claus, who more, even, than Dickens has sold the world on gaudy Christmas. To be sure, the Christmas tree came from Strasbourg and the Christmas card (as well as the *Christmas Carol*) from London,[1] but Santa's stocking has been the cornucopia. To probe that bulging stocking to the toe would satiate the reader as Santa has satiated many a pampered child. Consequently, as we approach N's demise I limit the topics to a necessary few.

A theme of biographers expressed in this volume is that a great life is a tragedy, that heroes perish from their own excesses. N, who rose to fame on the melodic strains of the Reginolds and the Moores and on the merchandizing powers of New Roman emperors and Crusading popes, who in hoary age could still do a turn to *Santa Claus Is Coming to Town,* nevertheless could not survive the latest rage, product of our merchant kings: *Rudolf the Red-Nosed Reindeer.* Those verses were composed as a commercial in 1939 for Montgomery Ward. The Second World War then intervened, and not until 1949 were they set to the tune which now determines our Christmas custom. Its theme of the triumph of handicap and absurdity, some sociologists maintain, is far more congenial to current taste than the N tradition of omnipotence and ubiquity. At all events, Rudolf's route around the world is on the track that Santa blazed.[2]

It would be laborious to demonstrate that Father Christmas, Père

Noel, the Weihnachtsmann, and other images of that demiworld are at present but reflections of the Knickerbocker Santa Claus; but a bewildering variety of evidence embodied in images and artifacts and other remains confirms the fact.

A CBS Christmas broadcast from Finland, 1939, started: "William L. White, speaking to you on this Christmas night from Finland, the country where our legend of Santa Claus and his reindeers first began. Reindeer still pull sleighs in the north of Finland tonight, carrying supplies to the little nation's army which is fighting to press back the great army which would come in."[3] This was propaganda: the Russian army was at Finland's gates in unprovoked aggression. We had already sentimentalized Finland for "paying its War Debts"; why should not SC be another emotional tie, joining a home of real reindeer with a Knickerbocker image? The propaganda worked beyond the wildest hopes. In September 1966, a foreign correspondent reported to the American papers that in Finland "Santa Claus is busy already. Mail addressed to him from all parts of the world has started to pour in to . . . Liisa Jantuonen, secretary to Santa Claus. Liisa is . . . the official Santa Claus or Father Christmas of the Finnish Post Office. . . . Every letter with a legible return address gets a note from Santa Claus. These used to be individually hand written, but today are printed in several languages, but mainly in Finnish, Swedish, and English. Tove Jansson and Kylli Kosi, two of Finland's best known modern story writers, compose the letters."[4] To be sure, N had been a venerated saint in Finland in the Middle Age,[5] and a lovely Latin N sequence had been composed there. But both cult and sequence had long been forgotten. SC apparently was first heard of in Finland about 1930.

N's ancient skill of operating on the enemy's border, discussed in chapter 2, was revived in this century. When Germany invaded the Netherlands in the Second World War, Holland found him an ideal propagandist. Immediately the government began to cultivate its common ties with America. The *Washington Star* on N Day 1940 described with elaborate specificity the annual visitation of N and Black Peter in Holland, even to verses in both Dutch and English:

> Look, the steamer from Spain
> Is nearing again;

It brings us Saint Nicholas,
  Oh, look, there he is!
How gaily his pony
  Is prancing on deck;

And banners are flying
  Way up to the stack.
His valet looks dandy
  And grins with a nod:
"Good children get candy,
  But bad ones the rod."

This was but the mockup. Before Christmas 1941, the Dutch had founded *The Knickerbocker Weekly* (first issue 15 Dec., a kind of mean between 6 and 25 Dec.), with a photograph of N, an old gentleman dressed as a bishop, mounted on a white charger, parading down Fifth Avenue. The white horse was led by a colored boy in a fantastic costume, and immediately behind these two apparent eccentrics came two coaches filled with children in Dutch costumes who blew loud blasts on their horns. According to the caption: "For the second year, this Dutch Santa Claus made his appearance in New York, the former New Amsterdam where St. Nicholas Eve was once celebrated in the traditional style of the Netherlands. There are only two countries that actually have a Santa Claus, and the tradition came to the United States from the country of its origin, the Netherlands." The same issue transcribed a radio talk for 6 December, beamed by G. J. Simons to the West Indies and South America, calling for faith, under the common bond of N and Black Pieter, in the release of Holland from German occupation and terror.[6] *The Knickerbocker Weekly* survived into the postwar reconstruction period, assisted by the now rather aged New York Saint Nicholas Societies, by the Holland House Corporation, the Dutch government, etc. A new film, *Dutch Tradition,* prepared for gatherings, parades N and Pete in all the major cities, coast to coast.[7] The Netherlands Museum in Holland, Michigan, and other Dutch centers presented a three-act drama written by a member of the Hope College faculty which "depicts the experience of a typical Dutch family as they prepare to receive St. Nicholas and 'Zwarte Piet.'"[8] The clergy of the Reformed Church, very active otherwise in war support, rather belligerently refrained from these N rites.[9] N and

Piet visited the Royal Netherlands Flying School at Jackson, Mississippi, creating "a new tradition which undoubtedly will be observed in Jackson long after the Netherlanders have gone back to wrest their territory from enemy invaders."[10] More than one wag described N's lessons in flying. The "new tradition" died long since.

Perhaps because of American ethnic sensitivity, Black Piet dropped out of the legend. The *Knickerbocker* explained in 1946 that N "always leaves Black Peter behind in Holland in view of the allegedly overcrowded condition of American hotels."[11] N continued to ride his white horse on special occasions such as at Irving's Sunnyside in 1952 and Philipse Castle in 1953, under joint sponsorship of the Sleepy Hollow Restorations Inc. and the Holland Saint Nicholas Committee of New York; their promise of annual repetition has not been kept.[12]

With characteristic Gallic rationality, the French weekly *Paris Match* stated in its issue of 25 December 1965: "Despite his white beard and bent back, the Father Christmas who nowadays distributes toys to our youngsters is one of the youngest persons in modern mythology. Our grandparents knew nothing of him. In France we began to speak hesitantly of him about 1920, and not until in 1949, according to the ethnologist Claude Lévy-Strauss, did the French, only gradually recovering from the war, openly adopt him. He came straight out of the U.S.A." But in fact he was not quite that new, for the *Magasin catholique* in December 1856 reported the American N's invasion of parts of France, aided by a third column "tendresse des mères et l'ingeniosité des marchands de bimbeloterie."[13] Recent Gaullism has somewhat dampened French ardor. The photographer of *Match,* as ingenious as the merchants, caught an unposed shot of a fisherman, amazingly like Irving's Santa Claus, riding an ass along the strand of N's Patara in Asia Minor, and a baubled conifer stuck in the sand. The text mourned, "Here as well, inside ten years there will be another Saint-Tropez."[14]

In 1827, about the time of Moore, when the *Knickerbocker History* 83 was captivating England, *Gentleman's Magazine* reported that the custom of conveying presents to children secretly on Saint Nicholas Eve "although unknown to us, is still retained in some parts of the Continent and in America."[15] Granted that Dickens *made* the modern English Christmas, Santa merchandized it. In 1854 James Nisbet published in England *A Christmas Stocking,* originally edited in New York.

The dramatic device is a Christmas stocking which Santa Claus fills
with toys, each of which has a story to tell. Two excellent English
scholars, Thurston and Attwater, reported that Santa was "apparently
introduced into this country by Bret Harte."[16] The botanist Edwin
Lees (commemorated in *rubus Leesii*) in 1879 described in detail the
Santa Visitations in Herefordshire and Worcestershire, and reported
hearing the same mummery in Devonshire.[17] The fact of an American
source of SC was embodied in *Chamber's Encyclopaedia,* which not
everyone consulted; for the historian and novelist J. S. Fletcher (1916)
was glad that he had no such German saint as "Santa Claus": "Our
Christmas presents were found in stockings and put there by Father
Christmas. I have a suspicion that Father Christmas is not very old
among us. Was he not the result of an attempt to naturalize Santa
Claus, whose name sounds Italian rather than German?"[18] From such
background arise odd combinations of fact and fancy. The poet Allen
Ramsay, who was Master of Eton, where N had once been patron
saint, composed these academic sapphics, made up of some Reginold
of Eichstätt and some Irving of Knickerbocker:

> *Nicola, clemens pater atque custos,*
> *Quem colit laetis puerilis aetas*
> *Risibus, sero referente Nonas*
> > *Sole Decembres,*
> *Sic eas fausto pede per caminum*
> *Nec tibi voltum maculet jocosum*
> *Foeda fuligo gelidoque barbam,*
> > *Rore micantem,*
> *Da novum follem mihi, da sonorum*
> *Tympanum et fictos pedites trochumque;*
> *Da pium pectus, precor, et mereri*
> > *Matris amorem.* [19]

> Nicholas, benevolent guardian father, whom
> youngsters invoke with shouts of joy when
> the aged sun returns 5 December, may you
> come down the chimney with so light a step
> that no grimy soot befouls your happy smile
> or beard all sparkling with frost. Give me a
> new leather bag; give me a resounding drum,

> toy soldiers, and a hoop. Give me a thankful
> heart, I pray, and conduct worthy of
> a mother's love.

From similar academic antecedents came Benjamin Britten's quite lovely cantata *Saint Nicholas.*

The Nazis attempted hardest to naturalize SC. Of course pure Aryans contemned N, and SC was almost equally disliked. Yet he found some office in the Third Reich. Goebbel's bureau militantly tried to convert his custom and iconography to Aryan orthodoxy. Der Weihnachtsmann, who like Father Christmas and le Père Noel had virtually disappeared when mumming disappeared, was revived in the fat, belted costume of New York's Santa Claus. During the Second World War, at government expense the pamphlet *Der Weihnachtsmann* brought to bombed-out families politically acceptable two-tone cheer on recycled paper.[20]

N had lost his patronage of Western sailors in the seventeenth century when new modes of navigation replaced the old, and freebooting pirates like Drake were devout Protestants. Then and thereafter few ships were named *Saint Nicholas;* as we have seen, the figurehead on the *Goede Vrouw* is a myth. American patriots, however, revived the dedication many times during and after the Revolution. The last important instance was the packet ship *Saint Nicholas,* launched in New York City 6 December 1841 for the Havre service. The Honorable Egbert Benson, third president of the Saint Nicholas Society, dressed in "Dutch" costume for the occasion, broke a bottle of Dutch schnapps across the bow. Doddering N protected the ship for twenty years, but then she foundered on the shoals of Sable Island with loss of captain and eight men.[21] A model of her, gift of the Society, is now in the Marine Museum of the City of New York. Nearby is a model of the Liverpool packet ship Washington Irving, built 1845, which met a more kindly fate.

But N, no longer patron of the seas, still might be regarded as patron of the modern post. In 1852 some settlers in Indiana met on Christmas Eve to choose a name for their settlement. The chosen name was Santa Claus. In 1856 John Specht became its first postmaster. The enterprising postmaster James Martin (1914 - 1935), at first by answering children's mail himself and then by enlisting the local

American Legion in the task, built up the trade toward its eventual nearly four million pieces annually.[22] One of these letters to Santa Claus read:

Dec. 24. 1901
Dear Santa Claus ●

I Havent Had Any Christmas Tree In 4 Years
and I Have Broken All My Trimmings And I
Want a Pair Of Roller Skates And A Book I
Cant Think Of Any Thing More I Want You
To Think Of Something More
Good By ●
   Edsel Ford[23]

Around the post office grew the tourist haven "Santa Claus Land," with sideshows ranging from acrobats to zoos. Its Chamber of Commerce sells memberships to anyone anywhere without discrimination as to race, creed, or color. One benefit is a regular monthly dinner, not wholly unlike those of the Saint Nicholas Society.

No commercial success continues long without siblings. The most prosperous, perhaps, was "Santa's Workshop at North Pole." In the Adirondacks near Lake Placid, visited by over half a million people each year, it is possibly best known for making the bumper sticker what it is today. It has, or had, the largest herd of true reindeer below the Arctic regions—a portion of 150 animals kept in stock along with "65 very attractive gnomes and elves in unique costumes working in his shops."[24] Nearly all other SC shrines and zoos substitute North American white-tailed deer.[25] The products of the shops were anything but given away, though an annual benevolence of the corporation was lavish and well publicized.

N's hold upon the mail has led to a ZIP Code number 99701, inducing Arthur Hoppe to answer a fictive letter from a little girl: "I am 8 years old. Some of my little friends say there is no 99701. Please tell the truth. Is there a 99701? Yours truly, Virginia 09426." Hoppe concludes his extensive answer: "No 99701! Thank Efficiency, he lives, and he lives forever! A thousand years from now, 09426, nay, ten times ten thousand years from now, he will continue to make glad the hearts of bureaucrats. Just as surely as there is a 558-18-4454 up there in 08702."[26] This whimsy is, of course, based on the famous reply in the *New York Sun,* 21 September 1897, of Francis P. Church to Virginia O'Hanlon's letter: "Please tell me the truth, is there a Santa Claus?"[27] N's connection with the mails extends to stamps—Christmas Seals of many years[28] and postage stamps of many countries.

What is good for trade is good for society, say officials of bourgeois states, and SC has visited presidents and governors. Lincoln once scoffed but, like Irving, stayed to pray. Harrison was the first president on record to attempt personification: "We shall have an old-fashioned Christmas tree for the grandchildren upstairs in the White House," he reported to the press in 1891, "and I shall be their Santa Claus myself. If my influence goes for aught in this busy world let me hope that my example may be followed by every family in the land."[29]

But he was not followed by all, for private enterprise took over. Santa's Helpers, Inc. in New York employed over fifty actors each year as trained Santas for private visitations to families whose fathers were not bold. Each visit was based on an advance questionnaire filled out by the parents about Junior's habits—a return to N's questioning of the youngsters in the mumming period, but without the switches. Not all visitations were successful.[30] The old *New York Graphic* landed a well-advertised Santa, an actor named Will Malory, by parachute from a plane in Central Park. He was frozen to the core and angrily tore off his beard and stalked away cursing, while the assembled children gaped to hear such unsaintly language. Melvin Freud, head of the Toy Guidance Council, in 1952 said, "The Frankenstein of the toy business has always been Santa Claus."[31] But Norman Rockwell, for Hallmark Cards, endowed senile N with a halo that in his prime of life he seldom could afford.

VI PSYCHOANALYSIS

The sheer materialism of old N's world has troubled the Puritan conscience.[1] Here are a few lines from a CBS-TV script (1962):

MR. SEVEREID: Today, Santa Claus keeps pace with modern tastes through the help of men like New York artist Saul Steinberg. The rooftops that beckon to Santa Claus are many, but he will always seem particularly at home in the true city of his growth and development, New York.

MUSIC: "We Wish You a Merry Christmas."
MR. SEVEREID: And there he goes—helping us to spread the
presents: this year an estimated $7½ billion bagful wrapped
up in $150 million worth of paper and ribbon. We'll buy
presents for our families, our business associates, for ourselves, for people off the streets we see once a week, and for
people from across the continent that we haven't seen for a
dog's age. . . . We'll return for some further comments on
"The Spirit of Christmas Presents" after this message.
(Commercial)
MUSIC: "O, Tannenbaum."
MR. SEVEREID: Under the spreading Christmas tree all the
gifts will stand. Christmas trees spring up everywhere in
December, and it's lucky they do. They provide a much
larger dumping ground for Santa to unload than a simple
stocking would. . . . We asked how about the people who
annually complain over the growing pressure of giving gifts.
MISS GEESEE (a professional personal shopper): Well, you know,
the very people that say it—that gift giving is becoming such
a problem and so forth, they're the very ones that go out and
do it, you know.[2]

Such contradictions were implicit in the person of N from Childhood. The patron of mariners and merchants, whose world is the
common sense balance sheets of quid pro quo,[3] was also the un-
audited dispenser of bags of gold (Three Daughters 13). The destroyer
of Czar Nicholas chose for himself the name Nicholas Lenin. For
parents to practice anonymous benevolence disturbs many a psyche.
Not to demand social reciprocity is apt to seem to merchants a sign of
childishness or second childishness. The puerile and senile cannot
shoulder their way through the marketplace. According to de Groot:
"For birthdays and on other festive occasions we send presents with a
card bearing our name, which actually means to say do ut des, I give
that thou shalt give. Not so with St. Nicholas: he gives without wanting returns. He is—and this is the crux—the symbol of a higher
giving-power. The essential 'good things in our lives' come without a
dangling card attached."[4]
But this crux has always caused a kind of psychological crisis

among N's devotees. It haunts those dark days of the Winter Season; it coins the thieving, murder, boiling, pickling legends that always end in bursts of superhuman goodness.

In 1909 the *Chicago Daily News* used Santa as a symbol equivalent with Lady Bountiful in dealings with other nations, but this image of opprobrium in benevolence remained comparatively moribund until Franklin Roosevelt became president.[5] Almost at once That Man became a political image in some minds identical with N. Roosevelt's death during the pious unanimity of the Second World War left the aged N the surviving symbol; thereafter he alone personified the *Three Daughters* 13 legend of depersonalized benevolence. In W. W. Bauer's *Santa Claus, M.D.* (1950) dealing, of course, with "socialized medicine": "Surveys have demonstrated that belief in Santa Claus disappears on the average at the age of seven years—except in Washington." In the election year 1952 (Eisenhower-Stevenson), which was near the climax of public regard for Santa Claus, the publishers McGraw-Hill, self-described "Headquarters for Business Information," took a full-page ad in *The New York Times* that began:

SANTA CLAUS COULD DIE OF OLD AGE
No one shoots Santa Claus. This remark about a government which spends and spends and spends may well be true.
But it is also true that Santa Claus is an old man. At his age
overwork might well kill him.

It is with the possibility of working Santa Claus to death
that this editorial is concerned. No position is taken as between the contending political parties in the present campaign. Our concern is with the problem of protecting Santa
Claus. . . .

Higher government expenditures of worthless dollars
then could accomplish nothing. Santa Claus would be dead
from overwork. . . . Santa Claus, be it remembered, is no
youngster. If we continue our present improvident course,
he will be worked to death.[6]

In these dying moments of N's biography, we knit up some raveled threads of time: the Christian Year and the Winter Season; commerce and religion; juvenility and scholasticism; instantaneous thaumaturgy and earthly senility; amorality and legalism. Our attention is drawn to the schizophrenic tendency.

In the psychoanalytic period following Freud and Jung the dying N has been totally analyzed by practicing physicians.[7] They have sometimes justified their analysis by stating that they have observed a rising incidence of neuroses in their patients in the winter season. Yet it is a fact of record that not December but February and, next, November mark the admission peaks in psychiatric hospitals.[8] At all events, the operation of the imagination naturally attracts both critics and psychiatrists. Freud was a remarkable literary critic and Jung a mythologist and anthropologist; each in his way illuminated dark recesses of the mind by studying records of the past. To be sure, much that is published by even the best of both scientists and critics is banal. All mothers say that Christmas shopping drives them mad, and fathers that the merchants' bills are crazy. We all laugh at the *Red-nosed Reindeer* as sibling rivalry and wish fulfillment. For that we do not need a physician's special skill.

But the imagination is somewhat more complex than that. Dr. L. Bryce Boyer writes:

> In recent centuries, man has mastered the preservation of his crops and learned enough about the movements of the celestial bodies that worries concerning the reappearance of the sun have been determined to be unrealistic. Nevertheless, his infantile anxieties about starvation have not lessened. Apparently, the celebration of Christmas as a children's holiday is still an acceptable medium through which man can express those fears and attempt to deny their existence. He is able to give his children gifts (food) and through his identification with children feel that he himself is fed by a beneficent mother. Perhaps this explains why it has been possible to a varying extent for Santa Claus to displace God as the figure to be worshipped.[9]

And Dr. James Cattell writes:

> The holiday period between Thanksgiving and New Years Day is a time to be with one's family, a time for giving gifts, and a time for feasting. These are special occasions for emo-

tional closeness and intimacy with family and friends, with additional emphasis on the presence of father, God, Christ, Santa Claus, and Father Time

as producing a "holiday syndrome":

> diffuse anxiety, numerous regressive phenomena including
> marked feelings of helplessness, possessiveness, and in-
> creased irritability, nostalgic or bitter rumination about
> holiday experiences of youth, depressive affect and a wish
> for magical resolution of problems.[10]

The reader recognizes in such statements, however different the terms, a relation to the content of this book—to tension between *Stratilates 3* and *Three Daughters 13*. From about 1930 a chain of professional studies by Erich Fromm, Ludwig Jekels, Ernest Jones and others has appeared, involving N. "There are three possible cross-sections: psycho-analytical, historical and religious."[11] If by *religious* Dr. Jekels meant, as I think he did, the action of community imagination through symbol, myth, and legend, then this biography of N has treated the latter two cross-sections; for its purpose has been to show how N has governed history and how history has governed N. Psychoanalysis, then, may add a third, and necessary view. Dr. Jekels spoke of "the theme which is embodied in some of the greatest works of poets as well as in the countless myths, fairy-tales and legends, now in one symbolic guise, now in another."[12]

Both the methods and the language of critics and analysts differ enough to make correlation difficult. "Trauma" and "superego" seem to be in one world, "invocation" and "veneration" in another, although presumptively they are all aspects of *ens*. But in earlier times the differences were not so marked. The psychoanalytic approach to poetry, to folklore, to dreams, to myths, parallels if it does not duplicate the allegorical method of scholastic interpretation, originating in Alexandria. We recognize an earlier, scholastic method when Dr. Sterba writes:

> . . . fireplace and chimney signify vulva and vagina in the
> unconscious and the child-present thus comes out of the
> birth canal. He, no doubt, is a father representative, and the
> unconscious knowledge of the fact that the father has some-

thing to do with childbirth is indicated in this way. . . .
Thus Santa Claus with his fat belly is a pregnant woman and
he acts in a most natural way when he drops his presents
down the chimney *per viam naturalem.* [13]

John Scotus or Bernard of Chartres might feel at home with such
exposition.

It is not, therefore, surprising that psychoanalytic interpretation of
Christian hagiography has most closely attached itself to those saints
whose cult rose in popularity inside the medieval schools: Mary, N,
and Catherine.

The most thoughtful and extensive of these inquiries into images of
Saint Nicholas is that of Dr. Adrianus de Groot. "Modern psychology
and psychoanalysis," he writes, "have taught us not to accept apparently selfless declarations and acts at their face value, and have shown
that underlying even the noblest, happiest and most useful behavior
there are motivations of self-interest."[14] Like the medieval exegetes,
he stresses different "layers" of interpretation, with the specific and
concrete, the literal and historical, the superficial layers above and the
latent, subconscious drives which are (he does not use the ancient
phrase) "enucleated," the kernel, beneath the shell. Though not repeating the latent "meanings" of Peter Damian or Nicholas of Clairvaux, he does examine each discrete tale within the legend in terms of
Freud and Jung.

Jung pointed to the Sanskrit word *tejas,* denoting subjective intensity, so charged with energy that it fosters a wide range of subjective
meanings.[15] "In the St. Nicholas folk customs," follows up de Groot,
"whether sanctioned by the Church or not, all stages of the human
reproductive cycle are duly represented." N "protects not only the
child but the process of human reproduction and growth within the
family (the *kinderzegen*) in the widest sense, viz., *the entire cycle from first
courtship up to and including family life with the children,*"[16] as a kind of
Christian successor to a pagan god of fertility. "The symbolism could
hardly be more characteristic: the *riding* on the rooftops of *houses,* the
pouring down of *sweets* and other *presents* through the *chimney,* so that all
these good things fall into the *shoe* or *barrel* beside the *fire.*"[17] De
Groot interprets *Iconia 37* and *Substitute Cup 58,* then *Three Clerks 44:*

The treasure [which de Groot equates with man's semen] has been protected miraculously, retrieved from devilish thieves. Gold and coins play a repeatedly important role, particularly in many legends of Byzantine Greek origin. . . . The *three scholars,* representing the male triumvirate, visit an *inn,* a place of enjoyment where food is offered and wine flows freely, and which is situated in a *wood.* In this inn the three are robbed of *pieces of gold* and to this purpose they are *killed,* the "death" of the phallus. The aspects of "stiffening" and "burying" are present, although in a different causal relationship of course. The logic of the superstructure of the story also requires that their *bodies, cut to pieces* ("Zerstücke-lungsmotiv," the dismemberment theme—again a familiar feature, especially in myths), and not the gold coins are put in the barrel of brine, and that the three of them are resur-rected, or (re-)born. The bodies are *preserved,* there is a period of "maturation" in the barrel, from which, through the intercession of Nicholas, after a certain *period of time* they *arise* again, i.e., are (re-)born. . . .

As medieval patron St. Nicholas watched over the fair, or direct, giving-and-taking in each of three fundamental expe-riential situations: erotic love, family life, and 'trade.' All three—sexual, familial, social—are situations wherein the individual, here and now, has to act in interaction with others; all three require communication and intercourse (verkeer), and therein a self-extension to a more com-prehensible world.[18]

The languages of the physician and the critic meet only in the common subject. The American Santa Claus may not have come from the Netherlands in the seventeenth century, but this recent psychoanalytic treatment did.

VII EPILOGUE

Lord Dunsany once wrote that he found Ireland as much in the Irish mind as in the Irish fields: "Much may pass over a field and leave no trace, but what wonderful tracks we may see where a fancy has passed over the mind!"[1] This book has been a history of the passage of a fancy, the biography of a legend. Its justification is that when a fancy or image (I leave the distinction to the romantics) passes over our world it leaves wonderful tracks behind, more humane than a human. It is the business of a biographer to avoid either becoming sententious about his subject or imposing principles on inappropriate matter. This book began with words of Kurt Riezler and now terminates with other of his words: "The truth of an image is not the truth of a proposition. The truth of some images reaches far beyond the truth of most propositions. It is important that the peoples of the earth possess such images and through them be able to understand and recognize one another as human beings across all the diversity of their historical worlds."[2] The Freudian de Groot complained that Meisen's "historical method" was not sufficient to provide a harmonious portrait from the total complex structure of lines as they are presented by the rich historical materials. "He has for the most part found the right note, but he has somewhat ignored the timbre." Easy enough to imagine what Meisen's reply would have been, had he been alive! Mine has not been a historical but an allegorical method, falteringly adapted from the Schoolmen whom I have admired. In trying to avoid the poles of casuistry and sophistry—to avoid distortion by oversimplification—I have doubtless made the life of my subject seem interminably long. But if Lord Dunsany is right, and the fancies of the mind are truly the broad highway to humanity, then it is not too long.

If the reader believes that this quest has merely beat the dead dog of Elizabethan Platonism, he is right. All these pages are contained in one Spenserian:

> I well consider all that ye have sayd,
> And find that all things steadfastnes doe hate
> And changed be: yet being rightly wayd
> They are not changed from their first estate;
> But by their change their being doe dilate:
> And turning to themselves at length againe,
> Doe work their owne perfection so by fate:
> Then over them change doth not rule and raigne;
> But they raigne over change, and doe their states maintaine.[3]

On 6 December 1964 I visited N in his basilica at Bari. A few sentences from my diary read: "Walked the Old City (churches locked) to SN Mole. No effigies apparent. Very cold, with wind and snow straight down from Russia. King Usorius is sending no warm gifts from Serbia today. The squads of police assigned to herd the crowd at the Commemorative Mass in the Basilica stand idly; doubtless some bureaucrat composed their annual orders a century or more ago. The Cathedral up the way closed for this occasion. Inside the Basilica were many people, as services go these days. But some empty benches."

Five years after this cold reception, the Papal Court pronounced that N is no longer of general interest, whether alive or dead. The universal legend had conformed with universal man's experience in its time, but man and legend grow frail when their days are numbered. There is a reality in images, a life and perhaps a death, lacking in the truth of propositions. N walked beside humanity and was "with it." In the year that the Pope pronounced N moribund, an Associated Press dispatch from Tarpon Springs, Florida (18 Dec. 1969) read in part: "The pastor and parishioners of a Greek Orthodox church say an icon of Saint Nicholas is forming what appear to be tear drops. The pastor said he had assured parishioners who feared the phenomenon was a bad omen that 'it's just an act of God.'"

NOTES

Prologue

1. Presidential address, University College London, 5 January 1970; published in *Modern Language Review* LXV (1970), p. xli.

1 Infancy

§1 WAS THERE A HISTORIC NICHOLAS?

1. *Acta SS,* Propylaeum Decembris 1940, pp. 568 - 569.

2. Anrich II, 514; Meisen, pp. 51 - 52; Falconi, Prolegomena, pp. 32 - 60. A classic phrasing of this conventional defense of the historicity of accepted legend is Caxton's Preface to Malory's *Morte d'Arthur.*

3. "Nicolaus eolice victoria populi resonat" (*BHL* nos. 6111 - 3, 6163 - 7; Mombritius, p. 306). Franke, p. 12; Falconi, p. 126, Admonitis xv; Meisen, pp. 334 - 335; and current lexicographers (e.g. Webster's New International Dictionary, 2d ed., s.v.). Medieval Christians regarded it as Greek equivalent of Hebrew Balaam.

4. Eusebius, *Eccl. Hist.* VII, 18, based on Matt. ix, 20.

5. Delehaye, *Legends,* p. 109. Since the title of saint is now loosely associated with papal canonization in people's minds, I call attention that that rite only began to evolve from the end of the tenth century. Indeed, only with the Carolingians did the Church concern itself with control of saintly cult (Council of Frankfurt 794, MGH, Concilia II, p. 170), and then authority was consigned to provincial bishops. Previously there had existed a tradition of *elevatio,* locally observed, which was accorded to more than 350 in Gaul and Germany between the years 481 and 750 (according to Professor Ganshof).

See Hermann-Mascard, pp. 83 - 105.

6. Hamilton, p. 34.

7. Anrich II, 452, and Anm. 2.

8. Josephus, *Jewish War,* Penguin trans. pp. 106 - 107, 114 - 115.

9. Pauly-Wissowa, s.v., where only six are listed.

10. Acts vi, 5. G. Wohlenberg, "Nikolaos von Antiochen und die Nikolaiten," *Neue kirchliche Zeitschrift* VI (1895), 923 - 961.

11. Apoc. ii, 6 and 15; Epiphanius, *Adversus Haereseos* I, ii, 25; Eusebius, *Eccl. Hist.* III, xxix. Amann XI, i, 499 - 506; Fliche VII, 476 - 482.

12. James, *The Apocryphal New Testament,* pp. 341, 347.

13. Jerome, *Epistola* xiv (to Heliodorus), 9.

14. Beowulf, lines 1428 - 1430; Meisen, pp. 5 - 6, and sources cited; Anichkof, pp. 109, 115 - 116; *Notes and Queries* I, vi, 198; xii, 229; Sébillot 1886 II, 75 - 76, 98, 134. Buss, pp. 11 - 18, in exploring the sources of the modern German Klabautermann, makes no mention of influence of Nick or Klas.

15. Acts xxi, 1; xxvii, 5. Pauly-Wissowa XVI, i, 1083 ff.; A.H.M. Jones, pp. 96 - 110; Ramsay, pp. 294, 297 ff., 314, 316 ff. His exposition of Myra's position in the shipping lanes is helpful.

16. *BHL,* nos. 8020 - 8025; *Anal. Boll.* XLIII (1925), 49 - 57.

17. The survival is described, with illustrations, by P. Armando, P.P., "La Basilica di San Nicola a Myra," *Collana,* no. 3 (1964). See chap. 4, v - vi.

18. Scudamore in *DCA* and *DCB,* s.v. "Patron Saint." Delehaye, *Legends,* pp. 161 - 166, 170 - 171.

19. Marin, pp. 80 - 81.

20. Anrich II, 449.

21. Vasiliev, *Byzance et les Arabes* I, 60, n. 1.

22. The relic fever begins with the Invention of Stephen, popularized by Augustine (*De Civ. Dei* XXII, 8). *DCA* s.v. "Stephen."

23. Vacandard; Aigrain, p. 375; Seznec, pp. 11 ff.; Delehaye, *Sanctus,* pp. 180 - 181. On euhemerism see Isidore, *Etym.* VIII, xi. "Many parts, indeed, of divine worship are unduly used in showing honor to men" (Augustine, *De Civ. Dei* X, 4).

24. Jerome, *Contra Vigilantium* (*Pat. Lat.* XXIII, 339 - 352).

25. Aigrain, p. 181.

26. Cyprianus, *Epistola* xii, 2 (trans. Kemp, pp. 6 - 7).

27. Fliche IV, 586 - 590. Until the late fourth century the popular cult of saints was limited to those who had lost their lives for the faith, but then the Fathers began to preach that exemplary ascetic life was identical; see John

Chrysostom, *Ep. ad Hebraeos, Hom.* xi, 3 (*Pat. Gr.* LXIII, 93). Hermann-Mascard, p. 74.

28. Nilsson, *Religion,* pp. 11, 18, 112; Argenti and Rose II, 1064 - 1065.

29. "Sie [names of months derived from Poseidon] liegen alle entweder in der Zeit der rauhesten Winterstürme oder in der der Ernte." (Pauly-Wissowa, 43 Halbband [= XXII.1], 1953, p. 506.) Mommsen, *Heortologie,* pp. 96 ff., calculated the Attic month Poseideon as 12 December - 10 January for the year 432 B.C. See Nilsson, *Griech. Feste,* p. 82; Pauly-Wissowa X. 2 (1919), cols. 1568 - 1602, esp. 1582 - 1583, 1591 - 1594, art. "Kalender." Farnell IV, 73 - 96, has gathered the references that survive in writing.

30. Oxford MS Bodl. 309, fo. 117ʳ: Annus cccxvii Dormitio sci Nicholai. These annals are indebted to N, Angers; see chap. 3, ii.

31. Pauly-Wissowa, s.v. The legend of the archimandrite Nicholas of Sion, who died as bishop of Pinara 10 Dec. 564, became entangled with N. His Life ed. Anrich I, 3 ff.; cf. II, pp. 241 ff. For other Sion clergy named Nicholas, see Anrich II, 220, 251, 450.

32. Procopius I, vi, 10; cf. *Atlas of the Early Christian World,* no. 538; Janin, pp. 404 - 408 (cf. p. 370). The shadowy Priscus, whom *BHG* identifies only as one of the Forty Martyrs (A.D. 320), and Baring-Gould (1 Sept.) as follower of Saint Peter, soon was dropped from the dedication.

33. *Anal. Boll.* LXX (1952), 120 - 121.

34. ICA (41 L84 MBr G10, 28); Dalton, p. 19, no. 119. A reliquary in the Metropolitan Museum has been dated 7th - 9th cent.

§II LEGENDS

1. As *BHG* with listed number. Latin texts are enumerated in the companion volumes, *BHL.* Cf. *Anal. Boll.* XII (1893), 459 - 460.

2. Encomia, panegyrics, and the like. Cf. I Thess. v, 3; Rom. xiv, 19; etc.

3. Thucydides, *History* I, vi. Günter, *Legende,* p. 3, sets the sixth century as the end of evolution of pagan into Christian legend; but compare the remarks of Rosenfeld in *Reallexikon der deutschen Literaturgeschichte,* art. "Legende."

4. Falconi, *Acta Omnia,* p. 86. Michael's Preface ed. Falconi, p. 39, and the standard Western version pp. 112 - 113.

5. Delehaye, *Etude,* p. 12; cf. C. W. Jones, *Saints' Lives,* pp. 57 - 64; id., *Collection Latomus,* pp. 217 - 218.

6. Aristotle, *Rhetoric* ii, 1389a.

7. *BHG* no. 1348.

§III N AND THE PAGAN GODS

1. *Pat. Lat.* VI, 237.

2. Evidently evolving from the Asian cult of Cybele, also a moon goddess. Cf. Anichkof, pp. 112 - 113. On the Christian view see Arnobius in *Pat. Lat.* V, 986.

3. Pliny, *Historia Naturalis* II, lxxxvii, 201.

4. *Swan's Hellenic Cruise Handbook,* 11th ed., ed. Sir Mortimer Wheeler, 1974, p. 202. On N as banker, see *Iconia 34.*

5. Cochrane, pp. 114 ff.

6. Lalanne, *Curiosités des Traditions,* p. 167. Loomis cites about a hundred such idoloclasts, p. 87.

7. For the concentration of the Artemis cult at Myra, see Pauly-Wissowa, s.v. Artemis; Dawes and Baynes, pp. 14 ff.; cf. Baring-Gould XV, 143 - 144.

8. Metaphrastes, Life of Daniel, chaps. 14 - 19 (11 Dec.).

9. Dawes and Baynes, pp. 97 - 98; Anichkof, pp. 114 - 115.

10. Esp. in the Edict of Marcian and Valentinian 12 Nov. 451 (Justinian Code I, xi, 7); Fliche IV, 17 ff.

11. Rufinus, *Hist. Eccl.* XI, xxiii; Fliche IV, 24.

12. Bede, *Hist. Eccl.* I, xxx. The rededications seem to become less predictable: e.g., just outside Corinth in the Gulf is the long serrated form of Hera Akraea, now called Hagios Nikolaos, marked by his chapel.

13. In later legend N cut down the tree sacred to Artemis (dendrolatry); for examples in art see Réau III (1958), iii, p. 985. On the full circle, from apostolic leveling of temples to the Protestant leveling of churches, see Thomas, pp. 58 - 59.

14. Falconi, pp. 96 - 97.

15. Sulpicius, *Epistola ad Aurelium diaconum,* ed. Halm, *CSEL I.*

16. For the version of John the Deacon, Falconi, p. 118; Mombritius, p. clxv[v].

17. Byron, pp. 85 - 87, 279 - 280.

18. Lewis, *Naval Power,* pp. 18, 31 - 32.

19. Sébillot I, 96, 118.

20. "Quaesumus ut eius meritis et precibus a gehennae incendiis liberemur."

§IV N AS PATRON OF MARINERS

1. Delehaye, *Sanctus,* chap. 5, pp. 208 - 232.

2. Hamilton, p. 31, after Rouse, *Votive Offerings,* p. 37; see also Delehaye,

Légendes, p. 191; Anrich II, 415. For the church on Eleusa, see *DCB* IV, 41.

3. Mombritius, p. 300, lines 28 - 51.

4. Meisen, pp. 245 - 249; cf. pp. 29 ff.

5. Mantuan, *Fastorum liber* xii, quoted in Hospinianus, fo. 153; Brand I, 419.

6. Virgil, *Aeneid* xii, 766.

7. Horace, *Carmina* I, v, 13 - 16. Milton's translation.

8. Max Herzog zu Sächsen, in *Das Chfistliche Hellas,* ascertained that of 4637 Greek churches, 752 were dedicated to the Virgin (inc. 282 Dormition), 359 to N, 291 to George, and 189 to John the Baptist.

9. Marin, p. 89.

10. Meisen (see note 4 above).

11. Isidore, *Etym.* VIII, xi. Delehaye, *Légendes,* p. 180, notes this evolution, Poseidon to N.

12. Marin, pp. 137 - 140.

13. Runciman, *Civilization,* pp. 149 - 151; Lewis, *Naval Power,* pp. 25 - 26; Deanesly, pp. 134, 200; Dvornik, pp. 32 - 34; Ebersolt, *Orient,* pp. 40 - 42, 71 - 72.

14. Janin in *Echos d'Orient,* 1932, pp. 404 - 410.

15. Marin, pp. 118 ff.

16. Falconi, p. 98; Anrich II, 396.

17. Anrich I, 288 - 299; II, 396.

18. Meisen, pp. 249 ff.

19. Aebischer in *Archivum Romanicum* XV, 390.

§V *Stratilates* AND THE THEME OF CHURCH AND STATE

1. *Martyrologium Romanum,* p. 373; *Acta SS Propylaeum,* Dec., p. 568, viii id. Dec.

2. *BHG* no. 1350; *BHL* no. 6106. Cf. *Anal. Boll.* XII (1893), 459 - 60; Marin, pp. 122 - 36; Meisen, pp. 55 - 56, 220 ff.

3. Not identified. The mountainous southern reaches of Phrygia might strategically be breached by the valley of the river Cestus, to the east of Myra.

4. Edited by Meisen, pp. 527 - 30. The Greek version of Symeon is in Falconi, pp. 98 - 105; John the Deacon's version, ibid., pp. 119 - 122; Mombritius', pp. cxlv^v-clxviii^r.

5. *DCB,* s.v. "Ablabius."

6. Meisen, p. 400.

7. See Anrich's Sachregister (II, 583, s.v. "stratilatis").

8. Daniel xiv, 32 - 38. Gregory the Great, who had lived at Constantinople, adapted the incident to his Benedict of Nursia in the *Dialogues,* naming the prototype Habacuc. Elsewhere in the Dialogues (III, 37) he attributed to Saint John N's act of catching the sword on the backswing—a borrowing noted by Salimbene, *Liber de praelato* (*MGH, Scriptores* xxxii), p. 115.

9. Acts viii, 38 - 40.

10. On saintly travel through air and barricades, see Loomis, pp. 89, 91 - 92.

11. Pope, *Moral Essays* I, i.

12. Runciman, *Civilization,* pp. 113, 134; Baynes and Moss, pp. 86 - 105 (by Henri Grégoire); Vasiliev, *Histoire,* p. 196.

13. Genesis xiv, 18; cf. Pfeiffer, p. 161.

14. Bréhier, *Monde* II, 59, 65.

15. Socrates, *Eccl. Hist.* i, 13.

16. Sozomen, *Eccl. Hist.* i; 14.

17. Baynes and Moss, pp. 129 - 130.

18. Gibbon, chap. 21.

19. Runciman, *Civilization,* pp. 113, 134.

20. Baynes and Moss, p. 5.

21. Fliche IV, 538 - 540.

22. Labbé, V, 61.

23. Diehl, *Monde oriental* I, 102 - 104.

24. Baynes and Moss, p. 76.

25. *Pat. Gr.* LXXXVI, 946 - 947, 1086.

26. Ibid., pp. 1178, 1183.

27. Bréhier, *Monde* II, 17.

28. *Acta SS, Propylaeum Dec.,* pp. 568 - 569.

29. Bréhier, *Eglise,* pp. 22 - 23, maintains that the patriarchal authority, vis-à-vis Rome, seriously declined during Iconoclasm, esp. A.D. 726 - 737.

30. Du Broc II, 531.

31. Saint Nicholas in Carcere, founded "between the end of the sixth and the beginning of the seventh century" (Thurston and Attwater IV, 506). Frere, p. 19, states without citing evidence that the church was rededicated, Lawrence to N, in the 11th cent.

32. Anna Comnena, ii, 5. See note in Leib's edition, 1937, p. 77.

33. Meisen, p. 231. " . . . ad eripiendum inopem de manu fortorium eius,

sicut legitur fecisse beatus Nicolaus," wrote Gerloh of Reicherberg in the year 1137 (*MGH, Libelli de lite* III, 179).

34. *BHG* no. 1351; Vatican MS Gr. 821, p. 256; Falconi, pp. 34 - 38. Another parallel in Anrich I, 416. Janin, *Géographie,* p. 373.

35. Pitra, I, 355 - 358.

36. Lucretius iii, 307 - 309.

37. Schiller, *Das Kind in der Wiege.* " . . . le plus populaire des saints de l'Eglise grecque" (*Anal. Boll.* XL, [1922] p. 197).

2 Boyhood
§I BOYHOOD

1. Marrou, p. 199.

2. Shakespeare, *A Winter's Tale* IV, ii, 23.

§ II THE LIFES

1. The 9th cent. authors were reviving a tradition of Eusebius of Caesarea (4th cent.), who composed an assemblage of saints' lives, *Synagogus* (Aigrain, p. 320).

2. *BHG* no. 1348; Anrich I, 111 ff. (text); II, 262 ff. (criticism).

3. *BHG* no. 1352y; Anrich I, 140 ff.; II, 284 ff. Aigrain, p. 320.

4. Infra n. 19.

5. Vatican MS Gr. 2084, fos. 174^V-186^r, ed. also in Falconi, pp. 112 - 126; see Anrich II, 83.

6. *BHG* no. 1352z; Anrich I, 153 - 182. The author is unidentified, but may have come from the Greek peninsula (Anrich II, 298). On the panegyric form, see Delehaye, *Passions,* pp. 183 - 235.

7. *Pat. Gr.* CXVI, 317 - 356, taken from MS Coislinianus 147. See Delehaye's *Synopsis Metaphrastica* in *BHG;* Aigrain, p. 320; Anrich II, 177 - 178.

8. Obit 1446. The Latin translation (*BHL* no. 6128) was dedicated to his brother Lawrence, Patriarch of Venice; it appears in *Poetae christiani,* Venice (Aldine) 1502 (= Hain 15168), often republished, as at Mainz by G. Vicelius, 1541.

9. *Sanctorum priscorum patrum vitae,* Venice, 1551 - 1560, I, fos. 138^V-149^V. A popular reprint, somewhat abbreviated, Louvain, 1568, 1571, etc.

10. It is the Latin translation of Lipoman, *De probatis sanctorum historiis,* 6 vols., Cologne 1570 - 1575, VI (1575), pp. 795 - 810. Many subsequent editions.

11. *BHG* no. 1349t; Anrich II, 301.

12. Ed. in Pitra, *Spicilegium* I, pp. 355 - 358; Anrich II, 360 - 362.

13. Pitra I, 202 - 209; Anrich II, 362 - 363.

14. See *Joseph the Hymnographer 26.* Anrich II, 365 - 366, and Sachregister s.v.

15. *BHG* no. 1348c; Anrich II, 112.

16. Louis's queen saved the party from shipwreck off Cyprus by vowing a silver ship to N (Ludlow, p. 359). See below chap. 5, vii.

17. Delehaye, *Légendes,* p. 20.

18. *BHG* no. 1347; Anrich II, 214 - 217, 241 ff., 509 ff. Fissen, p. 4; Meisen, p. 50.

19. *BHL* nos. 6104 - 6117. The number of surviving Western MSS is legion. It was first printed by Mombritius (above, n. 9) II, 161 - 168; then Lipoman (above, n. 10) II, 238 ff. Falconi, pp. 112 - 122 and 126 (chaps. 14 - 22, pp. 122 - 125, are later additions); Angelo Mai, *Spicilegium Romanum* IV (1840), 324 - 339 (abridged); and many others. See C. W. Jones, *Liturgy,* chap. 4, pp. 42 - 46; Ebert, III, 206 ff.; Anrich II, 26 ff. and 84; Meisen, p. 61.

20. Besides the *Golden Legend,* I mention only that of Vincent of Beauvais, *Speculum historiale* (ca. 1254), printed at Strasbourg, 1473, XIV, 67 - 81.

21. Siegmund, pp. 195 ff. In a Neapolitan calendar of A.D. 821 - 841, N Day is listed; see esp. Leclercq in *DACL* II, 2 (1910), 1586 ff. with illustration 1591 - 1592; *Anal. Boll.* LVII, 5 - 59. The oldest Latin N hymns (e.g., *Solemne tempus vertitur* and *Debitas laudes Domino*), extant in the 9th-cent. MS Vatican lat. 7122, seem to have been composed at Naples (Meisen, p. 62). Their verse form is traditional Ambrosian dimeter, and their content is exclusively that of Methodios and John.

22. Delehaye, *Passions,* p. 233. Père de Gaiffier lists the kinds, uses, dissemination, and audiences of hagiography in Subsidia Hagiographica 43 (*Études critiques,* 1947), pp. 119 - 120 (reprint from École Nationale de Chartres: Positions des thèses, 1926).

23. *MGH, Scriptores Rerum Langobardicarum,* p. 277. Jones, *Saints' Lives,* pp. 62 - 63.

24. Cf. Prudentius, *Contra Symmachum* ii, 17 - 66. Large portions of his Peristephanon (Crowns of Martyrdom) were thus composed.

§III Their Content

1. Psalms i, 3.

2. Luke i, 5 - 25.

3. Falconi, pp. 86 - 87.

4. Neckham v, 635 - 638.

5. Dawes and Baynes, pp. 8, 88.

6. Loomis, p. 141, n. 102, lists a dozen; see also pp. 15 ff., 20, 23. Anrich and others believe the incident entered N from the Life of Saint Nicholas of Sion (Meisen, pp. 257 - 261).

7. Falconi, p. 87. Late versions have him also standing in his bath, praising the Lord. Parallel texts for Saint Catervus of Tolentino in *Anal. Boll.* LXI (1943), 11 - 17.

8. *Pat. Lat.* CCII, 880.

9. Wace, lines 45 - 80. As might be expected, this subject was especially popular with renaissance painters. See also Egbert, pp. 69 - 70.

10. The New-York Historical Society MS, Saint Nicholas Society, Box 5.

11. Marin, p. 76.

12. Falconi, p. 87.

13. Delehaye, *Sanctus,* p. 221.

14. Matt. vi, 1 - 4; cf. I Cor. iii, 21, I Thess. ii, 4 - 6, Ep. John v, 44.

15. I Kings ii, 8; Psalms cxii, 7.

16. Falconi, pp. 89 - 91. The version of John the Deacon in Mombritius' text is in Young II, 488 - 490. Anrich II, 420.

17. Maurice des Ombians in *Marches de l'Est* II (1910), 280 - 281.

18. Meisen, p. 59. The identification was first made by Gruneisen, pp. 490 ff. and fig. 85, p. 110; Album épigraphique, Pl. vii, no. 4.

19. Ferrari, pp. 114 - 115.

20. Ferrari, pp. 47 - 48. Of all N tales only *Three Daughters 13* is referred to by Dante (Purgatorio xx, 31 - 33) and Aquinas (*Summa Theologica* II, ii, 1073).

21. Birch p. 186; Urlin, p. 220; Wright and Lones III, 194; Meisen, pp. 236 - 245.

22. See chap. 5, vi.

23. Jacobus de Voragine, p. 22.

24. See chap. 6, vi.

25. Falconi, pp. 94 - 95. Cf. Marin, pp. 71 ff.

26. Pitra, p. 204, c. 6.

27. Loomis, p. 73, and refs.

28. Jeremiah iii, 15. See e.g. Agnellus, *Liber pontif. Ravenn.,* 17 (*MGH, Scriptores Langob.,* p. 285); Salimbene, *Liber de praelato* (*MGH, Scriptores* XXXII, 141).

29. Acts i, 24 - 26.

30. By his secretary Paulinus, *Pat. Lat.* XIV, 27 - 46. Cf. Lalanne, p. 346.

31. Dudden I, 215 - 222.

32. Above, chap. 1, v.

33. Manitius I, 95.

34. Ibid., pp. 689 - 695.

35. Indeed, as early as the earliest Life of Gregory, composed at Whitby, England, ca. 700, just when *Stratilates 3* was first circulating in its Latin form.

36. *Vita S. Gregorii,* 28 (Jones, *Saints' Lives,* p. 116; cf. p. 68).

37. Gregory's interlocutor in The Dialogues.

38. Jacobus de Voragine, 12 Mar. fin.

39. Falconi, pp. 97 - 98.

40. *Epistola* 229, xi *non. Iun.* 1097 (*Pat. Lat.* CLI, 495).

41. E.g., three *Citizens of Myra 2,* three *Stratilates 3,* three *Grainships 7,* three *Daughters 13,* and many more to be mentioned below. Cf. Meisen, p. 302.

42. Cf. Marin, pp. 82 - 86, 103 - 104.

43. Gelzer, *Patrum,* pp. 67, 73, 81, 151, 181, 316 and xli, lxix; Pauly-Wissowa s.v. Nicaea.

44. Marin, pp. 100 ff.

45. Pitra, p. 204.

46. Marin, pp. 105 - 106.

47. Réau III, iii, 985; Cahier I, 36; Saintyves, pp. 291 - 292, cites Bagatta 1695, I, 27.

48. Bralion, pp. 78 - 84.

49. *Revue de l'art chrétien* XXVII (1884), 49 - 50.

50. Reproduced in *Iapigia* VIII (1937), 451; see also p. 453.

51. Falconi, pp. 106 - 107.

52. L. Petit, *Bibliographie des acolouthies grecques* (Brussels, 1926), pp. xii, 216 - 219; Dawkins, 63 - 64.

53. Cf. Gen. xxvii, 27; II Cor. ii, 14 - 16.

54. Falconi, p. 124. A different version in *Cat. Cod. Hagr. Lat. Namur,* pp. 37 - 50.

55. Falconi, p. 124. This addition is at least earlier than Brit. Mus. MS Cotton Nero E 1, copied at Worcester just before the Norman Conquest.

56. *Pat. Lat.* CLVII, 379 - 381.

57. Strophe 4, ed. Pitra I, 203; cf. Theodore the Studite, strophe 8, idem p. 355.

58. Indeed, for Réau (p. 988) it is a total explanation. Hagiologists have created the distinction between corporeal and representative relics. Corporeal relics are the whole or parts of the original animate body: a head or a

finger bone. Representative relics share the spiritual power because of their close contact with the sainted being, but they cannot be finitely numbered: the milk of the Virgin, stones of Stephen, chains of Peter and Paul, the grille of Lawrence, the veronica, fragments of Martin's cloak. See Hermann-Mascard, pp. 41 - 49. N's myrrh possessed the spiritual attraction of such representative relics.

59. Dawes and Baynes, p. 261; Laroche, *Vie,* pp. 56 ff.; Scognamiglio, *Manna.*

60. *EB* II, 80A.

61. Cahier I, 128 - 129. See also Fliche IV, 553; Loomis, p. 43, nos. 87, 89 - 91.

62. I depend on the following: Hippolyte Delehaye in *Anal. Boll.* XXIX (1910), 117 - 149; XLIII (1925), 46 - 49; C.-M. Kauffmann, *Dritter Bericht über die Ausgrabung des Menasheiligtümer in der Mareotiswüste* (Cairo, 1908), trans. A. Hartmann, *La découverte des sanctuaires de Ménas* (Alexandria, 1908); Henri Leclercq in *DACL* I (1907), 426, 1116, 1725 - 1730; XI (1933), 325 - 409; J. B. Perkins, in *Papers of the British School at Rome* XVII (1949), 26 - 71; Paul Peeters, "Le tréfonds oriental de l'hagiographie byzantine," *Subsidia Hagiographica* 26 (1950) pp. 30 - 41; *Vies des saints* XI (1954), 328 - 337; Agostino Amore, in *Enciclopedia Cattolica* VIII, 667 - 668. I have not seen R. Miedema, *Die heilige Menas* (Rotterdam 1913). A second saint of the name, whose legend adds confusion, is treated by de Gaiffier in *Anal. Boll.* LXII (1944), 5 - 32. Gregory of Tours is explicit about Andrew: "Profert hoc est manna in modum farinae vel oleum cum odore nectare quod de tumulo ejus exundat." (*De gloria martyrum* i, 31, ed. *MGH, Script. rerum Merov.* I, and *Pat. Lat.* LXXI.) Contemporaries of Gregory make more or less ambiguous references to saints Demetrius, Fortunatus, Medard, and Perpetua, who may be conceived as myroblytes. Cf. Hermann-Mascard, pp. 47 - 49.

63. Delehaye, in *Anal. Boll.* XXIX, 118.

64. Leclercq, in *DACL* XI, 382. "The Egyptian Lourdes"—Delehaye, in *Anal. Boll.* XXIX, 119.

65. Peeters (see note 62 above), p. 33, n. 3, after Carver; Leclercq, in *DACL* XI, 345.

66. Krautheimer, pp. 85 - 86; Leclercq XI, 345 ff.

67. Leclercq, in *DACL* XI, 382; the inscription, col. 364.

68. Leclercq, in *DACL* XI, 385 - 390.

69. Delehaye, in *Anal. Boll.* XXIX pp. 132, 135. The theme of lamp oil was especially intense at this time, as evinced by the cult of Saint Martin (see

Hermann-Mascard, p. 47). The cathedral of Monza still possesses a collection which had been brought to the queen Theolinde by a devoted priest in the years 590 - 604 (idem, pp. 345 - 346, citing Martigny).

70. Ibid., pp. 118 - 121.

71. Ibid., p. 145; Amore (see note 62 above), p. 667. The Greek Acts with Latin trans. in *Anal. Boll.* III, 258.

72. Janin, pp. 333 - 335, 368 - 377.

73. Peeters (see note 62 above), pp. 39 - 41, has an ingenious explanation for the cult at Cotyaeum. Delehaye, pp. 126 - 127.

74. Delehaye, in *Anal. Boll.* XXIX, 117 ff. (text p. 146 f.), 139 - 141.

75. Ibid., p. 120.

76. Ibid., pp. 127 - 135. Note that the author of the Cotyaean Passion borrowed just as directly from Basil's Encomium for Saint Gordius (Leclercq XI, 341).

77. C. W. Jones, "Norman Cult," n. 54.

78. Hermann-Mascard, pp. 33 - 34.

79. Ibid., pp. 26 - 48, et passim.

80. Ibid., pp. 69, 149.

81. See above, n. 58.

82. Leclercq XI, 380 - 381.

83. As reprinted in Falconi, *Prolegomena,* p. 62; cf. Pauly-Wissowa XVI, 1, 1083; Anrich I, 451. A bull of Pope Clement V, 26 July 1306, encouraged pilgrims to Bari for myrrh (Meisen, p. 105). See Bralion; Marin, pp. 141 - 145; *Anal. Boll.* XLIV, 404.

84. Saintyves, pp. 31 - 33.

85. Monk of Bec's Life of N (*Cat. Cod. Hagr. Paris.* II, 414).

86. *Revue de l'art chrétien* XXVI (1883), 304.

87. Breviary of Amiens, 1554, as in Cahier, p. 660; Du Broc II, 532.

§IV THE BYZANTINE-ARABIC BORDER

1. Meisen, pp. 50 ff., summarizing Anrich.

2. Falconi, pp. 56, 78 - 81; Anrich I, pp. 168, 182. Even more extravagantly in the *Vita Acephala* (A.D. 980 - 1050)—see Anrich I, 269 ff., 275, and Meisen, p. 70.

3. *Pat. Gr.* XCVI, 1389, Od. ix, str. 6; Kayata, p. 69.

4. Vasiliev I, 55, et passim; I have freely used Louis de Mas-Latrie. However, Taormina was not lost until 902, after 75 years of warfare on the island.

5. Thurston and Attwater IV, 505.

6. Herzog zu Sächsen, pp. 324 - 326; *Anal. Boll.* XL (1922), 199.

7. The number for Athos is drawn from Halkin, Lake, *The Early Days of Monasticism on Mount Athos* (1909), and *Anal. Boll.* XXV (1906), 34; the number for Constantinople from Janin 1932 and Janin pp. 368 - 377 and 590.

8. Kondakov, pp. 45, 175; Rice, no. 123.

9. Diehl, *Manuel* II, 511; Leib, pp. 75 ff.

10. Schlumberger, passim.

11. Citarella, pp. 299 ff.

12. Ibid., p. 309.

13. *BHG* no. 1359. Anrich I, 169 - 182; II, 403; Falconi, pp. 69 - 74.

14. *BHG* no. 1350u. Anrich I, 144 - 146; II, 406.

15. Anrich II, 406 - 407; Falconi, pp. 67 - 69.

16. *BHG* no. 1353. Anrich I, 185 - 201, 273 - 275; II, 407; Falconi, pp. 58 - 65.

17. *BHL* no. 6167. *Anal. Boll.* IV (1885), 257 - 261; cf. variant in *Cat. Cod. Hagr. Brux.* II, 27 - 28; Meisen, p. 253. An early analogue in Gregory's *Dialogues* i, 10, on which see Dudden I, 337.

18. Anrich II, 412.

19. Ibid., p. 414.

20. Ibid., p. 414.

21. Ibid., p. 43; Laroche, pp. 158 - 159. The historical Leo is recorded to have died on Christmas night, A.D. 820.

22. Above, chap. 2, ii.

23. *BHG* no. 1357. Anrich II, 416; Falconi, pp. 66 - 67.

24. Anrich II, 416.

25. *BHG* no. 1353. Anrich I, 185 - 197; II, 417; Falconi, pp. 57 - 58. In the 15th cent. and later, it was believed that the N church next to Hagia Sophia stood on the grounds of Demetrios' house.

26. Anrich II, 418.

27. Anrich I, 144 - 146; II, p. 418. A variant of three Christian adults thrown into the sea, II, 419 - 420.

28. Anrich II, p. 423.

29. Ibid., p. 424.

30. Pitra I, 206.

31. See Index, "De cultu et veneratione SS. Imaginum," *Pat. Lat.* CCXIX, 986.

32. Drawn from Fliche IV, 551.

33. One is the legend of Angarus, k. of Edessa, as told by Haymo, *Pat. Lat.* CXVIII, 825. On the excesses, Sébillot, *Légendes,* pp. 349 - 354.

34. Pitra I, 357, str. 9.

35. Anrich I, 338 - 342.

36. II, 429 - 430; Meisen, pp. 62 - 64, 261.

37. A historical inspiration seems to have been the Saracen invasions of Calabria, A.D. 871 - 923.

38. Falconi, pp. 124 - 126; other versions in Otloh's (Namur) Life, 19 (*Cat. Cod. Hagr. Lat. Namur.,* pp. 37 - 50); Mombritius, pp. 306 - 307 (repeated in Young II, 491 - 492).

39. Hogarth in *EB* IX, 675; Smith and Fuller I, 782. Of course this was Hellenic custom, as at Delphi, Delos, etc.

40. Mansi III, 32 - 33; Martin, pp. 29, 98, 113. At Berytus, wrote ps.-Athanasius, a picture of Christ, stabbed by Jews, spouted blood and water (Martin, p. 143).

41. Martin, pp. 94 ff.; Marin in *Marches de l'Est* III (1911), 320; Ostrogorsky, p. 397; Henri Leclercq, *Histoire des conciles* (Paris, 1907 - 1938) 767; Mansi XIII, 33D-34.

42. Ostrogorsky, pp. 410 - 411.

§V VENICE

1. An N church was built there in the late 8th cent. by Duke Ericus of Friuli, Charlemagne's leader against the Avars. Meisen, p. 60; cf. p. 66.

2. Gregorovius III, 72 - 76. Cf. Hermann-Mascard, pp. 368 - 369. Her catalogue of Venetian thefts of relics is questionable in details.

3. F. Babudri in *Collana,* no. 4, p. 10.

§VI THE SLAVIC WORLD

1. Ortutay, p. 550.

2. For the historical milieu I depend primarily upon Dvornik.

3. Baynes and Moss, pp. 117 - 119.

4. Diehl 1944, pp. 324 - 325; Leib, p. 12; *CMH* IV (1966), pp. 123 - 125.

5. Ostrogorsky, p. 411.

6. C. Diehl, *Monde Oriental* I, 325 - 326; Dvornik, pp. 171 - 172; Muralt, p. 740.

7. Samuel H. Cross, *The Russian Primary Chronicle* (Cambridge, Mass., 1930), p. 146.

8. Schlumberger, *Epopée* I, 454.

9. See Index in Uspensky.

10. Masaryk, p. 7.

11. Dvornik, p. 106.

12. Ibid., pp. 57 - 58.

13. Anichkof, p. 109.

14. Equally pertinent anecdotes reported by Eugène Hins in *Revue des traditions populaires* III (1888), 319 - 326. Cf. *CMH* II (1966), 425.

15. Kayata, p. 156. Cf. Bond, p. 173.

16. Ortutay, p. 551.

17. Frazer VII, 233.

18. *Anal. Boll.* XXXIII, 380 - 420.

19. In Livonia there were more dedications to N than to Saint Peter (*Der Katholik* II [1904], 128 - 133).

§VII POPE NICHOLAS I AND PATRIARCH NICHOLAS MYSTICUS

1. Fliche VI, 369 - 395; Amann XI, i, pp. 506 ff.; Gregorovius VII, 115 - 155.

2. Cf. Meisen, chap. 4, pp. 71 - 93, and 335.

3. *MGH, Auct. Ant.* XIV, pp. 252 - 253; Manitius I, 196.

4. Meisen, p. 54.

5. Marguillier, p. 5.

6. Above, chap. 1, v. See *Anal. Boll.* L, 180.

7. Huelsen, pp. xci, 392; Bartoli, pp. 213 - 226; Meisen, p. 57; Duchesne I, 515.

8. Meisen, p. 229.

9. Meisen, pp. 56 - 58, who also describes less certain instances.

10. Mâle, *Churches,* pp. 81 - 85.

11. Meisen, p. 58. It seems probable that *Three Daughters 13* inspired the dedication to N of two Roman nunneries founded in the 10th cent.; see Ferrari, pp. 47 - 48; Huelsen, pp. 405 - 406.

12. *Pat. Lat.* CXIX, 760D; Grüneisen, pp. 341 ff.

13. Karlsruhe MS, Aug. 32, was written before that date. Usuard of Saint-Germain-des-Prés incorporated it in his Martyrology between 859 and 875 (Meisen, pp. 56, 74 - 75). The earliest certain transalpine mention of N is in verses by Hrabanus Maurus at Fulda in 818 (*MGH, Poetae* II, 206). Hrabanus later entered N's name in his Martyrology (*BHL,* p. 891; *Pat. Lat.* CX, 1183; Falconi, pp. 110 - 111).

14. His Life (*BHL* no. 6095) was composed for the Pontifical Book (ed. Duchesne) II, 151 - 167; Fliche VI, 369; Meisen, pp. 57 ff. and 176, n. 3.

15. Fliche VII, 63. Sergius IV (1009 - 1012) presumably was the first (Larousse).

16. However, his cult did not include *Bishop 14,* or he surely would have cited it in his *Epist.* xii (*Pat. Lat.* CXIX, 787).

17. *Vita* (*Pat. Lat.* CXIX, 763 D; ed. Duchesne II, 161, lines 24 - 25).

18. Armellini, p. 606; *Anal. Boll.* XLII, 128; but cf. Meisen, p. 54.

19. E.g., the Lateran chapel of N; see Duchesne II, 166, 176, 186.

20. Roy, *Nicholas,* pp. 50 - 52; Deanesly, pp. 450 - 452. He severely hampered the Western emperors' Italian campaigns (see Gay, p. 71).

21. *Pat. Lat.* CXXXII, 950, an. 868.

22. Amann XI, i, p. 523.

23. Greinacher, pp. 40 - 69; Roy, *Nicholas,* pp. 105 - 106, 113 - 115; Fliche VIII, 250.

24. *Annales Bertiniani,* anno 864.

25. Amann XI, i, pp. 524 - 525; Halphen, *Charlemagne,* chap. 4, pp. 375 - 395.

26. Gregorovius III, 154.

27. C. Diehl, *Monde oriental* I, 325 - 326.

28. Pp. 326 - 327; Baynes and Moss, pp. 109 - 111; Deanesly, pp. 426 - 428.

29. *Epist.* iv (A.D. 860), *Pat. Lat.* CXIX, 777 - 778.

30. Halphen, *Charlemagne,* chap. 4, pp. 375 - 395.

31. *EB* XIX, p. 649.

32. Duchesne II, 151.

33. Gregorovius IV, 155. The Vendôme Annals (Oxford MS Bodl. 309, fos. 120^r - 131^v) have only one obit of a pope, Nicholas I, before 1075 (fo. 104^v).

34. C. Diehl, *Monde oriental* I, 326 - 327.

35. Gay, pp. 80 - 82.

36. His Life in *Pat. Gr.* CV, 863 - 925; Baring-Gould, Feb., pp. 92 ff.

37. Amann XI, i, pp. 621 - 623; Fliche VII, 116 - 125.

38. Guilland, pp. 9 - 30.

39. His letters in *Pat. Gr.* CXI, 1 - 406.

40. Eutychius, *Annales* (*Pat. Gr.* CXI, 1150 - 1151); Baynes and Moss, pp. 111 - 112. In 911 a commission sent to Constantinople by Prince Oleg of Kiev was instructed in the true faith and shown the relics of the saints not by the patriarch but by the emperor himself (S. H. Cross and Wetzer, ed. and trans., *The Russian Primary Chronicle,* 2d. ed. [1953], pp. 65 - 69; *Anal. Boll.* LXXXIX, 1971, 153).

41. Citarella, p. 309; Karlin-Hayter.

42. Eutychius, *Annales (Pat. Gr.* CXI, 1152).

3 *Adolescence*
§1 ADOLESCENCE

1. I Sam. xvii, 42.

2. Matt. xix, 22.

3. *Thesaurus Linguae Latinae* I, s.v. "adulescens."

4. Meisen, pp. 75 - 76; text of *Stratilates 3,* pp. 527 - 530.

5. *MGH, Poetae* II, 206 (n. XLI, v), line 13.

6. Meisen, pp. 73 - 76.

7. *Pat. Lat.* CXXIV, 771.

8. R. S. Bour in *Annuaire de la Société d'histoire et d'archéologie de la Lorraine* XXXVIII (Metz, 1929), 514, n. 44, and p. 632.

9. Meisen, p. 77; a list of 10th-cent. German dedications, pp. 79 - 81.

10. From Vatican MS Lat. 1339: "Et beato confessore tuo Iubenali, Benedicto, Gregorio atque Nycolao necnon et beato Michaheli archangelo tuo et omnibus sanctis tuis, etc." (*Anal. Boll.* LIV [1936], 169).

11. *Pat. Lat.* CXV, 735 - 818.

12. Lalanne, pp. 167 - 168.

13. De Gaiffier, *Pellegrinaggi,* briefly summarizes relevant discussions of such topics as the meaning of the word *peregrinus,* the scriptural and apostolic inspirations, who participated, why, and the relations of pilgrimage and cult. See also Avril and Gaborit, and Labande, "Recherches." Gregorovius III, 77 - 78. "Every species of vice—adultery, theft, idolatry, poisoning, murder—was familiar to the inhabitants of the holy city" (Gibbon, chap. 23).

14. Bréhier, *Eglise,* p. 21; Lalanne, pp. 186 - 187.

15. *MGH,* Conc. II, 282, c. 45 (A.D. 813).

16. Peregrinatio Frotmundi (AA SS 24 Oct., Tom. X, p. 847 ff.).

17. Ebersolt, *Orient* I, 75; Bréhier, *Eglise,* pp. 32 - 33.

18. Glaber, *Histoires* III, i, 2. According to Labande 1958, p. 160, *peregrinus* "aurait été employé uniquement avec l'acception de 'voyageur' ou 'étranger,' à l'antique" up to the appearance of *Saint Alexis,* ca. 1040, and Peter Damien (*Pat. Lat.* CLXV, 579).

19. See chap. 3, vi.

20. Bréhier, *Eglise,* pp. 35 - 37; Lalanne, p. 188.

21. Glaber, *Histoires* III, 7; IV, 6.

22. Lalanne, p. 170.

23. Bréhier, *Eglise,* pp. 45 - 48; Lalanne, p. 189; Ebersolt, *Orient* I, 75 - 81.

24. Ebersolt, *Orient* I, 81.

25. Bréhier, *Eglise,* p. 33.

26. The several versions of his Clermont address are gathered in *Pat. Lat.* CLI, 565 - 82.

27. J. Chavanon, ed., *Relation de terre sainte* (1533 - 1534), Paris, 1902.

§II THE ANGEVIN COUNTS

1. Laurent LePeletier; Halphen, *Etude,* pp. 3 - 43; idem, "Catalogue d'actes des comtes," *Le comté,* pp. 244 ff.

2. Annals and chronicles of Saint-Aubin, Beaulieu, Saint-Nicolas, Saint-Sergius, Saint-Florent Saumur, Saint-Maxent Poitou (ed. Richard), Holy Trinity Vendôme (Oxford MS Bodl. 309), Chronica Rainaldi. Editions: Marchegay and Salmon; Marchegay and Mabille; Halphen, *Receuil;* Halphen and Poupardin, *Chroniques.* The Gesta Consularum Andegavensum, existing in five redactions of various dates, but the earliest two generations after Fulk's death, fully arranged and described by Halphen in *Etude.*

3. Glaber; Adémar de Chabannes.

4. Wm. Stubbs, ed., *Gesta regum Anglorum* (Rolls Series). Also Johel's N legend (see below n. 57).

5. *Comte Fulk Rechin,* ed. Marchegay and Mabille, pp. 378 ff.; Halphen and Poupardin, pp. 235 - 237.

6. Historiae abbatiae S.-Nicolai compendium, written 1678, in *Recueil des historiens des Gaules et de la France* XII, from Paris MS BN Lat. 11818, fos. 313 - 318. Salies composed a complete biography of Fulk but Halphen, *Le comté,* is more dependable. Compare Roy, *Mille,* pp. 101 ff.

7. Halphen, *Le comté,* pp. 211 - 212. The first certain use of the epithet is on the Beaulieu tomb, incised possibly as late as the 14th century (Salies, p. 455; cf. Halphen, *Le comté,* pp. 234 - 236): "Hic iacet exiguo tumuli sub marmore Fulco / Noera, potens proles Gryssogongelle tua."

8. Boussard, p. 308. Angers was sacked 853 and continuously thereafter for 12 years; see Halphen, *Charlemagne.*

9. Halphen, *Le comté,* pp. 3 - 4; Poupardin in *Mélanges d'archéologie et d'histoire de l'Ecole française de Rome* XX (1900), 206; Mabille, Introduction in Marchegay and Salmon, 1871, pp. liii - lxxvii; Boussard, p. 308.

10. Le Moy, pp. 52 - 72; compare in the same tenor Halphen, *Le comté,* p. 129; Salies pp. 6 - 15, 198 - 206, 208 - 223 (a good map of Fulk's Angers

showing the site of N abbey, opp. p. 317). The abbot and monks of Saint-Florent recorded his *immanitatem ferociae* (Halphen, *Le comté*, p. 353).

11. Loches (site of Beaulieu) was one of the earliest holdings of the Angevin counts (Halphen, *Le comté,* p. 4); Montrichard erected 1005 (Marchegay and Salmon, p. 107).

12. Fulk Rechin; see Halphen, *Le comté,* pp. 153 - 154.

13. Marchegay and Salmon, p. 377; Halphen, *Le comté,* p. 26; but see *Cahiers de civilisation médiévale,* no. 46, pp. 147 - 159.

14. Glaber II, iii, 3, pp. 30 - 32; Marchegay and Salmon, pp. 89 ff.; Salies c. IV, 26 - 31; VIII, 72 - 80.

15. Chabannes III, 34, p. 156; Halphen, *Le comté,* pp. 29 - 30.

16. Halphen, *Le comté,* p. 129; the account survives in a separate document, pp. 348 - 349.

17. Gregory of Tours V, 4.

18. Oxford MS Bodl. 309 (Vendôme Annals); Halphen 1903, pp. 60, 86.

19. Halphen, *Receuil,* pp. 4, 46, etc.

20. Annals of Saint-Aubin, an. M (Halphen, *Receuil,* p. 3).

21. Saint-Florent (ed. Halphen 1903, p. 117); Hist. Saint-Florent (ed. Marchegay and Mabille, p. 273). Others blamed Fulk's treason against Herbert of Maine (Chavannes III, 24, p. 206). Halphen, *Le comté,* p. 130; a second decimating fire in the year 1032, ibid., pp. 96 - 97.

22. Glaber III, ii, 7, pp. 56 - 59; Halphen, *Le comté,* pp. 32 - 33. King Robert, a musician, composed at her command a hymn which rapidly became famous, *O constantia martyrum;* since Constance knew little Latin she did not perceive the malicious double entendre (Larousse IV, 1015).

23. Halphen 1903, pp. 61, 86, 108, 118; 1906, p. 211. On the state of Jerusalem pilgrimage at the time see Labande, "Recherches," pp. 164 - 169; on criminals and homicides sentenced to pilgrimage, Vogel, pp. 78 - 82; on their insecurity, Vogel p. 91c, and Labande, pp. 97 - 98; for the penitential pilgrimage in history, society, and law, see Vogel, pp. 59 - 60, who treats Fulk and King Robert.

24. A.D. 1002/1003; 1008/1009; 1039. I follow Halphen, *Le comté,* chronology, pp. 130, 213 - 218.

25. Halphen, *Le comté,* pp. 83 - 86, 219 - 231.

26. Glaber II, iv, 4, p. 33; Halphen, *Le comté,* pp. 84, 118.

27. Glaber II, iv, 7, p. 34.

28. Philippe Labbé, *Nova Bibliotheca MSS Librorum* (Paris, 1653) II, 213; *Gallia Christiana* XIV, 668; Halphen, *Le comté,* p. 33.

29. *Recueil des historiens des Gaules et de la France* X, 476; Halphen, *Le comté,* p. 33.

30. Halphen, *Le comté,* p. 214, n. 3.

31. Marchegay and Mabille, eds., *Historia S. Florentii Salmurensis* (1869), p. 273.

32. Halphen, *Le comté,* p. 216. Cf. chap. 3, vii.

33. Bréhier, *Eglise,* pp. 35, 43. Even if Halphen's date for the journey prove wrong, Fulk's journey would be no less remarkable, for Hakim maintained the intense persecution to A.D. 1020.

34. This *ben trovato* is retold from the *Gesta consulum Andegavensum* and other late sources by Lalanne, *Curiosités biographiques,* pp. 172 - 173, and Salies, pp. 145 - 146. On the parallel journey of Count William of Angoulême, who departed 1 Oct. 1026 and arrived at Jerusalem in the first week of March, see Chabannes, pp. 189 - 190.

35. Chron. Cons. Andegav. Labande, "Recherches," p. 343.

36. Marchegay and Mabille, p. 273; Chronicon *Saint-Florentii Salmurensis,* ed. Martène, *Amplissima Collectio* V, 1115; Halphen, *Le comté,* pp. 214 - 215. Johel, historian of N-Angers, places the incident on the voyage out (*Cat. Cod. Hag. Lat. Paris* III, 159 - 160).

37. This incident told by Monachus Beccensis without notable variation about "quidam miles, genere Normannicus, vocabulo Ricardus, filius Fulconis senioris de Alnon," a crusader returning from the capture of Jerusalem (*Cat. Cod. Hag. Lat. Paris.* II, 429).

38. Halphen, *Étude,* p. 41; cf. Salies, p. 148. The canard recounts that Fulk freed the pope from the evil Crescentius by shooting him with an arrow from the ground as he paced the parapet of Angel Castle. Halphen believed that the legend was adopted to account for the relics of the otherwise unknown saints at Angers. The fable of Crescentius' death by an arrow from the street is more commonly attributed to Emperor Otto (see e.g. *MGH, Scriptores* XIV, 121 ff.).

39. Marchegay and Mabille, p. 275.

40. Halphen, *Le comté,* p. 86, n. 2.

41. Halphen, *Le comté,* pp. 86 - 87, 252; idem, *Recueil,* pp. 59, 106, 118. The charter in LePeletier, p. 7; *Gallia Christiana* III (1656), 688.

42. *MGH, Scriptores* IX, 318; cf. pp. 386 - 387.

43. LePeletier, p. 7; *Gallia Christiana* III (1656), 688; *Pat. Lat.* CLV, 481; CLVII, 92.

44. Halphen, *Le comté,* p. 87.

45. Halphen, *Le comté,* 1906, pp. 253 - 254.

46. Oxford MS Bodl. 309, ed. Halphen, *Receuil,* p. 61; Marchegay and Mabille, pp. 166, 188.

47. Le Moy, p. 90.

48. Marchegay and Mabille, pp. 134, 387.

49. Chronique de Foulque le Réchīn, ed. Marchegay and Salmon II, 373.

50. Cf. Milton, *Paradise Lost* XII, 64.

51. *Gesta regum Anglorum* III, 235 (ed. Stubbs II, 292).

52. Annals of Saint-Aubin, ed. Halphen, *Receuil,* pp. 4, 46; of Vendôme, p. 61; of Saint-Florent, p. 118; of St. Maxentius, ed. Marchegay and Mabille, p. 393; others ed. Marchegay and Salmon II, 117, 168, 330, 331. At the request of his wife Hildegarde, her son Count Geoffrey confirmed and added to the possessions of N d'Angers (Halphen, *Le comté,* p. 267 (Actes 76 - 78)).

53. Disinterred A.D. 1870; see Halphen, *Le comté,* pp. 234 - 236.

54. Laisses 70, 74, 151 - 152; Halphen, *Etude,* p. 31.

55. "MLX . . . obiit Gausfredis comes . . . monachili habitu prius suscepto a domno Adraldo abbate Sancti Nicolai."—*Vendôme Annals,* ed. Halphen, *Receuil,* p. 63.

56. Johel's account (see n. 57) 3, p. 158, records a gift to Saint-Nicolas d'Angers of "a portion of relics given by Emperor Henry of Germany to Geoffrey," and their deposit in the abbey; he makes clear that they were part of the corpse, not myrrh. See also *Chron. de gestis consulum,* ed. Marchegay and Salmon II, 133.

57. Transcribed from MS Lat. 12611 in *Cat. Cod. Hag. Paris.* III, 158 - 162 (*BHL* no. 6177, p. 895); *Histoire Littéraire de la France* VIII (1747), 445.

58. *Cat. Gen. des MSS* XXXI (1898), 222 - 223. Another is from Paris MS BN Lat. 12611. It contains the Miracle of Brientius, an adolescent boy restored to health at Saint-Nicolas by N on N Day, described at length. According to the legend for the Feast of the Translation in the same MS (transcribed in *Cat. Cod. Hag. Paris* III, 158 - 162), the German Emperor Henry (doubtless Henry III) gave to Count Geoffrey Martel relics of N which he deposited in Saint-Nicolas: "These the count with great joy and honor accepted, and he gave a part of them to the venerable abbot Harold of this monastery."

59. These and others are listed in a "Charter of the 'Empress' Matilda Relating to Diverse Churches in England," a text prepared by the abbot and convent in 1648. Matilda, d. of King Henry I of England, was mother of Henry II by the Angevine count Geoffrey IV (le Bel). They are all listed in

Dugdale; see E. Dupont, "Les donations anglaises," *Revue d'histoire de l'église de France* II (1911), p. 458.

§III EMPRESS THEOPHANO

1. Schramm, *Kaiser, Rom, und Renovatio,* chap. 3.

2. Dölger, "Theophano," pp. 646 - 658.

3. P. Karlin Hayter, "La mort de Theophano," *Byzantinische Zeitschrift* LXII (1969), 13 - 19.

4. On the literary interests of her entourage, Reto Bezzola, *Les origines et la formation de la littérature courtoise* I (Paris, 1944), 256 - 258.

5. John XVI, deposed by the Council of Pavia.

6. *MGH, Scriptores* XIV, 144 - 146.

7. Frey, p. 89; Meisen, p. 80.

8. Meisen, pp. 81 - 82.

9. Meisen, p. 82; a full-page reproduction p. 37.

10. *MGH, Scriptores* XIV, 131.

11. *MGH, Scriptores* VIII, 75 - 76 (Broadway Translation II, 76 ff.).

12. *MGH, Scriptores* XIV, 121 ff.

13. The abbey was chartered in 1024 (*MGH, Scriptores* XIV, 135).

14. Ibid., pp. 140 - 141.

15. Edited by H. Pabst in Pertz' *Archiv* XII, 192 - 200; *MGH, Scriptores* XIV, 145 ff.

16. A tooth of N was given to Brauweiler A.D. 1061 (Meisen, p. 86; see Caesarius VIII, 73). The miracle has been treated by de Gaiffier, 1967, pp. 194 - 225; he finds it in legends of saints Anthony, Brigette, Catherine of Alexandria, Fidole, Henry VI, James of Compostella, Jerome, Martin, and Nicholas of Tolentino, among others.

§IV REGINOLD AND THE N LITURGY

1. Portions of the remainder of this chapter are drawn from C. W. Jones, *Liturgy.* See also Silvestre, 1965, and Gaiffier, 1967.

2. However, the 9th cent. Amalarius used the term in a prototypical sense: ed. I. M. Hanssens III (*Studi e testi,* 140), p. 91, line 22; p. 93, lines 33 - 40.

3. P. Wagner, "Zu m.a. Offiziums-komposition," *Kirchenmusikalisches Jahrbuch* XXI (1908); *Analecta Hymnica* V (1889), 1 - 16; Bäumer, pp. 73 - 86; Auda, p. 52.

4. As early as the 11th cent. it was believed that Alcuin invented the form

by composing the Historia de Trinitate (Apel, p. 8, n. 6; Auda, p. 82); see e.g. Sichard's *Mitrale* (*Pat. Lat.* CCXIII, 385).

5. Gilbert Reaney in C. W. Jones, *Liturgy,* p. 142; Auda pp. 42, 52 ff.

6. Admonitio Generalis, 23 Mars 789 (*MGH, Legum sectio* II, t. I, pp. 60 - 61); cf. the decree of the Council of Aix, A.D. 816 (ibid. III, t. II, p. 413).

7. Burchard III, chap. 198, after Haito (*Pat. Lat.* CXV, 14).

8. *Études grégoriennes* IV (1961), 7; text in *Pat. Lat.* LXXVIII, 725 - 850, after the Maurist edition of Gregory's works, Paris, 1705.

9. C. W. Jones, *Liturgy,* pp. 52 - 55; Peter Wagner, *Einführung in die gregorianischen Melodien,* 2d ed. (Berlin, 1901), chap. 15; Auda, p. 148; Corbin, pp. 338 - 339. *Historiae* are found in *Analecta Hymnica* vols. 5, 13, 17, 18, 24, 25, 26, 28, 29, 55a.

10. *MGH, Scriptores* VII, 253 ff. (Reginold, pp. 256 - 257); also in *Pat. Lat.* CXLVI, 1003 - 1026.

11. Bernard Bischoff, "Reginold, Bischof von Eichstätt," *Die deutsche Literatur des Mittelalters,* Verfasserlexicon V (1955), 943 - 945.

12. *MGH, Scriptores* VII, 257.

13. Dom Germain Morin, in *Historisches Jahrbuch* XXXVIII (1917), 773 - 777.

14. Trier MS 5 (s. xi, Abinghof near Paderborn), fos. 104^v - 141^r, contains the offices of Willibald, Wunebald, and Walburga. Fos. 120^v - 121^v record a macaronic sequence in Latin, Greek, and Hebrew for Willibald, transcribed by Daniel and then by Morin from the 10th cent. MS CLM 14377, fo. 51^v. See also Père Coens in *Anal. Boll.* LXIX (1921), 361 - 362.

15. E.g. in the diocesan Pontifical Book of his successor Gundechar II (MS 48 in the Episcopal Seminar), ed. Suttner, pp. 136 ff.; Andrieu II, 117 - 118.

16. F. M. Stenton, *Anglo-Saxon England,* 2d. ed. (Oxford, 1947), pp. 174 - 175. Coens, pp. 363 - 373.

17. Bréhier, *Eglise,* p. 21.

18. See chaps. 2, iii; 3, vii.

19. *MGH Scriptores* VII, 257. See n. 14 above and Professor Bischoff's conclusions, n. 11 above.

20. John "Chrysostom" (i.e., "golden-mouthed"), archbishop of Constantinople (d. 407).

21. Despite his episcopal preeminence contemporary annalists mention only the historia of N as grounds of distinction in recording Reginold's obit: *Auctarium Gartense* (*MGH, Scriptores* IX, p. 567); *Annales S. Rudberti Salisb.* (ibid.

IX, p. 772); *Annales S. Trudperti* (ibid. XVII, p. 290). Cf. Paul Lehmann, *Erforschung des Mittelalters* IV (Munich, 1961), pp. 248 - 249. In the Pontifical Book (above n. 15) N is included among the bishop saints in *Ordo ad dedicandum aecclesiam*.

22. I based the edition of N Liturgy primarily on London B. M. MS Cotton Nero E 1, as the earliest witness. But equally revealing and possibly equally early is Vatican MS, Regin. lat. 586, s. xi, containing the neumed liturgy (fos. 66^r - 69^r).

23. Professor Gilbert Reaney has analyzed the "novelty" of the N Liturgy in Jones, *Liturgy*, pp. 145 - 151. He quotes Letald of Micy, who lived ca. 1000: "The novelty of some musicians does not please me, for they prefer to be different and disdain to follow the old authors."

24. My census of extant sources indicates that copies spread widely before the Translation. Further treatment in chap. 3, vii. Reginold did not compose a proper Mass, but one appears as early as Paris B.N. MS Lat. 820 (s. xi^2, from Vendôme), fos. 11^r - 12^v; Andrieu II (1931), p. 354.

25. Text in C. W. Jones, *Liturgy*, pp. 17 - 45.

26. Corbin, pp. 342 - 343, after Lambot and Fransen.

27. *DCB* s.v. "Blase"; Baring-Gould (3 Feb.).

28. *BHL* no. 6210, ed. *Cat. Cod. Hag. Brux.* I, 320 - 322. Used by Bishop James in the Golden Legend (Jacobus de Voragine, pp. 841 - 842).

29. "La Croix-en-Brie, dioc. Sens, Seine-et-Marne, cant. Naugis, arr. Provins, dép. La Charité, qui le cède en 1208 aux chevaliers de Saint-Jean de Jérusalem." (Guy de Valous in *Archives de la France monastique* XXXIX [1935], t. II, p. 196.)

30. The "ancient custom" represented by the *Responsale gregorianum*, imported to France A.D. 823; Apel, pp. 95 - 98.

31. Transcribed from C. W. Jones, *Liturgy*, pp. 47 - 49, translated from the text transcribed in *Cat. Cod. Hag. Paris.* I, 510 - 511, from Paris B.N. MS Lat. 5284, s. xiii.

32. The earliest record of N as patron of a Cluniac cloister is Arbin, in A.D. 1011.

33. A second recension of *The Cross Legend 41* is transcribed from Paris B.N. MS 5368, s. xiii, in *Cat. Cod. Hag. Paris.* II, 430 - 431, where it forms chap. 34 of the *Miracula S. Nicholai conscripta a monacho Beccensi*.

34. Meisen, pp. 394 - 395.

35. Meisen, p. 395.

36. *Anal. Hymn.* LIV, 95 ff., no. 66; *Oxford Book of Medieval Latin Verse,* 2d ed. (Oxford, 1959), no. 116; F. J. E. Raby, *Christian Latin Poetry* (Oxford, 1927), pp. 345 - 346; Young I, 186 - 187. The musical score ed. C. A. Moberg, *Über die schwedischen Sequenzen* II (Uppsala, 1927), no. 22.

37. Dreves dates the Saint Martial MS s. x (*Anal. Hymn.* loc. cit.); there are many s. xi MSS.

38. Chap. 4, iii.

39. Chevalier, *Repert. Hymn.* II, 310; Mone III, 450, no. 1088, from Saint Gall MS 380, p. 271, with neumes. See the valuable history by my colleague and adviser Richard Crocker, *The Early Medieval Sequence* (Berkeley and Los Angeles, 1978.).

40. Chevalier, *Repert. Hymn.* II, 321; Mone III, 453, from Vatican MS Pal. lat. 1671, fo. 36^v, etc. Manitius II, 557.

§V GODEHARD AND *The Three Clerks*

1. For N entries in German calendars and sacramentaries before the year 1000, see Meisen pp. 176 - 177.

2. E.g. CLM 21557, fo. 22^r.

3. Mayer in *Archiv für Liturgiewissenschaft* VI (1960), 469, n. 1; Coffman, "Note." N's spread from Eichstätt in a century is indicated by its red-letter day in Salzburg by 1075 (Anton Lechner, *Mittelalterliche Kirchenfeste und Kalenderien in Bayern* [1891], p. 138).

4. Ghellinck II, 184.

5. C. W. Jones, *Liturgy,* chap. 7, pp. 74 - 89.

6. *BHL* no. 6126; CLM 14419, fos. 21 - 42; *MGH, Scriptores* XI, 391; *Neues Archiv* X (1885), 407 ff.; cf. *Anal. Boll.* XVII, 205 - 209. Pope Leo IX dedicated an N altar and relic at Saint Emmeram A.D. 1052, possibly the occasion for composition of this Life.

7. *BHL* II, 891, no. 6127; *Anal. Boll.* II (1883), 143 ff.; cf. I, 501; Ronsjö, p. 9; Albrecht, pp. 14 - 15; Charles H. Beeson, *Classical Philology* XLII (1947), 84.

8. Probably the Life now preserved in Paris B.N. MS lat. 5285 drawn directly from Metaphrast (*BHG* no. 1349) including the Life of Nicholas of Syon (*BHG* no. 1347) as in the *Vita Compilata* (*BHG* no. 1348a). Vienna MS Lat. 739, fos. 174vb, 203^r - 203va (described in *Münchener Museum für Philologie des Mittelalters und der Renaissance* IV [1924], 135 - 138) contains a *Sermo de obitu* N translated from Greek by "infimus Iohannis presbyter et monachus." This may be John the Monk of a *Liber de miraculis,* ed. Michael Huber in

Sammlung mittellateinischer Texte, ed. Hilka, VII, 1913). At all events with the opening up of the Danube through Hungary, texts and ideas from Byzantium were penetrating the West.

9. *Anal. Boll.* II (1883), 151; Koblenz MS 5 (see Meisen, p. 268).

10. Transcribed by Meisen, pp. 530 - 531.

11. The full text (*Pat. Lat.* CXLVI, 357) translated in C. W. Jones, *Liturgy,* pp. 94 - 95.

12. *MGH, Scriptores* XI, 167 - 218; Manitius II, 313 - 318.

13. *MGH, Scriptores* XI, 207 - 208.

14. No. 7, ed. Jones, *Liturgy,* p. 19.

15. Meisen, p. 86.

16. Incorporated in both of Otloh's Lifes, but not in his hymn, which is limited to Reginold's subjects.

17. Philippe Aries, *Centuries of Childhood,* trans. Robert Baldick (New York, 1962), pp. 33, 128.

18. Coussemaker, pp. ix - x; Coffman, pp. 59 - 60; Young II, 310 - 311, 488; Arnold Williams, *Drama of Mediaeval England,* East Lansing, Mich., 1961, chap. 10; Albrecht, *passim.* The earliest hymn with unambiguous reference to *Three Clerks 44* is s. xii (*Anal. Hymn.* XXI, 85).

19. British Museum MS Add. 22414, fos. 3 - 4, ed. Ernst Dümmler in *Zeitschrift für deutsches Alterthum* XXXIII (1891), 401 - 407; thereafter by Young II, 324 ff.

20. The inscription may indicate ownership by the abbey of Saint Godehard (founded 1146), not by the bishop; but see C. W. Jones, *Liturgy,* p. 92. Internal evidence indicates that it is a copy, not an autograph of the anonymous composer.

21. *BHL* no. 6217. Treated in chap. 5, iii. It has had an unbroken history of dramatization; for example, a version was performed at Rouen in 1911 to celebrate the foundation of Normandy (Albrecht, p. 25), and the Columbia Broadcasting System has a script for presentation on radio at Nativity Season.

22. *BHL* no. 6219. Meisen devoted his chap. 11, pp. 289 - 306, to *Three Clerks 44* and school patronage.

23. Reginold's anthem ed. C. W. Jones, *Liturgy,* p. 38, no. 46.

24. From Peter v, 3 - 5; cf. Ps. lxvii, 14.

25. C. W. Jones, *Liturgy,* pp. 130 - 134.

26. Ibid., pp. 99 - 103.

27. Young II, 310 - 311.

28. C. W. Jones, *Liturgy,* p. 115.

29. See Otloh's tale of *multi histriones et quidam histrio et fama et dignitate caeteris praestantior* (*Liber visionum* 23, in *Pat. Lat.* CLXXXVI, 385). On mimes, balladeers, and histrions among clergy, monks, and pilgrims, see Vogel, pp. 74 - 75.

30. See chap. 6.

31. Hauréau, XXXII, 2 (1888), p. 327, as in Albrecht, p. 114.

32. Albrecht, pp. 23 - 43; *Revue des traditions populaires* III (1888), 335 - 337.

33. M. F. Ermini in *Studi medievali* III (1930), 111 - 120; cf. Aebischer in *Archivum Romanicum* XV (1931), 383 - 399.

34. Meisen illustrations, p. 332; cf. p. 227.

35. Possibly *Mariners* 6. Or in a tower (Cahier, p. 304).

36. Meisen, p. 339; ICA records instances.

37. E.g., Glaber, II, ix, 17, pp. 44 ff.; IV, iv, pp. 99 - 103. "There are records of forty-eight famines and epidemics in sixty-three years." (Roy, *Mille,* p. 81.) See *Pat. Lat.* XC, 243.12 ff., from Vatican MS Regin. lat. 755 (Sens), for the comets and famines of A.D. 868.

38. Sébillot in *Revue des traditions populaires* XI (1896), 188.

39. C. W. Jones, "Carolingian Aesthetics," esp. pp. 326 - 327.

40. Baring-Gould, 11 Nov. p. 240, after Metaphrastes.

41. MS 34, s. xii, ed. Young II, 335 - 336; cf. Albrecht, pp. 29, 31; *Cat. Cod. Hag. Brux.* I¹, 317; *Anal. Boll.* XXIV (1905), 459.

42. C. W. Jones, *Liturgy,* pp. 136 - 137.

43. Daniel iii, 24; the Song iii, 52 - 90.

44. E.g., *Pat. Lat.* CI, 468 - 469, 485 (Alcuin); CXXI, 434 (Alvar of Cordova); *MGH, Poetae* II, 529.205 - 216; 539.44 - 59 (Florus of Lyons).

45. Genesis xviii, 2 - 22.

46. E.g., *Anal. Hymn.* XLIV, no. 277; LV, no. 265.

47. "Greek fire," imaginatively tied to N as we have seen, above chap. 1, iii, was known in the West as *ignis trium puerorum;* see B. Bischoff in *Studien zur lateinischen Dichtung des Mittelalters* (Ehrengabe f. K. Strecker), 1931, pp. 6 - 7.

48. See chap. 2, iv, *"Iconia 34."*

49. Reproduced in Kaftal, fig. 863, p. 767.

50. " . . . sicut liberavit tres illos innocentes de laqueo mortis . . .ita filium nostrum revocabit."

51. See chap. 5, iii.

52. See Silvestre, p. 145, citing P. Rolland, *Histoire de Tournai* (1956). The one at Mons is signed by the Tournai sculptor Lambert.

53. Also the first indication of the pickling tub (Albrecht, p. 64); *Le pays lorrain* XXIV (1932), 571.

54. *Chanson de Nicolas,* lines 213 - 226. Haskins, *Studies,* p. 63, quotes a 12th cent. MS: "Hinc est quod pauperes clerici qui non habent qui figant illos in ecclesia Dei, beatum Nicolaum invocent."

§VI LOTHARINGIA AND EARLY ENGLAND

1. C. W. Jones, *Liturgy,* pp. 86 - 89; Pietzsch, pp. 110 - 113, 128 - 130; Lesne V (1940), pp. 341 - 413, esp. 349 - 361. Gaiffier, 1967, pp. 415 - 507, reviews the hagiographical traits of the region but confines himself to subjects of local origin and does not treat N.

2. Kurth, chap. 14 and p. 166; *Leodium* VII (Liège, 1908), 142 - 146; *Anal. Boll.* XXVIII, 318; *MGH, Scriptores* XXX, 821 - 822.

3. Silvestre, review, p. 145; Kurth, chap. 12 et passim, inc. p. 133. On the distinction between regular and secular clergy, see E. John in *Bulletin of the John Rylands Library* XLII (1959), 61 - 87, and *Revue Bénédictine* LXX (1960), 333 - 359.

4. *Moyen Age* LVIII (1952), pp. 27 - 30.

5. Pietzsch, pp. 128 - 130, 140.

6. Kurth, pp. 326 - 327.

7. Ca. 1050 the chapel of the new palace at Nijmagen was dedicated to N (W. Braunfels, ed., *Charlemagne* [Aachen 1965], no. 586, p. 415). For the major N foundations see *MGH, Scriptores* XI, 396 and 401; XII, 43; XV, 965; XXV, 69 - 70.

8. Kurth, p. 245.

9. Ibid., p. 307; cf. p. 310.

10. Meisen, pp. 84 ff.; Jean Lejeune, "A propos de l'art mosan," *Anciens pays et assemblées d'états* VIII (Louvain, 1955), 90 - 157, esp. p. 146, n. 20.

11. C. W. Jones, *Liturgy,* pp. 86 - 87; Kurth, pp. 101 - 103.

12. At least once at Liège he was cited as a Bavarian plotter (Kurth, p. 82).

13. A.D. 989 - 990; Kurth, p. 87.

14. Kurth, p. 291; but despite Notger's extreme secularity he was friend and helpmeet of abbot Odilon of Cluny (see Auda, pp. 80 - 81), and Cluniac influence (cf. *Cross Legend 41*) in Liègeois cloisters was marked.

15. Brussels MS 9932, fo. 26^r (from S. Laurent, Liège).

16. Diocesan Library MS 141, fo. 56^V (Andrieu I, 110).

17. Gilles d'Orval's Chronicle (*MGH, Scriptores* XXV, p. 69.51 - 54).

18. *Anal. Boll.* XX (1901), 430 - 431; cf. *BHL,* no. 6176a (*Anal. Boll.* XLV [1927], 409; *MGH, Scriptores* XXX, 1926, 821 - 822).

19. Halkin, pp. 207, 426.

20. Silvestre, review, p. 146.

21. For Greek studies at Toul, A.D. 92 - 994, see Roy, *Mille,* p. 150.

22. Laisses 137, 156, 232 (trans. Crosland, pp. 87, 99, 158).

23. Above, chap. 3, iii.

24. Below, chap. 5, vii.

25. C. W. Jones, *Liturgy,* p. i, n. 2, after Arnold-Foster.

26. "Exeter Book"; "Leofric Missal." DNB; Auda, pp. 39, 78, and refs.; Bannister II, 227; *Leofric's Collectaneum,* Henry Bradshaw Society Publications 56.

27. C. W. Jones, *Liturgy,* pp. 8 - 10.

28. William Stubbs, "Introduction," *The Foundation of Waltham Abbey* (London, 1861); *DNB.*

29. *DNB.* Both Walter of Hereford and Gisa were consecrated at Rome by Pope Nicholas II.

30. Wilhelm Levison in *Deutsches Archiv* XVII (1961), 448 ff.

31. *DNB,* s.v., Herbert, pp. 143, 146.

32. Th. Forester, trans., *The Chronicle of Florence of Worcester* (1854), pp. 161 - 164 (an. 1062).

33. MS Cambridge C.C.C. 391, ed. Anselm Hughes, *The Portiforium of St. Wulfstan,* 2 vols. Henry Bradshaw Society Publications (London, 1958, 1960), pp. 598 - 599.

34. London B.M. MS Cotton Nero E 1, Pt. ii, fos. 153^V - 155^V, ed. C. W. Jones, *Liturgy,* chap. 2, pp. 7 - 13.

35. Cambridge C.C.C. 9, 422, and 473; London B.M., Harley 2961 ("Leofric Collectar"). Neil Ker in *British Museum Quarterly* XIV (1940), 82; idem, MSS Containing Anglo-Saxon, p. 41; idem, English MSS after the Norman Conquest, p. 49.

36. C. W. Jones, *Liturgy,* p. 12, after E. S. Dewick and W. S. Frere, *The Collectar of St. Wulfstan* (Henry Bradshaw Society Publications 56).

37. E. S. Dewick, *The Leofric Collectar Compared with the Collectar of St. Wulfstan,* Henry Bradshaw Society Publications 56 (London, 1921).

38. London B. M. MSS Cotton Vit. A XII (from Exeter); Faustina A VIII; Arundel 60 and 356; Oxford, Bodl. Fell i, 4 (Salisbury); Douce 296; Hatton

113 (Junius 99); Magdalen Coll. 100. Francis Wormald, *English Kalendars before A.D. 1100* (Henry Bradshaw Society Publications 72, 1934), p. vii; *Kalendars after A.D. 1100* (76, 1934): These indicate that N red-letter days first appeared in the decade before the Conquest at Sherborne, Wells, and Worcester, and then spread through Britain with remarkable celerity.

39. Cambridge MS C.C.C. 303, pp. 171 - 185. Ker, MSS Containing A.-S., no. 57, p. 99.

40. Darlington, p. xxxviii, n. 2.

41. Ibid., *Vita Wulfstani* III, 9. 10. 13. 16. 17. Two letters of Nicholas to Eadmer ed. Stubbs, *Memorials,* pp. 422 - 424.

42. *DNB;* Darlington, pp. 56 - 57 (Vita iii, 17; cf. iii, 9).

43. Darlington, p. li.

44. Darlington, pp. 42 - 43, 90, 154 - 157.

45. *Acta SS,* Mai VII, p. 406; Janin 1969, p. 579. William the Conqueror died 9 September, precisely four months after N's Translation (Guéry, p. 67).

§VII THE NORMAN CULTS OF N AND SAINT CATHERINE

1. This section is adapted from C. W. Jones, "Norman Cults."

2. But the official title of King's College, Cambridge, is The College of Saint Mary and Saint Nicholas (Coulton, *Panorama,* p. 600). For N, see Meisen, and Young II, 324 ff.; cf. Coffman, *Theory,* pp. 17 - 20. For C, see Assion, *Mirakel;* for Britain, F. Bateson, *Cambridge Bibliography of English Literature* I, 169. On the priory of Sainte-Catherine des Ecoliers, for which Saint Louis laid the foundation, see *Vies des saints* XI, 863.

3. Arnold-Forster III, 321 - 457; Meisen; Assion, *Mirakel,* pp. 177 - 189; *Vies des saints* XI, 854 ff.; *Lexikon für Theologie und Kirche* VI (1961), 60 ff.

4. See chap. 1 above, pp. 15 - 16.

5. *Oxford Dictionary of the Christian Church,* p. 249.

6. Weigand, p. 279; see also Delehaye in *Anal. Boll.* XI (1922), 35 - 36, 85, 114 - 115, 124. The evidence of a Roman fresco, s. viii, uncovered in 1948 (Assion, *Mirakel,* pp. 105 - 106) is cloudy.

7. Varnhagen, *Geschichte,* pp. 1 - 9. The "ignorant and ill written" Greek text used by Metaphrastes (s. x), *Pat. Gr.* CXVI, 276 - 301, from a Vatican MS s. x/xi (BHG 30 - 32) was studied by Klostermann and Seeburg; they conclude that a Palestinian monk wrote both the Passio SC and the *roman* of Barlaam and Joasaph. These texts speak of the angelic transport, but not of the prepared tomb (*marmorea*). The Latin texts were surveyed by Knust.

According to Assion, *Mirakel,* p. 125, following Knust, Hugh of Flavigny (*MGH, Scriptores* VIII, 399) is the first to have mentioned the marble tomb; cf. Peeters in *Anal. Boll.* XXVI (1907), 11, n. 1.

8. Cf. Weigand, p. 281. Saint Symeon told his biographer Eberwin (AA SS Jn. I, p. 87) that when he went to Sinai it had long been deserted because of Arabic incursions. The only MS of the Passio written before his trip to Rouen is one dated s. x at Monte Cassino which unfortunately lacks the last folio (Bibliotheca Casinensis III, Florilegium, pp. 74 ff.) wherein any account of the Invention would have appeared, if at all. Scholars now assume, without substantial evidence, that the oil motif went from Sinai to Rouen rather than from Rouen to Sinai (e.g., Assion, *Mirakel,* pp. 257 ff.).

9. "The presence of some relics at Rouen in 1033 - 1054 furnishes us a *terminus ad quem* for the date at which took place the 'Invention' of the body of the saint at Sinai" (Fawtier, p. 368). Fawtier assembled the data for change of name of the Rouen cloister, p. 366; in addition, see Cheroul p. 8, ann. 1090; p. 15, ann. 1201; p. 20, ann. 1233; p. 23, ann. 1248; p. 24, ann. 1256; p. 26, ann. 1262. Thereafter the designation disappears. Note that in the 1262 entry C and N were the only nonbiblical saints to receive the highest degree of cult (12 lections) in the abbey.

10. So Fawtier, p. 357. The text was edited by Père Poncelet in *Anal. Boll.* XXII (1903), pp. 423 - 438: *Haec de sanctarum reliquiarum translatione necnon et coenobii in quo venerantur, constructione, paucis dixisse sufficiant* (p. 431). Cf. Assion, *Mirakel,* pp. 180 ff.

11. *Anal. Boll.* XXII, p. 427. Glaber, *Histoires* i, 5: "He [Duke Richard II] sent rich gifts to the holy churches nearly throughout the world, so that from the orientals, specifically the renowned Mount Sinai, monks came every year to Rouen who in turn brought many presents."

12. Assion, *Mirakel,* pp. 221 - 224.

13. Richard II died 1026; his son Richard III died 1027; Robert I, his brother, was duke 1027 - 1035. Robert is especially noted as founder and protector of monasteries; he relied for counsel on Abbot Richard of Saint-Vannes (*CMH* V [1926], 491). In 1034 he set up a trusteeship for his bastard William, and went to the Holy Land, dying at Nicea A.D. 1035. The first Norman rule in Italy and Sicily was established at Aversa A.D. 1030.

14. Sackur, *Richard,* pp. 93 - 98, and *Cluniacenser,* p. 233, established that Symeon was in Angoulême in June 1027 and left Trier with Abp. Poppo for pilgrimage to Palestine in 1028, after stopping at Verdun. His stay at Rouen was therefore brief and not in the year that the Anonymous stipulated.

15. 1 June 1035 (Eberwin's Life, ed. *Acta SS* Jn. I, pp. 87 - 101). Glaber, p. 20, records that the monks came to Rouen *per singulos annos.*

16. I cited the primary documents and weighed their value, C. W. Jones, "Norman Cult," pp. 220 - 221. I have since read Père Coens' reexamination of the data, *Anal. Boll.* LXVIII (1950), 181 - 196, which then escaped me. He brushed aside (p. 183) as apochryphal any appearance of Symeon in Rouen, primarily, I think, because it had no place in his theme. But his data do not disagree with what I cite here; the anonymous author must have had some tradition from which to start.

17. Richard, abbot of Saint-Vannes, a notable Cluniac reformer, and Eberwin met Symeon in Antioch in 1022. Richard sponsored Hugh's Chronicle, which records this story (Manitius III, 512). He died before the altar of his special patron, N (*MGH, Scriptores* VIII, 404). MSS from centers Richard controlled are rich in materials on this subject: e.g. Namur MS 53, s. xii, from Saint Hubert (Ardennes), contains both the Vita of Symeon and the Passio of Saint Kilian.

18. *Acta SS* Jn. I, p. 91.

19. Symeon told Eberwin (p. 87) about God's miracle of granting manna to the monks after prayer, but made no connection with Catherine.

20. Eberwin 14, p. 89.

21. Weigand, p. 288. The second part of the Anonymous is a series of postmortem miracles. The author testifies that Isambert himself was relieved of toothache by oil from the relics, calling as witnesses his claustral brothers, specifically Eudes (ed. Poncelet, section 7). Moreover, an early vernacular Life of C (John Rylands Library, Fr. 6) of different tradition, confirms this incident. William the Forester, abbot of Saint-Wandrille (1311), wrote a eulogy of Isambert in 20 verses, including:

> *In crypta iacuit primo Katherinae.*
> *Ad magnum templum fuit eius postea latum*
> *Abbatis corpus in primi tempore cantus.*

Cheruel, Appendix B: *Vitae Abbatum S. Katarinae de Monte Rotomagensi,* p. 39.

22. Weigand, p. 289.

23. Fawtier (p. 365) would extend Symeon's mendacity, suggesting that he had never been to Sinai at all, but as a wanderer fell in with Abbot Richard and Eberwin at Antioch and assumed a Sinaitic sanctity to ingratiate himself. Fawtier supports his pejorative view by noting that Symeon

obscured the tradition of Saint Martial at Angoulême. Even sympathetic but factually accurate Eberwin (c. 18) reported that Symeon was suspected of evildoing by contemporaries: *Causa periculi huius Symeoni imputabatur ab omnibus* (*Acta SS* Jn. I, p. 90C); cf. *Frequenter iniuriatus tamquam agnus mansuetissimus omnia pertulit* (Hugo de Flavigny, *Chronicon* ii, 26; *MGH, Scriptores* VIII, 399).

24. The work began A.D. 1024 under advice and direction of Gundulphus, dean of Saint-Wandrille. The new church of Saint-Wandrille and the cloister of Sainte-Trinité were dedicated on the same day (Fawtier, p. 363).

25. Weigand, p. 290; cf. Anonymous, ed. Poncelet, chap. 11, p. 435. The abbey was dissolved s. xvi (Henry IV) and the relics disappeared (Assion, *Mirakel,* p. 234, after Knust).

26. Pp. 344 ff. It should be unnecessary to refute Guéry's thesis that the Norman cult of N originated in the Translation, A.D. 1087 ("Origine du culte de Saint-Nicolas").

27. C. W. Jones, *Liturgy,* p. 65.

28. *Revue de chant grégorien* V, 4 (1896), 51; cf. III, 10 (1895), 147 - 149; IX (1900), 49 - 52. In the last he transcribed both words and music of both the Response *Ex eius tumba* and the Prose *Sospitati.*

29. C. W. Jones, *Liturgy,* p. 68. Text in *Analecta Hymnica* XLIV, n. 196, pp. 179 - 180 (Chevalier *Repert. Hymn.,* n. 19244). No. 19243 (*Anal. Hymn.* X, 224; *Anal. Liturg.* I, 485) with verbatim incipit and duplicative throughout is a Prose to C; there are 4 other C Proses with the same incipit (nos. 19239 - 19242).

30. Texts in C. W. Jones, *Liturgy,* pp. 30 - 31.

31. See chap 2, iii, *"Myrrh 18."*

32. C. W. Jones, *Liturgy,* pp. 64 - 68. Cheroul, pp. xiii - xv, demonstrates that there were three outstanding schools in Normandy: Saint-Wandrille, Bec, and Sainte-Trinité.

33. "He was generously imbued with both sciences [human and divine], and exceptionally skilled in versifying, modulating, and notating melodic songs. This can clearly be seen in the historiae of Kilian, bishop of Würzburg, and the virgin Catherine, and in many other musical compositions." Orderic, *Hist. Eccl.* IV, xix (ed. Le Provost II [1849], 392; *Pat. Lat.* CLXXXVIII, 368, c. xxiv). A tetrasyllabic rhymed sequence (Kehrein, n. 618, pp. 419 - 420; Daniel II, n. 116, pp. 89 - 92) on the Franconian missionaries Kilian, Colonatus, and Totanus, may be the composition referred to. The literary allusions to this missionary trio in Franconia induced a special

emphasis on Trinity (as did Daniel's Three Boys, above), which may have entered into the last-minute change in dedication of the Rouen abbey from Saint Andrew to Holy Trinity.

34. At Würzburg Isambert could have studied beside Heribert, who became bishop of Eichstätt (1021 - 1042), composer of several well-known N compositions. His successor at Eichstätt was Gebhard (1042 - 1057), who became Pope Victor II, an N devotee who was the first of the reforming popes responsible for the N chapel in the Lateran (see chap. 4, iii). His successor at Eichstätt was Gundechar (1057 - 1075), a myroblyte to be mentioned later in this chapter.

35. Anonymous, ed. Poncelet, p. 426: *Nam ad eius tumba rivus olei indeficienter manare videtur.* Assion, *Mirakel,* pp. 180 - 181, records later verbally similar texts. For the cult of Saint Andrew at Patra, *manna* is the common word; for Menas, *liquor.* The word-play μυρον-Μυρα doubtless accounts for the attachment of *myrrh* to N.

36. C. W. Jones, *Liturgy,* chap. 7.

37. E.g., Jacobus de Voragine (ed. Graesse, p. 794): *Ex cuius ossibus indesinenter oleum emanat, quod cunctorum debilium membra sanat.*

38. Chevalier, *Repertorium Hymnologicum,* 1892 - 1921. Indeed, only Mary and Peter surpassed C; even Stephen fell behind. She had four times as many compositions as Cecilia, 35% more than N or Barbara, twice as many as Lawrence and Margaret. Except for a hymn which he misdated, Chevalier cited no C hymn earlier than Isambert.

39. Once attributed to Adam of Saint Victor, but certainly composed around the year 1000.

40. *Oxford Book of Medieval Latin Verse,* n. 116, p. 160; *Anal. Hymn.* LXVIII, n. 66, p. 67.

41. *Anal. Hymn.* LV, 296 - 298; cf. n. 204, pp. 231 - 232, s. xii.

42. N. 10249, without evidence. Mone III, 456 - 458, lists several MSS of s. xii, none earlier; nor have I discovered earlier ones (cf. Daniel II, 252 - 254; V, 124).

43. It was the crusaders who created a demand for oil at Sinai, which then began to flow (C. W. Jones, "Norman Cult," p. 230). Mone III, no. 988, p. 353, lines 27 - 32; cf. no. 995, pp. 357 - 358, s. xiv. Van de Walle discusses evidences of Flemish pilgrims to Sinai where they were "tout heureux d'obtenir quelques gouttes de l'huile qui émanait de sa dépouille" (p. 120). But none of the pilgrimages was earlier than s. xv. Indeed, the one document transcribed in full (pp. 137 - 142), though most detailed and specific about

the relics, does not mention the oil. It may well be that Van de Walle drew his statement about the oil from other documents and descriptions cited in the notes pp. 119 - 121.

44. Though the C historia is extant, it has not been edited to determine original parts and accretions. Dom Pothier transcribed the words and music of the Response *Virgo flagellatur* from that Office (*Revue du chant grégorien* V, 4 [1896], 49 - 52); cf. Collette, pp. 147 - 148.

45. Fragments of fingerbone, for which an iconography was supplied by the N historia at hand.

46. *Cat. Cod. Hag. Brux.* II, 168, from MS 7917, s. xiv: "Sicque multi scholares et rectores affectati, devotissime huic gloriosae virgini servierunt, et historiam eius cum magna diligentia didicerunt et exposuerunt et suis temporibus usque solemniter decantaverunt."

47. *BHL* no. 1658. *Bibliotheca Casinensis* III, Florilegium p. 74, ca. an. 1000. Varnhagen, *Geschichte,* pp. 2 - 5.

48. *BHL* no. 1660. Bruxelles MS B.R. 9810 - 14, fo. 53^V, s. xii/xiii, from Saint-Laurent, Liège (*Cat. Cod. Hag. Brux.* II, 373 - 374). Ed. Varnhagen, *Geschichte,* pp. 10 - 18, from CLM 1133, fo. 50^V, s. xii^2. "Arechis" used a Greek Passio redone by pseudo-Athanasius, possibly later than Symeon (the earliest MS is s. xii): Assion, *Mirakel,* pp. 105 - 106, 112, 120 ff. Though telling of the angelic translation to Mount Sinai, pseudo-Athanasius said nothing of oil or marble tomb.

49. *BHL* nos. 1659, 1663. MSS Brux. B.R. 7917 and 7959 (both from Utrecht, s. xiv), *Cat. Cod. Hag. Brux.* II, pp. 175 - 177, give the N wording to C: " . . . ex eius tumba marmorea . . . oleum effluxit." They are the earliest MSS to give the legend of the Invention: "Fuit suae inventionis primum celebrata festivitas anno ab incarnatione Domini millesimo octogesimo quinto."

50. Varnhagen, *Geschichte,* pp. 2 - 3.

51. *Anal. Boll.* I, 78.

52. Cheroul, p. 3, ann. 1031. A Prince Arechis, evidently one responsible for the translation of Saint Martin of Montemarsico, is mentioned in the Vita S. Martini of Peter the Deacon (*BHL* no. 5604); see *Anal. Boll.* LXII (1944), 18, n. 2.

53. Père Coens, "Légende et miracles de S. Richard," *Anal. Boll.* LXIX (1931), 361 - 373. Günter, *Legenden-Studien,* p. 156; Thompson, V, 221.0.1.1. Hermann-Mascard, pp. 68 - 69 and n. 285, reports that a list of western myroblytes appears in M. D. Marchant, *Aspects economiques du culte des reliques*

du xie au xiiie siècle, Mémoire de maîtrise déposé à la Sorbonne en 1969, p. 18.

54. Mone III, n. 901, pp. 283 - 284.

55. Laroche, p. 303.

56. Jacobus de Voragine, CLXVIII, 4, p. 767.

57. Assion, *Mirakel,* p. 144, lists them; cf. pp. 177 - 189.

58. J. C. M. Laurent, ed., *Magister Thietmari Peregrinatio* (1857), p. 20, quoted by Assion, *Mirakel,* p. 147; cf. pp. 133 ff.

59. On C's scholastic patronage see Assion, *Mirakel,* p. 351.

60. Matthaeus Parisiensis, ed. Wats, p. 56; cf. Knowles, pp. 187 - 188. So important was the instance that London B.M. MS Cotton Claud. E IV, fo. 108, has a portrait of Geoffrey in the act of composing the play: "Ubi quendam ludum de sancta Katarina quem miracula vulgariter appellamus fuit." (Merryweather, *Bibliomania* [New York, 1900] , p. 256). Carlton Brown in *Studies in Philology* XXVIII (1931), 62 - 69.

61. *Revue d'ethnographie* VIII (1927), 210; in IX (1928), pp. 22 ff., Van Gennep records Saint Andrew school verses, e.g.: *Saint-André / Crucifié / Fais-moi voir / Mon amant.*

62. Haskins, *Normans,* p. 22.

4 Knighthood
§I KNIGHTHOOD

1. *American Heritage Dictionary* 1969, p. 1550, root *yeu*².

2. Isidore, *Etym.* XI, ii, 16.

3. Francis Bacon, "Of Youth and Age."

4. *Ferocitas iuvenum* (Cicero, *De senectute* x, 33); *fervidi iuvenes* (Horace, *Carmina* IV, xiii, 26).

5. Oldenbourg, pp. 14, 86.

6. "While knighthood was avoided by poor nobles, it was coveted by rich citizens" (*EB* XV, 859D). Warfare changed into a business as nationality developed (p. 860). *Neptunus equestris est, quem Graeci hippion vocarunt* (Tertullian, *Pat. Lat.* I, 641; cf. Augustine, ibid., XLI, 119, 207 - 212).

7. Quoted by Shears in Prestage, p. 60.

8. Chronicles of the Crusades were apt to be entitled *Gesta Francorum* whether the knights were Franks, Flemish, North or South Normans, or Lombards.

9. In a most popular early medieval textbook, *De temporum ratione,* cc. viii - x, Bede instructed scholars in the *octo species hebdomadis,* the eight kinds

of temporal sevens: the calendar week, the week of Creation, the pentecostal week ($7^2 + 1$). the annual week (of 1st, 3d, and 7th month), the seventh year of fallow fields, the Year of Jubilee ($7^2 + 1$), the weeks of Daniel, and the Seven Ages. A standard exposition of this medieval manner of thought is Erich Auerbach's essay "Figura."

10. Oldenbourg, p. 43.

11. Painter, chap. 2, pp. 30 ff.

12. Psalms A.V. cvii, 23 - 24 = Vulg. cvi.

13. Psalms A.V. cxlviii, 12 - 13. *Damiani Sermo lix, De S. Nicolao, vi Dec., Pat. Lat.* CXLIV, 835 - 839. See also Kressner, p. 34.

14. Bernard of Clairvaux, the voice of the Second Crusade, justified the combination of religiosity and rapacity in his *De laudibus novae militiae.*

15. Pope Urban II (Epist. cxxxvii, *Pat. Lat.* CLI, 410 - 412) lists some sixty churches and priories obedient to Cluny, not one dedicated to N.

§ II THE NORMANS OF SOUTHERN ITALY

1. The earliest Latin hymns were composed in Italy in the 9th century, one in rhythmic Horatian sapphics, the other in Ambrosian octosyllabics (A. F. Ozanam, *Documents inédites* [1850], pp. 232, 234; repr. *Pat. Lat.* CLI, 813 - 814. Cf. Albrecht, pp. 13 ff.). Two 11th-century hymnographers of note are Alphanus of Salerno (1058 - 1085) and Alberich of Monte Cassino (d. 1088). Meisen, pp. 67 - 69, gives a long list of N foundations inspired by Monte Cassino and follows with a list of other south Italian churches, pp. 69 - 70. On p. 59 he gives an incomplete list of N churches in the city of Rome of the 10th and 11th centuries.

2. Michael Huber, ed., *Johannes Monomachus, Liber de Miraculis,* A. Hilka, Sammlung mittellateinische Texte 7 (1913); Manitius II, 422 - 424.

3. "Ductus amore quesivi et inveni, et non in qualibuscunque scedulis sed in archivis et emendatis codicibus." Hofmeister in *Münchener Museum* IV (1924), 135 - 138, from Vienna MS Lat. 739, s. xii. There is also a Vallicelli MS of the same age in Rome.

4. Hofmeister says the name Magnentius may be a corruption of *magnatus.*

5. Citarella, esp. pp. 301 - 303.

6. *CMH* V, p. 167.

7. A church was dedicated to N and others in Arezzo 2 Nov. 1058 (Meisen, p. 60).

8. Edited with Italian translation by Mons. Carmine de Palma in *Iapigia* VIII (1937), 275 - 294, text p. 290. Cf. Babudri in *Collana,* no. 4, p. 7.

9. *Anal Hymn.* L, 330 - 338; *Pat. Lat.* CXLVII, 1228 - 1229; Chevalier no. 17500.

10. Gay, p. 378.

11. *CMH*, V, chap. 4; cf. Glaber III, i; Norwich, chaps. 2 - 3; Haskins, *Normans*, pp. 192 - 200.

12. Barlow, pp. 10 - 11.

13. Haskins, *Studies,* p. 95; Douglas, esp. chap. 6, pp. 110 - 29, 214.

14. According to the contemporary verse-chronicler, William of Apulia:

> *Cognomen Guiscardus erat, quia calliditatis*
> *Non Cicero tantae fuit aut versutus Ulixes.*

15. Haskins, *Normans,* pp. 192 - 200; Norwich, chap. 6; Yewdale, p. 3.

16. The Palermo Breviary accorded N red letter and 9 lessons (Giovanni di Giovanni, *De divinis Siculis officiis* [Palermo 1936], p. 355). Pitra studied 150 of 357 Sicilian communes and found only two dedications to N (*Anal. Boll.* XXI, p. 96).

17. *Art Bulletin,* December 1949.

18. For the Sicilian sea cult of Nicolo-Pesce, which inspired Schiller, see Anichkof, p. 115, n. 3.

19. Haskins, *Normans,* p. 202.

20. *CMH* II, 384. For Barian history I rely strongly on Petroni.

21. *MGH, Scriptores* VII, p. 17; Dvornik, pp. 33 - 34, 53; Deanesly, pp. 455 - 458. For Bari at the visit of Bernard the Monk (s. ix), see Avril and Gaborit, p. 298.

22. Schlumberger II, 308, 320 - 322.

23. Heyd I (1885), 96.

24. An Exultet Roll of ca. 1000 which has survived preserves a miniature of N. Gambacorta, pp. 490 - 491, gives as evidence of N cult in Bari before 1087 a church dedication, a court, and a city gate; opp. p. 496 a depiction of Saints Basil and N with Christ in a wind rota found in the Exultet Roll.

25. *Anal. Boll.* XXII (1903), p. 354.

26. Meisen, pp. 63 - 66.

27. Yewdale, p. 10.

28. Ibid., pp. 9, 22 - 23; Vasiliev II (1932), 9 - 11.

29. Anna Comnena, *Alexiad IV,* 5.

30. Ibid.; Yewdale, pp. 11 - 16; Dawes and Baynes, p. 105.

31. Norwich, p. 200.

32. Alexius, says Orderic, committed to their guardianship his principal

palace and royal treasure (*Orderici* IV, 3), trans. Forester.

33. Yewdale, pp. 23 - 24.

§III THE PAPACY

1. Amann, in Fliche VII, 98 - 101.

2. Norwich, p. 80.

3. Gastoué, pp. 89 - 90.

4. The year before he was ordained bishop (1027) he had accompanied Conrad II on his Italian expedition.

5. "Si audiret totius cleri ac Romani populi communem esse sine dubio consensum."

6. Norwich, p. 81.

7. The word was used in Cardinal Humbert's Bull of Excommunication, 1054, and may have spread from there.

8. Meisen, pp. 85, 507.

9. Donnet, *Origines,* pp. 112 - 113.

10. Amann, in Fliche VII, 98 - 101.

11. *Viarum premonstratores* = *marones.*

12. Glaber III, i, p. 53.

13. Donnet, *Origines,* p. 109.

14. Ibid., p. 124.

15. *Acta SS,* Jun. XV.

16. van Gennep in *Revue d'ethnographie* IX (1928), pp. 32 ff.

17. *Acta SS,* Jun. XV, p. 350: "Audiens post in scholis grammatica innumera relatari miracula S. Praesulis Nicolai, Mirae maritimae . . . Bernardus Menthonista suscipiens ipsius S. Nicolai exemplo, a praedictis montibus Iovis . . . . Et suscepit ipsum sanctum Nicolaum in sui patronum et directorem . . . . Quod quidem coenobium [Montis Iovi] et aliud in altero monti Columnae Iovis, ambo sub nomine S. Nicolai pro patrocinio . . .," etc.

18. *Acta SS,* Jun. XV, p. 557.

19. Fliche VII, 98 - 101.

20. Humbert, author of *Adversus simoniacos libri III,* was especially denunciatory. Fliche VII, 98 - 101; Norwich, pp. 97 - 105.

21. Bloch, p. 191.

22. Ibid.; Leib, p. xxxi.

23. Norwich, p. 110.

24. Amann XI, i, 526 - 531.

25. *Speculum* XLIV (1969), 485. Before he died in 1087, William began a munificent church of Saint Nicholas, to the north of the Abbaye-aux-Hommes, which is still standing.

26. *Vendôme Annals,* Oxford MS Bodl. 309, fo. 3ʳ; Traill III, p. 27.

27. Amann XI, i, 527 - 530.

28. Ambroise, p. 77; Amann XI, i, 527 - 530.

29. Haskins, *Normans,* p. 204; Norwich, p. 127.

30. *CMH* V, 179; Yewdale, pp. 19 - 20.

31. M. R. Vincent, pp. 94 - 95.

32. Haskins, *Normans,* p. 205.

33. Duchesne, *Liber Pontificalis* (Paris 1892), II, 323; Meisen, pp. 91, 111 - 113; J. B. de Rossi in *Revue de l'art chrétien* XXVI (1883), pp. 196 - 224. In the 12th and 13th centuries its remarkable monuments were subject of remark throughout Europe, but in the 18th century it was completely demolished. A painting in the most sacred position in the chapel depicted N, surrounded by popes Alexander II, Gregory VII, Victor III, Urban II, and Pascal II (de Rossi, p. 198). On pp. 199 - 201 de Rossi emphasizes how Peter of Pisa, in composing the Lifes of these popes, applied to Urban II the phrase drawn from the Pontifical Life of Nicholas I *bonus Christi athleta.* Monsignor Barbier de Montault treats the frescoes of the chapel in *Mémoires de la Commission des Antiquités du Département de la Côte d'Or* VIII (1893), 192 - 194.

§IV THE TRANSLATION

1. Lindsay, pp. 399 - 401; Leib, appendix, pp. 327 ff. For the general topic of theft of relics, see P. Heliot and M. L. Chastang, "Quêtes et voyages de reliques," *Revue d'histoire ecclésiastique* LIX (1964), 789 - 822, LX (1965), 5 - 32; Hermann-Mascard, pp. 364 - 402 (on the pillage of Constantinople, pp. 369 - 372).

2. *Epist.* lxxviii, 3 (A.D. 404), *Pat. Lat.* XXXIII, 268 - 269.

3. *Epist.* IV, xxx (ed. P. Ewald and Hartmann, *MGH,* Berlin, 1887). The empress had *demanded* that Gregory send her "the head of St. Paul or some other portion of his body."

4. Acts x, 34.

5. I Cor. xii, 8 ff.

6. Ibid.

7. Anrich II, 514 ff. Antioch fell to the Arabs A.D. 638, was recaptured by Nicephorus Phocas in 969, and was taken by the Turks in 1085. Ebersolt I, 74 - 75; Yewdale, p. 52.

NOTES TO PAGES 173 - 176

8. Meisen, pp. 84 - 87.

9. Anrich I, 450; Muralt, p. 392.

10. xxvi, 8 (Anrich II, 270 - 271).

11. Marin, pp. 149 ff.

12. Muralt, p. 612; Chalandon, *Règne d'Alexis,* pp. 148 - 149, 279 - 280.

13. J. B. Bury in *EB* XXIII, p. 515.

14. Dawes, p. 4.

15. Aigrain, pp. 186 - 189.

16. Gen. v, 22; Eccl. xliv, 16; Hebr. xi, 5.

17. Fliche V, 518; Laistner, p. 279.

18. Delehaye, *Sanctus,* pp. 202 ff.; Silvestre, "Commerce," pp. 731 ff.; de Gaiffier, "Hagiographie salernitaine. La translation de saint Matthieu," *Anal. Boll.* LXXX (1962), 82 - 110.

19. The Hieronymian Martyrology, 5th cent., the earliest documentary statement, puts his death in a city in Persia.

20. Bloch, pp. 213 - 214.

21. Southern, *Middle Ages,* pp. 247 - 248; Loomis, p. 97. Guibert of Nogent, *Autobiography* II, i, trans. C. C. Swinton Bland (London, 1926), pp. 104 - 110. Though Theofrid (d. 1110) published after 1100 and knew the events of the First Crusade, he pictured N's corpse as still in Myra (*Flores Epitaphii Sanctorum* iii, 5, *Pat. Lat.* CLVII, 380). In the N church at Marseilles are N bones from Myra "authenticated" 3 April 1867 (Kayata, p. 30).

22. T. Wright, pp. 33 - 34; Runciman II, 480. *The Travels of Sir John Mandeville* (14th cent.): "We go through many islands in the sea to the city of Patara, where St. Nicholas was born, and so to Myra, where he was chosen to be bishop" (Bohn edition and modernization, chap. 4).

23. Armando's groundplan and photographs of interior and environs are helpful. Leib, pp. 51 ff.

24. Bk. VII, chap. xii (*Pat. Lat.* CLXXXVIII, 539). It contains, col. 537, a "lament of the Myrans" in 20 distichs.

25. Matthew Paris, *Historia maior,* an. 1087, ed. Wats (1640), p. 13.

26. *Archaeological Journal* 1888, pp. 232 - 233, lines 321 - 374.

27. E.g. *Chron. S. Maxentii Pictavensis,* ed. Marchegay II, 409; *Chronicon Novalicense* in *MGH, Scriptores* VII; others in *Scriptores* IV, 21, 29; V, 62.

28. Trans. Ryan and Ripperger, Jacobus de Voragine, p. 765.

29. *BHL* no. 6179. I use as text Nitti 1937, derived from Vatican MS. Lat. 5074. The other readily available printed edition, in *Anal. Boll.* IV (1885), 169 - 192 [*BHL* no. 6186], transcribed from Ghent MS 289, compared with

Ghent MS 499, is a weird conflation of Nicephorus' with Archdeacon John's account, at times virtually incomprehensible because of its inflated rhetoric. The Vatican MS was used in the 18th cent. by Falconius, pp. 131 - 138. His text closely agrees with Nitti di Vito's, and I believe that they quite accurately represent what Nicephorus wrote. Falconius also edited the anonymous Greek account (abridged) and Archdeacon John's account as well. Another version, based on the Beneventan MS, edited by Putignani (Naples 1771), pp. 551 - 568, had wide circulation (see Anrich II, 171 - 173, et passim). Leib, chap. 3, pp. 51 - 74. For no convincing reasons the date of translation has been questioned; a full summary of the authenticating evidence appears in *Anal. Boll.* LIX (1941), 337.

30. Author unknown.

31. In 1362 a fleet of Pierre de Lusignan, a last Crusader, took the town of Myra and transported to Cyprus the image of N, supposedly this one, which is also at Antalya. Bréhier, *Eglise,* pp. 297 - 305, sketches the life of this fascinating man.

32. *BHL,* pp. 896 - 897, cites editions and paraphrases; however, it does not list the more recent edition of Francesco Nitti di Vito in *Iapigia* VIII (1937), 357 - 366, which I have used for any quotations here. It is derived from Vatican MS Lat. 477 (s. xii), fos. 29 - 38. To judge by the number of surviving MSS and use by later writers, John's account (*John the Archdeacon 51*) found wider circulation than did *Nicephorus' 50*. Additions to it snowballed, so that *BHL* lists it in eight parts with two variants (nos. 6190 - 6199), only the first of which I take to be John's original composition. Gambacorta, p. 490, says without substantiation that both Nicephorus and John wrote in 1088; but this comparatively late date must be based only on Ursus' death in February 1089. On Ursus see Masellis, pp. 88 - 89; Petroni I, 191. I have not accepted the theory cogently expressed by Gambacorta, that the translation was secretly planned during the preceding year by opponents of antipope Clement III (Guibert, archbishop of Ravenna), led by Elias, in opposition to the cathedral chapter, represented by Ursus: "E fu una preparazione fatta in segretezza, perché allora, negli anni 1086 - 1087 la cattedrale di Bari era scismatica, aderente cioè all'antipapa . . ." (p. 497); but interested readers should review the evidence which Gambacorta presents.

33. Ed. Nitti, "Leggenda," p. 361, lines 132 - 133.

34. Lalanne, p. 131.

35. Gambacorta, p. 490, says this *gerosolimitana* was composed saec. xiii^2. See Leib, p. 63.

36. *Archiv für Liturgiewissenschaft* X (Regensburg 1967), p. 175.

37. Bartolini, p. 3; Falconi, pp. 139 - 140.

38. I take what follows directly from Leib, pp. 66 - 74.

39. Thurston IV, 506.

40. Hooker, p. 93.

41. Nitti, *Pergamene* II, 64, 279 ff, replacing Petroni I, 199.

42. Nitti, *Pergamene* II, pp. 33 - 49.

43. Loomis, pp. 56 - 57, 88 - 89, 92, 265.

44. Dawkins II, 64.

45. Delehaye, *Sanctus,* p. 224.

46. *Orderici* VII, 12 - 13, pp. 384 - 395. Cf. below, *Monachus Beccensis,* chap. 5, i, n. 12.

47. Ed. Nitti in *Iapigia,* n.s. VIII (1937), p. 358; Falconi, p. 186.

48. Ronsjö, p. 13.

49. Labande, "Recherches," p. 344.

50. Distinctis viii, cc. 67 - 68.

51. Riant, passim; Sumption, passim (on sale and theft of relics, pp. 31 - 40).

§V BARI

1. The standard local history is that of Lupus Protospatarius, *Barensis Chronicon,* 855 - 1102, ed. *MGH, Scriptores* V, pp. 52 - 63.

2. Meisen, pp. 337 - 338; for pilgrimages to Italy, esp. Monte Gargano, Bari, Tarento, and Mons Aureus, see Avril and Gaborit.

3. See de Rossi, *Codici.*

4. Meisen, p. 338.

5. Meisen, pp. 61 - 62; cf. pp. 108 - 111.

6. Engel, pp. 38 - 39.

7. *Historia inventionis sancti Sabini,* as in Ruinart's *Vita Urbani* in *Pat. Lat.* CLI, 58 - 59.

8. *Revue de l'art chrétien* XXVI (1883), 289, 456; Bartolini, p. 14.

9. In the canopy of the altar is an unusual plaque of N crowning Roger.

10. Bartolini, p. 8; *Revue de l'art chrétien* XXVI, 279.

11. Hagenmeyer, p. 167. An excellent triptych of Virgin and Child with the Baptist (type of monasticism) and N (type of prelacy) in *Bari città*, p. 53. In the year 1102 Roger, king of Sicily and duke of Bari, issued a diploma forbidding "reliquiis corporis sancti Nicolai nullo aut quolibet ingenio extra-

here vel extrahi facere de civitate Bari vel omnem vel partem." (Hermann-Mascard, p. 332).

12. Meisen, pp. 95 ff.

13. *Chron. Mon. Casinensis* III, auctore Petro, 68 (*MGH, Scriptores* VII, 749 - 750). Fliche VIII, 176 - 177; Bloch, p. 218.

14. A specimen grant in Petroni I, 206, made by Maurelianus Proedrus [Προέδρος] and Catapan and Dominator *de loco rutiliano* before Elias became bishop. Excellent color reproductions of deeds of endowments in *Bari città,* pp. 41 - 47. Hermann-Mascard, pp. 275 - 296, treats the general topic of monetary income from relics.

15. Clapham reproduces several views.

16. For documents on the church see de Rossi, *Codici,* indexes s.v. S. Nicolai. Color photographs in *Bari città,* pp. 35 ff. See also Francesco Babudri, "La cripta di San Nicola a Bari sei suoi alti valori di storia e d'arte," *Collana,* no. 2, 1963 (with photographs).

17. "After the death of William, king of England [William the Conqueror d. 1087, the year of the Translation] William Pantoul made another visit to Apulia, and on his return brought with him the relics of the body of the holy Confessor of Christ, St. Nicholas, with which he enriched the church of Noron [Normandy]."—Orderic Vitalis V, 17.

18. Hooker, pp. 88 - 89, 93.

19. *Revue de l'art chrétien* XXVI (1883), 280.

20. See, for example, Dante's *De monarchia* II, iv, in which he unconvincingly tries to counteract its effect on his readers.

21. *Revue de l'art chrétien* XXVI (1883), 280.

22. Meisen, pp. 100 - 102.

23. Ibid., p. 105. See this vol., chap. 5, v.

24. Nitti, "San Nicola," pp. 321 - 328; *Revue de l'art chrétien* XXVI (1883), 294; XXVII (1884), 47 - 53; *Bari città,* p. 57, pl. 28 - 29.

25. *Speculum ecclesiae,* ed. 1531, fo. 290 f. Color photographs of myrrh bottles and containers from s. xvii - xix (Collezioni Giovanni Conte e Umberto Colonna) in *Bari città,* p. 58, pl. 30 - 32.

26. Meisen, p. 105.

27. *Revue de l'art chrétien* XXVI (1883), 297 - 298.

28. Cf. ibid., pp. 300 - 304.

29. Ibid., pp. 307 - 308.

30. Labande, "Recherches," passim. N had his own chapel in the basilica of Saint James at Compostella (ibid., p. 159, n. 4).

31. Meisen, p. 105.

32. Ibid., p. 123; Réau, p. 977.

33. Meisen, pp. 121 - 122.

34. Ibid., pp. 122 - 123.

35. June 2. *BHL* nos. 6223 - 6226.

36. Catedrale San Nicola Trani, consecrated A.D. 1143. "The structure is one of the few of the period whose architect is known—Nicolaus Sacerdos" (*McGraw-Hill Dictionary of Art* V, [1969] , p. 86).

37. C. 337 (*Pat. Lat.* CLI, 252); Petroni I, 217 - 221.

38. For the dolphin-rider theme see *Archeology* XXIII (1970), 86 - 95.

39. The Acts by Bartholomew ed. *Acta SS* Jn. II, p. 235; The Acts by Adelferius, p. 245. Urban's *Epist.* ccxv (*Pat. Lat.* CLI, 448) states the details.

40. A.D. 1097. This is an early instance of papal canonization; the first was in 993. We have treated the canonization of Symeon in chap. 3, vii. See also chap. 1, i, n. 5.

41. Réau, p. 988.

42. Leib, pp. 96 - 98.

43. *BHL* no. 6206. Edited by M. le Ch. Cangiano, *Leggenda agiografica della fine del secolo XI* (Benevento 1925), 36 pp. On relic-rivalry see below, chap. 5, i, n. 12.

44. *Anal. Boll.* L (1932), 179, 228.

45. See above, chap. 2, iii.

46. *Anal. Boll.* LXII (1944), 28 - 29.

47. *BHL* nos. 6200 - 6204. Falconi, pp. 140 - 144; *Recueil des historiens des croisades* V, 254 - 292; Leib, p. 56; Meisen, pp. 116 - 118.

48. McNeal, p. 39; Diehl et al., *Europe,* p. 126.

49. Chevalier, *Repertoire,* s.v. "Nicolas."

50. Meisen, pp. 116 - 118.

§VI POPE URBAN II

1. *Epist.* cvii (*Pat. Lat.* CLI).

2. On the climate of opinion, see Bréhier, *Eglise,* p. 54.

3. Yewdale, p. 31.

4. The patriarch of Constantinople with whom he negotiated was Nicholas III.

5. *Epist.* xxvi (5 Oct.), *Pat. Lat.* CLI, 307 - 309.

6. Mansi, *Concilia* XX (1775), 645 - 646; Meisen, pp. 96 - 97; *Revue de l'art chrétien* XXVI (1883), 286.

7. According to Orderic Vitalis.

8. Gathered in *Pat. Lat.* CLI.

9. Fliche VIII, 247 ff.

10. Ibid., p. 265.

11. Ibid., p. 284. However, as suggested below, it seems to have emerged at the Council of Clermont. In 1087, the year of N's Translation, Count Robert of Flanders swore fidelity to Emperor Alexius and supplied knights to help him (Bréhier, *Eglise,* p. 59).

12. The Letter of Convocation in *Pat. Lat.* CLI, 422; Crozet, pp. 271 - 310.

13. Ruinart in *Pat. Lat.* CLI, 158; *Epist.* 150, col. 425.

14. *Epist.* ccii (*Pat. Lat.* CLI, 472) dated at Saint Gilles, confirms the privileges of the great Spanish abbey of Ripoll, with chapel dedicated to N.

15. Fliche VIII, 270 ff.; Bréhier, *Eglise,* p. 62.

16. Harrison, p. 225.

17. Bréhier, *Eglise,* p. 63. Ruinart, cc. 204 - 206, discusses numbers (*Pat. Lat.* CLI, 163 - 168).

18. *EB* XXI, 378.

19. *Recueil . . . croisades* III, 727 ff.; trans. Munro, *Urban,* pp. 5 - 8.

20. *Epist.* ccxxii, *Pat. Lat.* CLI, 394, from Mansi XX, 713.

21. Bréhier, *Eglise,* p. 64; Ruinart, *Vita Urbani,* cc. 240 - 246 (*Pat. Lat.* CLI, 192 - 196).

22. His Acts, dated viii Id. and v Id. Feb. 1096, in *Pat. Lat.* CLI, 445 - 447. Halphen, *Recueil,* pp. 6, 89, 93; Marchegay and Salmon, pp. 380 - 381.

23. *Epist. Papae Urbani clxxv,* ed. Ruinart, c. 246 (*Pat. Lat.* CLI, 447 - 448). See the report of Fulk Rechin (*Pat. Lat.* CLI, 282).

24. Ruinart edition, c. 242 (*Pat. Lat.* CLI, 444).

25. At Fulk's request Urban translated Geoffrey's body from the chapter house to the new chapel (ibid.; Marchegay and Salmon, pp. 380 - 381).

26. Ruinart, c. 243 (*Pat. Lat.* CLI, 445).

27. Bréhier, *Eglise,* p. 65.

28. Ruinart, c. 244 (*Pat. Lat.* CLI, 446).

29. LeMoy, pp. 82 - 84.

30. *Pat. Lat.* CLXXI, 748 - 752.

31. Ruinart, c. 242 (*Pat. Lat.* CLI, 444).

32. Ruinart, c. 243 (ibid., col. 445).

33. Ruinart, c. 242 (*Pat. Lat.* CLI, 444).

34. *Revue de l'art chrétien* XXVI (1883), 289 - 291.

35. *Pat. Lat.* CLI, 273 - 276. He was still at Tours 25 March, issuing a privilege to Nicholas, abbot of Corbie (*Pat. Lat.* CLI, 202).

36. E.g. *Pat. Lat.* CLI, 206 (Neracus in Gascony).

37. On 29 April at Poitiers he addressed an encyclical to all Gallican bishops confirming the privileges of Saint Martin of Tours (*Pat. Lat.* CLI, 459, *Epist.* clxxxvi²); compare his effusiveness there with his measured statements about N. He had very recently (17 Oct. 1093) confirmed Cluniac possession of an N church "built outside the walls of Poitiers by Countess Agnes" in 1062 (Meisen, p. 128), *Epist.* lxxxvii (*Pat. Lat.* CLI, 367 - 368; cf. *Epist.* cxcii, col. 465). This is out of consonance with Note 1 above.

38. For documents, de Rossi I, 59 - 65.

39. Ruinart, c. 324 (*Pat. Lat.* CLI, 242).

40. Southern, *Middle Ages,* p. 251.

41. Ruinart, c. 315 (*Pat. Lat.* CLI, 236).

42. William of Malmesbury I, liii, p. 98.

43. Ruinart, c. 324 (*Pat. Lat.* CLI, 242).

44. *Eadmari Historia Novorum in Anglia,* ed. Martin Rule (Rolls Series, 1884), p. 104; Ruinart, c. 317 (*Pat. Lat.* CLI, 237).

45. Southern, *St. Anselm,* p. 36; Schmitt in *Revue Bénédictine* 1932, pp. 322 - 350, esp. p. 338.

46. Anselm, *Epist.* I, li (*Pat. Lat.* CLVIII, 1206).

47. Edited by F. S. Schmitt III (1956), 55 - 56.

48. Perhaps it is not amiss to note here an exceptional cult of N among archbishops of Canterbury. The blessed martyr Saint Thomas appeared to an exhausted officer of the royal navy in the midst of a tempest to assure him that he (Saint Thomas), Saint Edmund, and N had formed a triumvirate (or would it be a triunate?) to protect the royal navy from harm (Matthew Paris, *Historia maior an. 1190,* ed. Wats {1640}, p. 160).

49. *Revue de l'art chrétien* XXVI (1883), 286.

50. Ancelet-Hustache, p. 45.

51. Ruinart, *Vita Urbani,* c. 345 (*Pat. Lat.* CLI, 259).

§VII BOHEMOND AND THE FIRST CRUSADE

1. Yewdale, pp. 26 - 28; Norwich, p. 116.

2. Yewdale, p. 28.

3. Ibid., pp. 32 - 33.

4. Ibid., pp. 132 - 133.

5. "Complures per portum Sancti Nicolai Constantinopolim pervene-runt." (Marchegay and Salmon I, 382).

6. Franke, p. 9, after Du Méril, I, 172. Chevalier, *Répertoire* III, 407, nos. 30245 - 6.

7. Bréhier, *Eglise,* pp. 71 - 73; Marchegay and Salmon I, 382; Ruinart, *Vita Urbani,* c. 277 (*Pat. Lat.* CLI, 248).

8. C. W. David, p. 98; Hagenmeyer, pp. 166 - 167.

9. Yewdale, p. 34, after *Historia Regum* II (ed. Stubbs, Rolls Series, p. 390).

10. Ruinart, c. 292 (*Pat. Lat.* CLI, 226).

11. His army was small, often estimated at ca. 7500, probably with fewer than 500 knights (Oldenbourg, p. 86).

12. Anna Comnena, *Alexiad* x, 9 (p. 258).

13. According to Fulcher i, 2 (ed. Hagenmeyer, p. 167), Hugh's army joined at N's tomb in a fervent prayer for safe passage.

14. Marchegay and Salmon I, 380 - 381.

15. Bréhier, *Eglise,* pp. 71 - 73.

16. Setton I, 258 ff.

17. University of Pennsylvania Translations and Reprints I, 2, p. 22. This is also the story of Albert of Aix and Jacques de Vitry, but not others. *Revue de l'art chrétien* XXVI (1883), 306; Munro, p. 20.

18. Bréhier, *Eglise,* pp. 58 - 70. See a spurious letter of Urban II to Alexius, *Epist.* ccxii (*Pat. Lat.* CLI, 485).

19. *CMH* V, 275.

20. Guibert de Nogent, *Gesta Dei* II, iii.

21. Fliche VIII, 300; Oldenbourg, pp. 99 - 101. On his debt to the Genoese and Pisans, Yewdale, pp. 103 - 104.

22. See chap. 5, ii. Oldenbourg, pp. 108 - 111, 126. A very satisfactory treatment of this crusading incident is that of Runciman in *Anal. Boll.* LXVIII (1950), 197 - 209. He does not, however, mention N's part in the affair.

23. William of Tyre in *Recueil . . . croisades* I, 190.

24. Yewdale, p. 103.

25. Fliche VIII, 301.

26. Bréhier, *Eglise,* pp. 79 - 81; cf. *Anal. Boll.* XXVII (1908), 169.

27. Yewdale, pp. 102 - 106.

28. Ibid., p. 107.

29. Annals of Renaud, ed. Halphen, *Receuil,* pp. 89 - 90.

30. Yewdale, p. 115.

31. His tomb and the cathedral at Canosa are in the particular architectural style of the N basilica (*Revue de l'art chrétien* XXVI [1883], 279).

32. "Monastère," pp. 173 - 188.

33. Vincent, p. 365. *MGH, Scriptores* XXIII, 893. Bréhier, *Eglise,* p. 178.

34. Pernoud, p. 166.

35. *Histoire de Saint Louis,* ed. N. de Wailly (Paris, 1868), pp. 265 - 266.

36. *MGH, Scriptores* VI, 427. Bréhier, *Eglise,* p. 127. In the French legend of the Minstrel of Reims (c. 21) Saladin baptized himself as he was dying and was buried in that cemetery (Stone, p. 302).

37. Diehl, *Monde oriental* I, 514; Dawkins I, p. 93 #104 and p. 309 #324.

38. Dawkins I, 112 - 113, no. 127.

39. For example, Dante's two foremost enemies, Charles II of Anjou and Pope Boniface VIII, were outstanding devotees of N (see Meisen, pp. 102 - 106). Dante is quite obviously not a devotee.

40. Francesco Babudri, "San Nicola di Bari e il sui patronato sul mare nella storia e nel folklore internazionale," *Collana,* no. 4 (1964). Tobler reviews the total published and unpublished pilgrimage and crusade writing, A.D. 330 - 1866.

5 Maturity

1. Pope, *Essay on Man* ii, 13.

2. Robert Ulich, *The Human Career,* New York, 1955, p. 32.

3. Horace, *Art of Poetry* 166 - 168.

4. Paré, p. 19.

§1 THE LITERARY LIFES

5. *Cat. Cod. Hagr. Paris.* III, 158 - 162.

6. *BHL* no. 6178.

7. Perhaps the earliest of this class, Paris MS Lat. 18303, was probably written at Saint-Germain-des-Prés late in 11th cent. (*Scriptorium* IX [1955], p. 15).

8. *BHL* no. 6207 - 6208; *Cat. Cod. Hagr. Paris* II, 405 - 432. The Bec customary, recorded in a 14th cent. MS., gives the liturgy for N Day (*Consuetudines Beccensis,* 546 [*Corpus Consuetudinum Monasticarum* IV, 1967], p. 227).

9. Ch. 15, p. 413.

10. Ibid., chap. 20, p. 416.

11. Ibid., pp. 424 - 425.

12. Ibid., pp. 425 - 427; cf. above, chap. 4, iv, n. 46.

13. Ibid., p. 412.

14. *BHL* nos. 6214 - 6216. Ed. Th. Wright and J. O. Halliwell, *Reliquiae Antiquae* II (1843), 199 - 208, from which Du Méril, pp. 185 - 189; also Birch, pp. 223 ff.; Meisen, p. 77.

15. Cotton Tiberius B V, fos. 55^r-56^r, 73^{r-v}, 77^r.

16. Some hasty critics have interpreted *Post transitum Nicolai* at the opening of *Broken Staff 61* as *Post translationem* and asserted that therefore the version could not have been composed before 1087.

17. Rose Graham, *Archaeological Journal* XXXIII, i, p. 62. Heinrich Henel, *Studien zum altenglischen Computus* (Leipzig, 1934), p. 14, n. 41, suggests an Exeter origin.

18. The homeoteleuton here is not syllabic rhyme but assonance, as in Chanson de Roland.

19. Meisen, pp. 281 - 285; *BHL* no. 6133.

20. *Pat. Lat.* CLI, 814.

21. According to Meisen, a prose version existed in a Chartres MS almost contemporary with the Battle Abbey Life; but we cannot examine it, for all Chartres MSS were destroyed in a night bombing in 1944.

22. No. 15, ed. *Anal. Boll.* II (1883), 153 - 156.

23. *Anal. Hymn.* X, 277, str. 12a.

24. *Notes and Queries* XII, ii, p. 374.

25. *Don Quixote* ii, 45. *Broken Staff* appeared as early as 12th cent. in a Spanish Latin legendary now in the Royal Library (de Plancy II, p. 215).

26. An episode recently modernized in *Ellery Queen's Mystery Magazine*, Sept. 1964, pp. 97 - 98.

27. Cf. Giraldus Cambrensis, ed. Rolls Series 2, p. 156.

28. *Vita 24* (*Cat. Cod. Hagr. Paris.* II, 419 - 421). This is an early version of *Dazed Thieves 69*, to appear below.

29. Additional MS 18364, fo. 73^v.

30. Modern writers (e.g., Meisen) report that those three balls were the coat of arms of the Medici family. But the Medici arms were six red balls on a field of gold (*EB* XVIII, 31).

31. Meisen, p. 282.

32. E.g., in the chansons: *Bernier en jure le cors S. Nicolai* (Raoul de Cambrai 3162); *Son bon en fist, mais par saint Nicolai / Il n'en por rien, pas ne vous mentirai* (Anseïs de Carthage, 1844, ed. J. Alton, Tübingen 1892, p. 74).

33. Franke, pp. 5 - 6.

34. *BHL* nos. 6172 - 3. Meisen, pp. 276 - 280; Ronsjö, pp. 12 - 13. The

Namur MS 15 text in *Anal. Boll.* II (1883), 151 - 153.

35. List of Verbal Relics nos. 3, 4, 8, 19, 22, 29, 46.

36. *BHG* 1258.

37. Delehaye in *Anal. Boll.* L (1932), 180; cf. ibid. XXIX, p. 129. In the legendary of Metaphrast the Menas legend appears in the December section, very close to the Life of N (see *Pat. Gr.* CXVI, 367 ff.).

38. Without intending to catalogue examples, I list a few representative appearances of *Substituted Cup 62* among the extant artifacts:

SCULPTURE: Barga Cathedral, 12² c.; Winchester font (also Zedelghem), 12² c.; Lucca (2 scenes), 12² c.; Atri, 14 - 15 c.

WINDOWS: Civray (dioc. Tours), 12 c.; Tours Cathedral, 13 c.; Bourges Cathedral, 13 c.; Chartres Cathedral (2 windows: 27, 60), 13 c.; Cathedrals at Le Mans, Auxerre, 13 c.

PAINTED PANEL: Kakopetria, Cyprus, 14 c.

FRESCOES: Minuto, 12¹ c.; Assisi, A.D. 1316 - 1321; Florence, S. Croce, 14 - 15 c.; Montefiascone, 14 c.

TRIPTYCHS: Siena, A.D. 1336; Florence, Bargello, A.D. 1333; Berlin, A.D. 1334.

MINIATURES: Paris, Arsenal MS 5080, f. 309.

TEXTILES: Anagni, 13 - 14 c.

39. *Histoire Littéraire de la France* VIII, 445; Rouen MS Y. 41 (12 c.), fos. 305ʳ - 331ᵛ (see *Anal. Boll.* XXIII [1904], 224).

40. *Zeitschrift für das Alterthum* XXI (1877), Angaben p. 424.

41. *Bibliotheca Arnamagnaeana* XXV (1961), 17 - 33; *Scriptorium* XVI (1962), 226; Widding, pp. 326 - 327.

42. Meisen, p. 217.

43. Ed. Ronsjö, 1942. The sources dealt with by Ida Del Valle de Paz (1921) and Fissen (1921).

44. *En romanz dirat de sa vie*
   Et des miracles grant partie,
   En romanz dirai un petit
   De ceo qu'ai veü en escrit,
   Ke li lai le puissent aprendre
   Qui ne sevent latin entendre. [lines 38 - 43]

45. The contents, with line numbers, are:

Prologue 1 - 44

1. Parentage 10, 44 - 57

2. Lactation 11, 58 - 67

3. Education 12, 68 - 80

4. Three Daughters 13, 81 - 120

5. Bishop 14, 124 - 156

6. Boiled Infant 66, 160 - 194

7. Virtue as Bishop 1, 195 - 212

8. Three Clerks 44, 213 - 226

9. Mariners 6, 227 - 274

10. Grainships 7, 275 - 336

11. Diana 4, 337 - 444

12. Stratilates 3, 445 - 600

13. Miracles in general, death, and angels' appearance, Psalm: *In te Domine speravi* 67, 600 - 632

14. Tomb and Myrrh 18; Magnentius 49, 633 - 650

15. Iconia 34, 651 - 722

16. Broken Staff 61, 723 - 806

17. Substituted Cup 62, 807 - 934

18. Son of Getron 46, 935 - 1092

19. Murdered Merchant 65, 1093 - 1156

20. Lombard Son 64, 1157 - 1376

21. Stolen Tooth 69, 1377 - 1484

22. Healing Lamp-oil, 1485 - 1518

23. Exorcises Demon, 1519 - 1545

24. Epilogue of Mestre Wace, 1546 - 1561

46. Nos. 6, 13, 19, 20, 21, 22, and 23.

47. *Cat. Cod. Hagr. Brux.* I¹, p. 316, from MS 1960 - 62, 13 cent.

48. Dawes, p. 161.

49. Du Broc II, 530.

50. ICA 20 M5627 Ch Ni A1.

51. *Le pays lorrain* XXIV (1932), 565 - 566.

52. *Cat. Cod. Hagr. Brux.* I¹, p. 317 (MS 1960 - 62, 13 cent.). Meisen, pp. 286 - 288.

53. *Anal. Boll.* IV, pp. 202 - 203, from Ghent MS 499, 12/13 cent.; pp. 317 - 319 (= *Cat. Cod. Hagr. Brux* I, MS 1960 - 62).

54. For these struggles of N with the Devil, see Anrich II, 328 ff.; Meisen, pp. 269 - 275; and for background, Loomis pp. 74 - 77.

55. A secular outgrowth of the *ioca monachorum* (Lehmann, pp. 10ff.).

56. *De temporum ratione liber,* c. xv.

57. Mombritius, p. 297, lines 5 - 14.

58. *Vie Saint Nicolas, altfranzösisches Gedicht* (Erlangen 1897), from Paris MS B. N. Lat. 1555, 14 cent. A prose life in Arras MS, s. xiii²; see Vincent, p. 32.

59. Quatrains 97 - 106.

60. Reese, pp. 241 - 242, with bibliography; F. Bateson, *Cambridge Bibliography of English Literature,* s.v. "Godric."

61. Dronke, p. 63.

62. *Libellus de vota et miraculis S. Godrici* (Surtees Society 20, 1845).

63. *DNB,* s.v. "Godric."

64. EETS 235, 236 (1956), 244 (1959), ed. C. D'Evelyn and A. J. Mill. Görlach for MSS and printed editions; see esp. pp. 209 - 210.

65. Laud. Misc. 108, fos. 111^r - 115^v; Görlach, pp. 88 - 90.

66. I count "Julian the Confessor" and "Julian the Hospitaller" (both 27 Jan.) "bishop of Le Mans ordained by the Twelve Apostles," derived from the Golden Legend, as among the martyrs.

67. Nos. 6, 18, 19, 21, and 22.

68. The verse is seven-stressed (8 + 6) iambs in rhymed couplets.

69. No. 13.

70. Lines 301 - 314, minimally modernized.

71. Ryan and Ripperger, p. 21.

72. Purgatorio xxx, 82 - 84.

73. Lines 209 - 210. Another Middle English legendary, of different tradition, is in London B.M. MS Harley 2277, fos. 177^r - 182^v. For further instances see Bateson, (n. 60 above) I, 174 - 175.

74. English readers will hold in mind also John Capgrave's (d. 1464) *Nova legenda Angliae,* twice printed by Wynkyn de Worde (1516, 1527).

75. Westminster 1483; by Wynkyn de Worde 1493.

76. As the Golden Legend was vulgarized by the evangelical Order of Preachers, Vincent of Beauvais's *Speculum Maius* (an encyclopaedia written in 80 books of 9,885 chapters!) was disseminated through the universities. Vincent devoted *Speculum historiale,* book XIII, chaps. 67 - 81, to N's Life and Miracles and XXX, 83, to N's Translation. Book XIII, 81, is the *Cross Legend* 41. Bp. Petrus de Natalibus (Pier de Natali)'s paraphrase of the Golden Legend was very popular (see Anrich II, 179 - 180): I, 33 = vita; V, 65 = Translation. For other popular printed legendaries see Aigrain, pp. 322 ff.

77. Additions for the parish of Rillaer, near Brabant, in MS Bolland. 467, transcribed *Anal. Boll.* XXIV (1905), 465 - 467.

78. It entered western tradition in Walafrid's Life of Saint Gall, 25; cf. Gregory I, *Dialogi* I, 3; III, 14 and 22. An early instance of this tale is in the legend of Theodore of Sykeon, 34 (Dawes, pp. 111 - 112). See Loomis, pp. 55, 85 (n. 179, 180), 98 - 99.

79. *Annales Monastici,* ed. H. R. Luard (Rolls Series 36) II, 74 - 77; cf. Graham, p. 176.

§II AMONG THE POETS

1. The Golden Legend (trans. Ryan, pp. 193 - 195) gives a story of a knight named Nicholas who was corrected in Saint Patrick's Purgatory.

2. Some exegetes suggested that Nikolaos is the Greek equivalent of Hebrew Balaam.

3. See above chap. 4, vii, at n. 22.

4. *Historia Francorum,* c. xvii (*Recueil croisades* III, pp. 279 - 281).

5. Ed. Thurston in *Anal. Boll.* XXII (1903), pp. 225 - 319 from eight MSS, basically B.M. MS Cotton Cleo. CXI (s. xiii, Dore Abbey), fos. 49^r-69^v. Trans. in part by Valerian Paget (New York, 1909).

6. Thurston (n. 5 above), p. 228; see Becker, pp. 93 - 94.

7. It is best known for its dramatic *Visitatio Sepulchri,* an Easter representation with eschatological and demonological overtones (cf. E. K. Chambers, *Eynsham under the Monks,* Oxfordshire Record Series 19). *Cat. Cod. Hagr. Brux.* I, 314.

8. Dionysius, *De novissimis* IV, 47.

9. Repr. in *Arber's English Reprints* (London 1869), no. 18. An especially popular episode about a drunken goldsmith (chaps. 19 - 23, pp. 262 - 272) was often copied separately (Ward, *Catalogue of Romances in B.M.* III); trans. Coulton, *Life in The Middle Ages* I, 48 - 50.

10. Edmund Rich is the subject of at least two 20-century biographies (*Oxford Dictionary of the Christian Church,* s.v.). Between his posts at Eynsham and Canterbury he taught Logic at Oxford. There Saint Edmund Hall stands today, presumably on the site of Edmund's residence (it is the only surviving medieval hall in Oxford). After a contest with King Henry III, Edmund migrated and was buried at Pontigny (*DNB*).

11. Annus 1196, ed. Rolls Series 2, pp. 243 ff.; *Matthaeus Paris*, ed. Wats, pp. 182 - 189.

12. Ed. Hewlett, Rolls Series I, pp. 246 - 266; trans. J. A. Giles, *Roger of Wendover* (Bohn's Antiquarian Library, 1845), II, 148 - 164.

13. Savage, pp. 219 - 220. Roger Bacon spoke slightingly of Robert's knowledge of Greek.

14. As in Jude 9 and Inferno xxvii, 112.

15. Cf. Elizabeth Willson, *The Middle English Legends of Visits to the Other World* (Chicago 1917), passim.

16. *Matthaeus Paris,* ed. Wats, p. 115.

17. Despite the quite strong visionary tradition of N, Dante gives

him only the slightest possible reference (Purg. xx, 31 - 33), and that doubtless by inspiration from Aquinas (*Summa Theologica* II, ii, 107, 3).

18. The earliest was perhaps Nicholas of Otranto, abbot of Casole, ca. 1200 (Vasiliev II, 219).

19. Waddell, pp. 55 - 56.

20. Max Manitius, *Die Gedichte des Archpoeta* (Munich 1913).

21. Caesarius of Heisterbach II, xv; Waddell, p. 209.

22. On N as patron of millers, Du Broc II, 620.

23. The French vernacular Life (chap. 5, 1 above), quatrains 107 - 123, tells how N rescued an amorous young clerk from the murderous servants of his amour's wealthy father.

24. Above, chap. 3, iv.

25. Text in *Cat. Cod. Hagr. Brux.* I (1896), 320 - 322, from MS. 1960 - 62, fos. 63^V-66^V. English translation in C. W. Jones, *Liturgy,* pp. 57 - 62.

26. *Haserensis 39,* as quoted above chap. 3, iv.

27. Henry Adams, *Mont Saint-Michel and Chartres* (1905), chap. 14, esp. pp. 288 - 290.

28. Charles Muscatine, *Chaucer and the French Tradition* (Berkeley 1969), pp. 11 - 30.

29. *Canterbury Tales* VII, 513 - 515.

30. Frazer VII, chap. 5, pp. 150 - 154.

31. Interpretations of Chaucer's grain have been countless; see, e.g., Beichner's in *Speculum* XXXVI (1961), 302 - 307. Professor David J. A. Ross writes to me: The 'grainchild' is known in East Anglia as a 'corn dolly.' They are still made, though mainly for sale to tourists. The traditional form is entirely abstract and bears no resemblance to a human figure."

§III WORDS AND MUSIC

1. Above chap. 3, v.

2. Hauréau, p. 327.

3. Albrecht, p. 70, of *Three Clerks 44:* "How familiar this scene had become by the end of the 15th century is shown in a wood engraving in the edition of the *Legenda Aurea* published at Lyon in 1488 (Meisen, fig. 109). Saint Nicholas is presented making the familiar gesture of blessing the three students in the tub, even though the *LA* does not include the legend."

4. Hardin Craig, *English Religious Drama* (Oxford 1955), pp. 81 - 87; Coffman; O. B. Hardison, *Christian Rite and Christian Drama* (Baltimore 1965); Douhet, cols. 199 - 201; Meisen, p. 234; Chambers II, 58 - 60.

5. *Cat. Gen. des MSS des Bibliothèques Publiques de France* XII (1889), 108 - 109; ed. with neumes by Giampiero Tintori, *Sacre Rappresentazione* (Cremona: Instituta et Monumenta I, 2, 1958). Coussemaker, pp. 83 - 99, 3 Filiae; 100 - 108, 3 Clerici; 109 - 122, Iconia; 123 - 142, F. Getronis. See also Young.

6. Schroeder was the first of many to assert the Germanic character of the plays, *Zeitschrift für deutsches Alterthum* XXXVI (1892), 239.

7. Anrich II, 84, 420; Meisen, pp. 232, 235.

8. E.g., handsel, étrenne.

9. *Studies in Philology* XXVIII (1931), 595 - 600.

10. Meisen, p. 300, after Du Méril, *Poésies,* p. 54, from Bibliothèque Nationale MS 1139, fo. 46.

11. As stated above, chap. 3, pp. 137 - 138. This is another instance of a tale quite possibly arising from a hymnological ambiguity. An intermediate step between the *trium puerorum innocentium nex* of *Stratilates 3* and *Three Clerks 44* can be seen in the Namur Life, *Anal. Boll.* II (1883), 145, no. 8.

12. Fowler, pp. 257 - 258.

13. Meisen, pp. 289 - 306.

14. *Le pays lorrain* 1904, pp. 374 - 378; 1932, pp. 76, 571.

15. Demont, pp. 16 - 17.

16. Gerard de Nerval, *Les filles de feu* (1854); also 1896, 1904, 1970.

17. Published with full musical score in *L'Illustration* XXX (1857), 389 - 390. Also ed. Mancel, pp. 4 - 5 et passim. In English and French: A. de Croze, *Beautiful Folksongs of France* I (1925); A. T. Davison et al., *A Book of Songs* (1924); T. W. Surette and Davison, *The Home Community Song Book* (1931); etc. English alone, *Notes and Queries* III, ix, pp. 123 - 124 et passim.

18. First published in the Paris Christmas Number of the *New York Herald* in 1908, and thereafter incorporated in France's volume *Les sept femmes de la Barbe-Bleue.*

19. *BHL* no. 6221. Readily available in Charles Beeson, *Primer of Medieval Latin,* Chicago (1925), pp. 375 - 382. Ed. Young II, 351 - 358, with Mombritius's text II, 492 - 494. Young, p. 351, says that the Fleury script is the only known dramatization, but there is a 15th-cent. morality of Simon le Borgoys and his son (Albrecht, pp. 47 - 53). It was recently transcribed by Colin Sterne and presented at the University of California, Davis.

20. Hofmeister, p. 137.

21. Above, chap. 2, iv. Anrich I, 188 - 195, 199 - 201, 273 - 275.

22. Falconi, pp. 127 - 129; Anrich I, 199 ff., from Vatican MSS Lat. 1194 and 5694.

23. Meisen, pp. 253 ff.

24. Sr. Nicholas Maltman, "The Evil Characters in Medieval Cyclic Drama," dissertation, University of California, Berkeley, 1957.

25. Above chap. 2, iv; Meisen, pp. 261 - 269.

26. First edited by Champollion-Figeac, *Hilarii versus et ludi* (Paris 1838). Young II, 337 - 343, with facsimile of MS. Douhet, cols. 480 ff., gives modern French translation.

27. A macaronic French hymn ca. 1300 ed. in *Speculum* VI, 109.

28. Fifteen poems and two dramas, *Lazarus* and *Daniel*.

29. Frank, p. 54; Meisen, pp. 263 - 264.

30. Ed. A. Jeanroy, *CFMA* 1925; F. J. Warne 1951; et passim. *Romania* LXXXI (1960), 112 - 119; LXXXII (1961), 201 - 239; Fissen, pp. 72 ff.; de Foulou in *Mélanges offerts à G. Cohen* (Paris, 1950), pp. 55 - 66.

31. Idem, p. 238. P. R. Vincent, pp. 63 - 65, makes a strong case that *Jeu* "both expressed and stimulated the crusading spirit of the twelfth century."

32. Jean Bodel, *Le jeu de Saint Nicolas,* ed. Albert Henry (Brussels, 1962), lines 583 - 1190.

33. *Modern Language Notes* L, 9 - 13; *Medium Aevum* VIII, 50 - 53; *Romania* LXVIII, 421 - 423; etc.

34. Laurentian Library MS Ashburnham 115, edited by de Paz, pp. 125 ff.; cf. *Romania* LI (1925), 191 - 197 and LIII (1927), 297 - 299.

35. Lebègue, p. 69.

36. Though N plays were performed in Britain, no script has survived; see *Studies in Philology* XXVIII (1931), 62 - 69. The Guild of Saint Nicholas of Parish Clerks existed from 1233. The Greyfriars' Chronicle records, an. 1411: "This year began a great pley from the beginnyng of the worlde at the skynners' welle, that lastyd vii days contynnually" (Chambers II, 380 - 381). That guilds and confréries dedicated to N were exceptionally given to drama will be mentioned below.

37. This would be an absurd statement if tunes were not clearly related to lyrics; their phrases frequently appear in surviving texts, often as apparently unconscious echoes.

38. Chevalier, *Repertorium* VI (*Anal. Boll.* XXXVI - XXXVIII [1917 - 1919, 1920]).

39. These lists contain *prosae, proselli, tropi, sequentiae, rhythmi,* etc., for all

saints (73 listed for N); but they are popularly indistinguishable from *hymni*. Abbé Leroquais's *Les bréviares manuscrits des bibliothèques publiques de France*, 5 vols. (Paris 1934), lists roughly 400 N items in the index, derived from ca. 350 separate codices, overwhelmingly of the 14th cent. None is earlier than the 11th cent. As the title indicates, the census is limited to MSS held in French public libraries.

40. Including *Debitas laudes Domino canentur*, and *Solemne tempus vertitur*.

41. Ed. Jeanroy in *Speculum* VI (1931), 107. The stanzas treat: (1) Invocation, (2) *Lactation 11*, (3) *Three Daughters 13*, (4) *Bishop 14*, (5) *Stratilates 3*, (6) *Mariners 6*.

42. Britten composed the cantata for the centenary of Lancing College, 24 July 1948; he used a script of Eric Crozier based on a *vita compilata* like Otloh's in which N is confused with Nicholas of Sion. *Three Clerks 44* is also incorporated. N sings a "simple heartfelt tune, one of the most beautiful things in the work, which caused some raising of academic eyebrows when first heard," writes a critic in the *Gramaphone* XXXIII (July 1955), 63. Britten could not have been conscious of how much in accord the simple tune is with the popular melodies of Reginold's *N Liturgy 40* as revealed in *The Cross Legend 41*.

§ IV VISUAL ARTS

1. A duplicate is housed at UCLA.

2. Réau III, 976 - 988.

3. Caesarius of Heisterbach VIII, c. lxxv. Mrs. Anna Jameson, *Sacred and Legendary Art*, Boston (n.d., 1848?), pp. 57 ff.

4. At Fribourg the tympanum is a Last Judgment with a large N immediately below the judging Son—the two separated by a band inscribed, "Protegam hanc urbem et salvabo eam propter me et propter Nicolaum servum meum. 4 Reg. 19." This church inc. 1283 replaced an N church consecrated by the founder of the town, Berchtold IV of Zähringen. Van Gennep, *Manuel* I, 6, 2822, says that in 1870 there were 3,668 churches dedicated to Saint Martin in France. He goes on to insist that the cult is abnormal in that despite this evidence of official recognition there is less evidence of popular cult for Martin than for less revered saints—meaning, I believe, N. However, there were a remarkable number of double dedications and paired altars and effigies, Martin and Nicholas (see Fournée, passim). I suspect that individualizing traits of Martin, too, had been reduced to virtual

extinction except for a kind of essential Frenchness.

5. The town of Saint Nicholas, 13 miles WSW of Antwerp, capital of ancient Waesland.

6. Paget Toynbee, *Dante Studies and Researches,* London, 1902, pp. 270 - 274, treats the medieval importance of port towns.

7. Peyster, pp. 77 - 78.

8. Modern tour guides at Wisby are apt to speak of a Greek Orthodox church there, but Professor Nils Lid, in answer to my query, doubted the connection. Orthodox churches in the Hanseatic towns appear to postdate the League.

9. *Archiv für Kulturgeschichte* XIII (1917), 243; *Anal. Boll.* XXIX, pp. 174 - 175.

10. "In England there is not a single city which does not have a chapel or church under N's invocation."—Du Broc II, 528.

11. British Museum MS Regius 2 B VII. They illustrate Verbal Relics nos. 10, 11, 13, 14, 17, 44, and 6.

12. A 13th - 14th cent. cope from Anagni Cathedral illustrates (sometimes with several scenes) the following episodes: Verbal Relics nos. 14^a, 44^a, 13^a, 5^a, 11, 14^b, 13^b, 62^a, 12, 62^b, 3, 64, 34, 66, 62^c, 44^b, 64, 62^d, 5^b, 5^c, 4.

13. Depicting the following documents (I use roman numerals for medallions, arabic for Verbal Relics): I, 11; II, 14; III, 10; IV, 12; V, 15; VI, 17; VII - VIII, 13; IX - X, 34; XI, 3; XII, 14; XIII, 65; XIV - XVI, 4; XIX - XX, 44; XXI - XXIII, 6; XXIV, 4; XXV, 15.

14. Window 27 has twenty-four medallions, of which the first five are restorations; the others are : VI, 11; VII, 12; VIII, 13; IX - XII, 14 and 15; XIV-XV, 6; XVI-XIX, 61; XX, 34; XXI - XXIII, 44; XXIV, 62. Window 53 has eighteen medallions, of which I and II are devoted to donor and family; then III to 3, IV to 14; scenes V - XVIII are all devoted to *Artemis 4* as follows: III, worshipers at idol with Diana's name inscribed on pedestal; IV, N preaching against idol; V, N destroying idol; VI, Devil and magicians; VII, magicians preparing oil; VIII, magicians' conjuration; IX, pilgrims disembarking; X, magician offering oil; XI, pilgrims embarking; XII, pilgrims sailing; XIII, pilgrims throwing oil; XIV, N beside boat; XV, Devil receiving oil from magicians; XVI, pilgrims arriving at Myra; XVII, N receiving pilgrims; XVIII, N blessing pilgrims. Window 60 has twenty-four medallions, of which the first three are devoted to the donors: haberdashers, pharmacists, and chapmen. Then: IV - X, 10; VI, 11; VII - VIII, 7; IX, 12; X - XI, 13; XII, 14;

XIII - XIV, 3; XV, 66; XVI - XVII, 62; XVIII, 15; XIX - XX, 44; XXI - XXII, 61; XXIII - XXIV, 34. In addition, Window 167 is a full-length N, donated by the tanners.

15. *Paradise Lost* I, 263 - 264; *Paradise Regained* II, 426.

§V ECCLESIASTICAL LIFE

1. "From the beginning of the MA to 1500, Meisen lists in Italy, Middle- and North Europe some 2300 cult monuments by name. This is an astonishing number but not the true representation. It would have been much greater with the Spanish peninsula, eastern Mitteleuropa, Scandinavia, and Great Britain. Also there is clearly missing most of the altar patronage and calendar notices, of which there are obviously a tremendous number. In the diocese of Münster alone, we know of not *eight* monuments but fifty before 1500. Of course these are only the monuments extant."—Börsting, pp. 178 - 180, who lists 65 evidences of cult in Westphalia (mapped p. 144). According to Mâle *Art,* pp. 327 - 333, N's popularity was equaled only by James and Martin.

2. L. D. Ettlinger, *The Sistine Chapel before Michelangelo,* London, 1965, p. 13.

3. Bolgia 3, Circle 8. "He is the first pope on whom contemporaries levelled in precise terms the accusation of nepotism."—Amann XI, i, 532.

4. Paget Toynbee, *Dante Dictionary* (Oxford, 1898), s.v.; Amann XI, 532 ff.

5. Huelsen, p. 392.

6. Ibid., pp. 389 - 408.

7. Cf. Meisen, pp. 111 - 114.

8. Armellini, p. 107. Lauer pl. III, shows mural of *Three Daughters 13* executed ca. 1280.

9. Vincent, p. 167. Above, chap. 4, iii.

10. G. B. de Rossi, *Esame storico ed archeologico dell' imagine di Urbano II papa e delle altre antiche pitture nell' oratorio di s. Niccolà entre il palazzo lateranense* (Rome 1881).

11. Luchaire in *EB* XX, 698.

12. According to my estimate, based on Meisen, pp. 126 - 171, with additions.

13. Graham, p. 209.

14. "Si pulsamur incommodis, Nicolaus ingeminatur" (Kayata, p. 69). "Nonne post memoriam Virginis singularis, tam dulcis pritas, vel pia dulcedo in cordibus fidelium observatur ut in die tribulationis nomen Nicolai teneatur

in ore, requiescat in cordo?" (Isn't it so that, excepting only the ideal of the matchless Virgin, such sweet reverence or reverent sweetness imbues the hearts of believers that in a time of tribulation the name of Nicholas shapes the tongue even as it stills the heart?) Sermo in die S. Nicolai of Saint Bernard (*Pat. Lat.* CLXXXIV) or Saint Peter Damian (*Pat. Lat.* CXLIV, 835) as quoted by P. R. Vincent, p. 32.

15. Coulton, *Middle Ages* I, 206.

16. Caesarius of Heisterbach VII, 46.

17. Marguerite Aron, *St. Dominic's Successor* (London 1955), pp. 40, 59, 63, 66, 72.

18. R. Van Marle, in *The Development of the Italian Schools of Painting* III (1924), 227 ff., 264, 409, 421, 424, figs. 131 - 135; idem, *Art Studies* III (1925), 19, 21 f., 29; E. Zocca, *Assisi* (1936), 47 ff., figs. pp. 49, 50; Igino B. Supino, *Giotto* (1920), pp. 296 ff., pl. ccxlvi, ccxlviii, ccxlix; idem, *La Basilica di San Francesco d'Assisi* (1924), 154 ff., figs. pp. 155 - 158.

19. I, 13; II, 6; III, 3; a fourth panel depicts John and Bartholomew. On the west vault: I, 2; II, 7; III, 3; a fourth depicts James the Lesser and Thomas. On the east wall: I, 64; II, 62; III, 46; a fourth depicts Peter, Andrew, and James the Greater. On the west wall I is 34, and the other three panels are destroyed.

20. *Prima Fundatio Fratrum Minorum Londoniae,* ed. J. S. Brewer, Monumenta Franciscana, Rolls Series, pp. 493 - 494; *New English Dictionary,* s.v. "Shamble."

21. *British Society of Franciscan Studies* IX, 47 - 51, 91, 212.

22. *Liber Pontificalis,* ed. Duchesne, II, 467; Gregorovius V, pp. 485 ff.; *Cambr. Med. Hist.* V (1957), 318 - 319.

23. The chronicles record the deposit of the first thorn *in capella regia Sancti Nicolai* at Paris by Saint Louis (IX) A.D. 1242: e.g., Cheroul, p. 21. He was also responsible for the N chapel at Compiègne.

24. Meisen, p. 351.

§VI PATRONAGE

1. Meisen, pp. 345 - 350. He lists (p. 350) 23 variants of family names and 78 variants of Christian names. Cf. Réau, p. 976.

2. Ewen 1931, pp. 292 - 293; G. Allen in *Cornhill Magazine* LXXI, 489 - 490. Spelling with *h* may be Norman; at all events Monachus Beccensis so spells it consistently in his N Miracula.

3. Ernest Langlois, *Table des noms* (1904), p. 485.

4. Frey, pp. 91 - 92.

5. Franke, p. 87.

6. Meisen, pp. 350 - 351.

7. De Groot, *Saint Nicholas,* p. 8.

8. *Childe Harold's Pilgrimage,* cxiv; cf. Gibbon, chap. 70.

9. Ernest Weekley, *Surnames* (1916), p. 308.

10. Meisen, pp. 347 - 348.

11. Ibid., p. 357.

12. In the 14th cent. N was next after John in Baden and in the 15th next to Hans in Switzerland (Meisen, p. 355). A list of godparents, A.D. 1384 - 1482, from Riga: Mary 0, Joseph 0, Paul 0, Andrew 20, Peter 56, Nicholas 101, John 282 (*Anal. Boll.* XXIII, 334, after H. von Bruiningk). I have casually observed in indexes that N as a given name runs exceptionally high in combination with place names (e.g., Niccolo da Uzzano, Nicolas de Biervliet, Nicolaus von Jeroschin, Nicolaus Cusanus, etc.), when compared with John and Peter. This suggests not only (as we know) the rise of the name in a feudal period but also centuries-long tradition in name giving within families.

13. Above, chap. 4, v.

14. Corrado Ricci, *Umbria Santa* (1926), pp. 159 - 165; Meisen, p. 257. Incidentally, the mother's name was Catherine (*Anal. Boll.* LXI [1943], 11).

15. Künstle, *Ikonographie,* p. 465; van Gennep in *Revue d'ethnographie* IX (1928), 38 - 39.

16. Lebègue, pp. 117 ff.

17. *The Benedictine Book of Saints* (4th ed., 1947) names 27 Saint Nicholases.

18. Bréhier, *Eglise,* p. 284.

19. E.g., A. S. Wood, *Luther's Principles of Biblical Interpretation* (1960), p. 25.

20. Stegmüller IV, 12 - 104.

21. Amann XI, i, 543, 601 - 612.

22. *CMH* I, 624, 628 ff.

23. Ibid., p. 599.

24. E. Cassirer, *Individuum und Kosmos* (1927), chap. 1.

25. John Addington Symonds, *Renaissance in Italy: The Revival of Learning* (London, 1875), pp. 126 - 130. Phyllis W. G. Gordan, *Two Renaissance Book Hunters: The Letters of Poggius Bracciolini to Nicholaus de Niccolis,* Columbia University, Records of Civilization, 91 (New York, 1974). For bibliography on Niccolò, see pp. 217 - 218, 220.

26. Pietro Rainalducci da Corrara was crowned antipope by Emperor Louis of Bavaria in 1328 as Nicholas V, but he resigned in 1330 and died in 1333.

27. Eugène Müntz, *Les arts à la cour des papes* I (Paris 1878), 68 - 189, is a

mine of information on this topic. Symonds (n. 25 above), pp. 161 - 166; Amann XI, i, 541 - 548.

28. *Camb. Mod. Hist.* I, 594. Today it has about 60,000 of the two classes.

29. Magnuson, 55 - 64, 351 - 362.

30. *Oxford Dictionary of the Christian Church.*

31. Alexander de Villedieu, *Ecclesiale,* lines 220 - 222.

32. *La revue critique* XIX (1912), 694. "Of all holy protectors Nicholas was probably the most popular."—*Nouveau Larousse Illustré* VI, 368; cf. Franke, p. 37.

33. Meisen, chap. 14, pp. 366 - 388.

34. For towns under invocation of N see Cahier II, 625, 636 - 673; Fournée, passim.

35. Imbart de la Tour I, 504 - 513. Crusaders' brotherhoods like the Templars and Hospitalers may have been the models.

36. Meisen, p. 379, cites many guild patronages in the Netherlands from the 12th cent.

37. Lebègue, pp. 4 - 5.

38. This growth esp. discussed by Marius Sepet, *Origines catholiques du théâtre moderne* (Paris 1901).

39. According to *EB* XX, 169B, wandering musicians began to settle in the cities and form guilds: "The oldest of these guilds was the Brotherhood of Nicolai in Vienna in 1288."

40. *Artemis 4, Boiled Infant 66.* Du Broc II, 626.

41. Meisen, chap. 14.

42. I draw much of what follows from the lists of Réau, pp. 978 - 980, de Schuyter, sects. 18 - 19, Meisen, pp. 366 - 388, Du Broc II, summarized p. 528, and Cahier II, 625, 636 - 673.

43. Burlet, pp. 10 - 18, credits N with 62 chapels, Catherine with 103. Compare van Gennep in *Revue d'ethnographie* IX (1928), 36 - 37.

44. *Cat. Cod. Hagr. Paris.* II, 414.

45. See the data given by Lebègue, p. 69; Grace Frank, p. 201.

46. Cahier II, 625, 636 - 673.

47. I, p. 85.

48. Du Broc II, pp. 599 - 631.

49. II, p. 533.

50. Réau, p. 979.

51. Du Broc II, pp. 626, 601.

52. Ibid., p. 621.

53. Ibid., pp. 613, 618; cf. Caesarius of Heisterbach VIII, 72, 73.

54. Thomas Dekker, *The Belman of London* (1616); *Notes and Queries* VIII, v, 274; cf. Brand I, p. 418.

55. See, e.g., *Cat. Cod. Hagr. Paris.* II, p. 405; Du Broc II, p. 619. There is an inscription at Archangel on the Arctic to N as "the great bishop of the sea" (Babudri in *Collana,* no. 4, p. 8). However, the Church of S.-N-du-Chardonnet, originally in a thistle-field, then vineyard, became the home and the inspiration for river boatmen as Paris expanded.

56. Du Broc II, 597 - 623.

57. Ibid., pp. 605 - 633. French rivers, esp. in Occitanie, were much less used than in modern times; see *Medievalia et Humanistica* XIII (1960), 68 - 80. So the N cult was light in the south. For the north, see Réau, p. 979.

58. Meisen, p. 386.

59. Du Broc II, 626.

60. Ibid.

61. P. 619. Bulletin de la Société des Antiquaires de France, 1879, p. 258.

62. Silvestre, p. 736.

63. Du Broc II, 601.

64. Demont in *Revue du folklore français* III (1932), 14.

65. Du Broc II, 598 - 625.

66. Confrérie Saint-Nicholas-aux-Epiciers.

67. Du Broc II, 598 - 620.

68. Ibid., 617.

69. Ibid., 633.

70. *Larousse XIXe siècle,* on what evidence I do not know, claimed the serfs among his votaries.

71. Du Broc II, 599, 631.

72. *Mémoires de la Société des Antiquaires de France* XLIV (1883), 9 - 10.

73. One of the coal docks at Quai du Louvre was named Saint-Nicolas.

74. Du Broc II, 605 - 607.

75. Crawford, p. 11.

76. Du Broc II, 618.

§VII SAINT-NICHOLAS-DE -PORT

1. Cahier, passim.

2. Above, chapter 3, vi.

3. *Le pays lorrain* XXIV (1932), p. 568; de Gaiffier 1967, pp. 452 ff.

4. I draw the data of this section primarily from Pierre Marot.

5. Edited in *Receuil des historiens des croisades,* V, 293 - 294.

6. *Strata publica que versus Sanctum Nycolaum ducit euntes.*

7. Marot, pp. 32 - 33.

8. They are now the city museum. The late story-windows in the cathe-dral depict their founding and dedication by Saint Louis and his brother Philip, King of Navarre.

9. Henry VI, ii, 73 - 121.

10. Meisen, p. 376.

11. The title page is reproduced in *Le pays lorrain* XXIV (1932), p. 66.

12. Illustrated description by Fourier Bonnard in *Le pays lorrain* XXIV (1932), pp. 49 - 62, and in his *Histoire* (1932). For a parallel instance of the Hospice Saint-Nicolas des Catalans at Rome, which has evolved into the national church of Spaniards, Santa Maria di Montserrato, near the Tiber, see Vielliard.

6 Old Age
§I DECLINE

1. Pp. v - vi.

2. Birch, pp. 188 - 189.

3. Coulton, *Medieval Faith,* pp. 224 - 225.

4. Loukovitch, p. 210.

5. See Delehaye, *Sanctus,* pp. 56 - 57, regarding the evaporation of ideals in popular transmission.

§ II THE REFORMATION

1. Imbart de la Tour I, 547 - 550.

2. Bax, pp. 140 ff. On the reaction against miracle-working saints which impelled men into magic, witchcraft, and the occult, see Thomas, *passim,* but well summarized pp. 631 - 640.

3. C. Dawson, p. 52.

4. Pimlott, pp. 22 - 25; Thomas, pp. 48, 70.

5. In general, Gardiner; but "he fails to see how much the decline owed to the rising tide of secularism, realism, and the Renaissance" (Henshaw, p. 34).

6. "Man could no longer count on the mediation either of reason or of other men in closer contact with the divine than himself"—(William Bouwsma in paper for the 4th International Luther Congress, Saint Louis, 25 Aug. 1971).

7. Article xxi (trans. *Library of Original Sources* V, 160).

8. Article xxii (*Sermons or Homilies Appointed to be Read in the Churches in the Time of Queen Elizabeth* [London 1817], p. 577).

9. Session xxv, *Concilium Tridentium*, ed. Societas Goerresiana (XII, 1930); *Oxford Dictionary of the Christian Church*, pp. 1207 - 1208; *Catholic Encyclopedia* VII, 671; Thomas, pp. 73 - 76. The core Scripture is Ps. cxlix; Mach. vii, 6.

10. Hakluyt, *Voyages* (Everyman ed. II, 99). *Bough* is doubtless "bog," meaning "God."

11. Aquinas, *Summa Theologica* IX, q. 7, a. 16.

12. *Realencyklopädie für die protestantische Kirche* VII, 555 - 559; *Dictionnaire de théologie catholique* II, 1642.

13. Martin, p. 245.

14. On the reforming decrees of 1634 (Urban VIII), see D'Ales IV, 1132 ff.

15. Exodus xx, 4.

16. Genesis vi, 5.

17. Erasmus, *Praise of Folly* (Traill III, i, 26).

18. *EB* XVII, p. 883.

19 Mather (1853), pp. 345 - 346.

20. Delehaye, *A travers trois siècles,* pp. 122 - 123.

21. N's particular association with papacy and prelacy made him especially vulnerable in the North; see Traill III, i, 42, 81.

22. The views of Catholic Humanists were often those of Jean de la Taille (1572): The perfection of the saints permits no variety of character (Loukovitch, p. 48; Lebègue, pp. 78 - 79).

23. Clichtove, *Defensio,* [A.D. 1518 (Imbart de la Tour II, 565 - 566)] .

24. *CMH* I, 610.

25. The content of these two paragraphs is drawn from Delehaye, *A travers trois siècles.*

26. "Mensonges forgez," "mensongères merveilles" (Loukovitch, p. 48).

27. *History of the Collegiate Church of St. Nicholas, Galway,* p. 3. The church was founded in 1320.

28. See Lalanne's brief census, pp. 123 - 124. On the relics seized from Constantinople in 1204 see the excellent century-old study of Riant. The duplication of relics is somewhat matched by duplication of Santa Clauses.

29. D'Ales IV, 927; cf. Lalanne, p. 124. Sir John Maundeville, *Voyages and Travels* (Bohn translation, chap. 6: "And close by that church (of the Nativity, Bethlehem) at a distance of sixty fathoms, is a church of St. Nicholas, where

Our Lady rested after she was delivered of Our Lord. And forasmuch as she had too much milk in her breasts, which grieved her, she milked them on the red stones of marble; so that the traces may yet be seen all white in the stones."

30. Naples 1620, 1633, 1642 (repr. 1645), Palermo 1659, 1672, Milan 1696, Rome 1701, Venice 1705.

§ III THE WINTER CALENDAR

1. Roy, *Nicholas I*, pp. 23 - 25.

2. Spelman, I, 391; Love, pp. 13 - 14.

3. Aigrain, p. 324, n. 1, scoffs at Dom Pitra's statement that Pope John XXII (A.D. 1316) found altogether 53,500 "crowned saints."

4. Coulton, *Europe's Apprenticeship,* p. 142; Richards, pp. 36 - 37.

5. Rodgers, pp. 96, 101.

6. Anastos, p. 251.

7. T. W. Simons in *University of Colorado Studies* XXIV (1936), pp. 65 - 66.

8. Amann XI, 599.

9. Rodgers, pp. 81 ff., 92 - 94.

10. No. 37 (Coulton, *Medieval Village,* p. 274).

11. Rodgers, p. 102.

12. In Delehaye's list, *Anal. Boll.* XLVI, 316 - 318; though other Days vary considerably, N Day is on every list.

13. See the edict of Henry VIII (Wilkins III, 823); Levy, pp. 97 - 98.

14. Luther *Werke* VI, p. 446; trans. Wace and Buchheim, *Luther's Primary Works* (London 1896), p. 213. Rodgers, pp. 109 - 110; cf. the Injunction of the Archbishop of York, Levy, p. 110.

15. Edward VI (A.D. 1552) had placed in the Preamble to the Book of Common Prayer a statement that work on any day was legal "when necessity shall require."

16. Holinshed, *Chronicles* (ed. 1807), I, 233 (Love, p. 29). The proscriptions against holydays often included Sundays throughout Britain and in rigid Calvinist provinces. Militant uprooting continued in England until the Restoration and in New England well into the 18th cent. See, e.g., C. H. Firth and R. S. Rait, *Interregnum* (London 1911), I, 954, Ordinance of 1647, leveling all traditional holydays for "scholars, apprentices, and other servants" to 12, i.e., the 2d Tuesday of each month. Cf. Levy, p. 241 et passim.

17. Hough, pp. 115 - 116, in describing the fairs and festivals in the Netherlands, says that they consolidated on two special days: Kermis (Feast

of Consecration of the local church) and N Day.

18. Lalanne, p. 136, n. 1.

19. Guibert of Nogent III, 18 (trans. John F. Benton, Torchbooks B 1471, p. 215).

20. E.g., MS Bibl. Bolland. 467, fo. 14ᵛ, in *Anal. Boll.* XXIII (1905), 465; the same legendary gives the year 1421 as date when lightning killed a plowman in the fields on N Day.

21. Richards, pp. 44 - 45.

22. Marx, *Das Kapital* I, 239, Anm. 124, quoted also Levy, p. 97, n. 1. The economic pressure can be measured in a law passed by Parliament in 1570 (18 Elizabeth c. 19) requiring everyone to wear a cap to Common Prayer on all Sundays and holydays purely to satisfy the Fellowship and Company of Cappers (Levy, pp. 137 - 139).

23. Wilkins III, 823; cf. IV, 3 ff. Also in John Foxe, *Acts and Monuments,* ed. Josiah Pratt V (1870), 164 - 165. Lennard, p. 89.

24. Van Gennep, *Manuel* I, 6, 2840 - 2841; W. Schulenberg, "Das Verbrennen des Niklaus," *Berliner Gesellschaft für Anthropologie, Verhandlungen* 1898, pp. 101 - 102. Thomas, pp. 615 - 623, offers some data on seasons and time governance in the Calendar of Saints.

25. Saint Martin's Day 11 Nov.

26. The straw costumes for N figures that appear in German lands (see chap. 6, v, "Animal Disguise") seem part of the season's fertility magic; see Frazer VII (*Spirits of the Corn* I), 131 - 170.

27. Banks III, 189.

28. Frazer XI, 325 - 326; Rodgers, pp. 50 - 52.

29. Meisen, pp. 486 - 501, has devoted a chapter to the N folkplay, especially popular in High Germany, a product of the winter mumming, though possibly taking some suggestion from the miracle plays.

30. Chambers I, 257 - 258. N's steed, of whatever kind, seems to have developed from the *palmesel,* a property ass used for carrying an impersonated Christ in Palm Sunday processional. It was frugally employed for the Boy Bishop on his Visitation, as still in Artois (Demont, p. 19).

31. Tittle, pp. vii - viii.

32. See Chambers I, chap. 17, "Masks and Misrule."

33. Chambers I, 243 - 244.

34. Bede, *De temporum ratione,* c. xv.

35. Britt, p. 112.

36. Nilsson, "Vorgeschichte," passim.

37. Frazer XI, 319.

38. Ibid., pp. 318 - 322.

39. Bell I, 50 - 65, et passim.

40. See refs. in Meisen, p. 311, n. 3.

41. Meisen, pp. 308 - 309.

42. Lehmann, pp. 19 ff.

43. Chambers I, 246; Douhet, col. 24. "There are four *tripudia* after Christmas. They are those of the deacons, priests, and choir-children, and finally that of the subdeacons, *quod vocamus stultorum*" (Chambers I, 275).

44. C. xix, after Douhet, col. 28. See the comparable edict of the Council of Basle in 1431 (Brand I, 427).

45. "For God has nothing to do with masked persons and Nicholas Bishops, since they teach nothing, yet hold a bishops office."—Luther, Erlanger Ausgabe XXVIII, p. 148, quotation, p. 328.

46. Ironically, the choirboys of Notre Dame hold a masquerade in Saint-Nicolas-des-Champs, where Budé and many other Humanists are buried, each 6 Dec. (Larousse XI, p. 990).

47. Meisen, p. 309.

48. See the accounts for Magdalen College an. 1481 - 1561, with N Day entries, digested by Chambers II, 248 - 250.

49. *Notes and Queries* 3, IV, 488.

50. Chambers I, p. 246, and elsewhere.

51. Conway II, pp. 17 - 19. But de Groot p. 10, properly objects to the folklorists' "reasonings by analogy and barely supportable inferences and suppositions," especially evident in their undemonstrable equation of N with Wodan.

52. An Aberdeen statute of 1508 invokes the citizens to ride in honor of N, Robyn Huyed and Litell Johne "quuilk was callit in yers bipast Abbot and Prior of Bonaccord, one every Sanct Nicholas day throw the towne." (Banks III, 189 - 193; cf. II, 164).

53. Walter Map's tale of Nicholas Pipe, the Water Man, is the earliest evidence I have found (*De nugis curialium* IV, 13, ed. Wright [Camden Soc., 1850], pp. 179 - 180).

54. Obit ca. 1179. *Sermo iii in die Nicolai* (*Pat. Lat.* CXCVIII, 1730). His text was Matt. xviii, Mark. x. The colleges which sprang up in the thirteenth century and eventually consolidated in Oxbridge were often dedicated to N, as at Salisbury (fd. 1261). "The difference between these colleges and the ordinary collegiate churches was simply that the former were *ad orandum et*

studendum and the latter *ad studendum et orandum"* (*EB* XXIV, p. 367).

55. Strasbourg MS E 60, fo. 91, gives a scholars' laud for N, composed A.D. 1404 specifically for the revels, ed. Mone no. 1103, vol. III, 465 - 466.

56. Cf. Meisen, p. 182.

57. Saint Nicholaus money used to give to Maydens secretlie,
Who, that he still may use his woonted liberalitie,
The mothers all their children on the eue do cause to fast,
And when they every one at night in senselesse sleepe are cast:
Both Apples, Nuttes, and peares they bring, and other things beside,
As caps, and shooes, and petticotes, which secretlie they hide,
And in the morning found, they say, that this saint Nicholas
brought.

—Thomas Naogeorgus (Kirchmayer), *The Popish Kingdome,* Englished by Barnabe Goodge, ed. R. C. Hope 1880, "The Fourth Booke," p. 86 (1st ed., London, 1570).

58. Conversely, on N Day students at Wye school, Kent, in the 15th cent. paid their tuition, the "usual offerings of cocks and pence" (*Gentleman's Magazine* 1790, p. 1076). See Harrison, p. 247, for a description of present customs on Saint Thomas Day (21 Dec.), which indicates what N Day customs would have been in earlier times.

59. The data in Loukovitch indicate that reformers tolerated drama of historical and hagiological subjects drawn from biblical and apostolic ages, but not thereafter.

60. Ekkehard IV, *Casus S. Galli* (*MGH, Scriptores* II, p. 84).

61. Classical schools were in session throughout twelve months, but with many holidays (Marrou, pp. 208 - 209).

62. On our ignorance of the medieval school calendar, see Paré, p. 109; knowledge of the ancient calendar is more precise (Marrou, pp. 208 - 209).

63. Trans. John F. Benton (New York, 1970), pp. 46 - 47.

64. Coulton, *Europe's Apprenticeship,* pp. 129 - 130; cf. Dyer, p. 433. *Festinatur a clericis / Et maxime scholasticis* (*Anal. Hymn.* XLV[b], no. 77).

65. Labbé XI, i, 79.

66. Douhet, col. 25.

§IV SPECTACLES ON NOSE AND POUCH AT SIDE

1. Good surveys in Chambers I, 336 - 371; Meisen, chap. 12, pp. 307 - 333; Ancelet-Hustache, pp. 73 - 84; Young I, 105 ff., and bibliography p. 552;

J. M. J. Fletcher, *The Boy Bishop at Salisbury and Elsewhere,* Salisbury, 1921; Wright and Lones, pp. 194 - 196.

2. Meisen, pp. 311 - 312; W. C. Miller, *The Boy Bishop* (London 1923).

3. Douhet, cols. 914 - 915; for analogues among other cults, Chambers I, 261. Dyer, p. 330, shows that the customs, shifted to Saint Andrew's Day, were persisting in the 19th cent.

4. Meisen, p. 311; note, p. 330, the edict of the Franciscans meeting in Barcelona A.D. 1401.

5. Meisen, p. 307.

6. Ibid., p. 313.

7. Douhet, cols. 28 - 32.

8. Ibid., cols. 914 - 915; Meisen, pp. 313 - 314.

9. Douhet, cols. 337 - 341.

10. Ibid., col. 338.

11. Meisen, p. 324; *Notes and Queries* 1, V, 557 - 621; 3, IV, 486 - 487; VI, 63, 110.

12. Elector of Cologne in 1662. " . . . detestabilis corruptelaque pueri a die s. Nicolai ad festum ss. Innocentium personatum Episcopum colunt." (Wetzer-Welte IV, 1400).

13. Banks II, 251; III, 189 ff.

14. Chambers I, 253.

15. Coulton, *Middle Ages* I, 242 - 243.

16. Brand I, 421 - 431; Edwards, pp. 323 - 324; Wright and Lones III, 196.

17. Meisen, chap. 12, p. 332.

18. Brand I, 426, translating Corvarruvias. Dr. Ephrem Compte informs me that at Montserrat, near Barcelona, the Boy Bishop was elected 22 Nov. (S. Cecilia) to serve on 6 Dec.

19. Meisen, pp. 326 ff.

20. Chambers I, 356 - 358; II, 287 - 289.

21. Banks III, 193 - 194, similarly lists payments for Edinburgh; for London see W. Sparrow Simpson, *Registrum . . . Sancti Pauli Londinensis,* n.d. pp. 92 - 93, including "a lytell chesebyll for Seynt Nicholas byssehop." Cf. Snell, pp. 42 - 46. Erasmus wrote one sermon (Concio de puero Iesu) for a Boy Bishop, and Dean Colet required attendance and a one-penny offering (Dyer, pp. 434 - 435; cf. p. 432).

22. Meisen, p. 324.

23. Ibid.

24. Peter Schott writing to the Nuncio A.D. 1497, trans. Coulton, *Middle Ages* I, 242 - 243.

25. Arnim and Brentano recorded an N masque ("Sankt Niklaus werde kommen / Aus Moskau") in *Des Knaben Wunderhorn,* transcribed Metken, p. 74.

26. *Notes and Queries* I, VI, 63.

27. In 1555 "the child Bishop of Paules Church with his company were admitted to the Queen's Privy Chamber, where he sang before her on Saint Nicholas Day and upon Holy Innocents Day" (W. F. Dawson, p. 119.)

28. Dyer, pp. 435 - 436; Warren, pp. 54 - 55.

29. James I (*Basilikon Doron,* 1598), still in Scotland, granted "good cheer if not unlawful" on Christmas "always provided that the Sabbath be kept holy" (Levy, p. 171). The effigy of the Boy Bishop in Salisbury Cathedral is well known, but Aubrey's words bear repeating: "The tradition of the Choirsters, and those that show the Church is, that this Childe-bishop being melancholy, the Children of the Choire did tickle him to make merry, but they did so overdoe it that they tickled him to death: and dyeing in his Office and Honour, here was this little monument made for him, with the episcopal ornaments, e.g., mitre, crosse, and cope."—*Remaines of Gentilisme and Judaisme,* by John Aubrey, R.S.S., 1686 - 1687, ed. James Britten, p. 171. The ritual for Salisbury is given in *The Antiquities of the Cathedral Church of Salisbury* (1723), pp. 72 - 80. In the south ambulatory are modern effigies of four saints: Aldhelm, Osmund, Francis, Nicholas (with three boys tubbed); the effigy honors Lt. Col. Balfour (d. 1936).

30. The 15th-cent. bejeweled and ornamented *episcopum conducere in domus* at Prague led a "Knightly Company of Saint Nicholas." An ordinance of 1494 attempted to regulate excessive pomp, but the festivity continued to 1776 (Meisen, p. 328).

31. Meisen, p. 411.

32. M. Stillger, *Allemagne* (Paris: Hachette, 1964), p. 540; Meisen, pp. 330, 411. In Namur children are still allowed to collect on N Day (de Schuyter, p. 11^v).

33. Meisen, p. 216: "ein so reiches und vielseitiges volkstümliches Brauchtum zu entfalten, wie es von keiner anderen Heiligengestalt bekennt geworden ist."

34. Brand I, 417, reports that English schoolboys cried Nic'las for truce in games of tag.

35. Meisen, p. 327.

36. But Lotharingian traditions are deep-seated and persistent; see Mar-guillier, pp. 6 - 7, who quotes Paul Claudel.

37. Also van Gennep, *Manuel* I, i, 183.

38. Meisen, pp. 324 - 328, for Netherlands laws against N Day customs.

39. Frazer VIII (1912), *Spirits of the Corn* II, p. 335.

40. Demont, pp. 14 - 19; de Groot, pp. 10 - 11; Meisen, pp. 390 - 392, 413 - 415, says the N custom in southern Italy was introduced from France. Is it sheer accident that the name of the renowned Bavarian crèche- or Krippen-maker was Niklas, A.D. 1800 (Rietschel, p. 58)?

§V THE SHRUNK SHANK

1. Whistler, p. 11 et passim.

2. Meisen, p. 408. This dualism even penetrates to European wines. The best (i.e., most expensive) is *Sanct Nikolas,* so named because the grapes are not picked until N Day; the poorest (i.e., most merchandized) is *Nicolas.*

3. Kurth, pp. 292 ff., has assembled texts on the use of the ferule in medieval schools.

4. *Anal. Hymn.* XXII, 207, no. 349, str. 10.

5. For Clement Moore, see below, chap. 7, iii. An English version of *Struwwelpeter,* with "great Agrippa" (a pun, I presume) substituted for "great Nicholas," but with Hoffmann's original illustrations, was reissued by Fred-erick Warne and Co., New York, as recently as 1962. A more standard version, with Nicholas in his own person, is *Slovenly Peter, or Cheerful Stories and Funny Pictures for Good Little Folks* (Philadelphia: Winston, n.d.).

Scottish records indicate that on N Eve the Bishop and his clergy in full canonicals were followed in their questing by "deblatis and ruffyis" (imps and satyrs), the latter in hairy costumes (Banks III, 190).

6. Meisen, pp. 361 - 364.

7. "This God of Unreason from whom the earliest Greek tragedy was supposed to have sprung . . . . The Bacchae of the rationalist Euripides" (Lucas, p. 5). "Apollo was regarded as supreme at Delphi nine months a year but gave way to Dionysus for the three winter months" (ibid., p. 357).

8. Gregory I, ii, 4.

9. De Schuyter, pp. 10 - 12.

10. De Groot, pp. 43, 51.

11. De Schuyter, p. 32.

12. Rietschel, pp. 110 - 120.

13. *Saturday Evening Post,* 20 Feb. 1960, p. 4.

14. De Schuyter, p. 12; de Groot, p. 43.

15. Franz Weineck, "Der Knecht Ruprecht und seine Genossen," *Nieder-lausitzer Mitteilungen* V (Guben 1897), has arranged a whole system of Christmas images derived, he argues, from heathen gods; I have drawn from him in this brief listing; also Meisen, pp. 6 - 7 and esp. 416 - 426; Tille, p. 7.

16. A. van Gennep, *Manuel* I, 6, 2840.

17. Meisen, pp. 439 - 441; Conway, pp. 110 - 113; Rietschel, pp. 101 ff.

18. Van Gennep in *Revue d'Ethnographie* IX (1928), pp. 37 - 38, after Hoffmann-Krayer in *Schweitzer Volkskunde,* 1911, pp. 94 - 95.

19. Van Gennep (n. 18 above).

20. So in Cyrano de Bergerac: "C'était un bon Nicolas, qui s'en allait devant lui hurluberlu." Children hurl the threat, "Nicolas, je t'embrouille" (Larousse XI, 986).

21. Appendix to de Groot, p. 190. Cf. Vicki Baum, *The Christmas Carp,* (New York: Doubleday 1941).

22. Geraldine de Conrey, *German Christmas Carols* (1936, repr. 1953), p. 11.

23. Conway, pp. 110 - 113.

24. Meisen, p. 352.

25. Chambers I, 195, 263; on other gift-givers, pp. 268 - 269.

26. W. P. Trent, ed., *Mr. Irving's Notes* (New York 1920), I, 141.

27. Tille, pp. 116 - 117.

28. *Deutsche Kriegsweihnacht 1944.* Rietschel, p. 108.

29. Tertullian, *De spectaculis* ix (*Pat. Lat.* I, 641).

30. The common Germanic theme of the *wilden Jäger* attached itself freely to most cults. *Das wütende Heer* is in Sweden *Odens Jagt* (H. M. Chadwick in *EB* XXVIII, 768).

31. Anichkof, p. 109. Common examples of disseminators: Hough, p. 125; Moran, pp. 19 - 20; Count, pp. 57 - 63; Fogel, p. 13. The origin of the N = Woden seems to be Dr. Adolf Wuttke (Prof. Theology, Halle), *Der deutsche Volksaberglaube der Gegenwart* (2d ed. Berlin 1869), who embodied the Higher Criticism and Romanticism inspired by the Grimms, inaugurating the method of finding analogues for all identifiable customs in ur-German. See Fritz Schakermeyr, *Poseidon* (Bern 1950), p. 99, who compares Elias and George. But Meisen (p. 416) quotes Karl Weinhold: "Keineswegs sind alte Götter darin zu spüren, sondern es sind die Reste der vermummten Teilnehmer an heidnischen Kultgebräuchen."

32. *Le pays lorrain* XXIV (1932), 571.

33. *L'Illustration* XXX (1857), 423 - 425.

34. Whistler, p. 2, cites the carol ca. 1450: "Hail, Father Christmas, hail to thee!"

35. Meisen, p. 10; Ortutay, p. 553.

36. *Deutsche Kreigsweihnacht 1944,* p. 27; Meisen, pp. 3 - 5.

37. "Le Christkindel et Hans Trapp en Alsace," *L'Illustration* XXXII (1858), 407 - 409; Harrison, pp. 212 - 213.

38. Rietschel, pp. 119 - 120; *Revue des traditions populaires* II (1887), 569 - 570, for N and Père Fouettard in Alsace; cf. *Le pays lorrain* XXIV (1932), 571.

39. So a Walloon formulaic invocation of N as rainbringer (Sébillot I, 120).

40. Rietschel., pp. 110 ff.

41. A good description of N Eve in the Low Countries is a story by Camille Lemonnier, trans. Edith Wingate in *The Massacre of the Innocents,* 1895, repr. in *Stories by Foreign Authors* (New York: Scribners, 1898), pp. 117 - 148.

42. Harrison, pp. 210 - 211.

43. De Groot, p. 41.

44. Harrison, p. 251.

45. De Schuyter, p. 9. Paul Rastelhuber, *Revue des traditions populaires* II (1887), 570, derives N from the Scandinavian god Niordr.

46. Meisen, pp. 3 - 4, et passim; see above n. 31.

47. *Revue des traditions populaires* III (1888), 651 - 653.

48. *Notes and Queries* 12, I, 174.

49. Harrison, p. 225.

50. Marguillier, p. 8; cf. *Marches de l'est* II (1910), 261, 277 - 278; Ortutay, p. 552. Paul Claudel has echoed several of these songs in his *Saint-Nicolas.*

§VI CHILDISH TREBLE

1. Ortutay, p. 553; Demont, pp. 14 ff.; *Notes and Queries* 1, XII, 118 for Belgian observances in 1855.

2. Meisen, p. 392.

3. Meisen, pp. 28 - 32 contain a number of proscriptive edicts from the Low Countries. I translate only the first (Grave, 3 Dec. 1614) as illustrative: "Since it has been observed that the celebration of sint Nicolaes puts many decent people to great expense and stimulates the youth in superstition, the magistrate of the town of Grave, wanting to prevent such abuse, has interdicted and forbidden, and interdicts and forbids herewith all citizens and inhabitants of this town to practice the mentioned superstition or have their

children do so or receive the shoes and wooden shoes from any children or have them bring these to or put these in any place. They who do otherwise will be punished by the highest possible fine according to the law on fines."

4. Nilsson, pp. 275 - 277.

5. Tille, in his chapter "Tabula Fortunae," pp. 107 ff.

6. Cf. Demont, pp. 14 - 15; Du Broc II, 529.

7. Meisen, p. 12.

8. The cakes and cookies are listed and described, de Schuyter, p. 13.

9. A writer in *Notes and Queries* 3, IX, 330 - 331, calls attention that N cakes in Brussels bakeshops are now identical with those depicted in the Heures d'Anne de Bretagne; cf. *Knickerbocker Weekly* IX, 6 (Dec. 1948), p. 21.

10. Hough, p. 130.

11. De Schuyter, p. 12^V. An N song runs: "Bring me a ship / Bring me a ship made out of sweets."

12. Ibid., p. 10.

13. Alofsen, pp. 14 - 17; Hough, p. 130.

14. Meisen, p. 352; Sébillot I, 127.

15. The shoes may have evolved from the paper ships (N the mariner) which appeared very early (full data in Meisen, pp. 405 - 407) and continue to the present. *Lebkuchen* is still called *Schiffeln*.

16. Alofsen, p. 12.

17. De Schuyter, pp. 19^V - 20. In France "cantiques spirituels" depicted garish N's; see *Le pays lorrain* XXIV (1932), 72, 76.

18. See above chap. 6, iii, n. 57.

19. Larousse XI, 987.

20. Brand I, 420.

21. Ibid.

22. Germ. *pumpern* = "to pass wind" = a rustic, boor, or booby. The term may well associate the form of leavening with the Westphalian N's dressed in corn shocks.

23. Lexicographers are apt to equate *nix, Nick, Nikolas,* and *nickel* with "demon" (e.g. *American Heritage Dictionary; Webster's New World Dictionary*). Cf. *Kupfernickel.* These coinages, though probably also traceable to N, have a somewhat different path of development from *pumpernickel.*

24. Van Gennep, *Manuel* I, i, 182 - 183.

25. Meisen, pp. 342 - 343.

26. De Groot, pp. 123 - 124. I borrow freely from Aebischer 1932.

27. As do mating and harvest rites (Frazer, *Spirits of the Corn* 1935, in I, 155 ff., esp. 162 - 163).

28. De Groot, pp. 18 - 19. A popular N pastry around Liège has a fully-dressed effigy of N, but with an especially large sugar navel exposed.

29. Demont, p. 21.

30. De Groot, p. 29.

31. So Caesarius of Heisterbach, ca. 1220: "Many wonders were wrought through it, especially in the case of women who were with child."

32. Sébillot III, 403.

33. Ibid. IV, p. 170.

34. Meisen, p. 245.

35. De Schuyter, p. 11ᵛ.

36. Van Gennep 1928, p. 36; Harrison, p. 213.

37. Van Gennep, *Manuel* I, ii, 577.

38. Meisen, p. 242.

39. Albrecht, pp. 24 - 25; Sébillot IV, 138; *Marches de l'est* II (1910), 261.

40. De Groot, pp. 126 - 127.

41. Van Gennep, *Manuel* I, i, 244.

42. From Naogeorgus (chap. 6, iii, n. 57 above).

43. C. xxix (*Cat. Cod. Hagr. Paris.* II, 423 - 424).

44. Van Gennep, *Manuel* I, i, 207 - 208.

45. Saint Flor (d. 1347) prayed to Notre Dame, Gabriel, the virgin martyrs, and N as special protectors of virginity and humility (*Anal. Boll.* LXIV, 1946, p. 25).

46. *Liber de praelato,* ed., *MGH,* pp. 131 - 133; he applied (p. 136) Job xxxi, 16 - 18 to Gregory the Great and added, "Hoc multum convenit beato Nicolao."

47. Nunnally in *English Language Notes* V, 2 (1967), 106 - 108.

§VII THE HYBRID COMPOSITION

1. Loukovitch, pp. 138 ff., shows a rise in hagiographical drama in France resulting from the Counterreformation; but though Catherine was still acceptable as a virgin martyr, N was totally neglected. In the main, historical instances like Joan of Arc were favored.

2. 25 Dec. 1652, also 1653.

3. Thomas Burton, *Diary,* as recorded in *Notes and Queries* 3, I, 246.

4. Levy, passim.

5. Note that the hymn tune *Saint Nicholas* still survives (no. 173) in the revised Episcopal hymnal.

6. Drawn from Arnold-Foster III.

7. Van Gennep in *Revue d'ethnographie* IX (1928), 36.

8. Bäumer II, 265 - 267.

9. Anrich II, 180 - 181; Bäumer II, 496.

10. Yet Sparks, pp. 2 - 3, could cite with approval the cardinal's doubt "whether there ever was any such man as S. George, or such a woman as S. Katherine." In 1606 the Congregation of Rites forbade the priests of Bari to carry myrrh with solemnity to the infirm, and in 1642 it denied the request of the collegiate church of Altamura to sign the people (sign of the cross) with myrrh (*Revue de l'art chrétien* XXVI [1883], 305).

11. Bäumer II, 395.

12. Mancel, p. 15.

7 *Second Childhood*

§I INTRODUCTION

1. Genesis ii, 2 - 3.

2. See, e.g., *Bedae Venerabilis In Genesim Liber* I, ed. C. W. Jones, Corpus Christianorum 118 A (1967), p. 39, with cited sources.

3. *King Lear,* IV, vii, 60.

4. *New York Times,* 10 May 1969.

5. Papal Decree, 1969, 80. The new calendar "elicited cries of protest"; for the official response of the Secretary of the Vatican Congregation for Divine Worship, see *New York Times,* 12, 14, and 31 May.

6. Horace, *Carmina* IV, vii, 16.

7. But even the Commission of Gregory XIV for rectifying the Breviary opined that no date or even Day for N was certain; see the minutes of Bäumer II, 266 - 267.

8. N. A. Cameron in *EB* (1962) XVIII, p. 690H.

9. *Hamlet* II, ii.

10. Some of what is written hereafter I once delivered at the annual N Day meeting of the New-York Historical Society, later published in its *Quarterly* XXXVIII (1954), 357 - 383.

§ II THE COLONIAL N

1. Founded by Bishop Arnold, A.D. 1126, at Gardar.

2. He landed 5 Dec. 1492. "The first of Columbus's New World names that has never been altered" (S. E. Morison I, 362 - 363).

3. *Herald Tribune Book Review,* 12 October 1952.

4. Washington Irving was founder and its first secretary. See the Address by President (Cornelius Vanderbilt) at the Semi-centennial Anniversary 28 Feb. 1885. Chauncey Depew, the main speaker on that occasion, said that the society had established a fund of $30,000 to aid indigent members, but since there had never been any the fund was as yet intact; cf. *An Hundred Year Record,* (New York, 1935), p. 35.

5. Booth pp. 192 - 195.

6. See, e.g., *Funk and Wagnalls' Standard Dictionary of Folklore, Mythology, and Legend* (1950), II, 967.

7. E.g., Pauli, pp. 100 - 101.

8. C. W. Jones, "Knickerbocker," pp. 362 - 363.

9. George R. Stewart, "Men's Names in Plymouth and Massachusetts," *University of California Publications in English* VII, 2 (Berkeley, 1948), pp. 109 - 137.

10. Hoffman, p. 24.

11. See Index of Manuscripts, New York, below.

12. *New York Hist. Soc. Collections* III, 88.

13. Samuel A. Green, *Diary of Increase Mather,* Cambridge, Mass., 1900, p. 54.

14. C. W. Jones, "Knickerbocker," p. 363.

15. On Saint Tammany's Day, 1 May 1783, Leacock sang to the Philadelphians:

> Of Andrew, of Patrick, of David, and George,
>
> What mighty achievements we hear!
>
> Whilst no one relates great Tammany's feats,
>
> Although more heroic by far . . . [Kilroe, pp. 78 - 79]

16. G. A. Morrison, p. 7.

17. Ibid., pp. 9 - 15.

18. Stokes IV, 679.

19. Ibid., p. 847.

20. *Pennsylvania Magazine of History and Biography* XXV (1901), 441; XXVI (1902), 17.

21. Furman MS.

22. See, e.g., John Trumbull's *M'Fingal, A Modern Epic Poem* (Philadelphia, 1775).

23. All this, and more of relevance, neatly expressed in Shakespeare's Henry V (V, i).

24. Myers I, 1 - 16.

25. Kilroe, p. 30.

26. William Penn secured land from him in 1683, 1684, 1694, and 1697, according to deeds in the Pennsylvania Archives.

27. "The Sons of St. Tammany of Philadelphia," *Penn. Mag.* XXV (1901), 433 - 451; Kilroe; Werner.

28. May 1 was Spring Day (the opening of the fishing season—see Kilroe, p. 37)—in Philadelphia, and partly in honor of Mr. Pole, mine host of the tavern where the Sons of Liberty gathered, a maypole was center of festivity. With acceptance of New Style, some wag suggested that Tammany Day had historically been 12 days later, so the Day was shifted to 12 May (Cabeen in *Penn. Mag.* XXVII [1903]; Werner, p. 4). The flag of the U.S. was first displayed 1 May 1785 at the Tammany gathering at Beveridge's, "ornamented with a fine figure of St. Tammany drawn by Mr. Wright. The flags of France and Holland were also in evidence" (Kilroe, p. 94; cf. p. 74).

29. Kilroe, pp. 30, 38. There were at least two ships named *Saint Tammany* (*The Register of the Times* [Friday 9 Dec. 1796] New York; Letter of William Lee to Francis Lightfoot Lee, Paris 11 Nov. 1777 [MS of NY Hist. Soc.]). The latter was a privateer.

30. Mrs. J. H. van Rensselaer, *Goede Vrouw,* pp. 291 - 292.

31. Hoffman, p. 24.

32. Furman MS. Cf. Chas. H. Rominger, *Early Christmases in Bethlehem, Pennsylvania,* Publications of the Pennsylvania German Folklore Soc. 6 (1941), p. 10.

33. Furman MS.

34. Henry P. Fairchild, *Immigration* (1930), p. 56.

35. At least as early as 1757 (*Transactions of the Grand Lodge . . . in New York* (New York, [1880], II, 120). Stokes IV and V, passim. The documents indicate to me that the Masons did not discriminate between the Baptist and the Evangelist.

36. *Dictionary of American English,* s.v. "Cincinnati"; Stokes I, p. 374.

37. Normally Saint Cuffee; see Kilroe, p. 30.

38. Cabeen, pp. 35 - 36; cf. Werner, pp. 6 - 7.

39. There was no uniformity among the Knickerbockers. Pintard wrote Saint Nicholas, Saint Claas, Saint Klas, etc.; Benson wrote Sanctus Klaas.

§III Knickerbocker Santa Claus

1. In 1773 there were two congregations of Huguenots in the city, pop. ca. 150,000 (*American Museum or Repository* [Philadelphia: Mathew Carey, 1789], VI, 302).

2. *Dictionary of American Biography,* s.v. "Pintard."

3. Wilson III, 76 - 78; T. E. V. Smith, pp. 112 - 113.

4. Kilroe, p. 61, suggests that the name of Saint Tammany, Louisiana, was due to Pintard.

5. For winter-spring 1975, as its observance of the Bicentennial, the New-York Historical Society held a Special Exhibition: "John Pintard and His Society." "More than 400 paintings, drawings, water colors and prints of Pintard and his friends and associates: Hamilton, Clinton, Audubon, Cooper, Jay, Livingston, Morse, and Washington Irving, reflecting the political, social, and artistic life of the state, 1785 - 1845."

6. *Penn. Mag.* XXVI (1902), 210. Kilroe, p. 32, says that the idea of forming a national society "is plainly traceable to John Pintard." He gives the constitution, pp. 103 - 105.

7. Stokes I, 373 - 374; Kilroe, p. 32.

8. Wilson III, 64 - 65; Blake; *Penn. Mag.* XXVI (1902), 462 - 463.

9. Letter to Belknap 11 Oct. 1790 (Belknap Papers III, 469 - 470).

10. Porcupine's Works I (London, 1801), p. 129.

11. Myers, I, 1 - 16.

12. Pintard I, 56.

13. The Tammany museum he established was given to Gardiner Baker, its curator, in 1795 (Myers I, 1 - 16). Eventually it became a part of Barnum's American Museum (Werner, pp. 15 - 16).

14. Minutes, 20 Nov. 1804. Facsimile in Wilson III, 178; *New-York Hist. Soc. Collections* I, 458.

15. C. W. Jones, "Knickerbocker," p. 369.

16. So also at a banquet of 5,000 persons at the Bayard country house celebrating the adoption of the Constitution (1788) (Wilson III, 41).

17. An evidence of the Dutch Revolutionary sympathy is that in the British occupation of the war years all three Dutch Reformed churches were closed down and used as stables; cf. Wilson III, 19 - 20, 100.

18. "Historical Sketch of the Society" 1841 (New-York Hist. Soc. *Collections,* N.S. I, p. 462).

19. Facsimile in C. W. Jones, "Knickerbocker," p. 371.

20. Pintard III, 83. For *Bilderbogen* see Metken, pp. 46 - 47.

21. From the legend of Saint Ambrose.

22. From "Domini-canes," the Dominican hounds of heaven.

23. Pintard III, 53.

24. 25 Jan. 1808, no. xx (Bohn's ed., [London 1853], I, 274 - 275).

25. Werner, p. 2; Kilroe, p. 47, indicates that the fables of this farce were incorporated in later social histories as reality, just as were Irving's fables of SC.

26. *Dictionary of American Biography.*

27. Stanley T. Williams. *The Life of Washington Irving* I (New York, 1935), 115.

28. *Old South Leaflets,* series 3, no. 69, p. 23.

29. Irving, *Knickerbocker's History* I, 115 - 117, 118, 155 - 157, 171, 201 - 202, 208; II, 60, 99, 110, 129, 139, 151, 163, 166, 182, 201, 214, 229, 231, 239, 256, 260, 269, 273.

30. The first *New York Directory,* prefaced by a General Description by Noah Webster, 1786 (Facsimile New York: H. J. Sacks and Co., 1905) should be compared with its equivalent for 1820 (Longworth's American Almanac). In the first, Andrew, Patrick and David find place, but not N; in the latter, N but not the others.

31. MS, New York Historical Society, Horner, p. 38. Cooper alluded to N as if a commonplace (*Pioneers*) (*Dictionary of American English* IV [Chicago, 1944], 2018).

32. Address at the semicentennial of the Saint Nicholas Society, 28 Feb. 1885.

33. *EB,* s.v. "Paulding." His father had been a violent anti-British patriot—perhaps a member of the original Sons of Saint Nicholas.

34. His son wrote *The Literary Life of James K. Paulding (New York, 1867).*

35. New York, 1836, containing stories from 1827 on. See esp. "The Author's Advertisement."

36. E.g., *The New Mirror for Travellers* (cited by Alofsen, pp. 5 - 6), 1826. In 1843 he published a sincere history of New Amsterdam. In the 1840s Morris and Willis published a serial, *The New Mirror,* inspired by Paulding; it describes N as "recently born again."

37. Reprinted by Patterson, pp. 11 - 12.

38. As late as 1839, "Communipaw" (reprinted in *A Book of the Hudson,* [1849], p. 14), Irving described N's appearance down the chimney on N Day, not Christmas or New Year.

39. *Clouds,* lines 615 - 619.

40. See *Loudon's New-York Packet* for 3 Jan. 1785 for description of the damage done by customary New Year revels, esp. indiscriminate use of guns.

41. Patterson's rather sentimentalized biography contains relevant documents and illustrations. *EB* printed 1,000 copies of Hosking, *The Night before Christmas,* as a kind of Carriers' Address; this slight volume, markedly factual, contains relevant illustrations, including a facsimile of Onderdonk's 1848 booklet of the *Visit.*

42. Patterson, pp. 17 - 18.

43. Ibid., pp. 112 - 113.

44. Ibid., pp. 19 - 21.

45. Patterson, pp. 66 - 68.

46. Ibid., pp. 118 - 119; H. L. West in *The Bookman,* Dec. 1920, pp. 300, 305; Horner (see note 31 above), p. 40.

47. Patterson, pp. 112 - 113.

48. His wife, Catherine Elizabeth Taylor, descended through the maternal line from Stephanus Van Cortlandt, mayor of the city in 1677 and 1687, and owner of an estate now Van Cortlandt Park in the Bronx (Patterson, pp. 64 - 66).

49. Columbia honored him with Ll.D. in 1829, aet. 50 (Patterson, p. 142).

50. The numerous verses in Patterson are a sufficient sample; see also *Century* LV, n.s. 33, (1897 - 1898) 201.

51. Horner (see note 31 above), p. 40.

52. Facsimile of the reindeer and the eight quatrains in Patterson, pp. 12 - 14; C. W. Jones, "Knickerbocker," p. 356.

53. Patterson has reproduced the New-York Hist. Soc. copy, pp. xiv - xvi; see p. 150. Another draft was sold in 1932 for $250.00; other holographs are listed among the Moore papers at the New-York Hist. Soc.

54. George A. Zabriskie, *A Visit from St. Nicholas* (Cliffdale N.J., 1930), p. 8. Patterson, p. 11, accepts this geriatric reminiscence somewhat too factually; see C. W. Jones, "Knickerbocker," pp. 380 - 382; Horner, p. 41.

55. *Life* XXI, 26 (23 Dec. 1946), pp. 14 - 16: "Using a stout apple-cheeked neighbor as a model, Moore transformed the gentle European saint into a bumptious little man with eight reindeer and a sleigh full of toys." The editors of *Life* had RKO Hollywood produce a series of stills with this cast: Papa—Henry Fonda; Mama—Barbara Bel Geddes; Little Boy—Ray Warren; Little Girl—Gale Warren; Saint Nicholas—Walter Slezak.

§ IV THE EMIGRANT WORLD OF THOMAS NAST

1. The New York *Daily Advertiser,* repeating daily to 25 Dec.

2. The *New-York Journal or General Advertiser* 18 Dec., repeated to 24 Dec.

3. Cf. above sec. iv.

4. One of Paulding's stories in the *Book of Saint Nicholas* was "Origin of the Baker's Dozen."

5. Horner, p. 38.

6. Ibid., p. 42. *Harper's* VI (1852 - 3), p. 276 (Editor's Drawer): "So twice in a sun, / Down the chimney I come, / With my treasures, and heart full of cheer; / You laugh as I call / 'Merry Christmas,' to all, / And you shout at my 'HAPPY NEW YEAR.' " Richards says "the movement toward general acceptance of Christmas was definitely under way by 1860." Christmas was not declared a public holiday until 1865 (Horner, p. 35).

7. *Gentleman's Magazine,* I, 407.

8. "St. Nicholas was born—and that is all I can tell you of the matter—on the first of January" (Quoted in Horner, p. 39).

9. 25 Dec. 1841.

10. Reprinted by Patterson, p. 20. Horner says 1829.

11. Reproduced in C. W. Jones, "Knickerbocker," p. 383; Patterson, frontispiece (cf. pp. 114 - 115).

12. Designed and engraved by Sherman and Smith; entitled "Santa Claus: The night before New Year."

13. As late as 1856 (*Santa Claus, or The Night Before Christmas* [New York: Mathews and Clasbach], frontispiece) he might have feathers in his cap.

14. Emelyn E. Gardner, *Folklore of the Schoharie Hills* (Ann Arbor, 1937), p. 305, n. 303. The switches lasted until at least 1873 (Broadside of C. F. A. Hinrichs, Toys, Park Place, New York). The Giftgiver had traveled full circle when in 1876 Thomas Zimmerman, Editor of the *Reading Times and Dispatch,* rendered Moore's verses in Pennsylvania Dutch (Reichard, pp. 11, 86).

15. Vinson, p. 41.

16. Paine wrote that Nast's 1862 depiction of SC so fixed the image in his 5-year-old mind that it never altered. When he was planning the biography, the elderly Nast said to him: "If we do this thing, I should like to put in some of my Santa Claus pictures."

17. Vinson, p. 39.

18. Ibid.

19. Ibid. The title page was his most circulated Santa Claus (facsimile in Patterson, p. 116).

20. Faust I, 583 ff.; Richards, pp. 95 - 96. When Dickens and Irving appeared together in New York on Valentine's Day 1842, they were equally lionized; see Wilson III, 371 - 372. Irving wrote to his daughter 29 Sept. 1853 (Irving, *Life and Letters* IV, 163): "The new St. Nicholas Hotel beats everything of the hotel kind I have ever seen."

21. *Christmas in Detroit a Hundred Years Ago* (Detroit Public Library, 1942).

22. Paine, p. 84.

23. James Fenimore Cooper, "The Towers of Manhattan," *New-York Hist. Soc. Quarterly* 1953, p. 47.

24. Paine, pp. 96, 319.

25. See above, p. 397. However, Rietschel, p. 141, reproduces a South German Schmutzi that is drawn in slightly similar fashion.

26. Wilson III, 377.

27. *Century* LV, n.s. 33 (1897 - 1898), 173 - 174.

28. Griffis in *Harper's* LXXXVIII, 217.

29. Wilson III, 442 - 443.

30. An earlier American *St. Nicholas,* a monthly, was published at Owego, N.Y., Apr. 1853 - Mar. 1854.

31. However L. Frank Baum, of *Wizard of Oz* fame, published "A Kidnapped Santa Claus" in the *Delineator* (Dec. 1904); it did not appear in boards until 1969 (Indianapolis: Bobbs Merrill).

32. Henry Steele Commager, *The St. Nicholas Anthology,* with an Introduction by May Lamberton Becker (New York, 1948), xxi + 542 pp.

33. Wagenknecht, p. 158.

34. New York: Holt.

§V THE NEW BYZANTIUM

1. Ca. 1880 (Gleason White in *The Studio,* Christmas 1894 Extra Number); Barnett, p. 18.

2. Barnett, pp. 108 - 114; *California Monthly,* Dec. 1967, pp. 12 - 13. Col. Ralph Gimbel has formed a collection on Rudolfana.

3. Becker 1941, p. 671.

4. Connie Soloyanis in *San Francisco Chronicle,* 4 Sept. 1966.

5. Aarno Malin and Towo Haapenen, *Zwölf lateinische Sequenzen* (Helsinki 1922), 24 pp.

6. *Knickerbocker Weekly* I, 42 (15 Dec. 1941), p. 38. The age of miracles has not passed. According to the report in that weekly (III, 44, [27 Dec. 1943], pp. 28 - 29) in 1943 Black Pieter had influenza and missed the Christmas Party 18 Dec. (sponsors Holland House Corporation and Netherlands Aid

Society); but that same day SC appeared with Black Pieter at another party at the City of New York Museum.

7. *Knickerbocker Weekly* III, 44 (27 Dec. 1943), p. 31.

8. Ibid.

9. E.g., the article by Rev. Dr. Auer, the clerical member of the editorial board, in the *Weekly* V, 41 (3 Dec. 1945), pp. 14 - 15.

10. *Knickerbocker Weekly* II, 43 (21 Dec. 1942), p. 10.

11. Ibid., VI, 42 (1946), pp. 1 ff.

12. The *Standard-Star,* New Rochelle, N.Y., 2 Dec. 1953.

13. Kayata, pp. 162 - 164.

14. *Match,* 25 Dec. 1965, pp. 38 ff.

15. *Gentleman's Magazine* I, 407.

16. In their edition of Butler's *Lives of the Saints* IV, 506.

17. *Notes and Queries* 5, XI, p. 66.

18. St. Swithin in *Notes and Queries* 12, I, p. 69; cf. pp. 173 - 174.

19. *Penguin Book of Latin Verse,* ed. Brittain (Baltimore, 1962), pp. 362 - 363.

20. *Deutsche Kriegsweihnacht 1944.*

21. Hon. Herbert L. Satterlee at the Ninety-third Paas Festival of The Saint Nicholas Society, Hotel Plaza, 18 Apr. 1938.

22. The post office at Christmas, Arizona, also does its principal business in December. It originated from discovery of a mine there on 25 December (George R. Stewart, *Names on the Land,* 1945, p. 318).

23. Facsimile in *Saturday Evening Post,* 16 May 1953, p. 39.

24. From the brochure.

25. As did North Pole, because of government regulations against disease; but eventually the owners discovered a legal herd in Alaska, from which they drew (*Sat. Ev. Post,* 19 Dec. 1953, p. 79).

26. *San Francisco Chronicle,* 20 Nov. 1963, p. 41.

27. In an advertising leaflet the *New-York World-Telegram,* successor to the *Sun*, described it as "the most famous editorial article that has ever been written. It has been reproduced in every conceivable form, in every quarter of the globe."

28. The first in the year 1912. Nicola Berardi, "Una corona di francobolli per S. Nicola," *Collana,* no. 1, 1963, has gathered a large number of instances, with facsimiles, from around the world.

29. W. F. Dawson, p. 313.

30. *American Magazine,* Dec. 1949, p. 103.

31. *The New Yorker,* 26 July 1952.

§VI PSYCHOANALYSIS

1. Richards, p. 155, sets the first warnings against commercialization of Christmas in the year 1899.

2. "The Spirit of Christmas Presents," Program Transcript, 14. Nov., Public Affairs Department, CBS.

3. So medieval Europe evolved the Klasholz and Klausenbein, on which children could record their Paternosters for N's visitation (Meisen, p. 408; de Groot, p. 40).

4. De Groot, p. 225.

5. *Dictionary of Americanisms* II, 1457.

6. *New York Times,* 1 Oct. 1952, p. 19R.

7. A satisfactory bibliography in Pollock, p. 131.

8. So, e.g., L. M. Boyd in the *San Francisco Chronicle,* 22 July 1972.

9. Boyer, p. 15.

10. Cattell, p. 39.

11. Jekels, p. 57.

12. Ibid., p. 63.

13. Sterba, p. 81.

14. De Groot, p. 228.

15. Jung, cited de Groot, pp. 91 ff.

16. De Groot, pp. 120 - 121.

17. Ibid., p. 154.

18. Ibid., pp. 146, 152.

§VII EPILOGUE

1. Lord Dunsany, *My Ireland.*

2. Riezler, p. 316.

3. *Faerie Queene* VII, 58.

Items for which an abbreviated reference is used are alphabetized according to the abbreviation which appears in brackets. Most publications referred to but once are omitted from this list and the bibliographic data are included at the point of reference. Manuscripts appear in the Index of Manuscripts Cited, p. 493.

Abrahams, Phyllis. *See* Albrecht.

[*Acta SS.*] *Acta Sanctorum.* Edited by the Société des Bollandistes (Socii Bollandiani). Antwerp and Brussels, 1643 - . Includes *Propylaeum Decembris* (Martyrologium Romanum), edited by Père H. Delehaye, 1940.

Adémar. *See* Chabannes.

Adler, Bill. *See* David, Jay.

Aebischer, Paul. *Une moralité de Monsieur Sant Nicholas.* Fribourg, 1940. Verse *Son of Getron 46* from Florence MS Ashburnham 115, from Avignon ca. 1470.

————. "Sur deux caractéristiques du culte populaire de Saint Nicolas." *Archivum Romanicum* (Geneva) XVI (1932), 125 - 134; cf. ibid. XV, 390.

Aigrain, l'abbé René. *L'Hagiographie, ses sources, ses méthodes, son histoire.* Paris, 1953.

Albrecht, Otto E., ed. *Four Latin Plays of St. Nicholas.* Philadelphia, 1935. See review by Phyllis Abrahams in *Medium Aevum* VI (1937), 216 - 219.

Amann, E., ed., continuator of A. Vacant and E. Mangenot. *Dictionnaire de théologie catholique.* Paris, 1903 - 1950.

Ambroise, G. *Les moines du moyen âge.* Brussels, 1946.

Ambrosi, A. C. "Il culto di S. Nicolao in Garfagnana e in Lunigiana." *Archivio storico per le Province Parmensi* 4 ser., xix (1967), 35 - 53.

American Magazine. New York, N.Y., 1906 ff.

Amplissima Collectio Veterum Scriptorum et Monumentorum Ecclesiasticorum et Dogmaticorum. Edited by E. Martène and U. Durand. 9 vols. Paris, 1724 - 1733.

[*Anal. Boll.*] *Analecta Bollandiana.* Edited by the Société des Bollandistes. Brussels, 1882 - .

[*Anal. Hymn.*] *Analecta Hymnica Medii Aevi.* Edited by G. M. Dreves, S.J., and C. Blume, S.J. 55 vols. Leipzig, 1886 - 1922.

Analecta Liturgica. Lille and Bruges, 1888 - .

Anastos, Milton V. "Plethon's Calendar and Liturgy." *Dumbarton Oaks Papers* IV (1948), 183 - 305.

Ancelet-Hustache, Jeanne. *Saint Nicholas.* Translated by Rosemary Sheed. New York, 1962.

Andrieu, Michel. *Les Ordines Romani du haut moyen-âge.* Spicilegium sacrum Lovaniense 2, 23, 24, 28. Louvain, 1931, 1948, 1951, 1956.

Anichkof, E. "St. Nicholas and Artemis." *Folk-Lore* V (1894), 108 - 120.

Anna Comnena. *Alexiad.* Translated by E. A. S. Dawes. London, 1928.

Annales Barenses. Edited by Pertz in *MGH,* Scriptores V.

Annales Bertiniani. Edited by Waitz in *MGH,* Scriptores I.

Anrich, Gustav. *Hagios Nikolaos.* 2 vols. Leipzig, 1913, 1917.

Apel, Willi. *Gregorian Chant.* Indianapolis, 1958.

Archaeological Journal of the British Archaeological Association. London, 1844 - .

Archaeology. Published by the Archaeological Institute of America. New York, 1948 - .

Archiv der Gesellschaft für ältere deutsche Geschichtskunde (Pertz' Archiv). Hanover, 1820 - .

Archiv für das Studium der neureren Sprachen und Literaturen. Brunswick, 1964 - .

Archiv für Kulturgeschichte. Berlin, 1903 - .

Archiv für Liturgiewissenschaft. Regensburg, 1950 - .

Archives de la France monastique. Ligugé, 1905 - .

Archivum Romanicum. 25 vols., Geneva, 1917 - 1941.

Argenti, Philip P., and Rose, H. J. *The Folklore of Chios.* 2 vols. Cambridge, 1949.

Armellini, Mariano. *Le Chiese di Roma dal secolo IV al XIX.* Rome, 1891.

Arnold-Foster, Frances. *Studies in Church Dedications.* 3 vols. London, 1899.

Art Bulletin. Published by the College Art Association of America. New York, 1913 -.

Assion, Peter. *Die Mirakel der Hl. Katharina von Alexandrien.* Bamberg, 1969. See review by Père de Gaiffier in *Anal. Boll.* LXXXIX (1971), 248 - 250.

————. "Die mittelalterliche Mirakelliteratur als Forschungsgegenstand." *Archiv für Kulturgeschichte* L (1968), 172 ff.

Aston, S. C. "The Saint in Medieval Literature." *Modern Language Review* LXV (1970), pp. xxv - xlii.

Atlas of the Early Christian World. Edited by F. van der Meer and Christine Mohrmann. Translated by Mary F. Hedlund and H. H. Rowley. London, 1958.

Auda, Antoine. *Etienne de Liège.* Mémoires publiés par l'Académie Royale de Belgique (Classe des Beaux Arts) 2. 1923.

Augustine, Bishop of Hippo. *De Civitate Dei (City of God), libri xxii.* Edited in *Pat. Lat.* XLI.

Avril, François, and Gaborit, Jean-René. "L'*Itinerarium Bernardi Monachi* et les pèlerinages d'Italie du Sud pendant le haut-moyen-âge." *Ecole Française de Rome, Mélanges d'archéologie et d'histoire* LXXIX (1967), 269 - 298.

Babudri, Francesco. "Sinossi critica dei traslatori nicolaiani di Bari." *Archivio Storico Pugliese* (Bari) IV (1950), 3 - 94.

————. *Il concilio di Bari del 1098.* Editore il Comune di Bari, 1959.

————. *La cripta di San Nicola a Bari nei suoi alti valori di e d'arte. Collana* 2. Bari, 1963.

————. *S. Nicola di Bari e il suo patronato sull mare nella storia e nel folklore internazionale. Collana* 4. Bari, 1964.

Banks, Mrs. M. M. *British Calendar Customs: Scotland.* 3 vols. London: Folk-Lore Society, 1937 - 1941.

Bannister, H. M. *Monumenti Vaticani di Paleografia musicale Latina.* 2 vols. Leipzig, 1913.

Bari città levante. Introduzione di Mario Sansone; testi di Manlio Spadaro e Pietro Marino. Bari, 1969.

Baring-Gould, Sabine. *The Lives of the Saints.* Rev. ed. 17 vols. Edinburgh, 1914.

Barlow, James William. *A Short History of the Normans in South Europe.* London, 1886.

Barnett, James H. *The American Christmas.* New York, 1954.

Barrett, Walter. *See* Scoville.

Bartoli, A. "S. Nicola in Carcere." *Atti della Pontificia Accademia Romana di*

Archeologia, 3 ser. V (1926 - 1927), 213 - 226.

Bartolini, Dominico. *Su l'antica Basilica di S. Nicola in Bari nella Puglia.* Rome, 1882.

Baudrillart, Alfred, and others. *Dictionnaire d'histoire et de géographie ecclésiastique.* 10 vols. Paris, 1912 - 1938.

Bäumer, S. *Histoire du Bréviaire.* Translated by Biron. 2 vols. Paris, 1905.

Bax, E. Belfort. *German Society at the Close of the Middle Ages.* London, 1894.

Baynes, Norman H., and Moss, H. St. L. B., eds. *Byzantium: an Introduction to East Roman Civilization.* Oxford, 1948.

Becker, Ernest J. *Medieval Visions of Heaven and Hell.* Baltimore, 1899.

[Bede, H.E.] *Baedae Venerabilis Historia Ecclesiastica Gentis Anglorum.* Edited by Charles Plummer. 2 vols. Oxford, 1896.

Belknap, Jeremy. *Belknap Papers III.* Collections of the Massachusetts Historical Society, 5 ser.

Bell, Mrs. Arthur. *The Saints in Christian Art.* 3 vols. London, 1901 - 1904.

Benedictine Book of Saints. See *Vies des saints.*

Berger, Leo Ernst. *Nikolaus-Werkbuch.* Munich, 1965.

[BHG.] *Biblioteca Hagiographica Graeca.* Edited by the Société des Bollandistes. Editio altera emendatior, accedit synopsis metaphrastica. Subsidia Hagiographica 8. Brussels, 1909.

[BHL.] *Biblioteca Hagiographica Latina Antiquae et Mediae Aetatis.* Edited by the Société des Bollandistes. Subsidia Hagiographica 6, 12. 3 parts. Brussels, 1898 - 1911.

Bibliotheca Arnamagnaeana: Icelandic and Old Norse Literature, History, and Art. Copenhagen, 1941 - .

Bibliotheca Casinensis. 5 vols. Monte Cassino, 1873 - 1894.

Birch, Walter de Gray. "The Legendary Life of Saint Nicholas." *Archaeological Journal* of the British Archaeological Association XLII (1886), 185 - 201; LXIV (1888), 222 - 234.

Blake, E. Vale. *History of the Tammany Society.* New York, 1901.

Bloch, Herbert. "Monte Cassino, Byzantium, and the West in the Earlier Middle Ages." *Dumbarton Oaks Papers* III (1946), 163 - 224.

Bohnstedt, Kurt K. Rud. *Vie Saint-Nicolas, altfranzösisches Gedicht.* Inaug. diss., Leipzig. Erlangen, 1897.

Bond, Francis. *Dedications and Patron Saints of English Churches, Ecclesiastical Symbolism, Saints and their Emblems.* London, 1914.

Bonnard, Mgr. Fourier. *Histoire de l'église de Saint-Nicolas in Agone de la Confraternité des Lorrains à Rome.* Paris and Rome, 1932.

The Bookman. New York, 1895 - 1933.

Booth, Mary L. *History of the City of New York, from its Earliest Settlement to the Present Time.* New York, 1859.

Börsting, Heinrich. "Liudger-träger des Nikolauskultes im Abendland." *Liudger und sein Erbe (Westfalia Sacra I),* pp. 139 - 181. Munster, 1948.

Boussard, Jacques. "L'Origine des familles seigneuriales dans la région de la Loire moyenne." *Cahiers de civilisation mediévale* V, 3 (1962), 303 - 322.

Boyd. *A Visit from St. Nicholas by Clement C. Moore. With original cuts designed and engraved by Boyd.* New York, 1849.

Boyer, L. Bryce. "Christmas 'Neurosis.' " *Journal of the American Psychoanalytic Association* III (1955), 467 - 488.

Bralion, Nicolas de. *La vie admirable de Saint Nicolas, archevesque de Myre, avec un discours sur la liqueur miraculeuse qui sort continuellement de ses s. reliques, appelée communément manne de s. Nicolae.* Paris, 1646 (repr. 1652, 1859).

Brand, John. *Observations on the Popular Antiquities of Great Britain.* Revised and enlarged by Sir Henry Ellis. 3 vols. London, 1877.

Bréhier, Louis. *La querelle des images (viiie - ixe s.).* 2d ed. Paris, 1904.

————. *L'Eglise et l'Orient au moyen âge: les croisades.* 2d ed. Paris, 1907.

————. *Le monde byzantin.* I: *Vie et mort de Byzance;* II: *Les institutions de l'Empire byzantin;* III: *La civilisation byzantine.* Paris, 1947, 1949, 1950.

British Museum Quarterly. London, 1926 - .

British Society of Franciscan Studies, Publications. Vols. 1 - 19. Aberdeen, 1908 - 1937.

Britt, Matthew, O.S.B. *The Hymns of the Breviary and Missal.* Rev. ed. New York, 1936.

Bulletin of the John Rylands Library. Manchester, England, 1903 - .

Burchard. *See* Haito.

Burlet, J. *Documents: Le culte de Dieu.* Académie des sciences, belles-lettres, et arts de Savoie 9 (Chambéry, 1922).

Buss, Reinhardt J. *The Klaubautermann of the Northern Seas.* University of California Folklore Studies 25. Berkeley and Los Angeles, 1973.

Byron, Robert. *The Byzantine Achievement.* London, 1929.

Byzantinische Zeitschrift. Founded by Karl Krumbacher. Leipzig, 1892 - .

Cabeen, Francis A. "The Society of the Sons of Saint Tammany of Philadelphia." *Pennsylvania Magazine of History and Biography* XXV, XXVI (1901, 1902).

Caesarius of Heisterbach. *Dialogus Miraculorum.* Translated by H. von Scott and C. C. S. Bland. 2 vols. London, 1929.

Cahier, Charles. *Caracteristiques des saints dans l'art populaire.* 2 vols. Paris, 1867.

Cahiers de civilisation médiévale. Poitiers, 1958 - .

Cambridge Medieval History. See [*CMH*].

Cambridge Modern History. Edited by A. W. Ward and others. 13 vols. Cambridge, 1902 - 1912.

Carhart, A. S. "Saint Nicholas: His life and miracles." A paper read before the Saint Nicholas Club of the City of New York. New York, 1884.

Catalogue général des manuscrits des bibliothèques publiques de France. Paris, 1849 ff.; new ser., 1886 ff.

[*Cat. Cod. Hag. Brux.*] *Catalogus Codicum Hagiographicorum Bibliothecae Regiae Bruxellensis.* Pars I, Cod. lat. Edited by the Société des Bollandistes. 2 vols. Brussels, 1886, 1889. (Appendix to *Anal. Boll.* II - VIII.)

[*Cat. Cod. Hag. Namur.*] *Catalogus Codicum Hagiographicorum Latinorum in Bibliothecis Publicis Namurici, Gandae, Leodii, et Montibus.* Subsidia Hagiographica 25. Brussels, 1948.

[*Cat. Cod. Hag. Paris.*] *Catalogus Codicum Hagiographicorum Latinorum . . . qui asservantur in Bibliotheca Nationali Parisiensi.* Edited by the Société des Bollandistes. 2 vols. Brussels, 1890.

Catalogus Codicum Hagiographicorum Latinorum . . . Vaticani. Subsidia Hagiographica 9. Brussels, 1909.

Catholic Encyclopedia. Edited by C. G. Herbermann. 15 vols. New York, 1907 - 1914. *New Catholic Encyclopedia.* Edited by the Catholic University of America. 16 vols. 1967 - 1974.

Cattell, James P. "The Holiday Syndrome." *Psychoanalytic Review* XLII (1955), 39 - 43.

Century Illustrated Monthly Magazine. New York, 1881 - 1930.

CFMA. Classiques français du Moyen Age. Paris, 1910 ff.

Chabannes, Adémar de. *Chronicon.* Edited by Jules Chavanon. Paris, 1897.

Chalandon, Ferdinand. *Essai sur le règne d'Alexis Ier Comnene.* Paris, 1900.

———. *Histoire de la domination normande en Italie et en Sicile.* 2 vols. Paris, 1907.

———. *Histoire de la première croisade jusqu'à l'élection de Godefroi de Bouillon.* Paris, 1925.

Chambers, E. K. *The Medieval Stage.* 2 vols. London, 1903.

Charanis, P. "Byzantium, the West, and the Origin of the First Crusade." *Byzantion* XIX (1949), 17 - 36.

Charbonnel (pseud. Chartrou), Josèphe. *L'Anjou 1109 à 1151: Foulque de*

Jerusalem et Geoffrey Plantagenet. Paris, 1928.

Cheroul, A., ed. *Normanniae Nova Chronica.* Caen, 1850.

Chevalier, Cyr Ulysse Joseph. *Répertoire des sources historiques. Bio-bibliographie,* 2 vols., 2d ed., 1905; *Topo-bibliographie,* 2 vols., 1894, 1903.

―――. *Repertorium Hymnologicum.* Bibliothèque liturgique 3 - 4. Brussels, 1920 - 1921.

Citarella, Armand O. "The Relations of Amalfi with the Arab World before the Crusades." *Speculum* XLII (1967), 299 ff.

Clapham, A. W. *Romanesque Architecture in Western Europe.* Oxford, 1936.

Classical Philology. Chicago, 1906 - .

[*CMH.*] *Cambridge Medieval History.* Planned by J. B. Bury, edited by H. M. Gwatkin and others. 8 vols., Cambridge, 1911 - 1936, and subsequent editions.

Cochrane, Charles Norris. *Christianity and Classical Culture.* London, 1957.

Coens, Père Maurice. "Un document inédit sur le culte de s. Syméon moine d'orient et reclus à Trèves." *Anal. Boll.* LXVIII (1950), 181 - 196.

Coffman, George R. *A New Theory Concerning the Origin of the Miracle Play.* Diss., University of Chicago, 1913. Menasha, Wisconsin, 1914.

―――. "A Note Concerning the Cult of St. Nicholas at Hildesheim." In *Manly Anniversary Studies,* pp. 269 - 275. Chicago, 1923.

―――. "A New Approach to Mediaeval Latin Drama." *Modern Philology* XXII (1924 - 1925), 239 - 271.

Collana di Studi Nicolaiani. Pamphlets issued by the Dominican Fathers of Basilica di S. Nicola, Bari, 1963 - .

Conway, A. *Histoire du Bréviaire de Rouen.* Rouen, 1902.

Conway, Moncure Daniel. *Demonology and Devil-lore.* 2 vols. New York, 1879.

Corbin, Solange. *L'Eglise à la conquête de sa musique.* Paris, 1960.

Cornhill Magazine. London, 1860 - 1943.

Corpus Consuetudinum Monasticarum. 5 vols. Siegburg, 1963 - 1968.

Coulton, George Gordon. *Life in the Middle Ages.* 4 vols., Cambridge, 1928.

―――. *Europe's Apprenticeship.* London, 1940.

―――. *Medieval Panorama.* New York, 1944.

―――. *Medieval Faith and Symbolism.* London, 1958.

―――. *Medieval Village, Manor, and Monastery.* New York, 1960.

Count, Earl Wendel. *4000 Years of Christmas.* New York, 1948.

Coussemaker, E. de. *Dramas liturgiques du moyen âge.* Paris, 1861.

Cox, Harvey. *The Feast of Fools*. Cambridge, Mass., 1969.

Crawford, Mary Sinclair. *The Life of St. Nicholas by M. Wace*. Diss., University of Pennsylvania. Philadelphia, 1924.

Crozet, René. "Voyage d'Urbain II et ses négociations avec le clergé de France." *Revue historique* CLXXIX, 271 - 310.

Crozier, E. *The Life and Legends of Saint Nicholas, the Patron Saint of Children*. Paris, 1949.

[*CSEL.*] *Corpus Scriptorum Ecclesiasticorum Latinorum*. Vienna, 1866 - .

Cyprianus, Thascius Caecilianus. *Epistolae. Pat. Lat.* IV.

[*DACL.*] Fernand Cabrol and H. Leclercq, ed. *Dictionnaire d'archéologie chrétienne et de liturgie*. 15 vols. Paris, 1907 - 1953.

D'Alès, D. *Dictionnaire de la foi catholique*. 4 vols., Paris, 1928.

Dalton, Ormonde M. *Catalogue of Christian Antiquities*. London, 1901.

Daniel, Hermann A. *Thesaurus Hymnologicus sive Hymnorum, Canticorum, Sequentiarum . . . Collectio Amplissima*. 5 vols. Leipzig, 1855 - 1856.

Darlington, Reginald R. *The Vita Wulfstani of William of Malmesbury*. Camden Soc. Pub. 3 ser., vol. 40. London, 1928.

David, Charles Wendell. *Robert Curthose, Duke of Normandy*. Cambridge, Mass., 1920.

David, Jay [pseud. Bill Adler]. *Children's Letters to Santa Claus*. New York, 1967.

Dawes, E., and Baynes, N. *Three Byzantine Saints*. Oxford, 1947.

Dawkins, Richard McG., trans. *Leontios Machairas: Recital Concerning the Sweet Land of Cyprus, Entitled "Chronicle."* Oxford, 1932.

Dawson, Christopher. *Medieval Essays*. London, 1953.

Dawson, William Francis. *Christmas: Its Origin and Associations*. London, 1902.

[*DCA.*] *A Dictionary of Christian Antiquities*. Edited by Sir William Smith and S. Cheetham. 2 vols. London, 1875 - 1880.

[*DCB.*] *A Dictionary of Christian Biography*. Edited by Sir William Smith and Henry Wace. 4 vols. London, 1877 ff.

Deanesly, Margaret. *Europe from 476 to 911*. London, 1956.

De Ghellinck. *See* Ghellinck.

De Groot. *See* Groot.

DeJong, Gerald F. *The Dutch in America, 1609 - 1974*. Boston, 1975.

Delehaye, Hippolyte, S.J. *A travers trois siècles: L'oeuvre des Bollandistes, 1615 - 1915*. Subsidia Hagiographica 24. Brussels, 1920.

————. *Les passions des martyrs*. Brussels, 1921.

————. *Sanctus: Essai sur le culte des saints dans l'antiquité.* Subsidia Hagiographica 17. Brussels, 1927.

————. *Les légendes hagiographiques.* Subsidia Hagiographica 18. Brussels, 1927.

————. *Etude sur le Légendier romain, Saints de novembre et de décembre.* Subsidia Hagiographica 23. Brussels, 1936.

————. *The Legends of the Saints.* Translated by Donald Attwater. New York, 1962.

————. *See* Meisen.

Demont, A. "La Sainte-Catherine et la Saint-Nicolas en Artois." *Revue de folklore français et de folklore colonial* III (1932), 1 - 22.

De Peyster, John Watts. *The Dutch at the North Pole and the Dutch in Maine.* New York, 1857.

Dergny, Dieudonné. *Usages, coutumes et croyances.* 2 vols. Abbeville, 1885, 1888.

De Schuyter. *See* Schuyter.

Deutsches Weihnachtsbuch, 1943. Deutsche Kriegweihnacht, 1944. Published by Hauptkulturamt der NSDAP für Reichspropagandaleitung.

Die deutsche Literatur des Mittelalters: Verfasser lexicon. Edited by W. Stammler. 5 vols. Berlin, 1931 - 1955.

Deutsches Archiv für Erforschung des Mittelalters. Marburg, 1937 - .

De Vries, Tiemen. *Dutch History, Art, and Literature for Americans.* Chicago, 1914.

Dictionary of American Biography. 21 vols. New York, 1928 - 1960.

Dictionary of American English on Historical Principles. Edited by Sir William A. Craigie. 4 vols. Chicago, 1938 - 1960.

Dictionary of Americanisms on Historical Principles. Edited by Mitford M. Mathews. 2 vols., Chicago, 1951.

Diehl, Charles. "Le Monastère de Saint-Nicolas de Casale près d'Otrante." *Mélanges d'archéologie et d'histoire de l'école française de Rome* VI (1886).

————. *L'art Byzantin dans l'Italie.* 2d ed. Paris, 1925.

————. *Justinian et la civilisation byzantine au vi^e siècle.* Paris, 1901.

————. *Etudes byzantines.* Paris, 1905.

————. *Byzance: Grandeur et décadence.* Paris, 1919.

————. *Byzantine Portraits.* Translated by Harold Bell. New York, 1927.

————. *Manuel d'art byzantin.* 3d ed. 2 vols. Paris, 1928.

————. *Les grands problèmes de l'histoire byzantine.* Paris, 1947.

Diehl, Charles, and others. *Le monde oriental de 395 à 1453.* 2 vols. Paris, 1944, 1945.

Diehl, Guilland, and Oeconomos. *L'Europe orientale de 1081 à 1453.* Paris, 1945.

[*DNB.*] *Dictionary of National Biography.* Edited by Leslie Stephen and S. Lee. 63 vols. 1885 - 1900, with subsequent supplements.

Dölger, Franz. "Wer war Theophano?" *Historisches Jahrbuch* 1949, 646 - 658.

Dölger, Franz, and Schneider, Alfons M. *Byzanz.* Berne, 1952.

Donnet, André. *Saint Bernard et les origines de l'Hospice du Mont-Joux (Grand Saint-Bernard).* Saint-Maurice, 1942.

————. *Le Grand Saint-Bernard.* Neuchâtel, 1950.

Dorn, Johann. "Beiträge zur Patrocinienforschung." *Archiv für Kulturgeschichte* XIII (1917), 9 - 49, 220 - 225.

Douglas, David C. *The Norman Achievement, 1050 - 1100.* Berkeley and Los Angeles, 1969.

Douhet, le comte de. *Dictionnaire des mystères . . . publié par M. l'abbé Migne.* Paris, 1854.

Dreves G. M., and Blume, C. See *Analecta Hymnica.*

Dronke, Peter. *The Medieval Lyric.* New York, 1969.

Du Broc de Segange, Georges F. L. *Les saints patrons des corporations . . . publié par L. F. Morel.* 2 vols. Paris, 1887.

Du Cange, Charles Dufresne. *Glossiarium ad Scriptores Mediae et Infimae Latinitatis.* 3 vols. fol. Paris, 1678. Many editions and revisions including a 10-vol. ed. by L. Favre, Niort, 1883 - 1887.

Duchesne, Louis. *Le Liber Pontificalis.* Bibliothèque des écoles françaises d'Athènes et de Rome, 2 ser., III. Paris, 1892.

Dudden, F. Homes. *Gregory the Great.* 2 vols. London, 1905.

Dufourcq, Albert. "Le passionaire occidental au viie siècle." *Mélanges d' archéologie et d'histoire* XXVI (1906), 27 - 65.

Dugdale, Sir William. *Monasticon Anglicanum.* Edited by Caley, Ellis, and Blandinal. 8 vols. London, 1846.

Du Méril, Edélstand P. *Poésies populaires latines du moyen âge.* Paris, 1847.

————. *Poésies inédites du moyen âge.* Paris, 1854.

————. *Les origines latines du théâtre moderne.* Leipzig and Paris, 1897.

Dvornik, Fr. *Les Slaves, Byzance et Rome au ixe siècle.* Travaux publiés par l'Institut d'études slaves 4.) Paris, 1926.

[*EB.*] *Encyclopaedia Britannica.* 11th ed. 29 vols. Cambridge, 1911.

Ebel, Uda. *Das altromanische Mirakel.* Studia Romanica 8: Diss. Giessen, 1964. Heidelberg, 1965.

Ebersolt, Jean. *Orient et Occident.* 2 vols. Paris, 1928, 1929.

————. *Monuments d'architecture byzantine.* Paris, 1934.

Ebert, A. *Allgemeine Geschichte der Literatur des Mittelalters im Abendlande.* 3 vols. Leipzig, 1880.

Echos d'Orient. Organe de l'Institut français d'études byzantines. Paris, 1897 - .

Ecole française de Rome. *Mélanges.* Paris and Rome, 1880 - .

Edwards, Kathleen. *The English Secular Cathedrals in the Middle Ages.* Publications of the University of Manchester, 301; Historical Series 82. Manchester, 1949.

[EETS.] Early English Text Society, Publications. London, 1894 - .

Egbert, Virginia Wylie. "St. Nicholas: The Fasting Child." *Art Bulletin* XLVI (1964), 69 - 70.

Ehrhard, Albert. *Überlieferung und Bestand der hagiographischen und homiletischen Literatur der griechischen Kirche.* 2 vols. Leipzig, 1936 - 1938.

Engel, Arthur. *Recherches sur la numismatique et la sigillographie des Normands de Sicile et d'Italia.* Paris, 1882.

Englehard, H. "L'abbaye Saint-Nicolas." *L'Anjou historique* 1955, 138 - 142.

English Language Notes. Boulder, 1963 - .

Etudes grégoriennes. Abbaye de Solesmes, 1954 - .

Etymologiae. See Isidore.

[Eusebius, *Eccl. Hist.*] *Eusebius: The Ecclesiastical History.* Edited and translated by Kirsopp Lake. 2 vols. London and Cambridge (Loeb), 1953.

Ewen, Cecil Henry L'Estrange. *A History of Surnames in the British Isles.* London, 1931.

Falconi, Niccolò Carminio. *Sancti Confessoris Pontificis et Celeberrimi Thaumaturgi Nicolai Acta Primagenia nuper Detecta . . . per Nic. Carminum Falconium.* Naples, 1751.

Farnell, Lewis R. *The Cults of the Greek States* IV. Oxford, 1907.

Faust, A. B. *The German Element in the United States.* Chicago, 1909.

Fawtier, Robert. "Les reliques Rouennaisses de sainte Catherine d'Alexandrie." *Anal. Boll.* XLI (1923), 357 - 368.

Ferrari, Guy. *Early Roman Monasteries.* Studi di Antichità Cristiana 23. Vatican City, 1957.

Fichtenau, H. "Zum Reliquienwesen im früheren Mittelalter." *Mitteilungen des Instituts für österreichische Geschichtsforschung* LX (1952), 60 - 89.

Fissen, Karl G. R. *Das Leben der heiligen Nikolaus.* Diss. Göttingen, 1921.

Fliche, Augustin, and Victor Martin, ed. *Histoire de l'église depuis les origines jusqu'à nos jours.* IV: *De la mort de Théodore a l'élection de Grégoire le Grand*; V: *Grégoire le Grand* (590 - 757); VI: L'époque carolingienne; VII: L'Eglise au pouvoir des laïques (888 - 1057). Paris, 1935 - .

Fogel, E. M. *Twelvetide.* Publications of the Pennsylvania German Folklore Society 6.5. Allentown, 1941.

Fournée, Jean. *Enquête sur le culte populaire de saint Martin en Normandie.* Travaux de la Société Parisienne d'Histoire et d'Archéologie Normandes. Nogent-sur-Marne (Seine), 1963.

Fowler, J. T. "Some Legends of St. Nicholas, with Special Reference to the Seal of Pocklington Grammar School." *Yorkshire Archaeological Journal* XVII (1903), 254 - 260.

Frank, Grace. *The Medieval French Drama.* Oxford, 1954.

Franke, Gertrude, "Der Einfluss des Nikolauskultes auf die Namengebung im französischen Sprachgebiet." Diss. Erlangen. *Romanische Forschungen* XLVIII, 1 (1934).

Frazer, Sir James George. *The Golden Bough.* 3d ed. 12 vols. London, 1911 - 1914.

Frere, W. Howard. *Studies in Early English Liturgy. I: The Kalendar.* Alcuin Club Collections 28. Oxford, 1930.

Frey, Johannes. *Heiligenverehrung und Familiennamen in Rheinhessen.* Giessener Beiträge zur deutschen Philologie 61. Giessen, 1938.

Furman, Gabriel. *See* Moore, Frank.

Gaiffier, Père Baudouin de. "Translations et miracles de S. Mennas par Léon d'Ostie et Pierre du Mont Cassin." *Anal. Boll.* LXII (1944), 5 - 32.

————. "L'Hagiographe du xie siècle et son public." In *Miscellanea L. Van der Essen.* Brussels, 1947.

————. Review of C. W. Jones, *The St. Nicholas Liturgy* (see below) in *Anal. Boll.* LXXXV (1967), 252 - 255.

————. *Etudes critiques.* Subsidia hagiographica 43. Brussels, 1967.

Gallia Christiana. Edited by the Maurist Fathers. Paris, 1870 - 1877.

Gambacorta, A. "Culto e pellegrinaggi a San Nicola di Bari fino alla primera crociata." *Pellegrinaggi,* pp. 485 - 502.

Gardiner, Harold C. *Mysteries' End: An Investigation of the Last Days of the Medieval Religious Stage.* Yale Studies in English 103. New Haven, 1946.

Gastoué, Amidie. *L'art grégorien.* Paris, 1911.

Gay, Jules. *L'Italie méridionale et l'empire byzantin.* Paris, 1904.

Gelzer, Heinrich K. G. *Patrum Nicaenorum Nomina.* Leipzig, 1898.

————. "Die Verhältnisse von Staat und Kirche in Byzanz." *Historische Zeitschrift* L, 193 ff.

Gennep, Arnold van. "Le cycle préhivernal dans les croyances et coutumes populaires de la Savoie." *Revue d'ethnographie et des traditions populaires* VIII (1927); IX (1928).

————. *Le folklore de la Flandre et du Hainaut.* Contributions au Folklore des Provinces de France 3 and 4. 2 vols. Paris, 1935.

————. *Manuel de folklore français contemporain.* Vol. I in 7 parts, 1937 - 48; vols. III, IV, bibliography. Paris, 1937 - 1948.

Gentleman's Magazine. Edited by Sylvanus Urban, gentleman. London, 1731 - 1907.

Ghellinck, Père J. de. *L'essor de la littérature latine au xiie siècle.* 2 vols. Brussels, 1946.

Gibbon, Edward. *The Decline and Fall of the Roman Empire.* 71 chapters. London, 1776 - 1788, and various dates.

Gilst, A. P. van. *Sinterklaas en het Sinterklaasfeest: Geschiedenis en folklore.* Veenendaal, 1969.

Glaber, Raoul. *Les cinq livres de ses histoires (900 - 1044).* Edited by Prou. Paris, 1886.

Golden Legend. See Jacobus de Voragine.

Görlach, Manfred. *The Text Tradition of the South English Legendary.* Leeds Texts and Monographs, new ser. 6. Leeds, 1974.

Grabar, André. *Martyrium: Recherches sur le culte des reliques et l'art chrétien antique.* 2 vols. Paris, 1946.

Graham, Rose. *English Ecclesiastical Studies.* London, 1929.

Gramaphone, The. London, 1923 - .

Gregorovius, Ferdinand. *History of the City of Rome in the Middle Ages.* Translated by Mrs. A. Hamilton. 8 vols. in 13. London, 1894 - 1902.

Gregory I (the Great). *Libri Quatuor Dialogorum de Vita et Miraculis Patrum Italicorum et de Aeternitate Animarum.* In *S. Gregorii Papae I Opera Omnia. Pat. Lat.* LXXV - LXXIX.

Gregory of Tours. *Historia Francorum. Pat. Lat.* LXXI. English translation by O. M. Dalton. 2 vols. Oxford, 1927.

Greinacher, Anton. *Die Anschauungen Papstes Nikolaus I über das Verhältnis von Staat und Kirche.* Abhandlungen zur mittleren und neueren Geschichte 10. Berlin, 1909.

475

Groot, Adrianus Dingeman de. *Saint Nicholas: a Psychoanalytic Study of His History and Myth.* The Hague and New York, 1965. Translation by the author of *Sint Nicolaas, patroon van liefde* (Amsterdam, 1949), revised.

Grüneisen, W. de. *Sainte Marie antique.* Rome, 1911.

Guerrieri, F. "Dell' antico culto di S. Nicola in Bari." *Rassegna Pugliese* XIX (1902), 257 - 262.

Guery, l'abbé Ch. "Origine du culte de saint Nicolas en Normandie," *Revue catholique de Normandie* XXI (1922), 65 - 72.

Guibert de Nogent. *Gesta Dei.* In *Pat. Lat.* CLVI, 702 ff.

Guilland, R. "Les noces plurales à Byzance." *Byzantinoslavica* IX (1947), 9 - 30.

Günter, Heinrich. *Legenden-Studien.* Cologne, 1906.

————. *Die christliche Legende des Abendlandes.* Heidelberg, 1910.

————. *Psychologie des Legende: Studien zu einer wissenschaftlichten Heiligen-Geschichte.* Freiburg, 1949.

Hagenmeyer, Heinrich. *Fulcherii Carnotensis Historia Hierosylimitana.* Heidelberg, 1913.

Haito, bishop of Basle. *Capitulare Ecclesiae Basileensis. Pat. Lat.* CXV, 14; repeated by Burchard, *Decretorum Liber, Pat. Lat.* CXL, 712.

Halkin, François. *Auctarium: Bibliothecae Hagiographicae Graecae.* Subsidia Hagiographica 47. Brussels, 1969.

Halkin, Jos., and Roland, C.-G. *Recueil des chartes de l'abbaye de Stavelot-Malmedy* I. Brussels, 1909.

Halphen, Louis. *Recueil d'annales angevines et vendômoises.* Paris, 1903.

————. *Etude sur les chroniques des comtes d'Anjou et des seigneurs d'Amboise.* Paris, 1906.

————. *Le comté d'Anjou au xie siècle.* Paris, 1906.

————. *Charlemagne et l'empire carolingien.* Paris, 1947.

Halphen, Louis, and Poupardin, R. *Chroniques des comtes d'Anjou et des seigneurs d'Amboise.* Paris, 1913.

Hamilton, Mary. *Greek Saints and Their Festivals.* Edinburgh, 1910.

Harper's Weekly. New York, 1857 - 1916.

Harrison, Michael. *The Story of Christmas.* London, 1951.

Haskins, Charles Homer. *The Normans in European History.* Boston, 1915.

————. *Studies in Mediaeval Culture.* Oxford, 1929.

Hastings, Hugh, editor and publisher. *Ecclesiastical Records. State of New York.* 7 vols. Albany, 1901 - 1916.

Hauréau, Barthélemy. *Notices et extraits de quelques manuscrits latins de la Bibliothèque Nationale.* Paris, 1890 - 1893.

Heinerth, Hans C. *Die Heiligen und das Recht*. Freiburg, 1939.

Henry Bradshaw Society Publications. London, 1888 - .

Henshaw, Millett. "A Survey of Studies in Medieval Drama." *Progress of Medieval and Renaissance Studies* XXI (1951), 7 - 35.

Hermann-Mascard, Nicole. *Les reliques des saints: Formation coutumière d'un droit*. Société d'histoire du droit: Collection d'histoire institutionelle et sociale 6. Paris, 1975.

Herzog zu Sächsen. *See* Sächsen.

Heyd, Wilhelm von. *Histoire du commerce du Levant*. Translated by Furey-Renaud. 2 vols. Leipzig, 1885 - 1886; repr. 1959.

Hieronymus. *See* Jerome.

Histoire littéraire de la France; Ouvrage commencé par des religieux bénédictins de la Congrégation de Saint-Maur, et continué par des membres de l'Institut (Académie des Inscriptions et Belles-Lettres). 40 vols. Paris, 1865 - 1974.

Historisches Jahrbuch. Bonn: Goerres-Gesellschaft. Münster, Munich, Cologne, 1880 - .

Hoffman, Charles Fenno. *The Pioneers of New York*. Address delivered to the Saint Nicholas Society of Manhattan, 6 December 1847. New York, 1848.

Holland Society of New York. *Year Book*. 1886 ff.

Honorius of Autun. *Speculum Ecclesiae*. Pat. Lat. CLXXII.

Hooker, Katherine. *Through the Heel of Italy*. New York, 1927.

Hornauer, Siegfried. *Lüge, Kitsch oder Fest? Ein Werkbuch zur Gestaltung von Nikolausfeiern*. Vienna, 1966.

Horner. *See* Manuscripts Cited, New-York Historical Society.

Horstmann, C., ed. *The Early South-English Legendary or Lives of Saints*. EETS, orig. ser. 87. London, 1887.

Hosking, Arthur N., *The Night before Christmas*. New York, 1971.

Hospinianus, Rodolphus. *Festa Christianorum: hoc est, de origine, progressu, ceremoniis et ritibus festorum dierum Christianorum*. Zürich, 1593.

Hough, P. M. *Dutch Life in Town and Country*. New York, 1901.

Houvet, E. *Cathédrale de Chartres*. 7 vols. Chelles, 1926.

Huelsen, Christian C. F. *Le chiese di Roma nel medio evo*. Florence, 1927.

Huizinga, J. *Herbst des Mittelalters*. German translation by T. Jolles Mönkeberg. Munich, 1924. Also in English trans., *The Waning of the Middle Ages* (Doubleday Anchor paperback).

Iapigia. Organo della R. Deputazione di storia patria per li Puglie. Bari, 1930 - 1946.

[ICA.] Index of Christian Art. Princeton University. Duplicate at University of California, Los Angeles.

477

Illustration, journal universal hebdomadaire. Paris, 1843 - 1944.

Imbart de la Tour, P. *Les origines de la réforme.* 2d ed. by Yvonne Lankers. 2 vols. Melun, 1946.

Irving, Washington. *The Life and Letters of Washington Irving.* Edited by Pierre Irving. 4 vols. New York, 1862 - 1864.

————. *Salmagundi; or The Whim-Whams and Opinions of Launcelot Langstaff, esq.* London: Bell, 1883.

————. *Father Knickerbocker's History of New York.* 2d ed. London, 1821.

{Isidore, *Etym.* } Wallace Martin Lindsay, ed. *Isidori Hispalensis Episcopi Etymologiarum sive Originum Libri XX.* Oxford, 1911.

Jacobus de Voragine. *Legenda Aurea,* or *Lombardica Historia (The Golden Legend).* Edited by T. Graesse. Dresden, 1846. Translation by G. Ryan and H. Ripperger, London, 1941.

James, Montague Rhodes. *The Apocryphal New Testament.* Oxford, 1924.

James of Voragine. *See* Jacobus.

Janin, R. *La géographie ecclésiastique de l'empire byzantin.* 2d ed. Paris, 1969.

Jekels, Ludwig. "The Psychology of the Festival of Christmas." *International Journal of Psychoanalysis* XVII (1936), 57 - 72.

Jerome (Eusebius Hieronymus Stridonensis). *Contra Vigilantium. Pat. Lat.* XXIII.

————. *Epistolae.* Edited and translated by F. A. Wright as *St. Jerome, Select Letters.* London (Loeb), 1933.

John the Deacon. *Vita S. Nicolai. See* Falconi.

Joinville, Jean, sire de. *Histoire de Saint-Louis.* Edited by Natalis de Wailly. Paris, 1865.

Jones, A. H. M. *The Greek City from Alexander to Justinian.* Oxford, 1940.

Jones, Charles W. *Saints' Lives and Chronicles.* Ithaca, N.Y., 1947.

————. "Knickerbocker Santa Claus." *The New-York Historical Society Quarterly* XXXVIII (1954), 356 - 383.

————. *The Saint Nicholas Liturgy and its Literary Relationships. With an Essay on the Music by Gilbert Reaney.* University of California English Studies 27. Berkeley and Los Angeles, 1963. *See also* Sylvestre.

{Jones 1975.} "Carolingian Aesthetics: Why Modular Verse?" *Viator* 1975, esp. pp. 326 - 327.

————. "The Norman Cults of Sts. Catherine and Nicholas, saec. xi." *Collection Latomus* CXLV (Hommages à André Boutemy, Brussels, 1976), 216 - 230.

Jones, Ernest. "The Significance of Christmas." In *Essays in Applied Psychoanalysis* II, 212 - 224. London, 1951.

Jonsson, Ritva. *Historia: Etudes sur la genèse des offices versifiés.* Acta Univ. Stockholmiensis, Studia Latina Stock. 15. Stockholm, 1968.

Kaftal, George. *Iconography of the Saints in Tuscan Painting.* Florence, 1952.

Karlin-Hayter, P. "Le synode a CP de 836 à 912 et le rôle de Nicolas." *Jahrbuch der österreichischen Byzantinistik* XIX (1970), 59 - 101.

Katholik, Der. Zeitschrift für katholische Wissenschaft und kirchliches Leben. Mainz, 1821 - 1918.

Kayata, Polycarpe. *Monographie de l'église grecque catholique de Marseille, et Vie de saint Nicolas de Myre.* Marseille, 1901.

Kehrein, Joseph. *Lateinische sequenzen des Mittelalters.* Mainz, 1873.

Keller, Morton. *The Art and Politics of Thomas Nast.* New York, 1968.

Ker, Neil R. *Catalogue of MSS Containing Anglo-Saxon.* Oxford, 1957.

————. *English MSS in the Century after the Norman Conquest.* Oxford, 1960.

Kilroe, E. P. *Saint Tammany and the Origin of the Society of Tammany or Columbian Order in the City of New York.* New York, 1913.

Kirchenmusikalisches Jahrbuch. Regensburg, 1876 - .

Kitzinger, Ernst. "The Cult of Images before Iconoclasm." *Dumbarton Oaks Papers* VIII (1954), 83 - 150.

Klostermann, Erich, and Seeburg, E. *Die Apologie der heiligen Katharina.* Schriften der Königsberger Gelehrten Gesellschaft, Geisteswissenschaftliche Klasse I, 2. Berlin, 1924.

Knickerbocker Weekly: "Free Netherlands" I - VII. New York, 1941 - 1947.

Knowles, David. *The Monastic Order in England.* Cambridge, 1949.

Knust, Hermann. *Geschichte der Legenden der keiligen Katharina von Alexandria.* Halle, 1890.

Kondakov, N. P. *The Russian Icon.* Translated by E. H. Minns. Oxford, 1927.

Krautheimer, Richard. *Early Christian and Byzantine Architecture.* Baltimore (Penguin), 1965.

Kressner, Adolf. "St. Nicolaus in der Tradition und in der mittelalterlichen Dichtung." *Archiv für das Studium der neueren Sprachen und Literaturen* LIX (1878), 33 - 60.

Kretzenbacher, Leopold. *Frühbarockes Weihnachtsspiel in Kaernten und Steiermark.* Klagenfurt, 1952.

————. *Bilden und Legenden.* Aus Forschung und Kunst, ed. Gotbert Moro, 13. Klagenfurt, 1971.

Künstle, Karl. *Hagiographische Studien über die Passio Felicitatis cum vii Filiis.* Paderborn, 1894.

————. *Ikonographie der Heiligen.* Freiburg, 1926.

————. "Eine wichtige hagiographische Handschrift." *Römische Quartalschrift für christliche Altertumskunde und für Kirchengeschichte* XXII (1908), 17 - 29.

Kurth, Godefroid. *Notger de Liége.* Paris, 1905.

Labande, Edmond-René. "Recherches sur les pèlerins dans l'Europe des xie et xiie siècles." *Cahiers de civilisation médiévale* I (1958), 159 - 169, 339 - 347.

————. "Eléments d'une enquête sur les conditions de déplacement du pèlerin aux xe - xie siècles." *Pellegrinaggi,* pp. 95 - 111.

Labbé, Philippe, and Cosart, G. *Sacrosancta Concilia ad Regiam Editionem Exacta.* 16 vols. Paris, 1671 - 1673.

Laistner, M. L. W. *Thought and Letters in Western Europe,* A.D. 500 to 900. Rev. ed. Ithaca, N.Y., 1957.

Lalanne, Ludovic. *Curiosités biographiques.* Paris, 1845. Repr. 1946.

————. *Curiosités littéraires.* Paris, 1845.

————. *Curiosités des traditions, des moeurs et des legendes.* Paris, 1847.

————. *Dictionnaire historique de la France.* 2d ed. Paris, 1877.

Laroche, l'abbé Jules. *Vie de Saint-Nicolas, Patron de la Jeunnesse.* New ed. Paris, 1890.

————. "La manne de saint Nicolas." *Revue de la Suisse catholique* 1890, 56 ff.

————. "Iconographie de saint Nicolas." *Revue de l'art chrétien* XXXIV (1891), 104 - 119.

Larousse, Pierre. *Grand dictionnaire universal du xixe siècle.* 17 vols. Paris, 1865 - 1890.

Lauer, P. *Le trésor du Sancta Sanctorum.* Monuments et memoires publiés par l'Académie des Inscriptions et Belles-Lettres, Fondation Eugène Piot, 15. Paris, 1906.

Lebègue, Raymond. *La tragédie religieuse en France: Les débuts, 1514 - 1573.* Bibliothèque littéraire de la Renaissance 17. Paris, 1929.

Legenda Aurea. See Jacobus de Voragine.

Lehmann, Paul. *Die Parodie im Mittelalter.* Munich, 1922.

Leib, Bernard. *Rome, Kiev et Byzance à la fin du xie siècle.* Paris, 1924.

Le Moy, A. *L'Anjou.* Paris, 1924.

Lennard, Reginald V., ed. *Englishmen at Rest and Play, 1559 - 1714.* Oxford, 1931.

LePeletier, Laurent. *Rerum Scitu Dignissimarum a Prima Fundatione Monasterii S. Nicolai Andegavensis ad hunc usque Diem Epitome.* Angers, 1635.

Lesne, Emile. *Histoire de la propriété ecclésiastique en France.* 6 vols. Paris and Lille, 1910 - 1943.

Levy, Max. *Der Sabbath in England.* Kölner Anglistische Arbeiten 18. Leipzig, 1933.

Lewis, Archibald R. *Naval Power and Trade in the Mediterranean, 500 - 1100.* Princeton, 1951.

———. *The Northern Seas: Shipping and Commerce in Northern Europe, A.D. 300 - 1100.* Princeton, 1958.

Lexicon für Theologie und Kirche. Edited by Michael Buchberger. 9 vols. Freiburg, 1937 ff.

Library of Original Sources. Edited by O. J. Thatcher. 10 vols. Chicago, 1908.

Life (weekly magazine). Chicago, 1936 - .

Lindsay, Jack. *Byzantium into Europe.* London, 1952.

Llewellyn, P. *Rome in the Dark Ages.* London, 1970.

Loomis, Charles Grant. *White Magic: An Introduction to the Folklore of Christian Legend.* Cambridge, Mass., 1948.

Loukovitch, Kosta. *L'évolution de la tragédie religieuse classique en France.* Paris, 1933.

Love, W. De Loss, Jr. *Fast and Thanksgiving Days in New England.* Boston, 1897.

Lucas, F. L. *Greek Tragedy and Comedy.* New York, 1967.

Lucretius. *De Natura Rerum.* Edited and translated by W. H. D. Rouse. London (Loeb), 1928.

Ludlow, James M. *The Age of the Crusades.* Edinburgh, 1897.

Mackinlay, James M. *Ancient Church Dedications in Scotland.* II. Edinburgh, 1914.

Magnuson, T. *Studies in Roman Quattrocento Architecture.* Stockholm, 1958.

Mai, Angelo. *Spicilegium Romanum.* 10 vols. Rome, 1839 - 1844.

Mâle, Emile. *L'Art religieux du xiiie siècle en France.* 6th ed., Paris, 1925.

———. *The Early Churches of Rome.* New York, 1960.

Maltman, Sr. Nicholas. "A Study of the Evil Characters in the English Corpus Christi Cycles." Diss., Univ. of California, Berkeley, 1957.

Mancel, M. G. *Saint Nicolas: Légende et iconographie.* La Société des Antiquaires de Normandie, Notice lue le 26 novembre 1857. Caen, 1858.

Manitius, Max. *Geschichte der lateinischen Literatur des Mittelalters.* 3 vols. Munich, 1911, 1923, 1931.

Manly Anniversary Studies. Chicago, 1923.

Mansi, Giuseppi. *Sacrorum Conciliorum Nova et Amplissima Collectio.* 31 vols. Florence, 1759 - 1798.

Marchegay, Paul, and Mabille, Emile, eds. *Chroniques des églises d'Anjou.* Société de l'Histoire de France. Paris, 1869.

Marchegay, Paul, and Salmon, André, eds. *Chroniques des comtes d'Anjou.* 2 vols. Paris, 1856, 1871.

Marches de l'Est. Paris, 1909 - .

Marguillier, Auguste. *Saint Nicolas, évêque de Myre.* Paris, 1917; 2d ed., 1930.

Marin, Eugène. *Saint Nicolas, évêque de Myra.* 2d ed. Paris, 1917.

Marle, Raimond van. *The Development of the Schools of Italian Painting.* 19 vols. The Hague, 1923 - 1938.

Marot, Pierre. *Saint-Nicolas-de-Port.* Les guides du pays Lorrain. Nancy, 1963.

Marrou, Henri-Irénée. *Histoire de l'éducation dans l'antiquité.* Paris, 1948.

Martin, Edward J. *A History of the Iconoclastic Controversy.* London, 1930.

Martyrologium Romanum, Gregoriae Pape XIII iussu editum . . . Editio IV Taurinensis . . . . Turin, 1944. See also *Acta SS, Propylaeum.*

Masaryk, T. G. *Russland und Europa.* Jena, 1913.

Masellis, Vito. *Storia di Bari.* Trani, 1960.

Mas-Latrie, Louis de. *Traités de paix et de commerce.* 2 vols. Paris, 1866; repr. 1965.

Paris-Match (weekly magazine). Paris, 1949 - .

Mather, Cotton, *Magnalia Christi Americana, 1702.* Edited by Thomas Robbins. 2 vols. Hartford, 1853, 1855.

Matthaei Paris Monachi Albanensis Angli, Historia Major . . . . Edited by William Wats. London, 1640.

McNeal, Edgar H. *The Conquest of Constantinople, Translated from the Old French of Robert of Clari.* New York, 1936.

Mecklin, John Moffatt. *The Passing of the Saint; a Study of a Cultural Type.* Chicago, 1941.

Medievalia et Humanistica. Boulder, 1941 - .

Medium Aevum. Oxford, 1932 - .

Meisen, Karl. *Nikolauskult und Nikolausbrauch im Abendlande.* Forschungen zur Volkskunde 9 - 12. Düsseldorf, 1931. See review by Delehaye in *Anal. Boll.* L, 176 - 181.

Meller, W. C. *The Boy Bishop and Other Forgotten Customs.* London, 1923.

Metaphrastes. *See* Symeon.

Metken, Sigrid. *Sankt Nikolaus in Kunst und Volksbrauch.* Duisburg, 1966.

[*MGH.*] *Monumenta Germaniae Historica.* Edited by G. H. Pertz and others for the Gesellschaft (afterwards Reichsinstitut) für ältere deutsche Geschichtskunde. *Scriptores,* 1826 - . *Leges,* 1835 - . *Poetae latini medii aevi,* 1880 - . *Legum sectiones,* 1882 - . *Scriptores rerum Merovingicarum,* 1885 - . *Auctores antiquissimi,* 1887 - . *Scriptores rerum Langobardicarum et Italicarum saec.* vi - ix, 1878 - . *Libelli de lite,* 1891 - . *Diplomata regum Germaniae ex stirpe Karolinorum,* 1932 - . *Scriptores rerum Germanicarum,* new series, 1922 - . *Hannover,* 1826 - .

Modern Language Notes. Baltimore, 1886 - .

Modern Philology. Chicago, 1903 - .

Mombritius, Boninus. *Sanctuarium. BHL* 6111 - 6113, 6136 - 6137. Milan, before 1480 (Hain, 11544). Repr. in 2 vols., Solesmes, 1910.

Mommsen, August. *Feste der Stadt Athen in Altertum.* Leipzig, 1898.

―――――. *Heortologie: Antiquarische Untersuchungen über die städtischen Feste der Athener.* Leipzig, 1864; repr. Amsterdam, 1968.

Monachus Beccensis. *Miraculae S. Nicolae.* In *Cat. Cod. Hagr. Paris.* II, 405 - 432.

Mone, Francis J. *Hymni Latini Medii Aevi.* 3 vols., Freiburg, 1853.

Moore, Clement C. *Poems.* New York, 1844.

Moore, Frank, editor. *Antiquities of Long Island by Gabriel Furman.* New York, 1875.

Moran, Hugh A. *The Story of Santa Claus.* Palo Alto, 1952.

Morison, Samuel E. *Admiral of the Ocean Sea: a Life of Christopher Columbus.* 2 vols. Boston, 1942.

Morrison, George A., Jr. *History of the Saint Andrew's Society of the State of New York, 1756 - 1906.* New York, 1906.

Moyen Age, Le. Paris, 1888 - .

Münchener Museum für Philologie des Mittelalters und der Renaissance. Munich, 1911 - .

Mulder, Arnold. *Americans from Holland.* Philadelphia, 1947.

Munro, Dana Carleton. *Urban and the Crusaders.* University of Pennsylvania, Translations and Reprints 1. Philadelphia, 1902.

Muralt, Edouard de. *Essai de chronographie byzantine.* Saint Petersburg, 1855.

Muscatine, Charles. *Chaucer and the French Tradition.* Berkeley and Los Angeles, 1957.

Myers, Gustavus. *The History of Tammany Hall.* 2d ed. 2 vols. New York, 1917.

Nast, Thomas. *Christmas Drawings for the Human Race.* New York, 1890.

Neckham, Alexander. *De Laudibus Divinae Sapientiae.* Edited by Thomas Wright for the Rolls Series. London, 1863.

Negri, Nicolò. *Vita del glorioso s. Nicolo vescovo, descritta in ottava rima.* Venice, 1604.

Nesbitt, John W. "A Geographical and Chronological Guide to Greek Saints' Lives," *Orientalia Christiana Periodica* XXXV (1969), 443 - 489.

Neue kirchliche Zeitschrift. Erlangen, 1890 - 1933.

Neues Archiv. See *Archiv der Gesellschaft für ä.d. Geschichtskunde.*

New-York Historical Society. *Collections.* 8 vols. New York, 1811 - 1859.

————. *Quarterly.* New York, 1917 - .

New Yorker. New York, 1925 - .

Niederlausitzer Mitteilungen. Niederlausitzer Gesellschaft für Anthropologie und Altertumskunde. Guben, 1890 - .

Nigg, Walter. *Grosse Heilige.* Zürich, 1946. English translation by William Stirling, London, 1948.

Nilsson, Martin P. *Griechische Feste von religiöser Bedeutung.* Leipzig, 1906.

————. *Die volkstümlichen Feste des Jahres.* Tübingen, 1914.

————. *Greek Popular Religion.* New York, 1940.

————. "Vorgeschichte des Weihnachtsfestes." *Opuscula Selecta* I, 214 - 311, repr. from *Archiv für Religionswissenschaft* XIX, 50 - 150. Lund, 1951.

Nitti di Vito, Francesco. *Le Pergamene di S. Nicola di Bari.* (= *Codice Diplomatico Barese,* edited by Commissione Provinciale di arch. e storia patria, IV, V.) 2 vols. Bari, 1901.

————. "Leggenda del monaco Niceforo." *Iapigia* n.s. VIII (1937), 336 - 356.

————. "San Nicola e l'Albania." *Iapigia* n.s. X (1939), 321 - 328.

Norwich, John Julius. *The Other Conquest.* New York, 1967.

Notes and Queries. Founded by W. H. Thomas. London, 1843 - .

Nouveau Larousse Illustré: Dictionnaire universal encyclopédique, publié sous la direction de Claude Augé. 7 vols. Paris, 1898 - 1904.

Oldenbourg, Zoé. *The Crusades.* Translated by Anne Carter. New York, 1966.

Orderici Vitalis Historiae Ecclesiasticae Libri Tredecim. Edited by Augustus Le Prevost. 5 vols. Paris, 1838 - 1855. Translated by Thomas Forester, 4 vols., London, 1853 - 1856. Translated by Marjorie Chibnall, 4 vols., Oxford, 1969 - 1975.

Ortutay, Jules. "Coutumes populaires de la Saint-Nicolas." *Nouvelle revue de Hongrie,* Budapest, 1938, pp. 550 - 554.

Ostrogorsky, Georges. "Les décisions du 'Stoglav' concernant la peinture d'images." In *L'Art byzantin chez les Slaves: Les Balkans,* ed. Théodore Uspenskij, II, 393 - 410. Paris, 1930.

————. *History of the Byzantine State.* Oxford, 1956.

Oxford Book of Medieval Latin Verse. 2d edition edited by F. J. E. Raby. Oxford, 1959.

Oxford Dictionary of the Christian Church. Edited by F. L. Cross. London, 1958.

Paine, Albert Bigelow. *Th. Nast, His Period and His Pictures.* New York, 1904.

Painter, Sidney. *French Chivalry.* Baltimore, 1940.

Paré, G., Brunet, A., and Tremblay, P. *La renaissance du xiie siècle: Les écoles et l'enseignement.* Publications de l'Institut d'Etudes Mediévales d'Ottawa 3. Paris and Ottawa, 1938.

[*Pat. Gr.*] *Patrologia Graeca Cursus Completus.* Edited by J. P. Migne. 162 vols., Paris, 1857 - 1866.

[*Pat. Lat.*] *Patrologia Latina Cursus Completus.* Edited by J. P. Migne. 221 vols., Paris, 1844 - 1864.

Patterson, Samuel White. *The Poet of Christmas Eve: A Life of Clement Clarke Moore.* New York, 1956.

Pauli, Hertha E. *St. Nicholas' Travels: A miraculous biography.* Boston, 1945.

Pauly, A., Wissowa, G., and Kroll, W. eds. *Real-Encyclopädie der klassischen Altertumswissenschaft.* Stuttgart, 1893 - .

Pays lorrain, Le. Organ of the Société d'Archéologie lorraine et du Musée historique lorrain. Nancy, 1904 - .

Paz, Ida Del Calle de. *La leggenda di S. Niccola nella tradizione poetica medioevale in Francia.* Florence, 1921.

Pellegrinaggi e culto dei santi in Europa fino alla I^a crociata. Convigni del Centro di studi sulla spiritualità medievale 3, Todi, 1963.

[*Penn. Mag.*] *Pennsylvania Magazine of History and Biography.* Historical Society of Pennsylvania. Philadelphia, 1877 - .

Perdrizet, Paul. *Le calendrier parisien à la fin du moyen âge.* Paris, 1933.

Pernoud, Régine. *The Crusaders.* Translated by E. Grant. Edinburgh, 1963.

Petroni, Giulio. *Della storia di Bari degli antichi tempi.* 2 vols. Naples, 1857 - 1858.

Pfeiffer, R. H. *Introduction to the Old Testament.* 2d ed. New York, 1952.

Pietzsch, Gerhard. *Die Musik im Erziehungs- und Bildungsideal.* Halle, 1932.

Pimlott, J. A. R. *The Englishman's Holiday: A Social History.* London, 1947.

Pintard, John. *Letters to His Daughter.* Edited by Dorothy C. Barck. 4 vols. New York, 1940 - 1941.

Pitra, Joannes Baptista. *Analecta Sacra Spicilegio Solesmensi I.* Paris, 1876.

Plancy, J.-A.-S. Collin de. *Dictionnaire critique des reliques et des images miraculeuses.* 3 vols. Paris, 1821.

Pliny the Elder. *Historiae Naturalis Libri XXXVII*. Edited by Jan; 2d ed. edited by Mayhoff. 6 vols. Leipzig, n.d.

Pollock, G. H. "Temporal Anniversary Manifestations." *Psychoanalytic Quarterly* XL (1971), 123 - 131.

Poncelet, Albert. "Sanctae Catharinae virginis et martyris translatio et miracula Rotomagensia saec. xi." *Anal. Boll.* XXII (1903), 423 - 438.

Pothier, Dom J. "Répons Virgo flagellatur de l'office de sainte-Catherine." *Revue de chant grégorien* V, 4 (1896), 49 - 54.

Prestage, Edgar, ed. *Chivalry*. New York, 1928.

Procopius. *De Aedificiis*. Translated by Aubrey Stewart. Palestine Pilgrim Texts, 1888.

Propylaeum: Martyrologium Romanum. See *Acta SS*.

Putignani, Niccolò. *Vindiciae vitae et gestorum S. Thaumaturgi Nicolai archiepiscopi Myrensis. Diatriba II*. Naples, 1757.

—————. *Istoria della Vita, de' miracoli e della traslazione del gran taumaturgo S. Niccolò, arcivescovo di Mira*. Naples, 1771.

Ramsay, Sir William Mitchell. *St. Paul the Traveller and Roman Citizen*. London, 1896.

Realencyklopädie für protestantische Theologie und Kirche. Founded by Johann Jacob Herzog. Leipzig, 1896 - 1913.

Reallexicon der deutschen Literaturgeschichte. Edited by P. Merker and W. Stammler. 4 vols. Berlin, 1925 - 1951. 2d ed. revised by W. Kohlschmidt and W. Mohr, in progress.

Réau, Louis. *Iconographie de l'art chrétien*. 5 vols. Paris, 1955 - 1959.

Recueil des historiens des croisades. Académie des Inscriptions et Belles-lettres. 16 vols. Paris, 1844 - 1906.

Recueil des historiens des Gaules et de la France. Rerum gallicarum et francicarum scriptores. 24 vols. Paris, 1840 - 1904.

Reese, Gustav. *Music in the Middle Ages*. New York, 1940.

Reichard, Harry Hess. *The Christmas Poetry of the Pennsylvania Dutch*. Publications of the Pennsylvania German Folklore Society 6.

Revue belge de philologie et d'histoire. Brussels, 1922 - .

Revue bénédictine. Abbaye de Maredsous, Belgium, 1884 - .

Revue critique des idées et des livres. Paris, 1908 - 1924.

Revue de chant grégorien, Grenoble, 1892 - .

Revue de folklore française et de folklore colonial. Paris, 1930 - 1942.

Revue d'histoire de l'église de France. Paris, 1910 - .

Revue de l'art chrétien. Lille, 1857 - .

Revue des traditions populaires. Paris, 1886 - 1919.

Revue d'ethnographie et des traditions populaires. 9 vols. Paris, 1920 - 1928.

Riant, le comte P. "Des dépouilles religieuses enlevées à Constantinople au xiiie siècle." *Mémoires de la Société Nationale des Antiquaires de France* XXXVI (1875), 1 - 214.

Rice, David Talbot. *Art of Byzantium.* London, 1959.

Richards, Katherine L. *How Christmas Came to the Sunday Schools.* Indianapolis, 1934.

Rietschel, Georg. *Weihnachten in Kirche, Kunst,und Volksleben.* Bielefeld and Leipzig, 1902.

Riezler, Kurt. *Man, Mutable and Immutable.* Chicago, 1950.

Robert of Clari. *See* McNeal.

Rodgers, E. C. *Discussion of Holidays in the Later Middle Ages.* Columbia University Studies in History, Economics, and Public Law. 1940.

Rohmer, Alice. *Nikolauslegenden.* Munich, 1963.

Rolls Series. *Rerum Brittanicarum Medii Aevi Scriptores.* Great Britain, Public Record Office. 254 vols. 1858 - 1911.

Ronsjö, Einar. *La Vie de Saint-Nicolas par Wace.* Etudes romanes de Lund 5. Lund, 1942.

Romania. Founded by Paul Meyer and Gaston Paris. Paris, 1872 - .

Rosenbach, A. S. W. *The Earliest Christmas Books.* Philadelphia, 1927.

Rossi, G. B. de. *Codice diplomatico barese.* Bari, 1897 - 1902.

Rott, Hans. *Kleinasiatische Denkmäler.* Studien über christliche Denkmäler, edited by Johannes Ficker, 5, 6. Leipzig, 1908.

Roy, Jules. *Saint Nicholas I.* Translated by Margaret Maitland. London, 1901.
————. *L'an mille.* Paris, 1885.

Rufinus. *Eusebii Historia Ecclesiastica Interprete Rufino Aquileiae. Pat. Lat.* XXI.

Runciman, Steven. *Byzantine Civilization.* London, 1933.
————. *A History of the Crusades.* 3 vols. Cambridge, 1951 - 1954.
————. "The Holy Lance Found at Antioch." *Anal. Boll.* LXVIII (1950), 197 - 209.

Ryan, G., and Ripperger, H. *See* Jacobus de Voragine.

Sächsen, Max Herzog zu. *Das christliche Hellas.* Leipzig, 1918.

Sackur, E. *Richard Abt von Saint-Vannes.* Breslau, 1886.
————. *Die Cluniacenser.* 2 vols. Halle, 1894.

St. Nicholas: An Illustrated Magazine for Young Folks. 66 vols. New York, November 1873 - October 1939.

Saint Nicholas Society of New York, *Record of the Semi-centennial Anniversary,*

February 28, 1885. New York, 1885. *The One-Hundred Year Record.* New York, 1935.

Saintyves, P. (Emile Nourry). *Les reliques et les images légendaires.* Paris, 1912.

Salies, Alexandre de. *Histoire de Foulques-Nerra, Comte d'Anjou.* Paris, 1874.

Saturday Evening Post (weekly magazine). Philadelphia, 1821 - 1969.

Savage, Ernest A. *Old English Libraries.* Chicago, 1912.

Schlumberger, Gustave Léon. *Un empereur byzantin au dixième siècle: Nicéphore Phocas.* Paris, 1890.

————. *L'épopée byzantine à la fin du dixième siècle.* 3 vols. Paris, 1896, 1900, 1905.

Schmitt, Franciscus Salesius, ed. *S. Anselmi Cant. Epi. Opera Omnia.* 6 vols. Edinburgh, 1946 - 1961.

Schnell, Eugen. *Sanct Nicolas, der heilige Bischoff und Kinderfreund.* 6 vols. Brünn, 1883 - 1886.

Schramm, Percy. *Kaiser, Rom, und Renovatio.* 2 vols. Leipzig, 1929.

————. *Kaiser, Könige, und Päpste* III. Berlin, 1969.

Schrijnen, Jos. *De heilige Nicolaas in het folklore.* Roermond, 1898.

Schug-Wille, Christa. *Art in the Byzantine World.* New York, 1969.

Schuyter, Jan de. *Sint Niklaas in de legende en in de volksgebruiken.* Antwerp, 1944.

Scognamiglio, Pio. *La Manna di S. Nicola nella storia, nell' arte, nella scienza.* Bari, 1925.

————. *Vita di S. Nicola di Bari.* Roma, 1930.

Scoville, Joseph A. [pseud. Walter Barrett]. Biographical Sketch of John Pintard, in *The Old Merchants of New York City.* 5 vols. 1863.

Scriptorium: Revue international des études relatives aux manuscrits. Antwerp, 1946 - .

Sébillot, Paul. *Folk-lore de France.* 4 vols. Paris, 1904 - 1907.

————. *Légendes, croyances et superstitions.* 2 vols. Paris, 1886.

Sereno, Renzo. "Some Observations on the Santa Claus Custom." *Psychiatry* XIV, 4 (Nov. 1951).

Setton, Kenneth M., ed. *A History of the Crusades.* 5 vols. 1955 - .

Seznec, Jean. *The Survival of the Pagan Gods.* Translated by Barbara Sessions. Bollingen Series 38. New York, 1953.

Siegmund, A. *Die Überlieferung der griechisch-christlicher Literatur.* Munich, 1949.

Silvestre, Hubert, review of C. W. Jones, *Liturgy,* in *Revue d'histoire ecclésiastique* LXV (1965), 138 - 146.

————. "Commerce et vol de reliques au moyen âge." *Revue belge de philologie et d'histoire* XXX (1952), 721 - 739.

Smith, George L. *Religion and Trade in New Netherland.* Ithaca, N.Y., 1973.

Smith, Thomas E. V. *The City of New York in the Year of Washington's Inauguration 1789.* New York, 1889.

Smith, William, and Fuller, J. M. eds. *A Dictionary of the Bible.* 4 vols. London, 1893.

Snell, Frederick J. *Customs of Old England.* New York and London, 1911.

Société Nationale des Antiquaires de France. *Mémoires.* 1817 - ; *Bulletin,* 1857 - .

Socrates, Scholasticus. *Ecclesiastical History.* Edited in *Pat. Gr.* LXVII, 9 - 842. Translated by A. C. Zenos in *Nicene and Post-Nicene Fathers,* 2 ser. II (1890).

South English Legendary, The. Edited by Charlotte D'Evelyn and Anna Mill. EETS 235 - 236. 1956.

Southern, R. W. *St. Anselm and His Biographer.* Cambridge, 1963.

————. *The Making of the Middle Ages.* London, 1953.

Sozomen, Salaminius Hermias. *Ecclesiastical History.* Edited in *Pat. Gr.* LXVII, 843 - 1630. Translated by Hartranft in *Nicene and Post-Nicene Fathers,* 2 ser. II. (1890).

Speculum. Quarterly Journal of the Mediaeval Academy of America. Cambridge, Mass., 1925 - .

Spelman, Sir Henry. *Concilia, decreta, leges, constitutiones in re ecclesiarum orbis britannici.* Edited by Sir William Dugdale. 2 vols. London, 1636, 1664.

Stark, Freya. *The Lycian Shore.* London, 1956.

Stegmüller, Friederich. *Repertorium Biblicum medii aevi.* 7 vols. Madrid, 1940 - 1961.

Sterba, Richard. "On Christmas." *Psychoanalytic Quarterly* XIII (1944), 79 - 83.

Stokes, Isaac N. P. *The Iconography of Manhattan Island.* 6 vols. New York, 1915 - 1928.

Stone, Edward N., trans. *Three Old French Chronicles.* Seattle, 1939.

Stubbs, William, ed. *Memorials of St. Dunstan.* Rolls Series 63. London, 1874.

————. *William of Malmesbury. De gestis regum Anglorum libri quinque. Historiae novellae libri tres.* Rolls Series. London, 1887 - 1889.

Studi e testi. Rome, 1900 - .

Studi medievali, nuova serie. Turin, 1928 - .

Studies in Philology. Chapel Hill, N.C., 1906 - .

Subsidia Hagiographica. Monograph series of the Société des Bollandistes (cf. *Acta SS.*).

Sumption, Jonathan. *Pilgrimage: An Image of Mediaeval Religion.* Totowa, N.J., 1975.

Surius, Laurentius. *Historiae seu Vitae sanctorum.* 13 vols. Turin, 1875 - 1880.

Surtees Society, Publications. London, 1834 - .

Symeon Metaphrastes. *Menologion.* See above, p. 45, and *BHG* 1909, pp. 267 - 292. Edited in *Pat. Gr.* CXIV - CXVI.

Thesaurus Linguae Latinae. Edited with the authority and supervision of the German Academies of Berlin, Göttingen, Leipzig, Munich, and Vienna. Leipzig and Munich, 1900 - .

Thomas, K. *Religion and the Decline of Magic.* London, 1971.

Thompson, Stith. *Motif-Index of Folk-Literature.* Revised and enlarged. 6 vols. Bloomington and Copenhagen, 1955 - 1958.

Thurston, Herbert, S.J., and Attwater, Donald. *Butler's Lives of the Saints.* 4 vols. New York, 1956.

Tille, Alexander. *Geschichte der deutschen Weihnacht.* Leipzig, 1893.

Tittle, Walter. *Colonial Holidays.* New York, 1910.

Tobler, Titus. *Bibliographia Geographica Palaestinae.* Leipzig, 1867.

Traill, Henry Duff, and Mann, J. S. *Social England.* 6 vols. London, 1901 - 1904.

Urlin, Ethel L. H. *Festivals, Holy Days, and Saints' Days.* London, 1915.

Uspenskij, Théodore. *L'art byzantin chez les Slaves.* 4 vols. Paris, 1930 - 1932.

Vacandard, Elphège. *Origines du culte des saints.* Etudes de critique et d'histoire religieuse, 3 ser. Paris, 1912.

Van Gennep. *See* Gennep.

Van de Walle, B. "Sur les traces des pèlerins Flamands, Hennuyers, et Liègeois au monastère Sainte-Catherine du Sinai." *Annales de la Société d'Emulation de Bruges* CI (1964), 119 - 147.

Van Rensselaer, Mrs. Schuyler. *The Goede Vrouw of Mana-ha-ta at Home and in Society.* New York, 1898.

―――. *History of the City of New York in the Seventeenth Century.* 2 vols. New York, 1909.

Varnhagen, Hermann. *Zur Geschichte der Legende der K. von Alexandria.* Erlangen, 1891.

―――. *Eine lateinische Bearbeitung der Legende der K. von Alexandrien in Distichen.* Erlangen, 1892.

Vasiliev, A. A. *Histoire de l'Empire byzantin.* 2 vols. Paris, 1932.

―――. *Byzance et les Arabes.* 2 vols., Brussels, 1935, 1950.

Vendôme Annals. *See* Manuscripts Cited, Oxford Bodl. 309.

Vielliard, Jeanne. "Notes sur l'hospice Saint-Nicolas des Catalans à Rome au moyen âge." *Mélanges d'archéologie et d'histoire de l'Ecole Française de Rome* I (1933), 183 - 193.

Vies des Saints et des Bienheureux selon l'ordre du calendrier avec l'histoire des Fêtes par les RR. PP. Bénédictins de Paris XI - XII. Paris, 1954 - 1956.

Vincent, Marvin R. *The Age of Hildebrand.* London, 1897.

Vincent, Patrick R. *The "Jeu de Saint Nicolas" of Jean Bodel of Arras.* Johns Hopkins Studies in Romance Literature and Languages 49. Baltimore, 1954.

Vinson, John Chalmers. *Thomas Nast: Political Cartoonist.* Athens, Ga., 1967.

Vogel, Cyrille. "Le pèlerinage pénitential." *Pellegrinaggi,* pp. 39 - 94.

Volpicella, Luigi. *Bibliografia storica della provincia Terra di Bari.* Naples, 1884.

Voragine. *See* Jacobus.

Wace. *Life of St. Nicholas.* Edited and translated by Mary Sinclair Crawford. Philadelphia, 1923. *See also* Ronsjö.

Waddell, Helen. *The Wandering Scholars.* 7th ed. London, 1934.

Wagenknecht, Edward Charles, ed. *The Fireside Book of Christmas Stories.* New York, 1945.

Ward, H. L. D., and Herbert, J. A. *Catalogue of Romances in the Department of MSS in the British Museum.* 3 vols., London, 1883 - 1910.

Warne, F. J. *Jean Bodel, Le Jeu de Saint Nicolas.* Oxford, 1951.

Warren, Frederick E., trans. *The Sarum Missal in English.* Alcuin Club Publications 11. London, 1913.

Weigand, Edmund. "Zu den ältesten abendländischen Darstellungen der Jungfrau und Martyrin Katharina von Alexandria." In *Pisculi: Studien zur Religion und Kultur des Altertums, Franz Joseph Dölger dargeboten,* pp. 279 - 290. Munster-in-W., 1939.

Werner, Morris R. *Tammany Hall.* Garden City, N.Y., 1928.

Wetzer, Joseph, and Welte, Benedikt. *Kirchen-lexikon; oder, Encyklopädie der katholischen Theologie und ihrer Hilfswissenschaften.* Freiburg, 1847.

Weydig, Otto. *Beiträge zur Geschichte des Mirakelspiele in Frankreich: das Nikolausmirakel.* Diss. Jena, 1910. Erfurt, 1910.

Whitmore, Eugene R. *Saint Nicholas, Bishop of Myra.* Washington, 1944.

Whistler, Laurence. *The English Festivals.* London, 1947.

Widding, O.; Bekker-Nielsen, H.; and Shook, L. K. "Lives of the Saints in Old Norse Prose." *Mediaeval Studies* XXVI (1964), 294 - 337.

Wilkins, David. *Concilia Magnae Britanniae et Hiberniae.* 4 vols. London, 1737.

William of Malmesbury. *Gesta Pontificum.* Edited by N. E. S. A. Hamilton. Rolls Series. London, 1870. See also Stubbs, *William of Malmesbury.*

Williams, Stanley Thomas. *The Life of Washington Irving.* 2 vols. New York, 1935.

Wilson, James Grant. *The Memorial History of the City of New-York* III. New York, 1893.

Wright, A. R., and T. E. Lones, *British Calendar Customs* III: *Fixed Festivals June-December.* Publications of the Folk-Lore Society 106. London and Glasgow, 1940.

Wright, Thomas, ed. *Early Travels in Palestine.* London, 1848.

Wright, Thomas, and Halliwell, J. O., eds. *Reliquae Antiquae.* 2 vols. London, 1841, 1843.

Yewdale, Ralph Bailey. *Bohemond I, Prince of Antioch.* Princeton, 1924.

Young, Karl. *The Drama of the Medieval Church.* 2 vols. Oxford, 1933.

Zeitschrift für deutsches Alterthum und deutsche Literatur. Leipzig, 1841 - .

INDEX OF MANUSCRIPTS

This list does not include manuscripts incidentally mentioned, known to the author only through a secondary source. Manuscript numbers are *italic*, page references roman.

LIST OF VERBAL RELICS

On the page listed, the text of the verbal relic or a description
of it is signaled in the margin by the symbol N̈

GENERAL INDEX

(See also N Index, above)